CRIMINOLOGY

CRIMINOLOGY

FOURTH EDITION

Donald R. Taft

Professor of Sociology, Emeritus
University of Illinois

Ralph W. England, Jr.

Associate Professor of Sociology
University of Rhode Island

HV
6025
T12
1964

The Macmillan Company, New York
Collier-Macmillan Limited, London

33678

THE MACMILLAN COMPANY, NEW YORK
COLLIER-MACMILLAN CANADA, LTD., TORONTO, ONTARIO

Printed in the United States of America

Preface to the Fourth Edition

The fourth edition of this book retains the same general organization as the third and the same theoretical emphasis that crime in the United States is fundamentally an expression of our general culture.

Part I discusses the relationship of our crime problem to our somewhat unique culture, examines the nature and sources of criminal statistics, and describes briefly the history of criminology as a science. We begin Part II with a discussion of the futility of viewing crime wholly as a manifestation of individual traits, contending that as a social phenomenon crime must be explained at a societal rather than an individual level. Next we examine a variety of specific social conditions and processes relevant to an understanding of crime. Part III is concerned with the agencies of our society charged with the responsibility of suppressing crime, apprehending and trying suspects, and dealing with convicted persons. The strengths and weaknesses of these agencies we see as explainable in large measure by their positions in our political and social systems.

Substantial portions of the book are new, and we have found it possible to cover the essential material in fewer words. The chapters have been reduced in number from 37 to 29. This shorter book will be more suitable for one-semester courses. The least changed are Chapters 2 and 3, since they present the general approach made by this text; both authors feel that nothing in our recent social history has reduced the validity of this approach. Chapter 16, A Theory of Crime, has been reorganized and considerably rewritten both to give a greater cogency to our theoretical statement and to emphasize that our approach is intended more to explain the presence of antisocial norms and values in American society than to explain how particular individuals come to conform to these norms and values.

For all but the first three, the chapter bibliographies have been replaced with shortened annotated lists of items. The subject of crime has long been so exceedingly popular with professional writers, practitioners, and scholars from numerous disciplines that the field suffers from a plague of words, most of which might better have gone unsaid. In selecting the bibliography we looked upon the remaining words and from them chose what we thought undergraduates would find interesting and stimulating.

For their many services to the authors in the preparation of this revision, we express our thanks to Miss Mary MacDonald of the University of Illinois Library and to Francis P. Allen, Librarian, and Franklin Talbot, Reference Librarian, both of the University of Rhode Island. Numerous unpleasant details and much typing were cheerfully handled by Mrs. W. Russell Bottomley. The junior author is deeply grateful to his wife, Edith T. England, for the hundreds of selfless hours she spent typing and proofreading the manuscript.

DONALD R. TAFT
University of Illinois

RALPH W. ENGLAND, JR.
University of Rhode Island

Table of Contents

PART I

The BACKGROUND of CRIMINAL BEHAVIOR

CHAPTER 1

Crime and Criminology

To remind ourselves that crime is a major American problem
would seem superfluous. Daily our newspapers and broadcasts
bring to us with our breakfast coffee a diet of murders, robberies,
sex attacks, chicanery in high places, and so on. This diet can, in
fact, become so overwhelming as to obscure our awareness that
conformity to the law is vastly more prevalent than law-breaking.
But in certain sectors of life, illegal activity dominates the lives
of large numbers of people. Criminalistic behavior is well-nigh
implicit, for example, in extreme business competitiveness as well
as in the search for monopolistic advantages. Somewhat unfairly,
it seems, a few criminologists have even tried to show that a large
proportion of our college students have committed rather serious
crimes. We, the authors, shall attempt to show that if all people are
not criminals, most of us are elements in processes which comprise
the crime problem.

Crime concerns us when it touches our own lives. Most Americans probably have been victims of crime and exploitation, either
directly and consciously or, more often, indirectly in ways of which
we are not aware. We worry about crime also when we realize its
increase and its costliness. Our crime statistics are not wholly
accurate, but criminal behavior seems to have greatly increased in
our decade of great prosperity, and it appears to have shifted its

3

locus a bit. We have long thought of crime as decidedly behavior of the lower class, and burglary, robbery, rape, and similar crimes probably are still found more frequently in the slum than on the boulevard, because the unsuccessful are exposed disproportionately to conditions which produce these particular kinds of crime. Yet the new trend is seen in the increased involvement of middle- and upper-class youths even in such predatory offenses.

But racketeering, white-collar crime, and what we call non-criminal exploitation are not the acts of the poor, and this is a period of prosperity. Recently the morning paper was headlined: "U.S. Charges G.M. Price Plot," and not long ago General Electric was among some 32 of our largest electrical corporations convicted of extensive violations of the anti-trust laws. A few of those concerns' near-top executives were sent to jail for acts which most informed people believed are the established, if not the admitted, policy of many other industrial concerns. The layman wonders how widely the business and labor sectors of our population have become involved in the criminal world.

Certain philosophers have concluded that the moral tone of our society has declined, while certain intelligent criminals have cynically asserted that "everyone has a racket." And criminal behavior begins early these days. Our children and adolescents have increasingly appeared in court. In certain sections of our great cities women fear to walk the streets alone because of youthful predators. Some drug addiction among juveniles is but the most sensational and, fortunately, the least representative example of this trend.

J. Edgar Hoover's estimates of the total annual cost of crime now run into tens of billions of dollars. The FBI "time clock," which records each major felony committed, jumps very fast, though its speed creates fears of unwarranted dimensions, since its chief explanation is that ours is a very populous and rapidly growing country. Some decades ago the National Commission on Law Observance and Enforcement published a multivolume study of crime. Its last huge volume dealt with the cost of crime. After reading its final page, the informed reader knew what he knew on page one: crime is a very costly problem, but nobody knows how much it costs. We cannot measure and we should not exaggerate the very real seriousness of the American crime problem.

Specific crimes come to public attention. Sensational attacks by miscalled "sexual psychopaths" are publicized, and large-scale robberies, like the Brink armored truck holdup and the Cape Cod robbery, are naturally headlined. If it be true that "crime does not pay," an occasional crime pays handsomely in monetary return, though probably not in terms of lifetime satisfaction. But typical professional crimes do not begin to hurt our pocketbooks as seriously as "takes" like those perpetrated by the electrical corporations. The various rackets to which the Kefauver Committee has so vividly called attention are immensely costly. They have also demoralized not a few police organizations and corrupted not a few municipal governments. The gambling racket is only the largest of a long list of these, and that racket is based upon the fact that millions of Americans want to gamble.

Fear of Communism is rightly or wrongly the most widespread fear in our country today—a fear possibly exaggerated by public and private propaganda. American liberals, however, are more concerned over threats to basic freedom and unjust injuries to some of our best citizens than over dangers from a small group of Communists, serious though the occasional acts of some of them are. We seem to be right if we hold that war problems, labor unrest, racial discrimination, or population pressures are more serious than the crime problem. But the criminologist is correct in stressing crime as a major threat and in indicating that its source is by no means confined to what is popularly considered the predatory underworld nor restricted to city slums or some minority groups.

Crime and the Criminal

SOCIAL INJURIES AND CRIMES ARE SUBJECTIVE AND RELATIVE

Crime is but one form of social injury. Injuries are defined in terms of the values cherished in any society: in nearly all societies life and property are valued; to steal and to kill are therefore rated as injuries. Being thus defined by group opinion, injuries are subjective concepts. They vary at different periods in any changing society, and they vary between societies. Injuries are thus relative as well as subjective concepts. To kill a public enemy is held a praiseworthy act. To pay less than value received for labor in effect "steals" property, yet it was once considered simply good business policy. If we fail to pay taxes on the full value of our personal property, we in a sense "rob" the government, yet to pay in full is perhaps more likely to bring ridicule than approval in some quarters. Moreover, the same act may be defined as an injury by one group and tolerated or approved by another. Lynching is abhorred in most American communities, South as well as North, but at a moment of tension has been condoned in a few of them.

Similarly, even in the same group, values may pass from the approved to the disapproved category or vice versa with the passage of time. To promote the socialistic state in Czarist Russia was considered treasonable, while to promote a return to capitalism is so defined in Soviet Russia. To accept interest on a loan was once considered immoral, while to criticize such a practice today would be generally regarded as an indication of radical tendencies. Similarly, social status may at one time or place be awarded for behavior which will be excluded from group approval at another time or place.

Parents injure children when they quarrel or show preference for one child over another, punish too much or too little, fail to serve as confidants, and so forth. Employees are deprived of property rights by employers who exploit them. Employers and the public may be exploited by labor unions which use monopoly power to extort more than a "just" wage. Patriots, with the best of intentions, injure their country when their chauvinism endangers world peace. Such acts, however, are not crimes in most American jurisdictions.

SOME LEGAL DEFINITIONS

Legally a crime is an act made punishable by law. A criminal is one who has committed such a legally forbidden act. Yet there are other criteria which determine whether a person may be dealt with as a criminal.

(1) Regardless of his act, he must be of *competent age*. Under English common law a child under seven could not commit a crime because he was held not capable of feeling a sense of guilt—and so was not responsible. In American states the age of criminal responsibility is fixed by statute or constitutionally considerably above the common law limit. Very young children may of course be dealt with in juvenile courts. They may be punished as well as treated constructively under the fiction that the court acts *in loco parentis* (as a parent would act) and in the best interests of the child.

(2) Criminal acts must also be *voluntary* and engaged in without compulsion. Compulsion as defined by courts must be evident and immediately related to a particular criminal act. Impulsion toward a life of crime may have extended over a long period of time in the form of the influence of parents, associates, or conditions. But such indirect influences of the past, however compelling, will not be recognized in court as destroying that voluntary nature of acts which is requisite to criminal behavior.

(3) Especially in the case of serious crimes, the criminal must be shown to have had *criminal intent:* he must have meant to do wrong. Usually

criminal intent is tested in terms of his knowledge of right and wrong and of the nature and consequences of his behavior. If it can be shown that a man who killed another did not know that it is wrong to kill or that death may result if one points a loaded gun at another and pulls the trigger, he will be judged irresponsible, being without *mens rea*.[1] Though in the case of some simple crimes, like running a stop light, the question of intent will not be raised, intent must be present to constitute most serious crimes. A wrongful *motive* need not be shown. A motive is the reason for crime; it is the subjective aspect of the causation of crime. Bigamy is no less a crime when the accused is actuated by religious motives, and euthanasia, the killing at the request of or for the benefit of the killed, is murder. On the other hand, a man who, intending to make hog feed, produced illicit corn whiskey, was held not guilty of crime.[2]

(4) Our criminal law also often recognizes *degrees of intent* as necessary to constitute particular crimes. Thus to carry a heavy penalty an assault may have to be shown to have been perpetrated "maliciously" or "wantonly," or a personal injury to have resulted from negligence.

(5) Finally, to constitute a crime an act must be classed legally as an *injury to the state* and not merely as a private injury, or tort. In ancient societies many acts now defined as crimes were considered only private injuries to be avenged by the injured party or by his family or friends. But as society became more and more complex, a large number of acts once considered torts became crimes. It is indeed increasingly difficult to discover acts without general social consequences. We still have a vast number of injuries dealt with through private suit under the civil law, in which the court acts as the arbitrator between the contestants and awards damages. Some offenses may be tried either under the civil or the criminal law. We shall later discuss white-collar crime, which is usually tried under civil procedure but may be tried as crime. In the United States, with its puritanical heritage, there has been a tendency to define as crimes many forms of personal behavior which on the European continent are rarely treated as crimes. That tendency has created the problem of unenforceable law and has set the stage for serious rackets created when satisfactions forbidden by law, such as gambling or prostitution, are nevertheless in wide demand by at least a large minority of the people.

[1] Sir James Fitzjames Stephen, *A History of the Criminal Law in England*. Quoted in Albert J. Harno, *Cases and Other Materials on Criminal Law and Procedure* (Chicago: Callaghan, 1939), p. 30.

[2] Justin Miller, *Handbook of Criminal Law* (St. Paul, Minn.: West Publishing Co., 1934), pp. 68ff.

From the *social point of view,* the legal definition of crime may be less important than other considerations. Two aspects of the social view of injuries and crimes may be noted.

1. Injurious acts are defined by group mores, either derived from the past or from the more current opinions of the people or of dominant subgroups which set patterns, define the moral code, and award status to those who keep the code and deny it to those who do not. Criminal law has been much influenced by these group definitions of morals but is not synonymous with them. Socially disapproved acts may be looked upon as immoral, sinful, unconventional, or criminal. Tested by the awarding of social status, it is not even clear that acts made punishable at law are held the most serious types of social injuries. Fornication is traditionally an immoral act, but it is punishable as crime in only something like half of the states and actually punished in a very small percentage of cases. On the other hand, the white-collar crimes of businessmen are made punishable as crimes at law, and yet those who indulge in false advertising or gain monopoly advantages over others usually do not lose status in their social groups. As a general label, the term "unconventional" is less damning than the term "criminal." But many a hostess might prefer to invite to her party a man who had a past record for some forms of criminal behavior, rather than one who, though with a clean crime record, nevertheless shovels his food indecorously into his mouth. A man without church affiliations may laugh if he is called a sinner, but he who cherishes his membership in an orthodox religious group will cringe when so labeled. Thus, from the societal viewpoint the seriousness of acts is defined by their effects upon social status. When one discovers the seriousness of some noncriminal acts, he gains perspective. He will be less ready to generalize that all criminals are our most dangerous citizens.

2. Secondly, in our traditional criminal law, a criminal is one who *in the past* committed, generally with evil intentions, an act made punishable by law. From the societal viewpoint we are more concerned to protect society against future acts than to requite the criminal for past acts. The concern is not with past wickedness but rather with possible *future dangerousness.* Of course the societal definition does not neglect a man's past behavior, since past behavior may suggest his possible future behavior. But socially the future is always the major consideration. *From the societal viewpoint the purpose of punishment is not to balance accounts or to take vengeance upon a criminal, but to assure that he will not repeat his crimes.*

Punishment will be used when it is the only way to prevent repetition or when it will deter others from committing crimes. If future crime can be prevented through constructive treatment without encouraging criminal acts by other, it is both more effective and more socially satisfying than is punishment.[3]

It is a nice question how far a state may shift to this emphasis on the future. Actually every constructive program, such as probation or parole, and every crime prevention program implies some concern over the future. Some states are successfully using paid specialists to estimate, on the basis of past records, the relative possibilities of different types of parolees repeating if they are released.[4] Criminologists are in general agreement on the soundness of the trend toward concern for the future with its emphasis on the individualization of treatment.

Yet if this trend is to succeed we must also be aware of difficulties, needs, and dangers involved. (1) We need increased knowledge of the causes of crime. (2) Criminology is not opposed to punishment *per se*. When the changes needed in the lives of criminals are known, it does not follow that their lives may be adequately controlled to bring these changes about. John may need a new wife, but where is the lady willing to take the chance? Jack would be a safe risk if he could change his residence from slum to avenue, but the change is too costly. Jim will succeed if he can be employed at a satisfying job and if he is not hounded because of his past record, but these needs are not easy to bring about. (3) Too great control over the future of our citizens is inconsistent with democracy and smacks a bit of authoritarianism. Such control has been most complete in totalitarian states. We cannot push men about like pawns on a chessboard without endangering liberties which may be held more precious than the absence of crime. (4) Much of the general public and many influential groups have not yet accepted the validity of concern for the future and the desirability of constructive aid to criminals. The public still relies principally upon deterrent punishment. Moreover, the typical criminal himself accepts the traditional view and defines justice as equal treatment of men for the same acts, rather than in terms of an estimate of their future needs and behavior.

The principle of concern over future dangerousness appears to be sound, and most criminologists are eager to see the difficulties named overcome. To this end indeterminate sentence laws, which leave the nature of punishment or treatment open, to be determined by administrative authorities after thorough study of each case, are advocated and are already

---

[3] For further discussion of the effectiveness of punishment, see *infra,* pp. 293–295.
[4] Cf. *infra.,* pp. 504–506.

in use. Indeed, the *individualization of treatment* of criminals has become the earmark of effective effort to protect society against crime. The word "individualization," however, should not be taken as meaning treatment as an individual, for the use of group methods is increasingly proving its value, and the delinquent is seen as very largely a group product.

The social conception of the nature of the criminal implies less concern with his intent as a measure of his wickedness and less search for responsibility. We are, of course, concerned with intent in the sense of the attitude of the criminal. A man who meant to commit a crime may continue to do so as long as his antisocial attitude remains. But intent may be no index of dangerousness. Those who habitually drive recklessly without intending to hit anyone are often more dangerous than men who deliberately and intentionally commit some kinds of crime. Most of the legally insane are not dangerous but pitiably diseased, but some few with delusions of persecution but without antisocial intent are extremely dangerous. Professional killers are rare, but they are clearly greatly to be feared. Typical murderers, however—public opinion to the contrary notwithstanding—are rarely dangerous in the sense of being likely to repeat their acts. Murder usually results from stresses and strains which are not often repeated in the life of one who murders. A robber or a forger, on the other hand, has often lived under social conditions which make change of attitudes and behavior difficult to bring about. That some of our most feared criminals are least often repeaters is borne out by statistics of parole.

Similarly, either the nature of a man's personality or the nature of his social relations may define him as a dangerous person, though he has committed no crime.

LEGAL AND SOCIAL ACCOMPLICES

Another type of dangerous person is the accomplice. At law an accomplice is one who takes part with another or others in the commission of a *particular* criminal act and in a way definitely defined in the law. He may have planned a crime he did not commit himself; he may have been the lookout who warned of the approach of police or the one who drove the car used by robbers; he may have received stolen goods. But if we are concerned with the causes of crime, and with future dangers as much as with past acts, the concept "accomplice" may reasonably be greatly expanded. From the social viewpoint an accomplice is *anyone who contributes to the general crime problem.*

Parents who neglect or injure children are social accomplices in their delinquencies. Members of a white majority race who discriminate against Negroes perpetuate one of the most important conditions contributing to the excess in Negro crime. Those who exploit advantages over others, though keeping within the limits of the law; those who insist on athletes winning games regardless of the ethics or legality of the winning; those who patronize gambling rackets and thus create the demand for them—are not these and others as truly accomplices in crime as those who fall nicely within the legal definition of the term?

There are a few professional killers who can be hired to kill a man. But these could not exist if it were not for another criminal element desiring to have men killed. In turn these gangsters—not themselves killers— could not exist were it not for illicit business interests or labor interests which they serve or exploit. Such illicit interest groups shade off imperceptibly into legitimate interests desiring, or well-nigh compelled, to seek protection from racketeers, and these in turn are dependent on unethical police, lawyers, or judges—not all technically criminal. Similarly, all of the above are more or less dependent on "respectable" but vote-seeking politicians, and many of these upon a citizenry obeying many laws fairly well but patronizing the services of those who disobey them. *Such a system of interlocking interests and social relationships is the crime problem.* Thus, if one starts out looking for accomplices in crime in this expanded social sense of the word, he is fortunate if he does not sooner or later find himself knocking on his own door.

Nature and Scope of Criminology

The term "criminology" is used both in a general and special sense. In its broadest sense criminology is the study (not yet the complete science) which includes all the subject matter necessary to the understanding and prevention of crime and to the development of law, together with the punishment or treatment of delinquents and criminals. In its narrower sense criminology is simply the study which attempts to explain crime, to find out "how they get that way." If this latter narrower definition is adopted, one must recognize related fields, including penology, concerned with the treatment of adult criminals, crime detection, the treatment of juvenile delinquents, and the prevention of crime. The treatment of delinquency and crime cannot be wholly separated from their explanation, since one of the reasons for crime and for its continuance into adult life is the damage done by ineffective treatment both of juveniles and adults. Parts I and II of this book will deal chiefly with the explanation of crime, Part III with treatment and preventative programs. Ultimately we shall hope to show that both crime and the treatment of crime are parts of dynamic processes of social relations, crime evoking punishment and other reactions and these reactions in turn evoking reactions of criminals as they are deterred, "reformed," or stimulated to further crime.

If any science is to explain any kind of phenomena consistently, these phenomena must be reasonably homogeneous. Criminology as a behavioral science or study faces an almost unsolvable difficulty because of the extreme diversity of types of behavior our legislators have seen fit to make punishable as crimes. To mention but a few of these types, does it seem logical that we should be able to explain in terms of a common theory behavior as diverse as the running of stop lights, the raping of women, robbery, huge racketeering syndicates, treason, murder, and the white-collar crimes of some businessmen? Not all of these crimes express the same attitudes of mind, not even a universal consciously antisocial attitude. Not all are conflict behavior, or exploitative behavior, or either wholly rational or wholly emotional behavior.

Facing this dilemma, criminologists have attempted various solutions. Valuable research has concentrated its attention on particular kinds of crime, such as professional thieving, embezzlement, murder, sex crime, and white-collar crime. Cressey [5] has gone further and believes he has arrived at sociologically meaningful subdivisions by isolating types of embezzlement. Cressey's plan would seem to lead us to theories as to the causes of specific crimes, rather than to any general theory of crime.

Other criminologists, such as E. H. Sutherland, have tried to discover processes or relationships which will explain all crime, in spite of its great variety. Thus we have theories of social disorganization and differential association, theories of delayed maturation, theories of economic exploitation, theories of anomie or normlessness, theories of subgroup influence, and so forth. We shall discuss some of these in Chapter 16. But we shall find that it seems that not all crime can be explained in terms of any given social process or relationship. However, this book will attempt to show that a vast amount of crime grows out of the nature of American culture and its attendant value systems.

Very many criminologists have given over the effort to find a single theory explaining crime without having abandoned the effort to discover

[5] Donald R. Cressey, "Criminological Research and the Definition of Crime," *American Journal of Sociology* (May 1951), pp. 546–51.

why men commit crime. Starting with evidence derived from case studies and many other sources, they list factors found in the life processes of criminals. They are able to determine fairly well the interrelationship of these factors in individual cases. They then find particular factors which often repeat themselves in many cases, such, for example, as gang membership, lack of status in constructive groups, tensions in homes, and sense of failure in competition. Discovery of such single repeating factors does not prove them causes of crime, since the meaning of any life experience may be different for one criminal than for another. This is because one factor or experience is, in different cases, combined with different accompanying factors which give the total *gestalt* and meaning which express themselves in criminal behavior. However, it is very significant when we find *clusters of factors* repeating themselves in many cases. The multifactor approach does seem to meet the dilemma of the criminologist in considerable measure. A large proportion of children in our type of society whose fathers have deserted the home, who have lived in city slums, who have experienced a sense of failure in competitive relations, who have lost status in constructive groups and joined juvenile gangs, who have come to believe that everyone has a racket, and whose early misbehavior has not been dealt with effectively either in the home or by schools and other social agencies—a large proportion of such children seem to appear continually in our juvenile courts, and many of them later in our adult courts. The discovery of repeated incidents of such combinations of experiences enables us to develop approximations to theories of crime. Such specific life experiences may often be shown to be by-products of the culture of our society.

SOURCES OF WRITTEN AND EFFECTIVE CRIMINAL LAW

It is important that we distinguish criminal law as set forth in our state and federal criminal codes from the law which is actually applied by our police and courts. In the first place, there is a considerable body of dead-letter laws in our codes which almost no one wishes to have enforced. Here we find the so-called "blue laws," including Sabbatarian legislation. Thus Barnes and Teeters [6] remind us of one Southern state where a man who fails to attend church on three successive Sundays commits a crime

[6] Harry Elmer Barnes and Negley K. Teeters, *New Horizons in Criminology,* 2nd ed. Quoted in Clyde B. Vedder, Samuel Koenig, and Robert E. Clark, eds., *Criminology—A Book of Readings* (New York: Dryden Press, 1953), pp. 91–92.

punishable with death, and of the persistence of our laws against blasphemy. More important are laws such as those penalizing gambling, which are supported by a part of public opinion and intermittently or locally enforced but which probably are violated by a majority of Americans.

Our criminal law itself is inherited in part from the *common law of England,* the principles of which are still applied in some of our states. Criminal law is further derived from *decisions of American courts.* Again, some crimes are defined in *constitutions.* But the great mass of American criminal law is an expression of the views of *legislatures,* and in most jurisdictions all criminal law is thus statutory. Since the police power rests with the states, most criminal law is state law and so varies considerably among the states. But increasingly, as the states have become more inter-dependent, the federal Congress, courts, and Constitution have defined a federal criminal law. Such federal criminal law must be passed under powers not reserved to the states, including the power to tax and to regu-late interstate commerce. Thus stealing a car is a state offense, but if the car is driven across a state line, the federal Dyer Act may be applied, and the FBI and other effective federal law-enforcement agencies come into play.

The effective criminal law, as distinguished from that set down in law books, is the law which will be enforced. Such law enforcement depends upon many influences. Though they must act within the law, the *police* have discretion to determine who shall be arrested. After an arrest the *prosecut-ing attorney* has tremendous power to decide who among the arrested shall be prosecuted and even for what offense. The *courts,* through judges, juries, and even minor officers, influence the effectiveness of the law, when they fail to convict or when they accept pleas of guilty to lesser offenses than those actually committed. Behind all these agencies is the force of *public opinion.* In a democracy, at least, the public influences the content of statute law and the effectiveness with which police, prosecuting attorneys, and courts enforce the law. This is true in spite of the fact that much of our criminal law itself is not an expression of public opinion, since with respect to many acts there is no public opinion. Partly for lack of such public opinion, *interest groups,* such as business, labor, or religious organi-zations, have played very important roles through their influence upon legislatures and through their pressures upon law-enforcement agencies. When law is studied historically, the changing role of such interest groups at different periods may be seen. Wide differences in penalties for the same crimes, and in the degree to which such penalties are actually in-flicted, reflect differences in the above-mentioned influences.

THE IMPORTANCE OF CRIMINOLOGY

Interest in the study of criminology is of course partly due to recognition of the *costliness of crime* already mentioned. Estimates of the cost of crime in the United States some years ago sometimes ran as high as $18 billion a year. They would probably run substantially higher today. But there seems little value in attempting even to guess at that cost, since the most serious costs cannot be measured in dollars and cents. Moreover, if such an effort were to include an assessment of the cost of white-collar crime and of exploitation not defined as crime but similar in nature, the figure would be enormously increased. The value of personal injuries defies calculation, even though it has to be decided by our courts. The psychological cost seen in fear of crime, worry over unguarded property, fear for personal security, the embittering effect of hatred and suspicion of one citizen for another in a society where mutual confidence, respect, and cooperation are so sorely needed—such costs are indeed great and incalculable.

Note should also be taken of *sentimental interest* in the crime problem. Fear, desire for revenge, a certain fascination, and a morbid interest either in the victim or the perpetrator of crime—such emotions help explain the prominence given to crime in the press and on television programs and even the large registrations in some college courses in criminology. It has been somewhat extravagantly said that morbid interest in crime expresses our unconscious desire to be criminals—a desire to throw off the restraints of civilized existence. It is clear that sentimental interest in crime, whether taking the form of negative hate or positive morbid sympathy, is not what is needed for the objective understanding and prevention of crime, and that its prevalence may be listed as a factor in the causation of crime.

When combined with understanding and a balanced consideration of all the values involved, *interest in the criminal is essential to the explanation of crime* and to intelligent protection against it. No child enters life a criminal. The attempt to unravel the processes by which what women call a "perfectly adorable baby" is warped and twisted by life's experiences into the personality of a calculating robber, burglar, kidnapper, or a Hitler, is a fascinating task which enlists the interest and challenges the intelligence of the criminologist.

This interest is enhanced by the discovery of the wide variety of human traits which the criminal possesses and the wide variety of types of which the criminal class is composed. Paradoxical though it sounds, one may hardly even describe criminals as a class as antisocial. Their criminal acts are indeed by definition antisocial, and no one would minimize the seriousness of some of them. Yet their criminal behavior on investigation is often found to be but one aspect of their total behavior. A typical prison population is largely made up of defeated men, overcome with apathy. Uninformed people are often astonished to discover that *some* prisoners love dogs, are fond of children, or will fight bravely for a cause. One finds, of course, morose and sullen specimens so soured by the consciousness that their behavior is despised, and by absence of genuine friendships, that they seem to be devoid of every human or kindly trait. But such are the exception. The senior writer once knew a forger with 35 years' experience who had served eight prison sentences but whom he would have trusted with a loan of $1,000. Robbers may be generous, murderers kindly, and prostitutes on occasion sympathetic. On the other hand, stress on the humanity of criminals may well be exaggerated. The fascination of the criminal personality for the student lies rather in the fact that study shows him to be even in his most ugly characteristics *a product* of life's experiences. As the student in criminology turns back the pages of such a life, as he would turn back the pages of a book, from the moment of the last terrible crime toward its beginning, sooner or later, if his analysis is complete, he finds an unsoiled page. The satisfaction of thus coming to understand life's failures is one of the fascinating rewards of the criminologist.

There are many types of criminals, if there is no criminal type. The farm hand of low intelligence who stumbles into delinquency literally not knowing how it happened is a common type which rarely "makes" the newspapers. The young city gangster, who has graduated from a juvenile gang far more naturally than he ever graduated from school, is a type differing radically from the farm hand. The pampered child of the rich, the kidnapper, the drunken sot, the brains of the underworld, the bank robber, the embezzler, the professional killer, the drug addict, the young girl sex delinquent—none of these are true types, because they vary so much within their groups. Moreover, more varied than the types of crime they commit are the roads by which they have entered crime. An understanding of the road to failure is of as great interest as is the story of the road to fame.

The study of criminology is also *background for a profession* and an opportunity for social service. Unfortunately, the difficult task of remaking character is still at times entrusted to untrained political appointees. But not always. Police staffs, lawyers, prosecuting attorneys, judges and jurors, probation officers, parole agents and members of parole boards, wardens and guards, statisticians, detectives, and a growing list of technically trained specialists, including medical men, psychologists, sociologists, social workers, psychiatrists, educators, directors of prison industries, recreational leaders—these and others constitute personnel who need training which includes a knowledge of criminology.

Some would say that the chief *value* of criminology to the student is not a knowledge of crime but a *positive or naturalistic philosophy of life* to be derived from it. The reader must decide for himself, as he proceeds, first whether that philosophy is true, and secondly whether it makes for human weal or woe. In this context we might mention that there are two extreme philosophies with reference to the explanation of human behavior. At one extreme is the position that human behavior is essentially unpredictable because man is free to choose the course he will pursue. This view conceives of the offender as choosing to be social or antisocial, criminal or noncriminal. Its proponents go through life classifying people in accordance with their behavior as "sheep" or "goats." The line between the two categories is conceived of as easily drawn and basically significant. The explanation of crime in terms of this philosophy is simple, because it is not pushed beyond the fact of bad choices; since the choices have no causes, they exist in their own right and are not products. From this viewpoint the task of preventing crime consists in the apprehension of the "goats" (criminals) and in showing them that bad choices are costly. From this viewpoint also, justice consists in requiting the doers of bad deeds in proportion to the badness of their acts, and every crime has its just and proportional punishment.

The opposite philosophy is equally concerned over the danger of crime. It implies equal willingness to punish when, and only when, punishment seems the only way to protect society. It conceives of crime and the criminal, however, as products. To the determinist the prevention of crime must always consist in creating conditions which will make for socially useful behavior as surely as different conditions produce crime. To him punishment as a process of balancing accounts with criminals is futile, though pain as a method of influencing behavior is useful when it is the most efficient means of social defense and when the end is worth the cost of punishment. Criminology in conjunction with other sciences of behavior at least *tends* toward a deterministic position. In so doing it creates many problems, but it also relieves us of the rational basis for praise, blame, hatred, and remorse. *If* such a philosophy is desirable, it is a chief argument for the study of criminology. Its implications for criminology will appear as we proceed. Its implications for still larger problems we discuss in the final chapter of this book.

CHAPTER 2

Law-Making and Law-Breaking in the American Setting

Law and Crime As a Conflict Relationship

Most, but not all, crime is an expression of a conflict relationship. Considered most immediately, the conflict is between the criminal and his victim.[1] The victim, however, may be either active or passive at the moment of the crime; the victim may not even be conscious of being victimized. At times a crime may be the end result of a long process of continuing tension, as when criminal violence breaks out in a long-term dispute between labor and management or when murder is the end result of increasing conflict between husband and wife. At other times, there may have been no such previous conflict relationship. Occasionally the criminal may also be unconscious of any antisocial attitudes in committing his crime. Usually, however, when a man steals, he consciously commits a crime against private property. In some criminal abortions and by rare exception in euthanasia, he consciously seeks to benefit his "victim." In the gambling racket he violates the law to his profit but may also feel that he is rendering a service to the millions who want to gamble. Hence no theory designed to explain all crime can be wholly a theory of conflict.

[1] Cf. Hans von Hentig, *The Criminal and His Victim* (New Haven: Yale University Press, 1948).

18

But the two-sided conflict aspect of the crime problem is generally evident.

Behind the immediate conflict relationship between criminal and victim lies the conflict between law-breakers and legislators, the police, and other agencies which make, enforce, or administer the criminal law. To understand the crime problem, then, we must understand both the processes through which laws and other parts of the enforcement machinery come to exist and those through which laws come to be broken. Both processes are rooted in the motives and attitudes and values which characterize American society and in changing social conditions and relations. These two processes are not independent of each other. Laws are made and criminals punished or treated because criminals injure society; in less obvious ways crimes are committed partly because of the conflict situation which criminal law expresses. Punishment itself may produce anger and stimulate further conflict and crime. Both criminal law and crime in the United States express social values, even though not all specific laws are implementations of the mores of the people generally. Sometimes two sets of values are in conflict; sometimes crime and non-crime are different expressions of the same values. Group loyalty, for example, may be loyalty to a criminal gang or to a community. In American society restricted group loyalties are expected and approved. The property owner wishes to keep his property, the thief to take it away; but both value property, both presumably seek the prestige which comes from possessing property, and both crave status in their immediate groups. In a society where material success is a major requisite to social status, there will be more crimes against property and more laws for the protection of property than in a society where less material bases for status are dominant.

But we shall discover that neither law-making or law-breaking exist independently of other social processes—of other institutions and social relations which characterize our society. When roots of widespread crime in our society are discovered, crime ceases to appear as merely a unilateral and unexplained act of a criminal against a victim or against society as a whole. It ceases even to appear as expressing a simple bilateral conflict relationship between the criminal and his victims or between him and the agencies which protect society against him. The crime problem is then rather seen as part of multilateral, dynamic, social relationships—of general social processes which constitute the whole of human experience in any society. Moreover, American society is both complex and in process of change, and simple and static societies have less law and less crime than do complex and dynamic societies like our own. The basic thesis of this book is that crime in America is the product of social processes of which the most important element is American culture.

Every society has its characteristic laws and crimes. Regional differences in culture and crime in the same or similar jurisdictions within one country also affect the influence of culture on law and crime. A frontier or rural society has values, laws, crimes, and reactions to crime somewhat different from those found in a highly industrialized urban society. The values of modern industrialism are everywhere different from the values of a feudal or peasant or frontier society.[2]

The fact that crime and its treatment are rooted in the general culture seems to have been somewhat neglected.[3] Men do not warm to the idea that that which hurts them comes from a society of which they are a part. Men have persisted in thinking of crime as just something done *to* society, rather than as an aspect of social relations. Many still think of the criminal as an abnormal deviate, whose unusual behavior is to be explained in terms of his personal peculiarities, without seeking an explanation of his personality or looking elsewhere for the roots of crime.

Laws and attitudes toward laws are often taken for granted but are actually, of course, historical products and dependent on other aspects of our society. Racketeering is an expression of the desires of at least large minorities among the general public. White-collar crimes of businessmen are so closely related to prevailing practices and values that the guilty businessman rarely loses status in his own group and often is not thought of as a criminal in society generally. The relationship of predatory crimes, such as larceny or robbery, to the general culture is more indirect and less evident, yet real. We shall not insist that all crime is rooted in the general culture nor that, in this sense, each society gets *exactly* "the criminals it deserves." But clearly we cannot understand the American crime problem without understanding American society. We must know why we have the laws we have and the institutions we have to know why we have the crimes we have. We turn, then, to preliminary consideration of the general nature of our society and its culture.

[2] Cf. Paul Meadows, *The Culture of Industrial Man* (Lincoln, Neb.: University of Nebraska Press, 1950).

[3] There are, however, exceptions. The very title of Milton L. Barron's text on juvenile delinquency, *The Juvenile in Delinquent Society* (New York: Alfred A. Knopf, 1954), indicates an emphasis similar to that in the present book. E. H. Sutherland, Donald Cressey, and Mabel Elliott devote chapters to the function of the general culture but do not seem to make it basic to their theories. Even some psychoanalytically inclined psychiatrists refer to society generally or changes in it as one source of the mental conflicts they emphasize.

Preliminary Considerations

Effort to explain crime may begin at either end of the criminogenic process. One may start with the criminal act and trace backwards into the criminal's past to see out of what roots it has grown. Or one may begin with an analysis of the nature of a society and trace the processes by which its characteristics imply or eventuate in crime. In this chapter we follow the second course.

Before we begin, however, we should mention that to attribute crime partly to the nature of our society is not necessarily to indict that society. If elements within our society tend to produce crime, it is because of an understandable process of evolution and not because of any inherent or self-determined differences between the American people and other peoples. Moreover, the reader must accustom himself to finding some of the roots of crime in values and situations which he accepts and with some of which he presumably would not willingly part even in the interest of less crime. Most of us prefer social change to social stagnation, yet change promotes maladjustment and crime. Probably the majority wish women to play more active roles than we expected of them 75 years ago, yet the freer life of women has exposed them to conditions which make for crime and has presumably increased the adjustment difficulties of both sexes. It is questionable whether democracy or totalitarianism is the more criminogenic in the sense of being more productive of internal disorder, yet few Americans would embrace the police state even if by so doing it could decrease crime. On the other hand, the reader may conceivably come to feel that some rather basic changes in our society may be required if the deeper roots of crime are to be cut.

AMERICAN CULTURE: A DEFINITION

By the culture of a people we mean the sum total of their material and nonmaterial achievements, with emphasis on their value systems as expressed in their basic institutions. The characteristics of American culture we shall mention are not necessarily unique to the United States. Many of our values are those of most industrialized societies. American culture is the product of pre-existing and coexisting cultures, modified by the distinctly American scene. Nor need we confine our attention to patterns of behavior which characterize *all* Americans. It is perhaps legitimate to include as "American" even minority traits, if these are prevalent in the

United States or if they characterize an influential social class with prestige. For example, property still counts in determining the differential treatment of the well-to-do and the underprivileged in the administration of the law. Also, within any characterization of American culture, it is legitimate, it would seem, to include traditions which may not be conspicuously followed today, provided those traditions are thought of as American by Americans and have also influenced either law-making or law-breaking. For example, Puritanism affects both law and its enforcement, although the practice of the Puritan code has declined. The Supreme Court, interpreting the Constitution of the United States (itself a great repository of tradition), has recently insisted on greater equality in the treatment of our Negro minority than public opinion in the South or even perhaps in the North desires.

For our purpose, then, American culture is culture deemed relatively prevalent in the United States, characterizing or accepted by large or influential groups and not confined to values limited to what is technically considered the criminal class. Its significance consists largely in the following fact: its values are those the acceptance or practice of which determines status in large subgroups or in American society as a whole. Some behavior contrary to these values has been defined as crime; some is tolerated; some approved and made a basis for acceptance and status in subgroups. For example, honesty in business is a general value, but a considerable degree of misrepresentation in advertising is expected and tolerated, and full honesty in business would put certain types of men out of business. Patriotism is demanded, but the man who pays taxes on the full value of his personal property probably loses status in his group more often than he gains it.

The church and business both implement the importance placed on individualism. In business circles men lose status if they do not show approval of "rugged individualism" as expressed in "free enterprise." The church member is generally expected to accept his "individual responsibility before God." The juvenile gang is often composed of those who have failed in individual competitive relations in conventional groups, and yet it may itself accept the value of individualism. Less direct is the influence of attitudes of Americans toward values related to race preferences, sex relations, and the home and other institutions, which are implemented in our laws and expressed in our enforcement or lack of enforcement of law.

THE STRUCTURE OF SOCIETY

In the United States, the democratic political structure is a valued institution. Law-making and law-breaking will be different in a democratically structured society than in an authoritarian regime. Popular attitudes toward laws which the public has a hand in making are not the same as attitudes toward laws imposed upon them by a totalitarian government. Yet enthusiasm for democracy and hence respect for its laws may somewhat wane when political corruption becomes evident. Our democratic society is divided into classes and other subgroups which may become pressure groups, so that on occasion interests other than those of the people as a whole become dominant. But class-made law is less generally respected; thus the existence of racial and cultural minorities in a society creates conflict between them and the larger society.

Law and crime are further affected by the *relatively static or dynamic and relatively simple or complex nature of a society*. Change creates problems of adjustment which sometimes express themselves in violations of law. The complexity of American society has led to the use of law to cover antisocial acts which in simpler societies are more effectively dealt with through mores and public opinion. Here is involved the difficult decision as to how far social control shall be left to local communities, where relative agreement is to be expected, or entrusted to the state and national governments, whose standards may not be accepted in all regions or localities.

The institutional structure of a society is reflected in law-making and law-breaking. The more socially stabilizing aspects of these institutions are written into our laws and tend to support obedience to law. Their less stabilizing aspects help explain violations of law. Thus, some types of broken homes, failure in economic competition, cultural conflict between immigrants and natives, the effect of the alleged decline of the influence of religion, political corruption, lack of or the wrong kind of education, scandals in the fields of sports—these help explain criminal behavior. In later chapters the emphasis will be upon the abnormal aspects of these activities, but we shall repeatedly trace these to the nature of the normal or general society and its values. In considerable degree, we shall thus see the unusual growing out of the usual: abnormal crime as a by-product of the nature of normal society.

Characterizations of American Society and Culture

The effort to characterize American society and American culture is beset with so many difficulties that some would abandon it. America is not a consistent whole. Such expressions as "American ideals," "the spirit of America," and "the American way of life" imply a homogeneity in the

American scene which never existed, whatever the current trend. The old distinction between the North and the South has recently been accentuated. The frontier is gone, but some sections of the country are relatively like the frontier, and the influence of the frontier on American individualism and revolt against restraint is evident. Contrasts between rural and urban life are especially obvious, and yet the metropolitanization of values in the small town and on the farm has progressed apace. The religiously orthodox live in a mental world rather different from that of religious liberals, and the gap between the relatively uneducated and the intelligentsia remains in spite of the increased proportion of college graduates. The workingman sees life through spectacles somewhat different from those of the capitalist, although the former often owns shares of stock himself and for the most part accepts our brand of "relatively free enterprise" because he hopes to rise to a higher plane of living. Important Negro, immigrant, and other minority groups imply somewhat varying points of view, but assimilation and/or that acceptance and integration of cultural variety known as cultural pluralism testify to the unifying effects of relative democracy and relatively equal opportunity. America has her common bonds but is far from being a cultural entity in any exact sense of the words.

To characterize American culture is further difficult because, although described today, it is sure to be something different tomorrow. The most prominent characteristic of American society is its dynamic quality, especially in the material field.

Moreover, to understand the criminal, it is more important to describe American culture in terms of varying values which determine status in subgroups than in terms of traditions to which only lip service may still be given. The practices of those immediate groups mold character and create new and conflicting behavior patterns, including some which help cause crime. Traditions of Puritanism or other past trends in American history have become crystallized in our laws, court practices, and our family and other social institutions, and remain after patterns inconsistent with them have become prevalent.

HISTORICAL ROOTS OF AMERICAN CULTURE

The earlier settlers in Colonial America brought an English culture of lower middle-class origin. To these English values, institutions, and conceptions of right and wrong, the colonists and their successors added others more original, as a result of the new environment, of the influence of non-English elements in the original population, and of the coming of the later immigrants. As compared with England, Colonial society feared too much law, was suspicious of centralized government, and, partly because of the Revolution, suspicious of law-enforcement agencies. The earlier American culture was relatively stable. Like modern Americans, the colonists sought economic success, but prestige among them came more as a result of individual effort rather than from the control of the work of others (apart from slavery), ownership of capital, or monopolization of a market. The influence of intimate primary groups was great. The family was still a religious, moral, social, and to some extent economic unit. The small community practiced neighborliness and cooperation. It also controlled its members largely through gossip and denied social acceptance to those considered "immoral."

The dominant moral philosophy in early America was Puritanism, and hence our law and our persisting moral codes today reflect the stern values of Puritanism. Changes in the application of that code have been great, but they have usually been rationalized in terms of the old code. Americans still attempt to justify themselves in terms of some moral code. Political democracy, love of liberty, relative localism, religious freedom, idealization of work, rudimental materialism yet with spiritual values uppermost, individualism, importance of primary relations, and the stern morality of Puritanism—these were some of the characteristics of early American society. That society was also relatively static, rural, isolated, and simple in structure. It implemented the "faith of our fathers," to which homage is still done, long after practice has deviated far from its basic principles because of vast changes, internal and external, in our society. Most of the changes we mention will appear throughout this book as parts of the explanation of some kinds of violations of codes of ethics by non-criminal elements and of law by the criminal elements in our society, unethical noncriminal behavior setting patterns for the criminal.

TRENDS IN AMERICAN SOCIETY AND VALUES

Crime has been in part an expression of problems of adjustment to change. The following effort to characterize changes in American society and culture should help us to understand both law-making and law-breaking in American society today.

The trend has been from the static to the dynamic, from the rural toward the urban, from the religious toward the secular. From exacting moral codes approaching asceticism toward the relative freedom and group conflicts of "the new morality." From bigotry in religion toward partial tolerance, made necessary by the coming of the Catholics and the Jews and the splintering of Protestantism into literally scores of sects. From the view that pleasure is sin to what Sorokin has called a sensate society, with various forms of immediate happiness as its goal—with sports, for example, possibly the most evident center of interest of the rank and file of the population. From other-worldliness toward this-worldliness. From the lesser individualism of Puritan New England, through the extreme individualism of the frontier, toward a relatively private and even public collectivism, which nevertheless calls itself "free enterprise," sometimes defines government planning as its foe, and almost always [considers] communism as its arch enemy. From the direct, local, political type of democracy of the New England town meeting, albeit with restricted suffrage, through the wider, indirect, representative political democracy of a huge nation, toward a never fully achieved social democracy. Latterly the trend has been in the direction of a still very remote approximation to totalitarianism in our fear-filled modern world. From a stable family less paternalistic than in some parts of Europe, yet where woman's place was in the home, to the relatively unstable and divorce-threatened type with women relatively free to enter active political and social life outside the home and to compete with men in industry.

[Urbanization and industrialization have been two of the basic processes which account for these and other changes in American social life. Further trends may be noted:] From the family as the recognized center of child upbringing and education to a considerable degree of substitution of other agencies and subgroups as controls, training schools, and sources of status demanded by children and youth. Generally from close-knit, primary, personal association in families, churches, neighborhoods, and small communities to the impersonal secondary relations of a large, complex, formally structured society, in spite of earnest efforts to repersonalize some aspects of life. From isolation and isolationism to membership in the United Nations and a still incomplete consciousness of informal membership in the Great Society. From localism, states' rights, and regionalism to nationalism, and yet toward a still rare and remote cosmopolitanism perhaps never to be achieved.

The trend has also been from what would today be called almost universal poverty and relative classlessness, in spite of some aristocratic elements, toward the table that groans and the tremendous national wealth of mid-twentieth-century America, with the gap between rich and poor still yawning, but with marked improvement in the level of living of the workingman. From individual bargaining and the gross exploitation it implied, to powerful unions ever demanding more, often coercing employers and not seldom causing genuine in-, convenience to the general public, yet generally accepting the basic principles of "free enterprise" because leaders and even rank and file have hoped—sometimes mistakenly—to be successful in the competitive struggle. From a farm-centered to a factory-centered economy, and yet with a reminiscent rural influence which politicians cannot safely disregard. From small, self-sufficient farms, local crafts, little shops and factories, through larger manufacturing and commercial units, to tremendous industrial giants whose power has been but slightly limited by persistent "trust-busting" campaigns. Yet the fear of the breakdown of a great interlocking national and world trading and financial system, which has had prolonged depressions, remains among our more pessimistic economists. From dedication to the dignity of personal work to reliance on profits based upon the often remote control of the work of others, who, nevertheless, increasingly have gained certain stakes in enterprise through stock ownership. From self-reliance to the willingness of business to depend upon government protection and favors and of unemployed workers to look to the same paternally protecting Uncle Sam when hard times come, or even in good times when organized blocks of voters can successfully demand public aid. From success or failure based upon a mixture of hard work and lucky possession of good soil, mineral wealth, or other natural resources to success or failure based upon a mixture of hard thinking and lucky advantage in relationships with fellow men as competitors or purchasers. From simple wants growing out of a simple life to a welter of advertising-created yet compelling desires, dictated by personal enjoyment or eagerness to follow the crowd. From the intimate isolation of each domestic scene to radio-broadcasted "fireside chats" by our presidents and a televised world scene where commercially controlled selections of reality and unreality expose millions to the same visualized scenes and threaten any genuinely private life of man. From the view that Indians are inferior beings, through the long struggle over Negro slavery, to regional heritages of degrees of racism and the more general "American dilemma." That dilemma consists in the fact that while all give lip service to the principle of race equality, yet discrimination between the light- and dark-complexioned continues, North and South, to be one of the most evident if irrational bases of preferment—this in spite of a World War fought ostensibly to destroy the extreme racism of Nazi Germany.

American history has also involved a trend from the political impotence of scattered colonies struggling for existence to the position of the mightiest of World Powers, with a partially recognized obligation to save the rest of the world from self-destruction. The story has passed from local Indian wars to great world cataclysms and a cold war seemingly without end and appearing to threaten the mighty achievement of the past. From the confidence in life which comes from making a rocky soil produce and which erects a successful defense against local dangers, we have passed to the sense of personal impotence which overcomes thoughtful individual men, swept on, as they feel, by forces they cannot comprehend, and each made conscious of his own personal insignificance. Thus as the United States has waxed strong, the individual American has become feeble.[4]

MORE SPECIFIC ALLEGED CHARACTERISTICS

From the above "motion picture" of general trends in American society, we turn to more specific characteristics of the American people or of American society which are alleged to be widespread or distinctive.

American culture is dynamic. As indicated above, the very dynamic quality which complicates a definition of American culture also hinders

[4] Adapted from Donald R. Taft and Richard Robbins, *International Migrations: The Immigrant in the Modern World* (New York: The Ronald Press, 1955), pp. 448–51. Copyright 1955, The Ronald Press Company, and used with permission of the publisher.

interpersonal and social adjustment and promotes crime. The typical American, finding new technologies, new contacts, new excitements, and new social values at every turn, is faced with unprecedented problems of adaptation and adjustment. Invention compels revised standards and new controls. The wrong of yesterday is the right of today. We scarcely dare train our children to any fixed behavior patterns, because the only certainty is that tomorrow will require a revision of the code if it is to fit the changed world which is to be expected. Crime is correlated with social change. Our dynamic culture is criminogenic.

American culture is complex. Repeatedly in our later discussion we shall see crime as the product of culture conflict, and culture conflict rooted in the vast variety of the American scene. Immigration, internal migration, and improved communication have brought into intimate contact groups with varying outlooks on life and varied patterns of behavior. The Southern Negro has migrated to the unaccustomed Northern metropolis. The Kentuckian has changed residence and brought his individualistic traditions with him and into conflict with groups where self-reliance is not carried to such extremes. Conservative and radical, the religiously orthodox and religious liberal or agnostic, rural farm hand and urbanite, advocates of the old and of the new morality—all have been brought into contact. Newspapers, magazines, radio, motion pictures, and television have exposed to our willing or unwilling attention a medley of conflicting ideals and patterns of behavior. Myriad ways to be good or to be bad, to manage a home "properly," to worship a god "piously," to make love "decently," have attracted but also confused the people. Such confusion breeds unadjustment and, for some, crime.

American culture is materialistic. American culture is, even if decreasingly, the embodiment of materialism. The dollar is dominant if not almighty. The symbol of success is still what Veblen called conspicuous consumption. Honest dollars may be preferred to dishonest dollars, but not a few unearned dollars *have* brought prestige.

In this materialistic culture, the successful businessman is given prestige, and his success is based somewhat increasingly upon financial gain similar to that of the banker or speculator rather than upon that of the old-fashioned industrialist whose fun was in the day's work.[5] Whatever the economists may say, speculative gains look more like luck than hard work and more nearly approximate the something-for-nothing philosophy of the pickpocket.

[5] Lewis Mumford, *The Culture of Cities* (New York: Harcourt, Brace, 1938), chap. 4.

Eagerness for material gain has even put a strain on business ethics. The compelling urge to sport a fast car or a "swell dame" is not infrequently the beginning of a professional criminal career on the part of those who have failed to achieve monetary success through legal activities. *Speaking generally, the underprivileged and unsuccessful accept the same values as the successful and aspire to imitate their success.*

The pressure to participate in conspicuous consumption is strengthened by the arts of publicity and advertising. The typical televised commercial forbids the simple life. Important in all this economic activity is the element of intense competition. Our society accepts verbally at least the value of "individualism." We approve competition, though actually most attempt to escape from competition and to take advantage of their competitors. Basically this struggle is for social status and enhanced prestige. Men strive not so much for wealth as to get ahead of the Joneses. Similarly, loss of social status tends to demoralization and indirectly to crime. And some must lose social status. Competition implies that many must experience relative failure. In general, to get ahead of the Joneses means that the Joneses must fall behind relatively.

Increasingly, perhaps, material success has been derived from some monopolistic advantage. Some monopolies are criminal under our antitrust laws, but no law will ever be drafted which will cover all types of advantage.

In a later chapter we shall view the slum as a cause of crime and the slum as a product of our culture. Slum dwellers having the same urge to emulate the consumption of the successful must either do without or obtain success by illegal means. They resent their relative failure as much in the prosperous sensate society of our day as in earlier less prosperous periods. The slum collects the failures of our society. Crime enables a few of them to taste "success" for a time.

American social relations are increasingly impersonal. We shall note later that primary groups, such as the family, function to socialize and control their members and that it is within such primary groups that personality and character are developed. Men prize social status and dread —perhaps beyond all else—the disapproval of their fellows in such intimate groups. Hence it is vastly significant today that life has become increasingly impersonal and primary relations in family and neighborhood have declined in relative importance. Efforts to recreate the old neighborhood have a socializing influence but have been bucking the larger tendency toward a more personal existence.

American culture fosters restricted group loyalties. In spite of the trend just mentioned, men tend to identify themselves with limited groups, to develop loyalty to them, and to exclude, disparage, and even hate representatives of the out-group. While we shall find this restricted loyalty a major characteristic of criminal gangs, it is a value almost universally accepted and even taught as a virtue in our homes, schools, and some churches. Preference for men, not wholly because of their personal qualities but because they are natives, neighbors, Masons, or of our race, class, or creed, is widespread and not essentially different in quality from gang loyalty. The loyalty of businessmen to their class associates or of laboring men to their fellow unionists weakens their opposition to some types of antisocial or exploitative behavior by their associates, such as false advertising by some merchants or tolerance of violence or racial discrimination in some unions. Another expression of group loyalty is, of course, nationalism and considerable animosity to the alien. An extremely dangerous type is seen in racial discrimination. In chapters on the Negro and crime, on the gang, and elsewhere, we shall be concerned with this prevalent value.

Survival of frontier values. The American frontier is gone, but some regions are relatively like the frontier. Its tradition of extreme individualism and the tendency of frontiersmen to take law into their own hands persist both in some sections and in times of crisis everywhere. The assertiveness of the Kentucky mountaineer, violent resistance to integration in the Deep South, violence on both sides in connection with labor disputes, attacks upon the "reds"—these are some of the evidences of possible mob or direct-action methods among minority and even local majority groups. Even certain police activities smack somewhat of this frontier tradition, especially when there is strong popular demand for crime repression or when a fellow policeman has been attacked.

Lack of the viewpoint of social science. It cannot be said that the scientific viewpoint, which sees the criminal as a product, is yet dominant in the United States. Particularly lacking is recognition that crime is chiefly a group rather than an individual phenomenon. Still more rare is the major emphasis of this book that crime is basically implicit in the nature of our society and in many of its cultural values. The contrary view, that these criminals are self-generated and individually responsible for their behavior, dies hard. That view is written into our basic laws and even more significantly "written" into the attitudes of the average citizen. The view that the criminal is a product does not, however, preclude the use of punishment when really needed for the protection of society. It permits the use of some of our most effective constructive efforts to protect society against crime.

Faith in law without expecting or even approving obedience to all laws.

Through the Revolution which made the United States independent of England, Americans recognized values more basic than respect for law. Indeed, in that sense the United States is founded on treason. We have noted how extreme individualism, born of the struggle with the frontier, fostered at least a local disrespect for law. Yet, in spite of all this, Americans have tended to rely greatly on the penal law to solve their problem of crime. Indeed they have tended to extend the law to penalize even some personal vices, the control of which European continental tradition leaves to educational forces and to the power of group approvals and disapprovals. The extension of law into areas where there is a great demand for that which is prohibited, such as gambling or sex vice, fosters powerful rackets, and often police, political, and other agencies become corrupted. Thus, paradoxically, faith in law tends toward disrespect for law.

Moreover, it cannot be said that unqualified obedience to law is approved, except verbally, in the United States. It is an exaggeration, but only an exaggeration, to say that *most* conservative people believe that *other* people should obey *most* of the *most* important laws *most* of the time! Hence we shall see that our more intelligent criminals do not distinguish themselves from noncriminals as *law-breakers* in a society of *law-keepers*. Rather they feel the distinction lies in the types of laws broken and the boldness and frankness which characterize their behavior as compared with that of a considerable number of the general public. There is rationalization in their excuse-making, but it also has much basis in fact.

Such values as those discussed above reach the individual through his own primary groups in a more or less altered form. In the following chapter we emphasize how any unsocial values accepted or denied by prestiged groups influence the values and behavior patterns of criminals and potential criminals. Clearly there are also socially oriented values which similarly spread and tend to prevent crime. In Chapter 29 we shall consider how such socially oriented values may become the basis for a program of delinquency prevention and also how we may be led to attempt change in some criminogenic aspects of our culture.

CHAPTER 3

Pattern-Setting by Prestiged Groups

Criminal and Noncriminal Patterns

Subgroups which confer or deny status are the channels through which some of the more general values of American culture reach the potential criminal. These more or less prestiged subgroups in the United States set patterns of behavior which influence criminals and potential criminals, including our children. These include, among others, lawyers, politicians and government agents, businessmen, labor groups, physicians, clergymen, teachers, and groups active in sports. The ideals and practices of such groups influence and are influenced by law-making and law enforcement and also help determine the nature and effectiveness of agencies of social control other than the law. A society in which such groups profess and practice complete honesty and respond to wholly social motivations will have less crime than one in which attitudes, values, and especially practices are antisocially motivated or aimed toward competition and conflict. General ethical codes and traditions may somewhat channel and control competition and conflict behavior, but practices which bring status in specific groups are more effective influences on behavior than mere verbalized standards. Prestiged groups set patterns for those of lower status, and taken together, such groups define "the moral tone of a society." Obedience

32

or disobedience to law, acceptance of social or antisocial values, the playing of conflict or cooperative roles, the narrowness or breadth of group loyalties found in these prestiged groups—these characteristics are contagious in any society. May it not also be assumed that hypocrisy involved in fairly frequent verbal acceptance of social aims which are not practiced is also criminogenic? Paradoxically, equal opportunity and discrimination are values simultaneously found in our society.

Pattern-Setting by the Legal Profession

IMPORTANCE OF THE ROLE OF LAWYERS

The specialists who administer the system of justice in our courts are the organized legal profession. They are men learned in the law, but like the rest of us they have been exposed to American culture and have adopted some of its values. During their training in our more conservative colleges of law, they have been taken aside, so to speak, to live in a world of logic and abstract legal principles. One of these principles involves the contentious system of justice. Guilt or innocence is to be determined in court by the outcome of a battle of wits. Lawyers take part in this contentious system as they prosecute or defend cases. In so doing they come into contact with the human aspect of the judicial process, with the power of discretion, which introduces the human equation into the treatment of criminals, and with the pressure of individuals and interest groups striving to use the system for their own purposes. Lawyers themselves have their own personal goals, pursued in terms of the values of the real world outside the courts, as modified by the codes and practices of the organized legal profession. As men of learning applying traditional, often religiously sanctioned conceptions of justice, lawyers have gained considerable prestige. Some become judges and governors. Because criminal lawyers make contact with the criminal directly, they become important sources of behavior patterns.

INFLUENCES UPON THE PROFESSION

But the behavior of lawyers is a product as well as an influence on others. Americans evidence a curious mixture of respect and disrespect for law and for those who make and administer it. Early Americans desired to limit the powers of government, against which they had revolted, and to retain popular controls over this courts. This tended to humanize the court process whether for good or for ill. There has also developed in America a tendency to meet problems, especially the problem of crime, by making new laws to cover them and by increasing the severity of penalties. So long as concern was over the wickedness of past acts, criminal law was based on abstract legal principles, which lawyers and judges had to know. They were required to interpret the law to fit concrete cases through logical deductions from these principles. Justice consisted in equal treatment of all accused in terms of these principles, with as little attention as possible given to individual differences among them or to the conditions surrounding or preceding their acts. The symbol of justice was a woman blindfolded so that she might not see differences between litigants or between social situations.

But the courts actually deal with human beings, and lawyers and judges are human. Even the fact of guilt, if not the facts about the lives of litigants, had to be determined through human machinery. The contentious system of justice pits against each other the wits of men trained in argument as well as in law. Victory in that argument, moreover, came to depend on ability to appeal to the sentiments of the human beings involved. The introduction of the jury also humanized the courts of justice. The emotions of the market place and the fireside simply could not be completely excluded from the court drama in the interest of abstract justice. Indeterminate sentence laws required the court or some administrative body to know varying social conditions and differences between convicted persons, and to temper the punishment to those differences. The very definition of justice came to be partially altered, and concern over the future behavior of the accused increased. The bandages of the blindfolded goddess of justice had slipped a bit, without eliminating wholly the older concept of justice as equal treatment of all under similar circumstances.

We are concerned then with the effect of this system of justice on the legal profession as represented by prosecuting attorneys, attorneys for the defense, and judges. Clearly the members of the legal profession play not one but several social roles, involving different aims and standards of behavior. In their purely legal role they must have some knowledge of the law, and a few will gain distinction thereby, especially in our so-called higher courts of appeal, where the court process is most nearly isolated from the realities of social life. More immediately influential on lawyers is their role of winning cases for clients, upon which their reputation and financial success so largely depend. Straining to win cases, lawyers use or misuse their powers of argument, including their powers to bargain with prosecuting attorneys and to persuade judges and juries. The temptation to unethical behavior in this area is very strong. One often hires a lawyer for his skill in winning cases rather than for his ethics. But lawyers also play roles as members of bar associations and clubs, whose approval they cherish and to whose code of ethics they subscribe. Surely exceptional are the lawyers who play no commercial role, seeking to win esteem through material success; the legal profession, as almost all professions, has tended toward commercialization. Yet lawyers also play social roles as civic leaders. On the one hand, the behavior of lawyers thus reflects values and patterns dominant in their groups. On the other hand, they themselves set patterns and contribute to the moral tone of society.

Patterns set by those charged with the administration of justice should logically be of especial significance in determining respect for and observance of law in the United States. Here appears a considerable divergence between written codes and overt practices of some lawyers and judges. In the 1947 edition of the report of the American Bar Association's Committee on Professional Ethics, some 47 canons of professional ethics for lawyers, 36 canons of judicial ethics, and 274 opinions of the Committee are set forth. We arbitrarily select from among these canons those which seem most significant here, recasting them in popular language.

1. Lawyers should use their influence to prevent political influence in the selection of judges.
2. They should not attempt to influence a judge to give special consideration to their side of a case.
3. Their fees should be related to the value of service rendered, and no effort should be made to collect larger fees just because of the ability of a client to pay. [However, the force of this canon would seem to be greatly weakened by an opinion which states that no question of ethics will arise with reference to such fees unless they are "flagrantly excessive."]
4. It is right for a lawyer to defend a client even if he thinks him to be guilty, but it is not the lawyer's duty "to do whatever may enable him to succeed in winning his client's cause." A client is entitled to every legal remedy.
5. A prosecuting attorney should aim not at conviction but at justice.
6. It is unprofessional to curry favor with the jury.
7. In general, splitting of fees is unethical.
8. A lawyer should keep most confidences from clients sacred, but this does not include a client's announced intention to commit a crime.
9. A lawyer should not receive outside compensation without consent of his client.
10. A lawyer should not induce a witness to suppress the truth.

Similarly, the following canons are included among those intended to guide the conduct of judges.

1. They should not use their prestige to promote their candidacy for office.
2. They should make their own conduct exemplary.
3. They should appoint on merit only.

4. They should not enter business relations inconsistent with their impartiality in judging cases.
5. They should avoid political activities.
6. They should not accept presents from litigants or lawyers.
7. Trials should be dignified, and photographs should not be permitted in court.
8. The administering of oaths should be dignified.

The above codes are concerned with the role the lawyer plays in court and in his relations with judges, clients, other lawyers, and the public. The influence of personal ambition and politics is to be excluded from the halls of justice. But the contentious system of justice, with its temptations to unethical behavior, is accepted in the code itself. The commercialization of the legal profession, though discouraged, is also accepted. On the whole, the lawyer may charge what the traffic will bear for his services. Powerful interest groups can sometimes pay a great deal, while poor litigants can pay but little.

It is impossible to measure statistically the observance or nonobservance of these canons, although their very existence may have some significance. The record of disbarment proceedings shows that some of them are not mere verbalizations, and probably most of them are sincerely subscribed to as ideals by the majority of the legal profession. Nevertheless, it is notorious that some are widely violated and that every one of them has been violated by not a few criminal lawyers and judges. The exigencies of our contentious system of justice daily put a strain upon most of them. It may be true that few lawyers could become financially successful if they literally obeyed rules which hinder their success in winning cases.

The most effective deterrent against unethical conduct within the legal profession, as elsewhere, is presumably the desire for status among one's own associates in local or wider bar association and in the more or less extended social circle within which the lawyer lives. Apparently, merely knowing the codes accomplishes little: whatever their interest in ethical principles, the primary concern of law students is to pass the bar examinations. In 1951 only 39 of 87 law schools replying to a survey made by a committee of the Association of American Law Schools were offering separate courses in legal ethics.[1] Dean Harno has argued [2] that the goal of the codes is to be achieved rather by efforts to develop the personal character of lawyers. That character comes not from knowing law or memorizing the above not wholly socialized codes. Rather it comes from

[1] Cf. Albert J. Harno, *Legal Education in the United States* (San Francisco: Hancroft-Whitney, 1953), p. 195.
[2] *Ibid.*, p. 155.

taking stands on great social issues of the day, as the American Bar Association's Committee on Prelegal Education urges. Social studies lead to a sense of professional responsibility. To interest law students in social science courses suggests, however, that knowledge of their subject matter be tested in the bar examinations. Those examinations include questions on legal ethics but require little knowledge of modern society.[3]

One may give full credit to great altruistic lawyers. One may hold that there are far more honest than dishonest lawyers. Yet there are enough cases of violations of the code of the lawyer that each interest group may well be permitted to get its share out of the general grab bag. When interest groups do favors for individual Congressmen or others, there is always the assumption that there will be something in return. The opportunity and temptation to act in some private interest has greatly increased. Graham emphasizes the general lack of action by fellow Congressmen when some of these abuses have been exposed.[4] He points out that the public is more impressed with the gift of one mink coat than with a Congressman's participation in profits or his lucrative employment by a business concern after his retirement from political life.[5]

Senator Douglas of Illinois and others have listed the following points of strain on political morality: (1) the letting of huge contracts to private concerns; (2) the collection of large taxes; (3) the granting of loans by public agencies; (4) the fixing of prices or other rates; (5) the selection of those who may engage in a particular industry; (6) the allocation of raw materials to concerns; and (7) the payment of subsidies, such as those which maintain the price of silver or permit ships to operate at high costs and still make profits.[6] Congressmen and administrators engaged in such activities are apt to find their loyalties shifting perhaps unconsciously from the communities they represent or the country as a whole to individuals and groups who in one way or another do them favors. Outside influences take many forms, including gifts and entertainment in Washington or state capitals, provision of lucrative employment opportunities, opportunities to make money in side lines while serving as representatives of the public, and the sale of influence by legislators to interested parties.

[3] According to press accounts, a study sponsored by the Missouri bar and based on interviews with about 3,000 laymen and lawyers found that people who have never employed a lawyer hold the legal profession in higher esteem than those who have, and that there is a "shocking lack of confidence" among the citizenry on the possibility of getting a fair trial in American courts. ["The Lawyers' Shrinking Image," *New York Herald Tribune* (July 27, 1963), p. 10.]

[4] Cf. George A. Graham, *Morality in American Politics* (New York: Random House, 1952). Also Paul H. Douglas, *Ethics in Government* (Cambridge, Mass.: Harvard University Press, 1952).

[5] Graham, *op. cit.*, p. 93.

[6] Douglas, *op. cit.*, pp. 22–23.

Douglas also recounts (8) the demoralizing influence of the need to get funds in order to run for office and (9) temptations connected with the conduct of Congressional investigations. Graham adds (10) the grave danger of misuse of power in the cold war's search for Communists and subversives, which may be turned to political advantage at the cost of honesty and decency.

The above characterization of unethical behavior patterns furnished by some of our public servants may seem to exaggerate their prevalence. But such practices need not be universal or even dominant to affect seriously the behavior of the general citizenry and of its potentially criminal elements.

Codes and Practices of Business Groups

For a century or more a major force shaping the ethical codes of American culture has been the pressures arising from the exigencies of successful commercial activities. Even before the transition of our society from an agrarian to an urban-industrial one, frontier land speculation, Civil War profiteering, and financial manipulations related to westward railroad construction produced numerous quickly made fortunes and awakened in the minds of many dreams of similar achievement. In time, as increasing numbers of individuals successfully found their livelihoods in the secondary, secularized marketplace of town and city rather than in essentially agrarian pursuits, broad gaps appeared between the tenets of the Judaeo-Christian ethic and those appropriate to the impersonal world of business. The homely virtues of candor, honesty, pride of workmanship, concern for communal welfare—all functional in sacred societies—gave way to the shrewd, opportunistic ruthlessness by which means fortunes were made. Although the tide of nineteenth-century economic buccaneering had considerably receded by the mid-twentieth century, it reshaped the terrain of our social conscience by making the accumulation of wealth a basic yardstick of individual worth and by producing a rationale appropriate to such accumulation. Moreover, the "reach of the business spirit," as Max Lerner has put it, extends to every area of American culture and has given a "synthetic cohesion to the far-flung diversity of American life." [7] It makes a difference, therefore, for law-making and law-breaking whether business is honest or dishonest.

Organized businessmen are not inclined to be specific in defining the

[7] Max Lerner, *America as a Civilization,* I (New York: Simon and Schuster, 1957), pp. 311, 312.

right ways to conduct business. They realize the need for better public relations, find concern for the public welfare often good for business, and hold that in large measure the public interest and long-term business interests coincide. But many specific ethical questions remain unanswered. A few of these include the following: How truthful should advertisers and sellers feel obligated to be in telling of the merits of their goods, and should they tell the whole truth about their products? What shall be done about temptations to manipulate finance in the interest of insiders? Must a merchant tell of the defects of his goods or indicate the merits of competing brands? How far, in general, is it legitimate to exploit the ignorance of buyers or the weaknesses of labor in bargaining? All in all, the patterns set by business groups are confused, to say the least. The "free" in free enterprise has social implications, but the "enterprise" tends to put a strain on the rules of the game which business groups subscribe to and, in the form of the search for advantage or even monopoly, to become far from "free." Seeing greed, rather than service, exemplified in the behavior of some businessmen, the potential criminal may rationalize his own unlawful behavior as not essentially different.

Codes and Practices of Labor Groups

Labor unions and their opposite numbers, the employers' associations, are primarily fighting organizations. The unions' codes are primarily codes of fair dealing with one another, which are threatened when in jurisdictional disputes conflict between skilled and unskilled trades or other intense competition puts a strain upon them. The type and intensity of the combat with employers varies greatly: laws have set limits to the weapons which shall be legal; the realization of common interests between labor and capital has increased; various types of agreements have been entered into to preserve at least temporary peace.[8] But the general pattern set by unions and employers' associations alike is one of often serious combat, in which each side has tended to use whatever weapons proved most effective. Extremely friendly, cooperative, and even selfless patterns have characterized internal relations among the membership of certain unions; competitive, criminalistic activities have predominated in their relations with employers. Our most serious labor disputes have exemplified on both sides not only unethical behavior but also violence and considerable disregard for the interest of the general public. Even peaceful arrangements with

[8] Frederick H. Harbison and John R. Coleman, *Goals and Strategy in Collective Bargaining* (New York: Harper & Brothers, 1951).

employers have occasionally taken the form of combination of both sides to maintain monopolistic advantages contrary to the public interest. Recognition of common interests in production has not necessarily implied recognition of common obligation not to exploit society generally.

And yet organized labor has increasingly recognized its wider social obligations, sometimes as a sort of trust, sometimes through the realization of the importance of favorable public relations for success in its battle with employers.[9] The support of the public has been necessary if labor was successfully to push its lobbying for favorable legislation. This broadened social consciousness, as well as government's recognition that labor must have a voice in policy-making, has led to pronouncements and practices quite outside of labor's role as a fighting organization. Thus labor has held that collective bargaining has a social justification and that it "humanizes" employer-employee relations. With some justification it has been held that organized labor ". . . has been interested to promote the welfare of all the people of the United States. And in later years it has broadened its activities in behalf of the peoples of the world" [10] and co-operated increasingly with the International Labor Office and even with foreign groups with somewhat socialistic programs.[11] The American labor movement has itself supported the so-called free enterprise system but has had somewhat to avoid the narrower implications of those words in its relations with organizations abroad. American labor has stood for the dignity of human life and for the welfare state, has accepted both competitive enterprise and government interference, and has held that economic and political democracy are inseparable.[12] Thus as a partial counter for organized labor's exemplification of intense competition and strain in using extreme combat measures, a pattern of concern for the general welfare has also been evident. Yet the general public, and hence most of the potentially criminal element, apparently are more impressed with the more unsocially oriented functions of the labor union. Moreover, a "seamier side of unionism" [13] has certainly appeared in its part in the two-sided use of violence, in occasional combinations against the public interest, in the

[9] Cf. Gordon H. Cole, "The Union's Public Relations," in J. B. S. Hardman and Maurice F. Neufeld, eds., *The House of Labor* (New York: Prentice-Hall, 1951), pp. 205–09.

[10] Jacob B. S. Hardman and Maurice F. Neufeld, *The House of Labor* (New York: Prentice-Hall, 1951).

[11] Cf. David Dubinsky, "World Labor's New Weapon," *Foreign Affairs* (April, 1950), pp. 7–10.

[12] *Ibid.,* p. 7.

[13] Cf. Jack Barbash, *Labor Unions in Action* (New York: Harper & Brothers, 1948), pp. 223–24.

involvement of unionism in very serious racketeering, and in the willingness of some labor leaders, like some employers, to exploit, not only their opponents, but the general public and even their own followers. Extremely significant in this connection is Barbash's defense that this seamier side of unionism "reflects the seaminess of the total society," for such is a major contention of the present chapter. Particularly important has been labor racketeering, which we discuss in a later chapter. In defending the social role of labor organizations, leaders stress that the days of "skull-and-knuckle" alley rules in labor conflict are largely gone and that the labor movement is antiracketeering as well as anti-Communist.

That both labor crime and exploitative behavior falling short of crime are one of the antisocial but influential patterns of our society is logical to believe. Yet one wonders on the one hand whether "featherbedding" is legitimate tactics or an example of exploitation of employers and the public by labor unions. On the other hand, what responsibility do employers have for the suffering and unemployment caused by labor-saving automation?

Codes and Practices in Sports

It is a nice question whether Americans are more money-minded or sports-minded, though commercialization of sports includes both interests. Enjoyment of sports generally requires reasonable confidence that the rules of the game will be observed. Good sportsmanship in the broadest sense of the word has been widely considered one of the major constructive values characterizing Americans. Prominent athletes are among the principal heroes worshipped by young America, and a large section of older America follows their careers and supports the home team with equal zest and loyalty. Participation in sports is acclaimed not only as a wholesome enjoyment but also as a source of moral education and as a substitute for the use of spare time in more "irresponsible" or less socially structured ways. Then enjoyment of good fellowship with teammates and their supporters, and even at times with competitors, is considered an important source of socialization.

For these very reasons, which are at least partly sound, decline in the social value of "good sportsmanship," the intrusion into sports of dubious practices, and sometimes even their acceptance and advocacy, weaken an important source of socially oriented patterns of behavior. Moreover, since the field of sports is pre-eminently the domain of youth, its moral values are effective with youth. In America all "regular guys" are emotionally absorbed in sports.

The two most basic influences in sports significant to our discussion have been the intensity of the desire to win games or have them won and the tendency of amateur as well as professional sports to become commercialized or to be used for momentary gain by others than the actual competitors. Passionate eagerness for victory and powerful if less passionate eagerness to profit financially tend to submerge the desire for nice conformity to rules or, on occasion, to laws. Allison Danzig, writing in the *New York Times*,[14] recounts both favorable and unfavorable trends in the practice of good sportsmanship. He concludes that "a winning team is still held more important than ethics." Similarly, the desire to make money out of sports has not only motivated the gambling racketeer and the gambler himself, but also not a few coaches, players, spectators, alumni, and— perhaps most significantly of all—educational leaders in some of our major high schools and colleges. Surely it is significant if even a part of our seats of learning compromise with moral principles even in the interest of their supposedly primary goals of education and citizenship training. Richard I. Miller begins his book, *The Truth About Big-Time Football*,[15] by saying that "big-time football is big business." He holds that it has been the practice of most large universities in some degree to cheat on the grades of athletes in order to attract them or keep them on their team. Not a few athletes have therefore held that they are only following a pattern set them by the universities if they also cheat on their examinations. Scandals at West Point some years ago provided evidence of this particular evil, and not everyone blamed the athletes or their coaches. Actual bribery of basketball players was perhaps at its worst in 1951, and Miller holds that approximations to such bribery were to be found in football. In such cases players were not always bribed to cause their team actually to lose, but sometimes only to keep the score below the margin upon which betting odds had been placed, so that organized gamblers might reap profits. Players could thus be dishonest and yet feel they were still loyal to their college and associates. Intensity of the desire to win has also tended to increase the roughness of games. Much slugging is concealed, and the line between legitimate hard play and illegitimate violence has been difficult to define and more difficult to enforce. The public seems to enjoy hard-hitting practices, and they help win games. In scouting, all sorts of pressure have been exerted to induce star high school players to enroll at some university or college. Some athletic

[14] March 22, 23, and 24, 1954.
[15] New York: William Sloane Associates, 1953.

scholarships have been but a thin disguise for the demand for athletes rather than for students. Not least among the means through which superior athletes have been retained has been the existence of "snap" courses sometimes deliberately made easy in their interest. Courses in physical education itself have naturally been most suspect, but the lowering of standards has not been confined to these. Students have acquired "not transferable" tickets and reaped minor illegitimate profits from extensive ticket-scalping.

Attempting to assess the character-building influence of competitive sports, Miller presents a mixed picture. On the one hand, teamwork, good sportsmanship, varying with the character of the coach employed, self-control, and increased if still incomplete racial tolerance are listed as morally valuable. On the other hand, the teaching of deception is thought to encourage fraud.

Miller and others have traced the demoralization of sports to several sources. Coaches, knowing that their jobs and their outside income depend on winning games, have at least secretly opposed the movement to de-emphasize sports. Organized and unorganized alumni have seemingly been more concerned over winning teams than over education or ethics, and they remain the most difficult group to control. Universities have at times found legislators or private donors (who reflect public attitudes) more ready to provide money if the football team has been successful. Behind the scenes the opinion of a not infrequently wildly sports-minded public has probably been the most basic influence. From this public the tendency to put a successful sports program first, or almost first, has seeped down the line through alumni, merchants, who find a winning team profitable, fraternities, student bodies, spectators, coaches, and players. Gamblers and legitimate business interests have made the most of the opportunity.

The Process of Behavior-Patterning

In this chapter we have found tendencies toward both uncooperative and criminal behavior rooted largely in the nature of certain goals and values accepted by large elements among both the technically criminal and the technically noncriminal sections of the population. Both have eagerly sought social status and followed patterns of behavior which would bring them approval in their several primary groups. Both have sought success largely through competitive striving, whether in economic, social, recreational, or moral endeavor. To both, competition itself has been a generally approved value, though among both are found efforts to avoid competition through seeking special advantages over others. This approved value, competition, has of necessity implied relative failure for large numbers of competitors. When success and status have not been obtainable in legal ways, there has been a tendency to seek success through illegal activities. Criminals and noncriminals both have developed all sorts of in-group prejudices and preferences through their association in primary groups, which have most immediately patterned the behavior of their members. These primary groups have been influenced strongly by values characteristic of the larger society and by patterns set by prestiged subgroups. *While criminal acts are by definition antisocial, criminals have not been alone in having antisocial attitudes* and have not been wholly antisocial in all their social relations.

We have suggested that the influence of prestiged groups has even tended to compromise the generally socializing effects of the family, church, school, and community, as they also have sought self-preferment and competitive success. Moreover, we have noted, among many significant trends in our society, the decline of the primary-group socializing character-building roles of the family and intimate neighborhood, and their partial replacement by impersonal, less intimate, and hence less socializing social relationships or by gangs or other groups in conflict with society. Such a process of impersonalization and of splintering into subgroups, each with its limiting social boundaries, has enhanced the pattern-setting influence of prestiged groups.[16]

The not wholly justified view that "everybody's doing it" is effective, even if not quite everybody is doing it. Conscious of this prevalence, both the criminal and the noncriminal exploiter evaluates himself less adversely because he sees himself in a goodly company of fellow exploiters.

It has not been implied that all men are dominantly exploiters of their fellow men. The social nature of man is at least as evident as the unsocial. But even our social motivations and "good deeds" are often restricted to narrow in-groups or directed to publicized individual cases, or categories of cases, which arouse our sympathies. Among the drivers of automobiles, courtesy is no doubt more evident than lack of concern for the life and welfare of the other fellow partly because "the life you save may be your own."

The sum total of the effects of the pattern-setting roles of our various

---

[16] Compare the analysis of this process of out-group reference in Robert K. Merton and Alice S. Kitt, "Contributions to the Theory of Reference-Group Behavior," in G. E. Swanson, Theodore M. Newcomb, and Eugene L. Hartley, eds., *Readings in Social Psychology,* rev. ed. (New York: Henry Holt, 1952), pp. 430–44.

subgroups in the United States creates what we vaguely call the "general moral tone" of our society. It results from a complex of interacting group relations. In its dynamic aspects it constitutes the social process or processes of our day. The general implication of this chapter is that if people generally grow more unsocial, suspicious, and exploitative of one another, those forms of injury and exploitation defined as crimes should logically increase. On the other hand, the spread of "courtesy" in the broadest sense of the word, based on realization of human interdependence, should furnish the most basic protection against crime. Undoubtedly prestiged groups spread both types of patterns. At the end of this book we consider possible changes in American values which might lead to changes in the nature of patterns set by our prestiged groups.

CHAPTER 4

Criminal Statistics

A basic process in modern scientific procedure is that of *quantification:* counting, measuring, and collating the phenomena under study. Without this process research efforts would consist of little more than impressionistic observation and highly imprecise experiment, both of which today's scientists increasingly eschew.[1]

If we would explain scientifically that part of social phenomena regarded as *crimes,* we must be able to perform the elementary step of counting crimes in order to relate them to time, place, and circumstance. To what extent does the magnitude of crime change in a day, a year, a decade? What is the distribution of crimes in cities, states, regions? Within which segments of the social structure do particular kinds of crime cluster? We must also know and count the characteristics of criminals of all types in order to know with what personal traits crime is associated. The available official criminal statistics, unfortunately, are of such dubious significance as to make this elementary step extremely hazardous to the unwary.

Unreliability of Criminal Statistics

There are several reasons for the unreliability of criminal statistics in the United States.

[1] The most notable exception to this in the behavioral sciences is probably found in psychiatry, where impressionistic operations are still acceptable.

Diversity of definitions. Despite their common ancestry the 52 criminal law jurisdictions in the United States (including those of the federal government and of the District of Columbia) embrace 52 somewhat differing sets of definitions of crimes—in addition to the fact that these jurisdictions differ as well in the *number* of crimes they define. Even within the eight ancient common law felonies inherited from English jurisprudence— murder, manslaughter, rape, sodomy, burglary, robbery, larceny, and arson—there exist sufficient differences so that such a felony committed in one state may not be quite the same kind of act bearing the same label in another state. Indiana, for example, defines first-degree burglary as "breaking and entering into any dwelling with intent to commit any felony or to do any act of violence or injury to any human being." The neighboring state of Illinois, however, not recognizing *degrees* of burglary, defines this crime as "wilfully and maliciously and forcibly breaking and entering, or wilfully and maliciously, without force (the doors or windows being open), entering into any dwelling, shop, warehouse, railroad car, or other building, with intent to commit murder, robbery, rape, mayhem, or other felony or larceny." Statistically, housebreakings in Indiana are the same kinds of acts as stealing from freight cars in Illinois!

Diversity of sources. Criminal statistics are collected by several thousand police departments, county sheriffs, state police units, magistrates', criminal, and juvenile courts, correctional institutions and agencies, local, state, and federal regulative bodies, federal police agencies, and other groups. Only some of these statistics ever appear in published form usable for research purposes, but those which do appear are collected with greatly differing degrees of efficiency, allowance for which can seldom be made by those using them.

Much crime is undiscovered. For a crime to become a statistic it must be discovered by someone and reported to some statistic-collecting body. Some crimes by their very nature are highly noticeable, for they can only occur in the immediate presence of victims or other observers: armed robbery, forcible rape, rioting, aggravated assault. Other crimes, typically committed by stealth, are much less noticeable: pocketpicking, evading taxes, burglary, selling adulterated foodstuffs, poaching. *All* crimes are known only to the Great Recorder; mortals can become aware only of a *portion* of this total.

Much crime is not reported, even though discovered. Armed robbery of floating crap games, a crime highly profitable to its practitioners and highly noticeable to its victims, tends not to be officially reported because such games are illegal in most places. Other crimes entail varying degrees of likelihood of being reported, depending upon the circumstances in which they occur. Among the least reportable would be such acts as stealing from prostitutes' customers, rapes committed by the victims' boy friends, badger games, shoplifting by "respectable" women, thefts and assaults within kin groups, and fish and game law violations by farmers.

Not all reported crime is properly recorded by the police. The Chicago police department reported that there were 69,122 major crimes known to have occurred in the city in 1959. The corresponding number reported in 1960 was an incredible 129,742—an increase of nearly 83 per cent! But instead of indicating a crime wave, the 1960 figures resulted from improved statistical procedures made at the instigation of the city's new police superintendent, Orlando W. Wilson.

If *all* crimes were discovered and *all* discovered crimes were reported and *all* reported crimes were verified, recorded, and presented as statistics within homogeneous categories, then and only then would the extent, kinds, distribution, and trends in crime be known. This ideal state of affairs does not, of course, exist, and as long as it does not, our statistical images of crime are distortions of reality. But if we are to make any use at all of official crime statistics, we are obligated to assume that the distortions are not great enough to render the image meaningless—that something akin to what the statistics show to be happening is actually happening.

Kinds and Sources of Criminal Statistics

It is convenient to think of three ascending ranks of public agencies from which official criminal data come, with the first rank consisting of those closest in procedural time to actual offenses (the police), the second the next closest (the courts), and the third the furthest removed (correctional agencies).

POLICE STATISTICS

Citizen John Smith discovers one morning that his car's four hubcaps have been stolen. He reports his loss to the police, who are now aware of one more larceny in their precinct. Added to the other crimes about which the police have learned from complaining citizens, from their own observations, and from other sources, a set of statistics of *crimes known to the police* accumulates in their files. No information on the perpetrators of the crimes is necessarily involved. Figures on crimes known to the police constitute our basic data on the kinds, extent, and distribution of crime in our communities and rural areas. If the police make one or more *arrests* in connection with the hubcap theft, the record of these, added to those already recorded in connection with other offenses, constitutes a second kind of police statistic, but it should be noted that this statistic is procedurally a step removed from crimes known. Arrests correspond only imperfectly in kind and magnitude to "crimes known" data and are not as numerous. The age, race, and sex of arrested persons are also usually recorded by the police and become a part of police statistics.

There are more than 8,000 law-enforcement agencies in the United States collecting data of the above kinds. While interested individuals might gain a spotty and piecemeal picture of criminal and police activity by obtaining annual reports from the police agencies which publish them, the task of collecting comparable data from those remaining would be monumentally difficult. Fortunately, this task is being performed by the Federal Bureau of Investigation (FBI) of the Department of Justice. Following pioneer statistics-collecting efforts of the International Association of Chiefs of Police, the Bureau took over in 1930 the responsibility of receiving, tabulating, and publishing reports submitted by voluntarily cooperating police agencies. Its *Uniform Crime Reports* [2] for 1962 included statistics of crimes known to the police received from nearly 8,000 law-enforcement agencies representing 94 per cent of the United States population. Besides crimes known, *Uniform Crime Reports* includes arrest data, facts about police forces, detailed breakdowns of certain offenses, and other information. The discrepancy between crimes known to have occurred and arrests made in connection with them is apparent from the fact that only 26 per cent of the 1,359,820 known offenses occurring in 1,655 cities in 1962 were "cleared by arrest" (that is, by nabbing promising suspects). [3] The rates of clearance, however, vary considerably by types of offense, as can be seen by the following percentages: murder and non-negligent manslaughter, 93; forcible rape, 72; robbery, 40; aggravated assault, 77; burglary, 28; larceny, 20; auto theft, 27. The significance of arrest statistics as indices of crime trends will depend partly upon the honesty and efficiency of the police and upon their policy in arresting or not arresting in certain types of cases. No one wants all the laws enforced.

The FBI warns readers of its reports that it does not guarantee the

[2] "Uniform" alludes to the fact that crimes are uniformly defined for reporting purposes by the agencies involved, in accordance with an FBI handbook used by the cooperating bodies.

[3] U. S. Department of Justice, *Uniform Crime Reports: 1962* (Washington, D. C.: 1963), p. 87.

accuracy of its data and that comparisons of crime rates between cities without first allowing for socio-economic differences can be misleading. Newspaper treatment of the FBI's releases seldom include these warnings or give other reasons why the data should be interpreted with caution. Consequently, intercity and temporal comparisons made in editorials commenting critically on crime rate differences between neighboring cities may result in unfair criticism of local police departments.

COURT STATISTICS

Judicial or court statistics are concerned with the number of offenses prosecuted, the number convicted and the method of procedure followed in determining guilt, the number not convicted and the point in the procedural process at which these cases are eliminated and under whose responsibility. Court statistics also account for the number found guilty and the type of sentence imposed upon these persons.[4]

While it is still possible to know in a few states, by examining their Attorneys General reports or similar sources, how many criminals have been charged by the courts and what have been the results of trials, it is not possible to know this for the entire nation. Statistics of this sort were collected and published annually for the years 1932 through 1945 by the United States Bureau of the Census, but the effort was abandoned on the grounds of insufficient demand for them. (Data on the activities of federal courts, however, are published annually by the Administrative Office of the United States Courts.)

Prosecuting attorneys largely determine what cases shall be brought to trial, as well as what charge shall be lodged against those accused. The most honest prosecutor will not and indeed cannot press all charges. The policies of state's attorneys, their efficiency, the efficiency of judges and juries—all vary among counties. They vary also in the same counties with changes in social conditions—including public opinion—and in personnel. All these factors affect the value for comparative purposes or as indications of trends of statistics of court disposition of cases.

Beginning in 1927 the United States Children's Bureau began publishing juvenile court statistics derived from some 200 courts. Since 1956 the reports have been estimates based on a national sample of 502 juvenile courts. A further refinement was made in 1957, when traffic cases handled by juvenile courts were no longer lumped with general cases but were

[4] U. S. Bureau of the Census, *Judicial Criminal Statistics, 1935* (Washington, D. C.: 1937), p. 2.

reported separately, in recognition of the fact that most traffic offenses do not involve what is usually connoted by the term "juvenile delinquency." Like the FBI, the Children's Bureau warns that its figures can be misleading when used to make comparisons between communities, in view of differences in local attitudes toward delinquency. Much discretion in funneling children into juvenile courts rests with parents, teachers, social agencies, police, and court intake officers. In communities where the juvenile court is viewed as "legitimately" dealing only with violations of law, its business will tend to be limited to such cases; where the court is valued in addition as a "helping" agency, children presenting other kinds of difficulties will bulk larger on court rosters.

In Figure 1 is reproduced a trend curve on delinquency in the United States since 1940. Interpretation of the rise in the curve since 1948 is still being debated. One opinion, voiced by law-enforcement officials, social workers, some members of Congress, and others, holds that the apparent increase not only is real but that increasingly serious offenses characterize juvenile misdeeds. Another opinion, held mainly by scholars wary of the duplicity of statistics, is that the apparent increase partly reflects a post-World War II step-up in juvenile court activities and that property thefts and vandalism, rather than felonious crimes against the person, still comprise most of the court cases. In the course of a critical evaluation of juvenile court statistics, Professor Herbert A. Bloch made the following comment, with which we concur: [5]

. . . a vast amount of our data concerning delinquency is not so much a measurement of what transpires on the national scene concerning the misbehavior of the young, *but rather a description of the volume of traffic through selected children's courts.* The data, therefore, represents perhaps, the zeal and conscientiousness, and especially the working philosophy, of a given court, rather than an accurate portrayal of the amount of delinquency in the area in which the court functions.

CORRECTIONAL STATISTICS

In the United States adult felons are, with few exceptions, incarcerated in state-operated institutions; counties and municipalities generally operate the facilities for lesser offenders. From the latter, statistics of prisoners are rarely available in usable form; we quite literally have no dependable figures—or even dependable estimates—on the number of county and municipal prisoners serving sentences throughout the country.

[5] Herbert A. Bloch, "Juvenile Delinquency: Myth or Threat," *Journal of Criminal Law, Criminology and Police Science,* **49** (Nov.–Dec. 1958), p. 305. Italics are his.

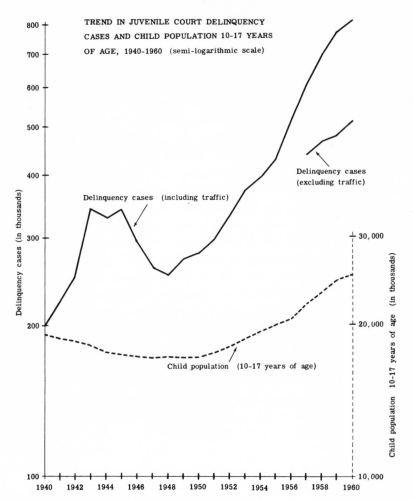

FIGURE 1　Trend in juvenile court delinquency cases and child population 10–17 years of age, 1940–1960 (semi-logarithmic scale). *Source:* U.S. Children's Bureau: *Juvenile Court Statistics: 1960.*

With respect to felony prisoners the statistical picture is considerably better. Formerly collected by the Bureau of the Census, state prisoner data have been collected and published by the Bureau of Prisons since 1950 as *National Prisoner Statistics.* The August, 1962, report showed that 196,633 prisoners were present in state institutions on December 31, 1961, of whom only 7,000 were women. Federal felony prisoners numbered 23,696, including 890 women. During the same year 93,590 prisoners were received from the courts, 13,517 of whom went to federal institutions.

The number of offenders commited to prison will vary with the wide differences in the disposition of cases in different jurisdictions. Between two-thirds and three-quarters of Rhode Island's convicted felons annually are placed on probation instead of being incarcerated, giving the state the second lowest commitment rate in the country, after New Hampshire.[6] In Pennsylvania and Massachusetts many felony prisoners serve their sentences in county institutions and hence are not counted in the Bureau of Prison statistics. Besides weaknesses of these kinds, institutional statistics have all the weakness of statistics collected at earlier stages of contact with the criminal, for the effects of error are cumulative. On the other hand, institutional figures are much more accurate counts than those of the police or courts, where recording mistakes will not come dramatically to light in the manner possible when prisoners are miscounted. Thus our most accurate statistics are our least significant for measuring crime, and those which would be the most significant, were they accurate, are the least reliable.

By far the most reliable way to know the amount and trend of crime is by making intensive local studies. If such studies are fortunate enough to reveal no significant changes in policies governing procedures at the various stages, and if the personnel involved are reasonably honest and efficient, one may be able to estimate quite accurately crime trends in that particular community. Short and Nye suggest that, instead of relying at all on published statistics to measure crime, data could be obtained directly by interviews with appropriate segments of the population, using systematic sampling techniques.[7] But comparisons still could not be made between a community in which this technique was used and others, unless equally careful procedures were used elsewhere and unless the significant socioeconomic factors were allowed for.

PROCEDURAL ATTRITION

The risks involved in using statistics obtained from levels above that of the police for purposes of measuring crime were shown two decades ago by C. C. Van Vechten, who measured criminal case mortality in moving through seven levels of procedure, from *crimes known* to *prisoners received*. Table 1 is an abridgment of his data pertaining to attrition in the District of Columbia, Minnesota, and the United States. Besides the striking uniformity in attrition rates among jurisdictions, the fragment of

---

[6] Federal Bureau of Prisons, *National Prisoner Statistics,* No. 24 (July 1960), Table 3A.

[7] James F. Short and F. Ivan Nye, "Reported Behavior as a Criterion of Deviant Behavior," *Social Problems,* 5 (Winter, 1957), pp. 207– 13.

persons charged who end up as prisoners shows not only the uselessness for measurement purposes of prisoner data but also demonstrates that prisoners constitute a poor sample of persons who become embroiled with the law on criminal charges.

Table 1   CRIMINAL CASE MORTALITY IN PART I
OFFENSES, 1939

	Dist. of Columbia		Minnesota		United States	
Procedural Level	Number	% of Crimes Known	Number	% of Crimes Known	Number (thousands)	% of Crimes Known
Crimes known	14,029	100.0	20,487	100.0	2,000	100.0
Offenses cleared	5,011	35.7	7,134	34.8	500	25.0
Persons charged	2,671	19.0	——	——	400	20.0
Judicial prosecutions	1,046	7.5	1,448	7.1	140	7.0
Convictions	828	5.9	1,318	6.4	110	5.5
Sentenced to prison	524	3.7	637	3.1	70	3.5
Prisoners from courts	506	3.6	701	3.4	75	3.8

Abridged from C. C. Van Vechten, "Differential Criminal Case Mortality in Selected Jurisdictions," *American Sociological Review,* 7 (December 1942), pp. 833–39.

Facts about arrested, tried, convicted, and imprisoned persons, as distinguished from facts about crime, are theoretically attainable at various stages. In practice, only at the point in the judicial process where *presentence investigations* are ordered on convicted persons [8] is information in quantity and detail first collected. Similar facts are also gathered by prison classification boards and sometimes by parole boards. Data at the judicial and correctional stages suffer, however, from lack of uniformity and from the fact that they are often derived from unverified statements of the individuals involved. The conclusions of studies based wholly or in part upon such data stand on shaky ground.

Some years ago the National Conference of Commissioners on Uniform State Laws drafted a Uniform Statistics Act, which has up to now been adopted only by California. This Act provides for the centralized collecting, within each state, of criminal statistics. The State Departments of Correction in New York and Massachusetts collect data on the arrest and disposition of prosecuted persons; a similar function is performed by Minnesota's Bureau of Criminal Apprehension, which in addition obtains reports on certain felonies from law-enforcement agencies in the state.[9]

[8] Such investigations are nearly always limited to felony cases and then only in courts served by probation officers. .

[9] Ronald H. Beattie, "Criminal Statistics in the United States—1960," *Journal of Criminal Law, Criminology and Police Science,* 51 (May–June 1960), p. 61. This article contains an excellent critical review of the present state of criminal statistics.

The Crime Trend in the United States

It is unlikely that accurate estimates of the trend of crime in the United States can be made in view of the unreliability of criminal statistics. Such estimates must be made on the following assumptions: (1) that all significant factors affecting the recording of crime statistics remain reasonably constant through a period of time; (2) that these factors are similar in nature throughout the country; (3) that the various sources of inaccuracy somehow cancel out when one deals with large areas and numbers; and (4) that the inclusion of the large numbers and kinds of crime not covered by the statistics (including white-collar crimes) would not significantly alter the apparent trend. The truth of any of these assumptions is open to question. The following discussion necessarily refers to the *apparent* trend of the more serious types of predatory crime, since data on lesser offenses over wide areas is practically non-existent.

National crime figures of reasonable scope were unavailable prior to 1931, when FBI statistics became available; trend estimates before then were based on scattered data from a small number of jurisdictions. Discussing trends in the first quarter of the present century, Gehlke and Sutherland concluded that, measured by arrest data, crime underwent a gradual increase from 1900 to 1925, broken by a partial downturn in the period 1917–1920. Despite popular concern over the alleged criminogenic influence of immigration and prohibition, they found no evidence of "crime waves" during the quarter-century studied by them.[10] If one attempts to carry the Gehlke-Sutherland study forward from 1926 to 1931, when the FBI statistics became available, the best data are certain Massachusetts arrest figures, the only long-time series of its kind. Between 1926 and 1931 these figures show an irregular increase in the index of total crime and a great increase in the robbery index in 1931, which was 65 per cent higher than that of 1926.

Our knowledge of crime trends since 1931 is based on FBI statistics on seven offenses: murder, forcible rape, robbery, aggravated assault, burglary, larceny over $50, and auto theft.[11] It is assumed that these seven constitute an index to changes in magnitude of the many other crimes not reported on by the FBI. With the exception of murder and non-negligent

[10] *Recent Social Trends in the United States,* 1 vol. ed. (New York: McGraw-Hill, 1933), pp. 1126–28.

[11] Prior to the report covering 1958, *Uniform Crime Reports* included figures on non-negligent manslaughter; larceny included thefts of $50 and under; rape included statutory rape. Because of these changes, rates for 1958 and later are not comparable to those for earlier years.

manslaughter, neither of which showed any consistent upward trend, per capita rates for the index crimes increased irregularly between 1932 and 1957. Since the FBI data subsequent to 1957 constitutes virtually a new series, Table 2 is given to show the reported trends for 1958–1962. Note that the total crime rate rose in that period from 896.9 to 1,102.3 per 100,000 population, most of it accounted for by the increases in burglary and larceny.

Table 2   ESTIMATED CRIME RATES PER 100,000
POPULATION, 1958–1962

	1962	1961	1960	1959	1958
Offenses	1,102.3	1,052.8	1,037.9	896.0	896.9
Murder	4.5	4.7	5.1	4.8	4.7
Forcible rape	8.8	8.8	8.7	8.3	8.4
Robbery	51.3	50.1	49.6	40.3	43.5
Aggravated assault	75.1	72.7	72.6	67.3	65.5
Burglary	480.4	466.0	457.9	385.9	392.4
Larceny $50 and over	290.5	272.3	264.8	227.0	226.0
Auto theft	191.6	178.3	179.2	162.3	156.4

Compiled from *Uniform Crime Reports* for years indicated.

Amount and Kinds of Crime in the United States

The United States is the fourth most populous nation on earth, after China, India, and the Soviet Union. In totting up the activities—legal or illegal, laudable or scandalous, routine or extraordinary—of our nearly 190,000,000 people, very large whole numbers are forthcoming. If the size of the parent population from which such numbers arise is not kept in mind, the impact on the imagination of such numbers can be highly misleading.

Uniform Crime Reports for 1962 informed the public—through newspaper releases—that 2,048,370 "serious" crimes were estimated to have occurred in that year and that the "crime clock clicked off four serious crimes per minute." [12] This intelligence is followed a few pages later by graphs of seven "time clocks," one for each crime. These show that murders took place at the rate of one each hour, forcible rapes at 32-minute intervals, and larcenies $50 and over at one per minute. The manner of presenting this data may leave naive readers with the impression that we

[12] *Uniform Crime Reports: 1962,* p. 1.

are swamped with crimes and that immediate and heroic efforts to prevent inundation are called for. But several points should be kept in mind by the student of criminology as he contemplates information of this kind.

(1) Some question exists as to whether the United States is as plagued with ordinary crime to an extent experienced in several other countries, especially when one considers the enormous quantity of personal property owned by Americans, much of which is parked casually and trustingly on the streets in the form of automobiles and their contents. In certain other Western cultures, notably Latin America, niggling thefts are so frequent that property owners are obliged to take what appear to us extraordinary measures of protection: defenses against home burglary and larcenous trespass, even in "good" neighborhoods, include barred first-floor windows and locked fences; the owners of cars parked in public even for short intervals remove windshield wipers and hubcaps or else hire street urchins to stand by; bicycles, often the most valuable item owned by the working class, are chained to stands and posts or kept within dwellings at night; crimes of personal violence among the masses of urban poor are accepted by police as matters of course and often receive only the most cursory investigation.

(2) The image of thousands of skulking murderers, rapists, and robbers conjured up by the usual manner in which crime statistics are released will be seen to have little foundation in fact upon more detailed scrutiny of the FBI's crime data. Listed below are the Bureau's 1962 estimates of the seven crimes upon which it reports, with the percentages of the total for each of the seven:

Murder	8,400	(0.4)
Forcible rape	16,310	(0.8)
Robbery	95,260	(4.6)
Aggravated assault	139,600	(6.8)
Burglary	892,800	(43.6)
Larceny $50 and over	539,900	(26.4)
Auto theft	356,100	(17.4)
Total	2,048,370	(100.0)

About 87 per cent of 1962's serious crimes consisted of property-taking which involved little, if any, personal violence; a substantial proportion of this 87 per cent apparently consisted not of sinister activities of master-minded criminals but of thefts related to automobiles: stealing them or removing their contents or accessories.[13]

---

[13] *Ibid.,* p. 88. Most "stolen" autos are actually taken for use without their owners' permission, much of this being for the purpose of joy-riding. More than 90 per cent of stolen autos are eventually returned to their owners.

(3) The risks of being victimized by direct criminal acts are unevenly distributed within American society. Murder, rape, and aggravated assault, for example, are concentrated particularly in the slum jungles of our large cities; the operators of small retail businesses face a greater robbery risk than do wage-earners; hotel and apartment dwellers are more likely to lose valuables to burglars than persons living in detached houses.

(4) The *configurational* nature of criminal activities is not apparent in published statistics. Many offenses arise in conjunction with companion crimes: nearly all burglaries are performed in the course of an act of theft; aggravated assaults are related to personal brawls or to attempted robberies; most murders appear to arise from quarrels and disagements which become violent; larcenies run a gamut from unplanned car thefts by boys at play to highly organized white-collar crime adjunctive to sharp business practices.

(5) The real significance of crime in American culture cannot be shown from FBI statistics. Labor racketeering, organized traffic in illicit liquor, prostitution, gambling, narcotics, and stolen goods, and the intricate inroads of crooked commercial and financial practices in legitimate business are far more costly in time, money, and social well-being than the piddling amounts stolen by honest thieves and robbers.

Suggested Readings

Eaton, Joseph W., and Polk, Kenneth. *Measuring Delinquency: A Study of Probation Department Referrals*. Pittsburgh: University of Pittsburgh Press, 1961. This book can be appreciated both as a description of delinquents and delinquency based wholly on probation records, and as a primer on the perils encountered in the use of social statistics. The knotty problems of statistical artifacts created by police and agency administrative practices are given particular attention.

Juvenile Delinquency. Washington, D. C.: United States Children's Bureau. Our only source of nation-wide delinquency statistics, this sketchy annual report is based on local court data.

National Prisoner Statistics. Washington, D. C.: Federal Bureau of Prisons. The Bureau publishes annually, under the above title, *Prisoners in State and Federal Institutions, Personnel in State and Federal Institutions,* and *Executions*.

National Probation and Parole Association Journal (July 1957). Most of this issue is devoted to nine articles on the nature and sources of criminal statistics.

Schwartz, Edward E. "A Community Experiment in the Measurement of Juvenile Delinquency," *National Probation Association Yearbook*, 1945, pp. 3–27. This study of delinquency statistics and their sources in Washington, D. C., underscores the problems encountered in using such data to measure trends.

Uniform Crime Reports. Washington, D. C.: U. S. Department of Justice. Issued annually, with briefer reports twice yearly, the *Reports* are a major source of national criminal statistics but must be interpreted with care.

CHAPTER 5

Backgrounds of Criminology; Modern Approaches and Methods

The Classical School and Its Background

The values, ideals, and institutions of contemporary Western civilization were profoundly influenced by the social and cultural changes which gave rise to the so-called "intellectual revolution" of the seventeenth and eighteenth centuries. The restrictive cosmology of medieval philosophers, with its image of a static universe whose nature and purpose were transcendental, was gradually replaced by one which saw natural phenomena as orderly and predictable events occurring in conformity with immutable natural laws. Both the practical exigencies of adapting to changing social and economic circumstances and the deliberately systematic observation and experimentation by a growing number of secularized scholars taught vast new lessons in astronomy, chemistry, physics, and biology, and in the applied arts of agriculture, animal husbandry, metallurgy, mining, ballistics, and medicine. The educated strata of European society became increasingly impressed with the possibility that mankind, for the first time in history, could wrest new means of well-being from what had up to then been a generally sparing, if not inhospitable, environment. Practical reasons for continuing to place human welfare entirely in the hands of supernatural powers diminished as human hands became increasingly versatile.

60

While Western educated men by no means jettisoned the role of Godly forces in human affairs, they did have to deal with the question of where and in what manner these forces impinged on man in a universe governed by impersonal natural laws. The answer which proved most satisfactory to the temper of the intellectual revolution was supplied by René Descartes (1596–1650). Descartes acknowledged that natural laws governed not only events external to man but also events occurring *within* him, that is, his own bodily processes of growth, sustenance, and decay. Then wherein lay man's divine uniqueness? In answering this, Descartes produced a doctrine which helped shape the eventual reformation of criminal law, provided an important rationalization for punishment, and produced an image of man's mental workings which prevails popularly to this day. Man's uniqueness, he said, rests in his possession of a "thinking substance" (probably located in the pineal gland) which makes possible the functions of memory, imagination, reasoning, and willing. These functions are "free" in the sense of being insulated from bodily operations and from dictates arising from external influences and consequently do *not* perform in accordance with natural laws. The powers of reasoning and willing are divine gifts, setting man apart from all other forms of life. This doctrine, conceptually separating mental from bodily processes, is known technically as the Cartesian dichotomy.

The doctrine of free will did not, of course, originate with Descartes, but he produced a theory of its place in the scheme of things which was palatable to the increasingly secularized and religiously skeptical educated people of his and later times. The hand of God does not tinker with His laws, but the hands of men, guided by man's divine gift of reason, could exert increasing mastery over nature for man's earthly comfort and well-being. In the scheme of things, human autonomy waxed, while Godly autonomy was seen as influencing human affairs indirectly rather than directly by providing the orderly physical universe in which man lived, meanwhile leaving him free to adapt as best he could to that universe. Human reason, thus ennobled, was the means for man's earthly salvation.

It was within this set of conceptions that English Utilitarianism developed, under the leadership of the legally-trained philosopher, Jeremy Bentham (1748–1832). In seeking a basis upon which to construct a system of ethics and of legislation appropriate to this "enlightened" view of reality, Bentham engendered the so-called "Classical school" of criminal law. Almost totally divorced from theological dogma, this school maintained (1) that the seriousness of crimes should be measured by their respective social harm rather than by their "sinfulness" or other transcendental qualities and (2) that crime is caused by the *rational* efforts of men to augment their pleasures and to minimize their pains. By establishing for each crime a punishment whose pains would outweigh any possible pleasure to be gained from them and by assuring the certain and swift administration of justice, rational men, deterred by the realization that a net loss will inevitably result from a criminal act, will refrain from breaking the law.

A bit later the neoclassical school, starting from the same premise that men are free to choose criminal or noncriminal conduct, made certain exceptions. They held that children under seven years of age were incapable of crime because they were incapable of understanding the difference between right and wrong. Further, they recognized certain mental diseases which might impair responsibility. Extenuating circumstances were also recognized as depriving an accused person of the power to control his behavior. This neoclassical school did not initiate scientific criminology. It is significant to criminology, nonetheless, for two reasons: first, their exceptions to the free-will principle did imply causation, though their attitude of mind was not scientific; secondly, much of our modern criminal law and policy is founded upon neoclassical principles. Indeterminate sentence laws, probation, parole, constructive treatment of criminals, and social preventive programs, however, imply the scientific view of the positive school that crime has causes.

Beginnings of a Scientific Criminology

In attempting to establish scientific principles pertaining to any class of phenomena, we must assume that the phenomena are based upon orderly sequences of events whose underlying patterns can be discerned and that the events cannot occur without the interplay of particular sets of circumstances. As long as capricious forces in the form of miracles, "uncaused" acts of willing, and so on, are presumed to intrude into the natural order, nexes of circumstances cannot, with confidence, be described. For a science of human behavior to exist, then, "willing," "deciding," "thinking," and "acting" must be considered just as much natural events as rainfall or chemical reactions, and the postulation of capricious forces must be eschewed. The doctrine that human behavior is an irrevocable part of natural processes is known as "determinism." While the student need not accept determinism as a philosophic truth, he must understand that it was the ground upon which a science of criminology took root and that the ground scarcely existed prior to the nineteenth century.

However satisfying Bentham's ideas about human behavior may have been to legal reformers, political philosophers, and the educated general public, the data accumulating from the burgeoning biological and social sciences of that century forced a revision in the scientific interpretation of humankind's place in the scheme of things. The researches of naturalists and other students of the life sciences steadily forged links between *homo sapiens* and "lower" life forms; psychologists explored the anatomical and physiological bases of mental phenomena; social statisticians showed the existence of behavioral "currents" in human affairs. To the consternation of many, particularly those with vested reasons for believing otherwise, evidence mounted that man, including his mental behavior, was part of the natural order and that the Cartesian dichotomy was an untenable metaphysical figment serving only to perpetuate a last glimmer of man as a unique product of a divine creation.

Credit for the specific application of quantitative methods to the study of crime seems to belong to the statisticians of the first half of the nineteenth century.[1] The beginnings of modern national census-taking had made possible the use of social statistics for the study of the geographical distribution and trends of social phenomena, including crime. Correlations were then found between crime and social conditions. Adolphe Quetelet[2] has been called the "first social criminologist."[3] ". . . Society," he writes, "prepares the crime and the guilty is only the instrument by which it is accomplished." Quetelet's importance for us consists in his early use of quantitative measurements in the study of crime and his social rather than individual emphasis.

A. M. Guerry's *Moral Statistics* and other publications first made use of shaded maps to show the ecological distribution of crime.[4] Such methods of study came into wide use in England between 1830 and 1860, and the concentration of crime in deteriorated areas of large cities was observed. Work of this type had its effect upon correctional policy, especially upon the development of juvenile reformatory institutions.

[1] Cf. Alfred Lindesmith and Yale Levin, "The Lombrosian Myth in Criminology," *American Journal of Sociology* (March 1937), pp. 653–71; "English Ecology and Criminology of the Past Century," *Journal of Criminal Law and Criminology* (March–April 1937), pp. 801–16.

[2] Frank H. Hankins, *Adolphe Quetelet as Statistician, Columbia University Studies in History, Economics and Public Law*, **XXXI,** No. 4 (New York: Longmans, Green & Company, 1908), p. 41.

[3] C. Bernaldo De Quiros, *Modern Theories of Criminality*, translated by Alfonso de Salvio (Boston: Little, Brown, 1911), p. 10.

[4] Lindesmith and Levin, "The Lombrosian Myth in Criminology," *loc. cit.*, p. 655.

Very different origins of criminology have been found in studies of physiognomy and phrenology; in the beginnings of anthropology and the work of Gall and Broca; [5] in Pinel's work in psychiatry; and in Morel's theories of moral degeneracy as "a kind of retrogressive natural selection." [6] These developments, together with the interest in criminal law aroused in Italy by the eighteenth-century work of Beccaria and the vogue of the new evolutionary doctrine, account for the origin of the Italian branch of the positive school.

LOMBROSO AND THE DOCTRINE OF THE CRIMINAL TYPE

This Italian school, beginning in the last third of the nineteenth century, utilized a primarily anthropological approach. Cesare Lombroso (1835–1909), for 30 years a professor of psychiatry and anthropology at the University of Turin, had been struck, while an army physician, by the relatively greater frequency of tattooing and the relative indecency of the designs found upon "vicious" as compared with "honest" soldiers. [7] This led him to study the physical characteristics of patients and later of criminals. He was especially impressed by abnormalties found through autopsies on a number of notorious violent offenders. Then, studying a series of 383 skulls of criminals, Lombroso recorded the percentage of frequency of a considerable list of abnormalties of teeth, skull capacity, shape of forehead, and so forth which he discovered. Comparison with savage and prehistoric skulls led him to emphasize the born criminal as a physical type explicable as a reappearance in modern times of traits characterizing primitive man and even animals. He broadened his study to include the anthropometry and physiognomy of 5,907 criminals. Lombroso also found the criminal to have less sensitivity to pain and therefore, he reasoned, less sensitivity to the suffering of others. Individuals possessed of five or six of the physical characteristics constituted for Lombroso the criminal type. One-third of criminals he classed as born criminals for whom little or no environmental handicaps were required as stimuli to crime. Lombroso also held that born criminals were epileptics, although not all epileptics were born criminals. Thus Lombroso clearly inaugurated a biological or anthropological school, emphasizing an hereditary criminal

[5] Gabriel Tarde, *Penal Philosophy*, translated by Rapelje Howell (Boston: Little, Brown, 1912), p. 47.

[6] De Quiros, *op. cit.*, pp. 6–7.

[7] See Lombroso's Introduction to his daughter's summary of his work contained in Gina Lombroso Ferrero, *Criminal Man* (New York: G. P. Putnam's Sons, 1911), p. xii.

type. Yet his later modification of the theory of atavism, his recognition that environment affects even the born criminal, his interest in such rehabilitory efforts as the reformatory movement in the United States, and his own program of crime prevention show him as less narrow than some of his critics have maintained.

The importance of Lombroso's work consists in the great influence it had upon criminology and also upon penal practice. He has long been erroneously considered the father of scientific criminology. He did inaugurate the use of quantitative measurements in the study of the person of the criminal. This led to a tremendous overemphasis upon the physical aspect of the personality and upon the factor of heredity. Lombroso is criticized even by some biologists for his lack of knowledge of genetics, his apparent belief in the inheritance of acquired characteristics, his faulty statistical methods, and his incomplete knowledge of the nature of primitive peoples. The vogue of Lombroso and his followers even today seems to stem from the popularity of any view which conceives of the criminal as very different from the rest of us.

GAROFALO AND INNATE DEFECTIVE MORAL SENTIMENTS

Raffaele Garofalo (1852–1934) was a lawyer, prosecutor, and magistrate who shared Lombroso's anthropological approach but who produced his own distinctive theory of crime. Knowledge of right and wrong, he maintained, was bred into the human race by evolutionary processes: [8]

. . . it is certain that every race today possesses a sum of moral instincts which are not due to individual reasoning, but are the inheritance of the individual quite as much as is the physical type of his race. . . . But since the moral sense is a psychic activity, it may be subject to change and infirmity, may become diseased, may even become entirely lost. It may be wanting from birth as a result of some psychic monstrosity which . . . we are compelled to attribute to atavism.

Criminals, he contended, are innately defective in the sentiments of *pity* and *probity,* the former lack explaining crimes against persons and the latter explaining crimes against property.

FERRI AND THE SOCIAL AND MULTIFACTOR APPROACH

More modern and more scholarly than either Lombroso or Garofalo was a third member of the Italian school, Enrico Ferri (1856–1929). As

[8] Raffaele Garofalo, *Criminology* (Boston: Little, Brown, 1914), pp. 7–9.

a pupil of Lombroso, he made a place in his own theories for the anthropological factor. As a socialist, however, Ferri naturally emphasized environmental influences, and his chief book is called *Criminal Sociology*. Ferri contended, however, that crime is the synthetic product of three major types of factors: physical or geographic; anthropological and psychological; and social. In terms of these three groups of factors Ferri stated his famous law of criminal saturation:

As a given volume of water at a definite temperature will dissolve a fixed quantity of chemical substance and not an atom more or less; so in a given social environment with definite individual and physical conditions, a fixed number of delicts, no more and no less, can be committed.[9]

This law, though in reality nothing more than a statement that the law of cause and effect applies to criminal behavior, is of the greatest significance as an indication of the scientific point of view.

In accordance with these views Ferri treated punishment as but one of the possible ways of influencing behavior and stressed an elaborate program of crime prevention through the removal of the conditions making for crime. Indeed, he calls crime prevention measures *equivalents of punishment.* To Ferri the criminal was in no way responsible for his acts, since he was conceived as the inevitable consequence of the conditions which had played upon his life. But for the concept of responsibility Ferri substituted that of *accountability,* holding that even irresponsible criminals are accountable to a society whose interests transcend those of any individual.

A great many other schools of criminological thought have been distinguished. It will be more helpful to us, however, to pass to a discussion of theories of today as implied in current approaches to the explanation of crime.

Approaches to the Explanation of Crime

From the beginnings of scientific criminology in the first half of the nineteenth century two separate streams of research and theory have persisted. The "subjective" approach, stemming mainly from the biological tradition, has sought for explanations of crime in the form of abnormalities or aberrations existing primarily *within* the criminal. This approach has perpetuated an image of the offender as one who deviates from standards

[9] Enrico Ferri, *Criminal Sociology* (Boston: Little, Brown, 1917), p. 209.

of presumed psycho-physical normality in ways adversely affecting his capacity to conform to acceptable standards of conduct. The "objective" approach, stemming from the social sciences, has assumed—at least tacitly—that offenders are normal beings upon whom have played *external* criminogenic forces. The subjective approach has promoted the study of individual offenders; the objective, the study of groups, social processes, and institutions as productive of deviant behavior. The former approach has "discovered" the ultimate causes of crime to lie in genetic, congenital, or developmental conditions; the latter, in broader social forces.

We may then distinguish as subjective approaches the physical or anthropological, the medical, the biological, the physiological, and the psychological, psychiatric, and psychoanalytical. Among objective approaches we find the geographical, ecological, economic, social, sociological, and cultural. The approaches, defined below, clearly overlap. Their proponents are getting together increasingly in the task of explaining crime. This is seen most strikingly in the work of the clinic, where representatives of many disciplines not only participate in the diagnosis of behavior but often have to arrive at a joint conclusion as to programs of treatment. To a lesser degree, unfortunately, they are uniting in cooperative research and in the organization of university curricula.

SUBJECTIVE APPROACHES [10]

The anthropological approach is illustrated by the work of the Italian school and the researches of the late Professor Hooton [11] of Harvard and of William Sheldon.[12] It attempts to discover whether the criminal is significantly different in his physical structure from the noncriminal. It examines the effect of physical traits upon behavior.

The medical approach, of course, seeks to study the influence of physical disease on crime.

The biological approach attempts to relate crime to heredity.

The physiological and biochemical approach correlates crime with both normal and abnormal physiological functions and types. Together with other disciplines it studies, for example, the developmental history of

[10] Merely characterizing most of these approaches here, we give slightly more space to one or two which are not illustrated in later chapters.
[11] E. A. Hooton, *The American Criminal, An Anthropological Study* (Cambridge, Mass.: Harvard University Press, 1939).
[12] William H. Sheldon *et al., The Varieties of Delinquent Youth* (New York: Harper & Brothers, 1949).

children, the maturation of adults, the cycles of change appearing in women, and the functioning of the ductless glands.

The psychological approach analyzes motivation and diagnoses personality deviations. Psychology tends to stress the individual rather than the group, yet we also have social psychology, which only the meticulous distinguish fully from sociology. Psychological research has contributed chiefly facts concerning deprivations in human needs and desires and individual deviations in personality. Clinical psychology has had a great recent development. In addition to the use of other methods psychologists give intelligence, emotional, personality, educational, occupational, and character tests.

The psychiatric approach originally specialized in the diagnosis of mental disease. Increasingly, however, psychiatrists have extended their activities into the analysis of all degrees of personality deviation and even of normal behavior. One of the major assumptions of psychiatry is that the origin of behavior difficulties is to be found in emotional tensions originating early in life in conflicts in the family. Moreover, behavior patterns established then are thought of by the psychiatrist as relatively fixed and permanent. His approach formerly was likely to be via the individual rather than the group.

In recent years some psychiatrists have recognized the influence of culture on the personality. Many have shown their leanings toward things sociological by frequent use of group therapy. Yet typically, psychiatrists utilize artificial groups made up of problem cases, in which the specialist himself may or may not be included. The sociologist might also do this, but he is especially concerned with the relationship of "natural" groups which arise spontaneously among delinquents. But it must be emphasized that the above characterization does not apply to an increasing number of psychiatrists who utilize sociological principles.

The psychoanalytical approach, based upon the Freudian theory, traces behavior deviations to the repression of basic drives. This repression is occasioned by the mores or demands of civilized life and produces a conflict between the super-ego, or conscience (the "introjected social traditions"), and the basic drives, such as sex and hunger. Another conflict is between desire for success and limited life opportunities. The source of these mental conflicts is unknown to the victim. Either early deprivations or long indulgence diminish his resistance to the tensions arising out of repressed tendencies.[13] He seeks release from conflict either by some mental

---

[13] Franz Alexander and William Healy, *Roots of Crime* (New York and London: Alfred A. Knopf, 1935), p. 279.

substitute, such as daydreaming and some other flight from reality, or by overt compensatory behavior, which may be criminal. Crime thus is seen as an unconscious effort to solve an emotional problem. Some of the principles of psychoanalysis have been accepted by representatives of other disciplines. Others seem to them to be as yet without factual basis. Dealing with the unconscious, the psychoanalyst must perforce rely on successful treatment for validation of his views, though even the successful use of his techniques is sometimes challenged because the cure may have been due to influences exerted by the practitioner but not necessarily dependent on the soundness of his theory.

OBJECTIVE APPROACHES

The geographical approach attempts to show the influence upon behavior of such factors as climate (including temperature, humidity, barometric pressure, changes in the weather, and so on), topography, natural resources, and geographical location. Such factors are largely beyond human control. Long ago Quetelet showed the tendency for crimes against property to increase in winter and for those against persons to increase in summer. This does not necessarily show a physiological influence of the seasons, however. An American sociologist has studied the effects of weather changes on crime.[14] Geographers like Ellsworth Huntington have tried to show the effect on morality of life in the tropics as compared with life in temperate zones. Geographical factors, of course, partly underlie economic and cultural influences.[15]

The ecological approach shows the influence of the spatial distribution of men and institutions upon behavior patterns. Ecology concerns itself with the biotic groupings of men, particularly those resulting from migration, competition, and division of labor. Ecologists use spot maps to compare the spatial distribution of crime with that of other social phenomena. Thus one studies the types of social conditions which characterize areas where crime is concentrated.

The economic approach. To those who subscribe to the economic interpretation of history the economic approach is basic to every other. Apart from this, economic conditions more directly related to crime include, of course, direct economic motivation; poverty; resentment over economic

[14] Cf. Edwin G. Dexter, *Conduct and the Weather* (New York: Macmillan, 1899).

[15] For a significant discussion of geographical factors, see Joseph Cohen, "The Geography of Crime," *Annals of the American Academy of Political and Social Science* (Sept. 1941), pp. 29–38.

exploitation; the effects of commercialized entertainments; child labor; the employment of women; unemployment; the economic basis of social prestige and behavior patterns; and many more.

The social, sociological, and cultural approaches. The social approach, in its general sense, includes assessments of those forces resulting from man's collective survival efforts, with emphasis upon his institutions: economic, familial, educational, political, religious, recreational. The sociological approach is concerned with the influences on behavior of group life, including roles and statuses, social classes and social mobility, subcultures, cliques, and social change. By culture is meant social attitudes, values, and norms characteristic of the several groups and strata within a society; the term is sometimes used to include as well arts, skills, language, philosophies, and the material aspects of social existence.[16]

Methods Used

THE THERAPEUTIC METHOD

Though criminology is not yet and may never be a science, it is scientific in viewpoint and in its attempt to use scientific methods. Clearly, criminology can use the experimental method only to a very limited extent. There are no convenient test tubes within which human beings and their environments may be confined and controlled. The therapeutic method most nearly approximates the conditions necessary in experimentation. Sometimes particular factors in the life of an individual may be manipulated, as when a probation officer tests the influence of the disorganized home by placing a delinquent child in a different home. Similarly, Clifford Shaw, by experimenting with neighborhood reorganization, tested his hypothesis that the disorganization of delinquency areas in Chicago produces crime. When treatment alters behavior, the soundness of the theoretical assumption is at least in part validated.

STATISTICAL METHODS

Statistical comparisons between criminals and noncriminals. A significant source of our knowledge of crime causation is found in statistical

[16] The thoughtful student will realize that *social, sociological,* and *cultural* are analytic categories whose referents cannot practically be considered apart from one another.

comparisons between both the traits of criminals and noncriminals and the conditions under which criminals have lived and those which have surrounded noncriminals. Here, however, we face the unavoidable difficulties that only apprehended delinquents are available as samples of criminals and that the control group of noncriminals may contain many who have broken the law without detection. For example, differences between the intelligence of arrested criminals and the not-arrested population almost certainly exaggerate the stupidity of criminals, because the less intelligent are more likely to be arrested. By holding certain factors constant—such, for example, as age, nationality, income class, and the like—differences between prisoners and nonprisoners with respect to one significant characteristic may be made more evident.

Statistical correlations between crime and other conditions. Correlation may be simply defined as the degree to which two variables vary concomitantly. By the method of correlation may be discovered what other conditions vary with crime, provided adequate indices can be obtained for both sets of phenomena. Significant correlations in criminology may be found in time or in space. Thus one may discover to what degree crime indices rise and fall with changes in density of population or with the ups and downs of the business cycle.

Again, the home addresses of delinquents and of recipients of relief may be spotted on maps, and coefficients of correlation between delinquency and dependency computed. However, it does not follow that a high correlation proves a causal relationship. Correlation studies of this type are only the beginning of the search for causes.

THE USE OF CASE HISTORIES

A good case history involves a much more thorough knowledge of an individual criminal than statistics can ever give. Some of the most significant of life's influences cannot be measured quantitatively. Statistics cannot show adequately the relationship between many factors which influence one another or the varied meanings of life experiences. Certain types of findings derived from many case studies may indeed be treated statistically, and conclusions drawn from the results. Actually some knowledge of criminogenic processes is derived from case studies by a sort of commonsense deduction from the observed influence of many factors, interpreted in the light of experience with similar cases.

Important as are case histories to the criminologist, they have serious limitations. Their use assumes that certain facts are known to the case himself; that he is able and willing to tell them; and that other informants, such as social workers, relatives, school teachers, officers of the law, and companions, are also informed and willing to tell the truth. In addition case histories, since they do involve subjective interpretations by the investigator, are likely to be colored by his prejudices. Even trained case workers are prone to find the facts they expect to find.

The types of facts sought by case historians vary considerably. In earlier editions of this book a case history outline was presented at this point which is not repeated here for lack of space. The use of formal outlines has come into some disrepute among case workers on the ground that they tend unduly to formalize the relationship with clients. For research purposes, however, it is important that comparable information be derived from all case contacts. While investigations made by busy probation officers cannot always be as complete as those called for in research studies, they should be as complete as possible, and an outline helps assure that no pertinent questions remain unanswered. Case outlines sometimes may include the following major headings: identifying information, description of behavior, family history, developmental history, medical history, personality traits, home past and present, neighborhood, social and recreational opportunities, group experiences and preferences, occupational opportunities and activities, school life, companionship, interests, attitudes, and life goals. Perhaps because of the psychiatric orientation of many social workers today, many truly sociological data seem often to have been under-investigated. Thus with respect to each of the activities listed above we need especially to know the attitudes, group values, affiliations and statuses, exclusion from groups, and roles the individual has played. Such an investigation underlines the importance of social relations in the development of the personality. For repeatedly, delinquency is found to result from association, exclusion from prestige groups, gang membership and patterning, loss of status or desire to achieve status, the attitudes of others toward the delinquent, and his attitudes toward a host of situations and values. No· inadequate generalization is, perhaps, less inadequate than the generalization that delinquency is a group product. After a case history is seemingly complete, to review it in terms of the attitudes and social status of all pertinent people involved is worthwhile. A social fact of little sociological significance can be illustrated by the discovery that a family seems indifferent to filth. Dirt by itself probably never led any boy or girl into crime. But if the boy lives in "the dirtiest house in the neighborhood" and is labeled "dirty Jim" in consequence, or if a girl will not bring her friends home because she is ashamed of its filthy condition—in such cases we have a sociological fact of social relationships and status of the type often found as part of the background of delinquency.

THE USE OF LIFE HISTORIES

Life histories are documents written by delinquents or criminals themselves. The individual's interpretation of life experiences may be significant, even when based upon error. The assertion sometimes made, that it is unimportant to check on the accuracy of statements is clearly in error, however.

The life history has obvious limitations. It can be written only by fairly well-educated delinquents. It is worth little unless the full confidence of the writer is secured. It cannot describe unconscious motivations, though these may sometimes be inferred through skilled analysis by others. If the investigator gives the delinquent no suggestions as to what to write, the latter may unwittingly leave out the most vital parts of his story. On the other hand, if the specialist suggests what it might be well to include, he may well be suggesting the interpretation of the case which he expects to find and may unduly warp the story in that direction. Prisoners who have been asked to write such histories have been known to get great enjoyment out of faking their material. Yet when proper precautions are observed, very valuable material is obtainable by this method.[17]

THE METHOD OF THE PARTICIPANT OBSERVER

This method is difficult, not to say dangerous. In it the student participates as nearly as possible in the experiences and group life of the delinquent. He may become an active or honorary member of a juvenile or even professional gang. He thus comes into such close contact with the delinquent experience that he can see many of its aspects which he could never understand otherwise.[18] In addition to the difficulty of arranging such opportunities and even the possibility of becoming involved in crime, the method does not usually allow the use of other more carefully controlled techniques.

[17] Cf. Clifford Shaw, *The Jack Roller* (Chicago: University of Chicago Press, 1930); *The Natural History of a Delinquent Career* (Chicago: University of Chicago Press, 1931); *Brothers in Crime* (Chicago: University of Chicago Press, 1938).

[18] Cf. Frederic M. Thrasher, *The Gang,* rev. ed. (Chicago: University of Chicago Press, 1936); John Landesco, "Organized Crime in Chicago," Part III of Illinois Association for Criminal Justice, *The Illinois Crime Survey* (Chicago: The Association, 1929), pp. 815–1087.

LONGITUDINAL METHODS

Case histories and life histories, revealing as they are, involve the difficulty of reproducing the past after some of its events have been forgotten or some sources of information have ceased to be available. If an elaborate program of recording significant events in the lives of representative individuals *at the time of their occurrence* could be devised, some of these difficulties could be overcome. Suppose adequate funds were provided to continue for a generation studies of a sample of the children passing through the school system of some large city. Such a study would begin even before entrance to the school and continue until, say, the age of 30. Ideally, it would involve the use of all the approaches and all the methods we have listed. At the age of 30 comparisons would be made between those who had and those who had not seriously violated the criminal law. Clearly, the difficulties involved are many. The expense is great. The plan assumes a community not only vitally interested in the crime problem but willing to wait possibly a little less than a generation for the formulation of a program of prevention. Changes in social situations during the period would complicate the interpretation of results. Moreover, there would need to be almost universal willingness on the part of the parents of "good" children to submit not only their children but themselves to intimate investigation in the interest of science and delinquency prevention.

Suggested Readings

Brinton, Crane. *Ideas and Men.* New York: Prentice-Hall, 1950. Chapter 11 contains a superb description of the Enlightenment and its child, rationalism.

Mannheim, Hermann, editor. *Pioneers in Criminology.* Chicago: Quadrangle Books, 1960. Essays on 17 historical figures important in the development of criminology and penology. The pieces on Bentham, Maudsley, Lombroso, Garofalo, and Ferri are germane to the chapter.

Randall, John H., Jr. *The Making of the Modern Mind.* New York: Houghton Mifflin, 1940. As a survey of today's intellectual backgrounds, this masterpiece is without parallel. Book I, "The Intellectual Outlook of Medieval Christendom," is an illuminating starting point for understanding the roots of transcendental ideas on crime causation.

Vold, George B. *Theoretical Criminology.* New York: Oxford University Press, 1958. An excellent review of the main currents in criminological theory, past and present.

The EXPLANATION of CRIME

In the first two chapters of Part I we characterized those general aspects of American society which seem to us germane to an understanding of crime in the United States. In Part II we discuss a number of the more immediate causes of crime; the student should be continually mindful, however, of the dependence of these causes upon the more basic attributes of our society. For example, if the physical and moral decay of certain neighborhoods is causally related to crime and delinquency, the fact must not be overlooked that such neighborhoods are themselves by-products of larger social processes of competition and conflict. In its interstate aspects, its forms of organization, its quest for money and power, and its need to accommodate political groups, syndicated crime, as a second example, has evident parallels with individual businesses, corporate structures, trade associations, and labor unions. All are in turn adapting to social and economic forces set going a century or more ago. And just how sharp a moral distinction can be made on the one hand between the crime rings purveying abortions, bootleg liquor, pornographic party films, off-track betting, and compliant girls, and on the other hand the multitudes of "respectable" citizens eager to further their pursuit of happiness by purchasing such goods and services? Is law-breaking by business and professional men and union officials in the course of their occupations the result of "criminal" motivation, or is it instead consistent with and perhaps encouraged by our admiration for the go-getter who seizes opportunities for gain? Are alcohol and drug addiction merely personal problems, or do their rather singular demographic distributions suggest causal forces inherent in the social structure of American society?

The next 11 chapters, then, will examine in some detail the possible relationships between crime and immediate socio-cultural forces; but while scrutinizing these trees, the student is urged to remember the forest they are part of.

CHAPTER 6

Subjective Theories of Crime

Theories of crime having in common the assumption that criminals are distinguishable from noncriminals in individual peculiarities and abnormalities began accumulating early in the nineteenth century as outgrowths of discoveries in the burgeoning sciences of biology and psychology. The purpose of this chapter is to indicate certain characteristics of the subjective approach in general and to examine with more brevity than we would prefer some of the specific theories arising from it.

The notions that criminals are a class of being set apart from the rest of mankind, and that crime is somehow a manifestation of inner peculiarities, antedate the nineteenth century. Scholastic theorists regarded felons as wilfully evil persons who succumbed to satanic blandishments; the ignorant had long believed crime to be due to "bad blood," ill fate, the evil eye, demonic possession, and so on. But nineteenth-century students of crime, eschewing such explanations, set themselves the task of discovering what was "really" different about the criminal. Offenders (by then conveniently sequestered in prisons instead of hung or dispatched to colonial holdings) were studied by men whose scientific training was mainly biological and medical and who worked under the ancient premise that *something* must be characteristically peculiar to the inner beings of law-breakers. From the sociologists' standpoint, their work contributed less to the understanding of crime than to a thorough muddling of both popular and scientific ideas about it.

Subjective theories of crime, ever since their somewhat theatrical beginnings in phrenology,[1] have enjoyed an immense popularity among the literate masses as well as with scholars in the natural sciences, law-enforcement officials, and prison administrators.[2] In addition to a historical readiness to accept any theory which would emphasize distinctions between criminals and the law-abiding, other reasons can be given for the popularity of these approaches.

(1) Subjective theories of crime function as adjuncts to class prejudices by underscoring the general belief that inherent qualitative differences underlie social stratification. While this observation is probably more pertinent to the nineteenth- than to the twentieth-century social scene, it is still valid *vis-à-vis* the widely held notion among white Americans that Negro criminality is due to peculiarly Negroid traits of temperament and predisposition. Subjective theorizing got off to a biased start: the educated and cultured minority from which were recruited most of the nineteenth-century scholars of Great Britain and the Continent constituted a privileged élite insulated by old social barriers from the peasant and urban proletariat whose progeny filled the prisons. A gentlemanly scholar's direct contacts with the "lower orders" were limited mainly to impersonal transactions with untutored servants, rustics, and tradesmen whose servile ways were interpreted even by Herbert Spencer as evidence of biological inferiority.[3] Men engaged in criminological research were predisposed by their image of the submerged classes to regard criminals as an especially accursed substratum. The direct evidence of the senses, moreover, supported such a view: unwashed, bedraggled hordes of offenders crowding the criminal courts; cowed, queerly-clothed prisoners peering from the dark confines of their cells; "dangerous" chained felons working in silence on quays or in prison shops.

(2) Subjective theories do not challenge established social institutions. If the causes of crime are traced to biological and psychological factors inherent in the offender, the problem of crime control becomes primarily one of attention to these rather than to social forces. With a few exceptions,

---

[1] George B. Vold, *Theoretical Criminology* (New York: Oxford University Press, 1958), pp. 47–48.

[2] To this day medically trained men—usually psychiatrists—are often the ranking members of treatment teams in correctional settings, and their pronouncements on crime are the ones to which the public listens with the most respect.

[3] Herbert Spencer, *The Principles of Sociology* (New York: D. Appleton and Company, 1897), III, pp. 346–48.

notably those of the socialist Enrico Ferri of the Italian School and some members of the neo-Freudian group, representatives of the subjective approach did not voice needs for basic revision in existing social arrangements. Private ownership of property, the class system, exploitative patterns in economic activities, racial segregation, disparaties in the distribution of wealth, differential social and economic opportunities—all of which have received critical attention from other branches of criminology—need not be called into question.

(3) The apparent simplicity of subjective theories has been a factor in their popularity. Crime during the last century and a quarter has been variously "explained" as being the direct result of: overdeveloped brain lobes governing certain animal propensities; moral insanity; innate criminal tendencies; deficiencies in inherited moral sentiments; glandular malfunction; deficient intellects; general biological inferiority; psychopathic personalities; unresolved conflicts between instinctive forces and social demands. The crucial question of just how such traits relate to the acquisition of learned attitudes, values, and rationalizations which underlie criminal motivation was seldom explored; it sufficed that criminals were "different" and that these differences accounted for their behavior being different.

Weaknesses in the Subjective Approaches

As we pointed out in Chapter 1, the definitions of acts considered as criminal vary by time and place according to the exigencies faced by particular cultures. No scientific evidence exists that a "natural sense" of right and wrong is part of *homo sapien's* inborn equipment or that social norms arise from any other source than socio-cultural processes. Therefore individual conformity or nonconformity to criminal codes are as much socio-cultural phenomena as speaking or failing to speak grammatical English and are not necessarily indicative of the possession of abnormal biological or psychological traits. A persisting naiveté concerning this point has long been characteristic of subjective criminologists, who apparently assumed without question that deviations from legal or other social norms were "pathological" in the same sense as deviations from anatomical, physiological, or mental health norms.[4] Moreover, laboring under a latter-day

---

[4] Examples of this tendency can be found in Cesare Lombroso's contention that anarchists and leaders of political bloodbaths are "nearly all" criminal types [*Crime, Its Causes and Remedies* (Boston: Little, Brown, 1911), p. 434]; in Raffaele Garofalo's

version of the medieval tenet that evil effects must have evil causes, they sought to explain the pathology of crime by tracing it to antecedent pathologies. A criminal, in short, "must have something wrong with him."

This expectation has caused subjective theorists typically to ignore the possible causal interplay between observed personal abnormalities and factors external to the offender. Once some trait presumably distinguishing criminals from noncriminals has been isolated, the search for cause ends. This creates first the possibility of inversion of cause and effect. A trait may conceivably be a factor in the causation of crime, or to the contrary it may be a result of a criminal career. Are some delinquents such because they are emotionally unstable, or are they emotionally unstable because of the worries and stresses resulting from crime and its punishment? Again, a presumably criminogenic personal characteristic and criminal behavior both may be a product of a common factor. For example, a culturally deprived background may account for low test-intelligence and also for a youth's finding antisocial paths to social status. Finally, we may define in similar terms a criminal and an individual with some abnormal characteristic and thus get an identity of no significance for causal explanation. This prevalent difficulty is illustrated by the frequent use of the label "psychopath." By definition a psychopath is a chronically unsocialized, egocentric individual who does not recognize obligations to others. Similarly, persisting criminality indicates an antisocial attitude of mind, and such behavior is thus "psychopathic."

As Professors Korn and McCorkle have pointed out, most etiological research in criminology has sought to discover *how criminals differ from noncriminals* rather than *how criminals differ from one another*.[5] Failure to put the second question first has obscured the range of data which a crime-causation theory should explain. Those subjective theories attributing crime to physical characteristics are especially incapable of predicting, for example, that the preponderance of known criminals are young, urban males of low socio-economic background or that non-whites appear disproportionately among known offenders. Such theories also are utterly inadequate to explain how it is that much of the behavior of even hardened offenders is conventional and law-abiding.[6]

---

theory that offenders against the person are deficient in an inherent sense of pity [*Criminology* (Boston: Little, Brown, 1914), pp. 23ff.]; and in Max G. Schlapp's generalization that defective human chemistry accounts not only for crime, but for poverty, divorce, horse-race betting, and radicalism [*The New Criminology* (with Edward H. Smith) (New York: Boni and Liveright, 1928), pp. 188–89]. Smith was a commercial writer of crime books.

[5] Richard R. Korn and Lloyd W. McCorkle, *Criminology and Penology* (New York: Henry Holt, 1959), pp. 316–18.

[6] *Ibid.*, pp. 319–20.

Heredity and Crime

Strictly speaking, the only truly subjective trait is heredity—is some quality characterizing the genes. All else save the genes and indeed the expression of the genes themselves is relative to the entire past and future experience of the individual. Yet such hereditary traits vary greatly in rigidity or pliability. Eye color seems truly genetic. Temperament, if it have any genetic basis, can be proven to be subject to radical change in spite of its frequent persistence throughout life. Occasionally, though rarely, the possible indirect connection between a trait believed to be genetic and some type of criminal behavior may be seen, as when some physical defect injures a man's social status.

By far the nearest approach to evidence of an hereditary factor in criminal behavior has come from studies of twins. Because other sources of information are so obviously defective or inconclusive, we shall largely neglect them. Thus evidence from the breeding of plants and animals cannot safely be carried over into the explanation of human behavior. Studies of families of "degenerates," such as the Jukes and Kallikaks, have shown crime running in families. Charles Goring [7] measured the resemblance of parents to children and brothers to brothers with respect to crime but did not thereby prove crime to be hereditary. Healy and Bronner,[8] studying thousands of cases, have emphasized the infrequency with which delinquent children have had delinquent sibs or parents with criminal records. Other researchers, including Sheldon and Eleanor Glueck, to whose important studies we shall refer repeatedly, have found somewhat larger proportions of cases where more than one member of the family is delinquent. The English psychologist Cyril Burt, however, found that in only 19 per cent of his cases were relatives of young delinquents known to have committed serious crimes.[9] Such a finding tends to minimize the possible influence of heredity on crime. Moreover, the evidence from embryology has shown that many inborn traits, such as a good deal of feeble-mindedness, are not hereditary but products of prenatal influences. Abundant facts also demonstrate how a single very emotionally toned

[7] *The English Convict* (London: His Majesty's Stationery Office, 1913). For a criticism of Goring's research, see E. H. Sutherland, *Principles of Criminology,* 3d ed. (Chicago: J. B. Lippincott, 1939), pp. 35–36. In his study of 3,000 English prisoners, Goring thought he had shown about the same correlation between the criminal behavior of fathers and sons as had been found between their physical traits.

[8] William Healy and Augusta F. Bronner, *Delinquents and Criminals, Their Making and Unmaking* (New York: Macmillan, 1926), p. 99.

[9] Cyril Burt, *The Young Delinquent* (London: University of London Press, 1938), pp. 50–51.

experience may modify behavior previously thought of as having an hereditary basis.[10]

Studies of identical twins are of special significance because, if correctly identified as identical, the two members of any pair have the same genetic traits. Hence behavior differences between them must be the result of experience. On the other hand, when two identical twins separated early in life continue in very similar behavior, that fact has been held to be evidence of the influence of heredity. The results of such separation have been variously reported,[11] and the evidence is inconclusive, though tending to emphasize the relativity of heredity to experience. One study,[12] though involving but one pair of twins, is of interest because one member of the pair was an "aggressive psychopath," a personality type almost synonymous with one type of criminal prevalent in prison populations, while the other, though genetically identical, had a totally different personality. In an article [13] addressed to geneticists, Dr. John Spencer takes a very cautious and objective position and even reports cases where identical twins reared in the *same* family have shown personality change at an early age.

On the other hand, studies of a second type, which have compared identical and fraternal twins as to similarity of behavior, have very generally shown greater similarity between the two members of pairs of identical twins. Table 3 combines several studies of this type, all of which concerned twins where one member of each pair was a criminal. Taking the table as a whole, it appears that whereas, in the case of 145 pairs of identical twins, both members were criminal in three-fourths of the cases, only one was criminal in the other fourth. This finding only gains significance, however, when compared with the finding that in the case of fraternal twins both were criminal in only three-tenths of the cases. Mention should be made that while this general situation was found in all the studies, the degree to which it pertained varied greatly, showing at least the need for much further study. Newman, Freeman, and Holzinger found the degree of similarity of identical twins as compared with fraternal twins to be

[10] Cf. William I. Thomas and Dorothy Swaine Thomas, *The Child in America* (New York: Alfred A. Knopf, 1928), p. 505.

[11] Cf. Barbara Stoddard Burks, "The Influence of Environment on the Intelligence, School Achievement and Conduct of Foster Children," *Yearbook of the National Society for the Study of Education*, pp. 139–40.

[12] Lorna Whelan, "Aggressive Psychopathy in One of a Pair of Uniovular Twins," *British Journal of Delinquency* (Oct. 1951), pp. 130–43.

[13] "Delinquent Behavior, Some Unanswered Questions," *Eugenics Review* (April 1954), pp. 29–37.

greatest "in physical traits . . . and least in tests of personality and temperament." [14]

Table 3

| | 145 Identical Twins | | 138 Fraternal Twins—One Sex | |
	Both Criminal	*Only One Criminal*	*Both Criminal*	*Only One Criminal*
Lange	10	3	3	15
Stumpfl	11	7	7	12
Kranz	20	11	23	20
Legras	4	0	0	5
Newman, Freeman, and Holzinger				
Adult criminals	25	12	5	23
Juvenile delinquents	39	3	5	20
Total	109	36	43	95
Per cent	75%	25%	31%	69%

This table is derived from Paul Popenoe, "Twins and Criminals," *Journal of Heredity* (Oct. 1936), p. 399; Aaron J. Rosanoff, Leva M. Handy, and Isabel Rosanoff, "Criminality and Delinquency in Twins," *Journal of Criminal Law and Criminology* (Jan.–Feb. 1934), pp. 925 and 928.

The above studies show inconsistencies, and the numbers studied have been inadequate. Apart from these two defects, several arguments have been presented tending to deny that such data prove an hereditary influence on crime. It is said that only by being present at the moment of birth can one be certain that twins are identical. It is pointed out that the physiological process of twinning may produce abnormalities in identical twins which may be important for criminal behavior in some situations. More significantly, it is argued that in our culture we welcome identical twins and provide for them a more similar environment than in the case of twins who do not look alike. Whether such considerations do or do not render such studies invalid as proofs of an hereditary influence is impossible to determine.

Very significant is the fact that many geneticists make no extreme claims for the influence of heredity on mental traits or crime.[15] Yet

[14] Horatio H. Newman, Frank N. Freeman, and Karl J. Holzinger, *Twins: A Study of Heredity and Environment* (Chicago: University of Chicago Press, 1937), p. 352.

[15] Cf. Adrian M. Srl and Ray D. Owen, *General Genetics* (San Francisco: W. H. Freeman, 1952), pp. 537–38.

apparently any heritable physical trait, disapproved or ridiculed by a group, will deprive one of social status and thus indirectly affect criminal behavior. In testing the hypothesis that a relationship exists between general social behavior and facial attractiveness, Corsini asked 1,000 prisoners to rank in comeliness the photographs of 108 white offenders of similar ages divided into six offense categories. He predicted that burglars, whose crimes are stealthy, thereby bespeaking contact-shyness, would be judged less physically attractive than robbers, who boldly face their victims. The results bore out the prediction. The robbers were judged the most attractive in all cases, followed in order by forgers, rapists, and murderers. Vying for last place were burglars and child molesters.[16]

The following tentative conclusions seem in order. There is no way of separating heredity from environment and proving its exact influence on crime. Some specific mental states, such as manic depressive insanity or manic tendencies of a lesser degree, may have some direct effect on certain kinds of crime and may be in part heritable. Some physical characteristics are known to be hereditary, and if any of these are such as to prevent admission to prestige groups, they may indirectly be factors in the causation of crime. But every hereditary influence is relative to experience and nobody is conceived with a tendency to steal your watch or rob a bank.

Race and Crime

The confluence in the nineteenth century of physical and social anthropology, Darwinian theory, and post-Napoleonic German racist doctrines led to a belief among scholars that an evolution of temperamental and psychological characteristics parallels social evolution. "Civilized," "barbaric" and "savage" societies were respectively seen as peopled by humans having innate qualities appropriate to each of the three evolutionary stages. The White, Yellow, Black, and other races were pegged at various rungs on the ladder of bio-social evolution. Directly upon these assumptions Lombroso built his theory of atavism. In discussing civilization and barbarism he states that

there are two forms of criminality manifesting themselves in our day side by side: atavistic criminality, which is a return on the part of certain individuals of morbid constitution to the violent means of the struggle for existence now suppressed by civilization, such as homicide, robbery, and rape; and "evolutive"

[16] Raymond J. Corsini, "Appearance and Criminality," *American Journal of Sociology* (July 1959), pp. 49–51.

criminality, which is no less perverted in intent but more civilized in the means employed, for in place of violence it uses trickery and deceit.[17]

Race, definable as a group of people relatively closely related genealogically and possessing certain inherited physical similarities, came to be confused with *nationality,* which connotes a group bound together by a we-feeling based upon cultural elements held in common and which usually identifies itself with a particular land area. The result of this confusion was that purely cultural traits characteristic of national groups came to be regarded as having a racial (i.e., biological) basis. Lombroso devoted an entire chapter of *Crime, Its Causes and Conditions* to the influence of race on crime, quite evidently using race interchangeably not only with nationality, but with language groups, regions, districts, and even villages. Despite a virtual abandonment by modern scholars of nineteenth-century racial theories, popularly-held remnants exist today. We still speak of Italian, Latin, German, English, Jewish, Gypsy, and what not "races," and tend to assume that the stereotypes of Sicilian violence, Gypsy thievery, English perfidy, Jewish greed, and so forth have biological bases.

Alternative explanations are available for presumably racially based behavior patterns. It is alleged, for example, that southern Italians—predominantly of Mediterranean stock—have a "hair-trigger" temperament which makes them easily offended at trifles, resulting in the well-known excess of crimes of violence among some immigrant groups from Italy. American-born sons of Italians, though involved in predatory crimes, are not usually violent in their offenses. In other words, this supposed racial trait passes in a single generation. The past lack of strong government in southern Italy created a demand for self-defense. The tradition developed that a red-blooded man will not go to court but will draw his stiletto at the slightest imagined affront to his traditionally jealously protected wife or daughter. His American-born son, however, has become Americanized in his crimes, loses much of his father's violence, and becomes a burglar or robber who seeks financial gain rather than personal honor in his criminal activities.

Belief in the superiority of one race over others is challenged by historical comparisons of the relative achievements of the different races at different periods of history. Isolation seems to have prevented the full development of the capacities of some racial stocks. But in what century should one compare the civilization of the Chinese with that of European Caucasians? And who shall say which civilization indicates the greater

[17] Lombroso, *op. cit.,* p. 45.

capacity to achieve, the recent industrial development of Europeans or the religious, philosophic, and artistic accomplishments of the Chinese while most of the rest of the world's peoples were culturally stagnant?

Finally, a word should be said of the trend of most geneticists toward an approximately equalitarian conception of racial capacities. In spite of their tendency to emphasize individual heredity, most geneticists today find approximately the same mental potentialities in all races. As Srl and Owen put it: "Evidence is lacking for association between particular characteristics and [even] the common heritable physical traits by which certain racial groups are identified." [18] What Ashley-Montagu calls "man's most dangerous myth" [19]—the belief in racial superiority and inferiority— is, according to most geneticists [20] wholly lacking in factual basis. That danger includes the danger that discrimination against a minority race, such as the Negro, rationalized in terms of fallacious belief in racial inferiority, will lead to crime. Indeed, few more evident contributing causes of crime exist than such discrimination.

Neo-Lombrosian Theories

In the view of many scholars, Lombrosianism was laid to rest by the monumental researches of an English prison official named Charles Goring, who compared the anthropological measurements of 3,000 imprisoned recidivists with those of large numbers of university students, hospital inmates, and soldiers. Using, for that day, highly refined statistical procedures, Goring found no significant anthropological differences of the kinds Lombroso's theory would predict.[21]

[18] *Op. cit.,* p. 540.

[19] Montague Ashley-Montagu, *Man's Most Dangerous Myth* (New York: Columbia University Press, 1942).

[20] Apparently the chief and perhaps the only exception to this statement is seen in the publications of Reginald Gates and his students, who still seem to hark back to a polygenetic theory of the origin of races, which is consistent with belief in the existence of distinct biological differences among them. Cf. Reginald R. Gates, *Human Ancestry from the Genetical Point of View* (Cambridge, Mass.: Harvard University Press, 1948). A noted physical anthropologist, however, has recently given additional support to this theory (Carleton S. Coon, *The Origin of Races,* New York: Alfred A. Knopf, 1963).

[21] Goring, *op. cit.* Goring was no environmentalist: he substituted his own theory of inherited biological inferiority for that of Lombroso. Goring's status as a slayer of the Lombrosian dragon depends in part upon one's orientation to criminology. The neo-Lombrosian E. A. Hooton accused Goring of "using his statistical genius to twist the results of his investigation so that they would conform to his [anti-Lombrosian] bias." [*The American Criminal* (Cambridge, Mass.: Harvard University Press, 1939), I, p. 19.]

In its heyday Lombrosianism enjoyed a wide vogue, especially in Italy and in Latin America, where some prison systems to this day make anthropological examinations of incoming prisoners as part of routine classification procedures. Even American prisons were not immune to his influence. Elmira Reformatory between 1881 and 1897 tailored its program partly in accordance with Lombrosian principles.[22] Lombroso himself published at least 23 articles in American periodicals between 1890 and 1910.[23] In terms of scholarly research in this country, however, the path carved by the Italian has been followed by relatively few, the principal figures being Ernest Hooton, William H. Sheldon, and Sheldon and Eleanor Glueck.

Hooton, late professor of anthropology at Harvard, completed an ambitious study of the physiques of 13,873 American criminals and 3,203 noncriminals.[24] With respect to the native white criminal of native parentage, he found that "criminals are inferior to civilians in nearly all of their bodily measurements." [25] "Low foreheads, high pinched nasal roots, nasal bridges and tips varying to both extremes of breadth and narrowness, excess of nasal deflections, compressed faces and narrow jaws, fit well into the picture of general constitutional inferiority." [26] He also found what he considered significant differences between offense groups. Findings regarding physical inferiority he felt were principally significant because associated with mental defects. This physical inferiority he interpreted tentatively as due to heredity.

E. H. Sutherland [27] and others have criticized the Hooton claims. The following statements from various sources, with some additions of our own, seem justified.[28]

1. Prisoners are not fair samples of criminals, but a selected group, and this selection no doubt may show in physical as well as social characteristics.

2. Hooton's civilian sample is inadequate, both in size and composition. The fact that he included in his civilian group a fair number of policemen and firemen is only the most extreme example of his failure to use a true norm for comparison with prisoners.

[22] Stanley E. Grupp, "Criminal Anthropological Overtones: New York State Reformatory at Elmira, 1876–1907," *Correction* (May–June 1959), pp. 9–17.

[23] Seminar paper by Charles Taylor, University of Illinois, 1958.

[24] Hooton, *op. cit.,* p. 35.

[25] *Ibid.,* p. 229.

[26] *Ibid.,* p. 306.

[27] *Journal of Criminal Law and Criminology* (April 1939), pp. 911–14.

[28] For a different view of Hooton's work, see William B. Tucker, "Is There Evidence of a Physical Basis for Criminal Behavior?" *Journal of Criminal Law and Criminology* (Nov. 1940), pp. 427–37.

3. He obtained, but largely disregarded, contrasts greater than those he found between criminals and civilians. Differences between samples in different states, differences between occupational groups, and differences according to the individual who did the measuring are among these. He did not correct such errors.

4. His 11-pound difference in weight between civilian and prisoner groups may well have been caused by prison diet.

5. Hooton implies that certain physical traits are "superior" to others but does not make clear by what criteria he so evaluates them. He suggests that they are related to mental defects but does not realize that the older view that criminals are disproportionately of low-grade intelligence has been exploded.

6. Really significant physical differences, not subject to a difference interpretation, were found only with respect to submedium helixes and somewhat longer, thinner necks, and this is a very inadequate basis for proof of "degeneracy."

Building on the work of the German psychiatrist Ernst Kretschmer,[29] who sought to relate bodily conformations to personality traits, William Sheldon published in 1949 his highly controversial book on physique and delinquency.[30]

Sheldon felt that he had distinguished three types of human physical structure: endomorphic (which may be roughly characterized as soft and round); mesomorphic (with predominance of muscle, bone, and connective tissue); and ectomorphic (with predominance of linearity and fragility). Though the types overlap, Sheldon relates these to three types of temperament: viscerotonia (characterized by general relaxation, sociability, and love of the approval of others), the digestive tract being "king"; somatotonia (seen in vigorous assertiveness and lust for power); and cerebrotonia (seen in inhibition, desire for privacy, and hyperattentiveness). Finally Sheldon presents three roughly corresponding psychiatric types: manic-depressive, paranoid, and heboid. The basic classification, however, is by physical type, though the transition from structure to function involved in relating somatotypes to temperament, psychiatric char-

---

[29] E. Kretschmer, *Physique and Character,* translated by W. J. H. Sprott (London: Kegan Paul, Trench, Trubner & Company, 1936).

[30] William H. Sheldon *et al., Varieties of Delinquent Youth* (New York: Harper & Brothers, 1949). Those seeking a thorough understanding of this book should also consult Sheldon's two earlier works: *Varieties of Human Physique* (New York: Harper & Brothers, 1940) and *Varieties of Temperament* (New York: Harper & Brothers, 1942).

acteristics, and finally to delinquency is, of course, crucial to his analysis. This last step Sheldon attempted in a study of 200 of what he speaks of as "delinquent youths" at a Boston institution called Hayden Goodwill Inn. Though each of the traits varies in frequency in a continuum, Sheldon insists he has identified an hereditary physical type which could be used in identifying potential delinquents at the age of six. Delinquents tend, he says, to be mesomorphic or endomorphic rather than ectomorphic. The connection between mesomorphy and delinquency Sheldon did not see as a deterministic one, however. Mesomorphy of build, presumably conductive to energetic vitality and freedom from inhibition, produces delinquency only when it occurs in social settings in which these qualities are likely to find few conventional avenues of expression.[31] Sheldon suggests that politicians, generals, and successful fiction writers typically are mesomorphs.[32]

As part of their study of 500 delinquent boys matched with 500 non-delinquents, Sheldon and Eleanor Glueck[33] had their 1,000 subjects somatotyped with the guidance of William Sheldon. The Gluecks did not use these data in developing their prediction scales, on the ground that physical anthropologists have not yet proven that somatotypes remain constant or can be distinguished at the age of six. They do, however, take their findings in this area very seriously. Their delinquents proved to be predominantly mesomorphic (muscular, solid), while nondelinquents showed a considerable incidence of ectomorphic traits. The Gluecks apparently even accept Sheldon's emphasis on hereditary factors of a physical type as "fundamentally related to differences in natural energy-tendencies."[34] They hint also at an early malfunctioning of endocrine glands as a possible explanation. Using the anthropological data collected for *Unraveling,* the Gluecks in 1956 published a monograph[35] reporting apparent relationships between physical build and a host of personal, social, and behavioral factors.

It is perhaps not unreasonable to expect muscularity to be associated with some forms of crime, and possibly certain kinds of fat deposit are prevalent in other types of delinquents. But the complete inadequacy of

---

[31] *Varieties of Delinquent Youth,* pp. 744–45.
[32] *Ibid.,* p. 745.
[33] *Unraveling Juvenile Delinquency* (New York: The Commonwealth Fund, 1950).
[34] *Ibid.,* p. 274.
[35] *Physique and Delinquency* (New York: Harper & Row, 1956). This book is dedicated to E. A. Hooton.

the Sheldon research to establish such expected facts and its even greater inadequacy to prove their hereditary basis is probably best set forth in Sutherland's scholarly if blistering analysis of this research.[36] Space permits us to list only the most important of his arguments:

1. Sheldon's research has no significance for the study of delinquency because he defines delinquency in terms of "disappointingness" (meaning behavior which disappointed Sheldon) and not in terms of violation of the law.

2. His method of scoring delinquents is also subjective and unreliable, as, for example, when he defines "first order psychopathy" in terms of subjectively determined interference with adjustment, which is apparently the same as his "disappointingness."

3. The varieties of delinquent youth he presents are themselves overlapping and inconsistent and do not differ from each other significantly in their somatotypes or psychiatric indexes, and these last, though somewhat concentrated in what Sheldon calls the endomorphic and mesomorphic areas, have no evaluative meaning. This is because their relation to social fitness is not made clear.

The population providing the somatotype standard against which the 200 boys were compared should be questioned. The 4,000 males comprising the standard were college students, "drawn mainly" from Harvard, Oberlin, and the University of Chicago.[37] Considering the predominantly northwestern European ethnic backgrounds of students at these schools prior to 1940 (when they were somatotyped) against the heavy interlarding of other ethnic stocks among the Boston boys,[38] any tendency toward heavier-set, mesomorphic build among the latter stocks would produce among the boys a physical bias toward mesomorphy, irrespective of their behavior. That such a tendency exists is suggested by the fact that of the 32 boys in the study both of whose parents were Caucausians of other than northwestern European background, 75 per cent (24) were mesomorphs; of the 121 boys of wholly northwestern European descent, 59 per cent (71) were mesomorphs.[39]

[36] Edwin H. Sutherland, "Critique of Sheldon's *Varieties of Delinquent Youth*," *American Sociological Review* (Feb. 1951), pp. 10–13.

[37] *Varieties of Delinquent Youth*, p. 726.

[38] One or both parents of 50 boys had descended from Caucasian stock other than northwest European; 13 other boys were wholly or partly Negro. Derived from *ibid.*, Table II, p. 721ff.

[39] *Ibid.*, derived from the biographies, pp. 114–718. Only cases unequivocally classified by Sheldon as mesomorphs were counted as such by the present authors.

The Endocrine Glands and Crime

Advances in biochemistry and related fields led to the emergence, during the 1910's, of the science of endocrinology, which is concerned with the influence upon bodily development and function of certain glandular secretions. Subsequent rapid discoveries in this field showed the dramatic effects which hypo- or hyper-secretion can have upon growth and behavior. While the great body of endocrinological findings were reported and interpreted with traditional scientific restraint, a number of workers in the field, perhaps caught up in their own enthusiasm, began sensationalizing their science by advocating its application as a panacea for social problems. Socially, the times were ripe: problems of urban adjustment were severely aggravated in the years before and after World War I by the vast "new immigration" from the rural regions of southern and eastern Europe. The spoils of bootlegging and vice were being fought over in our cities by ruthless gangs of these immigrants and their children. Problems of dependency among the newcomers arose, similar to those existing today among Negroes. Criminals, the unsuccessful, the socially inadequate, the impoverished, the psychologically disturbed—all were seen by some endocrinologists as the products of malfunctioning glands.

Dr. Max G. Schlapp, a professor of medicine and director of a New York children's clinic in the 1920's, represents the extreme approach in applying the new science to crime:

[We hope] to establish that such aberrations from the norm of conduct as we call crime are explicable under pathology, that there is in fact a Criminal Imperative, an inner drive which impels these forbidden and extraordinary human acts, and that this drive is to be completely accounted for under physico-chemical laws.[40]

With no controls, systematic presentation of his data, or statistical analyses, Schlapp supports his thesis by impressionistic descriptions of 30-odd cases of immigrant women who produced defective and delinquent children after arriving in the United States. His image of how a thief works shows his utter indifference to the role played in crime by sociological forces:

[A thief] sees a purse lying on a table and knows that it contains $50. The normal man might feel the desire for $50. He might need it sorely enough. But

[40] Schlapp and Smith, *op. cit.*, p. 28.

his intellectual control would at once advise him that the money was not his and he would draw away from the temptation without trouble. But the thief is emotionally disturbed and this is the dominant fact. He goes toward the coveted prize and then draws back, his intellectual center cautioning him with a wave of fear. He struggles between this fear and his desire. The contending impulses flow back and forth. Finally a wave of emotion sweeps the thief. He moves forward. He takes the bag. He flees. This thief has very likely tried to resist. . . . But before the reactions of his chemically disturbed bodily mechanism all willing and all fear have broken down.[41]

We do not indict endocrinological criminology on the basis of Schlapp's work, although it does show tendencies common to most subjective approaches (1) to confuse criminal behavior with abnormal behavior and (2) to overlook the operation of antisocial attitudes and values in criminal activities.

A number of researchers have found little or no connection between endocrine dysfunction and crime. A series of studies by Dr. Matthew Molitch and associates at the New Jersey State Home for Boys gave mixed and largely negative results when delinquents with endocrine disorders were compared with a control group of normal delinquents.[42] About equal proportions of delinquents and nondelinquents in the Glueck study showed external signs of glandular disturbances.[43]

Of some special interest is the possible relationship between glandular imbalance or dysfunction and sexual crimes of the more extreme types. Individuals probably differ physiologically in the power of the sex drive, but these differences have not been satisfactorily measured and are greatly influenced by cultural factors.[44] In some instances homosexuality seems to have a morphological and physiological basis, but it also has social roots. Possibly because we have not yet uncovered all the social correlates of some of our most "inhuman" crimes of violence as completely as in the case of other offenses, we cannot disregard the possible influence of physiological factors upon them.

[41] *Ibid.,* p. 202.

[42] Matthew Molitch, "Endocrine Disturbance in Behavior Problems," *American Journal of Psychiatry* (March 1937), p. 1179. Cf. also Matthew Molitch and Sam Poliakoff, "Subclinical Hypothyroidism in Children," *Endocrinology* (Nov. 1936), p. 820; "Pituitary Disturbances in Behavior Problems," *American Journal of Orthopsychiatry* (Jan. 1936), pp. 125–33; "Gonadal Disturbances in Behavior Problems," *American Journal of Orthopsychiatry* (Oct. 1936), pp. 553–61.

[43] *Unraveling Juvenile Delinquency,* pp. 177–78.

[44] Cf. Lowell S. Selling, "The Endocrine Glands and the Sex Offender," *Medical Record* (May 18, 1938), pp. 441–44.

Intelligence and Crime

With the great vogue of intelligence testing some decades ago, no explanation of crime was more investigated and no interpretation more generally accepted than the correlation between low-grade intelligence and crime. It was held that if we could only get rid of the stupid people in the world, we should largely eliminate the bad people in the world. In later years more refined research and especially the discovery of how stupid the rest of us are have made less significant the "stupidity" of the criminal.

Various difficulties are involved in correlating intelligence and crime. No one is quite certain what intelligence is. Test results have varied greatly according to whether they have been designed to measure general abstract intelligence, ability to comprehend concrete materials, or mechanical or other specialized capacities.[45] It has become increasingly evident that no device can completely eliminate the effect of learning and opportunity upon test scores. It is difficult to separate intellectual from emotional qualities. A major difficulty also lies in the fact that to measure the intelligence of the delinquent you must first catch him. Arrested criminals should be less clever than those who avoid arrest. Finally, study of delinquents has shown that, if stupidy causes one man to blunder into crime, it incapacitates a second for crimes requiring cleverness. The feeble-minded tend to continue in a rut, whether it be the rut of simple crime or the rut of simple virtue. Some folks don't know enough to sin!

In 1928–29, Sutherland analyzed some 350 studies of intelligence and crime.[46] He showed that, whereas earlier studies graded as many as 50 per cent of criminals feeble-minded, the average finding had dropped to about 20 per cent, but that even in the later period results varied greatly with methods used.[47]

[45] Florence L. Goodenough has pointed out that when different intelligence tests supposed to measure the same thing are given to a homogeneous group of children, it is hard to find any two which will yield intercorrelations as high as 0.87; that proportions of juvenile delinquents found feeble-minded have dropped from as high as 80 per cent to as low as 12 per cent; and that therefore mere intelligence tests are not enough. We must devise means to include in our measurements the conditions under which the delinquent functions. Cf. "The Relation of Mental Growth to Personality and Adjustment," *Mental Hygiene* (April 1937), pp. 243–54.

[46] E. H. Sutherland, "Mental Deficiency and Crime," in Kimball Young, ed., *Social Attitudes* (New York: Henry Holt, 1931), pp. 357–75.

[47] Cf. Clara Frances Chassell, *The Relation Between Morality and Intellect* (New York: Teachers College, Columbia University, Bureau of Publications, 1935), p. 134 and *passim*. Her study possibly combines too freely studies of varying types and of varying value.

We can perhaps conclude that, if allowance could be made for the selective effect of arrest and incarceration, little distinctive difference in intelligence would be found between delinquents and nondelinquents, although speaking generally, juvenile delinquents, women delinquents, and the typical jail population, with some exceptions, usually score low on such tests. On the other hand, felons in criminal courts or imprisoned in state institutions have often been shown to approximate the test scores of the army draft or other control group.[48] An Illinois survey covering over 10,000 men and 153 women prisoners confirms this last conclusion.[49] Some years ago only 2.4 per cent of more than 9,000 criminals examined at the Court of General Sessions in New York City were classified as mentally defective.[50] This percentage is lower, it is true, than that found by some other psychologists, and much depends on definition. When studied by type of offense, wide differences are found, with men guilty of fraud, embezzlement, and forgery scoring high and sex offenders at the bottom of the list. Here, too, sex offenders who are caught probably are more highly selected than are forgers who are caught. Stanley D. Porteus, the inventor of the Maze intelligence tests, has recently concluded that too much attention has been attached to the mental level of the delinquent.[51]

If we ask *how* does lack of intelligence affect crime, there is more agreement among students. Doll [52] says the feeble-minded as a class are not aggressively antisocial or aggressively sexually promiscuous, but passive and timid. They are easily led because they do not foresee the consequences of their behavior, are unable to cope with the difficulties of modern life, and are unable to see the difference between right and wrong or to realize the danger of detection.[53] They often seem merely to stumble into crime. Higher-grade defectives may be influenced by their relative failure in life. In any case, however, feeble-mindedness accounts for a very small proportion of delinquency.[54]

[48] Cf. Carl Murchison, *Criminal Intelligence* (Worcester, Mass.: Clark University, 1926).

[49] Simon H. Tulchin, *Intelligence and Crime* (Chicago: University of Chicago Press, 1939).

[50] Charles B. Thompson, M.D., "Some New Aspects of the Psychiatric Approach to Crime," *Mental Hygiene* (Oct. 1936), p. 533.

[51] "Setting the Sights for Delinquency," *Federal Probation* (June 1953), pp. 43–47.

[52] Edgar A. Doll, "Social Adjustment of the Mentally Subnormal," *Journal of Educational Research* (Sept. 1934), pp. 36–43.

[53] Milton Harrington, "The Problem of the Defective Delinquent," *Mental Hygiene* (July 1935) pp. 429–38.

[54] For a very different discussion of mental deficiency and crime in terms of social roles, see Edward J. Ferentz, "Mental Deficiency Related to Crime," *Journal of Criminal Law, Criminology and Police Science* (Sept.–Oct. 1954), pp. 299–307.

After reviewing British and American studies of intelligence among delinquents, Mary Woodward concluded that not only does low intelligence play little or no part in delinquency causation but that apparently lower I.Q.'s among delinquents are accounted for by the association with delinquency of constellations of cultural factors which adversely affect test scores.[55]

Personality Characteristics and Crime

PERSONALITY AS A SOCIAL PRODUCT

In a sense we all become human in the family and in other primary groups which socialize, culturalize, and determine status.[56] On the other hand, individual "constitutional" differences, even if social products themselves, also affect the personality and the role the individual will play in a given group or in a given culture. With a given physical and psychological make-up a man will succeed in one culture but fail in another. Yet any particular group awards or denies status differently to different types of personality.

The type of personality a child will have is largely determined before his arrival by the nature of the general culture and by the nature of the interpersonal relations in the particular family into which he is born. The family will be the medium through which the larger culture impinges upon him in early childhood. In the family also the temperament of the child is influenced by the temperament of parents. Thus Jimmy conceivably becomes emotionally unstable and selfish partly because of his own original equipment, but more because of quarreling, nagging parents who teach him the importance in our culture of successful competition but give him little preparation for such success. Some [57] have distinguished rather sharply between traits which are psychogenetic and those which are cultural. The former are held to be relatively permanent characteristics of the personality and to have their origin in familial interpersonal relations. Our own view is that such sharp distinctions cannot be made, since even traits called psychogenetic, such as egocentricity, reflect in part the general culture

[55] Mary Woodward, "The Role of Low Intelligence in Delinquency," *British Journal of Delinquency* (April 1955), pp. 299–300.

[56] For further discussion of the role of the family in these respects, see below, Chapter 9.

[57] Cf. Edward Sapir, "Personality," *Encyclopaedia of the Social Sciences*, Vol. XII, pp. 85–87; and especially Ernest W. Burgess, "Personality Traits of the Brothers," in Clifford Shaw, ed., *Brothers in Crime* (Chicago: University of Chicago Press, 1938), pp. 326–35.

as mediated by the family and, though relatively permanent, may and do change as a result of later social experiences. Clearly, personality affects behavior, but in doing so it is the medium through which present and past social situations operate.

Elements in personality especially significant for the explanation of crime include interests, beliefs, opinions, habits, and attitudes. Thus so-called antisocial attitudes, interests which conflict with those of society, habits which are socially condemned or interfere with normal social relationships—these are but a few of the specific elements in personality believed to be significant for crime.

Most researchers attempting to find connections between criminal behavior and traits of personality have shared with subjectivists a tendency to regard criminal behavior as symptomatic of deviations from physical or psychological norms on the part of offenders. The apparently insurmountable difficulty of getting adequate samples of criminals and delinquents which has plagued the subjective approaches from their beginnings continues, however, to dog the work of personality researchers. Juveniles, and the thieves, robbers, and burglars unlucky enough to be imprisoned, are virtually the only offenders studied in sizable numbers. From the kinds of research requiring direct contact between investigator and subject, almost no knowledge has been obtained of the traits of white-collar offenders, crooked politicians, syndicate bosses, labor racketeers, and craftsmanlike lesser offenders whose wealth, influence, or shrewdness keep them out of prison but whose depredations constitute an important share of our crime problem. This limitation on data should be kept in mind particularly in considering studies of offenders' personalities, because such studies emerge from the principal remaining subjectivist stronghold, buttressed in recent decades by the determined guardianship of psychiatrists and psychologists.[58] As a subjectivist approach, the personality approach to crime causation is open to the precautionary remarks made at the beginning of this chapter.

THE USE OF PERSONALITY TESTS

No doubt the most complete knowledge of the personalities of criminals and delinquents has been derived from long experience in association

[58] Michael Hakeem, "A Critique of the Psychiatric Approach to Delinquency and Crime," *Law and Contemporary Problems* (Autumn 1958), pp. 650–82. Among similar remarks by other psychiatrists, Zilboorg and Henry are quoted as saying that "criminology today, like demonology of yesterday, is a battlefield for the rightful possession of which the psychiatrist is still fighting" (p. 655). As a branch of medicine, psychiatry views crime as a symptom of disease. For a careful discussion of the weakness of this position, see A. G. N. Flew, "Crime or Disease," *British Journal of Sociology* (March 1954), pp. 49–62.

with them and from case and life histories. These sources of information have the advantage of showing how one personality trait is related to others and to varying social situations, past and present. From such detailed studies of many individuals, statistics of the prevalence of specified traits among criminals may be derived. In addition various types of personality tests have been developed for this purpose. There is a long list of characteristics which help explain human failure or revolt or nonadjustment to life. There are types of interests, attitudes, capacities, and so on, the degree of group disapproval of which helps account for nonadjustment. At the moment, however, we are rather concerned with testing of intellectual, emotional, or personality traits found most nearly distinctive of criminals as compared with noncriminals.

A brief résumé of a few of the most important among such tests by Carlton W. Orchinik [59] is useful here. The New Revised Stanford-Binet Tests of Intelligence are still widely used. Since education gives a distinct advantage in the achievement of high scores on these tests, they are supplemented by the use of performance tests like the Porteus Maze Test,[60] the Pintner-Patterson Scales, the Wechsler-Bellevue Intelligence Scale, and others, though all are in varying degrees influenced by varying opportunities which those tested have had. In certain types of cases we need to know the intellectual ability of delinquents, but as we noted above, feeble-mindedness is now known not to distinguish criminals as a whole from noncriminals. Some delinquents would not have stumbled or been led into crime had they not been so stupid; others could not have been successful in crime had they not been so bright.

Delinquency is often associated with delayed maturation of children. Hence the Vineland Maturity Scale is found useful. Tests attempt to reveal such characteristics as annoyance, conflict, aspirations, consistency, introversion or extroversion, euphoria and happiness, frustration, honesty, punctuality, degree of social acceptance or social nonadjustment. Some of these, such as social nonadjustment, are so nearly synonymous with delinquency that test scores proving that criminals are less well adjusted than noncriminals have little meaning. Equally obvious is the finding that the chronically unsocialized—the psychopaths—are extremely numerous among delinquents. Nor is it strange that a good many delinquents are found to be frustrated or in conflict with other individuals and groups or with society as a whole.

---

[59] As reported in Negley K. Teeters and John Otto Reinemann, *The Challenge of Delinquency* (New York: Prentice-Hall, 1950), pp. 269–73.

[60] For a recent discussion of use of these tests by Dr. Porteus himself, see Stanley D. Porteus, "Setting Our Sights for Delinquency Research," *Federal Probation* (June 1953), pp. 43–47.

Since some significant characteristics of delinquents may not be realized by them, or may be of such a nature as to bring shame, or for other reasons may be concealed, so-called projective techniques for their discovery have been developed. One such test, widely debated and widely used, is the Rorschach test. Asked to indicate what ink blots "could be" or "look like," the subject supposedly reveals significant emotional aspects of his personality. Rorschach test results have been more fully validated with mental patients than with delinquents. Yet Sheldon and Eleanor Glueck [61] feel that they have proven to be diagnostic of criminality in their comparison of 500 delinquents with 500 nondelinquents. The Rorschach test has, however, been severely criticized as a diagnostic tool.[62] The Thematic Apperception Test differs from the Rorschach in that it presents actual social situations in the form of pictures. The subject tells the story of the situation, the feelings of the characters, and the final outcome. In so doing he reveals some of his own emotions, motives, and attitudes which may be indicative of past delinquency or which may cautiously be used for prediction of future behavior.

We may emphatically state that none of the above-mentioned tests clearly distinguishes all criminals from all noncriminals. The traits they are designed to measure exist in some degree among nondelinquents as well. Probably the most serious challenge to the significance of the tests was published in 1950 by Schuessler and Cressey.[63] They examined the findings of all the studies to that date which had compared criminals with noncriminals. In only a little over two-fifths of the 113 studies examined did they find that the test differentiated the two groups.[64] Although their findings were extremely negative, they would agree that some qualifications are called for. The following briefly summarizes their major conclusions.

With certain qualifications these authors found that testing has not shown criminals to be distinctively emotionally unstable, emotionally immature, emotionally disturbed, temperamentally contrasted with noncriminals, nor different in total personality or even in character. They do add,

[61] *Unraveling Juvenile Delinquency,* Chapter XVIII.

[62] Hakeem, *loc. cit.,* pp. 665–66.

[63] Karl F. Schuessler and Donald R. Cressey, "Personality Characteristics of Criminals," *American Journal of Sociology* (March 1950), pp. 476–84.

[64] The authors of the critique did *not* prove or pretend to prove that no personality tests have distinguished any types of criminals from any types of noncriminals. Nor should the Schuessler-Cressey findings be interpreted as meaning that, even with improved techniques, testing will always be useless for the understanding and treatment of delinquents and criminals. Indeed, and by way of example, they themselves found that (*ibid.,* p. 477) four studies using the Porteus Maze Tests did differentiate criminals from noncriminals. Finally, the Schuessler-Cressey critique was written before a number of significant studies using, for example, the Rorschach and the Minnesota Multiphasic Personality Inventory had been more fully tested.

however, that perhaps attitudes studies, when more completely developed and used, may partly differentiate the criminal from the noncriminal population.

The Minnesota Multiphasic Personality Inventory,[65] which uses no fewer than 550 items, seems to have been proven in considerable degree to distinguish delinquents and "predelinquents." The Inventory reveals the delinquent as differing from the nondelinquent chiefly with respect to mental deviations of the psychopathic or the manic type. That delinquents are thus found to be characteristically unsocialized or to have less control than nondelinquents over their emotions does not seem surprising. Fairly obvious though this fact may be, the tests may nevertheless be valuable where adequate knowledge derived from fuller study of individuals is not available. Deviations in the direction of the symptoms of certain other mental diseases are also found relatively prevalent among delinquents. In addition, young male adolescents are shown to have fewer feminine interests than have delinquents. Patients whose profiles, however, resemble those of the neurotically depressed, hypochrondriacal, or psychasthenic are shown to be less likely to become delinquent than those similar to the psychotic and psychopathic. Hathaway and Monachesi recognize that "not all of the MMPI scales discriminate adequately between delinquents and nondelinquents," but they are able to show that some do so. It is not certain whether the MMPI tests point out true causes of delinquency or not, nor whether they suggest proper programs of treatment or prevention. Their usefulness for prediction has been questioned also.[66] We must emphasize the far greater importance that social relations underlying such mental states be discovered. These may be more important causes of delinquency than the mental peculiarities themselves, although such peculiarities do often prevent acceptance in constructive groups, and lack of such acceptance will be shown to be a major cause of delinquency.

PERSONALITIES AND SOCIAL RELATIONS AND ROLES

Professor Reiss [67] has taken a significant step in the direction of identifying social relations which are correlates of some of the psychological types discovered by psychologists. Reiss divides his delinquents into three

[65] Cf. Starke H. Hathaway and Elio D. Monachesi, *Analyzing and Predicting Juvenile Delinquency with the MMPI* (Minneapolis, Minn.: University of Minnesota Press, 1953). For a briefer statement, see their article, "The Minnesota Multiphasic Personality Inventory in the Study of Juvenile Delinquents," *American Sociological Review* (Dec. 1952), pp. 704–10.

[66] See *infra,* Chapter 29.

[67] Albert J. Reiss, Jr., "Social Correlates of Psychological Types of Delinquency," *American Sociological Review* (Dec. 1952), pp. 71–81.

types: the relatively integrated, the delinquent with markedly weak ego controls, and the delinquent with relatively defective super-ego controls. He suggests that differences in socio-economic status distinguish these three psychoanalytically labeled types. (1) Integrated delinquents come from families well integrated into the local life of their communities and which have good marital relations, teach moral ideals to their children, and have effective methods of controlling them, but which live in the less desirable areas of the city. These delinquents may be individual offenders or members of delinquent groups. They are less often repeaters than the two other types. (2) Delinquents with faulty ego controls, on the other hand, were found to be insecure persons with low self-esteem, or persons highly aggressive toward others in their environment. These come from economically better areas but from families which have been mobile. They less often participate in peer groups, such as gangs. In their homes there is frequently marital conflict, and their parents less often have conventional ideals. Their problem is more apt to be associated with the anxieties and conflicts of their parents. (3) The defective super-ego delinquent (the one without a disturbing conscience) has characteristics approximating those of the psychopath. He has not internalized the larger community's prevailing symbols of conventional control, nor has he become socialized, and he therefore does not experience a sense of guilt over his delinquencies. He has grown up in unconventional situations. He usually lives in areas of high mobility, such as the rooming-house district. Yet the families of such delinquents are less mobile than those of the second type. Hence the delinquents have had time to absorb patterns prevailing in their immediate neighborhoods rather than those of the larger society. They tend to reject the school and other conventional institutions. They often come from homes broken by desertion, divorce, and separation. Their parents are often in conflict and often lack effective means of control or of teaching moral ideals. These delinquents are very frequently gang members, and their acts are rationalized and approved by these peer groups. Their acts thus bring them less mental conflict and fewer feelings of guilt.

The significance of Reiss's study for the explanation and prevention of delinquency seems to us great indeed. Chapters which follow will furnish additional factual bases for his emphasis on social correlates of personality types.[68]

[68] For another significant effort to relate types of delinquent personalities to social situations and social relations, see Lester Eugene Hewett and Richard L. Jenkins, *Fundamental Patterns of Maladjustment: The Dynamics of Their Origin* (Springfield, Ill.: state publication, 1946). This significant study distinguishes "three fundamental patterns of maladjustment": the unsocialized aggressive, the socialized delin-

Characterization of personality may be helpful in the identification of predelinquents. It often does furnish an immediate but superficial explanation of crime. Offender A, for example, appears to have been impelled to crime because as a paranoid type his suspicions that others dislike him express themselves as a violent assault. Offender B is extremely self-centered and disregards the rights of others in ways defined as criminal. Offender C has always been considered "odd," and his oddness has excluded him from social relations which might have kept him from delinquency, or he reacts to exclusion in delinquent ways. In none of such cases, however, does the nature of the personality itself explain how the personality was acquired. Nor does it tell us whether the cause of misbehavior is in the personality or in social relations which have been experienced. Therefore characterization of personality furnishes an inadequate basis for prevention or treatment.

Suggested Readings

Lombrosianism

Ferrero, Gina Lombroso. *Criminal Man.* New York: G. P. Putnam's Sons, 1911. Written by his daughter, this English-language abridgment of Cesare Lombroso's principal book is hardly an adequate portrayal of the great man's scholarly researches, but it contains his main ideas and conclusions.

Ferri, Enrico. *Criminal Sociology.* Boston: Little, Brown, and Company, 1917. Ferri's socialist sympathies show clearly in this book. An interesting early attempt at eclectic criminology.

————. *The Positive School of Criminology.* Chicago: Charles H. Kerr and Company, 1913. A brief but brilliant statement of the Italian School's intellectual foundations.

Lombroso, Cesare. *Crime, Its Causes and Remedies.* Boston: Little, Brown, and Company, 1911. Lombroso's final book. An excellent example of matured Italian school thought.

Neo-Lombrosianism

Glueck, Sheldon and Eleanor. *Unraveling Juvenile Delinquency.* New York: The Commonwealth Fund, 1950. A comparison study of 500 Boston

---

quent, and the overinhibited. The first two are the more significant in connection with delinquency. These are related by the authors to parental rejection and parental negligence and exposure to delinquent patterns respectively. Their personalities are, however, subclassified into a variety of characteristic traits, and their social relations into a variety of relations. Useful as such classifications have proven, it must be borne in mind that less than half the delinquents could be classified as falling wholly within any one of these categories.

delinquents and 500 nondelinquents. It incorporates William Sheldon's neo-Lombrosian theory and was the springboard for renewed interest in delinquency prediction. Its multitude of factual social findings are valuable.

Hooton, Earnest A. *The American Criminal, An Anthropological Study.* Cambridge, Mass.: Harvard University Press, 1939. Massive anthropometric study of 14,000 prisoners. Neo-Lombrosianism is energetically defended in the early sections.

————. *Crime and the Man.* Cambridge, Mass.: Harvard University Press, 1939. A shortened, popularized version of *The American Criminal.* It should not be read as a substitute for the original.

Sheldon, William H., *et al. Varieties of Delinquent Youth.* New York: Harper and Brothers, 1949. Two hundred "disappointing" Boston youths somatotyped, with thumbnail biographies. Sheldon is a forceful and amusing writer; if his data do not convince you, his charm might.

Freudianism

Brill, A. A., translator and editor. *The Basic Writings of Sigmund Freud.* New York: The Modern Library, 1938. A collection of six of Freud's monographs. These should be read in preference to Mullahy or Hall. Interpreters can never do full justice to the interpreted.

Bromberg, Walter. *Crime and the Mind.* Philadelphia: J. B. Lippincott Company, 1948. Neo-Freudian principles are used in this interesting attempt to interpret a wide variety of crimes psychoanalytically.

Hall, Calvin S. *A Primer of Freudian Psychology.* New York: The New American Library, 1954.

Mullahy, Patrick. *Oedipus Myth and Complex.* New York: Grove Press, 1955. Together, these books are a clear and impartial exposition of Freudian psychology.

Other

Abrahamsen, David. *The Psychology of Crime.* New York: Columbia University Press, 1960. An excellent example of the almost purely psychopathological approach to crime. To Abrahamsen crime is a symptom of psychological disorder: "A general characteristic of . . . people who commit crime is that they possess to an overwhelming degree abnormal emotional affects" (p. 106). He presents only anecdotal evidence to support this contention.

Burt, Cyril. *The Young Delinquent.* New York: D. Appleton-Century Company, Incorporated, 1933. An English psychologist studies 197 children via case histories and finds 15 interrelated causal factors. An example of the multiple factor approach.

Law and Contemporary Problems, Autumn, 1958. A symposium of 10 excellent articles on crime and correction, including critiques of the legal, psychiatric, and sociological approaches.

Every student of the social sciences should become acquainted with *Law and Contemporary Problems;* its contents are invariably in the best scholarly tradition.

CHAPTER 7

The Negro and Crime

Those concerned with the problem of crime among American Negroes seem inclined to veer toward one of two extremes of sentiment, both of which are rooted in ideological orientations rather than in empirical assessments of Negro crime. The first of these positions is occupied by persons who are "pro-Negro" in the sense that they feel keenly about the second-class social and economic status of American Negroes, are concerned that equal rights shall prevail without regard to skin color, and take strong stands against the various forms of racial discrimination. To this group, Negro crime is a direct responsibility of whites, for it is seen as a by-product of the discrimination practiced by whites. To some in the group, the apparently high rate of Negro crime is an artifact arising from discriminatory law-enforcement practices, themselves a product of anti-Negro feelings among policemen, judges, juries, prosecutors, prison authorities, and parole boards. A simple tenet consequently emerges from this position: Negro crime is "caused" by discrimination; the possibility that some Negro crime might arise from etiological processes unrelated to discrimination is seldom entertained.

The other extreme position is that of the "anti-Negro," found among persons subscribing to the troglodytic image of the Negro as a primitive, subhuman, oversexed, lazy, happy-go-lucky, irresponsible being. This image of the Negro was, of course, one promoted avidly during slavery days to render that "peculiar institution" more palatable to what was ostensibly a Christian culture, and this idea is still doing yeoman service as a rationale for the continuance of segregation and other forms of discrimination. To this school, Negro crime is an expression of biological necessity: the Negro's primitive elemental passions and inadequate mentality render him unsuitable to the demands of complex urban living.

The authors of this text should make clear their own position between these two extremes. The first we find untenable for two reasons: (1) a monistic explanation is no more acceptable for Negro crime than for white crime, but "explaining" Negro crime in terms of discrimination is monistic thinking; (2) if we separate pious beliefs from scientific knowledge, the assumption inherent in the first position that biological differences have *nothing* to do with differences in behavior between races is untenable because we do not as yet have sufficient unequivocal information to make such a flat statement. The second extreme we reject as naively biological, arising not from reputable scientific researches but from a need to justify slavery and its post-bellum child, discrimination. Our stand is, however, closer to the first extreme than to the second. We believe (but cannot prove) that the position of Negroes in American society is much more significant in understanding Negro crime than are possible biological differences, but we also believe that attention to social forces unconnected with discrimination is necessary. After all, white crime can scarcely be accounted for by racial discrimination: both races are responsive to the criminogenic elements in our general culture, and some Negroes would undoubtedly commit crimes even if discrimination did not exist.

The Negro Minority in American Society

In Chapter 2 we saw American society largely as an integration of European cultures with a dwindling core of Puritanism. We have seen the peoples who brought those cultures seeking various goals, predominantly the not wholly harmonious goals of liberty and material profit. The various nationalities and races which came created a pattern of minorities involved in some degree of culture conflict. That conflict of cultures, though permitting contributions from each element to a richer whole, partly accounts for problems of adjustment and crime in the United States. But because American economic opportunity and American freedoms have been fairly generally open to all these European minorities, they have come to be bound together by common material and nonmaterial aims into a cultural pluralism which is modern America.

Most of the early settlers and most of the more recent immigrants came here voluntarily. But when King Cotton came to the South, the search for profits proved dominant over American dedication to human freedom. Northern shipping interests and Southern plantation owners imported large numbers of unwilling migrants—the Negro slaves. Thus was created the largest and most persistent of American minorities, defined by their lowly status as "second-class Americans," used and discriminated against and permitted to be in, but hardly of, American society. Sometimes almost accepting their low status, but increasingly revolting against it, the Negro population has also been defined as a minority by their own attitudes and sense of being apart. It is ironic that a tenth of the population of the United States today carries the heritage of slavery in the "land of freedom." Therein lies the essence of what Myrdal [1] calls "the American dilemma": a genuine tradition of freedom and equality combined with the stubborn fact of actual unequal Negro status, held necessary to rationalize, if not to justify, continued discrimination and exploitation.

In that continuing if declining discrimination lies the major explanation of the apparent excessive contribution of the Negro minority to the American crime problem. It also helps explain the crimes of whites which grow out of their relations with Negroes. Race discrimination is not, however, a result of any inherent difference between the people of the North and the people of the South. Negro crime is even more excessive in Northern cities than in the rural areas of the old South. Indeed, the isolating caste system of the South created at least temporarily a pattern of coexistence between the races which prevented some of the more open forms of aggression. By the same token, however, it tended to perpetuate the basic cause of the difficulty. Today that pattern is breaking down. The breakdown has probably immediately increased some tensions, while ultimately undermining the basis for the discrimination which is the root of the differential between Negro and white recorded crime rates. We say "recorded" advisedly, because we shall find that the contrasts in relative arrests, for example, do not correctly measure actual differences in criminal behavior.

STATISTICS OF NEGRO CRIME

The difficulties encountered in general criminal statistics are increased when attempts are made to measure the relative amounts and kinds of crime

[1] Gunnar Myrdal, *An American Dilemma* (New York: Harper & Brothers, 1944).

committed by Negroes. As we pointed out in Chapter 4, our best national statistics on the extent and kinds of crime are found in the F.B.I.'s data on crimes known to the police. These data cannot, by their nature, give information on the individuals responsible for committing the crimes. The earliest statistic-gathering point in the law-enforcement process where such information becomes available is in *arrest* data, but these reflect imperfectly the ages, races, and sexes of the offenders responsible for the "crimes known" because of the vagaries—both avoidable and unavoidable—present in the process of nabbing suspects. The feeling is widespread among criminologists, race relations experts, Negro leaders, and others that the Negro crime rate is exaggerated because of discriminatory arrest practices on the part of police agencies. (Extremists of the "pro-Negro" group, in fact, are inclined to attribute to police discrimination *all* the disproportion in Negro arrest statistics.) Negroes are more liable both to be suspected of and to be arrested for certain crimes than are whites. Drag-net arrests and illegal arrests are more likely to occur when Negroes rather than whites are involved. In the absence of reliable data on the extent of police discrimination, however, to estimate what disproportion from this source distorts Negro arrest statistics is impossible. In view of the disorganized, frustrating, and spiritually impoverished existence of the great mass of our urban Negro proletariat, we think it unlikely that the actual (although unknowable) rate of ordinary crimes against property and person would not be considerably higher among Negroes than among whites. It would then follow that the arrest disproportions shown in Table 4, while undoubtedly reflecting to some degree the uneven application of police powers, may bear enough relationship to reality to provide an approximate guide to the kinds of crimes committed by Negroes.

A recent survey of statistical studies made during the last 50 years on the extent and kinds of Negro crime concluded that Negro crime rates are "considerably" higher than white rates in murder, manslaughter, assaults, burglary, and gambling; "probably" higher for auto theft, drug offenses, robbery, larceny, and prostitution; and "equal to or less than" white rates in kidnapping, alcoholic offenses, and forgery.[2] These findings are roughly similar to the rates indicated in Table 4, which presents for 1961 a rough approximation of the degree to which Negroes figured in urban arrest statistics disproportionately to their percentage in the 1960 urban population of persons 14 years old and over. Thus, on gambling charges, Negroes were arrested nearly six times more than their 12.2 per cent "quota" in the

[2] Leonard D. Savitz, *Crime and the Negro: A Critical Review of the Literature* (Philadelphia, mimeographed, 1962), p. 24.

Table 4 PROPORTIONATE EXCESSES OF NEGRO OVER WHITE ARRESTS IN 2,759 CITIES, 1961

Gambling	5.78	Stolen property	2.72
Aggravated assault	4.98	Burglary	2.64
Murder	4.78	Larceny	2.55
Robbery	4.40	Liquor laws	2.39
Carrying weapons	4.38	Vagrancy	2.23
Forcible rape	4.15	Other sex offenses	2.17
Prostitution	3.83	Drunkenness	2.02
Other assaults	3.45	Auto theft	1.74
Disorderly conduct	3.14	Forgery and counterfeiting	1.44
Narcotic drugs	3.00	Embezzlement and fraud	1.42
Offenses against family		Drunken driving	1.28
and children	2.76		

Computed from *Uniform Crime Reports: 1961* (Washington, D. C.: U. S. Department of Justice, 1962), p. 97. Totals for non-whites other than Negroes were negligible, except for 60,000 Indian drunkenness arrests; these were eliminated from the computations.

total arrests for gambling would call for. Moreover, the further from "arrests" a racial count is made, the greater is the excess of Negro over white rates: the disproportion grows as the count moves through the stages of indictment, trial, conviction, and imprisonment. The proportion of Negroes executed in 1961 was no less than five times their 10 per cent proportion in the total population.[3]

Contrasts in types of crimes committed are probably influenced in part by the fact that the Negro has less opportunity to commit some crimes. Owning fewer cars, lacking driving skills, and living where fewer cars are owned by others, he steals fewer. Not being to as large an extent in business, crimes associated with white-collar employment (embezzlement, fraud, price-fixing, and so on) are less distinctively in his line. Being largely semi-skilled and unskilled in vocational preparation, he is less likely to counterfeit money or forge documents. Living in a subculture where interpersonal violence supplements mere noisy verbal exchanges when differences arise, he very often gets into trouble for carrying weapons and committing assaults, some of which lead to second-degree homicides.

[3] U. S. Department of Justice, *National Prisoner Statistics,* No. 28 (April 1962), Table 1. A recent statistical analysis of commutation and execution of death penalties in Pennsylvania suggests that in that state since 1914, "Negroes have not received equal consideration for commutation of the death penalty." [Marvin E. Wolfgang, Arlene Kelly, and Hans C. Nolde, "Comparison of the Executed and the Commuted Among Admissions to Death Row," *Journal of Criminal Law, Criminology and Police Science* (Sept. 1962), p. 311.]

The crimes which police tend to overlook if perpetrated against other Negroes are apt to be the relatively petty ones, except where they wish to apprehend Negroes for other reasons. This must give an exaggerated impression of the proportion of serious crimes for which Negroes as compared with whites are arrested. Moreover, crimes probably are often defined differently in cases involving Negroes, especially, perhaps, in the South. What homicides shall be held to be premeditated? What assaults are "aggravated"? What sex relations are really rapes? Against whom shall laws penalizing gambling be enforced? Given the tendency to blame the Negro, and given the Negro's relative lack of influence politically and socially, the exact crimes for which he will be prosecuted and punished are often very different than in the case of white men committing similar acts.

A BIOLOGICAL RACE FACTOR UNPROVED

The overwhelming evidence of the role of cultural factors in Negro crime argues against the role of biological factors. In eschewing the ideologically-based "pro-Negro" position, however, we likewise eschew another tendency within it, namely, to deny flatly and vehemently that racial biological differences play *any* role in Negro behavior, although in our opinion nothing in the way of convincing evidence which would belie such denial has been adduced by contemporary research. Both mental defects and mental disease may quite possibly be more prevalent among Negroes than among whites because of the observed association between low social status and high psychopathology rates,[4] but such association does not constitute proof of genetic or other biological factors in the etiology of such mental conditions. Moreover, neither low intelligence nor mental disease accounts for a large proportion of crime.

ECONOMIC HANDICAPS OF NEGROES

In a later chapter we shall minimize poverty as a direct influence on crime but shall emphasize other economic influences and the indirect effects of relative poverty. For example, failure in economic competition explains much crime; indirectly, relative poverty explains life in city slums, and slum life is conducive to crime. In spite of marked improvement in his lot, the Negro is still relatively unsuccessful economically, and he, though thousands

---

[4] August B. Hollingshead and Frederick C. Redlich, *Social Class and Mental Illness* (New York: John Wiley & Sons, 1958).

are exceptions, characteristically lives in the slums of our cities. It is therefore pertinent to examine the relative economic status of the Negro minority.

The low economic status of the Negro is indicated by wage, income, unemployment, and occupation statistics. In 1959 an appreciably larger percentage of Negroes (11.5) was reported as unemployed as compared with whites (4.6), a circumstance associated, of course, with the Negro's proportionally greater employment in occupations particularly affected by economic fluctuations.[5] The 1960 Census report on the occupational distributions of urban males showed nearly three times as many whites than Negroes employed at the professional and semi-professional level. These figures were reversed at the level of unskilled laborers.[6] Sharp declines between 1940 and 1960 have occurred in the proportion of Negroes employed in stabilizing (if impoverished) agricultural pursuits. In the earlier year 23.1 per cent of employed male Negroes were farmers or farm managers; by 1960 the percentage was a mere 5.7. The corresponding figures for farm laborers or farm foremen were 19.9 and 8.9 per cent respectively.[7] While some gains have been made in the proportion of Negroes employed in white-collar occupations, only 14.0 per cent of urban male Negroes as against 34.7 per cent of whites were so employed.[8]

Studies have found the Negro exploited in obtaining credit through installment purchases or loan companies. Moreover, owing partly to these economic handicaps and partly to the more direct effects of race prejudice, members of this race are obliged to live in deteriorated and delinquency areas of our cities, where many other social handicaps and incitements to crime exist. White criminal gangs often have headquarters in Negro neighborhoods. Though at any given moment some Negroes may themselves accept and profit from vice located in their vicinity, those who wish to be rid of it find action difficult to secure because the Negro often lacks political influence.

Negroes in industry have suffered from lack of union organization, for the "unity of labor" breaks down at the color line. The 1955 constitution of the AFL-CIO contained a racial disclaimer, and a Civil Rights Department was created to deal with union discrimination. Although integration is proceeding in many industrial unions, the trade and craft unions—whose

---

[5] Charles F. Marden and Gladys Meyer, *Minorities in American Society* (New York: American Book Co., 1962), p. 321.

[6] U. S. Department of Commerce, *U. S. Census of Population, 1960,* Final Report PC (1)–1C, Table 88.

[7] Marden and Meyer, *op. cit.,* p. 320.

[8] *U. S. Census, op. cit.*

members constitute a labor elite—have generally resisted the admission of Negro apprentices.[9]

In 1962, after a fairly consistent rise in individual Negro incomes as compared with those of whites, the estimated median income of non-white families was only $3,330, or slightly over half that of white families, $6,237.[10]

There still remains considerably more child labor among the Negro population. Increased employment of Negroes in manufacturing, trade, and transportation in recent years has both made possible their improved economic status and increased their adjustment problems and consequent incidence of crime. Increased employment in skilled and semi-skilled work and a substantial decline in employment as private household servants are important indices of improved economic status.

ASPECTS OF THE FAMILY SITUATION

The daily life of many Negro families, including much of their sex life, is indistinguishable from that of whites. Nevertheless, among other Negroes there are distinctive features which help explain their unusual involvement in crime. Recent studies of family desertion with racial comparisons are rare, but no data have been found to cast doubt on the significance of older Chicago and New York studies which showed that Negroes had considerably above their proportion of deserted families.[11] Thus we find not only that Negroes suffer disproportionately from broken homes but that the type of break—desertion—which is most frequently associated with juvenile delinquency is much more prevalent among them.

The relative disorganization of the Negro family today seems to be related both to the type of family characteristic of the African tribes from which the slaves came and to reinforcements and modifications of that type brought about by slavery in the United States.[12] The African family structure differed from that traditionally sanctioned by American whites for their own group. Survivals of polygyny under slavery were seen in a form of so-called progressive monogamy where a woman lived monogamously with more than one man successively, as the man moved from one plantation

[9] Marden and Meyer, *op. cit.*, p. 322.

[10] Bureau of the Census, *Current Population Reports,* "Consumer Income," Series P–60, No. 40 (June 26, 1963), Table 2.

[11] E. Franklin Frazier, *The Negro Family in the United States* (New York: Macmillan, 1957).

[12] Melville J. Herskovits, *The Myth of the Negro Past* (New York: Harper & Brothers, 1941), pp. 167*ff*.

to another. Under such conditions the illegitimate child was not handicapped in his own group by adverse attitudes, and the attachment to the mother became stronger than that to the father. Common-law relationships might take on a fair degree of stability, and little sense of guilt might be involved on the part of either parent. Nor was it held especially immoral to remarry without the formality of divorce, which was deemed an extravagance. Under these circumstances also were colored women who desired children but did not care to share responsibility for them with a husband.

Had the life of the Negro in America been that of a free man, the structure of his family and accompanying attitudes would, no doubt, have been changed more readily in the direction of the approved American institution. The actual change has, of course, been in that direction. In other words, the relative disorganization of the Negro family, which is significant for crime, is to be explained largely as a result of slavery and of postslavery conditions. Slaveowners differed in their desire to keep families together. As slavery was a profit-making institution, the increase of the slave population was often more desired than the protection of the morality of the slave home. Sexual license among the slaves was often tolerated and not infrequently desired. Not a few slaveowners and their sons themselves violated the Negro family. Negro women had no protection. They were property. It was said in 1854:

> Among the slaves, a woman, apart from mere bashfulness, has no inducement to be chaste; she has many inducements the other way. Her person is her only means of purchasing favors, indulgences, presents . . . [Connections with white men are] as much esteemed among slaves as an advantageous marriage would be among the free . . .[13]

Considering what has been said, it is not surprising that illegitimacy is more prevalent among the colored group. Illegitimacy rates in 1958 were reported as 223.7 per 1,000 Negro births and 20.6 for births to white women.[14] Though there is reason to believe that such births are much less completely reported for whites, some significance may be found in the fact that non-white rates never have been less than eight times white rates since 1938. Such differences reported are related to a complex of factors. Though important to both races, illegitimacy involves less stigma in some Negro groups. Moreover, the moral teachings of the whites have been handicapped by inconsistency. There was a different code for white men and white

---

[13] Quoted in Arthur W. Calhoun, *The Social History of the American Family* (Cleveland: Arthur H. Clark Co., 1917–1918), p. 293.

[14] *Vital Statistics of the United States, 1958* (Washington, D. C.: National Office of Vital Statistics, 1960), Table 3-V.

women. The male code of freedom with Negro women was sternly denied to Negroes with relation to white women. These family problems have had special significance for conflict attitudes and crime under the strained relations between the two races. Given these tensions, harsh repression of sexual advances by Negroes was to be expected.

EDUCATIONAL HANDICAPS OF NEGROES

In the vicious circle of forces surrounding the Negro in American society has been that of a level of educational attainment inadequate to prepare him for successful acheivement in our competitive society. Being undereducated has contributed to the Negro's continued disproportionate sojourn in the demoralizing urban slum and in occupations at the bottom of the prestige-income pyramid.

In 1962 the median of school years completed by white persons 25 years of age or older was estimated to be 11.8, while the comparable figure for non-whites was 8.6.[15] Among the nation's eight million persons with fewer than five years of schooling, about two million were non-white.[16] At the upper end of the educational spectrum the proportion of high school graduates among whites over 25 years of age was 29.6 per cent; among Negroes, 16.4. The corresponding percentages with college educations were 6.2 and 3.0.[17] Despite a recent sharp increase in the school enrollments of non-whites,[18] educational attainments of the American Negro population are considerably below those of whites, a factor significant to the Negro's struggle for economic betterment and particularly to his need for leadership within his race.

In 1954 a momentous and unanimous decision of the United States Supreme Court declared exclusion of Negroes from public schools where white students are educated to be unconstitutional. A little later in that year the Court announced that a period of delay for compliance with the law would be permitted. At that time no less than 40 per cent of public school pupils in the country lived in areas where school segregation was required by law. According to the *New York Times,* reactions to the Court's decision of 16 of the 17 states involved had in 1954 been as follows: four were strongly opposing compliance with the decision; seven were seeking post-

[15] Bureau of the Census, *Current Population Reports,* Series P–20, No. 121 (Feb. 7, 1963), Tables 2 and 3.
[16] *Ibid.,* p. 1.
[17] *Ibid.,* Tables 2 and 3.
[18] Bureau of the Census, *Current Population Reports,* Series P–20, No. 115 (Feb. 7, 1962), p. 1.

ponement of integration; three were awaiting court action before complying; and two were proceeding with the admission of Negroes to the public schools. The eight years since the decision have seen evasive maneuvers among some of the 17 which had been practicing legal segregation, early if grudging compliance in others, and last-ditch recalcitrance in a few, but with such notable exceptions as Little Rock in 1957 and Oxford, Mississippi in 1962–63, outbursts of violence directly connected with school desegregation were fewer than some observers predicted. Progress has, nevertheless, been very slow and uneven. By 1962, only 7.8 per cent of the South's 3¼ million Negro school children were in schools containing white pupils. Alabama, Mississippi, and South Carolina had yet to integrate any schools below the collegiate level.[19]

DISCRIMINATION CONTINUES

The 1947 report of President Harry Truman's Committee on Civil Rights painted a dismal picture of discrimination: lynchings were still occurring, with the murderers usually going scotfree; the threat of peonage continued; Southern voting qualifications and poll taxes disfranchised thousands of Negroes; restrictive covenants were widely used to keep Negroes from obtaining property in white neighborhoods; 20 states compelled segregation on public conveyances; discriminatory practices in both public and private work were openly followed; parks and beaches were generally closed to Negroes in the South. Aided by key court rulings, civil rights legislation, and vigorous efforts by the U. S. Department of Justice, events of the past decade—freedom rides, bus boycotts, the partial integration of schools, libraries, pools, beaches, and other public facilities, increased Negro voting registration, and so on—suggest not only a gathering momentum of change in the coloreds' second-class status but also a new determination among Negroes themselves that their days of acquiescence in that status shall be numbered.

Nevertheless, discrimination against the Negro in broad areas of private and public life continues to be a prominent feature of American culture and a source of shame and embarrassment to millions of white citizens. The rationalizing stereotypes of the past die hard, especially if they are functional in the present. Definitions of the Negro as the white man's biological and psychological inferior continue to serve their ancient purpose of salving

---

[19] *Southern School News* (Dec. 1962), p. 1. In the academic year 1962–63 the University of Mississippi and Clemson College (South Carolina) each admitted one Negro.

what would otherwise be anguished consciences among those whites directly or indirectly abetting discrimination. Without having precise data, the authors of this text are astonished by the continuing number of *Northern* college students who, although not distinctively "anti-Negro" in their thinking, appear calmly to accept as valid the notion of Negro inferiority. If this misunderstanding exists among some college students, it likely is much more pervasive among the lesser educated general population.

The position of the Negro, however, is not simply that of a minority experiencing economic and social deprivation. The Negro's unique history as chattel and his subsequent century of "freedom" as an oppressed agricultural peasantry and urban proletariat have produced what may be appropriately designated as a Negro socio-cultural system, account of which must be taken in understanding the problem of excessive Negro crime.

Negro Culture and Its Criminogenic Influences

In explaining the behavior of any group, one must consider its dominant or prevalent culture values. The African heritage was largely obliterated through experinces under slavery. But Herskovits [20] insists that the slaves came from a rather restricted area in Africa; that the culture of their tribes was fairly homogeneous; that the scattering of tribes and families in America did not prevent the preservation of certain culture traits; and that the presence of priests among them favored such preservation.

The following alleged African tribal attitudes and values, of which Herskovits reported remnants, are selected because of their possible relationship to crime. (1) Indirection, subterfuge, and a certain lack of frankness often observed today betray the African past. (2) The extensive use of whipping in the punishment of children was habitual in Africa. (3) Great interest in the supernatural, emotional displays in religious ceremonies, elaborate rituals, and the phenomenon of possession by spirits have been sources of the white man's sense of the Negro's strangeness. (4) Perhaps as significant for the criminologist as any element in African culture is the view of life which does not recognize a sharp dichotomy between good and evil in the realm of the supernatural. Thus good and bad magic involved almost the same techniques. (5) The already-mentioned maternal type of family may foster some juvenile delinquency. By no means all anthropologists follow Herskovits in his emphasis upon the preservation

[20] *Op. cit., passim.*

of these traits and mores among minorities of Negroes in the United States. He undoubtedly discovered them in some localities, but they are not to be thought of as in any sense characteristic of the majority of Negroes in this country and certainly not as "race" traits.

While some of these cultural traits were tolerated under slavery, the Negro slave was expected to adopt many of the values of the white man. These were enforced upon him whenever the white man saw fit. After emancipation the Negro was expected to abide by white mores and laws more than the slave had been. For example, in the North especially, petty stealing by a Negro maid is less likely to be condoned than it was under slavery on a Southern plantation. In addition new aggravations have seemed to the Negro to justify such stealing. The white man, whether as exploiter or condescending patron, has at times been held fair game.

In general the Negro in America took on the white pattern of values but with a difference. The difference grew out of the isolation of the Negro from the status-producing elements in American culture. He was in American culture, but because of his inferior status he was not of America. We must therefore examine the effect of American culture values upon a non-participating minority group assigned a most inferior role in that culture. What is the effect of democratic ideals of equality of opportunity upon a group denied such equality? What obedience to law is to be expected from Negroes in a culture where they can hardly feel the law to be their own because they have not shared proportionately in its making, and where they see this law often applied with discrimination against them? What conception of the "sanctity of property rights" does a group acquire whose grandparents have themselves been property? What view of the "sanctity of the home" would Negroes be expected to entertain when they had no sense of family possession or pride under slavery and when both during and after slavery their own homes were at times invaded by the white man without possibility of redress? What depth of significance for present-day behavior could religious values be expected to attain for them when their masters taught them to find solace in religion because in the next world injustice would be replaced by justice and they would no longer be "inferior beings"? In a culture which rewards with preferred status those who achieve material success, what is the effect of denying to a tenth of the population, by reason of race membership, a fair opportunity to achieve?

Probably the most effective crime preventive in America today is the fact that for the most part criminal behavior brings loss of social status. In such a society, what is the effect of denying a large group such status whether they avoid crime or not? The Negro is asked to be virtuous without the chief reward of virtue—the grant of social status. The Negro is rated first as a Negro—only secondly as a good Negro. What does it do to this race to deny them outlets for ambition, when only "men of ambition" are respected? What is the result of assigning a static role to a race in the midst of a dynamic culture? What, finally, is the effect when a dominant majority is the chief source of morality and ideals for a depressed minority and then itself presents such an inconsistent philosophy?

The general answer to these questions is obvious. Under such circumstances the Negro acquires an attitude of rebellion *or* a sense of defeat. The Negro finds himself in a perpetual state of conflict which he can never fully resolve. Dollard [21] sees five ways in which the Negro may react to this chronic state of frustration: by overt aggressiveness against whites, as in insurrection, which is dangerous and has always failed in the past; by suppressing his aggressive tendencies and adopting passive, submissive attitudes as he did for the most part under slavery; by directing his aggression toward members of his own group, which is a frequent occurrence; by giving up competition with whites, accepting his lower status and the compensations involved, such as expressing sex and other impulses which must be inhibited if one is to achieve status in white society; and finally by raising his *class* position in his own caste society and competing for values there similar to those in white society. This last the educated middle-class Negro often strives to do.

A very large proportion of Negro crime is against other Negroes. Much of such aggression in the South is due to the fact that the law does not protect the Negro's personal security as well as the white's. Gambling, along with much banter and boasting, is also said to be a cause of violence among Negroes. The former may be related to general discouragement with the possibility of getting ahead legitimately, and the latter to inferiority feelings, both partly products of discrimination. The Negro also comes to admire the man who engages in personal violence. The conflict situation of the Negro is further shown in a certain amount of direct aggression against whites.

This conflict situation, which helps explain Negro crime, is, of course, constantly aggravated by violent acts and provocations against Negroes by whites. Violent behavior short of lynching, including whippings, assaults, violent language, failure to observe etiquette when dealing with Negroes, use of first names, use of the term "nigger"—these and many other evi-

[21] John Dollard, *Caste and Class in a Southern Town* (New Haven, Conn.: Yale University Press, 1937).

dences of disrespect constantly keep in the mind of the Negro his low status and constantly stimulate conflict or potential conflict. Significant reduction in the criminal record of the Negro awaits the elimination of racial discrimination—the development of racial color blindness.

INEFFECTIVENESS OF CALVINISTIC INFLUENCES

The Negro's long sojourn in a subordinate caste status has not only kept him from participating in the "American dream" of moving from low beginnings to middle-class respectability and affluence, but it has served as well to make meaningless to him important normative elements of that dream: the necessity for denying immediate pleasures in the interest of greater future returns; for being prudent in expending time, money, and energy; for preparing carefully for one's "calling"; for learning manipulative social skills useful in the marketplace. With relatively few instances among the race of the achievement of middle-class status in legitimate occupations,[22] and with no real expectation of such achievement for the many, Negro culture has long since institutionalized an apathetic, non-achievement ideology in which immediate sensual gratifications of kinds within economic reach—sex, cheap liquor, gambling, music and dancing, spontaneous (if coarse) expressions of self—constitute the chief rewards of existence. This ideology is not unusual in human history, tending, in fact, to emerge among powerless, non-vertically mobile lower strata wherever they may exist in stratified societies, but the presence in Western urban-industrial countries of a large racial minority which cannot move from its lowly position *is* unique and helps provide the United States with a crime problem having unique aspects.

URBANIZATION, MIGRATION TO THE NORTH, AND
WAR EXPERIENCES

Recent decades have given the Negro two new experiences which have affected race relations and hence his attitudes and behavior. Large numbers of Negroes have migrated out of the Southern tradition, so to speak, and into that of the North. This migration, together with a similar movement within the South, has involved urbanization—a process which has spelled

---

[22] Even this achievement has been derided by one Negro writer as a movement into an over-Puritanized make-believe world in which a shabby parody of white "Society" is enacted. [E. Franklin Frazier, *Black Bourgeoisie* (Glencoe, Ill.: The Free Press, 1957).]

nonadjustment for whites and blacks alike. In addition a considerable number of Negroes have participated in two world wars. This has brought them into contact with Europeans, who received them as they received other younger cousins from America. Moreover, the second of these wars was ostensibly fought in protest against the ruthless application of a not wholly "un-American" Nazi doctrine of racial superiority.

Between 1900 and 1960 the percentage of non-white population which was urban increased from 22.6 to 74.2, of white population from 43.0 to 69.5, the largest percentage increase being during or after World War II. Urbanization makes for crime. While Negroes long settled in these cities remained fairly well adjusted, the newcomers produced friction, as their arrival brought contacts with people of the slums not accustomed to the race problem. Further, the unaccustomed relative freedom in the North frequently caused maladjustment. In the North there was greater freedom in personal relations. The Negro could ride with whites on the subway but could not count on the tolerance and personal interest of a white patron. Moreover, Negroes have complained that the North is going Southern. Thus while the migration of Negroes may well mean an eventual improvement in their status in both North and South, its immediate effects must be listed as further explaining the excess of Negro crime.

In World War II the Negro for the most part volunteered or accepted the draft and participated in other wartime experiences, much as did the white majority. Tension and riots on the one hand, increased cooperation and mutual appreciation on the other, characterized the association of the two races as soldiers. Some Negro leaders expressed the view that their race had little to hope for in the war. There was general recognition, however, that if the Nazis won, there would not even remain the theory of equal opportunity. Hearty appreciation, welcome, entertainment, and even association between the sexes which Negroes experienced in Europe contrasted in their minds with the color line in America. Returning home, the Negro had mixed experiences. Post-war renewed interest in civil rights is evident both in the United States and the United Nations. The future of Negro crime is tied in with the future of liberalism in the country and in the world.

Suggested Readings

An understanding of the Negro's position in American society is necessary to understand Negro crime. The following books are among the best for achieving this prerequisite.

Drake, St. Clair, and Cayton, Horace R. *Black Metropolis.* New York: Harcourt, Brace and Company, 1945. The Negro in Chicago. The chapter on "Bronzeville" is a classic portrayal of day-to-day living.

Frazier, E. Franklin. *Black Bourgeoisie.* Glencoe, Ill.: The Free Press, 1957. First published abroad in French, this remarkable book "exposes" the alleged sham and self-delusion of the middle-class Negro whose shaky prosperity Frazier attributes to white indifference to the Negro market.

————. *The Negro Family in Chicago.* Chicago: University of Chicago Press, 1932.

————. *The Negro Family in the United States.* New York: Macmillan, 1957. Definitive works by the late Howard University sociologist. The matriarchal nature of the lower-class Negro family is stressed, and its implications for child training explored.

Myrdal, Gunnar. *An American Dilemma.* New York: Harper & Brothers, 1944. A Swedish sociologist surveys the Negro's position in America.

Wright, Richard. *Black Boy.* New York: Harper & Brothers, 1945. The late novelist's bitter story of his early years in the South. As an ambitious youth, he collided repeatedly with white determination to keep the Negro in his "place."

CHAPTER 8

Crime and Economic Conditions

In this and certain of the following chapters, attention is given to the relationships between crime and selected social institutions. It is both conventional and convenient to conceive of society, for analytical purposes, as clusters of norms and values centered respectively around survival needs common to all human groups. These clusters are often labeled "social institutions." Norms and values pertaining to reproduction and socialization of the young are subsumed under the rubric "family"; those of producing and distributing goods and services under "economics"; patterns of maintaining internal order under "government"; dealings with the problems of man's orientation to his own existence under "religion"; and the processes of transmitting his culture to new generations under "education." [1] Of course, slicing the pie of society into such "institutions" may be misleading because segmenting social reality in this way focuses attention upon the segments rather than upon the totality. The mature student of sociology will realize, however, that institutions interrelate and interpenetrate to such a degree that their boundaries cannot "really" be discerned: the existence of the pie as a whole must always be recognized. But can the flavor of one

[1] These five by no means exhaust the possible list of institutions: "war," "communication," "recreation," "science," and others have been listed by various writers. The five named here are those commonly designated in American sociological writings.

part of the pie dominate the remainder? Without granting the inevitable primacy of one institution over the others (as "religious" or "economic" or other determinisms would do), the authors' conviction is that factors peculiar to American history have caused our institutions to be more heavily influenced by economic forces than is usually the case. Among these factors would be listed: the rapid settlement of our vastly rich land areas by individuals and kin groups motivated by a wish for material betterment; the relative ease of vertical mobility as waves of immigrants wedged up earlier arrivals; unique political and economic alignments which successfully militated against more than rudimentary control over economic activity; and the absence of any serious competition from such non-materialistic sources of values as a landed aristocracy, an established church, or vicinal loyalties.

The Nature of Economic Motivations

The old individualistic, rationalistic economics of Adam Smith is at least half dead. Smith's economics implied that man is a rational animal who seeks material satisfactions or utilities in competition with his fellows. To Adam Smith this selfish, competitive search for personal gain was socially beneficial and should be left unhindered by government. Led as by an unseen hand, he urged, the individual seeking his own welfare will achieve the welfare of the nation. And individualistic competition no doubt has produced a vast quantity of goods to be shared by all. But later study has shown that Smith's view misinterpreted the real nature of human motivation and underestimated the social ills resulting from unregulated individualism. Research into the actual behavior of men seeking a living, and the influence of psychology and sociology, have largely undone the economics of Smith. Even in their business activities, men have been discovered to be perhaps as often emotional as rational, and as eager for power and the approval of their associates as for full stomachs, elaborate shelter, and a superabundance of material satisfactions. Moreover, the social nature of man, though often given little chance for expression, is now known to be as real as his individual goals. Even in our materialistic culture, men are observed to get joy through cooperation. In our society and in most other societies, however, men may act from more purely individual economic motives up to the point when their basic physiological needs are met. Perhaps in the face of some social disapproval most starving men would take food and most freezing men would take clothing or seek shelter which did not belong to them. Yet at least a man who is not at the moment suffering the torments of long-time lack of food may sincerely declare that he "would rather starve then steal." Even in the days of government handouts and "relief as a right," the papers occasionally tell us of individuals who *have* starved rather than become dependent.

In the light of such considerations we must revise our notion of an economic factor in the causation of crime. An economic factor in the causation of crime is some influence relatively closely associated with the efforts of men to make a living. The behavior involved need not show purely rational, materialistic motivation. Men seek material satisfactions. Men are dissatisfied with incomes which leave unsatisfied needs of which they are conscious, with incomes lower than those they have been accustomed to, and with incomes below those of other men with whom they customarily compare themselves. Under these three situations men suffer economic discomfort, and an economic motive for action arises. In addition, in a culture which gives prestige on the basis of material success, men have positive ambitions even when not suffering actual discomfort. They seek to raise their plane of living. Men for the most part openly strive for economic advantages to gain status or to avoid loss of status. The importance of economic conditions as causes of crime grows largely out of the fact that materialism is approved in our culture.

If a man steals because he is starving; if a man blunders into crime because of idleness through lack of occupation; if a child becomes delinquent because of the nature of the street trade at which he is employed; if a family on relief become demoralized because they develop the notion that society owes them a living; if a man acquires an overpowering sense of inferiority because of failure in business or profession; if crime develops because a family finds it impossible to keep up with the Joneses; if low income means life in the slums, and slum life means criminalistic associations; or if simply in the course of a man's efforts to raise his standard of living he crosses a line fixed by the law—in these and hundreds of other types of cases we may recognize an "economic" factor in crime, though social influences may be equally or more important.

Individualism, competition, and specialization operating through trade relations have created economic interdependence. Family, community, nation, region, and world are today interdependent. Criminal and noncriminal alike are largely unconscious of this interdependence. The hard-headed economist of today is telling us that in the interest of our personal and national economic welfare, we may well strive to raise the standard of living of the underprivileged at home and in distant lands. Thus the rational economic man will recognize interdependence and be less likely to exploit the other fellow. Not all crime is based on rational elements. But to the extent that man is a rational economic being, failure to recognize interdependence is one of the major indirect causes of crime.

Crime and Business Depressions

The long business depression in the early 1930's gave some opportunity to test the effect of unemployment and greatly decreased incomes of millions upon the incidence of crime. In the United States vast sums were spent on relief, however, so that the depression did not test here, as in some other countries, the effect of actual threat of starvation.

The American experience still has theoretical significance for today. But unless a crash comes unexpectedly before these lines are printed, younger readers can hardly realize what widespread unemployment means. Some decades of prosperity have followed the end of the big depression here. Optimistic businessmen, optimistic political leaders of any party in power during prosperity, and an only slightly less optimistic wing among the economists are saying that the United States may not have another prolonged depression, but, at the worst, only temporary recessions. No large funds have been set aside for use in government works to provide employment, but various devices have been used to create greater financial and economic stability. Meantime marvelous new technological improvements have produced an extraordinary high standard of living in this country. Though people realize that a wholly "unplanned," as compared with a partially or fully controlled, economy involves some danger of unemployment, they have difficulty believing in times of prosperity that another big depression could occur.

At any rate, because the subject of the business depression is of less timely interest today, we shall give it less attention than in previous editions of this text. The lack, already noted, of reliable indices of crime trends and the fact that we are not sure how hard times affected the repressive policies of police and courts have made it difficult to be certain just what the depression of 1930–35 did to crime in the United States. Unemployment did not have a full adverse effect because of government relief and government-provided work.[2] However, the Social Science Research Council published a large number of studies throwing light on special aspects of the

[2] Cf. Thorsten Sellin, "Research Memorandum on Crime in the Depression," *Social Science Research Council Bulletin No. 27, 1937.*

situation. Most of the brief summary which follows is based upon these studies.

1. Neither American, English, nor European research has shown any clear relationship between depression and crime generally.
2. Evidence of relationship between nonviolent crimes and depressions is wholly inconsistent.
3. Many studies have shown that robbery and other property crimes with violence do increase when there is a large amount of unemployment.
4. Some studies have shown crimes against morals to decrease.
5. There is no evidence that crimes against the person generally increase.
6. Recent studies have tended to show that crime generally has increased in good times. In 1946, for example, speaking of juvenile delinquency in Los Angeles, David Bogen wrote: "We have had unprecedented economic activity in this area in recent years and likewise an unprecedented volume of delinquency." [3] The disturbing increase in 1953 and 1954 came in a time of continued prosperity although also of some slight increase in unemployment.
7. Perhaps influenced by the immediate situation, more criminologists today seem to stress the adverse effects of a "sensate society," with its tendency to undermine certain social values, than to emphasize the acknowledged, occasional, direct, and very general indirect effects of economic adversity. In other words, it is not an immediate decline in accustomed material well-being but a continuance of or change in *relative well-being* which is frustrating and sometimes results in criminal reactions. This finding thus emphasizes the last of the three situations we mentioned above: dissatisfaction because of blocked ambitions and the fact that others are more successful may stimulate crime more than sheer want or a temporary decline in an accustomed standard of living. This seems to have been the case in the United States. Lack of evident increase in crime between 1930 and 1935 also throws the emphasis upon non-economic influences. We shall speak of these later. Here we may note that if crime has increased since 1950, the increase seems to be connected with such changes as continued urbanization, long-term effects of World War II, and the demoralizing consequences of the continued "cold war," together with the emphasis on violence, preparation for war, and mutual suspicion which it has engendered.[4]

[3] In a letter to the senior author.

[4] Two Philadelphia studies may be cited by way of example of partial lack of consistency in findings. Wagner, in an investigation where other factors were fairly well controlled [Albert C. Wagner, "Crime and Economic Change in Philadelphia, 1925–1934," *Journal of Criminal Law and Criminology* (Nov.–Dec. 1936), pp.

A tentative general conclusion concerning business depressions and crime may be stated as follows: Very serious threat of starvation probably will drive most men to petty crime, but, at least where there is reasonable provision of relief, this does not occur. If law violation generally were chiefly due to unemployment or to a substantial reduction of customary income, there would have been such a great increase in crime in the United States between 1930 and 1935 that there would be no doubt of its source. There is such doubt, and on the whole the weight of the evidence to date is that crime has been more a phenomenon of prosperity than of adversity in the United States. Poverty in the usual sense of the word does not seem to be a *direct* cause of crime. But relative poverty, by requiring some elements in the population to experience the criminogenic social relations involved in slum life and other non-economic sources of dissatisfaction, *is* important. This kind of poverty also affects a man's attitudes toward those less successful than he is and toward the law which protects their property rights.

The above conclusions are based on statistical findings and are concerned with direct influences of the depression. They are confirmed, however, when one considers indirect effects or when one uses case evidence. The indirect effects of the depression were ambivalent: some were consistent with increased, some with decreased, delinquency and crime. The following may be noted:

1. During the depression the gap between the rich and the poor was generally narrowed, though some few made money out of the hardships of others.
2. Unemployment meant idleness and people could spend far less on recreation, but spare-time activities provided by municipalities or other public agencies were greatly expanded. Many radios were purchased and people played more at home.
3. Very important, no doubt, was the marked decline in migration to the city, although at first some rushed there to look for work, while a larger

---

483–90], found no significant correlation between the business depression and arrests, and a remarkable negative correlation of –0.922 to –0.955 for burglary. Dealing with juvenile delinquency, Reinemann [John Otto Reinemann, "Juvenile Delinquency in Philadelphia and Economic Trends," *Temple University Law Quarterly* (April 1947), pp. 576–83] found a high delinquency rate associated both with the depression period 1930–35 and the period of war prosperity of 1941–45.

Somewhat to the contrary, Bogan [David Bogen, "Juvenile Delinquency and Economic Trend," *American Sociological Review* (April 1944), pp. 178–84], dealing with the situation in Los Angeles, showed that delinquency decreased during the depression and increased in later years of prosperity.

and increasing number of people went back to the old farm homestead.

4. The family was weakened by the lowered prestige of the father, by doubling up of families to save expense, and perhaps by increased family discord, but there was a trend toward retreat to the old close family unit, and divorce, being expensive, decreased. The period of parental responsibility for children was increased.

5. Considerable effort failed to uncover marked effects upon either religion or sex morals.

6. Studies of attitudes during the depression came to similar mixed results. For example:

   a. Most Americans neither blamed the government nor the economic system for their misfortunes, though there were local instances of increased membership in radical organizations.

   b. The stigma of being on relief did not wholly disappear but declined as more and more found themselves in that situation. Some clients came for aid rejoicing that Uncle Sam would care for them; some with a defiant attitude that relief was their right; some terribly ashamed because, for the first time in their experience, resort to public aid was necessary.

On the whole, the incomplete material on attitudes during the depression seems to confirm our statistical and indirect evidence. Not uniform and criminogenic but varied attitudes resulted from the depression experience.

In a recent study using techniques rather more refined than those customarily applied in attempts to measure the associations between crime and economic conditions, Glaser and Rice [5] tested two hypotheses for which some support had existed in earlier researches but which were contradicted by conflicting findings. The hypotheses were (1) that the frequency of crimes committed by juveniles varies inversely with unemployment rates and (2) that the frequency of property crimes committed by adults varies directly with unemployment rates. Computing coefficients of correlation between age-specific arrest and unemployment rates both nationally and with reference to three large cities, Glaser and Rice obtained data supporting their hypotheses. The avenues via which fluctuations in employment rates influence arrest rates (assuming, of course, that the observed concomitances are causally related) are still undetermined however.

[5] Daniel Glaser and Kent Rice, "Crime, Age, and Employment," *American Sociological Review* (Oct. 1959), pp. 679–86.

The Ecology of Crime and Economic Conditions

It can hardly be shown that the economically poorer sections of the United States have the most crime. For example, industrial cities have much crime but are wealthier than rural areas.

Within cities, recorded crime is in general spatially associated with low income and dependency, but the correlation is far from perfect. The concentration of delinquency in industrial slums is, as we shall see, associated with mobility, anonymity, culture conflict, and change as well as with low economic status. Moreover, the great bulk of poverty-stricken people are known not to be criminal.

The Economic Status of Criminals and Delinquents

At this point the student should again remind himself that our knowledge of the criminal and his economic status is of necessity derived from those who have been apprehended only. Just as the relatively stupid, and groups, such as the Negroes, who are discriminated against, are especially apt to find themselves caught in the meshes of the law, so with the relatively unsuccessful economically. The communists are clearly wrong in attributing frustration and crime almost wholly to class membership, but the conservative is in error unless he underlines the great handicaps which the poor man faces when his lower-class status adds to suspicion of his guilt or determines his greater likelihood to be arrested, tried, convicted, punished, and retained in prison. Poverty is what makes it more difficult for him to secure bail and so exposes him disproportionately to the demoralizing influences of the jail. Poverty assigns him an inexperienced lawyer instead of a highly skilled and expensive defense attorney. Often poverty, or rather lack of influence on the part of his parents, prevents his felony charge from being reduced like that of the rich man's son to the level of a violation of a city ordinance, carrying a light fine instead of imprisonment. These disadvantages of the poor are very real, in spite of the sincere efforts of our best judges to provide even-handed justice and occasionally to show sympathy for the poor man. These selective factors are at least real enough to justify the generalization that our statistics of punished criminals probably overstate the relationship of low economic status to crime. Nevertheless, there is significance in the large number of studies which have compared the economic backgrounds of criminals and noncriminals.

Healy and Bronner, reviewing their experience with thousands of cases of delinquents in Chicago and Boston, found "poverty" present in about one-fifth of the cases but concluded that its frequency was about the same as among the general population. The careful studies of Sheldon and Eleanor Glueck [6] found only a small proportion of their delinquent children and reformatory men dependent, but over two-thirds of them in marginal economic circumstances. The economic status of their 500 delinquent women was, if anything, still lower. Cyril Burt, summarizing his English juvenile cases, found that in only 3 per cent of the male delinquents and in not one female case could the effects of poverty be called the prime condition leading to delinquency. He adds, "Our general conclusion, therefore, on the influence of poverty must be this. If the majority of delinquents are needy, the majority of the needy do not become delinquents." [7]

Among their 1,000 juvenile delinquent boys in Boston, the Gluecks found mothers employed over four times as frequently as were married women in the country generally.[8] Mothers of delinquent women were employed [9] in still greater proportion. One-eighth of the Gluecks' delinquent boys were themselves employed at the age of 10 or younger,[10] and over nine-tenths before they were 15, the average age at first employment being just over 13. Irregularity of employment characterized Massachustts reformatory men, over half having held their longest job less than a year.[11] They had characteristically never made planful industrial adjustments and never received the rudiments of vocational guidance. Equally unplanned had been the work of delinquent women. Though over half of them had had factory work, more than one-fifth had been in domestic service working out and 9 per cent more in domestic work but living at home. Three-fifths

[6] Sheldon and Eleanor T. Glueck, *1,000 Juvenile Delinquents* (Cambridge, Mass.: Harvard University Press, 1934), pp. 68–72; *500 Criminal Careers* (New York: Alfred A. Knopf, 1930), pp. 113–14; *500 Delinquent Women* (New York: Alfred A. Knopf, 1934), p. 67.

[7] Cyril Burt, *The Young Delinquent,* rev. ed. (London: University of London Press, 1938).

[8] *1,000 Juvenile Delinquents,* p. 71. A somewhat different relationship between delinquency and employment of mothers was found to exist in a study of 780 youngsters in three small cities [F. Ivan Nye, *Family Relationships and Delinquent Behavior* (New York: John Wiley & Sons, 1958)]. Among the 411 families involved, whether the mothers worked was found *not* to be significantly associated with delinquency when socio-economic variables were held constant, although the apparent association was in the direction found by the Gluecks (*ibid.,* pp. 58–59). These findings are not necessarily contradictory, however, for the Gluecks' cases were court delinquents from a big city, while Nye's were self-revealed delinquents (via questionnaires) from small cities.

[9] *500 Delinquent Women,* pp. 66–67.

[10] *1,000 Juvenile Delinquents,* p. 89.

[11] *500 Criminal Careers,* p. 135.

had been but irregular workers. In using such early studies the reader should bear in mind, of course, that wages have risen since and that child labor has greatly declined.

The relatively low, though not startlingly lower, economic status of apprehended delinquents has been borne out by more recent studies even where the control group of nondelinquents was drawn from the same or similar neighborhoods.[12] In spite of some possible methodological difficulties, a more recent study of Dr. and Mrs. Glueck's is very significant here.[13] They compared 500 institutionalized juvenile delinquents with 500 "nondelinquents." The following findings are calculated from their tables and are ratios obtained by dividing percentages for delinquents into those for nondelinquents, with reference to specified economic circumstances. For example, the data below show that 2.4 times *as large a proportion* of nondelinquents as of delinquents were rated as in comfortable economic circumstances, but only about three-fifths (58 per cent) as large a proportion were dependents. This last fact could be stated in reverse to the effect that one and three-quarters (1.7) as large a proportion of delinquents were dependents.

RATIOS OF NONDELINQUENTS TO DELINQUENTS

Economic Condition

Comfortable	2.4
Marginal	1.14
Dependent	.58

Sources of Family Income

From other sources than family	1.2
Entirely from nonfamily sources	.4

Average Weekly Income of Family per Person

$11 and over	1.7

Mothers Contributing to Family Income   1.2

Nature of Employment of Father

Own business, clerical, and public service	2.1
Unskilled work	.8

[12] Cf. treatment of this subject in Negley K. Teeters and John Otto Reinemann, *The Challenge of Delinquency* (New York: Prentice-Hall, 1950), p. 134.

[13] Sheldon and Eleanor Glueck, *Unraveling Juvenile Delinquency* (New York: The Commonwealth Fund, 1950), pp. 84–88.

Thus this latest of the important Glueck studies shows delinquents to be economically handicapped in most respects. Judging from such studies, the typical delinquent as compared with the total nondelinquent population of the society has begun work while still a child, been relatively poorly paid, worked irregularly, suffered much from unemployment, and been subjected to a relatively poor economic experience. Yet the contrast between his economic status and that of others in the same economic class who are not delinquent is not necessarily great. Moreover, a selective factor clearly operates to give a false notion of the importance of poverty as related to crime. Statistics therefore exaggerate the poor man's relative criminality as compared with the rich man's. Finally, racketeering and white-collar crimes are the crimes of the well-to-do. Such crimes, as we have previously noted, are notoriously underrepresented in our crime statistics.

Crime as the Product of an Economic System

The broadest approach to an economic explanation of crime is that which derives specific factors such as unemployment, exploitation, and others discussed above from the over-all nature of an economic system. So intense is the current conflict between "communist" Soviet Russia and "free enterprise" America, with their respective allies, that it colors the interpretation of every problem, including that of crime. The popular notion in socialist as well as Communist states is to attribute most crime to the capitalist system. But even if this interpretation were conceded to contain the least element of truth, most Americans would prefer to have more crime in order to escape from the totalitarian slavery which they associate with the word "communism." Extreme systems and the labels attached to them have also come to be values in themselves, and the stereotypes of the communist or the "bloated capitalist" are no doubt not far from the stereotype of the criminal. At least advocacy of or assistance to the Communist cause today, even if not in ways strictly defined as crime, evokes hostility far more violent than the acts of typical predatory criminals or racketeers do. It is therefore difficult in the United States today to discuss dispassionately whether a communist state would have more or less crime than a capitalist one. The objective student may well agree, however, that the merits or demerits of these two systems are by no means to be determined simply in terms of their relative criminogenic influence.

Before analyzing further the relative effects of extremely individualistic versus extremely collectivistic economic systems, one further point may help clear the air. Economic systems as they exist today are relatives, not absolutes. Neither extreme free enterprise nor extreme communism exists. Moreover, it is arguable that every society needs and has some sort of balance between individualism and collectivism. If these points are well taken, the practical question of the day is not whether one prefers a non-existent communist society or a nonexistent free capitalism, but what degree of government interference with economic activity one desires and in which direction—toward or away from free enterprise or communism—does one wish to proceed? Might not one arrange existing or proposed economic systems as a continuum beginning at one end with that which least limits economic activity of the individual and ending with a communism more complete than any which exists today? Perhaps the labels might read somewhat as follows: anarchism; free enterprise of the extreme Adam Smith type; free enterprise restricted by conservative organizations of labor and all sorts of social legislation, such as tariffs, laws against monopoly, and labor laws; the so-called New or Fair Deal of the Democratic regimes; the Scandinavian middle-of-the-road economies; state socialism as advocated by the British Labour Party and as practiced when they were in power; the different types and degrees of communism practiced in Yugoslavia, Communist China, and the Soviet Union; and complete communism with complete government ownership and with economic rewards fixed by the state without any private property. Regardless of his own position, the thoughtful student will agree, incidentally, that this ordering by no means perfectly corresponds with degrees of other liberties permitted, such as freedom of speech, discussion, teaching, and religion. With these provisos we may characterize the socialist Bonger's effort [14] some decades ago to explain most, though not quite all, crime as a product of the capitalist system.

Crime, almost by definition, is an expression of human selfishness. Man has the capacity both for selfish and for altruistic conduct and at all periods of history has given some evidence of these capacities. However, some periods more than others have stimulated the selfish capacity of man. So long as production was chiefly for use, men were not brought into conflict with one another in their economic activities. When, however, modern industry and production for exchange developed, men worked not for themselves but to satisfy the wants of others. They were not conscious of their interdependence, however, for they produced for a market in competition with one another. This competition has become very intense and has four chief aspects: There is competition between the buyers and sellers, which stimulates selfishness by the struggle

[14] Cf. W. A. Bonger, *Criminality and Economic Conditions,* translated by Henry P. Horton (Boston: Little, Brown, 1916), *passim.*

of sellers to sell for as high a price as possible and of buyer to purchase at as low a price as possible. Likewise there is competition between sellers of the same or similar commodities, each trying to undercut the other and even to injure the other in the struggle to capture lucrative markets. Thirdly, there is competition between labor and capital. Employers try to purchase labor at the lowest possible wage; workingmen try to sell themselves for the highest obtainable price. Since the commodity for sale is human, this competition no doubt involves still more intense emotions of hostility, and the methods used at times are unscrupulous. Finally, as by-products of this economic competition, there are two parasitic classes which evidence motives as selfish perhaps as those of men actively engaged in the struggle. At the bottom of the social scale are the dependent classes, who live upon the efforts of others; at the top of the scale are the idle rich, who are equally parasitic.

Such being the general nature of our competitive system, Bonger goes on to describe in more detail certain of its more specific aspects and institutions, emphasizing the significance of each for crime. Thus the system entails child labor. Child labor takes the young person out of the home and away from the socializing influence of his parents and other members of the family and exposes him to the criminogenic atmosphere of modern industry. Moreover, it puts children, at their most impressionable age, into the midst of this tooth and claw economic struggle and makes of them selfish beings, potential criminals. Similarly, the system takes woman out of the home—woman upon whom society peculiarly depends to teach its children the social lessons necessary for cooperation. This not only means the lack of parental care for children, but it exposes the homemaker to the selfishness-stimulating influences of modern industrialism. Likewise this system produces actual need through the exploitation of labor; it also creates those great inequalities in reward which stimulate the jealousy and hatred of the less privileged classes. Poverty has scores of direct and indirect influences upon crime. Perhaps most important of all, this unplanned economic system periodically breaks down, since markets fail, factories overproduce particular commodities, and underpaid labor underconsumes. Unemployment causes crime by greatly increasing poverty, inequality, and resentment, and also through the well-known criminogenic effects of idleness and dependency themselves.

If these are some of the more direct economic effects of capitalism significant for crime, there are, Bonger reminds us, many more indirect effects. For example, the institution of the family is demoralized and homes quasi-commercialized. The schools are debauched by the necessity of preparing children to compete in this economic struggle, and every other social institution is colored by its dependence upon its economic base. These influences, Bonger points out, no doubt affect different kinds of crime differently, the connection with predatory crimes being the most obvious. But sex crimes, pathological crimes, and political crimes are also influenced, though some crime resulting from individual causes is relatively little affected by these economic factors. A dominant economic system which stimulates the selfish criminogenic nature of man at the expense of his cooperative potentialities—this system, to Bonger, explains crime.

That there is much truth in Bonger's argument is almost self-evident. That his approach is one-sided and inadequate will also be clear to all except those who attribute the whole of social life and culture to its economic aspect. The reader will note that some parts of this argument are included in our characterization of American society in Chapter 2. But he will also note this marked contrast. We have by no means presented a wholly economic characterization of our society. For example, race discrimination in our society is not conceived of as primarily an economic phenomenon. In Chapter 16 we develop a process and cultural theory of crime in which economic values have a large but by no means wholly dominant place.

The argument of Bonger, based upon Marxian principles, is naturally similar to that accepted by the earlier leaders of Soviet Russia.[15] The Soviet leaders contended that, since crime was an outgrowth of class struggle, it would largely disappear in a classless society. The Russians also at first derived from Marxian doctrines a philosophy of determinism, leading them to put into effect a penal system which, so far as it affected civil rather than political prisoners, approximated an application of scientific criminological principles. Later when an increase of crime and political changes led to a basic modification of this penal system, the change was justified by a reinterpretation of the teachings of Marx and Lenin.[16] Revolution and outside pressures imply political crime. After reasonable stability was established and outside pressures had decreased, some kinds of crime appeared to decrease, but others, including political crimes, increased. While a certain amount of information about crime in Russia at a later date is available, its reliability may be questioned. A considerable shift away from communism has prevented Russia from furnishing a good test of Bonger's theories. Nor did the semisocialistic system of England under the Labour Party provide a test, partly because of its short duration but also because of other complicating factors.

Summary

The above discussion has shown many ways in which economic conditions may result in crime. Speaking generally, however, the evidence has

---

[15] Cf. Mary S. Callcott, *Russian Justice* (New York: Macmillan, 1935), chap. 2; Harold J. Laski, *Law and Justice in Soviet Russia* (London: Hogarth Press, 1935), *passim*.

[16] Cf. John N. Hazard, "Reforming Soviet Criminal Law," *Journal of Criminal Law and Criminology* (July 1938), pp. 157–69; and "Trends in Soviet Treatment of Crime," *American Sociological Review* (Aug. 1940), pp. 566–76.

stressed less the direct effect of poverty than the indirect effects and has emphasized economic competition rather than sheer lack of economic necessities. Imperfect statistics and other evidence seem to show that during hard times some types of crimes increase while others decrease, and, if anything, modern crime in the United States seems rather to be associated with prosperity.

In cities crime does appear concentrated in areas of low incomes, but concomitants other than low income appear there as possible cultural rather than strictly economic explanations of crime. While many students have stressed the poverty of delinquents and criminals, some of our better-controlled surveys which have compared their economic status with that of the general population have found rather slight differences or have explained them in terms of the selection of the relatively poor for arrest and punishment. If criminals who are punished somewhat rarely come from homes of comfort, it is equally true that the vast majority of the poor do not become criminal. However, the combination of poverty and certain other handicaps is clearly significant for crime. Unemployment, irregular employment, child labor especially of certain types, and probably the employment of mothers—these economic handicaps are relatively frequent among delinquents. If the analyses of socialists have at times overstressed the importance of the capitalistic system generally, nevertheless the competitive nature of the economic system is clearly an extremely important source of sense of failure, resentment, and delinquent patterns. American culture is materialistic; but that is just one and possibly not the most criminologically significant of its characteristics. The system which Bonger characterizes is really the system of Adam Smith, and such a free economy does not exist anywhere today, even in the United States. Everywhere it has been modified in the direction of "socialistic" state controls. Moreover, apart from state regulations, the American system of today has been aptly called not free enterprise but "private collectivism" because of the degree to which business itself has interfered with the free flow of competition. This in itself, however, does not necessarily weaken the force of Bonger's argument. The Bonger analysis seems especially significant in so far as it calls attention to the mental set of capitalism, which may be called criminalistic because it is individualistic and exploitative rather than social and cooperative. Relative failure in competition resulting from such individualism is one of our best-documented causes of crime, but that failure is by no means always economic failure. One may consistently emphasize this fact and yet, if he so desires, admire and defend our productive economic system on other grounds. What most Americans tend to defend on moral grounds is competitiveness restricted both by law and by codes of ethics.

Whatever the truth or falsity of this point, apparently Americans generally do not find fault with the basic nature of their economy. Even some of the relative failures seem to prefer its competitiveness. Like the man who plays the slot machine conscious that it is set, say 40 per cent, against him, most workers, when they consider themselves underpaid, prefer the gambling chance for great success to a more secure and "just" reward without such a chance. Moreover, most men are conscious of, and approve of, the marvelous productivity which modern capitalism has developed and which provides a larger product to be shared by all social classes. But the gambling attitude of mind, which keeps men hoping for better days, is one of the most conservative elements in our culture. Some would doubtless rather have crime than greatly to change the economy.

Suggested Readings

W. A. Bonger, *Criminality and Economic Conditions,* translated by Henry P. Horton (Boston: Little, Brown, and Company, 1916). The best statement on the possible relationships between crime and socio-economic conditions is still that of Bonger, the late Dutch socialist and criminologist. He was grinding an ideological axe but struck a good many bright sparks in the doing.

CHAPTER 9

The Influence of the Family

The infant does not enter the family as a social being; he *becomes* social through his interaction with the family group. In the home the child learns that others besides himself have rights to which he must make concessions. The family, then, is the first great training school in behavior or misbehavior.

The family is not only the first but it is the most homogeneous, unified, and intimate social group to which the child is likely to belong. Hence the child may there develop genuinely cooperative attitudes. On the other hand, the very intimacy of life in the family increases the points at which friction may develop, while the strong emotional tone created by these intimate experiences gives to this friction peculiar significance for the developing personality which is then at its most malleable stage.

The family is also the channel through which the child becomes familiar with his culture and competent or incompetent to live in it. Among the values which the child living in our culture thus is supposed to acquire we may include respect for the rights of others, respect for property, neighborliness, good sportsmanship, courtesy, and conventions of good manners, truthfulness, and reliability. We list these values as absolutes. Actually they are usually relative. For example, if the community itself approves and exemplifies "fair play" *except* for members of the minority races, and

136

if the family also excepts these groups, this qualified value, and not fair play for mankind generally, will be what the child learns.

Highly important among the numerous factors which condition the content and quality of the family's socializing role is that of *social status*. A child's values, attitudes, motivations, and perspective on life are intimately related to his parents' position in the social structure of their community. A youngster's socialization experience will generally be "appropriate" to his family's status, and, while experiencing certain socio-psychological processes found in all families (identification, role-learning, and the like), he will normally emerge from the family nest prepared to behave most effectively only within the stratum occupied by his parents. The significance for crime of this "differential socialization" would lie not in parental failure to implant "conventional" norms in their children, as the earlier sociological researchers emphasized, but in the circumstance that some cultural elements functional to a particular stratum supply motivations interpreted as having "criminal intent" when viewed from the perspective of another stratum.

Thus, Professor Marvin Wolfgang's research on Philadelphia homicide led him to hypothesize the existence of a "subculture of violence" among certain lower urban classes, the behavior of whose members will more likely be violent in proportion to the degree of their integration into this sub-culture.[1] Direct, non-symbolic patterns of interaction are functional in strata where the diplomacies of polite verbal exchange are limited. A boy brought up on kicks, slaps, and crude language may transfer this mode of interaction to the larger world, some segments of which—for example, a high school teacher assaulted by an angry teenage slum boy—define such behavior as "criminal."

In terms of Mead's [2] conception of motivation, the family is the medium through which the "generalized other" (the super-ego of the psychoanalyst) is acquired. Though it will be modified by later "others" derived from social experiences wider than those of the family, the self or personality gets started in the home. The delinquent has often been the child who has never learned in the home what is needed for status in our society, or who, learning this, has not been taught that others have rights, or who has scarcely ever experienced the personal enjoyment which comes from cooperation with others and from mutual helpfulness.

[1] Marvin Wolfgang, "Subculture Of Violence: An Interpretive Analysis of Homicide" (unpublished paper read before the American Sociological Association, New York, Aug. 1960).

[2] Cf. George H. Mead, *Mind, Self and Society*, introduction by Charles W. Morris, (Chicago: University of Chicago Press, 1934), pp. IX–XXXV.

The Family Meets the Basic Needs of Children

It has been said that a primary need of the child is *to be wanted,* to arrive as a planned and joyous event rather than the more or less accidental consequence of marital relations. Certainly the unwanted child can become the delinquent child. Fortunately, many children who do not arrive because they are wanted sell themselves to their parents and come to be beloved.

The family also satisfies the child's basic needs for *security.* Beyond the supplying of food and clothing and shelter, economic security is not the most vital type. The child feels secure in a normal family because it is a member of a group where somebody cares for it for its own sake—because it is a member—and not because of its unusual abilities or qualities. Such economic security, affectional security, and sense of being understood are normal needs of the child.

Similarly, the family gives the child *recognition.* His accomplishments need not be unusual to bring him the commendation which all children crave and which is assured by the affectionate interest of parents to whom his every achievement and virtue take on exaggerated importance because he is their child.

The family with other children also is a special asset to the developing child. Relationships with brothers and sisters require the child to adjust to more or less friendly rivalry. This experience serves him well in the more complex relationships outside the family.

More or less involved in the above considerations is the fact that the normal family gives the child *status.* As Plant says,[3] it answers the child's basic question, "Who am I?" and in this culture of ours it is all-important that each individual *belong*—that he be *someone.* Even if the child achieves recognition in other groups, this inadequately compensates for lack of status in a family group peculiarly his own. Moreover, status in the family is a ticket for admission to status in other constructive social groups. Delinquency is thus often a symptom of unmet needs of childhood.

Delinquency and the Changing Family Role

The contemporary family has been changing rapidly, and in those changes the family has ceased to culturalize, socialize, and supply the needs

[3] J. S. Plant, "The Child as a Member of the Family," *Annals of the American Academy of Political and Social Science* (March 1932), p. 69.

of children as adequately as formerly, in spite of greater material resources. Family ideals and patterns of behavior are less uniform than before. Moreover, groups outside the home compete today, often successfully, for the pattern-setting role. The children are out of the home much more, and the parents, especially the mother, spend far less time in the home than in the past. The home may still train the child to inhibit his emotions, but it is also a growing source of emotional tension. Every force noted below which has weakened the stability of the home threatens that intimate personal sympathy which constitutes the true hominess of home. In recent decades there came to be fewer children in the home to furnish socializing influences and to provide training in adjustment to competition. Since 1935, however, the larger, though not the extremely large, family has come into style again. The home is different, and its role is declining in importance.

The home has lost much of its socializing function because it has lost many of its other traditional functions. Instead of cooperating in a common task of making a living as a relatively self-sufficient family group, the adult members of the family have employment in different industrial activities, each implying an outside interest competing with loyalty to the home. Employment of women has sometimes taken away and subjected to the strains of business competition that member of the family whose socializing function was most important. The family atmosphere has become increasingly competitive rather than cooperative because of an increased strain to keep up with the Joneses. Greatly increased mobility has brought the traditional family into contact with many different norms of behavior. The family has also become more independent of the larger kinship group, which tended to pass on a common tradition. The commercialization of recreation has taken it out of the control of the family, given members less need of one another, and tended to lower standards to those believed most financially profitable. The city home affords less room for the child to play and drives him to the street. Patronage of restaurants has restricted the socializing function of the family meal. The hospital, clinic, and public health service are called upon in time of sickness. Aid in the peculiarly "domestic" processes of birth and care for children, the making and laundering of clothing, the safekeeping of savings, and provision for religious needs are all far less home duties than formerly. These services bound the members of the family together in a community of interests which strengthened affection and gave power to the family as an agency of social control, and hence reinforced the basic socializing function of the home. Not all of this is gone, but it has changed radically. Even the home as the center of monopolized sex satisfactions and physical, conversational, and social intimacies is threatened by the not infrequent extension of these activities outside its "sacred shrine." The wife is no longer so much a domestic servant. Her husband no longer rules the family and gives consistency if not always wisdom to its morality. The family itself has come to stress and exemplify the desire for self-expression rather than the spirit of cooperation. Radio and television have somewhat offset these tendencies by keeping children at home, but as we shall note later, these influences are sometimes thought of as injurious to children, and they tend to discourage interaction of the family members as such. At any rate, for good or for ill, the family's power over the destiny of the child has been lessened by these changes. Before considering specific influences of the family on delinquency, let us summarize the findings of an important study which, among other things, compared the family situations of 500 institutionalized delinquents with an equal number of "nondelinquents," matched for age, national origin, general intelligence, and residence in underprivileged neighborhoods.

Homes of Delinquents and "Nondelinquents" Compared

In interpreting this study [4] the reader should bear in mind that this piece of research, fine as it is, seems nevertheless to suffer from a few methodological defects.[5] Two of these may somewhat affect the full validity of the comparisons which follow. The control group of nondelinquents may not be entirely representative, and facts unfavorable to these children were probably somewhat less frequently uncovered as compared with the institutionalized delinquents. If this is so, the contrasts indicated below may exaggerate some types of differences. The ratios we have computed below from the Glueck tables do not necessarily imply that the characteristic in question is highly prevalent among the delinquents. They refer to relative and not absolute prevalence. For example, most of both delinquents and nondelinquents (1) lived with both parents, (2) lived in homes relatively lacking in cultural refinement, (3) were characterized by lack of ambition, (4) had "poor" family standards of conduct, (5) rather rarely had adequate provision for recreation for the family as a unit, (6) were usually fairly well accepted by their brothers and sisters whether delinquent or not, and (7) had not had their futures definitely planned by their parents. In other words,

---

[4] Sheldon and Eleanor T. Glueck, *Unraveling Juvenile Delinquency* (Cambridge, Mass.: Harvard University Press, 1950), especially pp. 107–33.

[5] Cf. Donald R. Taft, "Implications of the Glueck Methodology for Criminological Research," *Journal of Criminal Law, Criminology and Police Science* (Sept.–Oct. 1951), pp. 300–16.

these characteristics were those of a relatively underprivileged section of the general population and therefore are not to be thought of as distinguishing all or most delinquents from nondelinquents. Nevertheless, the degree to which even these conditions were found among delinquents as compared with nondelinquents remains significant. The ratios given below were obtained by dividing percentages among nondelinquents into those among delinquents, except in a few cases where, as indicated, the nondelinquents were the dividends. All the comparisons should then be read somewhat as follows: "Families rated as wholly lacking in 'cohesiveness' were 31 times as prevalent among delinquents as among nondelinquents. (Yet such families made up slightly under a quarter even of the delinquents and less than 1 per cent among the nondelinquents.)" In the statements which follow, then, the figures in parentheses represent ratios between the proportions with which a given characteristic or condition was found among delinquents as compared with nondelinquents or among the latter as compared with the former:

1. A larger proportion of delinquents were not living with their own father (1.7) and mother (2.2).
2. A larger portion showed no "self-respect for their families" (4.3).
3. Conjugal relations were poor in larger proportion (2.1).
4. Supervision of children by the mother was more often "unsuitable" (4.9).
5. Delinquent families were much more often reported as totally without cohesion (31.0).
6. Nondelinquents were more apt never to have changed households (1.8) and changes of eight times or over were much more frequent among delinquents (11.6).
7. Warm affection of the father for the boy was half as frequent among delinquents (.5) and hostile fathers were much more prevalent (5.1).
8. There was warm affection of mothers for sons more often among nondelinquents (1.3) and hostility of mothers appeared much more often among delinquents (6.7).
9. The father was rated as an unacceptable pattern for his son more often among delinquents (4.4).
10. Hostility or indifference toward brothers on the part of brothers and sisters was also more prevalent among delinquents (3.9).
11. Both lax and overstrict discipline was reported more prevalent among delinquents (4.9 and 2.7 respectively), while firm but kindly discipline was much more apt to be found in the homes of nondelinquents (9.7).

12. Parents of delinquents were more apt than parents of nondelinquents to employ physical punishment (1.6 for fathers, 2.0 for mothers).

To what do these contrasts add up? The Gluecks concluded that "the environment in which the delinquent boys grew up was less conducive to the wholesome rearing of healthy, happy, and law-abiding children than that in which the nondelinquent boys grew up." As regards affectional relations between the parents and the boys, the Gluecks state that the "delinquents were much more the victims of the indifference or actual hostility of their fathers and mothers, and were, in turn, less attached to their parents. . . . This greater emotional deprivation is further reflected in a greater feeling on the part of the delinquent boys that their parents were not concerned about their welfare." [6]

Clearly the family continues to be an important influence on delinquency in spite of its declining role, and that influence shows itself in specific characteristics of the homes of delinquents. We may now examine some of the more specific types of influence in somewhat greater detail.

Possible Ways in Which the Family Influences Delinquency

THROUGH FAMILY DISORGANIZATION

Homes are broken by death, desertion, separation, divorce, or the institutionalization of one or both parents. Data indicate that about 11 per cent of children under 18 in the United States are living other than with both parents,[7] death probably accounting for five times as many breaks in the home as all other causes combined. Obviously the older the children, others things being equal, the greater the possibility that the home will have been broken. A break in a home functioning as a socializing agency will tend to weaken this function. The greatest contrast in the above Glueck list is the tremendously larger proportion of homes of delinquents rated as lacking in "cohesiveness," though that term is not used as synonymous with "broken home." The stability of the family varies greatly among different racial and national groups.[8]

[6] *Unraveling Juvenile Delinquency*, pp. 115–16, 133.

[7] Computed from Metropolitan Life Insurance Co., "Statistical Bulletin" (Feb. 1955), p. 5.

[8] Cf. Clifford R. Shaw and Henry D. McKay, "Social Factors in Juvenile Delinquency," *National Commission on Law Observance and Enforcement,* "Report on the Causes of Crime," *Publication No. 13,* Vol. II (June 26, 1931), pp. 266–67.

The prevalence of broken homes found among juvenile delinquents in other studies has ranged generally from 30 to 50 per cent.[9] Clifford Shaw found 42.5 per cent of 1,675 delinquent boys to come from broken homes, the ratio between these and his control group of school boys being 1.18, a difference which he considered unimportant.[10] This study of Shaw's, however, seems not to have proved broken homes unimportant for delinquency. For example, Maller, using Shaw's data, compared delinquents from broken and unbroken homes [11] and found significant differences in the proportion. It has been pointed out (1) that Shaw did not distinguish between the different ways in which homes are broken; (2) that Shaw considered mainly gang offenders, whereas the effects of family tensions more often appear in individual rather than group delinquents; (3) that Shaw's control group of school children contained an undetermined number of delinquents, especially in the high delinquency areas. This would tend toward an understatement of the relatively greater incidence of broken homes among delinquents. Moreover, analysis of certain New Jersey juvenile court data suggests that the impact upon children of broken homes varies by age, race, sex, and rural-urban setting, and that the Shaw-McKay findings of an apparent slight relationship between delinquency and broken homes resulted from their failure to allow for this possibility.[12]

However, the broken home does not always cause delinquency; how and when the home was broken and the effect upon family relationships and the attitudes of the children make a great difference.

Death is a fairly normal experience. It may, indeed, remove a kind father's influence and it often means serious economic hardship. But it

[9] In an early and much-quoted study, Breckinridge and Abbott found, of 14,183 delinquent children brought into court between 1899 and 1909, that 34.1 per cent came from broken homes, the figure for girls (47.1 per cent) being higher than that for boys (31.0 per cent). See S. P. Breckinridge and Edith Abbott, *The Delinquent Child and the Home* (New York: Russell Sage Foundation, 1912), p. 91. Still greater differences between the incidence of broken homes among delinquent boys as compared with girls were more recently found by Caldwell and Lumpkin in their Wisconsin studies, the figures being 37.4 per cent for boys and 63.5 per cent for girls. Sullenger's Omaha study showed about the same figure for girls (64.1 per cent), but a higher one for boys (45.2 per cent). Sheldon and Eleanor Glueck found, among 1,000 juvenile delinquents, 42.7 per cent from homes broken early in childhood. Of 510 men from the state reformatory they found that in at least 60 per cent of their homes an abnormal situation existed prior to their commitment because of the absence of one or both parents from the home. In 58.4 per cent of the families of 500 reformatory women there had been a break before the girls reached the age of 21. A similar excess of broken homes among delinquents was found in their later study.

[10] Shaw, *op. cit.,* p. 276.

[11] Cf. discussions of Shaw's study by K. F. Lenroot, H. M. Shulman, J. B. Maller, and J. C. Colcord in *Social Forces* (May 1932), pp. 525–33.

[12] Jackson Toby, "The Differential Impact of Family Disorganization," *American Sociological Review* (Oct. 1957), pp. 505–12.

involves no connotation of friction in the home, as is found in separation, divorce, and desertion, and no sense of shame, such as may follow imprisonment. The reaction of children to such imprisonment is not uniform. Some may defend their parent and develop a lifelong grudge against society. Some may passively accept the community's evaluation—that "the Joneses ain't much good anyhow"—and act consistently with that evaluation. Some may develop more subtle inferiority feelings and compensate through delinquency. Which will be the result will depend upon the circumstances preceding and surrounding the parental offense.

If divorce deprives the child of the loving care of one or both parents, it is, of course, a serious evil. But the emotional tension preceding the divorce, or the necessity of taking sides with one parent, has usually caused the damage to the child's personality. Divorce has generally increased in the United States. In 1910 there were about nine divorces per 100 marriages in the same year, in 1955 about 25 per 100.[13]

Desertion is serious because it is usually a crime in itself, and it peculiarly involves feelings of injustice and hatred, as well as serious economic handicaps for the deserted family. The National Desertion Bureau has estimated that no fewer than 4,000,000 estranged mothers and children are not adequately cared for by fathers. Some 46 states have adopted the Uniform Reciprocal Enforcement of Support Act, but reportedly [14] a deserting father may avoid the law by moving to another state.

But in all this what is important to know is just what is the effect of the break in the home on the attitudes and social status of its members. Delinquents apparently come somewhat disproportionately from homes broken in ways more socially disorganizing than death.

BY TRANSMITTING CONFLICTS OF CULTURES

The home can transmit cultural values to the oncoming generation effectively only if the attitudes of the two parents are in harmony with each other and with the accepted codes of the general community. In our heterogeneous culture such harmony is by no means universal—some would say it is the exception rather than the rule. The views of those who work for a living conflict with those of the leisure class. The religiously orthodox cannot understand the religiously emancipated. The man to whom the traditions of

[13] William M. Kephart, *The Family, Society and the Individual* (Boston: Houghton Mifflin, 1961), p. 601.

[14] "Juvenile Delinquency," *Interim Report of the Committee on the Judiciary* U. S. Senate, published as Senate Report No. 61, 84th Congress, 1st Session (March 14, 1955), pp. 46–49.

the Puritans are still sacred looks upon the man of the world as immoral. The newly arrived immigrant does not understand American ways, and immigrant ways are almost as varied as their national origins. Such culture conflicts are part of the distinctive stuff of which America is made, but they are also part of the stuff of which maladjustments, mental conflicts, and crime are made. The family is one of the important battlefields upon which this struggle goes on.

AS AN AGENCY OF CRIMINALISTIC CONTAGION

The most obvious evidence that a family situation may promote delinquency is where delinquent patterns are known to be acquired within the family circle itself. Three degrees of this influence may be noted: the most extreme is where the parents deliberately teach children to commit crimes; a second is where, without direct teaching, the children acquire delinquent patterns through imitation of similar behavior by parents or other members of the family; while less direct is the acquisition of other behavior patterns tending toward antisocial behavior. In many neighborhoods it has been common for mothers to send children to pick up coal along the railroad tracks, to punish them if they bring home too little, and to be at least indifferent if they take it more efficiently off rather than from under the cars. Professional thieves often train their children to the vocation. The three earlier Glueck studies [15] give evidence of the second type of criminogenic contagion in the family. Among juvenile delinquents, women delinquents, and male felons, they found over four-fifths having other delinquents as members of their own families. Even without considering drunkenness this was true of three-quarters of the male felons. Studies which, unlike the Gluecks', have considered official records only have naturally shown a somewhat less striking situation.

AS THE SCENE OF EARLY EMOTIONAL TENSIONS [16]

Children whose basic needs have not been met in the home suffer stress and may become delinquent. Nondelinquent children who have suffered from similar stress may have found some compensatory satisfaction other than delinquency. Moreover, delinquents are frequently children who have not formed strong emotional ties with anyone who has been presented for

[15] *1,000 Juvenile Delinquents*, p. 79; *500 Criminal Careers*, pp. 111–12; *500 Delinquent Women*, p. 72.

[16] Cf. William Healy and August F. Bronner, *New Light on Delinquency and Its Treatment* (New Haven, Conn.: Yale University Press, 1936), *passim*.

emulation socially satisfactory patterns of behavior. Findings of the later Glueck research noted above in the numbered list greatly emphasize—probably overemphasize—the importance of emotional tensions in the interpersonal relations of parents and children in the home. Children may have been taught moral ideals, but their effectiveness depends upon the emotional values attached to them, and these are derived from relations with personalities or groups. Healy and Bronner [17] found inferiority feelings among delinquents as compared with nondelinquents in the ratio of 38 to 4; hyperactivity 46 to 0; emotional disturbances generally 91 to 13.

Some of the sources of such emotional tensions and frustrations in the home include the following:

They may arise out of physical deprivations, such as failure to provide allowance money when other children have this means of spending for their own pleasure or of playing the role of "good fellows" by treating others.

They may be rooted in feelings of jealousy often growing out of the real or imagined preference of a parent for one child over another or out of rivalry between siblings as each new child appears to disturb the privileged position of his predecessor. Similarly, tensions may be produced by relations with grandparents and in-laws. The attitudes and relations of mothers and fathers regarding sons and daughters may be inconsistent and cause stress.[18]

They may be seen in a desire for revenge because of parental injustice, real or imaginary.

They may be the result of quarreling between parents. The Gluecks [19] rated the relations between parents of their juvenile delinquents as either actually broken or showing gross incompatibility in 38 per cent of the cases, while the corresponding figure for their delinquent women was 52.1 per cent.

They may result from a sense of being unwanted or otherwise rejected.

Children in the family are sometimes subjected to emotional discomfort so unbearable that an effort is made not to face it but to repress it or forget it. Powerful sex interests conflict with Puritanical family ideals. Compelling need for self-respect and family status may come to grips with the knowledge of one's own illegitimate origin. The psychoanalyst believes he has a theory to explain certain subtle types of cases (or even all cases), a method of analysis to uncover the unconscious sources of conflict underlying delinquent behavior, and a therapy which will sometimes improve behavior

---

[17] *Ibid.,* pp. 128*ff.*

[18] For fuller discussion of these and other aspects of social relations in the family, see James H. S. Bossard, *The Sociology of Child Development* (New York: Harper & Brothers, 1954).

[19] *1,000 Juvenile Delinquents,* p. 73. Cf. also Shaw and McKay, *op. cit.,* pp. 288–343.

by bringing the source of conflict into consciousness or otherwise reducing its baleful influence. Lack of fully adequate proof for his theories and the frequent availability of simpler explanations still prevent the sociological criminologist from giving full credence to these views of psychoanalysis. The very fact that the victim is unconscious of the source of his difficulty precludes his direct testimony as evidence. The analyses of the psychoanalyst, designed to discover the unconscious motivations, therefore either must be taken on faith or must be tested in terms of the success of therapy. Moreover, the number of cases analyzed is limited by the fact that a full analysis of a case is very time-consuming, ideally requiring something like 200 interviews. Finally, where success is demonstrable, the question may still remain whether success was due wholly to the correctness of the analysis or to other influences—such as the personality and the understanding attitude of the psychoanalyst.

In spite of these difficulties, students of criminology should know something of the nature, achievements, and potentialities of psychoanalysis as applied to delinquents and criminals. While our own emphasis is sociological, part of it is not wholly inconsistent with the following brief attempt to characterize the psychoanalytical approach to the study of family influences and delinquency.[20]

The psychoanalytical approach finds the roots of delinquency in the frustration of drives common to mankind. All men, for example, have the impulse to kill. Whether they kill or not will depend upon how early family experiences have brought about frustrations and the determined reactions to frustrations. The later environment also plays a real but secondary role in the causation of delinquency. In later life, however, the individual may be wholly unconscious of the source of his frustrations and conflicts. The drives frustrated are those of sex and aggression. These drives normally mature with age, and the normal child is seen as passing through certain phases characteristic of successive periods of life. The delinquent child is seen as one who often is *immature* because he has not progressed from one stage to the next as other children do and as they are expected to by society. If traces of the earlier stages remain, they form the basis for the development of various "perversions" which were natural to those earlier stages.

Some degree of frustration characterizes every stage of development, including that of the early parent-child relationships. The child then not only wants food but to touch his mother. He fears her absence. Experiences of being weaned (whether from breast or bottle), of being left alone, or of being required to develop toilet or other habits of cleanliness are all frustrating, as is the possible arrival of another baby competing for affection, attention, and care.

[20] This statement is largely derived from Kate Friedlander, *Psychoanalytical Approach to Juvenile Delinquency* (New York: International Universities Press, 1947).

Delinquent acts at an early age are, then, normal manifestations of the drives and experiences of the child. But the child's pleasure-pain principle of life must in some measure be replaced by the adult's reality principle, which takes into consideration the mores and the demands of social life. At a later age the repressed child returns (regression) into the immature behavior proper at an earlier period.

At an early age the child also has incestuous desires, and when his hostile tendencies have been directed toward himself, rather than toward his father or mother, conscience has appeared. There is often manifest or latent homosexuality. Conflicts associated with these repressed desires may result in neurosis or delinquency. At the Oedipus stage of development, children are supposed to have incestuous wishes, which are socially taboo. These are repressed and cannot be remembered later in life. Yet these repressed desires function in later life. Their expression in disguised and symbolic form may at times consist of acts which transgress the law. For there is a censor which polices the human mind more effectively and imperiously than any policeman pounds his beat. To that censor, even in mid-twentieth-century American society, transgressions of the code of sex are taboo. To that censor—or so the psychoanalysts tell us—violations of that code call for sterner disapproval than violations of the criminal code such as theft or mayhap even murder. What, the sociologists might interject, are changes in the sex mores of our culture doing to the policies of this censor?

The source of the code is found in the child's identification with his parents and the internalization in his character of their personalities. Later the super-ego, which earlier had reflected the parental image, is modified as the personality comes to mirror the images of other associates, and it becomes the partly rational conscience.

Feelings of guilt are brought about by the conflict between the super-ego and the personality. A prevalent source of this conflict is the practice of masturbation, which, though almost universal as a temporary practice, is still verbally frowned upon. Another source is remnants of the old Oedipus complex or emotional relationship to the mother, and the need to change love objects is seen in a revolt against the parents. Severity with one's self alternates with self-indulgence. There is a search for new heroes or heroines. Changes in the character of heroes call for changes in the child's ethical standards. Where the super-ego is too weak to control the ego, latent delinquency develops. In the case of delinquents there is said often to have been a history of inconsistency in the parent's handling of children's behavior. This inconsistency is said rarely to have appeared in the cases of neurotics as opposed to delinquents. Thus, to the psychoanalyst, early parent-child relationships are the primary causes of delinquency. Later environmental experiences are only secondary causes. The attitudes of parents are thus of major importance. Dr. Friedlander seems to grant that delinquency may be based upon different degrees of the relative influence of early and later events.

Delinquent behavior may be the symbolic expression of unconscious guilt feelings. For example, the stealing by a girl "kleptomaniac" was interpreted is symbolic gratification of her aggressive impulse toward her mother. Her punishment satisfied her feeling of guilt over this impulse. Similarly antisocial acts at puberty may be designed to hurt the feelings of a father—an urge rooted in an early desire for revenge upon him.

More or less consistently with their analysis, some psychoanalysts distinguish four techniques for dealing with delinquencies of this sort: (1) Transference, where an emotional relationship established with the specialist playing the role of substitute parent is relied upon gradually to change the urges themselves. (2) Free association or hypnosis, the former being designed to bring the "real," deeper sources of the problem into consciousness and reduce the demands of the super-ego. For example, guilt feelings are reduced by showing the prevalence of masturbation or other sources of guilt feelings or by providing other outlets for sex or other drives and so sublimating them. The frequency of such successful sublimation has been questioned, however. (3) Psychotherapy, on the other hand, aims at pushing the conflict back into the unconscious. (4) Manipulation of the environment has sometimes proven helpful. Thus in a book often referred to by psychoanalysts, Aichhorn [21] allowed a group of institutionalized boys free rein to express their aggressive impulses. After a very difficult period these boys are reported to have begun to feel guilty over their antisocial aggression, because they came to "want to be loved" and because they discovered for themselves the social consequences of their acts. Thus they were said to have accepted the need for social control and to have become mature, losing their immature tendencies to act according to pleasure-pain principles. Though allowing free rein to impulses may well be criticized, this last group method is more acceptable to sociologists.

Other psychoanalysts have somewhat different emphases. Thus Lindner [22] gives somewhat greater weight to later cultural and other environmental influences. His analysis is thus more acceptable to the sociologically minded criminologist. Elsewhere in this book [23] we emphasize the importance of the increased use of group therapy and distinguish between the psychiatric and sociological types. We have presented the above summary at this point to illustrate the psychoanalytical approach because it is so much concerned with family situations.

The reader may well go over the above analysis and ask which parts of it are consistent and which inconsistent with the cultural and sociological

[21] August Aichhorn, *Wayward Youth* (New York: Viking Press, 1935).
[22] Robert M. Lindner, *Stone Walls and Men* (New York: Odyssey Press, 1946), chaps. 5–8.
[23] Cf. *infra*, pp. 478–80.

emphasis characterizing the present book. The following brief critique is intended merely to illustrate a few differences in emphasis.

Apparent evidence exists that motivations are often unconscious and that early emotional experiences, including those in the home, are important and often permanent. No argument is needed to prove that sex drives and impulses to aggression are often quite compelling. However, the strength, direction, form of expression, and possibility of inhibiting these drives is largely given in the culture. They are not, it seems, so universally dependent upon a particular type of interpersonal relationship in the family. The source of mental conflict today is at least as often found in conflicting group patterns as in the struggle between a physiological drive and a forbidding super-ego. The sociologist is more likely to speak of group mores than of the super-ego and of group patterning rather than personal identification as the source of morality. He thinks of personality as more often modified by later experiences. The sociologist is much interested in the increasing use of group therapy by psychoanalysts, though he would urge increased use of natural as well as artificial groups. He is quite certain that by no means all gang boys in our great cities have joined up because of mental conflict or because of an unusual passivity in their personalities, for he finds joining a gang the prevailing mode of boys growing up in our slums. Moreover, he observes the gang frequently undoing the work of the family and even achieving an internalization of behavior patterns and standards of its own.[24] The sociologist knows there is such a thing as symbolic behavior, but he finds it difficult to accept some of the more extreme explanations of behavior in terms of symbolic expression of unconscious wishes.

THROUGH FAMILY DISCIPLINARY POLICIES

The indifference of parents to children's behavior, too great severity in discipline, too great laxity, or inconsistencies in disciplinary policies—each, when combined with other factors, has its own peculiar relationship to misconduct. Parents who have been the subjects of severe punishment in their own childhood frequency use the same unsuccessful methods with their children. Unconsciously they are "getting back" at their children for their own earlier suffering. Punishment frequently reveals the poverty of the parents' other devices for control, or may be an expression of their desire to dominate.

[24] Cf. Richard A. Cloward and Lloyd E. Ohlin, *Delinquency and Opportunity. A Theory of Delinquent Gangs* (Glencoe, Ill.: Free Press, 1960).

Healy and Bronner [25] found 40 per cent of their 4,000 cases to come from families with lack of discipline. In their earlier studies, the Gluecks found "unsound" discipline, involving either extremely lax or extremely rigid control, in the families of about seven-tenths of criminal men and nearly two-thirds of delinquent women.[26] Differences in disciplinary practices were found a major contrast between delinquents and nondelinquents in their later research, and "father's discipline" became one of five social-factor categories used by the Gluecks in constructing their now-famous prediction instrument.[27]

Finally, the effect of punishment in the home upon the child will vary greatly with the other parent-child relationships. Some children reduced to tears by a spanking inflicted by affectionate parents frequently have their arms around the punisher's neck a few minutes later, while each added chastisement of other children makes the sufferers more sullen and bitter. Where parents are predominately sources of friendliness and happiness, occasional punishment merely serves to impress upon the child that the loved one is displeased, while in families where there are few if any friendly contacts competing with the influence of the beatings inflicted, the punishment is worse than useless, because it only confirms the child's impression that the parent is hostile. In a later chapter [28] we shall point out the general ineffectiveness of punishment as applied to adult criminals. Yet it is expected in the case of adults, while often criticized in the case of children.

BY INJURING THE STATUS OF THE CHILD IN THE COMMUNITY

The status of the family in the community or its subgroups is significant for the character and behavior of its individual members. This status depends upon the characteristics which bring social approval locally and upon the *relative* condition of the home. Dirt *per se* probably never led to crime; but to live in the dirtiest house in the row is morally dangerous. It is not so much the dirt in Mary's home as the fact that it is looked upon as dirty by her schoolmates that makes her ashamed to bring her boy friends there. It is not at all the fact that Gus is an illegitimate child, but the fact that his playmates know of it and taunt him with it which affects his behavior. Alfred's father is profane, and that no doubt is too bad, but it is what the neighbors

[25] William Healy and Augusta F. Bronner, *Delinquents and Criminals, Their Making and Unmaking* (New York: Macmillan, 1926), p. 125.
[26] *500 Delinquent Women*, p. 72.
[27] *Infra*, pp. 521–23.
[28] *Infra*, pp. 293–95.

say about his father which determines Alfred's own language, behavior, and hence relations with others. Similarly, criminal behavior in the home is a factor determining the social status of the family and therefore the attitude of the child toward his family and toward his own role in the community or its subgroups—which in other words determines his self-respect, which is a reflection of what some group thinks of his family and of himself.

Suggested Readings

Glueck, Sheldon and Eleanor T. *Unraveling Juvenile Delinquency.* New York The Commonwealth Fund, 1950. Chapters 8 to 11 contain extensive data contrasting the home conditions of delinquents and nondelinquents raised in similar neighborhoods.

Nye, F. Ivan. *Family Relationships and Delinquent Behavior.* New York: John Wiley and Sons, Incorporated, 1958. An empirical attempt to trace family factors in delinquency based on questionnaire data obtained from 3,000 high school students in three small cities.

CHAPTER **10**

The Ecology of Crime

Human or social ecology is concerned with the relationships which exist between people who share a common habitat or local territory and which are distinctly related to the character of the territory itself; it is a study of social structure in relation to the local environment.[1]

The ecology of crime may be studied in terms of the location of criminal acts themselves, of the residences of delinquents and criminals, or of some other supposed influence upon crime which has distribution in space. Delinquent acts of little children may occur near their homes, and in that case their correlation in space may conceivably have some significance for causation. But adult professional crime in these days of easy transportation will occur wherever opportunity for profitable activity is greatest, which may be hundreds of miles away from the criminals' homes. Hence maps of the home addresses of adult criminals at the time of their acts and maps of the locations of their acts need not even suggest possible causal influences.

All such studies are subject to serious difficulties. Without accurate and complete criminal statistics, perfectly reliable crime maps cannot be constructed. Political boundaries do not coincide with culture areas or with social relations significant for crime

[1] Terence Morris, *The Criminal Area* (New York: Humanities Press, 1957), p. 1.

153

causation. Even in small areas we must be sure that crime is similarly defined throughout the given region. Police policies and those of social agencies vary. What we really need to locate is not necessarily the current residence of a criminal but the location of the causes of his criminal patterns of behavior. Criminals are very mobile. Yet with due care the spatial distribution of some kinds of crime in some limited areas may be approximated. Map-making may well be the beginning of the search for causes; it cannot be the end. Proximity of crime and social conditions does not in itself establish causal relationships between them. Moreover, the location of delinquency-producing agencies, such as houses of prostitution, in a particular neighborhood merely makes contact with them convenient. The influence of such nearness on children in the neighborhood may indeed be considerable, but patrons and various people other than residents are involved.

Regional Distribution of Crime in the United States

Federal reports of crimes known to the police seem hardly accurate enough for the construction of fully reliable maps of the regional distribution of crime in the United States. However, the general conditions making for regional differences in crime are better known than the amount of the differences. Thus Lottier [2] speaks of the racial caste system in the South as accounting for the concentration of homicides there. He explains the family feuds in the Southern mountains as growing out of a former need for self-help and the enfeebled enforcement of the law. The North is characterized by industrialism, the fusion of corrupt politics, and Puritanical legislation. It is therefore the home of racketeering and the gangster, the former being not a little due to emulation of the methods of large-scale business. In the West the tradition of the frontiers once accounted largely both for the activities of the desperadoes who broke, and of the vigilantes who enforced, the law. Even today, Lottier holds, a desperado of the Dillinger type could hardly carry on his depredations in Massachusetts, because his operations require the wide-open spaces and a minority who tolerated or even admired his bold, dangerous criminal exploits.

The following table, though based upon *Uniform Crime Reports* data of somewhat uncertain accuracy, is presented for what it is worth. In this table the figure 1 means the lowest crime rates, and the figure 9 the highest. The causes of such differences may lie in genuine regional cultural factors.

[2] Stuart Lottier, "Distribution of Criminal Offenses in Sectional Regions," *Journal of Criminal Law and Criminology* (Sept.–Oct. 1938), pp. 331–33.

They may, however, reflect partly statistical inaccuracies or other difficulties already noted. The favorable ranking of New England is roughly confirmed by the fact that insurance against certain crimes carries low rates for that region.

Table 5   RANK ORDER (*1 = lowest crime incidence*) OF GEOGRAPHICAL DIVISIONS FOR OFFENSES KNOWN TO THE POLICE PER 100,000 INHABITANTS, 1961

Geographical Division	Murder, Non-negligent Man-slaughter	Robbery	Aggra-vated Assault	Burglary, Breaking, Entering	Larceny	Auto Theft	Rank for Sum of Ranks
New Eng.	1	1	1	2	3	6	3
Mid. Atl.	3	6	4	3	7	5	4
E. No. Cen.	5	9	5	6	6	7	7
W. No. Cen.	2	4	2	4	2	2	2
So. Atl.	8	5	9	5	5	3	5
E. So. Cen.	9	2	6	1	1	1	1
W. So. Cen.	7	3	7	7	4	4	6
Mountain	6	7	3	8	8	8	8
Pacific	4	8	8	9	9	9	9

Computed from *Uniform Crime Reports, 1961*, pp. 34–37.

Urban and Rural Areas and Crime

Speaking generally again, crime is more prevalent in cities than in rural areas. Nevertheless, improved transportation and a lessening of the differences between city and rural life are reducing this contrast.

Crimes committed in rural areas may then originate in urban situations. The vast majority of rural crimes, however, are committed by country folk. The rate for crimes against persons, like crime rates generally, is higher in urban areas, but the proportion of all crimes committed which are of this type is higher in rural communities. Not only is crime concentrated in cities, but with some exceptions the larger the city the greater the per capita crime rate. For example, in 1961 the urban complaint rate for robbery rose regularly from a low of 12.9 per 100,000 inhabitants for cities with less than 10,000 population to a high of 152.8 for cities of over 250,000. With unimportant exceptions, the same tendency was reported for the other seven serious felonies for which the FBI publishes information.[3]

[3] *Uniform Crime Reports, 1961*, pp. 81–82.

Police are generally less efficient in the smaller places, but informal social control by community influences is more effective. Rural sociologists have pointed out that country populations usually show high moral homogeneity and that rural moral control is concentrated in fewer agencies and especially in the family and community. Occupational data show farmers and farm laborers to have relatively low crime rates. Arson, cattle stealing, infanticide (not including abortion), and various acts against the use of land are predominantly rural offenses. Racketeering and white-collar crime are concentrated in cities but cannot be measured statistically.

Rural areas show these generally lower crime rates in spite of their smaller wealth. Yet the gap between rich and poor, the intensity of economic competition, and group pressure to emulate the successful are also less in rural areas. The more stable rural family, the greater homogeneity of the rural population, its lesser mobility, less dense population, less opportunity for criminals to hide away, and so on are certainly factors to be emphasized.

Ecological Studies of Urban Delinquency and Crime

In characterizing American society in Chapter 2, we stressed the trend away from primary toward secondary relations, the increasingly impersonal nature of life except where special efforts to repersonalize are made, and the decline in the functions of such significant groups as the family and neighborhood. The last-named neighborhood trends deserve careful study.

The most important urban ecological studies of crime have been those of Clifford Shaw and his associates at the Institute for Juvenile Research in Chicago. Shaw indicated on spot maps the home addresses of no fewer than 55,998 delinquents divided into eight groups, comprising juveniles, youthful felons, adults, and delinquents of both sexes. Data from as early as 1900 and as late as 1927 were included in his first study. Later maps, such as those we reproduce on pages 157 and 158 show a roughly similar distribution. Shaw found that delinquency was very unevenly distributed in the city of Chicago. For example, in 1926 some areas showed no complaints of juvenile delinquents by police probation officers, while in one area 26.6 per cent of boys of juvenile court age had been complained of in that single year.[4] Again, Shaw found that delinquency rates varied inversely with distance from the Loop, except where outlying industrial areas in-

[4] Clifford R. Shaw and Henry D. McKay, *Juvenile Delinquency and Urban Areas* (Chicago: University of Chicago Press, 1942).

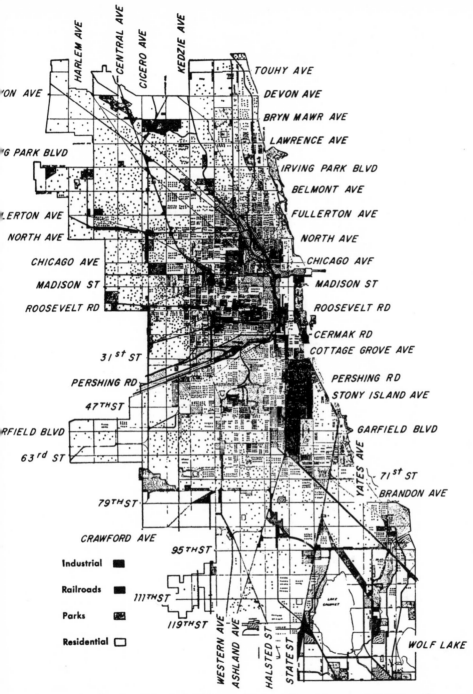

FIGURE 2   Outline Map of Chicago. Places of residence of 9,860 male delinquents brought before the juvenile court of Cook County during the years 1934–1940. Reproduced from Clifford R. Shaw and Henry D. McKay, *Juvenile Delinquency and Urban Areas*, p. 56, by permission of the University of Chicago Press.

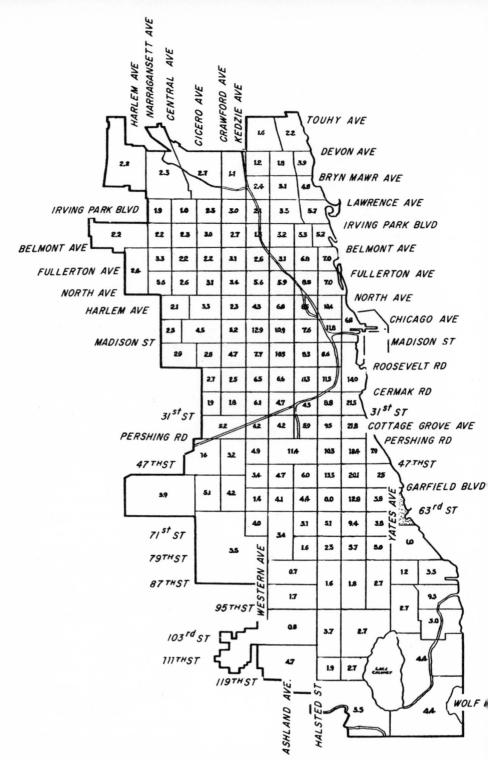

FIGURE 3   Map of Chicago. Boys brought before the Cook County Juvenile Court, per 100,000 residents. Reproduced by permission of the University of Chicago Press.

158

creased the rates locally. The same areas had remained the most delinquent for over 20 years in spite of radical changes in the nationality and racial composition of the population with the influx of Italians, Poles, Negroes, Syrians, and other minority groups. Shaw and McKay found a somewhat similar pattern of distribution in six other American cities.[5]

Areas where delinquency was concentrated were found to be characterized by proximity to industry and commerce, physical deterioration, decreasing population in a period when the city as a whole was growing rapidly, dependency, absence of ownership of homes, presence of Negroes or recent immigrants, and absence of constructive agencies intended to promote well-being and prevent maladjustment.

To Shaw, however, the major explanation of this concentration of delinquency was rather to be found in the deterioration of the neighborhood as an agency of social control. As the city grew and became industrialized, former residential areas were invaded by industry or commercial establishments. Population became mobile. People lost interest in the appearance and moral reputation of the neighborhood because their residence was shorter. Neighborliness declined. Immigrant groups brought conflicting patterns, and conflicts between the first and second generation multiplied. The neighborhood ceased to be a primary group defining and regulating behavior in the interest of a common standard. It became indifferent. Hence patterns differed widely, and criminal groups could exist side by side with noncriminal. Finally a stage was reached in some areas where certain types of delinquency, such as violations of laws against the sale of liquor or against vice, came to be approved. The area then became in a new sense a delinquency area. Shaw has given us additional convincing proof of his thesis in a series of case studies and life histories. Perhaps no more effective criminological literature of its type exists than his books, now to be considered classics, *The Jack-Roller, The Natural History of a Delinquent Career,* and *Brothers in Crime.*[6]

Criticisms of Ecological and Neighborhood Studies

Many others have made neighborhood studies similar to Shaw's. Hayner[7] showed that the Japanese, though living in deteriorated areas, were

---

[5] Clifford R. Shaw and Henry D. McKay, "Social Factors in Juvenile Delinquency," U. S. National Commission on Law Observance and Enforcement, *Report on the Causes of Crime,* Vol. II (June 26, 1931), chap. 5.

[6] Written in cooperation with his assistants and published by the University of Chicago Press in 1930, 1931, and 1938, respectively.

[7] N. S. Hayner, "Delinquency Areas in the Puget Sound Region," *American Journal of Sociology* (Nov. 1933), pp. 314–28.

able to keep their children from delinquency. Davie [8] has concluded that the Shaw-Burgess pattern of delinquency, declining as one passes toward the outskirts of a city, does not apply to New Haven, Cleveland, and various other cities. Mowrer, who himself makes extensive use of the ecological approach, has noted that significant changes in the ecology of delinquency in Chicago took place from time to time. He also points out that the pattern of distribution varies considerably among different types of offenses.[9]

Shaw's studies are of major importance and have led to very promising programs of prevention through neighborhood organization.[10] Certain critical comments may be added, however.

In the first place, Shaw seems to have rather neglected the possible effect of selective migration to and from delinquency areas. The neighborhood undoubtedly is a sort of factory manufacturing delinquents, but it is also a receptacle into which drift both delinquents and potential delinquents. A delinquent who has lost status in a neighborhood may not remain and live it down but rather seek a residence elsewhere where he is not known, frequently in a delinquency area. Such neighborhoods receive also other social waste—congregations of life's failures. The economically down and out, the relatively unintelligent, the discouraged, the minority group which is unfortunately not welcomed in more reputable areas, and not a few of the genuinely pathological—these types drift to the slum, to the delinquency area. Though migrants are more often adults than children, such adult migrants as parents may influence adversely the behavior of their children born in the slum. Similarly, the more successful tend to move out of delinquency areas. Though a few of these are no doubt successful in crime, this movement generally tends to drain off the noncriminal and potentially noncriminal. Statistical evidence of such selective influences was found in the Danville, Illinois, crime survey.[11] Evidence of a high degree of mobility among Danville criminals and of many persons residing temporarily in rooming-house areas tended to support this finding.

All this does not, of course, indicate that neighborhood influences are unimportant. Moreover, as Sutherland says,[12] those who enter delinquency areas may have come from similar areas elsewhere, but this is not necessarily

[8] Maurice R. Davie, "The Pattern of Urban Growth," in George Peter Murdock, ed., *Studies in the Science of Society* (New Haven, Conn.: Yale University Press, 1937), pp. 133–61.

[9] Ernest R. Mowrer, *Disorganization, Personal and Social* (Philadelphia: J. B. Lippincott, 1942), p. 131.

[10] Cf. *infra*, pp. 531–32.

[11] For detailed evidence of such selective migration, see Donald R. Taft, "Testing the Selective Influence of Areas of Delinquency," *American Journal of Sociology* (March 1933), pp. 699–712.

[12] *Principles of Criminology*, 6th ed., revised by Donald R. Cressey (Philadelphia: J. B. Lippincott, 1960), p. 161.

so. McKenzie has stressed the process of selective migration within the city as follows: "Each formation . . . within a community serves as a selective or magnetic force attracting to itself appropriate population elements and repelling incongruous units, thus making for biological and cultural subdivisions of a city's population." [13] Shaw does not tell us how long delinquents had resided in the areas of concentration. Thus his study may neglect the influence of family relations, subgroups, and other causes of delinquency other than the neighborhood before migrants left their previous homes. Disorganized neighborhoods certainly are, as Shaw and McKay contend, factories manufacturing delinquents, but they are also receptacles attracting and having forced into themselves life's relative failures—moral as well as economic failures. The underprivileged, exploited, and discriminated against tend to be swirled into the slum.

Again, the breakdown of neighborliness [14] stressed by Shaw, far from being confined to delinquency areas, is a general characteristic of recent trends in the entire country. Few areas are less neighborhood consciousness than our fashionable apartment-house neighborhoods, yet there is little evidence that such areas are centers of delinquency as popularly defined, though occasionally a successful "big-shot" gangster rents an apartment there. If high-rent apartment house residents are indeed relatively free of crime, this is not because they are immune from the demoralizing effects of the decline of neighborliness. Rather their behavior is patterned in other status-determining groups—the church, the club, the business organization, the informal social group. We cannot reiterate too often that racketeers and white-collar offenders almost certainly have an ecology nearly the opposite of that of lower-class crime. Shaw's maps could not show the residences of these criminals. Yet undoubtedly neighborhood disorganization combined with other criminogenic conditions in the slum produces much crime.

Shaw's claim that changes in the racial and national composition in a neighborhood have no effect upon its crime rate also seems unproved. Some nationalities possess cultures which make adjustment difficult. It probably never has been a matter of indifference for the prevalence of crime whether such nationalities, or groups with cultures more favorable to adjustment, have entered a neighborhood.

Miss Robison [15] has shown that public records of delinquency (for various reasons) are not fair measures of the relative amount of delinquency

[13] R. D. McKenzie, "The Ecological Approach to the Study of the Human Community," in Robert E. Park, Ernest W. Burgess, and Roderick D. McKenzie, eds., *The City* (Chicago: University of Chicago Press, 1925), p. 78.

[14] Cf. Peter H. Mann, "The Concept of Neighborliness," *American Journal of Sociology* (Sept. 1954), pp. 163–68.

[15] Sophia M. Robison, *Can Delinquency Be Measured?* (New York: Welfare Council of New York City, Columbia University Press, 1936), *passim.*

in different neighborhoods. She also discusses the difficulty of determining the geographical limits of delinquency areas and criticizes reliance on arbitrarily determined mile-square areas or census tracts.[16] She concludes that the ecological method is invalid and its approach not very useful. No doubt Miss Robison's criticisms are partly sound. Yet criticisms of any sort have not shaken seriously the most significant contributions of men like Shaw and McKay. Granting sources of error, delinquency areas can be located. The essential soundness of their analysis is established by the apparent success of the crime-prevention program they have set up.[17]

One of the crudest and least justified criticisms of studies like Shaw and McKay's is the point often made that neighborhoods and neighborhood disorganization cannot be the cause of delinquency because not all children who live in such disorganized neighborhoods are delinquents. The same type of criticism might be brought against practically any other "cause" of delinquency, such as the broken home or parent-child relations which are found to help explain crime. Not all of those who have been exposed to them commit crimes. But the fact that not all children living in disorganized neighborhoods become delinquents suggests that criminogenic influences within such areas operate selectively. The most notable attempt yet made to examine this hypothesis is that by Walter Reckless and his colleagues through their studies in Columbus, Ohio. In comparing two groups of 12-year-old white schoolboys living in high delinquency areas, Reckless obtained evidence that "good" boys are insulated from delinquent pressures by their self-concepts as conventional and law-abiding. The concepts in turn apparently result from adequate socialization of the boys by their parents.[18] It is possibly a minor theoretical criticism of Shaw and McKay that emphasis seems to be shifting somewhat away from the neighborhood to subgroup relations of various kinds which more closely and significantly pattern the behavior of their members. Yet, as Shaw and McKay have shown, such gangs are in part the products of neighborhood situations.[19]

[16] We note in that connection that, were population data available, delinquency areas should be determined by the density of delinquency itself, regardless of the shape of the area so marked out.

[17] For discussion of this Chicago Area Project, see *infra,* pp. 531–32.

[18] The Columbus studies are reported in a series of five articles published since 1956, summarized with concluding observations in Simon Dinitz, Frank R. Scarpitti, and Walter C. Reckless, "Delinquency Vulnerability: A Cross Group and Longitudinal Analysis," *American Sociological Review* (Aug. 1962), 515–17. The insulation is not completely successful, however, for by the time they were 16, the "good" boys had committed an average of 1.3 delinquent acts apiece for which they apparently had never been caught (*ibid.,* p. 516).

[19] Evidence of the importance of such subgroups which cut across neighborhood lines and the discovery, in cities smaller than Chicago, of neighborhood conditions not unlike those studies by Shaw and McKay have resulted from many other studies, including the Danville Crime Survey mentioned above.

A study of delinquency areas in Baltimore, using statistical procedures considerably more refined than those commonly found in ecological studies, resulted in a sharper focus on the variables related to area rate differences. Bernard Lander applied to Baltimore data partial correlation techniques to determine the relative associations with delinquency rates of education, rentals, overcrowding, substandard housing, home ownership, and population composition. Only the last two of these were significantly associated with rates. Home ownership, which Lander regards as an index to neighborhood stability, was negatively correlated with delinquency. Maximum social instability (and highest delinquency rates) he found to be located in areas where Negroes and whites approach equality in numbers.[20] When the proportion of Negroes moves above this, delinquency rates decrease.

A replication in Detroit of Lander's Baltimore study supported his finding concerning home ownership but revealed that education and overcrowding were, in addition, independently associated with delinquency.[21] The economic variables of income, rent, and housing value were found not to be associated.

Although neither of these studies purport to demonstrate *causal* ties between delinquency and particular variables, their findings suggest that only a limited number of those conditions conventionally labeled "bad" are causally important. Moreover, individual cities might show somewhat differing congeries of factors associated with delinquency, since cities differ in population composition, land-use patterns, intergroup relationships, and so on.

Finally, Shaw and McKay would have agreed that their research does not in itself tell us why we have slums and disorganized neighborhoods. There are deeper levels of causation which need to be studied. Disorganized neighborhoods remain, however, one of the most important "proximate" influences on crime, even in a society where neighborliness has rapidly declined. In a later chapter we shall indicate the great importance of organizing the neighborliness which remains and of stimulating the growth of that which is potentially avialable, if we would effectively prevent delinquency and crime.

Importance of Neighborhood in Delinquent Careers

Even without ecological studies, there is abundant evidence that delinquency is influenced by the neighborhood.

[20] Bernard Lander, *Towards an Understanding of Juvenile Delinquency* (New York: Columbia University Press, 1954), p. 65.

[21] David J. Bordua, "Juvenile Delinquency and 'Anomie': An Attempt at Replication," *Social Problems* (Winter, 1958–59), p. 236.

The dominant role of the neighborhood in the development of some delinquent careers has been clearly demonstrated in *Brothers in Crime,* the last of the series of life histories by Clifford Shaw and his associates. Its authors recognize, of course, that family, play group, and gang also had their share in the process, and that all of these were but elements in the larger community culture.[22]

The five Martin brothers whose life histories are analyzed in this volume had served a total of 55 years in correctional and penal institutions, had been arrested at least 86 times, had been brought into court 70 times, and so on. They had committed over 300 burglaries, in addition to other crimes. The neighborhood where they lived illustrates many of the characteristics of delinquency areas we have already mentioned. It was adjacent to heavy industry, "a drab, unattractive, and deteriorated community." Dwellings were old and dilapidated structures, and many had been condemned for demolition or repair. These structures made junking an easy neighborhood practice. It was an area of declining population; of poverty, unemployment, dependency, and economic insecurity. Residents were thus handicapped in providing their children with educational opportunity. Yet the neighborhood was "exposed to the luxury standards of life which are generally idealized in our culture but which are beyond their attainment." "Very often crime and the rackets offer the only means of achieving even the minimum of economic security." Yet the delinquent children came from families of very divergent economic status. Therefore, Shaw concludes, the effect of economic conditions was a relative matter dependent on many other factors in the situation.

Again, the neighborhood was one of confused moral patterns. Theft was sanctioned in some groups, condemned in others; brought prestige in some, ostracism in others. This confusion was seen in the "disparity of interests, standards, and philosophy of life as between parents and children," largely because children were not receptive to the old-world standards adhered to by their fathers and mothers. To deal with the resulting conflicts, parents of the neighborhood frequently resorted to severe corporal punishment. This was ineffective largely because the children, through their wider contacts, were better adjusted to the larger community and more sophisticated than their parents. As indicated, this conflict was partly cause and partly result of the fact that the children belonged to street crowds, play groups, and gangs where patterns at variance with those of the home were taught. While the preponderant attitude of individual parents toward delinquency was one of disapproval, some were indifferent to, tolerated, or tacitly approved stealing, and some were directly involved in their children's criminal behavior. Resident professional fences purchased goods stolen by children.

The neighborhood also possessed a delinquency tradition resulting from the long prevalence of crime there. This tradition was assimilated by boys' groups and disseminated to other succeeding groups. Each year about 12 to 15 per cent of the boys aged ten to seventeen were dealt with by the police for

[22] The following condensed summary is from chap. 5 of *Brothers in Crime.*

delinquency, and general crime rates among young men were high. Local and less serious crimes were committed by younger boys; downtown and more serious crimes by the older young men. Thus, despite varied attitudes toward crime in the community, the boy who "engages in delinquency may be regarded as a 'right guy' but from the standpoint of the court he is regarded as a law-violator and a delinquent."

Types of Delinquency Areas

Seven types of neighborhoods significant for their influence on delinquency may be distinguished, though they are not entirely mutually exclusive.

(1) The first is the simple area of poverty and fairly normal family organization relatively uncomplicated by other influences. The great bulk of poor people are by no means delinquent, but petty stealing is relatively prevalent in such areas.

(2) A second type of neighborhood is the slum. Here poverty is complicated by heterogeneity of population and other factors. The slum, Zorbaugh [23] tells us, is a region of dark alleys and damp cellars, of freedom and individualism, of undesirable elements from among immigrant groups, of poverty-stricken and broken families, of human derelicts and a heterogeneous mass of the unsuccessful from among the ranks of unskilled labor, of hoboes and criminals, of pauperization and not merely dependency, of drug addicts and drunkards, of mobility and anonymity, of overcrowding, and of the absence of community controls and constructive influences. Particularly the slum is an area of cosmopolitanism based upon common failure rather than upon that recognition of achievements of others which characterizes cosmopolitanism at higher levels. Social distance is reduced to a minimum in the slum. This means that any chance acquaintance may become an intimate. The people have little or nothing to lose and no pride in the past which has seen their failure. Hence the slum breeds crime.[24]

(3) The term "interstitial area" is somewhat useful, but it overlaps with the concept of the slum. An interstitial area is one which is shut off from conventional society by some physical or social barrier, perhaps a mass of railroad tracks, a river or canal, a large industrial area, or, just as often, a color line or the animosities of rival nationalities. An interstitial area created by social barriers lies between two better-organized neighbor-

[23] Harvey W. Zorbaugh, *The Gold Coast and the Slum* (Chicago: University of Chicago Press, 1929), chap. 7.

[24] Cf. also William F. Whyte, *Street Corner Society* (Chicago: University of Chicago Press, 1943).

hoods—a no man's land separating the region where Poles predominate from the Puerto Ricans, or Little Italy from the land of the Slavs, or white from Negro. Any such marginal region is a battleground of conflicting cultures and at times a literal battleground of gangs representing them. Such conflicts of cultures make interstitial areas seedbeds of crime.

(4) The rooming-house area is a goodly portion of the slum but not all of it, and the higher-type rooming houses are outside the slum. Zorbaugh pictured this region in the near north side of Chicago.[25] It was known by its "rooms for rent" signs, its unconventional customs and unconventional people. In the area he surveyed 71 per cent of the homes kept roomers, and the population was divided into 52 per cent single men, 10 per cent single women, and 38 per cent couples living with or without the sanction of marriage. It was thus a childless area and an area of highly mobile population. At least half of the *keepers* of the rooming houses, to say nothing of the roomers, had been at their then residence six months or less. It was a region of impersonal relations. Inquiry of the keeper concerning a roomer of a few weeks back discovered that she had entirely forgotten his identity. He was a source of income and almost a number, scarcely a name. The keepers of such rooming houses care little what goes on so long as other roomers are not too much disturbed, and the man in one room has perhaps never recognized the occupant of the room across the hall.

In such a region of anonymity varied patterns of behavior are found. Neighborhood control is nonexistent. There is no community tradition, no common definition of situations or generally accepted morals, no public opinion. There is complete political indifference, at least so far as local government is concerned. It is naturally an area of personal and social disorganization. The wish for security is unsatisfied in such a locality, for family and friends are left behind, and in the rooming house nobody cares. The wish for intimate response and friendship is starved. The wish for new experience may be satisfied, but new experience finds its charm only when it is a diversion from more stable life. The wish for recognition cannot be satisfied unless perhaps in groups where status depends upon the very personality traits which have meant failure before. A man or woman remaining in the rooming-house area becomes a restless lonely dreamer or expresses his dissatisfaction in unusual and often criminal behavior.

(5) A certain type of ghetto—or neighborhood inhabited by any single minority group—may also be a center of crime, although, as we have seen elsewhere, the ghetto, preserving homogeneity and primary group control, often protects from crime and is usually far less delinquent than

[25] *Op. cit.,* chap. 4.

the heterogeneous slum. However, where a national or other culture group cherishes values and practices behavior by its nature criminogenic in any culture, the ghetto may have a high delinquency rate. In the ghetto, moreover, there is the conflict between parents and children if the latter attend American schools.

(6) Vice areas are usually slums, but not all slums are vice areas. These areas are characterized by police-protected commercialized vice such as prostitution and gambling. Not only do these violations of law center there, but they attract more dangerous criminal exploiters. The struggle between rival vice lords may even result in gang murders. Such areas corrupt city politics. Patrons of vicious resorts, however, come in large proportion from the outside. The number of children resident there may be small, but those living in the area or on the fringe are adversely affected by associations there and by the knowledge that crime is protected.

(7) Finally, we note certain types of rural areas which are criminogenic influences. There is the community which serves as a hideout for city gangsters. There is the very different run-down village from which the more enterprising elements have departed for the city perhaps and where lack of enterprise and demoralization obtain. Former mill towns in New England and sites of abandoned coal mines in the Middle West are examples of such situations. Population and wealth decline, taxes are inadequate to provide for community needs, poorer teachers are hired in the schools, churches close, and shiftlessness and indifference to lapses from former behavior standards pervade the village life. Alert leaders are lacking to stimulate improvement. Such a village may not be a center of serious crime, but it is often characterized by neglect of variants and a drift into petty "immoralities" and delinqencies. Speaking generally, however, rural areas are not crime centers.

No doubt other types of delinquency areas might be distinguished, including some industrial or mining communities where strife between labor and capital or between rival unions leads to a disproportionate amount of violence.

A recent ecological study of crime in Seattle gives further support to the "area" concept. Analyzing areas where crimes are committed *and* areas where offenders reside, Professor Calvin Schmid found that both are generally characterized by most of the following factors: [26] low social cohesion and low socio-economic status, weak family life, physical decay, high population mobility, and personal demoralization. Schmid pointed out that

[26] Calvin F. Schmid, "Urban Crime Areas: Part II," *American Sociological Review* (Oct. 1960), p. 678.

although a number of empirically plausible hypotheses exist to explain the spatial distribution of crime, "a satisfactory theory of socially deviant behavior, which would encompass urban crime areas, lies a considerable distance in the future." [27]

Status-Determining Influence of the Neighborhood

The neighborhood determines what influences outside the family will be near the child as his personality develops. The influence of the neighborhood is therefore *in part* just the influence of the type of people, the type of families, schools, churches, play groups and gangs, social agencies, and other organizations located there. Yet more important are the attitudes and values of the inhabitants, which determine the atmosphere of the neighborhood itself.

This atmosphere is something more than the sum total of its constituent institutions. For the neighborhood is also influenced by its relationship to the larger community and the still larger general culture. The attitude of the larger community toward the particular neighborhood is important for its members. Thus the child's personality is influenced by the role he plays in the neighborhood and the status of the neighborhood in the community. A neighborhood where social values are identical with those in the larger community and with those defined by law and where achievement is roughly comparable will teach respect for law and will be relatively free from delinquency. To this statement there is the exceedingly important exception that white-collar crime is generally approved in well-to-do areas. But a neighborhood feeling itself in conflict with the values of the outside world will communicate that opposition to children growing up in its midst. Similarly, a neighborhood characterized by failure in terms of the goals of the larger society will instill a sense of failure in the minds of its children.

Whyte, in his *Street Corner Society*,[28] points out that while our society places a high value on the man who climbs the ladder of success, it is difficult for the Cornerville man to get onto the ladder, "even on the bottom rung." He sees that his district has become known as a disordered and lawless community. To get ahead he must move either in the world of business and Republican politics or in the world of Democratic politics and the rackets.[29] If he is recognized as successful in the larger society, that suc-

[27] *Ibid.*
[28] *Op. cit.*, p. 273.
[29] These local party labels are, of course, not essential to the point Whyte makes.

cess labels him as a sort of traitor to his district, its established ways, and its gangs. Success in the local world, on the other hand, means that he is an outcast in the world outside. To reduce delinquency in such a neighborhood, the status of Cornerville society as a whole in the larger external society must be raised. While in this particular Cornerville what was needed was the rise in the status of the Italian nationality in the United States, in slums generally areas housing the underprivileged must rise in the eyes of the more successful community outside of them. The slum type of neighborhood thus impresses its own lowly status upon its denizens.

American Culture and the Neighborhood

Neighborhoods where crime is concentrated are abnormal. Yet they are products of the normal. They result from the general processes of competition and segregation which characterize the larger society. Speaking generally, failure in social competition results in residence in delinquency areas. The slum results in part from the fact that Americans value individualism. Boys living in such areas would not feel themselves in conflict with the larger society were it not for the condescension with which Americans generally view the poor, the relatively unsuccessful, the Negro, the recent immigrant. The very conflict between slum children and their parents reflects changes going on in society generally. Some social values of the slum are in conflict with the general culture. But basic values, such as the urge for material achievement and the tendency to rate and be rated, to resent inferior roles, and to contest for supremacy, are American values.

Suggested Readings

Morris, Terence. *The Criminal Area.* New York: Humanities Press, 1957. The early sections of this study of crime in an English town contains a good review of British and American ecological work dealing with crime.

Motley, Willard. *Knock On Any Door.* New York: Appleton-Century-Crofts, 1947. A perceptive and highly informative novel depicting the impact of slum life on a Chicago family.

Shaw, Clifford R., and McKay, Henry D. *Delinquency Areas.* Chicago: University of Chicago Press, 1929.

————. *Delinquency and Urban Areas.* Chicago: University of Chicago Press, 1942. *Delinquency Areas* describes the spatial distributions of delinquents in Chicago; the second book, similar distributions in several other cities. Together they seemed to provide further factual support for the concentric-zone theory of urban growth.

CHAPTER 11

Association and the Juvenile Gang

Beginning at birth, humans undergo a series of conditioning experiences whereby the presence of other humans comes to be identified with the satisfaction of biological needs. Through subtle processes of elaboration, these purely organic requirements begin differentiating into psychological and social need-satisfaction patterns as the child's capacity for symbolic interaction with others develops, and these patterns become a part of "human nature." Thus individuals value the company of others not only because of infantile conditioning but also because one's sense of self and the "worthiness" of self are preserved by the reassurances resulting from sustained social ties. The shift in Western cultures toward the urban end of the folk-urban continuum has entailed among other changes considerable decline in the role of family and neighborhood affiliations in satisfying individual psychological and social needs, and their partial substitution by limited-interest groups. The part played by such groups in ordering and motivating the behavior of their members has led to extensive speculation and research by sociologists. It is with these functions, as they pertain to delinquency, that this chapter is concerned.

Types of Association Related to Crime

It is worthwhile to distinguish at least three kinds of association: personal friendship or the mutual companionship of two people; membership in passive groups; and association in interaction groups, such as clubs, play groups, and gangs. The influence of single companions, friends, and hero types is of importance. A dominant personality may induce crime in a more suggestible and weaker associate. Hero worship may lead to imitation or identification with the hero, and even in gangs the role of the leader is often almost dictatorial. Similarly, the offender's road away from a criminal career has occasionally been taken through the influence of an understanding friend; of a person less intimately related to him, such as a psychiatrist or other specialist, perhaps serving as a "substitute parent"; or of a hero whom he may take as a model or with whom he may identify.

As for the influence of passive groups, teachers and preachers almost have to assume that their lectures or sermons "get across" and somehow affect the behavior of their hearers, if, indeed, their purpose has, perhaps unwisely, been to bring about such a result. But except where the discussion method is used, or where there is group activity as well as passive listening, passive groups lack interaction. They are ephemeral, do not develop common codes of behavior, nor become sources of status craved by their members. Hence they do not usually result in either criminal or other behavior patterns. Such patterns are the product usually of the warmer continuing association in groups and gangs within which there is interaction. We saw in the last chapter that, while the neighborhood still has influence, the subgroups it contains, and in some measure creates, are increasingly recognized as the seedbeds of delinquency.

Evidence of the Importance of the Gang

The evidence of the importance of this type of association is overwhelming, whether the facts are derived from case studies or from statistics. Shaw and McKay [1] found that out of 5,480 offenders only 18.2 per cent had committed their offenses alone. Of the remainder, 30.3 per cent had had a single companion; 27.7 per cent, two companions; 10.8 per cent, three;

---

[1] Clifford R. Shaw and Henry D. McKay, "Social Factors in Juvenile Delinquency," National Commission on Law Observance and Enforcement, *Report on the Causes of Crime,* Vol. II (1931), pp. 195–96.

7.1 per cent, four; 3.9 per cent, five; 1.0 per cent, six; and 1.0 per cent, 7 or more. Stealing was particularly a group phenomenon, 89 per cent of the offenders charged with theft having been brought into court with accomplices. The Gluecks found that seven-tenths of 1,000 delinquents boys and nearly three-fifths of reformatory men had committed their offenses with companions, but they classed only 7.3 per cent as members of gangs. In their later and better-controlled study, however, they found gang membership of the greatest importance.[2] Healy and Bronner found companionship an associated factor in 62 per cent of 3,000 cases of delinquents in Chicago and Boston. British figures since at least 1920 "consistently show that the great majority of juvenile crime, i.e., between 8 and 17 years, is committed in company of others."[3] Burt, studying English children, found bad companionships an "outstanding" factor in 18 per cent of their cases, a minor factor in many more. Unlike Shaw, however, Burt inclines to the belief that the very fact that a boy surrenders to the lead of another boy indicates some mental abnormality. The weight of American evidence is against this interpretation, although in a recent book on New York City gangs Yablonski suggests that members of violent gangs are "sociopaths."[4] Rather personality, family tensions, and ganging appear to reflect deeper influences in our society, and the city child, though dissatisfied with his parents, learns his delinquent patterns in a majority of cases through gang association. In so doing he is expressing in a way characteristics of certain neighborhoods and the more general revolt of modern adolescents. Even when boys are arrested as lone wolves, their initiation into delinquency may often have been through the influence of companions or gang members. A gang is distinguished from a simple play group in that it is a conflict group in conflict with other gangs, the family, the school, the police, or other institutions in the larger community.

The juvenile gang, then, is a phenomenon of the pre-adolescent and early adolescent period and has been variously assigned by different authors to different age ranges. Thrasher speaks of adolescence as an "interstitial"' period between childhood and maturity,[5] and finds its location characteristically in the interstitial life of city neighborhoods.

---

[2] Sheldon and Eleanor T. Glueck, *1,000 Juvenile Delinquents* (Cambridge, Mass.: Harvard University Press, 1934), pp. 94 and 100–01; *500 Criminal Careers* (New York: Alfred A. Knopf, 1930), p. 152; *Unraveling Juvenile Delinquency* (Cambridge, Mass.: Harvard University Press, 1950), pp. 163–64.

[3] Peter Scott, "Gangs and Delinquent Groups in London," *British Journal of Delinquency* (July 1956), pp. 7–8.

[4] Lewis Yablonski, *The Violent Gang* (New York: Macmillan, 1962), chap. 12.

[5] Frederic M. Thrasher, *The Gang*, 2d rev. ed. (Chicago: University of Chicago Press, 1936).

Gangs originate spontaneously. Chance meeting on the streets, revolt from a conventional group, the combining of a play group meeting opposition, the organization of a poolroom group or of a number of truants—these and other such incidents occasion boys' gangs. Whyte tells us they rarely result from ordinary associations at school but often from street-corner contacts, although children in schools for disciplinary cases do often form gangs.

We shall better appreciate the influence of the gang on behavior patterns if we examine the origins of such patterns. In the case of the "good" child, distinctions between "right" and "wrong" behavior become internalized as a part of the personality through the processes of interaction in the family long before he can have had a gang experience. They then are not consciously derived from a social force outside him, but are a part of him.

In the child who has had such a "normal" moral education in the family, supplemented perhaps by the school, a certain resistance is set up against change of these moral values as a result of later experience. This, no doubt, is one reason why not all boys join gangs; why not all gangs are equally delinquent; and why many boys do not continue indefinitely the delinquent patterns learned in the gang. But the gang may and often does overcome such resistance. And where the child has lacked such internalization of traditional moral patterns in the family; where family and school norms have been in conflict as they may be in some immigrant families; or where for other reasons the appeal and contagion of the gang is especially strong—in such cases, the gang will be able to impose its own.morality. By processes not altogether different from those described above, reinforced by opposition from forces without, the gang may achieve an "internalization" of delinquent patterns until stealing becomes honorable and crime brings not shame but pride. Thus the gang may rival the internalization achieved by the family.

The Location of Gangs

The most significant analyses of the juvenile gang seem still to be those of Thrasher and of Whyte.[6] Thrasher produced a map of 1,313 gangs in Chicago some years ago. His conclusion was that gangs are concentrated "in the space between more stable residential areas and the growing domain

[6] William F. Whyte, *Street Corner Society* (Chicago: University of Chicago Press, 1943).

of business and industry; between immigrant or racial colonies; between city and country or city and suburbs; between continuous towns." [7]

During several years in crime-prevention work on Manhattan's upper west side, Lewis Yablonski observed differences between the "new" slums of this area and some of New York's older slums.[8]

The slums of the past, amply described in the literature, were characterized by a high incidence of crime, delinquency, assault, alcoholism, and mental illness. Despite this, within many of these older slum areas there was a "sense of community." The early gang's turf was not simply a thin rationale for a fight as it is for today's violent gang; it meant something to a youth, and his neighborhood was part of his identity. The earlier "high-delinquency" neighborhoods of New York—the Lower East Side and Harlem—had severe problems, but theirs was a "community" with some degree of cohesion.

*   *   *   *   *

The two types of slum described also appear to produce different deviant patterns: the stable slum creating a more normative delinquent adjustment and the disorganized slum a higher rate of violent behavior. With particular reference to gangs, the stable slum appears to produce more "delinquent" and "social" gangs, and the disorganized neighborhood "violent" gangs. It should be re-emphasized, however, that purely "stable" or "disorganized" slums seldom exist. Thus, currently, there seems to be a composite of these slum conditions, with the disorganized slum becoming the prevalent condition.

A study in Dallas found gangs in noninterstitial areas and situations, and some were found which, instead of being in conflict with community mores, seemed to be an expression of them [9]—in large part an expression of the view of the local area that the Negro is fair game and of the more widespread view that Negroes are inferior and should be discriminated against. Whether interstitial or not, the gang is a conflict group reflecting conflict between different elements in the body politic. Gangs reflect attitudes, prejudices, and lines of conflict in our society.

Local Causes of Gangs

Gangs exist because they satisfy various socio-psychological needs of boys living in gangland better than alternative opportunities. The gang may satisfy the wish for new experience so well that agencies opposed to it find themselves at their wits' end to plan recreational outlets which can compete

[7] Op. cit., p. 23.
[8] Yablonski, op. cit., pp. 172–74.
[9] Haskell M. Miller, "The Gang Boy in Texas," Southern Methodist University Studies in Sociology, Vol. II, No. 1 (Summer, 1937), pp. 22–24.

successfully. The gang in its antisocial escapades provides the joys of pursuit and escape dear to the heart of the boy. Yet the gang may also provide security in a dangerous world. It protects its members against the punishment threatened by rival gangs on the one hand, and by police, schools, and other agencies of the community on the other. The gang is the source of friendships for boys who may not have made friends elsewhere; it provides recognition for those who may not have "rated" in school or on the baseball field. Indeed, some of the very personality traits which hinder success elsewhere may bring the plaudits of fellow gang members. "Rowdy" behavior brings disapproval in school, approval in the gang.

The gang is also in part a neighborhood product. It reflects the conflicts which characterize areas of low economic status in juxtaposition to areas of comfort. It reflects the reproduction of old-world struggles between Pole and Jew or Italian and Slav. It reflects conflict-producing, new-world prejudices against the immigrant and the Negro.[10]

The Gang Code and Its Enforcement

Accepted attitudes and behavior patterns of the gang often include gambling, profanity, obscenity, vandalism, and sexual promiscuity. Loyalty is the gang's primary virtue and the traitor the arch-criminal. Thrasher found younger gangs in Chicago refusing to have anything to do with girls. Boys, rather than girls, form gangs, but the presence of girls in mixed gangs has apparently increased somewhat. The gang's methods of social control include applause, ridicule, preferment, ostracism, physical punishment, and imitation of "taking for a ride," as in older gangs. The use of epithets to secure conformity or to show scorn is general. "Yellow-belly," "snitcher," "baby," "sissy," and other taunts are more feared by the gang boy than is physical punishment. Rather than submit to these epithets, he will conform to the demands of the gang even when they call for acts which as an individual he would never attempt. If the reader doubts the effectiveness of such terms in inducing uniform behavior, let him substitute for them whatever label is most dreaded in his own primary groups.

[10] The existence of intra-ethnic gang rivalries, however, shows that ethnic and similar underlying social cleavages are not essential to the formation of such rivalries. One observer, in fact, believes that "geography and propinquity—not racial differences—lie at the heart of street combat." [Harrison E. Salisbury, *The Shook-up Generation* (New York: Crest Books, 1958), p. 15.]

Gang Leadership, Structure, and External Relations

The code and the activities of gangs follow a widespread general pattern in our ganglands. But the specific nature of a gang's behavior is dictated by its leader. The leader spends more money on his followers than they spend on him.[11] The relationship between leader and led is more nearly that of personal friendship and loyalty, however, than that of exchange of expected favors. While the leader must conform to the gang's conception of a hero, he need not be the most proficient in all types of gang activities.

The hierarchical organization of the gang, each of its members having his accepted place in the gang structure, has been well described by Whyte.[12] Similarly, in cases where the gang is locally accepted, it has its corresponding place in the hierarchical structure of the community. "The corner gang, the racket and police organizations, the political organization and . . . the social structure [make up] a hierarchy of personal relations based upon a system of reciprocal obligations." Such integration of the gang into the community structure is no doubt characteristic of some immigrant communities, such as the Italian neighborhood which Whyte describes, rather than of other types of areas where the gang is more at war with the local as well as the larger community.

Development and Decline of the Gang

The typical city boys' gang originates in a play group and is integrated by conflict with the police, the school, the family, and the conventional community generally. Shaw has shown how, beginning with truancy or undefined delinquency, the typical gang boy progresses to pilfering in the neighborhood and then breaking into neighborhood stores. Widening the radius of its activities, the gang may then engage in shoplifting in downtown department stores, jackrolling (stealing from drunks), stealing the accessories from automobiles, stealing the cars themselves, robbing with a gun, rape. It does not follow, however, that most members of juvenile gangs will become serious criminals or professional gangsters. On the contrary and fortunately, the gang usually breaks up long before a truly professional stage is reached. Families moving out of the neighborhood, boys going to work, members becoming interested in girls and marrying, arrest of gang

----

[11] For an excellent analysis of leadership in Italian gangs, both juvenile and those of later youth, see Whyte, *op. cit.*, chaps. 1 and 2, and his summary, pp. 258–68.
[12] *Ibid.*, pp. 262–63.

leaders and their imprisonment, or conventionalization of the gang in the form of a political or athletic club—one or more of these changes usually results in the breakup of the juvenile gang. Yet not a few of such gangs continue as professional groups, losing some early members and taking on outsiders who may not have had the juvenile gang experience. The juvenile gang may train its members for later professional crime, even when the gang as a whole breaks up.

Specific Gang Influences on Delinquency and Crime

The general trend of the juvenile gang toward crime is evident from its characteristics and usual development. Thrasher summarizes these influences as follows:

The undirected gang or gang club demoralizes its members. It aids in making chronic truants and juvenile delinquents and in developing them into finished criminals. It augments racial friction in some areas. It complicates the problems of capital and labor in certain fields. It organizes bootlegging and rumrunning into a profitable business. It contributes to perverted politics and governmental corruption. It promotes the corrupt alliance between crime and politics.[13]

More specific gang influences may be summarized as follows:

1. Through the gang the boy develops attitudes of conflict with the community and with its agencies of social control.
2. The juvenile gang teaches a general hoodlum pattern of destructiveness which may be adapted to the commission of many types of delinquency.
3. The gang teaches the technique of crime. Even simple theft requires skill if it is to be successful, and highly developed professional crime requires training which cannot be had in books or universities. Beginners must be shown how to take apples from fruit stands unseen by the owners; how to put their caps down on articles on store counters and pick up both cap and article; how to steal and dispose of junk such as piping from vacant houses; how to break a window without making a noise; how to pick a lock; how to jackroll a drunk; and many other skills.[14]
4. More important in criminogenic influence than the teaching of techniques is the gang's teaching of its code. The adult professional gang's hierarchy of approved behavior and its caste system may be accepted by the juvenile gang and beckon its members to bigger and better crimes.

[13] *Op. cit.*, p. 368.
[14] For an extended account of the technique of pickpockets, see E. H. Sutherland, *The Professional Thief* (Chicago: University of Chicago Press, 1936).

Enmity to the police is a natural element in the gang's code, as well as the importance of always refusing to tell gang secrets. The gang also has its own hero worship, for the "big shot" for his boldness and success, and the "right guy" for his loyalty and dependability.

5. The gang is again a medium of contact between beginners and more experienced delinquents, including especially those who have served terms in juvenile institutions.

6. Similarly, the juvenile gang serves as a medium of contact with older professional gangs. The order of development is frequently from play groups who admire and discuss their gang heroes, to juvenile gangs who imitate them, and finally to professional gangs who make a business of crime.

7. The gang also brings the delinquent into contact with the "fence," who will purchase junk and other stolen articles. The "fence" teaches the boy that crime, which has been a source of thrills, may also be a source of profits.

8. The older gang makes for continuance of crime by welcoming the ex-convict out of prison. Where such a man wishes to go straight, he often meets insuperable difficulties, and when he then is invited back by the gang, the temptation to accept the invitation is great indeed.

9. It is obvious that the gang stimulates crime through its very organization. Even juvenile delinquency of some sorts requires confederates to warn of approaching police, distract attention of spectators, and so on.

10. Loyalty and organization are the chief elements which the gang adds to the crime problem, and the two are interdependent. It is true that in the adult professional gang, quarrels over the spoils are not infrequent, and the temptation to "squeal" to save one's life is tremendous. Nevertheless, the cooperation and loyalty which are found even in professional gangs are often striking. Their essence is that the individual is esteemed and aided, not for his own qualities, but because he is one of a group.

11. As already observed and as indicated in the following chapter, the juvenile gang is sometimes a preparation for later adult professional crime and organized gangs.

Structural-Functional Gang Theories

Since 1955 several exceedingly interesting theories of delinquent juvenile collectivities have dealt with somewhat more subtle social and socio-psychological processes than those discussed by Thrasher and others of the

Chicago school. Professor David Bordua has aptly described Thrasher's processes as involving the pursuit of "fun, profit, glory, and freedom" [15] in urban areas where the agencies of social control are inadequate to the task of channeling youthful energies into law-abiding activities. A characteristic of the newer theories, in contrast, is their view of delinquency not simply as action-for-its-own-sake, but as action *systems* which are to be regarded most appropriately as products of systemic processes. Values, attitudes and norms defined as delinquent have meaning sociologically insofar as integral relationships to broader categories of values, attitudes, norms and institutions can be assumed to exist. This is not merely another way of recognizing that "things are interrelated" within a society; the Chicago writers were fully aware of this general principle. It is, rather, a considerable sharpening of this principle by focusing the sociologist's attention on the interplay of social forces within and between systems and subsystems. Seen in this way, delinquent behavior patterns are parts of complex social structures-in-process, and are thus "meaningful" to the structures. Three examples of these newer theories will be cited.

Professor Albert Cohen sees "non-utilitarian, malicious and negativistic" delinquency as arising from the need of working class boys to disavow the validity of middle class standards of conduct which they encounter in socially heterogeneous high schools and elsewhere.[16] Bloch and Niederhoffer interpret adolescent gangs as units performing the functional equivalents of primitive rites of passage. Adolescent striving for the attainment of adult stutus in societies lacking formalized procedures for status change leads to such age-restricted culture traits as hazing, colorful nicknames, tattooing and extreme clothing styles. The strong in-group loyalty often typical of youngsters sharing these traits may, under particular conflict conditions, sour into attitudes of hostility to the adult world.[17] In a refinement of Robert Merton's theory that criminality is a response to circumstances where legitimate means to affluence, power and esteem are severely limited, Cloward and Ohlin contend that illegitimate means themselves are not equally available within culturally deprived population segments. This differential accessibility can give rise to three kinds of delinquent subcultures—criminality, violence and drug use—depending upon

[15] David J. Bordua, "Delinquent Subcultures: Sociological Interpretations of Gang Delinquency," *Annals of the American Academy of Political and Social Science* (November 1961), p. 123.

[16] Albert K. Cohen, *Delinquent Boys: The Culture of the Gang* (Glencoe, Ill.: The Free Press, 1955). Cohen's theory, together with several others, is described more fully in Chapter 16, *infra*, but in a different connection.

[17] Herbert Bloch and Arthur Neiderhoffer, *The Gang: A Study of Adolescent Behavior* (New York: Philosophical Library, 1958), pp. 17; 161–64.

the distribution of certain neighborhood and personal-social characteristics.[18]

However intellectually attractive these and similar delinquency theories may be as products of the sociological imagination, none has been accompanied by a body of data comparable in quantity or relevance to that of the Chicago school. However quaint its delinquents may seem to us today, in their knickerbockers and cloth caps and pre-atomic innocence, they swarmed unmistakably through Chicago's transition zone in a noisy pursuit of happiness and adventure. Before we abandon entirely this image for one promoted by more recent theories, let us await further data.

American Culture and the Juvenile Gang

Though the seriously delinquent gang may be an abnormal phenomenon, the conditions which ultimately account for the prevalence of the gang and some of its criminogenic characteristics clearly are embedded in our culture. The slum which produces the gang is a by-product of our economic and social system. It is true that gangs are conflict phenomena and that some of their superficial values are directly opposed to those of the community. Yet the most basic values in our culture are accepted by both the gang and the larger society. We have already emphasized that the value of "gang loyalty" is a widely esteemed social virtue. Materialism, individualism, and competition are common to the gang and the society upon which it preys. Race prejudice is in our culture and helps determine the lines of much gang conflict. Not only are these values held in common, but the very existence of gangs and the slums which manufacture them may be said to result from the acceptance of some of them. The gang does not so much introduce new social values in conflict with society, as determine the form and direction in which common values shall be expressed. In our culture the unusual force of some of the gang boy's drives, especially perhaps the drive for social recognition, reflects the almost universal fact that Americans must at all costs belong and must strive for social recognition. Law-abiding Americans have many traits in common with gangsters, and ours is a gang-producing culture.

[18] Richard A. Cloward and Lloyd E. Ohlin, *Delinquency and Opportunity: A Theory of Delinquent Gangs* (Glencoe, Ill.: The Free Press, 1960), ch. 7.

Suggested Readings

The Chicago School

Shaw, Clifford. *Brothers in Crime*. Chicago: University of Chicago Press, 1938.
———. *The Jack-Roller*. Chicago: University of Chicago Press, 1930.
———. *The Natural History of a Delinquent Career*. Chicago: University of Chicago Press, 1931.
Shaw, Clifford, and McKay, Henry D. *Delinquency Areas*. Chicago: University of Chicago Press, 1929.
———. *Delinquency and Urban Areas*. Chicago: University of Chicago Press, 1942.
Thrasher, Frederic M. *The Gang,* rev. ed. Chicago: University of Chicago Press, 1936.
Zorbaugh, Harvey W. *The Gold Coast and the Slum*. Chicago: University of Chicago Press, 1929.
These seven books were products of the "Chicago School," which flourished during the '20's and '30's. It emphasized the role of community disorganization in social problems and is one of the main roots of today's sociological criminology.

Other

Annals of the American Academy of Political and Social Science (Nov. 1961). This issue is on the teenage culture: its nature, values, and ethnic variants. A valuable collection.

CHAPTER 12

Organized Predatory Crime, Racketeering, and White-Collar Crime

In perhaps no other area of lawless activity is the intimate association between crime and the general culture revealed than in that of organized crime. The organization of professional crime parallels a similar trend in business, labor, and other activities, and has greatly increased the seriousness of the American crime problem. Moreover, the lines between the "underworld" and the "upperworld" have become increasingly blurred as functional relationships joining the two worlds have burgeoned. The employer who connives with a crooked labor leader to win a "sweetheart" contract; the police judge who sets low bail and grants endless continuances which eventually exhaust the resources of prosecuting authorities; machine politicians who accept campaign contributions from underworld sources; the government bureaucrat, dined, partied, and enchanted by a sharpshooting wheeler-dealer, who fails to exercise proper scrutiny of his benefactor's operations—all are examples of such relationships.

The great army of petty thieves, drunks, disorderly persons, and what-not are, in total, of some importance from the point of view of social injury. Yet even *en masse* they do not greatly alter the distribtuion of wealth or the security of person in the country. They are important to society chiefly because of the large number of its citizens who assume the degraded status of the petty criminal.

Individual felons—murderers, robbers, and rapists—are serious enemies, of course, of the victims who suffer from their crimes. Yet even such dangerous but unorganized criminals do not injure large numbers of people or threaten huge proportions of the total national wealth. It is otherwise with organized crime.

Organization introduces into the field of crime those factors of leadership, group discipline and obedience, cooperation, and group planning which spell efficiency here as in our normal economic, political, and social life. Capone's criminal organization was efficient and dangerous for the same reasons that a huge industrial organization or a major political party is efficient and potentially beneficial or dangerous. In addition, the study of organized crime, particularly in the form of racketeering and white-collar crime, shows more clearly than does the study of individual crime that the problem is rooted in the general culture of which we are all a part. We shall see that rackets are due to the American tendency to extend law to penalize satisfactions which are in wide demand. We shall see that men who commit white-collar crimes do not often lose social status as a result, because their acts are not rated as crimes in certain prestiged groups.

Extent and Cost of Organized Crime

The very integration of organized crime into our political and economic life makes difficult the measurement of its extent and cost. Monetary estimates run into the billions and variously include losses to victims, protection money, the costs of the machinery of justice, gambling "takes," and tax losses on unreported illicit incomes. It is unlikely that over-all meaningful estimates can be had, since no agreement exists among experts as to what kinds of sums should be included. The following figures are given as examples of past and current estimates rather than because of any presumed intrinsic worth they have as measures of organized crime.

Nearly 30 years ago the Federal Trade Commission estimated that a single racket—the fraudulent sale of worthless securities—made $25 billion in a 10-year period.[1] Al Capone's annual income when he was czar of the Chicago underworld is said to have been about $30,000,000—tax free. Illegal slot machines may be taking in as much as $20 billion yearly.[2] As much as a quarter of a billion dollars annually may be going into numbers

[1] E. Jerome Ellison and Frank W. Brock, *The Run for Your Money* (New York: Dodge Publishing Company, 1935), pp. 3–6.
[2] Herbert A. Bloch, "The Gambling Business: An American Paradox," *Crime and Delinquency* (Oct. 1962), p. 362.

betting in New York City alone.[3] In a single city (Philadelphia) in a single month gamblers' protection payments to policemen were estimated to be $152,000.[4] If the monetary costs of organized crime defy calculation, the greater loss is fear, political corruption, lowered popular morals and morale, personal embitterment, to say nothing of not-infrequent murder—the "racket's bill"—is likewise incalculable.

There is no question but that the bank robber both exploits and threatens violence when he uses his sawed-off shotgun. But so does the racketeer with his threatened bomb, the agent of big business when he employs thugs or threatens discharge to "trouble-makers," the walking union delegate when he secures new members through threats, the politician who bleeds his protegés through his control of jobs, and even, on occasion, the agent of government when he protects racketeers or enforces a law passed ostensibly in the public interest but really favoring some restricted interest or class.

Types of Organized Crime

Organized crime is of two general types: (1) predatory crime and (2) service crime, or racketeering. Included in the first category are crimes systematically carried out for monetary gain by the cooperative action of two or more persons whose criminal actions benefit no one but themselves. In contrast to service crimes predatory crimes involve no element of the *quid-pro-quo* marketplace relationship, although certain "protection" rackets, confidence games, and dishonest gambling enterprises may initially involve an ostensible service to the unsuspecting victims. Among the major predatory crimes would be listed robbery, pickpocketing, car thefts, extortion, shoplifting, burglary, sneak thievery, blackmail, counterfeiting, confidence games, and dishonest carnival gambling. Because organized society has literally no use for these kinds of criminal activity, their perpetrators find sympathizers in the upper world only among a limited number of policemen, bail bondsmen, criminal lawyers, magistrates, and local political leaders. The classic "war with the underworld" is fought most enthusiastically with predatory criminals, for they find few champions willing to connive at weakening the forces of justice in their behalf.

Racketeering is organized crime in which the criminal elements purvey

[3] Ted Poston in Gus Tyler, ed., *Organized Crime in America* (Ann Arbor, Mich.: University of Michigan Press, 1962), p. 263.

[4] Estes Kefauver, *Crime in America* (Garden City, N. Y.: Doubleday and Company, 1951).

illicit goods or services to a consuming public which is engaged for the most part in legitimate activities. Since a good or service is included, the criminal behavior is not so completely or obviously exploitative as is organized predatory crime, though the total takings are far greater. The list of service crimes is large and would begin with the "Big Three": gambling in all its forms, traffic in illicit liquor, and prostitution. Of less importance but still big businesses would be receiving stolen goods, dealing in narcotics, abortion, phoney unions, pornography, and adoption rackets. The clientele of service criminals are sometimes convinced of the value of the racketeer's service, sometimes not. Oftentimes they even invite the service or welcome the racketeer when he approaches. In such cases there may be little violence involved. However, where there is resistance, violence and coercion may be very marked.

ASPECTS OF ORGANIZED PREDATORY CRIME

There is no demand for predatory crime, since no one wishes to be robbed, or burglarized, or raped. Hence the explanation of organized predatory crime need only account for the fact that a considerable number of people are all set, so to speak, to choose a predatory criminal profession. Incidentally, that explanation will also in large measure account for the supply of racketeers. But racketeering must, in addition, be accounted for in terms of some demand which cannot be satisfied legally.

We have seen how occasionally the juvenile gang continues intact as an adult professional organization and how more frequently individuals trained in a juvenile gang have later joined some other professional group. Contacts with the fence, hero worship for adult gangsters, neighborhood attitudes favorable to some form of organized crime, and direct contacts with adult gangs and with their members who are often neighbors and family intimates all tend toward the development of a permanent criminal career. As Landesco has well pointed out,[5] in some delinquency areas the choice of a professional career in crime is as natural to the criminal as the choice of a legitimate career may be elsewhere. The choice is between following in the footsteps of a father who had earned his pittance as a "poor working sap" or emulating the example of successful local gangsters. The achievements of these "big shots" are made evident by their expensive cars, "cool dressing," "classy dames," and prestige in the neighborhood. Moreover, the choice of crime is not inhibited by strong feelings of remorse, for

[5] John Landesco, "The Gangster's Apologia Pro Vita Sua," in *Illinois Crime Survey* (Chicago: Illinois Association for Criminal Justice, 1929), chap. 26, *passim.*

the gangster, though vaguely conscious of the opposition of legitimate society, does pretty much what is expected of him by his associates. The approval of such intimate associates is more effective than the disapproval of an abstract and distant legitimate society. This tendency toward a criminal career is even strengthened by the disapproval of police, school, or other institutions which gang members have long looked upon as enemies. Examples of unsuccessful gangsters there are, but these are offset by knowledge of the ease with which a fix is obtained and by the optimistic gambler's attitude which hopes for more luck than others have had. Moreover, as Landesco points out, the gangster is frequently perplexed if asked why he is in the racket. "Who hasn't a racket?" he replies. Exposed as he has been to rather unrepresentative examples, he feels that the policeman on the beat, the businessman or union delegate, the politician, the lawyer, and even the judge all have their rackets. At the least, the choice between crime and no crime is not presented to the slum-dwelling gangster as a clear-cut issue of white versus black, since he conceives of all men as at least gray.

Other professional predatory gangsters enter by way of the business world or by transfer from a racket to a more frankly predatory career. A father who has exploited labor or the public, yet kept wholly within the letter of the law, has nevertheless given his son an excellent training in crime. No change in attitudes, but only a lesser degree of caution or a technical difference in the definition of acts, need be discovered in order to explain why the son becomes a criminal. Undoubtedly, a police record, life in correctional institutions, and the gradual acceptance of the criminal's role as a result of being treated as a criminal help to turn juvenile delinquents and occasional adult offenders into professional gangsters. Moreover, in the underworld "big shots" have more prestige than "little shots," and petty thieves who confine their activities to snatching purses from old women are scorned. Hence there is social mobility among criminals. Sutherland has well described processes involved in the development of a criminal career. Beginning with early *maturation* of delinquent children toward increasingly more serious misbehavior, there is a process of *segregation* from the rest of society; of *progressive conflict* with established institutions and competitive *development of techniques* by police and criminals; of *organization, professionalization,* and the *development of a criminal code.* Along the line there may also be the appearance of *fashions* in crime. Such a process is not universal but is often repeated.[6]

[6] *Principles of Criminology,* 6th ed., revised by Donald R. Cressey (Philadelphia: J. B. Lippincott, 1960), ch. 12.

Discussing professional thieves in particular, Sutherland has pointed out also how personal crisis situations affect a choice of a professional career.[7] Undoubtedly, the number of boys who will choose a professional criminal career is affected also by the effectiveness or ineffectiveness of the punishment of crime at the time the choice is made. Where the beginner has observed the avoidance of punishment by those who have had a proper fix, the fear of punishment has had little deterrent effect. Moreover, criminals gamble on success.

THE EXPLANATION OF RACKETEERING

Racketeering springs up in response to demands which are not satisfied legally. American laws have been extended to penalize satisfactions which are in wide demand. For example, our law forbids many kinds of gambling to millions who want to gamble, and it penalizes abortion,[8] which may satisfy the need of the unmarried pregnant woman to escape disgrace among her associates. Similarly, our laws penalize businessmen who take some kinds of monopolistic advantage over competitors, and labor unions which at times utilize some methods of collective bargaining, such as the closed shop. In addition our laws permit the stimulation through group pressures, advertising, and so forth of many of the very desires which cannot be legally satisfied. The desires of many people must therefore either remain unmet or be satisfied illegally. Under these circumstances, the enforcement of law becomes difficult and there is much lawlessness. Moreover, in our dynamic sensate society, desires have expanded rapidly in all social classes, but opportunities for the equal satisfaction of these by all people have lagged behind. Paradoxically, at the same time that we may be called the richest nation of the world (with more desires satisfied), we may also be called the most starved nation (with more desires unsatisfied). We have tasted luxury. Our democratic ideal implies that *all* men are entitled to that luxury. High-pressure salesmanship and advertising create in each person the gourmand's insatiable appetite. Our advertising mechanisms for stimulating desires are the most perfect in the world. Hence there are concerted attempts to meet needs outside the realm of law. Our modern business tradition causes them to be met in an organized fashion. Our competitive system and philosophy justify the satisfaction of our ungratified desires through exploitation.

[7] E. H. Sutherland, *The Professional Thief* (Chicago: University of Chicago Press, 1937), p. 213.

[8] For an account of the operation of "the abortion mill" in Kings County, New York, see Jerome E. Bates, "The Abortion Mill, An Institutional Study," *Journal of Criminal Law, Criminology and Police Science* (July–Aug. 1954), pp. 157–67.

Thus our culture implies racketeering. Illegal, organized exploitation of our illegitimate desires *is* racketeering.

Unlike predatory crime, markets exist for service crimes, ranging in size from the millions of persons patronizing gambling, through the hundreds of thousands of abortion-mill clients, to the relatively few who find use for professional arsonists and killers. Because the general public's moral repugnance toward service criminals is more or less inversely proportional to the size of their markets—which is to say, the more customers a particular service crime has, the more difficult it is to enlist public opinion against it—cooperative relationships between service criminals and the law-enforcement agencies charged with suppressing them is infinitely more extensive, pervasive, and rationalizable than is the case with predatory criminals. The "interpenetration and fusion" between the upperworld and the underworld in the area of big-market service crimes have apparently reached such an extent in this country that there is great difficulty in finding just where the line separating the two worlds exists. And since the *customers* of service criminals are themselves usually committing criminal offenses when they solicit and/or purchase an illegal good or service, one notes with some irony that in the strictly legal sense service criminals can exist only with the connivance of another body of criminals—their customers.

Common Elements in Many Rackets

Rackets tend to have certain elements in common. First, there is a strongly felt desire or need. In our culture men need status almost as much as they need food. If money, avoidance of disgrace, or enhanced bargaining power are essential to status, the desire for them may be as compelling as what society generally calls a need. Secondly, there is the impossibility of satisfying the desire legally. Thirdly, there is, or is believed to be, opportunity to meet the need illegally through racketeers. Fourthly, the individual, business, or labor union often becomes dependent upon the racketeer. In the case of business or labor, a final step may be that the racketeer "muscles in" and comes to control the business. When this occurs, it is a matter of indifference to the racketeer whether he continues to satisfy the need, say, of a labor union or business concern, whether he turns traitor and serves its competitors, or whether he uses his power to exploit the public. An additional characteristic of racketeering of many types is the use of compulsion, sometimes involving serious violence or threat of violence.

In the cleaning and dyeing business some years ago, there was cutthroat competition. On the payment of a large membership fee to their organization, the racketeers would force one or more competitors out of business, since resistance might mean a bomb. A demand for the adoption of children in short supply, and difficulties involved in applying for them through an approved legitimate agency, have created an adoption racket. According to a United Press newspaper report, babies were recently sold in this way for as much as $3,500. There has recently been a considerable scandal over the pressure methods used by professional solicitors of money for philanthropies, over the large proportion of the money collected which often goes to the professional collectors, and over actual fraud in charity rackets. It is estimated that in 1953 no less than $120 million were fraudulently collected in charity rackets.[9] Professor Clinard has published a fascinating book about the wartime OPA racket, in which indifference to the needs of the country, plus a great desire for more than the legal amount of rationed goods, created a huge black market.[10] This last example, because of the tolerant attitudes of much of the public, constituted also an instance of white-collar crime, to be discussed more fully later.

We shall select for slightly fuller discussion two types of rackets, one a specific waterfront racket to illustrate a racket involving union-employer relations, and the other gambling in general, which is perhaps our most serious racket today.

Business–Labor Racketeering

IN GENERAL

In our competitive economic system, both labor and employers desire bargaining power; the former in the interest of high wages and other aims, the latter in the pursuit of profits. Both also gain satisfaction through the acquisition of power and the joys of victory. Labor's bargaining power is jeopardized by the activities of unorganized workers and of employers. Legal methods of strengthening and protecting this bargaining power, though more available than formerly, have partially failed. Labor racketeering is an attempt to secure desired protection by illegal means. In its struggle for improved status, labor had long been obliged to meet increasingly forceful opposition from employers and adverse decisions by conservative courts against the employment of some of their weapons, such as

[9] "Charitable Rackets," *Social Service Review* (March 1954), pp. 87–88.
[10] Marshall B. Clinard, *The Black Market* (New York: Rinehart & Company, 1952).

picketing and the closed shop. The urgent desire of workingmen to improve their welfare and power has hardly been diminished by the fact that their plane of living has risen greatly. The capitalist class is similarly not satisfied with partial success.

Because of the partial failure of legal collective bargaining, collective bargaining was sometimes made effective outside the law through violence. Louis Adamic recorded the story of this violent struggle between labor and capital in his appropriately titled book, *Dynamite*. With little hesitancy, organized capitalist interests used violence, frame-ups, and "judicial murders" in suppressing union growth among their workers. Labor retaliated as violently. Though the large national labor organizations declared officially against the use of violence and sincerely considered its use a mistaken method, they could not prevent violence on the part of all of their constituent unions, the building trades among others being often involved. However, violence often failed and led to severe penalties. Faced with this problem, some unions hired criminal elements experienced in the techniques of terrorism and in evading responsibility under the law. "Dynamiting operations were put upon a business-like, unsentimental basis." [11]

Then racketeers began to see how indispensable they were to certain labor unions. By fair means or foul, they secured their election to union offices. Once in control, the racketeers could make large profits for themselves from employers in return for protection against strikes. The employers, in turn, could often pass on the considerable money cost to the more or less unsuspecting consumer.

In *The Enemy Within,* U.S. Attorney General Robert F. Kennedy recounts the investigations during the 1950's of the Senate Select Committee on Improper Activities in the Labor or Management Field, which he served as Chief Counsel. After unearthing evidence that Dave Beck, "the president of America's largest and most powerful labor union, the Teamsters, was a crook," [12] the committee eventually turned its attention to Beck's successor, James Hoffa, who became the Teamsters' president in October, 1957, in a "rigged" convention fewer than 5 per cent of whose delegates "had any clearly legal right" to be voting participants.[13] Mr. Kennedy first met Mr. Hoffa in February, 1957, at the request of a third party who hoped to convince Mr. Kennedy that Mr. Hoffa "had reformed" and did not warrant investigation. Kennedy's view of Hoffa, however, was somewhat jaundiced, because just six days before their meeting Kennedy had gotten wind of a

[11] Louis Adamic, *Dynamite* (New York: Viking Press, 1934), p. 328.
[12] Robert F. Kennedy, *The Enemy Within* (New York: Harper & Brothers, 1960), p. 3.
[13] *Ibid.,* p. 118.

scheme of Hoffa's to plant a spy among the committee's investigators.[14] Kennedy's subsequent inquiries into Hoffa's affairs were pursued with energy and thoroughness and unearthed an incredibly sordid story of the betrayal of union members by their leader.

> We found that a close relationship existed between Jimmy Hoffa and employers. We found that he was more than willing to do favors for them. Big favors, such as settling strikes against the wishes of his men. And we found that employers were anxious to do favors for him. Big favors, such as setting him up in business so that he could reap big profits. He helped them. They helped him. And they always insisted that the exchange of favors was coincidence.[15]

Most unions and most employers have fought such racketeering. A high degree of labor peace has been secured in many industries, partly as labor has come to see advantages in cooperating with employers in a common aim to increase efficiency in a time of plenty. The conflict tends to recur if unemployment threatens, and a very serious problem of labor-capital racketeering remains in places, even in good times. In all this the nature of a system, more than the nature of the people and leaders involved, seems to have been the basic cause of racketeering. Two types of gangsters have been involved in labor rackets: [16] city-bred bosses from outside the labor movement and old-time labor leaders. The former are said to be trying to forget their hoodlum background; the latter to feel they own the union because some of them have come up the hard way by fighting with their fists. Gangsters such as Dutch Schultz are to be decidedly contrasted with labor leaders of high ideals such as David Dubinsky and Walter Reuther. The building trades unions were once peculiarly involved in crime and racketeering, and labor leaders often furnished so-called strike insurance to employers in double-dealing operations. Crimes of embezzlement, extortion, and assault were not infrequent.[17]

AN EXAMPLE: THE NEW YORK HARBOR WATERFRONT RACKETS

A number of conflicting needs and desires underlie the New York Harbor waterfront racket. The most basic of these is the need for rapidly unloading the cargoes and discharging the passengers of great ships. Delay through strikes reduces profit to shipping companies, hurts the importers,

[14] *Ibid.,* pp. 36–43.

[15] *Ibid.,* p. 104.

[16] In considerable degree our characterization of capital-labor rackets and part of our description of the New York waterfront racket are derived from Malcolm Johnson, *Crime on the Labor Front* (New York: McGraw-Hill, 1950). For a briefer account of the latter, see *Editorial Research Reports* (March 4, 1953), pp. 161–77.

[17] Johnson, *op. cit.,* chap. 4.

injures perishable goods, and causes great inconvenience to travelers and the general public. Hence threats of strikes may be effectively used to secure what the rather peculiar type of labor employed around the docks desires. But even when work is organized in an orderly way, a considerable surplus of labor on call is required, and in the New York region a floating labor supply of about 20,000 men came to exist, each employed only occasionally. In the interest of membership fees and personal power, it paid the union leader to increase this surplus.

A considerable number of ex-convicts, some just out of Sing Sing prison, were habitually employed. Most of these presumably just wanted work, and their relatively necessitous condition made them willing to engage in work which was far from constant. But the situation also lent itself to the employment of a few ex-convicts quite willing to continue a life of crime or near-crime, actually to steal, and to be parties to a regime of extortion. As the system was set up in the New York region, some employer groups learned how to use it to their own profit, and some of them even preferred the system. It tended to prevent strikes, and the costs could be added to the basis for the Governments' subsidy or passed on to the consumer. According to Johnson,[18] some employers feared most that the lucrative system would be abolished. Under this system, hiring bosses, some of whom were ex-convicts, had the power to pick whom they chose from a supply of workers in excess of those needed. Those chosen tended to be those who indicated by signals their willingness to support the racket by paying kick-backs to the labor bosses, paying high interest rates on loans, or paying high initiation fees to join the union. The hiring bosses were in practice appointed by the union. Workers making objection often learned by bitter experience, including slugging, to go along with the system and keep their mouths shut. The Senate committee investigating this situation discovered that, through collusion between the shipping interest and the union, names of nonexistent employees were carried on the payroll. Paychecks for such "phantom" employees were picked up by an International Longshoremen's Association official.

Resulting crimes and exploitations included organized theft, salary kick-backs, padded payrolls, listing men who do no actual work, charging excessive dues and initiation fees, bribery, and extortion. Rackets came to be considered necessary evils, out of which each should get what he could. Even the policy racket was connected with the system, and it is said that men who would gamble were more likely to be hired. Other evils included duplicate hirings, bookmaking, and smuggling of narcotics.

A combination of serious crime, strikes, and problems of political cor-

18 *Ibid.,* p. 107.

ruption demanded action. The government of the city of New York and the port authorities, the governors of the states of New York and New Jersey, the National Labor Relations Board, and the Congress of the United States were drawn in. In addition, the American Federation of Labor sought to discipline the International Longshoremen's Association, which had been in power in the region, and to provide a rival union pledged to get rid of the gangsters and later to cooperate in the reorganization plan set up by the Waterfront Commission of New York Harbor, created by bi-state legislation and ratified by Congress. A long fight between the ILA and the AFL unions ensued in which, to the surprise of many well-wishers of the long-shoremen, the old ILA union won out, though by a narrow vote margin.

Under the reorganization provided by the Waterfront Commission, supervised hiring centers have replaced the shape-up. The Commission has claimed that it no longer is necessary for men hired to pay a kick-back. This seems doubtful, since the Commission admitted in its first annual report that the influence of the underworld on the selection of men hired had not been eliminated. A surplus labor supply of some 15,000, in addition to the 20,000 needed, was said still to exist in 1955. At that time it appeared that the problem was not yet solved. The union was fighting the Waterfront Commission, and the Shipping Association seemed unwilling to give full cooperation to the reform movement. At that date the racket was exploiting the port and the public, but improvements in the system were planned. The longshoremen themselves appeared to be divided and confused, not daring to trust anyone from their immediate superiors to the shipping companies or the federal and state governments. They cling to the right to strike as their one seemingly reliable weapon—a weapon which the shipping companies would be glad to be rid of.[19]

Fulfilling Consumer Demands—Racketeering

GENERAL NATURE OF CONSUMER RACKETS

Wherever a strong consumer demand for any satisfaction exists among at least a considerable minority and may not be satisfied legally, racketeers will attempt to satisfy it illegally. A strong desire to win lucky gains on the part of some tens of millions (reportedly 57 per cent of the total adult

[19] Cf. A. H. Raskin, "Angry Longshoremen Allow Port No Peace," *New York Times* (Dec. 19, 1954), E, p. 8. In times of prosperity and the consequent relatively peaceful relations between labor and its employers, labor rackets temporarily decline, but consumer rackets may flourish. Cf. Daniel Bell, "Crime, an American Way of Life," *Antioch Review* (Summer, 1953), pp. 131–54.

population) explains the tremendous gambling racket in the United States. But no gambling racket would exist without a law against gambling or heavy taxation of gambling. It does not follow that repeal of laws by itself would solve the problem, however. Similar if less widespread demands for illicit satisfactions explain other consumer rackets.

THE GAMBLING RACKET

In Chapter 2 we hinted that among the many conditions which determine success in American society, there is a considerable element of luck. Indeed, a certain amount of such a luck element would seem to be inevitable in any type of social structure, though its degree will vary among types of societies. But there is also in the United States a considerable degree of acceptance of luck, tolerance of gains based upon luck, awarding of status for lucky achievements, stimulation of the desire to be lucky, and commercialized exploitation of the desire for lucky gains. On the other hand, there are types of chance rewards which are frowned upon, and there is a resort to law to penalize some forms of gambling. Anti-gambling laws are based in part on tradition, but they also seem to express a certain current, ill-defined distinction made by a considerable number of people between rewards for service rendered and rewards for mere chance gains. Yet Americans appreciate cleverness, sometimes even without clear-cut evidence that the cleverness leads to social benefits. Moreover, elements of sheer luck, of mere cleverness in seeking personal advantage, and of cleverness beneficial to a community or country are often intertwined to obscure the influence of luck itself. A farmer whose employee happens to strike oil on his land, a purchaser of real estate who correctly estimates the future site of a city, and a person who plays the ponies or shoots craps—these men in various degrees must thank Lady Luck. They will perhaps occupy different statuses in the hierarchy of local social approval, though to forget the source of success is easy in a society which gives prestige to the successful. Efforts wholly to eliminate the luck element in American competitive society are often considered radical and frowned upon. This is conceivably because we all must recognize that in some degree our own successes have been due to good fortune, and we perhaps hope for better luck in the future. Those forms of search for luck which are most obviously solely such we call gambling, because there is little element of social service involved. Yet because some of these, such as betting on horse racing, give great exhilaration to millions as well as a last chance for escape from financial ruin for a few, they are in great demand in spite of considerable opposition to them. The gambling racket is therefore deeply rooted in American desires, and very extensive.

Organized gambling in part is also an illegal service which racketeers furnish to satisfy a still more general desire of Americans to get something for nothing. Millions wager sums on the fortuitous distribution of cards, the casting of a die, the winning of a race, or the outcome of a prize·fight. The amount of money involved probably reaches into billions of dollars annually.

This demand for gambling has somewhat varied roots. Gambling for some men expresses a *belief* in luck derived from a prescientific age and persisting today for thousands. For others gambling expresses a *hope* that the laws of chance may favor the individual even if they recognize that most who, for example, play the slot machines must lose. Given either of these attitudes, motives ranging from desperate need to mere enjoyment of a game may lead to gambling. The experience of gambling is peculiarly exhilarating. Gambling easily becomes an obsession.

The use of sharp practice and cheating has aroused suspicion of gamblers and their trade. In a Puritanical culture, also, gambling is obnoxious as a form of mere pleasure-seeking, and legal penalties are looked upon as the appropriate means to prevent it. Moreover, apart from the serious crime of racketeering, gambling is often found to have been an important element in the development of a criminal career. A distinction must here be drawn between a friendly bet over the outcome of a game by two well-matched golfers and the unscrupulous fleecing of thousands of poor people in a policy racket or in the operations of any huge syndicate of racketeers. There is a distinction between honest and dishonest gambling, as well as between private charity lotteries and the public and commercialized varieties. Yet all of these forms are rooted in a common concern over luck.

Granting, then, that most gamblers are by no means criminals in the unusually accepted sense of the word, that much gambling is "just for fun," and that a code of good sportsmanship often enters in, yet the line between taking from another, just because one is lucky, and stealing from him may be one of the examples of "thin lines" [20] which separate criminal from non-criminal behavior. At any rate, a good many criminals seem to have histories of much gambling.

We are here primarily concerned, however, with the dangerous racket which laws, penalizing an activity in such widespread demand, have created.

[20] For a fascinating literary discussion of this "thin line" in a number of its aspects, see Edward Selim Atiyah, *The Thin Line* (New York: Harper & Brothers, 1952).

Unlike most others, the gambling racket is based upon a majority demand. It was estimated that in 1950 the gambling American public lost $20 billion through gambling.[21] The pari-mutuel turnover in 1962 amounted to over $4.0 billion.[22] Gambling is the principal source of income for organized criminal gangs in the United States.[23] While bookmaking for betting on horse racing ranks first in take, there are also gambling with slot machines, punchboards, roulette wheels, government and philanthropic lotteries, policy or numbers games, dog races, animal combats, ball games of various types, bingo games, and scores of other types. Pari-mutuel systems at horse-racing tracks, which are most widely legalized, serve to regularize betting and are supposed to favor honest gambling. Where such legal gambling is permitted at the tracks, bookmaking activities off the tracks have been widespread and generally illegal.

In November 1963, New York City voters approved by a 3-to-1 margin a proposal to study the possibility of legalized off-track gambling centers. Reactions to the proposal both as to benefits and problems have been decidedly mixed.

The public attitude toward gambling is reflected in the fact that the typical bookmaker seems to feel that his profits are earned and to have no qualms of conscience. Wide variety in the nature and scope of state laws reflects the general uncertainty as to what should be legalized and what penalized. Where, as in Illinois, the law has been so strictly drawn that technically even the giving of a prize at a bridge party at home could be prosecuted as a crime, even the most scrupulous and honest state's attorney is compelled to draw a line in his policies. In some counties that line seems to be drawn between commercialized and private gambling, while in others both have been protected with only weak and vacillating complaints from the public. Thus, gambling at country and social clubs may be protected. Where police administration is dishonest, protection money is collected.

The degree to which the system is locally organized or controlled by larger regional and national syndicates varies considerably. The Kefauver Committee found the gambling interests so powerful in some cities that they could dictate to governments and could corrupt police and other law-enforcement agencies. Violent struggles to monopolize this profitable racket have caused occasional murders and all sorts of more or less violent con-

---

[21] Hugh R. Manes, "Gambling and the Law," *Journal of Criminal Law, Criminology and Police Science* (July–Aug. 1951), p. 205.

[22] *Statistical Abstract of the United States* (Washington, D. C., 1963), p. 210.

[23] Mortimer M. Caplin, "The Gambling Business and Federal Taxes," *Crime and Delinquency* (Oct. 1962), p. 372.

flicts between rival gangs. Moreover, Senator Kefauver found that gangster racketeers had infiltrated into legitimate businesses and carried their violent and criminal activities with them. Another cover-up used by racketeers was to make contributions to worthy causes to fool uninformed people as to their real criminal and exploitative activities. Combining with honest business, racketeers were able to hide illegitimate gains within their reports of legitimate activities and so hinder prosecution for avoidance of income taxes. Further, under such conditions it had often become good policy for honest businesses to cooperate with hoodlums. Rackets cannot long exist without a fix with the police. When money can be used to fix a gambling case, it can also serve to fix other types of serious predatory criminal cases.

Nevada is the only state in the Union which has licensed and so legalized gambling. Legislation in the other states is varied indeed.[24] Abatement statutes in many states permit the removal and sale of gambling devices from enterprises violating the law and the padlocking of the premises, but owners of such establishments must usually be shown to have known of the violation. In Wisconsin the licenses of those serving food and liquor where gambling goes on may be revoked. Some states forbid the dissemination of racing information, but the law has been poorly enforced. A federal law to this effect was introduced into Congress in 1954.

Successful prosecution has too often required granting of immunity to some of the guilty. The effort totally to repress gambling lacks a supporting public opinion. Another major difficulty has been the desire of governments to secure large revenues from taxation of gambling, to which policy the public has not vigorously objected. It has even been said that governments have built up a greater stake than private interests in the maintenance of gambling. But the people do not want racketeer domination of government such as the Kefauver Committee uncovered. As a result, Congress in 1951 passed a law providing for a registration fee of $50 for bookmakers and a tax of 10 per cent on their gross receipts. This law has had important immediate effects, but its long-time effects on gambling generally seem not yet wholly clear. In states where the forms of gambling taxed by the law are illegal, the gambler becomes open to prosecution by local authorities. If he does not register and pay the tax, he risks prosecution by the federal authorities. In some areas very few registered. In New York City reportedly [25] the federal tax law had by mid-1954 resulted in the substitution

[24] Cf. Manes, *loc. cit., passim,* for a characterization of the situation as of about 1950, before the report of the Kefauver Committee.

[25] Don Mankiewicz, "How the Horse Industry Went to the Dogs," *Reporter* (Sept. 14, 1954), pp. 36–37.

of lone-wolf bookies for the former highly organized and protected syndicate. The bookie's clientele had been reduced, his danger of arrest increased, and most betting on horse races had been sent to the tracks or at least temporarily eliminated. Thus the tax law made *one channel* of gambling unprofitable. But pari-mutuel bets and slot machines were exempted, and other forms of gambling were not affected. By 1961, after 10 years' operation, federal taxes paid by gamblers amounted to slightly over $75 million, far less than the $4 billion estimated by the law's Congressional sponsors.[26]

The deepest roots of the gambling problem in the United States, then, seem to us to be two: (1) Americans like to gamble and are generally willing to permit men to accumulate rewards based on luck as well as rewards based on work; (2) yet, being opposed to some forms of gambling, they have made them illegal and so furnished the basis for our largest racket. Nevertheless, efforts are currently being made to penalize some forms of gambling while permitting and even legalizing others.

Suggested Solutions

Six different solutions have been suggested for the great problem of racketeering.

(1) It has been proven that rackets least supported by public opinion, such as prostitution, can temporarily be *repressed* successfully in a local community by an honest and efficient prosecutor, such as Thomas E. Dewey proved to be in New York City. The public is still waiting to see how much and how long the gambling racket, which is in much greater demand than is prostitution, can be repressed in this way. Most rackets have reappeared after the "heat" has died down, but control through wise taxation is an experiment worth watching.

(2) Numerous Congressional investigations carried out during the last 12 years into the interstate nature of organized crime generated considerable feeling in Congress and the general public that federal legislation to inhibit such crime was necessary. We have already mentioned the gambling tax laws of 1951. Of eight anti-racketeering laws proposed in 1961 by the Justice Department, five have thus far been enacted. Three of the five prohibit the interstate transmission of betting information by professional gamblers, ban interstate shipment of certain gambling equipment, and prohibit interstate travel for the purpose of promoting racketeering. The remaining

[26] Caplin, *loc. cit.*, p. 373.

two laws strengthened the Fugitive Felon Act and the Federal Firearms Act. Passing laws is one thing; their effective enforcement is quite another. The history of organized crime has demonstrated repeatedly the underworld's capacity for devising evasions or countermeasures in the face of new laws. As long as a huge market for the racketeer's services exists, motivation for surmounting legislation will continue to exist.

(3) There has been a fairly strong demand that satisfactions now illegal be *legalized*. The Nevada example of legalization of gambling does not seem to be a fair one, because a single state becomes the mecca for gamblers and exploiters and because of other local conditions and lack of other effective controls. In the absence of a high tax, legalization takes the profit out of rackets and in that way is effective, but the step is opposed by fairly large sections of the population.

(4) A racket is weakened when *the needs can be met* or the desires satisfied *in other ways*. Thus did baseball tend to replace cockfighting in the Philippines. Thus, for good or for ill, are new patterns of sex relations weakening commercialized prostitution.

(5) A few of those who are most distressed about the hold which racketeers have gained over city and even state governments lose faith in our political democracy and call for the more vigorous controls of *the fascist state,* forgetting the danger that the government itself may then become in effect the exploiting racketeer.

(6)   Others, seeing the problem rooted in deeper social and economic relations, would move toward greater *social and economic planning,* retaining full popular controls.

White-Collar Crime

The term "white-collar crime" was coined about 1941 by the late Professor E. H. Sutherland, who later presented evidence of its nature, extent, and significance through studies which in some respects may be called the most important criminological research undertaken to date.[27] More recently a number of other criminologists have contributed additional studies.[28]

A white-collar crime, says Sutherland, "may be defined approximately as a crime committed by a person of respectibility and high social status in

[27] E. H. Sutherland, *White Collar Crime* (New York: Dryden Press, 1949).

[28] Cf. Marshall Clinard, *The Black Market* (New York: Rinehart & Company, 1952); Frank E. Hartung, "White Collar Offenses in the Wholesale Meat Industry in Detroit," *American Journal of Sociology* (July 1950); Donald R. Cressey, *Other People's Money* (Glencoe, Ill.: Free Press, 1953).

the course of his [legitimate] occupation." White-collar crime includes, by way of example, such acts as promulgating false or misleading advertising, illegal exploitation of employees, mislabeling of goods, violation of weights and measures statutes, conspiring to fix prices, selling adulterated food-stuffs, evading corporate taxes, suborning justice (by lawyers), performing illegal abortions (by physicians), knowingly approving false claims (by insurance agents), and so on. Since Sutherland limits the concept to unlawful behavior engaged in for the purpose of furthering the financial or strategic interests of legitimate callings, crimes by respectable people committed for other purposes are not white-collar crimes: murder of his spouse by a businessman or bribery of a traffic officer by a motorist who happens to be a physician are not encompassed by the concept.

More than predatory crime or even racketeering, white-collar crime is closely related to attitudes and values in our general society such as we characterized in Chapter 2. The slum, which accounts for so much ordinary crime, cannot explain white-collar crime, since white-collar criminals live in our reputable neighborhoods. Feeble-mindedness, emotional instability, broken homes, a sense of failure, or loss of social status cannot explain the white-collar criminal, since he is characteristically intelligent, stable, and successful, and commands some prestige. Such considerations by no means invalidate studies of low-class crime. Since our penal and preventive programs have been primarily concerned with the crimes of the underprivileged, the treatment of burglary and robbery rather than breaches of trust or taking of rebates has properly been the concern of the penologist. Yet the existence and partial acceptance of white-collar crime as well as of noncriminal exploitation help account for the delinquencies and crimes of the slum-dweller. All three of these types of behavior, as well as the slum, are products of the general culture. But white-collar crime *is* crime, and its belated discovery by some criminologists has caused quite a stir in both the legal and criminological world. Our contention is that white-collar crime can be explained in terms of the major principles of our analysis; that no separate theory of crime is required; that white-collar crime is peculiarly closely related to the general culture; and that it is only the *form* of white-collar crime which calls for separate explanation.

White-collar crime is most distinctively defined in terms of attitudes toward those who commit it. White-collar crime is definitely made punishable by law. It is convictable behavior. However, it is generally regarded by courts and by sections of the general public as much less reprehensible than crimes usually punished by our courts, which may be designated "blue-collar crime." Blue-collar crime is the crime of the under-privileged;

white-collar crime is upper- or middle-class crime. Just what proportion or section of the population must condone this type of behavior to constitute it as white-collar is not, and perhaps cannot be, clear. Many courts and other authorities clearly distinguish between a man who illegally misrepresents the qualities of his products and a burglar or robber. Yet the very existence of the law penalizing the former type of act indicates an adverse attitude toward it, though ordinarily not of the same degree. The fact that white-collar crime is punished in less degrading ways than "ordinary crime" does not imply that the former is petty. Actually society loses huge sums through white-collar crime. Some of the rackets we described in an earlier chapter are white-collar crimes; some are not. As Sutherland defines the term, most racketeering by officers of a labor union would not be white-collar crime; nor, apparently, would the vice racket be so defined. Thus neither in terms of class status, business activity, attitudes, nor degree of seriousness can white-collar crime be wholly separated from other crime. Nevertheless, it is the somewhat distinctive attitudes and policies toward the offender in such cases which have given significance to discussions of white-collar crime. It appears that even outside of business circles, white-collar crime is less reprehensible than ordinary crime, because low-class people often aspire to be white-collar criminals. Or if not, they at least accept the same individualism and the same value of materialism which the middle and upper classes accept. White-collar crime is attractive because it brings material rewards with little or no loss of status.

Sutherland's research concerned 70 of our largest corporations. All were found to have been guilty of white-collar crime. Even if one considers only those convicted through criminal prosecutions, 60 per cent of these large corporations were guilty. Laws violated included among others: the Sherman Anti-Trust Law and related legislation penalizing restraint of trade; laws forbidding infringement of patents, trademarks, and copyrights; the National Labor Relations Act and others penalizing certain labor practices; the Securities and Exchange Act, regulating financial deals; the Federal Trade Commission Act and the Pure Food and Drug Act, making misrepresentation in advertising illegal; and the Emergency Price Control Act, fixing wartime prices under the OPA.

Sutherland makes clear the fact that the 907 adverse decisions he studied understated greatly the prevalence of such violations and that most corporations had been recidivists. For example, the Federal Trade Commission has estimated that one-third of advertising makes fraudulent claims.[29] Violations in the labor field include refusals to bargain collectively and the

29 Sutherland, *op. cit.*, chaps. 7 and 8.

unlawful interference with labor union methods, at times involving violence. The question whether business or organized labor is more involved in such crimes is unimportant. However, such acts when committed by the unions would not come under Sutherland's concept of white-collar crime. Yet presumably they are not looked upon as crimes by union members.

There is nothing new in the recognition of all these white-collar crimes *as social problems*. Muckrackers condemned such practices decades ago. Nearly all textbooks in labor problems, corporation problems, problems of finance, and so on condemn them. The new element is the recognition that they fall within the field of criminology, and even this was recognized before the term was coined. Sutherland's inclusion of white-collar crime in his criminology is entirely legitimate. However, certain legalists and some criminologists have raised objections.[30] In so far as these objections merely warn against the danger to liberty involved in the overextension of administrative discretion in dealing with crime, they may be well taken. Yet the white-collar criminal is protected by the favorable attitudes of our commissions toward him, where the traditional criminal has no such protection, for example, against the arbitrariness of a parole board. In so far as critics insist that white-collar crime is not properly crime, they appear to be wholly in error. Some of them have said that to consider white-collar crime as crime tends to blur the distinction between civil and criminal law. Considering the huge losses we suffer from white-collar criminals, such blurring would seem to be desirable from the social point of view. Moreover, white-collar crimes *are* crimes from the legal as well as the social point of view.

White-collar crime is also distinguished by differential treatment accorded by courts or administrative authorities. Though definitely criminal under the law, white-collar crime may be dealt with either under criminal or civil procedures at the pleasure of the court or commission. This alternative, and the fact that much white-collar crime is dealt with by administrative authorities, reflect a favorable attitude toward this middle-class behavior pattern. Adverse decisions by the Federal Power Commission or the Federal Trade Commission do not entail social stigma, such as follows conviction for burglary or grand larceny in a criminal court. In addition stipulations and cease-and-desist orders are normally used in cases of white-collar criminals. We do not warn the burglar to desist. We arrest him forthwith and send him to prison. Sutherland explains this favorable treatment

[30] Cf. Jerome Hall, "Criminology," in George Gurvitch and W. E. Moore, *Twentieth-Century Sociology* (New York: Philosophical Library, 1945) p. 351; Paul W. Tappan, "Who Is the Criminal?" *American Sociological Review* (Feb. 1947), pp. 96–102; Robert G. Caldwell, "A Reexamination of the Concept of White-Collar Crime," *Federal Probation* (March 1958), pp. 30–36.

of white-collar criminals as due to such factors as the following. (1) The white-collar criminal and the judges, legislators, or commission members belong to the same social class. (2) There is a trend away from the use of punishment. (3) Resentment against exploitation by white-collar criminals is not organized and so is ineffective. Opposition to such criminals is weak because the channels through which they injure us are devious, and losses are widely diffused among a large number of people. Moreover, Sutherland observes that newspapers, which might publicize white-collar crime, are controlled by businessmen. Pickpockets do not control newspapers.

There is some evidence from recent events that certain kinds of white-collar offenders can expect less sympathetic treatment in the courts than they have traditionally received. The plea of *nolo contendere* (no contest) by a person formally accused of a crime is a backhanded plea of guilty. For decades, businessmen accused of violating anti-trust laws have pleaded *nolo contendere* when the evidence against them was clearly overwhelming. Never, until 1959, did imprisonment follow such a plea. In that year, to their astonishment four Ohio businessmen were sentenced to jail for anti-trust violations. In February, 1961, 44 executives of 29 electrical equipment companies, including General Electric and Westinghouse, pleaded guilty or *nolo contendere* to charges of price-fixing and rigging bids on $7 billion worth of heavy electrical equipment. In addition to fines ranging up to $12,500, 23 executives, one of whom was a Westinghouse vice president, were variously sentenced to 30- and 60-day jail terms.[31] Most of these sentences were actually served. The extensive press coverage given this incident was apparently based not upon the enormity of the crimes involved, but upon nationwide surprise at the jail sentences meted out and upon the verbal reprimands uttered by the sentencing judge.

The facts about the backgrounds of white-collar offenders challenge prevalent views and certain theories concerning crime and its causes. While further study is needed, white-collar crime cannot be explained in terms of abnormal personality or unusual failures in life. Hooton's,[32] Healy's, Glueck's, and Shaw's theories of crime hardly explain white-collar crime. Bonger's notions [33] may help explain it, but only in part. Sutherland cautiously concludes that white-collar crime has not yet been fully explained. His own inclination is to suggest that differences between the behavior of the individual white-collar criminal and others may be due to differential

---

[31] "The Great Conspiracy," *Time* (Feb. 17, 1961), pp. 84*ff*. It is worth noting that *Time* put its report of this story in its "Business" department. This magazine usually reports crime news under "Crime."

[32] Cf. *supra*, p. 87, and *passim*.

[33] Cf. *supra*, pp. 131–33.

association and to his isolation from contact with those groups which condemn white-collar crime. From the social viewpoint, Sutherland tentatively explains white-collar crime as due to social disorganization, resulting in either lack of behavior standards or conflict between standards regulating such behavior.

Clinard studied wartime OPA violations affecting the sale of no fewer than eight million commodities. He found the general public and businessmen favoring government wartime controls in principle. Yet violations, though by no means the universal practice, were exceedingly numerous. Clinard does not attempt to explain fully this type of crime. He finds differential association significant in some cases but inadequate as a general explanation. He concludes that no single explanation is possible. He urges further study and somewhat surprisingly emphasizes the need to know the individual's "personality pattern."

Hartung's study of the wholesale meat industry in Detroit gives special attention to theoretical implications. He concludes that social disorganization does not explain the prevalence of these white-collar crimes as well as does social differentiation. To Hartung, not a disorganized society, but a society with common basic values and with subgroups and their differing values integrated in terms of these basic values, generates white-collar crime. Hartung's emphasis on common values seems sound and is in harmony with our emphasis on the underlying influence of values in the general culture.

More recent study of white-collar crime seems to have added little to the findings of Sutherland, Hartung, and Clinard. Systematic analysis of the policies and decisions of various government agencies is still a promising source of criminological investigation. A beginning of such investigation by a graduate student of the senior writer shows the Sutherland study to be apparently as valid today as it was two decades ago.

While the reasons why some businessmen do and some do not commit white-collar crimes have not been fully worked out, the following points have been made.[34]

1. Marginal concerns or those in decline are more apt to be involved in white-collar crime.
2. Occasionally, though not usually, businessmen have been ignorant of the law, and some have lacked legal advice as to how to avoid crossing the line between legal and illegal activities.
3. Different types of business have been in different degrees under group pressure to violate or not to violate the law, and there has been a vary-

[34] Cf. R. E. Lane, "Why Business Men Violate the Law," *Journal of Criminal Law, Criminology and Police Science* (July 1953), pp. 151–65.

ing lack of a definite code of business ethics in some business organizations.

4. The law itself is often ambiguous, so that a businessman may take a chance that he will not be held to violate the law because its definitions are not clear-cut.

5. Readiness to violate the law will vary with the character of leadership, and this will depend on many factors in the leader's life and business experience:

   a. Studies have varied somewhat in their findings, with a rather general pattern of behavior characterizing most firms in some lines of business, but with considerable variation in others.

   b. Firms may interpret the enforcement or lack of enforcement of law differently as it has varied in their line of business as compared with others. Past penalties have been observed to have some effect in changing behavior.

   c. All the influences which affect personal values, usually derived from group experience, will affect indulgence in white-collar crime.

6. Businesses vary in the degree to which they have been involved in a process of impersonalization. The more impersonal business becomes, the less does the influence of the personal ideals of leaders operate.

The study of white-collar crime is significant because it reveals varying attitudes toward different types of crime. Even more logically than other types of crime, we hold, may white-collar crime be seen to reflect the general culture. The *form* of crime or of exploitation results from membership in subgroups with varying subvalues. The businessman would not be a burglar, but he would violate the Labor Relations Act, because his own group tolerates or even approves such violation, and the larger society expects and does not vigorously condemn it. The burglar would violate the Sherman Anti-Trust Act but cannot because he has no opportunity to do so. His own group may or may not condemn such violation verbally but tolerates or approves of his burglary or confidence game as more open types of crime. The noncriminal exploiter accepts essentially the same values as the white-collar criminal. Individualism and approval of competitive achievement or of lucky breaks—these are values in our culture which are common to all three of these types of exploiters. The nonexploiter hardly exists in our system of "free enterprise" and individualism. Indeed, our system almost compels all of us to exploit if we would exist and/or gain social status. Our basic culture thus implies exploitation. The *form it will take* is determined by subgroups, and association in these groups may be called by Sutherland's term, differential association. Thus the significant source of crime, both white-collar and traditional, is the general culture. It is the same as the source of all exploitation. Such at least is our hypothesis. This hypothesis will be developed in connection with a general theory of crime in Chapter 16.

Suggested Readings

Organized Crime: General

Annals of the American Academy of Political and Social Science (May 1950). Seventeen articles on gambling, of which the six on forms of gambling are of particular value to sociologists.

Crime and Delinquency (October 1952). The entire issue is a 9-article symposium on organized crime, concentrating mainly on the purveying of illicit goods and services. Included is a 211-item bibliography, which is especially useful in that it lists official investigation reports.

Rice, Robert. *The Business of Crime*. New York: Farrar, Straus and Cudahy, 1956. A popular writer describes arson, traffic in narcotics, counterfeiting, immigrant-smuggling, and gambling, as carried out by notorious professional criminals, and relates these offenders to their times.

Tannenbaum, Frank. *Crime and the Community*. New York: Ginn and Company, 1938. This old text contains in its first 200 pages a masterful analysis of the interrelationships between crime and its larger social setting. The chapters on politics, the police, and crime are superlative.

Tyler, Gus, editor. *Organized Crime in America—A Book of Readings*. Ann Arbor, Mich.: University of Michigan Press, 1962. Descriptive and theoretical pieces of an unusually high order, given the subject. The editor's preface to Part II, "The Matrix of Organized Crime," states in part: "Indeed, the very strength of organized crime arises from the fact that it is a complex counterpart to our complex civilization, an ironic image in a mocking glass."

Bootleg Days in Chicago: the 1920's

Allsop, Kenneth. *The Bootleggers and Their Era*. Garden City, N. Y.: Doubleday and Company, 1961. A lengthy and reasonably temperate account of gang warfare, booze, and politics in Chicago during the 1920's.

Lyle, John H. *The Dry and Lawless Years*. Englewood Cliffs, N. J.: Prentice-Hall, 1960. Chicago bootlegging in the Capone Era as seen by a criminal court judge of the time.

Networks of Crime in the 1950's

Frasca, Dom. *King of Crime*. New York: Crown Publishers, 1959. An account of a New York Italian-American whom Frasca insists is the Mafia head in the United States. Contains some useful, if breathless, descriptions of the interpenetration between racketeering and politics.

Kefauver, Estes. *Crime in America*. Garden City, N. Y.: Doubleday and Company, 1951. A popular rendering of the Kefauver committee findings in its investigation of organized crime. Considerable emphasis on the venality of local law-enforcement officials and "Mafia-like" gangster operations, thus giving a fragmented view of this problem.

Sondern, Frederic Jr. *Brotherhood of Evil: The Mafia*. New York: Farrar, Straus and Cudahy, 1959. This somewhat sensational account of the shadowy Mafia contains useful descriptions of the importation and wholesaling of narcotics.

White-Collar Crime

Gibney, Frank. *The Operators*. New York: Harper & Brothers, 1960. The "growing habit of fraud" among otherwise respectable citizens is described, from expense-account padding to stock swindles. Gibney finds that the distinction between con men and businessmen is getting blurred.

Sutherland, Edwin H. *White Collar Crime*. New York: Dryden Press, 1949. This study analyzes 980 decisions against 70 large corporations for restraint of trade, false advertising, infringement, unfair labor practices, and rebates. An important antidote to the comforting idea that prosperous people do not commit crimes for gain.

Criminals' Own Stories

Hamilton, Charles. *Men of the Underworld*. New York: Macmillan, 1952. Forty-two autobiographical pieces by a wide variety of professional criminals, reprinted from popular books and periodicals.

Martin, John Barlow. *My Life in Crime*. New York: Harper & Brothers, 1952. This is an autobiography of a professional criminal as reported by Martin. Especially useful for showing techniques and rationalizations used by predatory criminals.

Mezzro, Milton, and Wolfe, Bernard. *Really the Blues*. New York: Random House, 1946. A fascinating account of the jazz musicians' sleazy world of addicts, alcoholics, and ceaseless mobility.

Sutherland, Edwin H. *The Professional Thief*. Chicago: University of Chicago Press, 1961. A classic study from which Sutherland got his idea about criminal behavior systems.

Others

Quennell, Peter, editor. *London's Underworld*. London: Spring Books, 1950. A reprinting of Volume Four of Henry Mayhew's classic study of London's poor. Dozens of criminal specialties are described, including some long vanished: dog stealers, mud larks, sweeping boys, river pirates. Mid-nineteenth-century scene.

CHAPTER 13

Media of Communication; Organized Religion

Communications Media

Any one individual's knowledge of the world beyond his primary groups is based largely on hearsay, for only a small fraction of that world can be known by direct experience. For the most part, the individual must rely on what is at best second-hand information. To the extent that one's actions are partly shaped by the presumed nature of things outside direct observation, the media through which symbolic representations of these "things outside" reach one must obviously have some influence on one's behavior. Among these media, the newspaper, radio, television, motion picture, and popular magazine are of particular relevance in considering the causes of crime, for they have mass audiences and comprise the principal means by which the larger world is communicated to the individual.

It is impossible for several reasons to generalize and say without qualification that such media cause delinquency. Newspapers, television programs, and moving pictures are not uniform. The influence of all three is apparently ambivalent—both toward and away from crime. Moreover, their effects cannot be isolated from those of other factors, as some have attempted to do. For their influence is limited by and combined with the effects of many other past and current experiences of those exposed. For this reason the influence of the media on behavior will vary with the type of listener or reader. It will vary at different periods of time and in different settings. The same movie or television program could even impel one person toward, another away from, crime. Furthermore, direct and immediate influences should be distinguished from indirect and delayed ones. The immediate influence of the media on crime may sometimes be shown. It does not follow that these media are independent of basic influences. Surely they are channels through which deeper forces in society operate and are themselves products of those forces.

NEWSPAPERS AND CRIME

Certainly newspapers vary greatly in their possible influence on crime. We find four types of papers in this respect: (1) papers such as the *Christian Science Monitor* print little or no crime news except for programs of crime prevention; (2) other conservative papers print relatively brief, unsensational accounts of crime; (3) large numbers of papers print much crime news, attempting not to offend average standards of good taste; (4) finally, not a few play up crime news because they believe their readers wish sensational thrills. Efforts to measure the effect of newspapers have not been very satisfactory.[1] We list below ways in which newspapers may affect crime.

By teaching the technique of crime. Clever methods of committing crime may be news. Newspapers have made known in this way, for example, how automobile thieves pick out the cars to be stolen, prevent their identification, secure their registration in other states, and dispose of them.[2] Accounts of insurance swindles have indicated just what error in method led to their discovery and so warned those not yet arrested. On the other hand, delinquents far more frequently find their technical training in the gang.

By making crime seem attractive, profitable, and exciting. As we saw in Chapter 4, most of the two million "serious" crimes coming to police attention each year are forms of larceny. Most of these, in turn, are relatively picayune or at least of little newsworthy interest. The fraction of the two million crimes reported in the daily press, however, represents highly

---

[1] For one of the more significant, see Susan M. Kingsbury, Hornell Hart, and associates, *Newspapers and the News* (New York: G. P. Putnam's Sons, 1937), part I.

[2] Leon Nelson Flint, *The Conscience of the Newspaper* (New York: Appleton-Century-Crofts, 1925), pp. 197–98.

selected samples: crimes of violence, large-scale thefts, chicanery in high places, constitute the bulk of crime news. This selection gives to the popular image of crime a dash and glamor which is in sharp contrast to the sordid circumstances, mean motives, and trifling gains involved in most crime.

In some cases the reading of a thriller may simply provide vicarious satisfaction of the compelling urges of adolescence. In other cases there is known to be a call to experience the thrill more completely through imitative action. Juvenile gangsters of the slum are surely more influenced by such accounts than are boys who have other satisfying sources of thrills or whose groups do not so effectively reinforce the invitation of the newspaper.

Occasionally there occur what are sometimes rather extravagantly called "epidemics" of some type of crime currently portrayed sensationally in the papers. On rare occasions children have been arrested with newspaper clippings in their pockets depicting a crime they had imitated. On the other hand, obviously few who read of crimes imitate them. The more vivid movies and television probably have a greater influence than newspapers in this respect.

By giving prestige to the criminal. Good men are supposed to seek publicity, and bad men to shun it. But this is by no means universally true. The delinquent banker who has enjoyed prestige in his own community fears what the newspapers will say more than he fears the hardships of prison themselves. The hardened criminal who no longer has prestige to maintain in any "respectable" group does not fear newspaper publicity. The juvenile gangster whose delinquent exploits bring him prestige in the gang is reported as eagerly inquiring the morning after his arrest: "Did I make the papers?" Newspapers might stimulate crime if they thus widen the circle of admirers before whom the delinquent parades. Even undesired publicity is demoralizing to the child, because it may lead him to adopt the role assigned him.

By attracting sympathy or hero worship for criminals. The man on the street probably likes to read in the newspaper Mr. J. Edgar Hoover's· colorful adjectives as applied to public enemies, including "scum from the boiling pot of the underworld," "public rats," "lowest dregs of society," "vermin in human form," and "the slimy crew who feed upon crime" [3]—in other words, the *uncaused* enemies of society. Yet one charge against newspapers is that they have often shown sympathy for certain types of criminals. Realizing the grip of the human-interest story, the papers have often played

---

[3] Cf. Newman F. Baker's editorial, "J. Edgar Hoover," *Journal of Criminal Law and Criminology* (Jan.–Feb. 1938), p. 627.

it up, apparently indifferent whether their readers weep over the sufferings of innocent victims or over those of the perpetrators of crime.

The sin of the newspaper here is that it is concerned not with giving the reader an understanding of a situation but with arousing an emotion. The need is neither sentimental sympathy nor blind hatred of criminals. On the whole, growing public concern over the crime problem seems to have reduced the newspapers' sentimental regard for bold male or gorgeous female offenders.

By reflecting crime-producing elements in our culture. If one accepts the view, suggested in Chapter 1, that crime is largely rooted in our system of values, it follows that the newspaper may promote crime directly or very indirectly by emphasis upon "criminogenic" values which may be widely accepted in our society. We are a sensation-loving people. We are a profit-seeking people. We are full of prejudice against the outsider and against racial and national minorities. We show elsewhere that these values help explain crime in the United States. These same values predominate in our newspapers. Newspapers reflect our culture.

Salmon also argues that newspapers stimulate "the exaggerated idea of their own importance given themselves and their families by the illustrations of schoolboys prominent in school athletics, of society debutantes, of prize-winning babies . . ." [4] These make possible that system of personal rating scales which characterizes our culture. Inability to stand the pace, failure to rate on the scale, resentment against unfairness involved in the struggle and the rating process, and resulting discouragement or revolt— these are causes of crime. Moreover, the build-up which newspapers thus provide, and which is eagerly sought after by many people, subtly reinforces the false view that criminals who are bad, girls who are beautiful, and enterprisers who are lucky deserve sole credit for their failure or success. One of the most significant findings of social science is the demonstration that such a personalized view of life is unrealistic and misleading.

Among the conventional practices in American crime reporting which contribute to this personalized view is that in which reporters at once seek a crime's motive. The more shockingly trivial the alleged motive, the more newsworthy it becomes, particularly where heinous offenses are involved. "I wanted to see what it was like to kill someone." "I stabbed Pa because he was always criticizing me." "We set fire to the school because the gym teacher bawled us out." Such verbalizations of motive—even accurately

[4] Lucy Maynard Salmon, *The Newspaper and the Historian* (New York: Oxford University Press, 1923), p. 410.

reported—are really gross oversimplifications of human conduct, for they obscure the complex of attitudes, values, and group influences necessarily antecedent in some degree to all overt action.

By ridiculing the machinery of justice, or through "trial by newspaper." [5] The ends of justice require that the law, the police, the courts, and prison administrators be respected. Yet newspapers have been known to question the desirability of laws and even condone their violation and to ridicule the administration of justice. Defenders of the press reply that democracy requires freedom to do just these things; that mistaken laws are passed; that police are often deserving of ridicule; that courts are not infrequently inefficient and occasionally corrupt; and that criticism is one of the chief duties of a public-spirited newspaper.

A related major criticism of newspapers has concerned the so-called "trial by newspaper." Newspaper handling of the trial of Bruno Hauptmann for the kidnaping and murder of Colonel Lindbergh's infant son was simply an extreme example of the indecencies to which some newspapers will stoop under such circumstance.[6] Hounding of defense attorneys for information prejudicial to one side or the other; newspaper predictions of the outcome of the trial; insistence that officials take sides; flashing of photographs in court and out; use of unfair methods to gain admission to court; assigning reporters to live with relatives of the accused—these have been some of the questionable methods used in such cases. Attorneys for the defense have sometimes insisted that they are more concerned over trial by newspaper than over the weight of argument in the courtroom.

The fact is, of course, that some types of criminal trials are of great, if morbid, interest to the general public; that both fact and fiction concerning them have been in great demand; that newspaper sales have increased markedly during such trials; that police, attorneys for prosecution and defense, and judges themselves have sometimes desired publicity in the interest of their professional advancement; that newspapers, even if they desired, would hardly dare refuse to advertise for a powerful prosecuting attorney; and that a judge who would refuse newspapers opportunity to obtain much of what they want might be in danger of defeat at the polls.

Freedom of the press and of public criticism may be of vastly more

[5] Thomas D. Thacher, "Trial by Newspaper," address revised for *Vital Speeches of the Day,* Sept. 15, 1936 (New York: City News Publishing Company), p. 779.

[6] The role of the press in the lengthy investigation of the kidnapping, and in the trial and appeal, was an inextricable element in these steps. For a recent new account of the entire case, see George Waller, *Kidnap: The Shocking Story of the Lindbergh Case* (New York: The Dial Press, 1961).

social significance than are the worst abuses of that freedom. The evil of trial by newspaper and related problems is inherent in our culture, our competitive economic regime, our widespread craving for status and publicity, our political system with its elected court officers, and the tremendous power of publicity in securing personal economic, social, and political advancement.

By advocating ineffective types of treatment of criminals. Newspaper advocacy of penal methods has generally reflected dominant popular opinion rather than pioneered for a new penology. Speaking generally, newspapers follow the average citizen in his assumption that crime results from the free and deliberately wicked and uncaused choices of bad men. In accord with that assumption, the cure for crime is to be found, according to the press, in honest but severe punishment in proportion to the wickedness of the particular act. A great many newspapers have apparently been suspicious of efforts to test the sanity of criminals; have inclined toward the determinate rather than the indeterminate sentence; have depicted probation as merely "giving another chance"; and have violently attacked parole as unwarranted softness. Where popular prejudices have been aroused or where vested interests have been involved, as in the Sacco-Vanzetti case in Massachusetts years ago or in recent trials of alleged communist subversives, newspapers have often shared popular prejudices rather than stood for impartial justice.

The newspaper practice of identifying certain arrested persons as "probationers," "ex-convicts," or "parolees" fosters the idea that such persons are criminal types especially likely to commit further offenses. It also reflects unfairly on the corrective measures to which offenders are subjected, for it does not similarly identify those recipients of treatment who make law-abiding adjustments. Good news is no news.

Standards of Crime News Presentation. Realizing the possible evils of sensational crime reporting, newspapers have shown uneasy consciences in a long series of codes of ethics intended to govern the newspaper profession. Like the drunkard's good resolutions, these codes are often broken by the very papers whose owners subscribe to the code. The following illustrate elements in such codes.

1. "The news should not 'offend the moral sensibilities'; it should not supply incentives to base conduct; it should not publish 'sordid details.'"
2. Crime news should deter others from imitating the criminal.
3. Unfair treatment of accused persons is to be condemned.

4. Reporters should not assume the duties of a detective agency.
5. Rumors, gossip, or assumptions of reporters regarding the accused should not be published.
6. Helpless offenders should be gently dealt with.
7. Laws and law-enforcement agencies should not be ridiculed.

Such codes have proved ineffective because the chief problem arises out of the general dominance of the profit-making functions, the tremendous power of and demand for publicity, and the varying demands of different levels among the reading public. We should not conclude, however, that professional codes are of no avail whatever.

The Personal Element in Crime Reporting. Students of the influence of the newspaper on crime have sometimes neglected the important element of the personal relationship between the crime reporter and his human sources of information. Given a paper desiring crime news, its representatives must establish a reputation as good fellows with police officers who can give them that news. "Come on, be a good guy and give me some dope, and I'll be a good guy and give you a build-up in the *Journal*" is the accepted line. Such an interpersonal relationship and understanding is the newspaper-police system in action. This fact is recognized by those who train reporters. So the reporter gets his scoops, sometimes through special pipe lines from police officers "in the know." In return, the reporter protects the record of his pals, the police, when he might sometimes comment on their inefficiency or mistakes or complain of the rather frequent use of the dangerous "third degree." A partial cure for this particular aspect of the problem is seen in the proper training of journalists. Textbooks in journalism often teach an ethics of crime reporting which puts the social interest above that of the reporter's personal profit or the economic welfare of the press. This ethical principle is indeed difficult to practice.

Another aspect of the personal element in crime reporting concerns the customary sources of crime news cultivated by reporters. While news-men are sometimes eye-witnesses to strikes, floods, political campaigns, riots, athletic events, and what not, they but rarely are direct witnesses to crimes and must consequently rely upon informants. The handiest in-formants are victims, court attendants, police officers, prosecutors, jail and prison wardens, and guards, all of whose outlooks are apt to be colored by a punitive or authoritarian bias. Seldom is crime news obtained from juvenile court referees, probation and parole officers, prison sociologists and psychologists, parole boards, police juvenile officers, or others whose positions in law enforcement entail commitment to a "treatment" point of view. Not only are these personnel often bound by professional ethics constraining them to silence, but their perceptions of criminal matters are less likely to yield up the tangy meat which goes to make up exciting crime news.

Conclusion and Suggestions. Newspapers have both contributed to crime and prevented crime. Professionalization of newspaper leadership and adoption of new codes of ethics seem to promise improvement only as the codes are supported by a better-informed public opinion. Government control with any degree of censorship which goes beyond libel laws might threaten an evil of interference with free expression far more serious than the crime problem. The newspaper is just what one would expect it to be in our culture. Yet something can be done. Newspapers can continue to experiment with the effect on sales of a policy of giving decreased prominence to crime and decreased sensationalism in the presentation of crime news. Previous experimentation [7] has been inconclusive. One of the most hopeful lines of attack today is through the popularization by the press of facts about the causation of crime and about the intelligent treatment of criminals. Men may like to read about crime, but speaking generally men do not favor crime. If newspaper readers can be shown the most promising ways of reducing crime, they will be interested. Increasingly, more adequate case studies of juvenile and adult criminals have appeared. Increasingly, feature articles have described some of our best preventive programs. Increasingly, also, really informing articles about the crime problem appear in popular magazines.

TELEVISION

The direct influence on children of such media as moving pictures, radio, television, and comic books is probably greater than that of the newspaper, partly because of their vividness and hence greater emotional appeal. With reference to the first three, we are obliged to confine our attention largely to television. Some rather good, if not wholly definitive, early research [8] at least suggested some of the probable influences of the movie screen on behavior patterns, although it probably overestimated the total influence. It further erred in throwing the blame too exclusively upon one specific medium. Relying less upon advertising than newspapers, radio, and television, the movies have been more directly dependent upon popular

[7] Compare, however, Baker, *loc. cit.*

[8] Cf. Herbert Blumer, *Movies and Conduct;* Herbert Blumer and Philip M. Hauser, *Movies, Delinquency, and Crime;* Charles C. Peters, *Motion Pictures and Standards of Morality* (New York: Macmillan, 1933).

taste. On the whole, the allegedly evil influence which the movie research uncovered has been partly corrected. Yet, in common with radio and television, the cinema has generally appealed to the interests of the masses in some ways which critics have not considered elevating. The influence of radio can be held to be generally similar to that of its new and popular rival, television.

The effects of television viewing have been the subject of a growing number of researches during the last decade, with particular attention given to children and television.[9]

Television represents but one element in the totality of a child's or an adult's complex life experience. Its meaning and influence on behavior patterns cannot be separated from that totality. Television helps set behavior patterns, but patterns set cannot be known simply by knowing a program content, because those patterns have so many other modifying sources. Through the study of content the so-called expert may more or less shrewdly guess the probable general direction of effects on behavior, but to do so he must always be concerned with the meaning of the program within the totality of the spectator's experience. As Siepman says, television is young, fluid, and unpredictable. Television reinforces current patterns; that it initiates many new ones is less certain. We can only guess what exposure to the whole of reality would mean to man. Television exposes us to not wholly representative sample scenes which are fictitious as much as real and which are designed primarily to market goods or convey ideas or emotions.

Television is an ideal medium to reach the masses, who make up the majority of the audience in spite of the costliness of television sets. Television does sell goods. Criminologists want to know how effectively it makes the spectator wish to "do something" as well as to "buy something." The

[9] A useful annotated bibliography of 52 items published between 1949 and 1960 on children and TV is contained in Wilbur Schramm, Jack Lyle, and Edwin B. Parker, *Television in the Lives of Our Children* (Stanford, Calif.: Stanford University Press, 1961), pp. 297–311. All but a few of these are empirical inquiries. The following brief discussion leans heavily on the following sources: Charles A. Siepman, *Radio, Television, and Society* (New York: Oxford University Press, 1950); Jack Gould, "What Television is Doing to Us," a series of seven articles in the *New York Times*, beginning with Jan. 24, 1951; Gilbert Seldes, "A Clinical Analysis of TV," *New York Times* (Nov. 28, 1954). We have also had the advantage of advice from Professor Dallas W. Smythe, formerly Research Director of the Federal Communications Commission, and of the late Professor J. W. Albig of the Department of Sociology of the University of Illinois. Some of the valuable content analyses of Professor Smythe, made for the National Association of Educational Broadcasters, concerns the presentation of crime on television programs, the types of heroes depicted, and so on. Smythe will properly insist, however, that such studies of content are only the beginning of research needed to answer the question as to what the media do to behavior patterns.

answer is not yet fully known. Writing at different periods, Gould, Siepman, and Seldes have given us significant content analyses. Television exposed gambling and police corruption in New York. Video has certainly kept the family at home and centered their attention on a common scene. However, by the same token it has tended to reduce their conversation and discussion and their recreational activities as a family group.[10] Television has collected much money for good causes and especially for individual sufferers dramatically presented. But this has been done selectively with an eye to publicity favorable to advertisers. Advertisers have been compelled to demonstrate their wares visually as well as to tell about them. They have not spoken of the often equal merits of commodities put out by their competitors, and the problem of misrepresentation in advertising has not been solved. Seldes especially praises the high quality of the longer dramas shown and the commendably dispassionate way in which some events, such as the Kefauver Committee's crime hearings, have been presented. In terms of such considerations, the potentially constructive educational influence of television may eventually outweigh its current adverse effects. But if this is to be so, the educators must win their case for programs independent of commercialized interests and must also agree among themselves as to what social values, if any, are to be taught.

Other adverse criticisms have been made. If the Kefauver Committee's hearings were well presented, they nevertheless tended to confirm the public in its interest in purely repressive programs of crime prevention. Seldes tells us that television has been a "godsend to the half-talented," enabling a few selected nonentities to rise from mediocrity for a few cherished minutes of popular applause. By the same token it has created a yearning for such undeserved applause which is scarcely social in its aim or effects. It has thus reinforced the general tendency for successful men to feel that their success has been the result of individual ability and merit, and the failures of others the result of their natural inferiority. In the name of giving people what they want, television gives them what they will accept without much complaint and, some would add, what they can be propagandized into accepting or believing.

Television programs occasionally have included discussion of the causes of crime and of constructive delinquency prevention, but this note has been exceptional. If one judges rather on the basis of the prevalence and provocative nature of crime programs, then television comes in for severe

---

[10] Hilde T. Himmelweit, A. N. Oppenheim, and Pamela Vance, *Television and the Child* (London: Oxford University Press, 1958), p. 383. The authors refer to a "spurious unity" created by television.

criticism. It is impressive to watch the attention with which children observe a faked wrestling match on television and the very real glee or horror with which its simulated sadism is received.

Empirical evidence is lacking, however, that television plays a direct role in causing delinquency. In their carefully controlled study of nearly 2,000 English children, half of whom watched television and half of whom did not, Himmelweit *et al.* concluded that there was no more aggressive, maladjusted, or delinquent behavior among viewers than among controls.[11] Among the conclusions reached by Schramm and his associates after studying the effects of television on some 6,000 children was the feeling that very little delinquency can be traced to television. At best, it is a contributory cause.[12]

In keeping with the general analysis of the present book, we similarly are inclined to emphasize television and the other media as making for crime indirectly through its reflection of criminogenic or unsocial values in the general culture and of the trend toward violence associated with the cold war even more than through the direct influence of the crime themes themselves.

In the hope of exerting a favorable influence upon television policies and programs, the organized industry has developed a code of ethics,[13] and the federal government has set up the Federal Communications Commission. As in the case of the newspapers, the codes are frequently violated. Such codes often seem to exist chiefly to quiet public clamor. The FCC was established as a protection to the general public, but pressure from industry has caused it for the most part to degenerate. It has tended to become mere machinery for providing the services of the media to agencies seeking them. Television policies are today almost wholly controlled by those who sponsor programs for advertising purposes.

Organized Religion

Criminology cannot wholly neglect to discuss the possible influence of religion and the church upon delinquency and crime. The majority of Americans are probably rightly called "religious," whether affiliated with a church or not. Religion is a value in our culture, and the church is one of

11 *Ibid.,* p. 215.
12 Schramm, *op. cit.,* p. 174.
13 For consideration of such codes, see Wilbur Schramm, *Mass Communications* (Urbana, Ill.: University of Illinois Press, 1949); *Process and Effects of Mass Communications* (Urbana, Ill.: University of Illinois Press, 1954).

our major social institutions. Most people respect the church and think of it as a protection against crime. In times of increased crime, religionists have attributed its increase to a decline in religion. "Get back to God," they have implored, "if you would get away from crime." Religion has supported morality and has made our mores allegedly more effective by sanctifying them. Crime has not only been seen as wrong in the eyes of the law and the court, but also in the eyes of God. We have space only to summarize some of the argument and evidence regarding the influence of religion and the church on delinquency and crime. We shall divide our brief discussion into three parts: (1) argument or evidence which appears to be neutral, (2) argument or evidence which supports the more general view that the church prevents crime, and (3) argument or evidence as to certain adverse influences of religion or church. In doing this we had best remember that there are many kinds of religion and many kinds of crime and also that the church is not by any means the only source of morals. These facts may appear to be disregarded in our brief comments below.

Neutral Evidence. If religion prevents crime, one would expect that criminals would be predominantly men and women without religion. Such is not wholly the case. Some years ago, Kalmar and Weir, Catholic priests, made a study of the replies of inmates at Joliet prison in Illinois to questions asked them on their admission there. They found that 87 per cent were registered as affiliated with some religious group, as compared with but 40 per cent of the general population.[14] Studies at the federal reformatory at Chillicothe disclosed that about one man in four claimed church membership. The Gluecks found but 8 per cent of 500 reformatory men had been regularly attending church before commitment, 88.5 per cent had attended irregularly, and 3 per cent were not church-goers.[15] Kalmer and Weir quite properly went behind the inmates' statements and found the men had not been performing their religious duties recently or regularly.

Some students have tried to show differences in the influence of various denominations upon crime, but their findings have proven little. If Protestants were inclined to criticize the Catholic institution of the confessional as tending toward crime by absolving from guilt, these Protestants often showed lack of appreciation of the benefit of the confessional as a relief of tensions which may lead to crime and of the role of the priests as counselors. Counseling is today proving one of the most constructive influences in dealing with criminals; clergy in all denominations have attempted to perform

---

[14] Leo Kalmer and Eligius Weir, *Crime and Religion* (Chicago: Franciscan Herald Press, 1936), p. 19.
[15] *500 Criminal Careers* (New York: Alfred A. Knopf, 1930), p. 131–32.

the role of the counselor with the advantage that some people will talk more frankly to a member of the clergy. Moreover, when considerable differences have been found in the criminal records of members of some denominations as compared with others, the contrasts in class membership, degree of urbanization, and exposure to other causes of crime have been found almost certainly to be the real explanation of these denominational differences. For example, since Baptists include a large number of Negroes, the Baptist crime record naturally reflects the rather high crime rates of that minority group. Only slight relationships have been found between church attendance of adults and Sunday school attendance of children and their relative criminal behavior as compared with that of non-attendants.

If one inquires as to the influence of the church on cruel punishments, one finds that historically that influence has been ambivalent, as we indicated in an earlier chapter. The medieval canonical church exerted some humanitarian influence but was extremely severe in the treatment of heretics. It introduced the modern principle of individualization in treatment but favored the clergy in this practice and did not of course use the factual basis for individual treatment which characterizes our correctional practices today. We owe to the Quakers, on the other hand, a tremendous emphasis upon constructive treatment of offenders, although their early emphasis upon isolation of offenders for purposes of religious meditation proved a mistake. Churches today often favor punishment, and yet their over-all influence has been to humanize the treatment of delinquents.

Similarly in our prisons today the chaplain has played an ambivalent role. In some of the old-line institutions the chaplain has been the only person to whom the inmate might go for sympathetic and understanding help. In others, the chaplain has been so obviously insincere, subservient to the prison administration, and lacking in understanding that he has lost his opportunity to transform his charges. Some chaplains have been opposed to the application of scientific principles in dealing with inmates; others may be of real assistance to the specialist.

Preventive Influence of the Church. There is abundant evidence of constructive influences of religious groups in the field of criminology.

The "Christian ideal" is almost the antithesis of what we think of as the criminal attitude of mind. The Christian ethic preaches the brotherhood of man. Both living and teaching such brotherhood consistently surely tends to reduce crime by setting examples of constructive, cooperative living. To stress this is not to deny that ideals are best taught in intimate primary groups rather than from the pulpit. Moreover the cooperative ideal is not confined to Christian groups but is espoused by Jews and other religionists and indeed is almost implicit in the exigencies of group life itself.

Throughout all human history religious belief has been an important agency of social control. As we said above, religion to the believer sanctifies morality. Belief in punishment in a remote but terrifying hell may conceivably influence the behavior of a devout member of an old-fashioned church. The Christian church personalized the Christian ethic in the character of Jesus, thus giving that ideal a driving personal power. The weakness of religious belief as a preventive of crime is of course that only so long as the belief itself is accepted is it effective. Today many hold that morality has a secular rather than a sacred origin. Thus faith in a sacred morality may be weakened and so cease effectively to prevent crime.

Religion gives men faith in God; science gives men faith in facts. But not all men have faith in science. Science has created the hydrogen bomb, which is difficult to use "in the Christian spirit." In times of great stress the wisest of "religionless" scientists may be overcome with a sense of futility and discouragement. On the other hand the man of religion may retain hope, since "God's in his heaven, all's right with the world." This seems to be what Harry Emerson Fosdick meant when he stressed the importance of religion as a source of morale and urged that without morale a man will not be moral.

Increasingly sociologists are finding that primary groups are the major immediate teachers of morality. The individual church congregation may function as a primary group. There men of similar beliefs and similar ideals communicate and develop common socialized life goals. Unfortunately the ex-criminal has not always found a warm welcome in churches. Primary group status may prevent crime; exclusion from the church primary group may be a source of resentment and consequent repudiation of moral values.

How the Church May Conceivably Aggravate the Crime Problem. Militant atheists and other devoutly anti-church people have long been inclined to find social "evils" of fundamental kinds either arising from or given impetus by organized religion, pointing out that religious bodies at various times have supported slavery, war, racial segregation, torture, oppressive political regimes, caste systems, and other conditions judged by the critics not to be in mankind's best interests. In so far as these social evils may be causally associated with others, such as crime, an apparent case can be made that organized religion contributes to the causes of crime. By the same reasoning, of course, other social institutions can be similarly indicted, since they too at divers times and places have supported such evils, but religious groups have been especially vulnerable to criticism because of their avowed role as moral mentors. Arguments of this kind eventually reduce to the general proposition that crime arises from social circumstances; the particular aspect of society one emphasizes is more likely to reflect the critic's particular value orientation than the result of dispassionate inquiry.

Possibly the most important way the church affects the crime problem is through its promulgation of an image of man as complete master of his own moral choices. Seldom has the typical church accepted a deterministic philosophy; its traditions of salvation and remorse seem inconsistent with the view that man cannot, by autonomous willing, control his ultimate destiny or his current behavior. This text has urged that the criminal is a product, that his behavior—like everyone else's—is the necessary result of antecedent forces. The authors feel that this view, or something very like it, is essential to the development of a scientific criminology. The opposite view introduces into behavior an element of caprice scarcely tolerable to the scientific approach.

To the extent that religious teachings promote an image of man as a creature having complete freedom of moral choice, there continues to exist in the public mind a pre-scientific metaphysical basis for the application of "pure" punishment. Moreover, this image may contribute to the existence of vindictive hatred toward certain offenders, affecting their trials, sentencing, and post-prison adjustment.

CHAPTER 14

Alcohol and Drug Addiction

Alcohol

Americans have been concerned about the "drinking problem" since at least the late eighteenth century, when the popularity of rum began to rival that of beer and ale in the communities of the Eastern seaboard.[1] An association between excessive drinking and low moral character—with causal forces operating in both directions—was early assumed to exist. This assumption came to be especially emphasized following the emergence of the temperance movement in about 1825, which identified alcohol with Satanic influences.[2] Along with the town freethinker and the town moron stood the town drunkard, whose improvidence, irresponsibility and "weakness" of character provided a living moral lesson for the young. However much later generations of secularized Americans may have abandoned the naive condemnation of Demon Rum appropriate to a rural sacred society, the fact remains that today's predatory crime, racketeering, car accidents, marital tensions,

[1] Raymond G. McCarthy, "Alcoholism: Attitudes and Attacks, 1775–1936," *Annals of the American Academy of Political and Social Science* (Jan. 1958), p. 13.

[2] *Ibid.,* p. 14.

economic failure, and many other human woes are very often closely related to the excessive use of alcohol, regarded by many as one of our major social problems.

One reason alcoholism is serious and difficult to prevent is that alcohol is for more than half of our population a source of pleasure which would not willingly be sacrificed. Of about 70,000,000 Americans who drink alcoholic beverages, an estimated 4,700,000 are alcoholics—chronic excessive drinkers.[3] While the occasional drinker may break a law because of lowered inhibitions, the alcoholics are the chief immediate concern of the criminologist. Yet the 70,000,000 are in a sense a part of the problem, because they, and especially the prestiged groups among them, set patterns of drinking which, if innocuous to them, are very dangerous to the alcoholic who may imitate them. It has been claimed [4] that the trend of alcoholic drinking in the United States during the past century has been toward "better balanced drinking" in that per capita consumption of spirits has declined, while that of wines has doubled and that of beer has increased eightfold. Over $9 billion are annually spent on alcohol, though this is a smaller proportion of the national income than formerly.

Alcohol, then, is a source of pleasure and conviviality for at least half of our adult population. It furnishes an opportunity to escape reality when men are overcome by a sense of failure, boredom, or unworthiness. The need or desire for such escape characterizes, not individuals alone, but handicapped classes and racial groups. The unskilled laborer, the domestically tormented husband or wife, the minority suffering from discrimination, the soldier facing probable death, as well as those who merely seek relaxation and pleasure—all sing the praises of alcohol.

Even when taken in small amounts, alcohol often weakens inhibitions. This weakening of inhibition in itself may be an immediate cause of some crime. For some individuals, alcohol produces a very real enslavement and gains a sway only less imperious than that of opiates over the drug addict. For a few, alcohol is the source of the development of a definite psychosis. A large minority, at least, are opposed to the consumption of alcohol. The wet–dry controversy is a real conflict in our society even today. Hence prohibitive legislation—local, state, and national—and a high tax policy after the repeal of such legislation create the basis for a huge racket. Through its effects on industrial inefficiency, poverty, domestic discord, relations be-

[3] Mark Keller, "Alcoholism: Nature and Extent of the Problem," *Annals of the American Academy of Political and Social Science* (Jan. 1958), p. 6.

[4] Cf. Gilbert Burek, "How Hard Do Americans Drink?" *Fortune* (March 1953), pp. 121–25ff.

tween parents and children, and so forth, alcohol has an indirect effect on crime. Drunkenness and disorderly conduct account for a larger proportion of arrests than any other type of offense, with the occasional exception of violations of traffic laws.

Motives for drinking may, of course, be mixed. Millions of people drink alcoholic beverages, especially beer or wine, with their food. Others drink because they think it gives them a lift. Actually this sensation results from the soothing, rather than any stimulating, effects of alcohol. Many persons feel with some reason that alcohol makes them more sociable because it lowers inhibitions and so is an aid to relatively unrestrained conversation and behavior. In many social groups one is expected to drink and to offer drinks to others. Rather pathetic millions drink because of a paucity of alternative opportunities to have fun.

CAUSES OF ALCOHOLISM

While attempts have been made to explain the alcoholic in terms of a neurotic or psychopathic personality, the consensus now is that there is no such thing as a unitary alcoholic personality. The alcoholic has been called immature and too childish to be able to sublimate his craving for alcohol. Yet we must also know *why* some remain immature. The explanation lies not in the label of the personality type but in the process which produced it. In recent years a group of specialists at Yale University, acting under the Research Council on Problems of Alcohol, have conducted excellent objective studies of alcohol, alcoholism, and its treatment. One of these investigations [5] discovered a series of phases through which the life cycle of the alcoholic tended to pass. In spite of some variation the following process of development was defined.

Dr. Jellinek's study discovered that only about 10 per cent of the 98 interviewees began with solitary drinking. Indeed, solitary drinking was an evidence that the alcoholic was some distance along on his road to the "lowest point" in his enslavement. At about the age of 25 the interviewees had begun to have blackouts. They would wake up after a party with no idea of what had happened. The blackout was thus an omen of alcoholism in the offing. Perhaps a bit later they would show dependence on drink itself by sneaking drinks beyond what was being served to people in the party generally. Say two years later the alcoholics began losing control. Some two years later still they began rationalizing their excessive drinking—finding unreal excuses for it. A year later,

[5] E. M. Jellinek, "Phases in the Drinking History of Alcoholics," *Memoirs of the Section on Alcohol, Laboratory of Applied Physiology, Yale University*, No. 5, pp. 7–78.

perhaps, they gave further evidence of losing control by beginning to take a drink in the morning to "get themselves going." This was a sign that drinking was becoming a compulsion. Not many years after, the alcoholic began going on "benders" where he might be absent from family, work, and duties for days. "The irresponsible behavior of the excessive drinker evokes rebuffs and ultimately rejection by his group, and he is thus driven into isolation. . . . The solitary drinking leads the alcoholic to brooding, to the creation of psuedo-problems, and to a centering of all thoughts on himself." [6] Antisocial acts develop in close connection with solitary drinking. Aggressive behavior is seen as in part a compensation for the humiliations he has suffered or imagines he has suffered. Remorse and "going on the water wagon" often appear as additional reactions. Especially significant to the criminologist is the development, some two years after the beginning of the "benders," of unreasonable resentments which show exaggerated self-importance and rejection of remorse. Protecting the supply of liquor, tremors, and indefinable fears characterize later stages of the process. Intoxication has become a goal and not merely a means. The alcoholic's egocentrism has become dominant. After three years of excessive drinking, resulting physical disease may lead him to seek medical advice or the consolations of religion. It usually takes five years for the alcoholic to admit that he is licked, and two years more to bring him to what he calls his "lowest point." Then he may join Alcoholics Anonymous. On the average it takes from 12 to 18 years to pass from the beginning of the "benders" to the lowest point.

The Yale studies and others have found various situations related to alcoholism. Failure in association may either precede or follow inebriety,[7] Bacon classifying four-fifths of some 1,200 arrested alcoholics as maladjusted to marriage. Oltman and Friedman did not find parental deprivations or broken homes more prevalent in the histories of alcoholics than in those of nonalcoholics.[8] Macrory [9] emphasizes the importance of the social function of the tavern in an urban community in spite of the trend away from the old saloon drinking. Jackson and Connor [10] have pointed out the influence of Skid Road culture on alcoholism, noting that alcoholics found there are much like other discouraged people and can be helped, provided they have not come to look upon themselves as permanent residents of Skid Road, the symbol of failure. Comparing the first drinking experiences of the addictive with those of normal drinkers, Albert

[6] *Ibid.*, p. 73.

[7] Seldon D. Bacon, "Inebriety, Social Integration, and Marriage," *Memoirs of the Section on Alcohol, Laboratory of Applied Physiology, Yale University,* No. 2, 1945.

[8] Jane E. Oltman and Samuel Friedman, "A Consideration of Parental Deprivation and Other Factors in the Alcohol Addict," *Quarterly Journal of Studies on Alcohol* (March 1953), pp. 49–57.

[9] Boyd C. Macrory, "The Tavern and the Community," *Quarterly Journal of Studies on Alcohol* (Dec. 1952), pp. 609–37.

[10] Joan K. Jackson and Ralph Connor, "The Skid Road Alcoholic," *Quarterly Journal of Studies on Alcohol* (Sept. 1953), pp. 468–86.

D. Ullman [11] has shown that the confirmed alcoholic began drinking later; more often became intoxicated at that time; drank away from home; and had parents who disagreed whether one should or should not use alcohol. In a later study of initial drinking experiences of 1,420 college students, Ullman found evidence supporting his notion that differential alcoholism rates among ethnic groups are associated with differential amounts of ambivalence toward drinking in the same groups. Ethnic groups which tend to regard drinking as a moral issue and consequently tend not to permit early parentally sponsored drinking by their children (Irish- and English-Americans) exhibit relatively high rates of alcoholism. On the other hand, ethnic subcultures for which the consumption of alcohol is scarcely more of a moral issue than is the consumption of food (Jews and Italian-Americans) and consequently allow early but moderate consumption of alcohol by their children at meals and on ceremonial occasions exhibit relatively low rates of alcoholism. For the former children alcohol achieves a shuddery fascination; its use, moreover, is identified with "being an adult" and thus is tied to status shifts.[12]

These are but samples of the Yale studies, which, though also dealing with physiological aspects of the problem, emphasize social relations as influential in initiating drinking habits, developing compulsive drinking, and suggesting possibilities of successful therapy.

ALCOHOLISM AND THE GENERAL CULTURE

Behind the personal experiences of the alcoholic lie deeper social forces which affect alcoholism by increasing the difficulty of social adjustment and creating a need to escape reality. Bacon, for example, has related alcoholism to the complexity of society:

. . . stratification, individualism, ignorance, intergroup and internal competition, all engendered by the complexity of society, enhance the function of alcohol. Complexity results in need for greater integrative functioning; relaxation of tension, uncertainty, and suspicion is necessary for this function; alcohol has been found useful in its accomplishment.[13]

This characteristic of our culture creates various personal problems of adjustment involving anxiety, tension, guilt, and the like. These feelings are connected with the individual's desire to have a good opinion of himself,

[11] "First Drinking Experiences of Addictive and 'Normal' Drinkers," *Quarterly Journal of Studies on Alcohol* (June 1953), pp. 181–91.

[12] Albert D. Ullman, "Ethnic Differences in the First Drinking Experience," *Social Problems* (Summer, 1960), pp. 45–56.

[13] Seldon D. Bacon, "Alcohol and Complex Society," *Alcohol Science and Society, Journal of Studies on Alcohol* (1945), pp. 179–200.

to gain and hold the respect and affection of others, to be secure, to achieve his life goals, to make satisfactory sexual adjustment. In all of these areas alcohol depresses inhibitions and anxieties and allows relaxation. "It has taken away the power from agencies of control which could once be efficiently used." [14] We may add that in much of our society it is held a mark of masculinity to drink and of effeminacy to refuse alcohol. Even drunkenness itself is a positive value at times in some groups, while in a few there is competition to see who can drink his fellow under the table.[15]

Devoting his book entirely to cultural influences on the use of alcohol, Patrick [16] has shown how group values and attitudes determine through what channels, alcohol or other, men will seek escape from anxiety. He especially notes that the function of alcohol is differently defined in different social classes. Straus and Bacon [17] have also shown the importance of distinguishing class differences in drinking patterns. The low-status alcoholic may rationalize: "If the college crowd can drink, why can't I?"

DRUNKENNESS AS A CRIME

Arrests for drunkenness in practice are arrests for disorderly conduct. Presumably the vast majority of drunks escape arrest. Fines or a sentence of a few days in jail will tend to deepen the pauperization of an already pauperized man. Probably hundreds of thousands of lower-class Americans would otherwise never have spent a night under the demoralizing conditions of the typical police lock-up or county jail. A large proportion of these return over and over again and get a reputation as jailbirds for no other reason than that they have craved escape from reality through liquor and have not been able to "take" as much as their more fortunate fellows. By contrast the drunken playboy rarely goes to jail unless his behavior has involved a serious offense.

In criticizing the contention that Skid Road alcoholics (who constitute a large proportion of persons arrested for public drunkenness) are best understood as sufferers from biological, psychological, and moral defects, Earl Rubington has emphasized that a Skid Road subculture can be identified, peopled by low-status men alienated from majority value patterns.

[14] *Ibid.*, pp. 194–95.
[15] Cf. Ralph S. Banay, "Cultural Influences in Alcoholism," *Journal of Nervous and Mental Diseases* (Sept. 1945), pp. 265–75.
[16] Clarence H. Patrick, *Alcohol, Culture and Society* (Durham, N. C.: Duke University Press, 1952), p. 62 and *passim.*
[17] Robert Straus and Seldon D. Bacon, *Drinking in College* (New Haven, Conn.: Yale University Press, 1953).

A certain proportion of the alienated find it convenient to fend together, and they do so by banding together and expressing their alienation as part of a pattern of organized behavior. Denied status in respectable society, they develop or seek out a social organization in which a role more suitable to their own needs is possible. If that role prescribes social drinking as defined on Skid Row, the alienated are quite willing to comply.[18]

ALCOHOL AS A FACTOR IN THE CAUSATION OF OTHER CRIMES

Case studies show that a considerable minority of criminals have been excessively intemperate.[19] Logic and case studies suggest that a genuine causal relationship between drink and crime often does exist. Occasionally, as when a man kills his best friend over a trivial situation, drunkenness appears as a direct and almost the sole factor. More often drunkenness is rather a complicating factor. Most men who are drunk do not commit serious crimes.

When alcohol is taken in excess, however, the personality may become completely disorganized. Psychological effects include ultimate destruction of memory, increased suggestibility, and lack of ability to plan and to inhibit impulses. The alcoholic thus easily becomes the tool of other criminals. The violence of the alcoholic may be unintentional, since he cannot judge the force of the blow he strikes. Assault is the most frequent crime of the alcoholic. The sex crimes of alcoholics are less likely to take the form of rape, and more likely to take the form of exhibitionism.

Shupe [20] indicates that men arrested for rape were sober in about half of his cases and that alcohol tends to repress rather than stimulate sexual impulses, though it does lower inhibitions. In two-thirds of all cases of crime, he found the man arrested was in some degree under the influence of alcohol, but this is not inconsistent with a figure as low as 25 per cent when a study is concerned with alcohol as a primary cause. Emphasizing the well-known prevalence of drunken driving and resulting homicide, Seliger [21] reports that most such killers have not been true alcoholics but have been classed as only moderate drinkers.

[18] Earl Rubington, "The Chronic Drunkenness Offender," *Annals of the American Academy of Political and Social Sciences* (Jan. 1958), pp. 67–68.

[19] Cf. Sheldon and Eleanor T. Glueck, *500 Criminal Careers* (New York: Alfred A. Knopf, 1930), p. 127; *500 Delinquent Women* (New York: Alfred A. Knopf, 1934), p. 86; George E. G. Catlin, "Alcoholism," *Encyclopaedia of the Social Sciences*, I, p. 626.

[20] Lloyd M. Shupe, "Alcohol and Crime," *Journal of Criminal Law, Criminology and Police Science* (Jan.–Feb. 1954), pp. 661–64.

[21] Robert V. Seliger, "Alcohol and Crime," *Journal of Criminal Law, Criminology and Police Science* (Nov.–Dec. 1953), pp. 438–41.

According to Banay [22] the immature alcoholic prefers certain behavior patterns of childhood, but if he follows them he will lose status in the community. Under the influence of alcohol, however, he may return to his tabooed earlier behavior patterns. In the psychopathology of aggression, Banay finds two distinct elements, hostility and lessened anticipation of punishment, both increased by alcohol. The alcoholic's behavior may be sadistic and cruel or at times masochistic and self-accusatory.

EFFORTS TO CONTROL ALCOHOLISM

Methods of control. Various devices have been tried for control of the sale of alcoholic beverages.[23] There were the earlier rather ineffective efforts of temperance societies to reduce intemperance through educational activities. Under the license system, local option laws were passed and, by 1906, 40 per cent of the people of the United States were living in dry territory. In 1918, principally as a result of state-wide prohibition, 90 per cent of the area of the nation, containing two-thirds of the population, was "dry." Other methods tried have included the dispensary system, under which the local community has a monopoly of dispensing spirituous liquors; the Swedish system, under which a limited-dividend corporation for the manufacture as well as the sale of drink is created, the people put on what amounts to a ration, and on-premise consumption except in eating places is forbidden; the Canadian system of government monopoly of retail sales; and in the United States somewhat similar state-wide government-controlled sales of packaged liquors, as in Michigan and Pennsylvania.

National prohibition. Growing dry sentiment and the great political power of the Anti-Saloon League, the partial failure of certain other experiments, and the association of the liquor traffic with some of the German elements in the United States led to the passage of the Eighteenth Amendment, which took effect in 1920. Such legislation gave opportunity for American moral ideals to find expression in laws [24] which the people, or at least many of the urban elements in the population, had no intention of obeying. It thus introduced an inconsistency between precept and practice which even today is an important cause of disrespect for law in the United

[22] Ralph S. Banay, "Alcoholism and Crime," *Quarterly Journal of Studies on Alcohol* (March 1942), pp. 686–716.

[23] Cf. Clark Warburton, "Prohibition," *Encyclopaedia of the Social Sciences,* XII, pp. 499–510; D. W. McConnell, "Liquor Traffic," *ibid.,* IX, pp. 504–05; Leonard Harrison and Elizabeth Laine, *After Repeal* (New York: Harper & Brothers, 1936), p. x.

[24] Cf. Harry Elmer Barnes, *Prohibition versus Civilization* (New York: Viking Press, 1932), p. 33.

States. National prohibition produced a huge racket. Violence, including murder, resulted as gangs contended for control of lucrative bootlegging.

The aim of prohibition, of course, was to reduce drinking, drunkenness, and the ill effects of alcoholism. The following table indicates a real decrease of alcoholic consumption, especially during the early years of the national experiment. It also shows, however, that the reduction came chiefly in beer drinking. Prohibition did mean a considerable drop in arrests for drunkenness. Deaths from alcoholism, however, rose nearly fourfold.[25]

Table 6   AVERAGE ANNUAL PER CAPITA CONSUMPTION
IN GALLONS IN THE UNITED STATES

Period	Spirits	Beer	Wine	Equivalent in Pure Alcohol
Local prohibition, 1911–14	1.47	20.53	0.59	1.69
Wartime restrictions, 1918–19	0.80	11.44	0.50	0.97
Early years of national prohibition, 1921–22	0.92	1.49	0.51	0.73
Later years of national prohibition, 1927–30	1.62	62.7	0.98	1.14

Clark Warburton, "Prohibition," *Encyclopaedia of the Social Sciences,* XII, p. 507.

More important for us is the fact that the law itself was imposed upon the unwilling cities and the still more unwilling minorities among the foreign-born and their children living in our city slums.[26] In the interest of enforcement it was necessary to limit some of our cherished civil liberties. Moreover, when many feel that a law does injustice, everyone begins to list the laws he will keep; those he will permit others to break; and those he will break in his own interest, to follow his group's pattern, or in order to demonstrate the evil of the law. Such a situation spelled a great opportunity for the gangster. He could make huge profits and secure the support of respectable people who ordinarily would have been his opponents. One of our large business enterprises thus became a great underworld activity. Police, legislators, and judges were corrupted. "During the twelve and a half years from the date when the National Prohibition Act went into effect up to June 30, 1932, federal prohibition officers arrested more than 750,000 persons, of whom more than 500,000 were convicted of violating

[25] Clarence Darrow and Victor S. Yarros, *The Prohibition Mania* (New York: Boni and Liveright, 1927), p. 231; Herman Feldman, *Prohibition: Its Economic and Industrial Aspects* (New York: D. Appleton & Company, 1927), p. 397.

[26] Cf. Peter H. Odegard, *Pressure Politics, The Story of the Anti-Saloon League* (New York: Columbia University Press, 1928).

the law. . . ." [27] Courts became congested, and cases were rushed through with fines assessed by the judge. This resulted in what amounted to little more than the payment of a moderate license fee. Prohibition certainly led to widespread violation of law.

Postprohibition control of alcohol. On December 5, 1933, the national prohibition experiment terminated with the repeal of the Eighteenth Amendment. Yet, just as the amendment did not solve the alcohol problem, so its repeal did not solve the problem of law violation. Heavy taxes upon the manufacture and sale of liquors made bootlegging again profitable. Estimates of the proportion of the liquor consumed which was illicit varied from 15 to 60 per cent. The Alcohol Tax Unit of the Bureau of Internal Revenue, charged with enforcement, had relatively little difficulty in collecting taxes from large dealers, but thousands of illegal stills were annually seized and thousands of individuals arrested.

Supported by a high tax and by local tradition in some areas, the racket continues today. State monopoly systems are said to produce even more revenue than does a licensing system. Governments seem to prefer to risk the dangers of racketeering rather than forgo billions in easily collected revenue. The liquor industry has grown to huge proportions and has perhaps gained respect in the public mind, in spite of continued opposition from the drys.

TREATMENT AND PREVENTION OF ALCOHOLISM

Specialists tell us that there is no cure for alcoholism in the sense that there is no way by which a true alcoholic can escape from the enslavement of alcohol and still continue to drink. But it has proven possible to help alcoholics give up drinking. Essential to this is that the man treated should be made first to want to recover and secondly to believe that recovery is possible. Three types of treatment may be mentioned: aversion treatment, psychotherapy and counseling, and resort to Alcoholics Anonymous.

In aversion treatment the patient is given something to make him vomit at the same time that he takes a drink of whiskey. Thus an undesired nausea is conditioned along with the satisfaction of the craving for alcohol. The method may be rather costly, since hospitalization may be required. Moreover, the effect is not always lasting, and treatment must be repeated. There are some favorable reports of the use of the drug tetraethylthiuram disulfide,[28] though it has been said that 70 per cent of the patients later trade the pills for the bottle.

[27] Warburton, *loc. cit.,* p. 506.
[28] Cf. Olaf Martensen-Larsen, "Five Years' Experience with Disulfiram," *Quarterly Journal of Studies on Alcohol* (Sept. 1953), pp. 406–17.

In psychotherapy the cure depends upon showing that the real problem is not the craving for alcohol itself but a more deeply rooted emotional problem, and upon finding a solution for that deeper problem. Various subsidiary methods of psychoanalysis may be added. Reports on their efficacy are not very encouraging.

Recently attention has rightly been directed toward the remarkable achievements of the organization known as Alcoholics Anonymous.[29] Founded in 1934, Alcoholic Anonymous consists of alcoholics banded together in order, through association, to gain an escape from compulsive drinking. As described by one of their number, Alcoholics Anonymous distinguishes some 12 steps in its program. Among these steps we mention the following: (1) admission that the victim is powerless over alcohol (i.e., that even one drink will set him off); (2) the decision to have God run his life; (3) admission to God, to himself, and to at least one other person that a wrong has been done; (4) a resolve to make amends for any damage to other people which has come from his behavior; and (5) work with other alcoholics, aiding them to be free from alcohol.

If one disregards for the moment its religious aspects, Alcoholics Anonymous uses a distinctly group or sociological method. A habit acquired presumably largely through group influences is overcome through group influences. The alcoholic has become a member of a group which has confidence in him and which will continue to have confidence even if he fails a number of times. Talking over his own problems with the group, he discovers that his problems are by no means unique. He also discovers that many have been enabled to keep away from alcohol. Members may go where alcohol is served and may even serve it to others themselves, but at A.A. parties only milk or soft drinks are available.

A.A. claims 75 per cent success for its members, 90 per cent if those who have dropped out within a short time are deducted. Specialists seem unanimous that A.A. shows a larger degree of success than any other method. Some stress the religious aspect of A.A. Yet the religious appeal itself is not new but very old, and backsliding in the past has been notoriously prevalent among the converted. Religion is no doubt an aid to A.A. members with strong religious beliefs, but group organization is the distinguishing characteristic of Alcoholics Anonymous. Like many criminals the alcoholic needs above all else to regain self-respect. His group, by giving him status and hope and a social goal, gives him the self-respect he needs. The success of Alcoholics Anonymous argues well for a wide extension of

[29] Cf. Anonymous, *Alcoholics Anonymous* (New York: Works Publishing, 1939); Charles Clapp, Jr., *Drinking's Not the Problem* (New York: Thomas Y. Crowell Company, 1949); Anonymous, *12 Steps and 12 Traditions* (New York: Harper & Brothers, 1953).

group organization methods in the treatment of life's failures, including among them thousands of criminals whether alcoholics or not. To some sociologists it suggests that the use of natural groups may be more effective than the not-too-well-validated efforts of individual-centered psychotherapy. Alcoholics Anonymous has been successfully introduced even into some of our "tougher" oldline prisons when it has been possible to secure permission from wardens to hold meetings without the presence of guards and to develop relations with chapters of the organization on the outside.[30] Prison conferences of A.A. have been held; tape recordings of meetings have been exchanged; inmates who are insincere have been screened out; provision has been made for membership in outside chapters after release; wardens have been convinced of resulting benefits in the form of better discipline on the inside; past members have been secured from the outside to testify to inmates of their success; and statistical evidence of that success, in spite of some failures, has been recorded.

There exists some evidence, however, that A.A.'s usefulness extends mainly to outgoing, sociable individuals who have previously come to define their drinking as a threat to the well-being of themselves and their families.[31] This may mean that A.A.'s program is inherently unsuited to some alcoholics, or that at the very least the acquisition of negative attitudes toward one's own drinking from some source other than A.A. is a precondition to willingness to become affiliated with the organization.

Apart from A.A., counseling and group therapy with alcoholics in jail has also been reported as successful, for example, in Los Angeles.[32] All in all, the best hope for the alcoholic seems to lie in group support for his efforts to give up alcohol.

Drug Addiction

The mere use of narcotic drugs for other than medical or scientific purposes is not technically a crime, although several states—among which are Kentucky, Michigan, and New Jersey—have made addiction a crime

---

[30] Cf. Anonymous, "Alcoholics Anonymous in Prisons," *Federal Probation* (Dec. 1954), pp. 17–20.

[31] Harrison M. Trice, "Alcoholics Anonymous," *Annals of the American Academy of Political and Social Science* (Jan. 1958), p. 113.

[32] See the following challenging articles by Dr. Arthur Lerner: "Male Alcoholic Inmates in a City Jail," *Quarterly Journal of Studies in Alcohol* (Sept. 1953), pp. 429–67; "Considerations of Content Material of Group Counseling with Jailed Alcoholics," *ibid.* (Sept. 1954), pp. 432–52; "An Experiment in Group Counseling with Male Alcoholic Inmates," *Federal Probation* (Sept. 1953), pp. 32–39.

per se.[33] Yet in the United States all addicts and most of those who provide them with drugs are of necessity criminals. The Harrison Act of 1914 forbade anyone to sell, purchase, or possess these drugs for their euphoric effect or merely to relieve pains due to the withdrawal of the opiate derivatives,[34] except, of course, when administered as part of a supposed cure for the habit. Moreover, the addict is both looked upon as a criminal and treated as such by probably the majority of the general public, by the United States Narcotics Bureau, and apparently even by some medical specialists who try to effect a cure. This attitude, as well as the contrary view that the addict is a physically, psychologically, or socially sick person, is important because the problem of drug addiction is highly controversial. Recognizing it as controversial and so largely a matter of opinion, the criminologist must deal with opposed views and even contradictory alleged facts presented by supposed specialists. Even the official government line has at times been somewhat different, for example, in England, Canada, and the United States, and there has been some controversy within United Nations circles. Specialists unconnected with government have often been in conflict with officials.

In their direct physiological effects, opium and its derivatives, such as morphine, heroin, and codein, do not incite to crime but rather tend away from violence, since they are depressants. But the memories of euphoric joys obtained from past indulgence and the experience or memory of terrible withdrawal pains when deprived of his drug practically compel the addict to break the law by purchasing drugs from the peddler, making him a criminal. While some control over the sale and use of such dangerous drugs clearly is required, nevertheless the Harrison Act is what makes it a crime to satisfy either of these compelling needs (the line between intense desire and the need being impossible to draw) and creates one of our most serious and lucrative rackets. This racket, plus the fact that an addict without funds will steal or commit other crimes to get drugs, constitute the criminal aspects of drug addiction.

[33] Rufus King, "Narcotic Drug Laws and Enforcement Policies," *Law and Contemporary Problems* (Winter, 1957), p. 128.

[34] An abstinence syndrome is a characteristic result of drug withdrawal among persons addicted to opium derivatives and barbiturates. Different drugs produce different syndromes. That of morphine, for example, includes sneezing, vomiting, yawning, sweating, diarrhea, and muscle-jerking, and may continue for a week or more. Barbiturate withdrawal produces insomnia and anorexia, at least, and may induce convulsions and psychotic episodes. The addict's intense need for his drug may arise more from his wish to avoid the syndrome rather than from the pleasant sensations which initially made the drug attractive to him. Certain drugs, including marihuana, mescaline, cocaine, and benzedrine, are not addicting strictly speaking, since they do not produce physical dependence. Like the others, however, they have detrimental effects on social relations by reducing the capacity for role fulfillment.

In addition, there is some slight direct relationship between the use of cocaine and crime and a disputed relationship in the case of marihuana. Cocaine, or cocaine mixed with morphine in a "speed ball," has sometimes given the professional criminal added bravado but is rarely used because its later effects are unpleasant and dangerous. Marihuana, smoked in "reefer" cigarettes, is occasionally a first step which may lead to the use of such a drug as heroin, though it is said that some two-thirds or more of adolescent addicts begin directly with heroin or other opiates. Marihuana can easily be grown in the United States, though a good deal comes from Mexico. It is fairly widely used in certain professional groups, such as jazz musicians, for whom the drug's effect on the user's perception of the passage of time reportedly enables the musician to perform more effectively.

The major crime problem is connected with the intense desire or need for the opium derivatives (mainly heroin and morphine) and certain new synthetic drugs, and the fact that it is a crime to buy or sell them. It takes on the three aspects mentioned: the racket, the crime of purchase, and other crimes committed to get money for purchase. These, it would seem, are not so much drug-created as law-created crime problems. This is true whatever one's view of the nature of the addict or the reasons he wants drugs. To some he is just a bad man; to some he is a weak character choosing the wrong way to seek joy and avoid pain and stress; to others he is basically like the rest of us but has become involved in intolerable stresses leading him to seek pleasurable escape from reality; to others he is a group product following a drug pattern which is part of a larger pattern of revolt from conventional society; to still others he is the indirect product of values in our general culture. This culture creates the need for escape; accounts for the gang's unconventional definitions of how to have a good time; produces the sense of conflict with society; engenders the drug peddler's eagerness to make a profit out of the needs and weakness of others; and even explains the typically American emphasis on repression and punishment as the traditional way of meeting this and other problems. The proponents of severe punishment and of compelling addicts to take cures no doubt often sincerely believe they are thereby benefiting the addict and protecting society. They say there would be more addicts if it were not for this repression. Their critics, though concerned about addiction and acknowledging the need for some control, hold that other methods are more humane and at least equally effective. After all, addicts, as such, hurt themselves and their immediate families and friends more than they hurt society. Some few even carry on fairly successfully and are unknown addicts. Possibly all of them have taken one of the most dangerous and enslaving ways of seeking happiness or avoiding intolerable strain, but all men seek these goals. The above statement leaves open important controversial questions as to what causes people to take drugs; what are the best methods of cure; how to reduce resort to narcotics; and what are the relative functions of threat of punishment, on the one hand, and constructive use of education and of licensing of physicians, clinics, and group organizations, on the other, in dealing with the problem.

ESTIMATED AMOUNT AND TREND OF DRUG ADDICTION

The United States Bureau of Narcotics had reported a marked decrease in drug addiction at least up to the end of World War II. They attributed this decline to prevention of smuggling and effective internal law enforcement.[35] As evidence of the earlier decrease, Harry J. Anslinger, former Federal Commissioner of Narcotics, reported a decline in the rate of army disqualifications by reason of addiction from one in 1,500 draftees in World War I to one in 10,000 in World War II.[36] Anslinger has estimated that there were 60,000 narcotics addicts in the United States in 1955, and 45,000 five years later.[37] A recent medical study put the number at nearly 1,000,000.[38] Unless we assume that one or both estimates are merely wild guesses, it is evident that the number of addicts arrived at is a function of differing criteria of addiction and differing sources of data.

CAUSES OF DRUG ADDICTION

Thousands of people who take drugs for medical reasons do not become addicts. Before patent medicines containing narcotic drugs were restricted by law, medication was a considerable source of addiction, and decline in addiction to a considerable degree may have been due to those needed laws. Nevertheless, addiction has resulted from physicians' prescriptions, and some 5 per cent of admissions to the federal hospital at Lexington, Kentucky, are said to have been medical cases. Maurer and Vogel [39] tell us that today most such medical cases result from the use of morphine in an attempt to cure alcoholism, the patient sometimes shifting from alcohol to the drug.

[35] *Traffic in Opium,* Report by the Government of the United States of America for the Year Ending Dec. 31, 1947 (Washington, D. C.: (publ.), 1948).

[36] Letter to the senior author, February 1, 1949.

[37] Edwin M. Schur, *Narcotic Addiction in Britain and America* (Bloomington, Ind.: Indiana University Press, 1962), p. 43.

[38] *Ibid.,* p. 44.

[39] David W. Maurer and Victor H. Vogel, *Narcotics and Narcotic Addiction* (Springfield, Ill.: Charles C. Thomas, 1954), p. 73.

A view popular with the medical profession and with law-enforcement officials who think of the addict as a criminal is that addiction is due to defects in the addict's personality. Extreme examples of this view are seen in Dr. David P. Ausubel's statement that ". . . only individuals with a very special kind of defect can become truly addicted to drugs," [40] and by the allegation by Chein and Rosenfeld that "all juvenile addicts are severely disturbed individuals." [41] Apparently more generally accepted is the characterization of addicts under such vague terms as "neurotics" and "psychopaths." The mere use of such terms does not help us understand addiction any better than it helps us to understand crime generally, unless accompanied by a careful analysis of the process through which the undesirable personality trait was acquired or which led the man under stress to seek this particular type of escape. On the other hand, there is much evidence that addiction very often has a social origin in the suggestion of other addicts, through attendance at parties where drugs are dispensed, or where euphoria is sought by a group in connection with sex experience or other entertainment. (It should be noted, however, that regardless of the purpose of a party, drugs in themselves tend to reduce rather than stimulate sex impulses.) Addiction among youth today has been proven to be a group pattern of revolt among adolescents already having accepted unconventional patterns. Some earlier addiction of adults, such as Dai studied, seems to have had a similar source. The matter is in dispute, but at least it may be said that there is no convincing proof that addicts, before addiction, are basically different as regards their physical or mental traits. They have often been delinquents before they were addicts. Their deviant personality traits and behavior patterns appear often as the result of conditioning in groups in which they have sought status.

Basic among stress-producing conditions is the nature of our competitive culture, which leads so many of the socially unsuccessful to seek flight from reality. Drug addiction may thus be viewed as one of the less socially approved avenues of flight. Studying the characteristics of opium addicts in Chicago, Dai found them to be irregular in employment with a considerable proportion from the ranks of those in domestic and personal service and commercialized recreation, not suffering unusually from disease, and not usually criminal before addiction. This last characteristic is not found true of our recent adolescent addicts. Ecologically, Dai found that drug addicts

[40] "An Evaluation of Recent Adolescent Drug Addiction," *Mental Hygiene* (July 1952), p. 374.
[41] Isidor Chein and Eva Rosenfeld, "Juvenile Narcotics Use," *Law and Contemporary Problems* (Winter, 1957), p. 59.

lived disproportionately in areas of mobility with an excess of male inhabitants and absence of social control through primary group relationships; and areas were found in other studies to be characterized by family disorganization, crime, vice, alcoholism, insanity, and suicide. Considering the social relationships of addicts, Dai found them associating with other addicts and either admiring them or engaged in some form of affectional relationship with them. Non-users had come to identify themselves with users, who might be the former's heroes, intimate friends, or lovers, and to follow their example.[42]

TREATMENT OF DRUG ADDICTION

Whatever the method used, all authorities report that, while physical health may be re-established without use of the drug, the percentage of relapses following treatment is extremely high—probably over 90 per cent. The federal narcotic institutions, however, report that about 30 per cent of patients treated are not known to have returned to drugs within three years. Even when desiring cure, addicts return to the drug when with cure their former restlessness and discontent recur.

On the other hand, as hinted above, it is arguable that medical and social care could check the abuse of drugs and prevent the suffering incidental to their denial. This, however, our law does not permit. A general physician's patient is supposed to be in the process of cure through withdrawal and to be directed to the federal hospitals at Lexington or Fort Worth. The past and possibly future use of clinics to provide drugs to addicts at cost and of the English system of specially licensing physicians are discussed below, and the argument appears to favor their use.

A unique movement in the treatment of addicts with long criminal records is that known as "Synanon." [43] Begun about 1958 in the Los Angeles beach area as a spontaneous gathering of alcoholics and addicts, about 15 of whom moved into the home of a former business executive, Charles E. Dederich, the movement has evolved into a form of autonomous communal colonies whose social structures apparently provide status-achievement on the basis of drug avoidance. A kind of "leaderless" group therapy is practiced in which merciless self-and-other critiques are vigorously carried out. Social control techniques in the colonies take the form of harsh reprimand, ridicule, and threat of expulsion. In the absence of careful follow-up studies

[42] Bingham Dai, *Opium Addiction in Chicago* (Shanghai, China: Commercial Press, 1937), p. 24.
[43] A term derived from an addict's mispronunciation of "seminar."

the success of Synanon is yet to be determined,[44] but it is a remarkable instance of self-help in which the "therapy" is almost exclusively sociological.

CONTROL OF DRUG ADDICTION

Public control of the drug problem may be attained through international, national, state, and local machinery. Public efforts at control have been made principally through penalizing the production of raw materials; the manufacture, transportation, and sale of the finished product; and its possession or use for other than medical and scientific purposes. Subsidiary methods have included the estimate of legitimate needs and licensing or otherwise regulating the ways in which they may be met.

International control of narcotic drugs is imperative, at least so long as there is a demand for such drugs and huge profits can be made from their illegal sale. In terms of agreements and administrative machinery, there has been a great development of international control, and today no fewer than 84 countries participate in some degree. Yet this control is still very inadequate. Some of the difficulties and problems include considerable disagreement on policies and methods. At least until the end of 1953, there had been failure to control the basic root of the problem in the cultivation of the poppy and other raw materials. There has been some little success in limiting the production and sale of heroin and synthetic drugs which are used for industrial purposes. Nations have resented accusations that they have violated agreements and that they are important sources of drugs. It has been hard to enforce agreements, especially when a few important countries have not been parties to them or have relied greatly on the sale or taxation of narcotics for revenue. Narcotics have been used as weapons of war. Since World War II, production of raw materials, manufacture, sale, and illicit consumption have increased. Recently mentioned as new sources of supply have been Mexico, Lebanon, Iran, and India.

International control agreements began with the Hague International Opium Convention of 1912, an outgrowth of a 1908 meeting in Shanghai of Western governments concerned about the opium traffic in their Far East territories. Between 1925 and 1948, under the sponsorships of the League of Nations and the United Nations, seven additional international agree-

---

[44] Nearly 400 addicts have been Synanon enrollees in the Los Angeles colony; 29 per cent of these are known to be off drugs. However, 86 per cent of 75 addicts who remained at least seven months are now non-users. See Rita Volkman and Donald R. Cressey, "Differential Association and the Rehabilitation of Drug Addicts," *American Journal of Sociology* (September 1963), p. 142. Cf. Lewis Yablonsky, "The Anti-Criminal Society: Synanon," *Federal Probation* (September 1962), pp. 50–57.

ments were reached, relating to such matters as suppression of opium smoking (1925, 1931); the opium trade (1925); manufacture and distribution of narcotic drugs (1931); suppression of illicit drug traffic (1936); control of synthetic drugs (1948). Adoption of a 1953 proposal to control cultivation of the poppy plant and the exportation of opium from the poppy-growing countries of the Near and Middle East met with strong opposition from certain of these countries, which foresaw threats to their economic interests. A single convention to replace all existing international agreements was prepared by the United Nations Commission on Narcotic Drugs, but the convention had not yet been adopted by the end of 1962.

Federal narcotics legislation in the United States has long been the subject of much controversy among legislation, law-enforcement personnel, biological and social scientists, physicians, and social reformers. Few informed persons are entirely satisfied with the federal narcotics laws, and some persons are outraged by what they regard as a reactionary and unnecessarily oppressive spirit prevading this legislation and its enforcement.

As a signatory to the Hague Convention, the United States government agreed to take steps to control narcotics production, sale, use, and traffic within and across its borders. The so-called Harrison Act of 1914 was the instrument by which these steps were to be taken. The Act, as amended, continues in force to date. Its most portentious provision proved to be one requiring that persons legitimately dealing in narcotics (importers, manufacturers, wholesalers, retailers, pharmacists, physicians, etc.) must register with the Treasury Department and pay an appropriate tax, consisting either of an impost of one cent per ounce or a vocational tax of up to $24. These taxes are not heavy, but the penalties for failing to register or to pay the taxes are severely so, and it is within this feature of the law that the Bureau of Narcotics ferrets out illicit users and underworld traffickers. Unfortunately, a series of early decisions upholding convictions under the Act of certain unscrupulous physicians had the eventual effect of scaring physicians away from the treatment of addicts whose therapy would require the administration of drugs. Although later rulings held that treatment in good faith is legitimate, the damage was done. One critic of the Harrison Act has stated that the Bureau of Narcotics persists to this day in misinforming physicians as to their rights in treating addicts by citing in its administrative instructions to them a "discredited" court ruling of 1919.[45] Threats by the

---

[45] King, *loc. cit.*, p. 123. The moving spirit behind the Bureau's enforcement practices was for many years Mr. Harry J. Anslinger, Federal Commissioner of Narcotics and chief of the Bureau. Mr. Anslinger retired in 1962 at the age of 70; his successor is Mr. Henry L. Giordano, an employee of the Bureau since 1941 and Deputy Commissioner since 1958. He is reported to share Mr. Anslinger's view that drug addiction is chiefly a problem of law enforcement [New York *Herald Tribune* (July 6, 1962)].

Treasury Department of criminal prosecution of persons establishing narcotics clinics closed down some 40 such clinics in the early 1920's; under Anslinger, the Bureau maintained a flinty opposition to the clinic idea, branding it "impractical, immoral, and downright subversive." [46]

Underscoring our American penchant for trying to solve social problems by legislating against them, Congress in 1952 passed the stringent Boggs Act, the chief provisions of which (1) require that *all* federally convicted narcotic drug offenders receive mandatory minimum sentences; (2) establish minimums escalated for first, second, and third convictions respectively of two, five, and ten years; and (3) prohibit probation for offenders convicted more than once. After conducting lengthy hearings throughout the country, a subcommittee of the Senate Judiciary Committee proposed yet heavier penalties; these became law as part of the Narcotics Control Act of 1956. A narcotics offender can now be fined up to $20,000 in addition to being imprisoned; peddlers and pushers face minimum sentences of five years, increasing to 10 years on two or more offenses; adults providing drugs to juveniles are to receive minimums of 10 years, or life imprisonment or death if the drug is heroin.

Apart from penal legislation, the use of public clinics, the English system of licensing physicians to give drugs to addicts, and educational programs are of chief interest. Clinics, which were once tried locally and which some advocate today, are intended not to cure addicts but to provide a legitimate source of supply at a price so low that illegitimate vendors must go out of business; to relieve suffering; to prevent victimization by underworld peddlers; and to prevent crime. The argument for the clinic rests upon the relief of unnecessary suffering, destruction of a vicious racket, elimination of necessity for the addict to steal in order to escape from the torment of withdrawal pains, and reduction of the expense involved in enforcing the Harrison Act. The defenders of the clinics hold that physicians can usually identify genuine addicts, can keep them in balance without pain, and can educate against the dangers of addiction. Treatment would be by specialists attached to general medical clinics, thus permitting confidential relations between addicts and physicians. It is difficult to see how such clinics properly administered would, as their opponents claim, create new addicts. An almost complete absence of an illegal supply of drugs, and of a profit motive to supply them, should aid control.

Britain's counterpart to the Harrison Act is the Dangerous Drugs Act of 1920, which ended more or less open traffic in narcotics and is the basic legislation within which the English system of addiction-treatment takes

[46] *Ibid.,* p. 125.

place. The official British position on the nature of addiction is that it is a health and not a moral problem, at least with respect to the use of morphine and heroin.[47] Addicts are not required to register as such in Great Britain and may seek assistance from private physicians under the National Health Act (i.e., "socialized medicine"). In treating addicts, doctors are guided by the report of a 1924 Parliamentary committee which studied medical and health aspects of the Dangerous Drugs Act. The report said in part that

. . . morphine or heroin may properly be administered to addicts in the following circumstances, namely, (a) where patients are under treatment by the gradual withdrawal method with a view to cure, (b) where it has been demonstrated, after a prolonged cure, that the use of the drug cannot be safely discontinued entirely, on account of the severity of the withdrawal symptoms produced, (c) where it has been similarly demonstrated that the patient, while capable of leading a useful and relatively normal life when a certain minimum dose is regularly administered, becomes incapable of this when the drug is entirely discontinued.[48]

Despite the fact that addicts under treatment are permitted to administer prescribed drugs to themselves in their own homes, apparently very few cases of doctors being tricked out of prescriptions have arisen.

As every sociology student knows, risks are entailed in transplanting traits from one culture to another. Those advocating adoption of the British system for the United States should be aware that Britain has such a small number of addicts [49] that the problem of addiction is nearly negligible, and that the socio-economic characteristics of British addicts differ considerably from those in the United States. American addicts are likely to be young males of minority-group status, living in a few large cities, whose addiction is associated with criminal activity; British addicts are likely to be older, female, law-abiding, representative ecologically and status-wise of the general population, and whose addiction is not associated with criminality.[50] Moreover, British narcotics use has not become a significantly institutionalized pattern within subcultures as it has in this country, where the consumption of narcotics is to some extent supported by subcultural norms.[51]

[47] Schur, *op. cit.*, p. 71.
[48] *Ibid.*, p. 76.
[49] The number reported in 1959 was 454 (*ibid.*, p. 119).
[50] *Ibid.*, pp. 122–29.
[51] On this, see particularly Harold Finestone, "Cats, Kicks and Color," *Social Problems* (July 1957), pp. 3–13. Finestone attempted to depict social types among 50 young male Negro heroin users in Chicago, concluding that the blasé, "cool," pseudo-sophisticated posing among these poverty-stricken youths is one of several possible reactions to their demeaned social status. Also see his "Narcotics and Criminality," *Law and Contemporary Problems* (Winter, 1957), pp. 69–85. Howard S. Becker's "Becoming a Marihuana User" *American Journal of Sociology* (Nov. 1953),

No system will be free of defects, but our present repressive policy with the suffering and racketeering it involves seems a major blunder. Provision of drugs at cost could kill the racket except, perhaps, so far as wealthy addicts might prefer to pay a much greater price if they objected to going to the clinics or the licensed physicians. With proper care, publicity could be avoided, however, and the stigma itself should decline with the dissociation of addiction from crime in the public mind.

Our culture produces relative failures. One escape from the reality of failure is by way of drugs. Hence our culture produces drug addiction. But some of our laws—also expressions of our culture—seem to make the situation worse. It is not claimed, of course, that the English system or clinics would eliminate "search" for euphoria or for escape from personal problems.

THE DRUG ADDICTION CONTROVERSY

Drug addiction is a highly controversial topic. There is disagreement as to the essential nature of the addict and even as to the definition of "narcotic." There is disagreement as to the relative importance of personal versus social causes of addiction. There is disagreement as to the curability of addiction, and as to the reality of some cures claimed. There is disagreement as to how far treatment methods infringe on personal liberties. There is disagreement as to the seriousness of withdrawal pains. There is even disagreement as to whether children should be taught the truth about drugs, the Narcotics Bureau apparently preferring ignorance plus information derived from the underworld to knowledge provided by teachers. There is especially disagreement over the effectiveness of repressive methods, though all recognize that some controls are needed. There is disagreement about the value of the Harrison Act, and more disagreement about its interpretation and enforcement. Many feel that the Narcotics Bureau conceives of the problem too largely as one of law enforcement. Critics complain that present policies compel addicts to be known as criminals in order to seek a cure.

The criminologist who is not a specialist in drug addiction cannot fully resolve these controversies. We have emphasized the social rather than the personal causes of addiction and have found some of its roots lying deep in the general culture. We agree with Professor Lindesmith [52] that the

---

pp. 235–42, analyzes the process through which a marihuana user learns of the habit from his group, especially the techniques to employ for the greatest enjoyment of the drug.

[52] Alfred R. Lindesmith, "Handling the Opiate Problem," *Federal Probation* (Dec. 1948), pp. 23–25.

interpretation and enforcement of the Harrison Act has been unnecessarily cruel to some addicts, and that physicians or clinics might well be permitted to administer drugs to keep addicts out of pain. We disagree with former Commissioner Anslinger when he says that the English system or these public clinics would neglect the cure of addiction and would increase the number of new addicts.[53] It is of great significance that the New York Academy of Medicine has published a report [54] extremely critical of the administration of our drug laws and strongly advocating the use of clinics where drugs may be furnished by competent physicians.

A vicious circle has been created by our present policies of suppressing the drug traffic: suppression drives up the price of drugs purchased illicitly; the consequent higher prices increase the profit-making possibilities and attract to the racket shrewder traffickers, who in turn must be outwitted by the authorities. The addict, faced with higher prices, must increase his efforts to support his habit; these may include not only spending a larger portion of his legitimate income (if any) for drugs, but exploiting with increasing desperation illegitimate sources, including armed robbery of physicians and druggists.

In our opinion, ending the illicit drug racket can best be accomplished by taking the profits out of the sale of narcotics through adoption of a suitably Americanized version of the British system of addict-supply, through public clinics, or through a combination of both. The treatment and prevention of addiction could then be redefined as a socio-medical rather than as a law-enforcement problem and dealt with accordingly.

Suggested Readings

Annals of the American Academy of Political and Social Science (Jan. 1958). Symposium of 16 articles on alcoholism.
Law and Contemporary Problems (Winter, 1957). Nine articles on narcotics.

[53] In view of this controversy the reader may be interested to contrast different discussions of this problem. For emphasis upon the need for repression and the danger of clinics, see H. J. Anslinger and William F. Tomkins, *The Traffic in Narcotics* (New York: Funk & Wagnalls Company, 1953). For emphasis on the medical aspects of the problem by experienced specialists and for a somewhat intermediate position toward policies, see the book by Drs. Maurer and Vogel already referred to. For critical views of our present repressive policies written by an academic specialist, see Alfred R. Lindesmith, *Opiate Addiction* (Bloomington, Ind.: Principia Press, 1947), and the article by the same author, "Handling the Opiate Problem," *Federal Probation* (Dec. 1948). See also the annual reports of the United States Bureau of Narcotics.

[54] "Report on Drug Addiction," by the Academy's Committee on Public Health, Subcommittee on Drug Addiction. Prepublication typewritten copy (New York: The Academy, June 7, 1955).

Lindesmith, Alfred R. *Opiate Addiction*. Bloomington, Ind.: Principia Press, 1947. An exploration of group influences in addiction, and a rejoinder to the claim that most addiction is a direct result of personality disorders.

Pittman, David, and Gordon, C. Wayne. *Revolving Door: A Study of the Chronic Police Case Inebriate*. Glencoe, Ill.: The Free Press, 1958. An analysis of sociocultural and sociopsychological characteristics of 187 chronic drunks in Monroe County, New York.

Rubington, Earl. "The Chronic Drunkenness Offender," *Annals* (Jan. 1958). The subculture and social functions of Skid Road are discussed.

CHAPTER 15

Sex Offenses

The category of "sex offenses" embraces a behavioral range of such breadth that we might well question the wisdom even of utilizing the concept for scientific purposes. The following list of sex crimes is incomplete but illustrates our point:

adultery
animal contacts
fornication
exhibitionism
incest
indecent assault
indecent shows and exhibitions
mutual masturbation
oral copulation by force
peeping
pornography

prostitution
public mating of certain
    animals
rape, forcible and statutory
seduction under promise to
    marry
sex contacts with corpses
sexual molestation of children
sodomy
using obscene language

Moreover, the 52 criminal law jurisdictions in the United States by no means agree on what sexual activities are appropriately designated as criminal. Even among those codes exhibiting agreement, wide differences are found in punitive measures attaching to them.[1] But the 52 codes share a common cultural ancestry, and

[1] An excellent summary of these differences will be found in Morris Ploscowe, "Sex Offenses: The American Legal Context," *Law and Contemporary Problems* (Spring, 1960), pp. 217–24.

taken together they bespeak past feelings that only conventional hetero-sexual relations carried on within marriage should be countenanced, since virtually every other imaginable form of direct or indirect sexual expression is prohibited in one or another of the codes.

The enforcement of sex laws, however, is quite another matter. Public sentiments toward enforcement vary from indifference to militant deter-mination and may basically depend less upon the nature of particular acts themselves than upon the degree to which other, non-sexual norms are violated during their commission. Compared to their probable incidence in the population, the crimes of adultery, fornication, "perverse" foreplay in heterosexual relations, and private homosexuality between consenting adults, are not crimes whose known or suspected existence results in any significant amount of reporting to the authorities. At the other extreme, however, are the far less frequent but actively abhorred offenses of rape, incest, indecent assault, exhibitionism, and child molestation. If, as sociologists, we eschew attempts to explain these differential attitudes by recourse to Freudian theory, to notions of degrees of sinfulness, and so on, and ask instead what non-sexual elements pertain respectively to the two groups of offenses, the answer suggests that the diversity of sentiments toward their enforcement might rest simply in pragmatic judgments of their social harm. For the most part, the offenses in the first group are performed privately on a basis of mutual consent and involve little, if any, of the "criminal-and-victim" rela-tionship. Public decency and order are not threatened, at least in the short run. Those in the second group, however, violate the general cultural proscriptions against victimization (particularly where the victim is of tender years), assaults on personal integrity and safety, and "public" ex-pression of physiological needs. Here, decency and order tend to be per-ceived as clearly and immediately threatened to a degree at which inaction is intolerable.

The criminologist is interested in sex crimes for several reasons. In the first place a substantial amount of organized crime relates directly or in-directly to the possibilities of profiting from disapproved concupiscent activities: prostitution, pornography, lewd movies and shows, pandering to men with extraordinary sexual proclivities, etc. In the second place vice, because it is usually underworld illicit behavior, tends to ramify to non-sexual crime in various ways. The vice area attracts and harbors elements engaged in more serious crimes than sex delinquency. Contacts with prosti-tutes and their exploiters and patrons may accustom children to sex delin-quency. Moreover, the prostitute herself and her pimp or procurer are sometimes confederates in non-sexual criminal gangs. Thirdly, sex offenses are partly a problem which is largely, but not wholly, attitudinal; that is, some aspects of the problem would disappear could attitudes toward sex be changed and agreement on the changes achieved. Finally, because of our attitudes, perhaps no aspect of penal and correctional treatment appears more irrational, unjust, and ineffective than the treatment of sex offenders.

History of Social Attitudes Toward Sex Behavior

Some primitive customs suggest a practically unlimited opportunity for sexual gratification,[2] permitting a trivialization of the sex function such as some modernists advocate for modern man. Yet the rich variety of primitive practices calling for inhibition of sex impulses prevents such a generalization. Primitive experience shows that man can live with some degree of satisfaction under widely different sex ethics. Margaret Mead [3] has told us both how the New Guinea tribes out-Puritan the Puritans in their restrictions upon sex and how the Samoans largely avoid psychoneuroses and worry over sex through a relative freedom for adolescents to follow their inclinations. It appears, however, that even the Samoan girl is sometimes frustrated [4] and that neither sex repression nor sex freedom is congenial to every individual. Primitive society at least presented to its young people more consistent sex mores than does modern society.

Hebrew insistence on continence [5] was more concerned with preventing relations with alien religious cults than with preventing extramarital intercourse between Hebrews. The Pharisees and Essenes, however, condemned sex vice.

Christian asceticism comes not so much from the teachings of Jesus as from the element of Oriental dualism, implying the antithesis of the moral and physical, found in the doctrine of St. Paul. Moreover Christians revolted against the sexual excesses of the Romans. Thus the Christian church came to comdemn all forms of sexual relations with the exception of life-long union of one man with one woman and also all stimuli which would

[2] Robert Briffault, *Sin and Sex* (New York: Macaulay Company, 1931), p. 91.

[3] Cf. *Coming of Age in Samoa, Growing up in New Guinea* (New York: Blue Ribbon Books, 1928, 1930).

[4] Ira S. Wile, *The Sex Life of an Unmarried Adult* (New York: Vanguard Press, 1934), p. 73.

[5] Cf. Geoffrey May, *Social Control of Sex Expression* (New York: William Morrow & Company, 1930), pp. 3–4, and George Ryley Scott, *A History of Prostitution* (New York: Greenberg Publishers, 1936), chap. 8.

arouse sex impulses. Practice departed, of course, from these standards. The story of the immorality of some of the clergy is well known, and there was a considerable development of concubinage. Prostitution was frowned upon but it was sometimes considered a necessary evil that protected woman's virtue.

Colonial New England inherited the Puritan sex morality from England, though her laws and their enforcement differed somewhat. Massachusetts Colony alone provided capital punishment for adultery, and three persons are known to have been executed. In Massachusetts, public opinion supported the laws, and there seems to have been relative obedience to them. Yet the many convictions for fornication showed the ineffectiveness of the penalties in spite of such popular support. Severity is said to have led to homosexual practices, and bundling became the recognized concomitant of courtship, at least among the poor. This Puritan morality is the basis of our law and tradition today.

Prostitution

Mores and laws repressing sex expression have created a demand for forbidden indulgence, which in turn has been met by prostitutes. The significant elements in prostitution are those of reward and promiscuity. Yet tolerance of marriage for money, easy divorce, and some promiscuity in sex relations short of intercourse show that these elements of reward and promiscuity do not completely distinguish prostitution from legal or even moral sex relations.

The history of prostitution shows the extraordinary persistence of vice in the face of intermittent efforts to abolish it. It also shows attitudes toward the institution varying from approval, through acceptance and tolerance, to violent opposition. Whenever the institution of marriage weakened, prostitution declined because gratification could be obtained without payment. Thus prostitution in a way is an index of "morality" rather than "immorality." Similarly, the attitude toward the prostitute herself has varied from the esteem in which some priestesses and the Greek *hetarae* were held to the scorn which virtuous women feel toward the modern prostitute. Generally speaking, however, in our society a stigma has been attached to the prostitute's calling, which has prevented her from escaping from it when she desired and has been the basis for her exploitation.

In the fifteenth and sixteenth centuries, venereal disease imported from the New World took firm hold on Europe, and a reform movement began which involved cruel persecution of prostitutes. There followed alternating periods of repression and toleration. On the Continent, prostitution finally came to be tolerated and regulated, and campaigns against it were considered futile, but anti-vice crusades continued in England and America. Recently, Continental countries have tended to adopt, on paper at least, repressive policies rather than merely regulatory policies involving licensing of prostitutes.

Laws against prostitution in America were only spasmodically enforced, while many cities came to license vice. Not until after some 30 investigations early in the twentieth century was the modern repressive campaign begun. Concentration of one sex in camps during both world wars tended toward an increase in prostitution, but repressive measures were also made more effective. The older attitude of military leaders that prostitution is inevitable in wartime and even essential to morale did not wholly disappear, but there was increased agreement upon policies of repression combined with efforts to provide substitute social activities. Attitudes toward prophylactic protection against venereal disease provided by the army varied. A very important development has been the use of penicillin, permitting quick cure for gonorrhea within a few hours and of the earlier stages of syphilis in a few weeks. This has meant reduction in suffering; it probably also has weakened the view that disease is a penalty for sin.

PROSTITUTION AS A BY-PRODUCT OF AMERICAN CULTURE

Prostitution expresses in part the profit-making interest in our culture. The girl herself, her pimp and other individual exploiters, and the large syndicate which at times organizes vice, all follow the larger pattern of struggle for material gain by more or by less fair and socially desirable means. The difficulties experienced in controlling prostitution when large minorities of individuals desire it, the abandonment of the prostitute herself to her fate, since she is conceived of as having freely chosen the "wrong" path, and her punishment for behavior secretly approved by many illustrate the American pattern of individualism with a minimum of sense of social responsibility. The whole is modified, however, by the persistence of moral patterns which condemn this source of profit-making but which increasingly tolerate related behavior. Thus respectable citizens may indulge in or tolerate sex behavior essentially like prostitution while scorning the prostitute herself. Prostitution reflects our culture; yet changes in that culture compete with it and are seemingly fatal to its existence.

NATURE AND PRESENT STATUS OF PROSTITUTION

The prostitute herself is indeed a sorry figure under our traditional mores. Prostitutes have been called "unspeakably degraded," but this term overlooks traits such as a not infrequent sympathy for others who, like themselves, have lost social status. They are at once protected and exploited by their pimps, who may have brought them into the game and toward whom many girls show a curious attraction and loyalty in spite of much abuse. The prostitute cannot appeal to the courts against exploitation, since her occupation is illegal. These girls are also both exploited and "mothered" by the madams who run the houses.

Formerly the prostitute was wholly an outcast. Once in the profession it was very hard to get out. More recently prostitutes have emerged through matrimony, obtained legitimate jobs, or even returned home, provided their former occupation was unknown or partially condoned in the home community. Prostitution thus is becoming more and more a temporary vocation for unadjusted girls and women. It is the less clever prostitute today who falls into the hands of the pimp, enters the organized house, or is prosecuted in our courts. These are the impressions of persons in close contact with prostitutes through police, public health, and rehabilitation work.

THE CONTROL OF PROSTITUTION

There is difference of opinion as to how far prostitution can be controlled, eliminated, or reduced. The American Social Hygiene Association has asserted: "The actual abolition of red-light districts and of single houses of prostitution outside of the district proved that commercialized prostitution can be destroyed." [6] On the other hand, Ernst, speaking of changing laws and attitudes with reference to vice, writes: ". . . the legislatures and the courts evidence their greatest ineptitude whenever they try to govern the emotional lives of men and women." [7] The contrast between these two statements is more apparent than real. In a small community, with opinion united, open prostitution and street solicitation can be stamped out. As a result clandestine vice increases. Clandestine vice is today the major sources of venereal disease. On the other hand, the number of contacts is reduced where open prostitution is eliminated. Even with changing

[6] *Social Hygiene Legislation Manual,* Publication No. 312 (New York: The Association, 1921), p. 7.

[7] Morris L. Ernst, "Changing Laws and Changing Attitudes," in Wile, *op. cit.,* p. 213.

patterns of behavior some prostitution will presumably remain for the gratification of old or unattractive men.

One thing is certain: the control of prostitution entails far more than the rehabilitation of individual prostitutes and the enforcement of laws against them. A substantial part of prostitution constitutes one branch of organized, syndicated crime, along with gambling, narcotics, and dealing in illicit liquor. Control measures which ignore this circumstance may suppress those prostitutes operating on an independent, hit-or-miss basis but are not likely to make a serious dent in syndicated prostitution.

REPRESSION, REGULATION, AND OTHER POLICIES

Prostitution may be tolerated without attempt at regulation; it may be virtually licensed with attempts at regulation; it may be repressed. The European system of registration and inspection has been generally condemned as ineffective, and the trend has been toward its abandonment. No system of control short of examination after every act could make promiscuous sex relations fully safe. It has been said that laboratory tests needed would require at least two days' time.[8] The incidence of disease is, of course, by no means the only consideration.

In the United States, cycles of toleration and almost hysterical attempts to enforce the law have been oft repeated. Surveys as late as 1954 by the American Social Hygiene Association showed conditions fairly satisfactory to them in a majority of centers, but unsatisfactory in a considerable minority.[9]

The experience of large cities like New York and Chicago in attempting to repress vice is illuminating. It has shown the impossibility of enforcing stringent laws against individual sex offenders; the possibility of reducing the more open forms of vice, including street soliciting; the resulting demoralization of policemen when they had to "make" a case against a woman; the impossibility of enforcing the law effectively against male patrons; the ease with which well-meaning private organizations assisting in repressive activities may be hoodwinked; the bribing or indirect involvement of police, prosecuting attorneys, and magistrates; the involvement in some cities of huge racketeering syndicates most difficult, though not

---

[8] Lieut. Colonel Thomas B. Turner, "The Suppression of Prostitution in Relation to Venereal Disease Control in the Army," *Federal Probation* (April–June, 1943), p. 10.

[9] See the files of their magazine, the *Journal of Social Hygiene,* which discontinued publication in 1954. The group changed its name in 1959 to the American Social Health Association. The long-time trend of prostitution is certainly downward, but that decline is not entirely, and probably not chiefly, due to repression.

impossible, to reach; flight of establishments to outlying suburban jurisdictions when "the heat was on," to return under a more lenient administration; the general failure of specialized women's courts to handle the problem effectively; and the occasional framing of innocent women.

The policy of repression involves the use of general and special legal machinery as well as of public and private agencies of a more socially constructive nature. These agencies include special vice squads within the regular police organization; women police; detention homes for women and girls; private agencies engaged primarily in assisting in the prosecution of sex delinquents or owners of property used for vicious purposes; special public defenders; girls' divisions of juvenile courts; womens' or family courts and courts of domestic relations; probation service for girls; child placement agencies concerned with exploiters of children and dealing by case-work methods with sex delinquents; private institutions for delinquent girls; clinics and hospitals for the venereally diseased; public institutions for delinquent girls and for adult sex offenders; parole or other after-care activities so far as they concern the sex delinquent; and special organizations for the repression of the traffic in women and children. In general, all these agencies still reflect primarily the old morality, though they have in varying degrees been influenced by the new. Vice control has been called the chief menace to police departments.[10] At a different level women police organizations play an important part in relation to sex delinquency.[11]

Some cities have developed specialized morals or women's courts for treatment of sex offenders.[12] These differ somewhat today in the relative success achieved, though it seems that none has fulfilled the promise of their early days. Their standards seem inadequate because they disregard our changed and conflicting sex morality. The failure of these courts is but a part of the failure of the whole system of penal treatment as applied to sex offenders in particular.

Private agencies concerned with the treatment of sex delinquents are of many types. Many, such as juvenile protective associations, protect adolescent girls against sex exploitation. Girls' Senior Leagues, child-placing agencies, and sundry religious organizations work with the individual girl with varying degrees of approved case-work methods. The American Social Health Association is the chief national organization in this field. There is no question of the value of the research, legislative, organizational, and

[10] Leonard V. Harrison, *Police Administration in Boston* (Cambridge, Mass.: Harvard University Press, 1934), p. 144.

[11] Eleanor L. Hutzel, "The Policewoman's Role in Social Protection," *Journal of Social Hygiene* (Dec. 1944), pp. 538–44.

[12] George E. Worthington and Ruth Topping, *Specialized Courts Dealing with Sex Delinquency* (New York: Bureau of Social Hygiene, 1925), pp. 396*ff*.

educational work of this organization. However, its philosophy seems to have been but little affected by changes in attitudes and behavior patterns discussed earlier in this chapter.

WHITE SLAVE TRAFFIC AND ITS REPRESSION

The control of commercialized vice has important international aspects. Foot-loose travelers, traders, sailors, and soldiers seek the prostitute. Men who are abroad feel less the restraints of group opinion. The foreign prostitute satisfies a certain desire for variety and she is less under control. Hence she is easily exploited. Hence the traffic in women and children and the efforts at its international control. Previous international agreements have been integrated and amended in the Convention for the Suppression of Traffic in Persons and of Exploitation of Prostitution (A–1164) signed in 1949 and which came into effect July 25, 1952. There is also a Convention for the Suppression of Circulation of Obscene Publications. The former of these conventions is notable because it abolishes the registration of prostitutes and obligates the states which are parties to it not only as previously to cooperate in the punishment of those engaged in the traffic but also to deal constructively with the women involved. International machinery has brought about coordination of research, the exchange of rather unreliable statistics and of information as to control methods, frequent conferences and efforts to control disease through the control of communication routes, and latterly efforts to rehabilitate and repatriate foreign prostitutes if they so desire. United Nations activities in this field center in the Social Commission of the Economic and Social Council and in the venereal disease program of the World Health Organization, not to mention the work of earlier organizations.

Drs. Guthe and Hume,[13] writing in 1948, held that the record of achievement at the international level had not been impressive. The disordered post-war situation found open prostitution widespread in much of the world. In a few countries, including Soviet Russia and Sweden, a dramatic fall in venereal disease was associated with experimentation with new and constructive methods of control and prevention.

AMERICAN WARTIME CONTROL OF PROSTITUTION

While war conditions greatly stimulate prostitution, the enforcement of repression is a bit easier in wartime. During World War II, the War Department (later the Department of the Army) laid down a policy of

[13] Thorsten Guthe and John C. Hume, "International Aspects of the Venereal Disease Problem," *Journal of Social Hygiene* (Feb. 1948), pp. 51–55.

venereal disease control. The Army officially emphasized the possibility and desirability of continence. In its propaganda but not always in its practice, it stressed a moral and spiritual approach to the problem and emphasized the individual responsibility of the soldier.[14] The commanding officer of a post was responsible for administering the policy. Prophylaxis was to be mentioned to the troops but not stressed. Infected men were put under a 30-to-90-day quarantine not intended as a punitive measure. The provost marshal enforced off-limits restrictions designed to keep soldiers from entering notorious areas. The prime duty of the Disciplinary Board was to reduce venereal disease. A major control measure was the May Bill, passed by Congress in 1941, which prohibited prostitution within designated, reasonable distances from military or naval establishments. The program against vice was organized under an Eight-Point Agreement. Soldiers who repeatedly exposed themselves might have their passes restricted. Control of the women who were the source of infection was left, however, in the hands of the police of the community. A system of confidential reports by soldiers concerning the contacts through which they had become infected enabled discovery and treatment of the women. Since the war, the work of the armed services and various agencies has been conducted under the Social Protection Division of the Federal Security Board. Control measures were and are supplemented by preventive programs of education and recreation. In spite of all this effort, clandestine prostitution cannot be stamped out, and noncommercialized sex relations are naturally very numerous.

SUGGESTED POLICIES

In the light of experience, dishonesty and corrupted police are well-nigh inherent in the repressive system. Repressive activities leave the basic problem untouched. Always they must be evaluated in terms of substitute sex activities which they may stimulate. These include clandestine prostitution, which today is a major source of venereal disease, unpaid sex relations, so-called perversions, and lesser degrees of intimacy tolerated or approved among many young people. In contrast there are those who still advocate licensed prostitution, but their number has declined. Social workers have urged that prostitutes themselves be dealt with as sick persons, that treatment be constructive, and that the women's court become a clinic.

[14] Cf. Major Louis N. Altshuler, "U. S. War Department Venereal Disease Control Program," *Journal of Social Hygiene* (June 1947), pp. 259–71. See also Commander George W. Mast, "Venereal Disease Control in the United States Navy," *ibid.*, pp. 272–78.

The trend is probably toward such a policy. The ultraliberal in this field faces a certain dilemma. On the one hand, it seems to him unjust that the prostitute be denied social status if her vocation is to be recognized. On the other hand, few liberals probably would wish their own daughters to enter the profession.

Within the limits of the present system, there would seem to be no complete cure for the problem. Only basic changes in attitudes, codes, social and economic systems, and philosophy of life would seem to be adequate, and even at such deep levels it is difficult to define the ultimate goal. Some forms of sex activity involving violence and exploitation simply cannot be tolerated, yet tolerance and understanding, rather than hypocrisy and punishment, seem generally to be called for, especially in a period of moral confusion. Meanwhile, medicine is curing and preventing venereal disease; prostitution has become a dying institution save under unusual conditions or for unusual people; and young people are introducing substitute sex activities.

THE PROSTITUTE

Although dozens of studies of prostitutes have been conducted by specialists in the several behavioral sciences, our understanding of this particular species of offender is still sketchy. Prostitutes are ordinarily "captured" for study only when they become enmeshed in a law-enforcement or correctional net, with the consequent likelihood existing that the captives are atypical of the sorority. While a few girls endowed with beauty, charm, and good connections enter the most select branch of prostitution— that of the highly-paid "call-girl"—the majority have gotten into a tawdry, dead-end livelihood in which they are at the mercy of pimps, madams, racketeers, corrupt policemen, and customers.

"Captured" prostitutes are a sorry lot. The Gluecks found in a study involving about 250 prostitutes that social backgrounds ranged from the sordidly wretched to "barely adequate": their parents were typically semi-literate members of the urban and rural proletariat who had not provided settings for the development of good character or constructive self-conceptions in their children. The girls had typically drifted away from home and school at an early age and had entered the labor market as unskilled workers in dull, underpaid jobs. Psychopathy, feeble-mindedness, and emotional instability were present among the girls to a disproportionate degree.[15] A

---

[15] Sheldon and Eleanor T. Glueck, *500 Delinquent Women* (New York: Alfred A. Knopf, 1934).

similarly dismal social-background picture emerged from a study of 530 Danish prostitutes, of whom only 29 per cent were judged to be "normal" in character or mentality. The presence of chronic physical disabilities (exclusive of venereal disease) had, in addition, contributed to this group's unsuccessful competition in the legitimate labor market.[16]

The most illuminating study to date of the process of induction into prostitution is that of an English inquiry based on interviews with 69 girls contacted by investigators in the girls' native heaths, the streets of London. The typical hustler drifts to London in her late teens or early twenties after experiencing unsatisfactory work and social adjustment in her home city. She obtains work as a waitress or counter girl and for a time lives a rootless, disorganized life without friends and without ties to stabilizing social institutions. During this crucial period she is tense, dissatisfied, bitter, and bewildered. Her drifting brings her into contact with established prostitutes, whose tinsel finery and seeming security she finds appealing. Her morale at low ebb, and hungry for at least a simulacrum of friendship and affection she accepts "dates" arranged for her by the prostitute (or by the latter's pimp). Her dawning awareness that she is moving outside the pale of lawful society is hastened by her first two or three arrests, after which these experiences come to be viewed as occupational risks. Eventually she becomes stabilized in her calling, finds her friends almost exclusively among the underworld, and acquires recognized status as a prostitute.[17]

Homosexuality

Sexual relations between persons of the same sex are punishable under statutes prohibiting sodomy, fellatio, and mutual masturbation regardless of the sexes of the parties involved. In practice, these statutes are seldom invoked where the parties are of differing sex, but English and American values are strongly set against their being practiced between persons of the same sex. Sodomy (sometimes called "buggery"), long an ecclesiastical offense, was prohibited by statute in 1533 and made punishable by death, while church canons forbade fellatio and mutual masturbation; all are the subject of statutory enactment in the United States.[18]

In recent years considerable discussion has occurred on the necessity or

[16] Tage Kemp, *Prostitution* (Copenhagen: Levin and Munksgaard, 1936).

[17] C. H. Rolph, ed., *Women of the Streets: A Sociological Study of the Common Prostitute* (London: Secker and Warburg, 1955).

[18] For a brief history of English homosexual legislation, see François Lafitte, "Homosexuality and the Law," *British Journal of Delinquency* (July 1958), pp. 8–19.

wisdom of enforcing these statutes when the prohibited behavior is engaged in privately through mutual consent by adults of the same sex—that is, homosexually. The stimulus to this dialogue is traceable in considerable measure to the first Kinsey Report, which informed the public that "at least 37 per cent of the male population has had some homosexual experience." [19] Kinsey himself contributed to the popular misinterpretation of this finding by referring to this percentage as being that of "the homosexual in the population" and to the 37 per cent as "homosexuals." [20] Careless reading of the report and still more careless publicizing of its findings produced the widespread impression that homosexuals constitute a large minority of the male population. In fact, however, Kinsey's data showed nothing of the kind. *One* sexual connection to the point of orgasm with a person of the same sex was sufficient to put a respondent among the 37 per cent; what proportion of his respondents reported more than one such experience cannot be determined from the published Kinsey data, nor are data presented on the proportion of the 37 per cent who were practicing homosexuals *at the time of their interviews*. That the proportion is less than 37 per cent is suggested by his finding that only 6.3 per cent of the orgasms experienced during the accumulated lifetimes of his respondents were derived from homosexual contacts.[21] Ten per cent of his respondents had been "more or less exclusively homosexual . . . for at least three years between the ages of 16 and 55," [22] but the definition of homosexual used in making this particular tally is not clear.[23]

At any rate, the Kinsey Report, along with several celebrated cases of blackmail of homosexual government employees in connection with East-West cold war espionage, and public concern over seeming post-war moral changes, have contributed to an awareness of the existence of homosexuality not seen in English-speaking countries since Oscar Wilde was convicted of sodomy in 1895. But in contrast with the unbending Victorian condemnations heaped upon Wilde and other homosexuals (then spoken of darkly as men of "unnatural desires"—about as specific as a Victorian could get) the latter-day dialogue is open, frank, and uniquely sensible. Of particular significance has been the development among some legal theoreticians,

[19] A. C. Kinsey, W. B. Pomeroy, and C. E. Martin, *Sexual Behavior in the Human Male* (Philadelphia: W. B. Saunders Company, 1948), p. 623.

[20] *Ibid.,* p. 626.

[21] *Ibid.,* p. 610.

[22] *Ibid.,* p. 651.

[23] *Ibid.,* pp. 639–41. "Psychic responses" of a homosexual nature as well as overt homosexual behavior were factors in ranking respondents on a scale of homosexual intensity, but no replicable details used in measuring "psychical response" or in combining this with overt acts are supplied the reader.

psychiatrists, clergymen, and others of the notion that legislation of private morals is an improper function of government when social harm resulting from presently illegal behavior cannot be shown to exist. In discussing the inconsistencies of present sex legislation, Professor Stanton Wheeler points out that some of the difficulty can be attributed to the existence of varying aims underlying this legislation. It attempts to (1) reflect the public's sense of revulsion and moral condemnation; (2) recognize the degree of social harm presumably inherent in sexual misbehavior; (3) express the degree of psychopathology characterizing the offender; and (4) take account of the difficulties of enforcing sex laws.[24] In both Britain and the United States substantial bodies of informed opinion now exist that (2) should be the primary basis for sex legislation and that (1) serves little or no useful purpose.

THE WOLFENDEN REPORT

In 1954 the British Home Secretary appointed a committee, under the chairmanship of a noted jurist, Sir John Wolfenden, to study the extent to which homosexual behavior and female prostitution should be regulated by law. In 1957 the committee issued its report.[25] Among 18 specific recommendations, the first, proposing that homosexual behavior between consenting adults in private be no longer a criminal offense, stirred much controversy on both sides of the Atlantic, striking as it did at the very heart of the centuries-old Anglo-Saxon interdiction against "crimes against nature." [26] At the present writing British law has not been altered in accordance with this recommendation, although a lively discussion of its implications and of the broader meanings and problems of homosexuality has occurred in connection with the work of the Wolfenden committee.[27] A public opinion sampling shortly after publication of the report showed that

[24] Stanton Wheeler, "Sex Offenses: A Sociological Critique," *Law and Contemporary Problems* (Spring, 1960), p. 261.

[25] Departmental Committee on Homosexual Offenses and Prostitution, *Report* (London: H. M. Stationery Office, 1957).

[26] Among others, the criminal codes of Sweden, Norway, Denmark, Belgium, and France either no longer punish sodomy between consenting adults or have made it punishable only in special cases. For the first four countries named, see Report of the Cambridge Department of Criminal Science, *Sexual Offenses* (London: Macmillan & Co., 1957), part 6. In 1961 the State of Illinois declared that homosexuality between consenting adults no longer involves criminal conduct.

[27] See, *inter alia*, the July, 1958, issue of the *British Journal of Delinquency*, which is devoted entirely to this matter; Eustace Chesser, *Live and Let Live* (London: Heinemann, 1958); Hervey Cleckley, *The Caricature of Love* (New York: Ronald Press, 1957); Peter Wildeblood, *A Way of Life* (London: Weidenfeld and Nicolson, 1956).

47 per cent of Britons opposed legalization of adult homosexuality, with 38 per cent favoring it and 15 per cent uncertain.[28] The American Law Institute, responding to currents of thought similar to those influencing the Wolfenden group, has recently proposed extensive changes in legislation regulating sexual offenses, including homosexuality.[29] If the tendency of Americans to out-Puritan the English again makes itself felt when popular response to the Model Code is eventually elicited, there is little likelihood that the proposals will find much support at the present time.

If adult consensual homosexuality is eventually accepted as socially harmless (a point which might prove exceedingly difficult to establish scientifically), interesting questions will arise concerning the extent to which this kind of behavior can continue to be looked upon as "abnormal." Those homosexuals who are vocal in defense of their "rights" to be homosexuals [30] without persecution from the Philistines are seemingly defining themselves as anything but abnormal. In this they received an assist from Kinsey, who holds that "it is difficult to maintain the view that psychosexual reactions between individuals of the same sex are rare and therefore abnormal or unnatural, or that they constitute within themselves evidence of neuroses or even psychoses." [31] On the other hand, homosexual conduct is viewed by many physicians and psychiatrists and by some psychologists as sexual aberrations arising from abnormal psycho-biological processes.[32] Legalizing homosexuality may have the further effect of reducing the defensive role of the homosexual subculture, which presently serves, among other things, to support the egos and relieve the anxieties of those sharing the culture.[33]

Trends in Attitudes Toward Sex Behavior

The old mores of sex which characterized Puritan New England still remain patterns approved at least in tradition. They may perhaps be summarized under the following statements:

[28] J. E. Hall Williams, "Sex Offenses: The British Experience," *Law and Contemporary Problems* (Spring, 1960), p. 355.

[29] *Model Penal Code, Tentative Draft No. 9*, 1959, Article 207.

[30] There are now published in the United States four homosexual periodicals: *One Quarterly, The Ladder, Mattachine Review*, and the League for Civil Education *News*.

[31] Kinsey, *op. cit.*, p. 659.

[32] Paul W. Tappan, *Crime, Justice and Correction* (New York: McGraw-Hill Book Company, 1960), pp. 106–07.

[33] Maurice Leznoff and William A. Westley, "The Homosexual Community," *Social Problems* (April 1956), 257–63.

1. Physical sex expression is basically evil, though necessary to procreation.
2. Sex expression for other purposes than procreation is especially evil, and its pleasurable aspects should be minimized.
3. There should be no sex intercourse outside of marriage and no voluntary physical sex expression by the unmarried.
4. Chastity, though enjoined upon both sexes, is peculiarly essential to women.
5. No special education or other preparation for married life is desirable other than that imparted by parents to children.
6. Sex being an evil, all stimuli intended to arouse sexual desire are immoral.
7. Venereal disease is a sort of punishment for sin, and the spread of information as to methods of cure and still more as to methods of prevention is dangerous, since it may increase promiscuous intercourse.
8. Intercourse between married couples being for procreation only, no knowledge of contraceptives is needed, and such knowledge should not be communicated because it would remove a deterrent to immoral behavior.
9. Though prostitution is immoral, it is preferable to illicit intercourse between those of the same social level and may even serve to protect innocent womanhood.

A significant trend characteristic of modern times has been the decline in the prestige of this code, the conflict with "the new morality," and the resulting moral confusion.

Conditions which have brought about these changed attitudes toward sex and changed patterns of behavior are many. Increased knowledge of biological facts and the decline of religious sanctions have undermined belief in the essential evil of sex. Modern industrialism has taken woman out of the home and given her as an alternative to marriage a career and a corresponding independence of masculine control. She has sometimes demanded among her "equal rights" the same opportunity as man to "sin or not to sin." Increased commercialization of all kinds of sex stimuli has had its influence.

Improved communications of all sorts have brought men into contact with varying types of moral and ethical values. The study of comparative ethnology has shown that sex morals have varied with the nature of the culture—that morals vary from place to place. The history of sexual ethics has shown that within the same culture what has been deemed right at one period has been labeled wrong at another and vice versa—that morals vary from time to time. These two discoveries have challenged the concept of absolute morality and substituted for it the notion that morality, though vitally important, is relative to the situation and the group.

Human migration has brought modern sex patterns into close geographical competition, compelling comparison and discussion and suggesting imitation. Puritan and Continental, East and Occidental, primitive and modern moralities have been brought into juxtaposition. Many persons have been disturbed by the belief that right and wrong are merely human valuations, implying the possibility of error which inheres in all the works of man. Disagreement and discussion have compelled a search for a more rational basis for morality on the part of the thoughtful few, while the thoughtless many have followed more and more their local group patterns.

If many families and church and school still preach the old morality, those primary groups whose approval young people most desire not infrequently have approved varying degrees of departure from it. Fear of venereal disease is less of a deterrent than formerly. Knowledge of birth control has made possible sexual indulgence with a minimum risk of its most important possible consequence. The very development of small groups practicing a new morality made it possible to violate the mores without complete loss of social status. Sex behavior has varied from indiscreet to illicit, and relations have been occasional or frequent, permanent or promiscuous, with close friends or casual acquaintances.[34] The double standard is said to continue to flourish, though the term is no longer fashionable. Today a new code of sex morality may be in process of development.

EVIDENCE OF SUCH TRENDS [35]

Have these changes in sex patterns shown themselves in the statistics of family life? A temporary increase in illegitimacy would be expected and appears in the not-too-dependable figures.

No evidence exists as to the trend of so-called perversions, but according to the Kinsey report discussed below, they are more prevalent than general opinion would expect, masturbation at an early age being well-nigh universal and homosexual activity characterizing a considerable minority. The trend of venereal disease appears to have been generally downward in the United States up to the end of World War II, with a rise in reported

[34] E. W. Burgess, "Sociological Aspects of the Sex Life of the Unmarried Adult," in Wile, *op. cit.*, pp. 126, 144.

[35] Kinsey, *op. cit.* See also footnote 38.

cases in 1945–46. Just what the trend has been since that time is uncertain. Some public health officials claim that venereal disease among juveniles is rising at an "alarming" rate, but difficulties in obtaining accurate statistics and the failure of agencies releasing such data to take demographic shifts into account make these claims dubious.[36]

The long-time trend of prostitution also seems to have been downward. The professional has met the competition of the amateur. This competition, rather than an increase in morality in the traditional sense of the word, and rather than any great influence of either repressive or constructive measures, would seem chiefly to explain the decline. Such a statement does not deny that repression may, under favorable conditions, immediately reduce open prostitution and make its large-scale organization at least temporarily unprofitable. Nor does it mean that efforts to provide recreation and substitute sources of social status are of no avail. These may affect both the prostitute and her potential customer.

Undoubtedly the most comprehensive and influential study of actual sex behavior is the recent work of Professor Alfred C. Kinsey already referred to. Its first volume concerns the behavior of some 5,300 men. Corresponding data on women showed a departure from the traditional sex code of similar nature but less in degree. The Kinsey report on men concludes that over 73 per cent of American males had had premarital intercourse by the time they were 20 and that only a small percentage remained virgin until marriage.[37] Similarly, Kinsey's later book [38] reports that "nearly 50 per cent of the females in the sample had had coitus before they were married," and that "among the married females in the sample, about one-quarter had had extramarital coitus by the age of 40." The two Kinsey volumes indicate a much greater percentage of the population violating the code through masturbation, premarital and postmarital intercourse, and homosexual activity than had generally been supposed. Publicity given to

[36] Celia S. Deschin, *Teen-Agers and Venereal Disease* (Atlanta, Ga.: U. S. Department of Health, Education, and Welfare, 1961), pp. 2–6.

[37] For a convenient but rather uncritical summary of the first volume of Kinsey findings, cf. Albert Deutsch, "The Sex Habits of American Men," *Harpers' Magazine* (Dec. 1947), pp. 497*ff*.

[38] A. C. Kinsey, W. B. Pomeroy, C. E. Martin, and Paul H. Gebhard, *Sexual Behavior in the Human Female* (Philadelphia: W. B. Saunders Company, 1953), pp. 287 and 416. This second volume appears to be methodologically an improvement over its predecessor. It recognizes that the following elements in the general population are underrepresented: rural groups; the southeastern quarter of the country; the Pacific Northwest and the Rocky Mountain area; Catholics; and previously married women, now widowed, separated, or divorced. The volume's most serious underrepresentation exists, however, with respect to Catholic women and to women with fewer than 13 years or more of schooling, the respective proportions of which were 12.3 and 20.1 per cent—far less than the actual percentages in the U. S. population of the time. Protestant and Jewish college students apparently constituted about half of Kinsey's sample (Table 1, p. 32).

this research will probably tend to reduce mental conflicts among those who had thought of themselves as unpardonably unworthy and abnormal because of code violations. This development might reduce crime. On the other hand, it is arguable that such publicity may also increase the frequency of violations.

On the basis of criticism [39] which cannot be fully verified, the following comments may be made:

1. It seems possible that the Kinsey study somewhat exaggerates the proportion of American men and women who have violated the code.
2. Its representativeness regionally, occupationally, educationally, and in terms of marital status may be open to some questions.
3. Kinsey's conclusion that there has been but little change in behavior patterns is open to question. At any rate we need and lack equally thorough studies for past decades.
4. While Kinsey's tendency to view petting as socially innocuous may be well founded, the basis for his evaluation has been challenged.

Even if all these criticisms are justified, the general conclusions of the Kinsey research remain unchallenged, and they have real import for an understanding of sex delinquency and for programs of prevention or treatment. Our treatment policies continue to implement the old morality, after our sex practices have departed greatly from its precepts.[40] At any rate various degrees of extramarital intimacy between the sexes are today tolerated, expected, enjoyed, and even demanded. The prevalence of these varying patterns among the general population seems to be one important reason why punishment of sex delinquents has been so ineffective. Even sex education which preaches the old sex ethic as the only proper one tends to seem hypocritical to them and is thus ineffective.

Causes of Sex Delinquency

In the light of the moral confusion and violations of the Puritanical sex code, the milder forms of sex delinquency seem almost normal. The juvenile apprehended for such violations and the girl who becomes an unmarried

[39] We are following rather closely here a scholarly review of the first Kinsey report: Lewis M. Terman, "Kinsey's *Sexual Behavior in the Human Male,*" *The Psychological Bulletin* (Sept. 1948), pp. 443–59.

[40] Even though actual behavior is at considerable variance with precepts, however, there is some evidence that attitudes toward premarital intercourse have not relaxed since at least the late 1930's. According to opinion-poll data, just 22 per cent of national respondent samples questioned in 1937 and in 1959 approved of premarital relations. See Stanton Wheeler, *loc. cit.*

mother come to appear as unlucky or ignorant rather than as distinctly deviant. The form of their behavior pattern, rather than its unsocial or immoral quality, is what needs to be explained. The types and degrees of behavior which appear must be explained also.

ALLEGED PERSONALITY DIFFERENCES

The very frequency of intercourse in extreme cases (reaching at least four or five experiences a day) argues strongly for individual differences in the strength of the sex drive. Biologists find variations in the nature and intensity of the endocrine influences. Yet the intensity of desire is also a cultural product, and we have no easy physiological explanation of sex delinquency. "The prostitute is seldom a nymphomaniac, though the nymphomaniac may become a prostitute." [41]

Apprehended sex delinquents are a highly selected group and logically should be less intelligent than the many who are not arrested. Similarly, minorities of sex delinquents have often been found emotionally unstable, psychopathic, neurotic, suggestible, or addicted to the use of tobacco, alcohol, or narcotic drugs. However, it has not yet been shown just how excessive are such traits among them as compared with control groups, nor that these characteristics are true causes of their delinquency.

ECONOMIC FACTORS

Fear of starvation seems to be a rare motive for entering the profession of prostitution.[42] Woolston concluded that prostitutes, before they entered the profession, had not earned wages conspicuously below those of other employed girls. He remarks: "In prostitution the ordinary woman can realize almost as much in one night as her meager abilities would enable her to earn [legitimately as a domestic] in a week. . . ." [43] To be considered also is the loneliness and lack of social life of the domestic, her inability to marry well, and her close association with, but aloofness from, an intimate family circle.[44]

Poverty also largely determines such factors as the type of neighborhood in which girls have to live, their companions, employment of mothers, room overcrowding, jealousy of those who have more of life's material satis-

[41] Scott, *op. cit.*, p. 6.
[42] Gladys Mary Hall, *Prostitution in the Modern World* (New York: Emerson Books, 1936), p. 86.
[43] Howard Woolston, *Prostitution in the United States* (New York: Century Company, 1921), p. 65.
[44] Hall, *op. cit.*, pp. 87–88.

factions, and so on. "The harlot's return," says Davis,[45] ". . . is primarily a reward for loss of social standing." This loss may or may not have an economic basis.

HOME AND NEIGHBORHOOD SITUATIONS

Many studies report sex delinquents coming disproportionately from broken homes (the proportion varying, however, in different studies from 23 to 69 per cent); from homes where mothers work outside; from crowded homes with members of both sexes sleeping in the same room, or having male boarders and roomers; from sweatshop homes; and from homes characterized by constant friction. "In many cases," says Scott, "the mother is a prostitute herself, the father is a pimp, and they send their daughter on the streets without the slightest compunction, often themselves initiating her in sexual intercourse." [46]

Patterns of sex behavior vary in different types of neighborhoods. In some sections of large cities early heterosexual experiences are prevalent and expected. In others they are less prevalent, secretive, and traditionally and currently disapproved. Neighborhoods where open vice is tolerated become inured to it, tolerate it, defend it against police raids, and so forth. In some such neighborhoods, pimps and keepers may even become leaders. Their vocations are then looked upon as acceptable and lucrative.

Where sex delinquents have lived in delinquency areas more or less isolated from contacts with the rest of the community, they have always to a degree been products of the patterns of their groups. Dr. Farnell says: "A great many of these girls are unmoral rather than immoral in that they have no code of [sex] morals." [47] Given patterns such as Kinsey describes as prevalent, the prostitute may well reason that her behavior differs from the ordinary only in degree of promiscuity or in the more frequent receipt of money as compensation rather than in being immoral.

THE INFLUENCE OF CONTRACEPTIVES

Prophylaxis has made possible sexual indulgence with reduced danger of VD infection. Contraceptives reduce the fear of pregnancy. The use of penicillin has robbed intercourse of a bit of its terrors, although it is argued

[45] Kingsley Davis, "The Sociology of Prostitution," *American Sociological Review* (Oct. 1937), p. 750.

[46] Scott, *op. cit.,* p. 32.

[47] Frederic J. Farnell, "The Social Evaluation of Psychosexual Deviations," lecture presented to the postgraduate students in sociology at the summer training class, New York Training School for Girls, Hudson, New York, July 25, 1934.

that fear of disease has never been a great deterrent under any circumstances. It is said also that the possibility of rather easy cure leads to reporting of cases formerly not discovered.

Other Sex Crimes

Thus far we have spoken mainly about two kinds of sex offenses, prostitution and homosexuality, which constitute but a fraction of the statutory prohibitions within the category of sex crimes. We shall, however, content ourselves here simply with some brief concluding remarks on the other sex offenses.

Many sexual offenses are morally repugnant and sometimes deeply shocking to most "conventional" citizens of middle- and upper-class backgrounds, particularly when the crimes combine violence with concupiscent actions lying far beyond their experience. It is consequently very tempting to attribute such behavior—motivations for which are scarcely present in middle-class culture—to individualistic aberrations of physical or psychological kinds, since the conventional citizen cannot readily empathize with the lower-class wrongdoer or imagine "how anyone could behave like that unless something is wrong with him." The idea is widely held, in fact, that only "disturbed" people could commit such acts as forced rape, incest, child molestation, paedophilic sodomy, exhibitionism, and so on. This conviction has, in the last 15 years, found concrete expression in the form of so-called sexual psychopath laws now existing in the statutes of 26 states and the District of Columbia.[48] These variously provide for the special handling of persons suspected or convicted of sex crimes, under the premise that such offenders are likely to be disturbed in ways not usually encountered among persons committing other kinds of crimes.

Evidence that sex criminals are dislocated physically or psychically is, however, open to question. In reporting a study of 200 consecutive sex offenders examined under New Jersey's Sex Offender Act, Ellis, Doorbar, and Johnston stress the point that "*sexual deviants who are rash enough in their behavior to get caught and convicted of a specific sex crime* are frequently exceptionally disturbed . . . ;" their psychiatric difficulties lead to "repetitive, compulsive, uncontrolled, and public sex acts" whose conspicuousness results in arrest and conviction.[49] The authors warn against

---

[48] Alan H. Swanson, "Sexual Psychopath Statutes: Summary and Analysis," *Journal of Criminal Law, Criminology and Police Science* (July–Aug. 1960), pp. 215–35.

[49] Albert Ellis, Ruth R. Doorbar, and Robert Johnston III, "Characteristics of Convicted Sex Offenders," *Journal of Social Psychology* (Aug. 1954), pp. 12–13.

generalizing to uncaught sex offenders the characteristics of those who are caught. They feel this to be particularly important in the case of Negroes, whose "distinctively different cultural sex patterns" may account for their finding that Negro offenders were significantly less disturbed than white offenders.[50]

Only recently have investigators with sociological training begun throwing some light on the possible role played by cultural factors in the etiology of sex crimes, although some of this has been incidental to broader investigations of such matters as subcultures and social classes. The confluence of aggressive, predatory attitudes toward females, subcultural traditions of violence in interpersonal relations,[51] and the possibility that some males in our culture misunderstand the nature of female sexuality [52] may be important in such crimes as self-exposure and forcible rape. Wheeler has suggested the role of limited means in producing certain homosexual patterns and in incest among rural people, and of tantalization by the victim in rape cases.[53] Promiscuous behavior among lower-class girls has been tentatively traced to adolescent subcultural factors wherein sexual intercourse is an expected part of dating.[54] Forcible rape by gangs, ostensibly instigated by "strongly sadistic" leaders, may involve a group process wherein the leader gets caught up so inescapably in the expectations of his followers that he will behave in daringly novel ways.[55]

Suggested Readings

Adler, Polly. *A House Is Not a Home.* New York: Popular Library, 1954. Autobiography of a New York sporting-house madame. Valuable for her accounts of recruitment into prostitution and her ties with political and underworld figures.

Karpman, Benjamin. *The Sexual Offender and His Offenses.* New York: The Julian Press, Incorporated, 1954. Exclusively psychopathological in approach, this large work is useful as a descriptive compendium of sexual offenses.

Law and Contemporary Problems (Spring, 1960). Symposium of nine outstanding articles on sex offenses and offenders.

[50] *Ibid.,* pp. 11, 14.
[51] Marvin E. Wolfgang, *Patterns in Criminal Homicide* (Philadelphia: University of Pennsylvania Press, 1958), pp. 328*ff.*
[52] Kinsey, 1953, chap. 16.
[53] Wheeler, *loc. cit.,* pp. 277–78.
[54] John C. Ball and Nell Logan, "Early Sexual Behavior of Lower-Class Girls," *Journal of Criminal Law, Criminology and Police Science* (July–Aug. 1960), pp. 209–14.
[55] W. H. Blanchard, "The Group Process in Gang Rape," *Journal of Social Psychology* (May 1959), pp. 259–66.

Sexual Offenses, A Report of the Cambridge Department of Criminal Science (London: Macmillan and Company, Limited, 1957. An exhaustive report of British experience with sexual offenders, including trends, victims, offenders' characteristics, recidivism, treatment, and legal problems.

Westwood, Gordon. *A Minority: A Report on the Life of the Male Homosexual in Great Britain.* London: Longman's, Green and Company, Limited, 1960. The homosexual behavior patterns of 127 volunteer interviewees are described both quantitatively and in anecdotal form.

CHAPTER 16

A Theory of Crime

Introduction

With this chapter we conclude Part II of this book, in which we
have attempted to point out those aspects of the American scene
which seem to us relevant in understanding our crime problem. In
Chapter 6, Subjective Theories of Crime, we reviewed the principal
approaches having in common the notion that crime is fundamentally symptomatic of individual peculiarities and abnormalities. In
rejecting this notion we contend, as would most sociologists, that
much crime—and certainly most crime for gain—is ordered social
behavior having characteristic norms, attitudes, values, and techniques. As with all actors within a society, the individual pickpocket, confidence man, burglar, robber, prostitute, pimp, drug
peddler, bookmaker, white-collar offender, labor racketeer, crooked
politician, or vice lord, in the commission of his crimes, follows
established social grooves. The individual offender may modify
these to a very limited extent according to his imagination, intelligence, and the exigencies of his situation, but the general outlines
of criminal ways persist over time as discernible patterns.

Considering the extent to which sociological criminologists in
recent years have stressed the relationship of crime to social structures and institutions, they have paid surprisingly little attention to

the question of *how criminal patterns come to be present in a social system in the first place.* By what processes are they generated? How are they interlocked with "legitimate" parts of the larger society? What accounts for their persistence through time? Far more attention has been given to the matter of how particular individuals come to follow criminal patterns; in short, we have been more interested in the etiology of criminals rather than the etiology of criminal patterns. The concern of the present text throughout Parts I and II has been more with the problem of criminal ways than with the criminal himself. Before turning to a general statement of the possible relationship between crime and American culture, let us examine briefly those few other theories which are concerned, as is ours, with the sources of criminal behavior patterns but which deal with specific kinds of patterns.

Professional theft and crooked carnival gambling. The late Professor Edwin H. Sutherland made an important contribution to criminology by pointing out in an early edition of his textbook the existence of what he called "behavior systems of crime." [1] He described these as integrated units which include, besides actual criminal techniques, the "codes, traditions, *esprit-de-corps,* social relationships among the direct participants, and indirect participation of many other persons." [2] Because these systems are shared by a large number of persons, "it should be possible to find causal factors and processes which are not unique to the particular individual." [3] As a move in the direction of finding such causes, Sutherland suggested that professional theft could be traced to such cultural factors as corrupt law-enforcement personnel who cooperate with thieves to defeat justice; the existence of a market for stolen commodities; the absence of a solid public front against theft.[4] Circus and carnival grifting he thought accountable for by dishonest town officials and show managers; the atmosphere of moral relaxation at carnivals; their "here-today gone-tomorrow" characteristic; and the "hard, unsociable," people who elect to work in circuses and carnivals.[5]

Delinquency among working-class boys. Focusing on the causes of juvenile-delinquency subcultures, which he asserts are characteristically productive of non-utilitarian, malicious, and negativistic behavior patterns, Professor Albert Cohen [6] has theorized that these patterns are the responses of

---

[1] Edwin H. Sutherland, *Principles of Criminology* revised by Donald R. Cressey (New York: J. B. Lippincott, 1955), chap. 13.

[2] *Ibid.*, p. 239.

[3] *Ibid.*

[4] *Ibid.*, pp. 242–43.

[5] *Ibid.*, pp. 245–46.

[6] Albert K. Cohen, *Delinquent Boys: The Culture of the Gang* (Glencoe, Ill.: The Free Press, 1955), especially chaps. IV and V.

working-class boys to their socially disappointing experiences in high-school settings. Unable to meet the qualifications for social achievement in the essentially middle-class school culture and threatened consequently with injury to their self-esteem, working-class boys tend to coalesce into truculent groups within which status is dependent upon disavowing the validity of the middle-class criteria of social success. This disavowal takes the form of norms indicating contempt for the things valued by middle-class youngsters: academic indifference, truancy, rudeness, property destruction, stealing. By thus changing the rules of the social game to fit their own limitations, working-class boys can obtain emotional and social need-satisfactions otherwise denied them.

An alternative theory of working-class delinquency is that of Walter B. Miller, who has suggested that certain "focal concerns" presumably indigenous to the general working-class culture motivate certain adolescents to adapt themselves to these; the adaptations take the form of behavior which denotes successful coping with these concerns: masculine toughness, an ability to dupe others, "living dangerously," showing contempt for external authority, and being able to manage trouble.[7]

Middle-class delinquency. With a theory not unlike Miller's, R. W. England[8] has sought to relate an increase in middle-class teenage delinquency to certain changes in the "function" of this age and class group in American society. In his view juveniles generally have occupied an increasingly ambiguous status in the social structure during the last 100 years as the productive roles of this group have diminished. Middle-class post-war prosperity and juvenile idleness conjoin to make "play" the new function of this population segment. In order to retain the need-satisfactions produced by this new status clarification, the segment's values and norms must support its play function by conforming to a hedonistic ethos and must neutralize non-hedonistic pressures from the adult middle-class world either by denigrating them entirely or by altering them to conform with the teenage culture. Thus thrift, hard work, self-denial, and other norms traditionally necessary for middle-class achievements are not useful to a hedonistic ethos. Automobiles, sex, the competitive spirit, and alcohol, among others, *are* highly useful and are adapted with alacrity. In the process of adaptation, however, the norms controlling these elements among adults tend to be sloughed off: cars are used recklessly; sexual intercourse becomes "smart";

---

[7] Walter B. Miller, "Lower-Class Culture as a Generating Milieu of Gang Delinquency," *Journal of Social Issues* (1958), pp. 5–19.

[8] Ralph W. England, Jr., "A Theory of Middle-Class Delinquency," *Journal of Criminal Law, Criminology and Police Science* (April 1960), pp. 535–40.

inter-high-school rivalries degenerate into mob behavior; alcohol is consumed to excess.

Confidence games. Limiting their discussion to one emerging variety of confidence game, Bloch and Geis have suggested the role of certain socio-cultural elements in the gulling of rich widows in the retirement resorts of California and Florida. These elements include the greater longevity of women; the rapid increase in the numbers of rich widows; the desirability of remarriage.[9]

Car theft. The same authors trace car theft, typically a youthful crime, to such general cultural elements as the high rates of car ownership; widespread driving and mechanical knowledge among boys; the American penchant for "tinkering"; and carelessness in safeguarding cars.[10]

Our concern here is not with the soundness or unsoundness of the preceding ideas but with the fact that they represent attempts to relate specific criminal behavior patterns to the general culture. They are *sociological* in that the causes of such patterns are sought in the interplay of socio-cultural elements, without recourse to metaphysical, biological, anthropological, psychological, or psychoanalytic premises, or to a presumed influence of individual pathological conditions in the population.

The question of why particular individuals come to enact the roles incorporated in criminal patterns is another matter. Here some cognizance must be taken of individual differences but without necessarily presuming that such differences must exceed the range of normal limits—that is, be "pathological." It occurs to us that the part played by individual traits in the "recruitment" of personnel into criminal behavior systems may be no *greater* than in the recruitment into noncriminal behavior systems, although the *configurations* of traits may vary. If impressions are a guide, it seems to us that seminary students tend to be myopic, mild-tempered, philosophic, and sympathetic; movie starlets, young, pretty, and pliable; sheriffs, mesomorphic, outgoing, congenial, and self-confident. In one sense, individuals "qualify" for these roles by possessing requisite traits of physique or personality. None of the traits listed above are "abnormal," nor could they reasonably be regarded as "causes" of role-occupancy; they might, at most, be thought of as minimum requirements of candidates for the roles. Similarly the roles of abortionist, burglar, and labor racketeer—no less parts of our social order than seminarian, starlet, or sheriff—may have their respective minimum requirements. But again we need not anticipate that they would

[9] Herbert A. Bloch and Gilbert Reis, *Man, Crime, and Society* (New York: Random House, 1962), pp. 578–79.
[10] *Ibid.*, p. 579.

include some abnormality, nor would we attribute an individual's occupancy of such a role to his possession of the requisite traits. It would be necessary, rather, to examine the social forces to which "qualified" persons were previously exposed. Thus the problem of explaining the entrance of individuals into those roles defined as criminal may be no less sociological than that explaining the occupancy of legitimate roles.

Our primary concern in this chapter, however, is with the problem of why criminal patterns in general have taken such firm root in American society, rather than with individual recruitment into crime. It is our thesis that our criminal patterns are products of our general culture, are vitalized by the same historical and social processes, and are just about what we can expect.

A Theory of Crime in American Culture [11]

Among the basic elements in any culture are social values. These have been developed out of the historical experience of each society. Experiences and behavior patterns which have brought the group satisfaction are positively valued. Experiences which have brought dissatisfaction are negatively valued. Sanctions are set up by society designed to encourage approved behavior and discourage disapproved behavior. These sanctions are embodied in the folkways, mores, conventions, religious ideals and taboos, public opinion, and laws of a society, and may be promoted through education. Every society has to decide what kinds of behavior shall be discouraged through law, and what kinds by appeal to other sanctions. We have seen in our society a great reliance on law and yet a considerable disrespect for many laws. Criminology is, strictly speaking, concerned only with acts which are made punishable under the criminal law.

The characteristics of American society, which we listed or implied in Chapter 2, include its dynamic quality, complexity, materialism, growing impersonality, individualism, insistence upon the importance of status, restricted group loyalties, survivals of frontier traditions, race discrimination, lack of scientific orientation in the social field, tolerance of political corruption, general faith in law, disrespect for some law, and acceptance of quasi-criminal exploitation. The list might be extended.

Now it is important to note that most of these attributes are accepted

[11] The statement following is a slightly modified version of that contained in the previous edition of this book [Donald R. Taft, *Criminology,* third edition (New York: Macmillan, 1956), pp. 336–43].

by Americans generally, criminal and noncriminal alike. For example, both criminals and noncriminals are individualists and materialists, characterized by in-group prejudices, and accept the principle of personal responsibility. But there are various antisocial groups to be explained: predatory low-class criminals who rob and steal; racketeers who perform or pretend to perform a service which is in demand at least by large minorities and furnish us with opportunities to gamble, drink, practice various other "vicious" habits, and secure protection through extralegal means from the exigencies of our competitive society; white-collar criminals, a part of whom are racketeers, who can commit their crimes with little or no loss of social status; and noncriminal exploiters who are not technically criminal at all but who perhaps deprive us of our property or threaten our welfare more effectively than any of the rest. Criminals who injure our persons are often involved in conflict over property, but many are the products of other elements in the general culture.

It has been contended that a society characterized by such values must expect considerable crime, though not necessarily more than some other type. The general structure and culture of our society have made for crime in several ways: (1) They have provided a differential and underprivileged experience for millions of people. Thus slums, gangs, broken homes, demands for escape through the use of alcohol or drugs—such experiences of the underprivileged are implicit in such values as individualism, materialism, the necessity to gain status in some group, and so on. In a society cherishing such values some individuals *must* be underprivileged—some *must* fail. Such differential experience involves differential association with others who have become relative failures or criminals, as Sutherland points out.[12] But differential association is implicit in the values and the structure of modern society. Blue-collar crime may largely be explained in this way. (2) Our society involves the relative tolerance, acceptance, and even the approval of exploitative behavior either of the white-collar crime type or that of the noncriminal exploiter. The values in the general culture explain these two types of unsocial behavior more *directly* than they explain the crime of the underprivileged. But the prevalence and acceptance of white-collar crime and noncriminal exploitation also help explain blue-collar crime. The prestiged classes hand on to the underprivileged the value basis of their crimes. In Chapter 3 we characterized the pattern-setting role of a few of many influential groups. The intelligent underprivileged man need have but slight qualms of conscience over his delinquencies, when he observes the prevalence and the tolerance of exploitative behavior generally. (3) There

[12] Sutherland, *op. cit.*, chap. 4.

are certain characteristics of our society which are not necessarily positively valued, but which exist and help explain crime. Among those listed above, the complexity of our society and the decline of primary relations seem to be of this type.

Thus far we have spoken of characteristics and values of society generally. Men especially crave approval and acceptance by prestiged groups in that society. Indeed, the imperative need or desire for status is more nearly universal even than the desire for money. Money is desired in our society largely because money brings prestige. But status is not derived most significantly from one's reputation in the United States as a whole—few indeed enjoy such a broad basis for their prestige. Most of us seek status in some intimate primary relationship of family, neighborhood, gang, club, church, school, or other small group. Hence the criminologist must pay attention to the influence of social classes and subgroups which determine status. These subgroups themselves are products of the general culture and accept the same general values as do the vast majority of Americans. The difference comes in the *form* which criminal or other exploitative and antisocial behavior takes in some subgroups as compared with others. American culture demands that we be individualists, conformers, materialists, and so on, but the *ways* in which we meet these norms are determined by the *ways* which are approved in these primary groups. The underprivileged slum dweller joining a criminal gang commits blue-collar crime. The businessman joining the entrepreneurial community becomes a noncriminal competitor if possible, but a white-collar criminal if such a course is essential to his prestige. Some fortunate people are able to achieve success without exploitation of their fellows, but these, we hold, are a minority, not a majority, because our system well-nigh compels many of us to be exploitative.

Given a culture dynamic, complex, materialistic, and admiring the successful in a competitive struggle but with many falling short of success, relative failures will collect in its slums and there develop patterns of behavior hostile to the interests of the general community but in harmony with the community's basic values. Assume such a society nominally approving democracy but in practice often rating its members not on the basis of individual virtues but on their accidental membership in such social groups as races, classes, nationalities, or cliques. Weaken in such a culture primary-group controls which prevent serious departure from approved traditional patterns. Develop in such a culture, through processes of social change, a confusion of tongues in definitions of morality and hypocritical rationalizations as to contrasts between the criminal and the noncriminal, the dangerous and the nondangerous. Permit white-collar criminals to receive but mild punishment and no status loss. Permit also gigantic social swindles and injuries to the body politic to go unpunished, while no more serious injuries, classed and treated as crime, result in severe punishment. Provide that often the power of the fix or the fear of political loss to those in power shall permit escape from punishment. Assume in this culture a holdover of frontier traditions involving approval of the use of force and mob action by "respectable" groups against those who oppose their interests or arouse their hostile prejudices. Grant the prevalence in that society of Puritanical traditions preventing the legal or "moral" expression of basic sex and other drives—traditions to which lip service continues to be given long after large minorities, at least, cease to follow them. Create thus a great gulf between precept and practice. Give prestige and important pattern-setting roles in that society to groups whose behavior is not infrequently exploitative. Observe in that society a much-publicized reliance for half a generation on massive deterrent force as an instrument of national policy.

Assume, in spite of all this, great faith in law as being effective to regulate behavior, so that the scope of law is extended to forbid satisfactions which are in wide demand. Observe in such a culture not only a competitive spirit and exploitation tending to restrict what one's fellows shall "earn," but tendencies to strive to obtain something for nothing (with consequent ready victims for fake mark-down sales, "easy" credit, and other sharp retailing practices). Involve in this situation the two important social institutions of family and church so that the sincerity and moral significance of their influence is brought into question. Make education subservient to preparation for participation in competitive activities. Develop there newspapers, commercialized entertainments, radio, television, and other agencies of communication and enjoyment through which the values of a competitive society may be propagated and the interests of minorities promoted.

In such a culture there will be considerable conflict, often taking the form of crime. Effort to make the punished feel unusual shame over their behavior, rather than mere regret that they were caught, will be ineffective. Under such conditions, indeed, the very process of punishment will appear to the punished as further evidence of hypocrisy and discrimination. It will tend to embitter rather than reform.

Such a culture will undoubtedly have a different behavior significance for the slum dwellers than for those who live in the suburbs, for the child from the broken home than for the child in the whole home. It may also impinge somewhat differently upon the emotionally unstable than upon the emotionally stable, upon the dull than upon the intelligent. But these differences will merely determine *the form* or degree of their competitive or exploitative behavior. Blue-collar crime, white-collar crime, and noncriminal exploitation will all tend to reflect criminogenic elements in the general culture. By and large, it is our contention, such a culture must expect considerable crime which can be attributed basically to its own inherent qualities. In this sense we get the criminals we deserve. When we "deserve" less crime, we shall have less of it.

PART III

The TREATMENT of OFFENDERS

In Part I we considered the general influence of American culture on crime. In Part II we dealt with certain more specific criminogenic forces, but in so doing repeatedly tried to trace their influence to deeper aspects of our society as a whole. We turn now to the practical area of the processing and treatment of offenders.

If we "get the criminals we deserve," we also apparently get the police we deserve, the courts we deserve, the correctional institutions and agencies we deserve, and the recidivism we deserve. These instruments of social defense, against crime are political step-children in our culture. With the possible exception of the public prosecutor's office, they are seldom avenues to political power or advancement, so that able and ambitious public servants are not drawn to them. Their leadership consequently has typically ranged in quality from fair to incompetent. Lacking prestige and power, the voices of police chiefs, sheriffs, wardens, and correctional commissioners have been faint in the budgetary hearings of city councils, county commissions, and state legislatures. With limited funds and consequent low salaries and generally dreary working conditions to offer prospective employees, even able and progressive administrators have been hard put to develop competent staffs, not to mention needed buildings and equipment.

This vicious circle is ultimately rooted in the ordinary citizen's general indifference to public agencies of all kinds which deal mainly with our social failures: the casualties of our competitive culture receive short shrift, whether they are deserted mothers, impoverished oldsters, roistering slum children, skid row drunks—or criminals.

In the next 13 chapters we examine our ways of handling the people who are drawn into the machinery of law enforcement and correction. Some parts of the mechanism are ancient; much of it was constructed in the eighteenth and nineteenth centuries; it has a few bright new gears among the rusty ones. By and large it does not run well.

CHAPTER 17

History and Efficacy of Punishment

Among the numberless customs acquired by man are many which persist partly because of man's limitless capacity for rationalizing his behavior. The custom of punishing wrongdoers is among these. While it *may* be true that punishment, real or threatened, is a necessary ingredient in maintaining conformity to group norms, most societies accept its usefulness without question. With a few possible exceptions established means of corporately inflicting some form of unpleasantness upon the wrongdoer are found in every society. At sundry times and places men have been branded, mutilated, torn apart, fed to beasts, slowly starved, burned, exposed in pillories to the insults of passers-by, enslaved in galleys, crucified, and pressed to death. Contemporary Western societies have largely abandoned these remnants of tribal punishment, providing instead that criminals be deprived of money or property, removed from the group, executed painlessly, or put to forced labor. Hardly less varied than man's *armamentum* of punitive measures are the reasons—simple and sophisticated, outrageous and logical—he has adduced for their application. In the pages following, some attention is given to these rationalizations, but it should be kept in mind that since virtually all antedate the behavioral sciences, they were derived from other than scientific inquiry into the reasons for human misbehavior.

The universality of the punitive weapon in the face of quite differing reasons given by its users has led some students of man to conclude that its roots lie deep in the human psyche, perhaps in the form of an elemental impulse to vengeful retaliation against any hurting agent, perhaps, as psychoanalysts would have it, in resentment against having our own suppressed wishes awakened by a malefactor's example. Whatever the "real" reasons, the rationalizations for punishment bear them no necessary relationship, for they are designed, as are most rationalizations, to ennoble rather than demean their creators: it is "better," for example, to imprison a rapist on the grounds that society will thereby be protected than to admit that our true motive may actually arise from anger at his concupiscent impudence.

History of Punishment

PUNISHMENT IN PRELITERATE SOCIETIES

In at least one curious way primitive man deludes himself less than his literate brethren: he seeks revenge against those who wrong him and makes no attempt to embroider his motive. To the primitive, that a personal injury deserves a rejoinder is simple justice. If my name is profaned by a neighbor, I profane his and perhaps work a spell on his yam-patch in the bargain— not to deter him in the future, or to placate the gods, or to re-establish group equilibrium, but simply because I want to get even. Such retaliation is not, of course, punishment in a corporate sense, nor even in an individual sense. The group may take no "official" notice of an exchange of injuries unless it erupts into a blood feud or other violence. The older notion that primitive "justice" was characterized by endless series of retaliatory exchanges has been modified; acts of retaliation and revenge are so destructive of ordered living that limitations upon them early in the development of human societies were essential. In commenting upon the legal historians' picture of primitive life as an "an arena of violence," the anthropologist Hoebel, an authority on primitive law, writes:

[The error in this] lies in the notion that there ever was a time when torts were not emendable or a time when blood feud prevailed unchecked. The factual data make it very clear that the societies of man have from the outset wrestled with the problem of maintaining internal peace and harmony. The lowly Andamanese flees to the jungle when he has committed a homicide within his local group. His headman intervenes to pour oil on troubled waters when it appears that a dispute may lead to violence. The Eskimo meets killing with killing, but men who let the killing impulse run to feud and so kill more than once are removed by common communal action. The song duel exists as a substitute for violence to close issues of dispute without recourse to steps that may lead to feud. The lowly Australians have no composition and they are plagued with feud, but regulated combat is used again and again in lieu of feud or to bring a standing feud to a close. . . .

What emerges from the data is this: within loosely organized tribes in which the local group is autonomous, trouble involving members of different local groups frequently brews physical violence which often leads to feuding; feud marks an absence of law, for the killing is not mutually acknowledged as a privilege-right; yet it appears that every society has some set procedure for avoiding feud or bringing it to a halt. . . .[1]

Elsewhere, Hoebel has advanced the interesting argument that acts of private retribution actually represent, sociologically speaking, a species of primitive justice undertaken with the implicit approval of the retributors' group.

The privilege of applying force constitutes the "official" element in [primitive] law. He who is generally or specifically recognized as rightly exerting the element of physical coercion is a splinter of social authority. It is not necessary that he be an official with legal office or a constable's badge. In any primitive society the so-called "private prosecutor" of a private injury is implicitly a public official *pro tempore, pro eo solo delicto.* He is not and cannot be acting solely on his own, his family's or his clan's behalf and yet enjoy the approval or tacit support of the disinterested remainder of his society. If the rest of the tribal population support him in opinion, even though not in overt action, it can only mean that the society feels that the behavior of the defendant was wrong in its broadest implications, *i.e., contra* to the standards of the society as a whole.[2]

If Hoebel's interpretation is correct, then the former distinction made by writers on primitive societies between private and public wrongs clearly requires modification: in an ultimate sense, there are only "public" wrongs. Nevertheless, only certain disapproved acts elicit overt group response, and this realm of threats to *corporate* safety is where preliterate practices are most relevant to the history of punishment. To primitives the struggle for survival is a perilous enterprise requiring constant vigilance to avoid numerous threats to life and health: injuries, diseases, food shortages, enemy attacks, hostile animals—not to mention innumerable and varied unseen beings of unearthly character. Keeping alive and well is, more commonly than not, such a touch-and-go matter that actions tending to endanger a

[1] E. Adamson Hoebel, *The Law of Primitive Man* (Cambridge, Mass.: Harvard University Press, 1954), pp. 329–30.

[2] E. Adamson Hoebel, "Law and Anthropology," *Virginia Law Review,* **32** (1946), pp. 836–54, as quoted in Morton H. Fried, ed., *Readings in Anthropology,* Vol. II (New York: Thomas Y. Crowell Company, 1959), p. 303.

group's safety by unnecessarily increasing the odds against survival are promptly and sometimes severely dealt with. Treason and "unauthorized" witchcraft are such actions; defiling sacred objects, cowardice in battle, and assault upon a ruler or holy man are examples of others. (This is not to say that the preliterates' rationalization for proscribing such behavior is based directly upon recognition that it is "dangerous to the group." Taboos are, on the contrary, alleged to spring from transcendental sources—an allegation by no means restricted to primitive societies.)

TRENDS OF PENAL THEORY AND PRACTICE IN PRESCIENTIFIC LITERATE SOCIETY

The civil state compounded of many tribes was no longer a primary group with the unity and intimate bonds of primitive society. Categories of conquerors and conquered, master and slave, nobleman and commoner, priest and layman, lord and serf, upper class and lower class, and later employer and employee became more definite and significant. These implied a stratified society with conflicting class interest and multiplied points of friction. This meant laws furthering class interests, weakened bonds of sympathy, less interest in the individual member of the enlarged state, more crime, and more punishment for crime. Moreover, the civil state, unable to tolerate the disorder resulting from blood feuds, interfered more and more in private disputes and developed elaborate machinery to promote order. Unwritten mores, though by no means the only source of criminal law, became written penal codes. Many private injuries or torts became public injuries or crimes. Individuals, rather than the groups of which they were members, came to be held responsible for crime. Penal practices, along with other social activities, were a bit less dominated by magical formulas.

Yet possibly the similarities between punishment in preliterate and literate societies are as worthy of emphasis as the contrasts. These we have illustrated above. Really significant changes in penal methods do not occur at the line between primitive and literate society so much as at the line between the prescientific and the not-yet-fully-achieved scientific era.

For these reasons there is little point in attempting to trace the history of punishment in detail through classical, medieval, and postmedieval times, except as we speak later of a theory of punishment. A few generalizations must suffice. The Code of Hammurabi (about 2300 B.C.) illustrates early composition of penalties. The various Hebrew codes down to the Talmud show a progressive secularization and social emphasis. Early Hebrew history also illustrates group responsibility for crimes, private vengeance, and efforts to avoid the ill effects of such vengeance through provision of holy refuges where the offender might obtain temporary protection from the pursuing avenger. Relatively to the divinities of some other tribes, the Hebrew God was conceived of as interested in "just" relations among humans. The prophet Hosea is said to have introduced the element of redemption into the older view of expiation for crime.

Greek justice illustrates many holdovers from primitive society, such as composition of penalties, vengeance attitudes, and outlawry. The harsh code of Draco, the oldest of Greek codes, is of interest as providing the same penalties for slave and freeman. Solon permitted any citizen to prosecute instead of the injured party only, thus showing the growing public interest in offenses formerly considered of private concern. Plato intimated that education might replace punishment as a protection against crime. The Romans, pre-eminent in matters legal, nevertheless contributed little of interest for the penologist of today.

Though factual evidence was gathered for medieval trials, the Middle Ages nevertheless are famous for the use of the various forms of ordeal which called in supernatural forces to demonstrate guilt or innocence. Crude as were these ordeals, they represented an alleviation of the bloodshed involved in private vengeance without trial. As a single example we cite the ordeal of the sacrament, based upon the belief that to the guilty the sacrament would be fatal. Abolished in church courts in 1215, the ordeal was retained longer in the secular courts. Another significant medieval institution was compurgation, in which men selected by the bishop might swear their belief in the innocence of the accused. The civil right to trial by compurgation existed in England until 1833, although it had long since become obsolete.

Medieval men conceived of reformation as a process of religious redemption. The sinner must not only pay a debt to society; he must get right with God. Penance exacted by the church was a process of spiritual regeneration through the performance of some painful pilgrimage or by making some sacrifice in the interest of the church. Penance tended to degenerate into the vicious system of indulgences, which, at their worst, permitted a man to anticipate a future sin by building up, through gifts to the church, a "treasury of good works" on the credit side of the books, against which forbidden pleasures might be debited. This institution suggests the modern notion, found among the punishing as well as the punished, that the criminal has through imprisonment "paid his debt to society."

The influence of the medieval church meant also the introduction of new crimes, including heresy, witchcraft, and certain sex offenses. The church's attitude toward the latter is of tremendous influence today. Recognition of the crime of heresy tended to justify the most cruel punishments, supposedly in the interest of the sinner himself. The crime of heresy has largely passed out the codes of today, but the principle of heresy survives in statutes penalizing some expressions of irreligion, such as blasphemy.

The most basic influence of the medieval church is seen, however, in its principles of free will and individual responsibility. Logically, a church which preaches the doctrines of eternal punishment, atonement, and spiritual conversion must justify its teachings by the assumption that the individual, had he so willed, could have acted differently than he did. This teaching still dominates modern penal practices. The Scriptures may be quoted to justify either a "powder-puff" or a "machine-gun" penal policy but rarely, if ever, to support a search for causes of behavior or a truly scientific crime-prevention program.

Neverthless, partly because of the humanitarian element in Christian teachings and partly by reserving clerics for trial in the canonical courts, the church exerted a certain influence toward milder punishments in an age of extreme cruelty. Its members having originally risen largely out of the slave and plebian classes in the Roman Empire, the early church also denounced certain class distinctions in punishment. Yet the institution of benefit of clergy implied a very genuine class distinction and led to serious injustices, of which Beccaria and the classical school of penology complained.

Law and penal practice in Puritan New England had a large medieval flavor. Punishment was even possible for offenses not defined in any law.[3] A seventeenth-cenutry Massachusetts code known as the Body of Liberties provided the death penalty for idolatry, witchcraft, blasphemy, and adultery (with qualifications), as well as for such offenses as murder. Governor Hutchinson expressed the opinion that probably Catholics could have been hanged as idolaters. Torture to extort confessions was not generally permitted, however, except in some cases of witchcraft, where it sometimes produced confessions to all sorts of communion with evil powers. Quakers were persecuted, and the New Englander could with complacency "see Quaker women tied to the cart's tail half clothed in mid-winter and whipped until their bare backs were raw and bleeding."[4] In New York and Virginia, but apparently not in New England, men were broken on the wheel. It was in New England that a village atheist who maintained that there was no God, no devil, and no hell, had his tongue pierced with hot iron. The Puritan

[3] Lois T. Merrill, "The Puritan Policeman," *American Sociological Review* (Dec. 1945), pp. 766–76.
[4] *Ibid.,* p. 768.

church supported the government in punishing for heresy and other religious offenses. Wood must not be chopped on Sunday even on the coldest day. "Captain Kimble of Boston was put into the stocks for two hours for his 'lewd and unseemly' behavior, in the language of the court, for 'publiquely' kissing his wife on the doorstep of his house upon his return on the Sabbath day from a three-year sea voyage." [5] Laws against the use of tobacco were in force between 1632 and 1647. The courts could penalize the lower classes for wearing unduly costly clothes. "Identification of man-made law with God-made law kept the Puritan under a livelier sense of the evil of criminal acts than is prevalent now." [6]

TREND TOWARD A SCIENTIFIC PENOLOGY

Before discussing classical and neoclassical theories of punishment which intervened between medieval and scientific penologies, we must find the roots of the latter in the slow decline of medievalism. Scientific penology could not originate in a medieval atmosphere totally inconsistent with it. The other-worldliness of the Middle Ages prevented attention even to the physical world. Men had to observe nature and its orderliness before they could observe human nature and the order in human relationships. A "rebirth" was required to emancipate man from the absolutist hold of the medieval church. The Reformation attacked that absolutism but substituted for it an almost equal slavery to a book. The Renaissance introduced gradually, not the scientific attitude of mind, but a skepticism toward the universe which permitted rational thought and replaced the dogmatic faith of the Middle Ages. The Renaissance disclosed a universe full of a variety of things, and only later did reasoning about and observation of this variety of things disclose order in their arrangements. Still later the order discovered in inanimate phenomena was found, though less demonstrably, also to characterize psychological and social phenomena. This scientific development grew out of discoveries, contacts, and inventions in the economic realm which produced the industrial revolution.

THE "NEW PENOLOGY"

The scientific point of view, though increasingly evident, does not yet dominate modern penal or treatment policies. Men have come to deal with the weather, mechanical and chemical problems, physical disease, and to some extent mental disease as products of precedent conditions, but most

[5] *Ibid.,* p. 772.
[6] *Ibid.,* p. 775.

men do not yet usually deal with human behavior and moral problems as the consequences of what has gone before in the lives of those who "misbehave." We still punish primarily for vengeance, or to deter, or in the interest of a "just" balance of accounts between "deliberate" evildoers on the one hand and an injured and enraged society on the other. We do not yet generally punish or treat as scientific criminology would imply, namely, in order to change antisocial attitudes into constructive attitudes.

In the chapters which follow we shall describe existing penal policies and practices. We shall find neoclassical principles, slightly modified by scientific principles basically inconsistent with them. We cannot wholly avoid evaluating these policies. In so doing we shall often compare them with the principles and policies of the "new penology." The words "new penology" might be used in two senses. They might refer to the most progressive penal systems actually in existence today, such as, perhaps, that of the federal government. Or the term might refer to an "ideal" penal system conceived to be implicit in a scientific criminology. Of course, so used, the "new penology" of one criminologist may differ somewhat from that of another. This is because it is not yet clear just what specific methods of treatment a scientific criminology implies.[7]

Briefly we shall use the "new penology" in the second sense to mean:

1. A penal or treatment policy which shall always look upon the criminal as a product of antecedant conditions.
2. One which shall distinguish between the need for repression when dangerous criminals are in action and deeper levels of the crime problem where more constructive methods are requisite to social protection.
3. Treatment adapted to the individual case.
4. Treatment utilizing as fully as possible the group approach, because the criminal is seen as largely a product of his group relationships.
5. Treatment recognizing that crime is also rooted in the very nature of the general culture, of which both criminal and noncriminal are a part.
6. Treatment which nevertheless calls upon every pertinent science to cooperate, because crime is seen as a synthetic product varied in origin.
7. Treatment which shall incorporate much which is appropriate and effective in specific existing practices and policies of the indeterminate sentence, probation, parole, reformatory treatment, and the like, but which will suggest changes in such policies where they appear ineffective or inconsistent with a scientific approach.

[7] The need for specifying these methods has been trenchantly discussed by Alfred C. Schnur in "The New Penology: Fact or Fiction?" *Journal of Criminal Law, Criminology and Police Science* (Nov.–Dec. 1958), pp. 331–34.

8. Operation of correctional institutions in such ways as will minimize the gulf separating the prisoner from the society to which he will eventually return.

Philosophies of Punishment

MEANING AND SIGNIFICANCE

Punishment policies have many sources. How far new philosophical principles normally precede the origin of any policy is open to question. Probably they are more often rationalizations of existing policies. Yet principles of punishment have been logically deduced from larger principles—for example, from the concept of abstract justice or divine will. Such principles have had an influence at least in perpetuating existing penal policies in the face of changed conditions. Thus the ghost of Hegel as well as the shadow of God may be discerned in many a modern courtroom.

TRANSCENDENTAL PHILOSOPHIES

Transcendental theories [8] are those based upon principles supposed to transcend experience and to be especially sacred because of assumed universal validity. They are ideas spun in the dream factory of the mind, rather than induced from the fact factory of scientific research. These transcendental theories of punishment have been subdivided into the following: (1) The theological view, which holds it a religious duty to punish criminals. (2) The expiatory theory of punishment, in terms of which we must punish because the nature of the mystical order of the universe is that we punish. Ours not to reason why. (3) Kant's theory of the moral law. Believing in an intuitive source of absolute morality, Kant insisted that there exists a categorical imperative to punish criminals who have violated this moral law. Punishment is an end in itself.[9] (4) The theory of Hegel that punishment is necessary to annul the injury produced by crime. ". . . Crime has to be punished because it postulates punishment as its necessary logical complement." [10] (5) The aesthetic theory of punishment. Our aesthetic sense rebels against the discord produced by crime.

[8] Heinrich Oppenheimer, *The Rationale of Punishment* (London: University of London Press, 1913), p. 181.
[9] *Ibid.*, p. 196.
[10] *Ibid.*, p. 215.

PENAL THEORIES OF THE EIGHTEENTH CENTURY AND LATER

Eschewing authoritarian sources of moral ideas, the eighteenth-century rationalists sought to derive ethical principles from more mundane sources. Jeremy Bentham, a chief expositor of the Utilitarian school of philosophy, held that since men are governed in their actions by rational assessments of the pleasures and pains to be netted by various courses of actions, punishment should be allotted in amounts just sufficient to produce a net loss (i.e., pain) for a person committing a criminal act. By thus putting its thumb on the scale used by men as they choose between alternatives, the state can, if justice is swift and sure, prevent crime. Ably and energetically propounded by Bentham and his followers in an age whose burgeoning capitalism taught daily lessons in the principles of profit and loss, utilitarianism had an enormous appeal. The rationale for today's graduated penalties derives largely from this doctrine, and one need only observe the public's reaction to proposals to modify punishment in order to realize the extent of its grip on the popular mind.

The neoclassical school, including such men as Garraud, Rossi, and Joly, started with the same principle of free will as the classical school but made exceptions in the case of little children, the insane, and those whose crimes were committed under extenuating circumstances. Thus punishment was to be based upon the degree of responsibility which the individual had at the time of the crime. The importance of this school in the history of punishment lies first in the fact that its theories *implied* causation and secondly in that upon its philosophy is based the bulk of modern penal law and practice, though both have increasingly been influenced by scientific principles derived from a later period.

As we saw when tracing the history of criminological as distinct from penological thought, the really significant and revolutionary change came when study of the conditions surrounding crime began. Since the early work of the social statisticians in France and England and Lombroso's measurements of the physical traits of criminals in Italy, evidence has gradually been accumulated tending to show that man's will is far from free and that crime and the criminal are products. The implications of this discovery for penal treatment were revolutionary, but the scientific view is not yet adopted by most of the people. The indeterminate sentence and probation and parole apparently have a sentimental rather than a scientific basis, or were largely put over by small groups rather than accepted by legislatures or public opinion. They exist today in the United States as very important but inconsistent adjuncts to an essentially neoclassical penal system.

Conditions Influencing the Effectiveness of Punishment

LABORATORY EXPERIMENTS OF PSYCHOLOGISTS

Little can be derived from the study of punishment in the laboratory which is significant for the problems of the penologist. Miss Strang, reviewing 88 such laboratory studies, concluded that they show reward almost universally beneficial, while punishment did harm twice as often as it did good.[11] The nature of the punished, the conditions surrounding punishment, and the meaning of punishment are not the same in the treatment of crime as the corresponding factors in the laboratory. A rat "deciding" whether to change his course to avoid an immediate, painful electric shock differs in myriad ways from a man "deciding" whether to kill his irritating spouse on the possibility (possibly one in twelve chances) that he may receive a very severe shock in the electric chair.

INDIVIDUAL AND SOCIAL FACTORS

We know something of the effectiveness of punishment from other sources. The following conditions affecting the influence of punishment on behavior should not be considered as universal but rather as fairly general, for they are altered by changes in group values and patterns of behavior which determine status in different cultures. Punishment, to deter from crime, must provide a pain greater than the pleasure involved in crime. Again, pain to be deterrent must normally come shortly after the act it is desired to prevent. Long-delayed justice interferes with such deterrence. Pain is not deterrent unless it appears as a fairly inevitable consequence of criminal behavior. Criminals are often experienced gamblers, and some have been known to remark that at any given moment the crime game is safer than playing the ponies and more nearly comparable to the danger from lightning in a severe electrical storm. Sooner or later the offender is caught, unless he has a fix or is engaged in a crime easily concealed. Yet there is probably no frequently committed crime so effectively punished that there is great risk *the next crime* will result in punishment.

Insistence that punishment *alone* cannot socialize a personality is quite

[11] Ruth Strang, "Contributions of Research to Discipline and Control," in National Society for the Study of Education, *Thirty-Seventh Yearbook,* Part II (Bloomington, Ill.: Public School Publishing Co., 1938), p. 216. See also William K. Estes, "An Experimental Study of Punishment," *Psychological Monographs,* Vol. 57, No. 3 (1944).

consistent with Jenkins' statement that ". . . children cannot be socialized without a discerning use of punishment, and society cannot exist without penal sanctions." [12] Such a statement is especially obvious if one emphasizes the word "alone" and extends the concepts of "punishment" and "penal sanctions" to include all degrees of personal and social disapproval. A society requires a certain amount of conformity. Society requires that its members aid one another. It must reward conformity and cooperative behavior at least by positive assignment of social status to those who conform or are helpful. This positive approval implies negative disapproval. Threat of such disapproval is the minimum "penal sanction." Under certain conditions this disapproval appropriately takes the form of punishment. Jenkins also holds that punishment, in addition to controlling behavior, sometimes relieves tensions, not only of injured parties but of the offenders themselves. However, a juvenile gangster may try his best to avoid capture and punishment, and yet the prestige which punishment brings him among his associates will make his suffering more endurable and perhaps pleasing in restrospect, even if he retains a certain vague sense of guilt.

Not a particular punishment experience, but the total situation, seems to determine the effects of punishment. A little child living in a home where she has experienced predominantly affection and satisfying social relations may be punished for some offense. It is not uncommon to find that a few minutes later she will throw her arms around the neck of the punishing parent. Because the general atmosphere of the home is constructive, the punishment appears as a minor temporary shock, acting as a reminder that those whom she loved were displeased with her behavior. In such cases punishment may be effective. In court and prison, on the other hand, the dominating experience is generally not only painful but productive of fear and hatred.[13] In such a situation punishment may be effective in deterring from *overt* crime, *so long as threat of punishment remains.* Yet it cannot create social attitudes. Indeed, it may strengthen and crystallize existing antisocial attitudes. Hence furtive antisocial acts thrive in prison.

The offender's attitude toward punishment largely determines its effect upon him, and this attitude in turn is largely determined by his group relationships. Thus punishment which expresses the hatred or anger of the disciplinarian may have some deterrent effect at the moment but can hardly lead to remorse or changed attitudes. There may be exceptional cases where

[12] Cf. Richard L. Jenkins, "The Constructive Use of Punishment," *Mental Hygiene* (Oct. 1945), pp. 651*ff*. See also Lester E. Hewett and Richard L. Jenkins *Fundamental Patterns of Maladjustment: The Dynamics of Their Origin* (Springfield, Ill.: 1946).

[13] Cf. discussion of prison discipline *infra*, chap. 24.

the punished have come to recognize the need for punishment and to accept the disciplinarian as a suitable source of authority or "parent-substitute," as some psychiatrists put it. It is held that punishment need not express either hatred or blame,[14] yet the closer one is to crime and physical punishment, the more difficult it is to inhibit one's emotions.

Punishment is also ineffective when it affords the offender enjoyment because of the trouble it is making for parents, schoolteachers, police, or prison administrators. Just as a nation may forget its own military losses by gloating over and exaggerating those of the enemy, so a criminal, though bruised and bleeding from combat with the police or languishing in a punishment cell in prison, may console himself with the injuries or annoyance he has afforded his captors.

Punishment is ineffective, too, if administered by one who is not respected.[15] Children will take much from parents they respect. The effectiveness of punishment in our penal system is reduced when staff are perceived by prisoners as brutal, stupid, or dishonest.

Finally, punishment fails when it raises the status of the punished in his group. This is often true in a gang. Moreover, continued avoidance of crime seems to call for group support. It seems almost correct to define a "reformed" criminal as one who has achieved status in some noncriminal group. Such group support seems to explain the success of group therapy and of less controlled groups, such as Alcoholics Anonymous.

Recidivism

The task of evaluating penal treatment in terms of the subsequent behavior of offenders is complex and difficult. Considering imprisonment and parole alone (excluding, thereby, probation, fines, judicial scoldings, and other punitive measures), the following procedural problems must be faced:

(1) What criteria shall be used to measure post-prison recidivism? Arrests? Convictions? A ne'er-do-well life? A bad reputation? Failure to meet family obligations? All of these have been used by various researchers. Clearly, results among studies applying differing criteria cannot be meaningfully compared.

(2) How much time after release is needed to allow the full effects of punishment to be measured? One year? Five years? Twenty years? And

[14] Lawrence Sears, *Responsibility* (New York: Columbia University Press, 1932), pp. 140, 146–47.
[15] *Ibid.*, p. 136.

will not allowing longer rather than shorter lengths of time likely permit factors extraneous to the prison experience to intrude in the offenders' lives? A famous 15-year follow-up study of 500 Massachusetts reformatory graduates found that two-thirds were involved in subsequent criminal behavior, although only one-third persisted in serious crime during the entire 15 years.[16]

(3) What kinds of prisons should be used in evaluating punishment? Maximum security? Minimum security? Reformatories? Old-line? Modern?

(4) How can allowance be made for the multitude of experiences released men severally encounter, thereby introducing variables other than punishment as factors in subsequent behavior?

(5) What categories of prisoners should be followed up? Hardened old men? Young and tractable? Urban? Rural? A study of 551 men released in 1954 from the Maryland State Reformatory found that 57 per cent of 304 released by expiration of sentence were convicted for new crimes within three years at most after getting their freedom, but all had been residents of Baltimore City or County at sentencing.[17] The recidivism rate would probably have differed had the study included substantial numbers of small-town or rural offenders.

No single post-prison study has satisfactorily met all of these procedural difficulties. The deceptively simple question—what is the extent of recidivism?—therefore cannot be answered except within the limitations of individual studies, most of whose findings are not comparable with each other. We have no meaningful "national recidivism rate"; most of the publicized rates covering individual states are based on parole violations and thus involve criteria besides additional criminal convictions.[18]

Difficult as it is to measure the effect of punishment upon criminals, the problem of assessing its effect upon potential criminals—quite possibly its real value—is probably impossible. Certainly fear of punishment is not the major force preventing most of us from serious crime as defined in the law. Fear of punishment is one element in crime prevention. On the other hand, it is an element for which substitutes may be provided. The people

[16] Sheldon and Eleanor T. Glueck, *Criminal Careers in Retrospect* (New York: The Commonwealth Fund, 1943), p. 121. This book was the last of a series of three reports, each covering 5-year post-release periods. The other two were *500 Criminal Careers* (New York: Alfred A. Knopf, 1930) and *Later Criminal Careers* (New York: The Commonwealth Fund, 1937).

[17] *A Follow-Up Study of Men Released in 1954 from the State Reformatory for Males by Reason of Parole and Expiration of Sentence* (Baltimore: Baltimore Criminal Justice Commission, June 6, 1958) (mimeographed), pp. 1, 6.

[18] For a discussion of additional problems involved in measuring recidivism, see Milton G. Pescor, "Factors in Measuring Recidivism as Presented in Annual Reports," *National Probation and Parole Association Journal* (July 1958), pp. 218–32.

undoubtedly have an exaggerated faith in punishment. Most of our crime commissions still attempt to prevent crime by making punishment more severe. Of course our police and court machinery should be effective. Punishment, however, does not create social in place of antisocial attitudes. Constructive methods alone have a permanent effect.

Capital Punishment

Perhaps during no period in the history of Western civilization were more frantic legislative efforts made to stem crime by the infliction of capital punishment than in the eighteenth century. Beset by a growing crime problem attendant upon rapid agrarian and industrial changes, a problem particularly evident in the burgeoning cities, England's Parliament added to the 50 capital crimes extant in 1688 no fewer than 190 between that year and the end of George III's reign (1810).[19] Moreover, the provisions of the statutes covering these offenses were so broad as to embrace three or four times the number of acts primarily indicated.[20] The intentions of Parliament, however, were blocked in part by the widespread tolerance by judges and prosecutors of innumerable dodges designed to help culprits escape the noose: conviction for an offense less than that stated in the indictment; failure to press grand juries to indict; "pious perjury," wherein jurymen appraised stolen property at amounts just under the felony limits, etc.[21]

If fewer crimes were punishable with death in our own colonies, the number was nevertheless considerable, ranging from 10 to 18. The federal government did not reduce its code's 17 capital offenses to three until 1892. Egalitarianism, humanitarian sentiments, and the fact that crime was observed not to increase after most crimes ceased to be capital, led to a questioning of the need of the death penalty for any crime. Pioneered by Michigan in 1847, six additional states became abolitionist: Rhode Island (1852), Wisconsin (1853), Maine (1887), Minnesota (1911), North Dakota (1915), and Delaware (1958). Before achieving statehood Alaska and Hawaii abolished capital punishment in 1957 and have retained abolishment as states.

[19] Leon Radzinowicz, *A History of English Criminal Law and Its Administration from 1750. The Movement for Reform 1750–1833* (New York: Macmillan, 1948), p. 4.

[20] *Ibid.*, p. 5.

[21] *Ibid.*, chap. 3. This chapter makes abundantly evident the fact that bourgeois Englishmen—so roundly castigated by Marx and other observers—were by no means unanimously determined to enlist the hangman's help in protecting their property and privileges.

The use of capital punishment among Western cultures has been declining during the last 100 years. Some 30 countries had outlawed it in peacetime up to World War II, although a few reintroduced it under totalitarian regimes or after that war. Not only was there no general post-war revival of its use in the United States, but a number of states with laws providing the death penalty have been increasingly disinclined to use it. In fact, a clear downward trend in its application is evident for the last 25 years.[22] Commencing with 1930, the average yearly number of executions by civil authorities in the United States for 5-year periods was: [23]

1930–1934	155.2
1935–1939	178.0
1940–1944	129.0
1945–1949	127.8
1950–1954	82.6
1955–1959	60.8

Over half of the 57 executions in 1960 took place in four states: New York, California, Texas, and Arkansas.[24]

A second trend has been toward a reduction of the number of offenses for which death may be the penalty. In practice, murder and rape are the principal offenses remaining for which persons are put to death in this country. Of 3,724 executions between 1930 and 1960, 3,225 were for murder and 434 for rape. The remaining 65 were scattered among armed robbery, kidnapping, burglary, espionage, and aggravated assault. A third long-time trend has been toward making the process of execution private, painless, and quick. From time to time one hears of a prosecutor inviting a murder victim's kin to observe the killer's execution, but usually only official witnesses may legally be present. Enraged citizens occasionally complain that a particular type of execution is "too good" for a certain offender, but the fact is that electrocution, hanging, lethal gas, and shooting are the sole means employed within the United States. Each is presumably painless, although the victims themselves are silent on this point.

DETERRENT EFFECT OF CAPITAL PUNISHMENT

Scott has said that the question of capital punishment falls between two stools: if it proves deterrent, it risks executing the innocent; if it protects

[22] Computed from United States Department of Justice, *National Prisoner Statistics*, No. 26 (March 1961), Table 1, p. 4.

[23] *Ibid.*, computed from Table 1, p. 4. The increase in 1935–1939 was due partly to executions following organized gang killings. This is the only period of the six during which more whites than Negroes were executed.

[24] *Ibid.*, p. 4.

the innocent perfectly, it is used so seldom that it fails to deter.[25] The question again is not merely whether capital punishment deters potential murderers but whether it does so more effectively than other penalties or methods. All thorough studies are said to have concluded that the death penalty is inconsequential as a deterrent.[26]

A number of nonscientific arguments have been presented for the death penalty. Thus it has been said to be justified by the Scriptures, to be a natural expression of the emotion of vengeance, or to be "just" in cases of murder in terms of the balanced-account theory of punishment.

If the death penalty really appreciably decreases murder, if there is no equally effective substitute, and if its by-products are not equally injurious to society, penology will support the death penalty. But its necessity is seriously questioned. The fear of death may be the most intense of all fears; but fear of death is fear of certain, imminent death, and courage is not confined to those who are engaged in meritorious deeds. One cannot argue from any terror of the murderer on the morning of execution to the deterrent effect of fear of problematic execution at the moment of the crime.

In the United States, homicide rates are generally higher in states with capital punishment than in those which have abolished it. The FBI *Uniform Crime Reports* shows an over-all rate among the 50 states of 5.1 per 100,000 population in 1960. Corresponding rates among the seven states without the death penalty were: Michigan 4.3, Wisconsin 1.3, Minnesota 1.3, Maine 1.7, Rhode Island 1.0, North Dakota 0.5, and Delaware 6.5.[27] The homicide rates in the four states leading in the use of capital punishment during 1960 were: New York 2.9, California 3.9, Texas 8.7, and Arkansas 8.6. Comparisons between contiguous states with and without the death penalty are also generally favorable to the abolition state.[28] The homicide rate has not consistently fallen with increased risk of execution.

Quantitative studies attempting to measure the alleged deterrent effects of capital punishment are slowly accumulating. None of them finds support for this allegation. The contention of police officials that armed desperadoes are more likely to "shoot it out" with the police in abolitionists states, thereby increasing the hazards of law-enforcement work, was tested by

[25] George Ryley Scott, *The History of Capital Punishment* (London: Torchstream Books, 1950).

[26] Karl F. Schuessler, "The Deterrent Influence of the Death Penalty," *Annals of the American Academy of Political and Social Science*, 284:54–62 (November 1952).

[27] *Uniform Crime Reports: 1960* (Washington, D. C.: United States Department of Justice, 1961), Table 2, pp. 34–37.

[28] George B. Vold, "Extent and Trend of Capital Crimes in the United States," *Annals, loc. cit.*, p. 4.

Sellin and by Campion. Sellin [29] found that the rates of fatal attacks per 100,000 police officers in 266 cities in abolitionist and non-abolitionists states were 1.2 and 1.3, respectively—a difference of no significance, although ironically enough in a direction contrary to that predicted by the deterrence theory. Campion [30] made a similar finding with respect to state policemen. Deterrence theory would also predict that newspaper publicity attendant upon convictions and sentencings for capital crimes would serve to remind would-be killers of the law's severity toward murderers and that the murder rate should decline immediately following a sentence to death. A study by Savitz [31] on homicides in Philadelphia for 8-week periods before and after four such sentencings in Philadelphia County courts found no significant changes in the murder rate.

Abolition of the death penalty has sometimes been followed by an increase in murder, sometimes not, and the important point is that changes in either direction have usually paralleled similar trends in states with the opposite policy. The state of Washington was without the death penalty between 1913 and 1919 and murder increased somewhat. However, when capital punishment was reinstated, the increase continued.[32] Only rarely, if ever, have men contemplating murder been known to drag their victims across state lines into an abolition state.[33] Indeed it has been said that criminals prefer to take their chances in Massachusetts with capital punishment than to be subjected to reputedly more certain conviction in Rhode Island without the death penalty. The truth is, however, that the typical murder involves no such rational forethought, but instead is irrational behavior. Even when the plot is more deliberate, the expectation of execution is slight. The death penalty possibly influences the rare professional killer more than the far more numerous nonprofessionals, but even this is uncertain.

It is also important to note that differences in the prevalence of murder vary greatly within any state, though the legal penalty is the same throughout its jurisdiction.[34] This fact supports the principal conclusion of all careful studies. The major cause of murder is not the presence or absence

[29] Thorsten Sellin, "The Death Penalty and Police Safety," *Minutes of Proceedings and Evidence, No. 20, of Joint Committee of the Senate and the House of Commons on Capital Punishment of the Canadian Parliament*, pp. 718–41, quoted in "Notes," *Journal of Criminal Law, Criminology and Police Science* (Jan.–Feb. 1959), pp. 465–66.

[30] Donald Campion, "The State Police and the Death Penalty," *ibid.*

[31] Leonard D. Savitz, "A Study in Capital Punishment," *Journal of Criminal Law, Criminology and Police Science* (Nov.–Dec. 1958), pp. 338–41.

[32] Cf. Norman S. Hayner and John R. Cranor, "The Death Penalty in Washington State," *Annals, loc. cit.*, pp. 101–104.

[33] Cf. *Report from the Select Committee on Capital Punishment*, London: H. M. Stationery Office, 1930, p. 71.

[34] G. B. Vold, "Can the Death Penalty Prevent Crime?" *The Prison Journal* (Oct. 1932), pp. 4–9.

of the death penalty, but social relations conducive to tensions preceding the act or strong desires to have someone out of the way.

Less significant are other arguments. Many criminals are said to be hopeless cases and better put out of the way instead of incurring expense to the state. The same argument, as Sutherland points out, would apply to many other dependent and pathological classes. It also applies to many criminals for whom capital punishment has never been suggested. It is usually a sufficient reply that the injury to humanitarian sentiments involved in wholesale killing of social ineffectives would far more than offset the saving in money.

There is common sense and some factual evidence to support the argument that juries are less willing to convict when the penalty is death. The Illinois Crime Survey[35] studying the disposition of murder cases in Cook County, Illinois, in 1927 and 1928 found that but 10 of 701 cases were sentenced to death and but 153 found guilty. This situation has changed somewhat since then. The claim that in England punishment is more certain than in the United States has but little factual basis. In 1948, 170 murders in England resulted in but 30 convictions and but 10 executions. Nor has capital punishment been more frequently carried out in England than, for example, in New York State.

Capital punishment has also been opposed on the ground that it is irreparable. The number of innocent among the accused who have been executed cannot be known. There have been authentic cases of such miscarriages of justice.[36] Their number has probably been very small in democracies like the United States, except, perhaps, in the case of the Negro, where the gathering of incontrovertible evidence may not have been as painstaking as in the case of whites. The number has undoubtedly been greater than is known, however, because prosecuting attorneys are presumably not inclined to give more publicity than necessary to their own mistakes of this sort. Pollak tells us that the causes of such errors, aside from prejudice against some minority group or class, have been use of circumstantial evidence, false identification, false confessions forced by mistreatment, false promises of immunity, and convictions of persons suffering from severe mental disorders.[37]

A prominent lawyer,[38] after careful study, has concluded the existence

---

[35] *Op. cit.,* p. 627

[36] Edwin M. Borchard, *Convincing the Innocent* (New Haven, Conn.: Yale University Press, 1932). Cf. also Florence L. Sanville, "When Justice Goes Astray," in Julia E. Johnsen *Capital Punishment* (New York: H. W. Wilson, 1939), pp. 38–44.

[37] Otto Pollak, "The Errors of Justice," *Annals, loc. cit.,* pp. 115–23.

[38] Herbert B. Ehrmann, "The Death Penalty and the Administration of Justice," *Annals, loc. cit.,* pp. 73–84.

of the death penalty tended to destroy the proper administration of justice and hinder its improvement. With the death penalty, sentences tend to be based on emotions rather than upon rational consideration either of facts or of the consequences of punishment or release. Capital punishment has stood in the way of such reforms in law and procedure as critics have recommended. This has been true because, with the death penalty, judges have been inclined to allow the accused otherwise indefensible technical defenses and to urge that these be retained in the law.

Finally, the effect of the death penalty on the general public is a most important question. Yet this effect can only be surmised. Not only a sane solution of the crime problem, but also a generally happy social existence, seems to depend not a little upon the reduction of hatred and violence to a minimum. Moreover, the society which values life should not readily take it. It would seem, then, that only absolutely incontrovertible evidence that the abolition of capital punishment will mean a significant increase in murder would suffice to justify its retention. The evidence, to say the least, is not incontrovertible.

Suggested Readings

Andrews, William. *Bygone Punishments.* London: William Andrews and Company, 1899. Descriptions of corporal and capital punishments. Profusely illustrated.

Annals of the American Academy of Political and Social Science (Nov. 1952). This issue contains 19 authoritative articles on various aspects of capital punishment, including statistical measures of effectiveness.

Atholl, Justin. *The Reluctant Hangman.* London: John Long Limited, 1956. The biography of a nineteenth-century English executioner.

Caldwell, Robert Graham. *Red Hannah.* Philadelphia: University of Pennsylvania Press, 1947. The history and contemporary operation of Delaware's whipping post law. The author dispassionately analyzes evidence for and against its use and presents a statistical analysis of 1,100 whippings, including the number of lashes given.

Earle, Alice Morse. *Curious Punishments of Bygone Days.* Chicago: Herbert S. Stone and Company, 1896. Corporal punishments in colonial America: bilboes, stocks, ducking stool, pillory, etc.

Ives, George. *A History of Penal Methods.* Philadelphia: Frederick A Stokes Company, 1914. Still one of the standard works on the subject. Especially good on punishments in classical and medieval times.

Teeters, Negley K. "Public Executions in Pennsylvania 1682 to 1834," *Journal of the Lancaster County Historical Society* (Spring, 1960). The English were not alone in their zest for public hangings. A well-known criminological historian examines Pennsylvania's quaint folkways at the gallows.

CHAPTER 18

Criminal Law

In Chapter 2 we considered law-making and law-breaking as aspects of conflict processes in our society. We also emphasized the importance of the legal profession as a pattern-setting group influencing potential criminals toward and away from crime. In the present chapter we consider the law more descriptively and shall not repeat evidence that law is an expression of American culture modified by the roles of subgroups.

Law may be thought of as a device for limiting discretion in the punishment of offenders. It limits the discretion of injured parties and prescribes a certain orderly procedure in determining guilt and assessing punishment. It sets limits to the discretion of constituted authorities in dealing with criminals. The police, prosecutors, courts, prisons, parole boards, and other agencies may differentiate in their treatment of offenders only so far as the law permits. Yet the trend is toward laws like probation and indeterminate sentence acts which permit a wide range of possible punishments or treatments, leaving specific treatment increasingly to courts or parole authorities. Nevertheless, the law still does prescribe specific punishments for large numbers of crimes, including some of the most serious.

Nature of the Criminal Law

As the Roman Empire decayed into barbarism, the Eastern Roman Empire continued for a time to preserve the values and institutions of the darkening West. Among its great legacies was the codification of law sponsored by the emperor Justinian, whose lawyers and jurists performed their difficult task of systematizing the disorderly accumulation of the previous millennium in the amazingly short time of six years (529–535 A.D.). The resulting Code of Justinian, known now more formally as Roman Civil Law, eventually became the basis of the legal systems of continental Europe, Scotland, and Latin America, a role it began playing when European rulers, aggrandizing their territorial hegemony, cast about for a basis upon which to build a coherent structure of law.

For uncertain reasons, the English chose a different path. Faced with a motley assortment of feudal custom, canon, and local, manorial, and commercial laws which interfered with his own hegemonic ambitions, Henry II (1133–1189) created a system in which London-trained royal judges, trying cases throughout the kingdom, began *writing* law in the form of judicial decisions. These decisions reflected—more or less—established English customs and values. This procedure contrasted sharply with that followed in other countries, which, under Roman Civil Law influence, often sought the bases of legislation in a body of abstract legal principles. The accumulated body of judicial decisions became known as the "common law," i.e., applying commonly throughout a territory. Eight common-law felonies were eventually spelled out: murder, manslaughter, sodomy, rape, robbery, larceny, arson, and burglary. The occasional archaic wording of American criminal statutes reflects the fact that after we achieved our independence from Britain our state legislatures usually followed the common-law definitions of crime, in some instances lifting them directly from the decisions reached by English judges in earlier times.

Along with the ancient common law [1] there exists "statute law," established by legislative bodies rather than by judges. The role of judges in Anglo-American countries nevertheless continues to be a vital one, for judges continue to interpret the law through decisions they must reach when disputed legal issues come before them. The net effect of this constant ad-

---

[1] Strictly speaking, ours is not a common-law country, because we have made explicit in statute form law which would otherwise exist in the form of collated decisions. Our jurists, however, still refer to "common-law offenses"; and despite the fact that modern criminal laws far exceed in number the eight felonies of olden times, these eight still constitute the bulk of felony actions in our courts.

judication is, among other things, the updating of laws to bring them into closer conformity with current conditions, reducing somewhat the need for updating through legislative action. Since judicial decisions themselves usually have the force of law (the so-called "law of precedent"), it is sometimes said that judges are the real law-makers in Anglo-American cultures. At any rate, a citizen seeking to learn where the legal boundaries of criminal conduct lie must do more than merely read the statutes; he must also know what decisions have been made concerning them.

Felonies and Misdemeanors

The word *felony* originally denoted in its English usage certain breaches of contractual obligations existing within feudal social structures. In time, *felony* acquired additional semantic baggage through its application, under common law, to offenses punishable by death or loss of limb, together with confiscation of lands and goods. Since these were crimes of a serious nature —"malicious, wicked, and base"—a *felony* was a crime embodying these unpleasant qualities, and a *felon* was a person with sufficiently malicious and evil intent to commit such crimes. It probably did not require many generations of such usage before proper Englishmen came to regard *felons* as a special category of human beings, even though their only distinguishing characteristic was the fact of their having been so labeled by a court. Although *felony* in contemporary usage has lost most of its earlier transcendental connotations, it is still current and is used to designate in general those offenses for which one may be incarcerated in a state institution for a year or more. Vestiges of its ancient significance still persist, as seen by the practice in many states of automatically stripping a convicted person of certain civil rights, which may be restored only through executive clemency.

A *misdemeanor* (literally, an act of misconduct) is any crime less than a felony, for which one may not in general be incarcerated for more than one year, usually in a county institution.[2]

In addition to felonies and misdemeanors, a third category of crimes, *summary offenses,* can be said to exist. These are best exemplified by city or county ordinances governing traffic, rubbish disposal, public nuisances, amusement places, and the like, breach of which can be punished summarily by justices of the peace, usually through fines and short terms of imprisonment ("ten days or ten dollars").

[2] Again, the student must keep in mind that generalizations are risky in the face of 52 criminal codes existing within and among the United States. Pennsylvania, for example, provides three years' imprisonment for certain misdemeanors.

The student must avoid assuming that conviction within any of these three categories is necessarily indicative of a convicted person's degree of dangerousness, need for rehabilitation, character, or any other attribute. Robbery is technically a more heinous offense than assault and battery (a misdemeanor), but many a would-be strong-arm robber has pleaded guilty to assault and battery and taken the milder medicine than he might have had to swallow had he stood trial for attempted robbery and been convicted. Many a man convicted of vagrancy (a misdemeanor) has had a long-standing need for rehabilitation, while many a man found guilty of embezzlement (in some states a felony) may be otherwise a solid citizen. Contemporary penological theory denies the diagnostic value of legal categories.

The Law of Insanity and Responsibility

BACKGROUND

Any system of criminal law must hew in some degree to the doctrine that individuals are more or less responsible for their own actions. Whether the law's purpose be to coerce, deter, extract revenge, punish, or placate the deities, its application to individuals would make little sense without this assumption. But early in the history of civilization recognition was made of the fact that the deliberateness of acts varies under different circumstances. Among the provisions of the oldest complete legal code known—that of Hammurabi of Babylon (about 1800 B.C.)—was one requiring that an eye probing into forbidden secrets be removed from its owner's head. But Hammurabi's lawyers, inheritors of many previous generations of Middle Eastern legal thought, whose authors had long recognized that an eye may so probe without its owner's deliberate intention, knew that its loss under these circumstances would be grossly unjust. The code took account, as civilized codes must, of the need to recognize such human shortcomings. It provided for lesser penalties when crimes resulted from carelessness or negligence rather than from deliberate intent.

But what of mental disorder and responsibility? The earliest codes took no cognizance of insanity as reducing blame. Only until the emergence of Mohammedan law in the seventh century A.D. do we find what appears to be the first clear distinction between crime (in this case, homicide) by the mentally sound and by deranged persons.[3] But this distinction found no

[3] John Biggs, Jr., *The Guilty Mind: Psychiatry and the Law of Homicide* (New York: Harcourt, Brace, 1955), chap. 2.

place in European laws until the first quarter of the nineteenth century, although judicial practice in England for at least 100 years had allowed defenses on the grounds of insanity. Not until 1843 was a definitive attempt made to achieve a concept of mental disorder free of the vagaries of those used in earlier litigation.

THE M'NAGHTEN RULE

In 1843 a Scotsman named Daniel M'Naghten tried to assassinate Sir Robert Peel, the Prime Minister, but, through an error in identification, killed instead one of Peel's secretaries, Edward Drummond. The testimony of nine medical men convinced a jury that M'Naghten was insane (he apparently suffered from some form of paranoia). His acquittal on this ground alarmed and angered Queen Victoria and her advisors, moving them to request from the judiciary a clear principle to be applied in future criminal cases. The so-called "M'Naghten Rule" was the result:

To establish a defense on the ground of insanity, it must be clearly proved that, at the time of the committing of the act, the party accused was labouring under such a defect of reason, from disease of the mind, as not to know the nature and quality of the act he was doing; or if he did know it, that he did not know that he was doing what was wrong.[4]

The application of these rules—known also as the "knowledge test"—soon became established practice in most Anglo-American legal systems. But as medical knowledge advanced, their inadequacy provoked mounting complaints from psychiatrists and interested laymen, who felt that the rules were founded upon a naive cognitive conception of mental disorder. One of the few exceptions to the use of the rules has been the state of New Hampshire, which since 1870 has allowed acquittal if it can be shown that a crime was caused by mental disease. In the celebrated case of *Durham v. United States*,[5] however, the District of Columbia Court of Appeals in 1954 reversed the conviction in a lower federal court of one Monte Durham, charged with housebreaking, who had sought to defend himself on the ground of mental disease. The higher court discarded the right-wrong test as inadequate for the determination of criminal responsibility ". . . in that (a) it does not take sufficient account of psychic realities and scientific knowledge, and (b) it is based upon one symptom and so cannot validly be applied in all circumstances." The court followed the New Hampshire

[4] 10 Clark and Finnelly 208 *et seq.;* 8 *English Reports,* Reprint, 722 *et seq.* (quoted in Biggs, *op. cit.,* p. 105).
[5] As set forth (214 Fed 2nd 862) in *Federal Reporter* (Oct. 4, 1954), pp. 862–76.

precedent and laid down the rule that ". . . an accused is not criminally responsible if his unlawful act was the product of mental disease or defect." It is not sufficient for the accused to be afflicted with a mental disease or defect. There must be a causal connection between this and his crime, and this is a matter for the jury to decide. In reaching such a determination, the jury may rely on psychiatric evidence about the character of the accused's mental disease or defect. The jury is not confined solely to considering whether or not the accused knew the difference between right and wrong.

The Durham decision was hailed by the psychiatric branch of the medical profession and by many practitioners in the behavioral sciences as being a long step toward a needed *rapprochement* between law and medicine. Although the only state so far to adopt legislatively the Durham rule has been Maine (in 1961), it has been pushed hard in other states. Opposition to the rule has come from many quarters. One of its most outspoken critics is Professor Herbert Wechsler of the Columbia Law School,[6] who finds prominent among its weaknesses the extreme difficulty of deciding whether a particular crime is *caused* by "mental disease or defect." The Model Criminal Code presently being drafted by the American Law Institute avoids this difficulty by providing that "a person is not responsible for criminal conduct if at the time of such conduct as a result of mental disease or defect he lacks substantial capacity either to appreciate the criminality [wrongfulness] of his conduct or to conform his conduct to the requirements of law." [7] The Model Code would thus provide a compromise between the cognitive nature of the M'Naghten Rule and the psychiatric view that mentally disturbed individuals may be fully aware of their acts but be volitionally non-responsible.

Another quarter from which the Durham decision has been attacked is that of one of sociology's most lively critics of psychiatry, Professor Michael Hakeem of the University of Wisconsin. Hakeem's opinion is that forensic psychiatry has succeeded in overselling itself to a substantial part of the legal profession. Because psychiatric testimony is necessary in any case where defense is based on a plea of mental illness, Hakeem urges the legal profession to take a hard look at psychiatry's claims of forensic competence.

[6] Herbert Wechsler, "The Criteria of Criminal Responsibility," *The University of Chicago Law Review* (Winter, 1955), pp. 367–76. In a letter to the senior author (March 21, 1955) Professor Wechsler said, "I do not think that the formulation of the court in Durham will or should receive general acceptance either legislatively or judicially." His most recent criticism is "On Culpability and Crime: The Treatment of *Mens Rea* in the Model Penal Code," *Annals of the American Academy of Political and Social Science* (Jan. 1962), pp. 24–41.

[7] American Law Institute, *Model Penal Code, Proposed Final Draft No. 1: Sentencing and Correction* (April 24, 1961), Sec. 4.01 (1).

At the conclusion of a detailed review of the contradictory statements within psychiatric literature, Hakeem bluntly states that: [8]

Psychiatric testimony should not be admissible in court. The courts have traditionally followed the principle that expert testimony and evidence that purport to be scientific will not be admissible unless their reliability and validity have been amply tested and unless substantial agreement among the appropriate experts has been demonstrated. When it comes to psychiatric testimony, the courts are acting in heedless disregard and flagrant violation of this eminently sound principle. It should be unmistakably clear on the basis of the evidence adduced here . . . that psychiatrists have not attained the level of competence and scientific reliability and validity necessary to make their testimony eligible for serious consideration by the courts.

While Hakeem's broadside is unlikely to stem the growing tendency of the courts to heed psychiatry's counsels, it can remind the student that these counsels are not unchallenged.

THE MODERN LAW AND PROCEDURE [9]

Many American states have added the irresistible-impulse test to the knowledge tests. Some states have also a special delusion test. The states are almost equally divided in putting the burden of proof to show insanity on prosecution or defense. The tendency is to require less proof of insanity than formerly. Though the court may exclude witnesses as nonspecialists,[10] often any practicing licensed physician may testify as to sanity, and if a witness qualifies as an expert, he need not be a physician. In 1937 the Conference of Commissioners on Uniform State Laws drafted the Uniform Expert Testimony Act, which eliminates many of the abuses often associated with the use of such witnesses, but the law has been only tardily copied by the states. The trend, however, is to require that experts be appointed. Experts base their opinion on a personal examination of the accused or on the testimony in the case, or, when the evidence is conflicting, they answer a hypothetical question based upon assumed facts involved in the evidence. Opposing attorneys, clever in framing such questions, can make an honest

[8] Michael Hakeem, "A Critique of the Psychiatric Approach to Crime and Correction," *Law and Contemporary Problems* (Autumn, 1958), pp. 650–82. This important article warrants study by every student of criminology.

[9] Cf. Manfred S. Guttmacher and Henry Weihofen, *Psychiatry and the Law* (New York: W. W. Norton & Company, 1952). This scholarly book is one of the best among many sources for the student of the much-argued issue of criminal responsibility.

[10] Cf. Winfred Weihofen, "Psychiatric Expert Testimony in Criminal Cases Since M'Naghten—A Review," *Journal of Criminal Law, Criminology and Police Science* (Sept.–Oct. 1951), p. 294.

expert give two different answers. In some states the court at its discretion
may appoint experts of its own, and in a few states such appointment is
mandatory upon the court. Several states wisely provide for commitment of
the accused, when suspected of being insane, to a hospital for a period for
observation.[11] If the question of sanity is not raised at the trial, a reviewing
court will not raise it on appeal. If the accused is found insane in court trial,
there should always be provision for committing him to a hospital. Procedure varies as to this and also as to release after recovery.

At the time of trial the accused must have power to understand the
proceedings against him and to make a rational defense. The burden of
proof here is usually on the defendant. If the trial had begun at the time of
finding the accused insane, he is returned for trial on his recovery. If he is
found insane after trial but before sentence, sentence is stayed until he becomes sane. If a man condemned to die is shown to be insane at the time set
for execution, execution is stayed.

THE PROCEDURE IN MASSACHUSETTS UNDER THE BRIGGS LAW

The insanity plea is frequently abused. Insanity is often feigned; unscrupulous lawyers will strive to prove mental disease when there is no
factual basis for its existence; specialists will frequently find it possible to
argue conscientiously for the side which employs them because of the doubt
which frequently surrounds the question of sanity.

Among more conservative methods of partially meeting this problem,
the Briggs Law and related procedures in Massachusetts [12] have been widely
advocated. This law as amended provides in sum that when a person is indicted for a capital offense or has been indicted or convicted for any felony
more than once, his mental condition shall be examined by the Department
of Mental Diseases. The department's report is available both to the court
and to the prosecuting and defense attorneys. It is not admissible as evidence, but its availability has tended to discourage useless wrangles in court.
No restriction is put upon either side calling experts of its own, but the
practice has largely ceased. Certain weaknesses in this law have been recognized, but they are not inherent in such a system. The law has avoided expense of costly trials, reduced "battles of experts," protected the rights of

---

[11] Guttmacher and Weihofen, *op. cit.,* p. 420. For an illuminating discussion of
Swedish practices, see Olaf Kinberg, "The Swedish Organization of Forensic Psychiatry," *Journal of Criminal Law, Criminology and Police Science* (July–Aug. 1953),
pp. 235–50.

[12] Winfred Overholser, M.D., "The Briggs Law of Massachusetts: A Review and
An Appraisal," *Journal of Criminal Law and Criminology* (March–April 1935), pp.
859–83.

he accused who is mentally incompetent, indicated a more socially useful disposition which may be made in such cases, and helped educate some of he judges to a more social point of view.

CRITICISM OF LEGAL METHODS OF DETERMINING
SANITY AND RESPONSIBILITY

Glueck and others have shown that the law fails to cover many types of mental deviation which do influence behavior, and have urged that a condition of partial responsibility be recognized in borderline cases.[13] Some hold that recognition of such partial responsibility is philosophically untenable and also that such a compromise delays a hoped-for disregard of "responsibility" and the substitution for it of estimated future dangerousness,[14] which is the real need. Similarly, the concept of temporary insanity seems to have little utility. Rather there is need that the court consider the effects of diverse immediate and earlier social experiences in assessing the future dangerousness of each individual. Recognized defects in current procedure also include lack of examinations before trial, lack of competent expert opinion, restriction of consideration to certain types of criminals, and inadequate protection of society in some states against the release of those found insane. In addition, altogether too much stress upon mental and too little upon social factors has been evident to the sociologist.

For the discovery of cases needing study, clinics attached to some of our metropolitan courts have shown themselves increasingly useful. Some have urged that employment of experts by either side in the case not be allowed, but such a measure would probably be unconstitutional. Some suggest that experts be required to consult and to give a joint report. Restrictions upon the compensation of experts would eliminate one evil. Some would wholly replace the jury with experts to determine sanity; but on the one hand, such a step would be unconstitutional at the present time, and on the other, psychiatrists can hardly pass upon the metaphysical question of responsibility.

Finally, a few students would abandon the search for responsibility and substitute estimation of the dangerousness of the individual. A tribunal of experts would investigate the mental state of the accused as but one element in his personality and conditioning and determine treatment in terms of his probable future.

[13] Sheldon Glueck, *Mental Disorder and the Criminal Law* (Boston: Little, Brown, 1925), chap. 12 and *passim*.
[14] Cf. J. Walter McKenna, "Criminal Law," *Annual Survey of Law* (New York: New York University, 1946), pp. 1049–50.

Trends in Criminal Law

APPLICATION OF POSITIVE PRINCIPLES

In an earlier chapter we noted changes in criminological thought away from classical principles of free will, equal responsibility, concern over past acts, and emphasis on punishment equated to the wickedness of the criminal as seen in his act. We noted modifications of these principles in the neoclassical school, which wrote our early codes of law, with concern for the principle that *mens rea* must be shown to constitute a criminal act. Later came the beginnings of the positive school, which looks for causes, limits or denies free will, substitutes the principle of accountability for that of responsibility, and aims not so much to balance accounts with criminals as to protect society through individualized treatment, rehabilitation, and constructive preventive efforts. For decades criminal law has been basically neoclassical but with a gradual trend toward implementation of positive principles. This trend has been seen in indeterminate sentence laws and the legal foundations of probation, parole, reformation, differential treatment of juveniles and youths, and new modifications of the treatment of insanity pleas in court. Changes in the law have also shown some willingness to delegate discretion to administrative authorities, who will study the individual criminal and deal with him in terms of his own personal characteristics and situation. This tends to deprive the court of part of the sentencing function. These changes have followed the development of the psychological and social sciences. The use of discretion by classification centers or parole boards has sometimes been extended without full legal definition of the limits of their authority. This expansion has led to fears that criminals may be deprived of the right of due process of law. The organized legal profession has rightly been concerned over such dangers.

Latterly, however, law itself has come to be thought of as an application of the growing science of human behavior. Today the most significant trend within the legal profession has been toward plans to alter the law in the light of the findings of psychological and social science, and even toward field research into human behavior conducted by the organized legal profession itself, albeit in cooperation with social scientists.

Writing in 1951, and concerned with the events of a century rather than solely with these recent trends, Dean Albert J. Harno [15] traced trends under

[15] "Some Significant Developments in Criminal Law and Procedure in the Last Century," *Journal of Criminal Law, Criminology and Police Science* (Nov.–Dec. 1951), pp. 427–67.

such topics as the following: less concern with *mens rea;* changes in the law of insanity; greater recognition of the criminal responsibility of corporations; expansion of the doctrine of conspiracy with possible threat to individual liberties; and substantive reforms, seen in indeterminate sentence laws and habitual criminal acts, probation and parole, the juvenile court movement, and the federal and state youth correction acts, together with procedural reforms looking toward less use of the grand jury and extension of waiver of petit jury trials. We deal with the effects of such trends elsewhere.

Currently, activities of the organized bar indicate law itself becoming more scientific and yet demanding legal authority for and limitations upon the treatment of criminals by administrative authorities. The American Law Institute is currently engaged in a very large project looking toward the development of a model penal code which will steer a middle course between the Scylla of an antiquated law out of touch with the realities of human existence and the Charybdis of denial of due process of law and dangers to individual liberty on the part of administrative authorities.

The Model Penal Code proposals for sentencing [16] embody several interesting departures in navigating between rock and whirlpool. *The role of legislatures* in determining sentences to imprisonment is limited to establishing three degrees of felonies from most to least serious; within each degree judicial sentencing latitudes are spelled out. *The indeterminate sentence* principle is adopted in so far as judges are obliged to assign minima and maxima rather than a fixed term within a minimum and maximum. Thus, a person convicted of a second-degree felony would receive a minimum term of anywhere between one and three years (as the judge sees fit) and a maximum of ten years (no choice),[17] the date of release being decided upon by a paroling authority within these limits. *Parole is built into the sentence* for those receiving more than one year's imprisonment and must be for at least one year and no more than five.[18] Provisions are made for *extended terms* to apply to professional criminals, aggressive offenders who are mentally abnormal, and multiple offenders. Again, three degrees of felonies are established, each with higher minima and maxima than for ordinary terms, but judges would not be *obliged* to give extended terms.[19] *Pre-sentence investigations* would be mandatory in all felony convictions, all convictions of persons less than 22 years of age, and extended sentence cases, whether a felony or misdemeanor is involved.[20] *The confidentiality*

[16] American Law Institute, *op. cit.*
[17] *Ibid.,* Sec. 6.06.
[18] *Ibid.,* Sec. 6.10 (2).
[19] *Ibid.,* Secs. 7.03, 6.07.
[20] *Ibid.,* Sec. 7.07.

of pre-sentence investigations is modified by requiring that defendants or their counsels be informed of the contents of such investigations and be given an opportunity to contravert them upon request. This would presumably obviate the danger of long sentences being based on misinformation.

The Model Penal Code thus recognizes the principle of individualized treatment while retaining the older concept that length of sentence should still bear some relationship to *offense,* as well as to offender, on grounds of the presumed deterrent effect of long sentences and on recognition of the public's feeling that "justice should be done"—i.e., that longer sentences be meted out for the more serious offenses. The reader will see that the organized bar faces the dilemma of a felt need to apply mutually inconsistent principles, any one of which might, perhaps, come to dominate in actual practice according to the predilections of those to whom discretion is given. This dilemma reflects, not so much the unwillingness of progressive lawyers to accept the new penology as basic attitudes, values, and concepts of justice which persist in our culture. It also reflects the incompleteness of our knowledge of the causes of crime and what to do about them.

EXPANSION OF THE AREA OF PENALIZED CONDUCT

Expansion of the scope of criminal law is seen in increased penalizing of acts believed to threaten government. During World Wars I and II and after, there was probably increased fear of movements threatening organized government. Recently the exigencies of cold war with the Communist world have led to defining as crime affiliation of men with groups known by them to advocate the violent overthrow of government. The doctrine of guilt by association has crept into the doctrine of conspiracy. We cannot go into the details of this knotty problem. Many have felt that such trends and the methods used to prosecute suspects have in some degree moved us in the direction of the very totalitarianism which, rightly or wrongly, has been thought of as almost synonymous with Communism. Some of these efforts have been changed by Supreme Court decisions protecting civil liberties. Our Department of Justice has a Civil Liberties Bureau. Its very existence indicates that American law still covers violation of civil liberties as well as protection of life and property.

Increased regulation of business and finance. Business practices formerly tolerated have been defined as crimes. Hall [21] says one effect of this

---

[21] Livingston Hall, "The Substantive Law of Crimes, 1887–1936," *Harvard Law Review* (Feb. 1937), pp. 616–18.

as been to make us all criminals. Examples of legislation in this field include the penalizing of false advertising, the misuse of trademarks, and conspiracies in restraint of trade, laws regulating labor-capital relations, and wartime OPA regulations. Violations of such laws have, as we have seen, often constituted what Sutherland has called white-collar crime. Embezzlement, false entries, and false reports are penalized. Statutes now forbid the receipt of funds while insolvent. There are also laws punishing insolvency caused by fraud or the negligence of the officers of a bank.

Laws controlling use of automobiles, radio, television, and other means of communication. The trend here has been toward administrative control through the issuance or denial of licenses. This new weapon of the state has great potentiality for effective crime repression, but it also contains the possibility of undue interference with popular liberties.

Strengthening pure food, drug, liquor, and racketeering laws. Our narcotic drug laws carry increasingly heavy penalties and are widened in scope. Partly as a result of the work of the Kefauver Commission, the law against gambling has been extended.

Effectiveness of the Criminal Law

The effectiveness of criminal law cannot be accurately measured. The law is but one of the agencies of social control. Custom, religious belief, current group approvals and disapprovals, the pressure of interest groups, and the influence of general public opinion constitute more efficient means of regulating human conduct than do the sanctions of the law. The law's capacity to protect from crime depends upon the operation of all these other agencies. The operation of the law itself is more immediately dependent upon the efficiency of its enforcement by police, prosecutors, courts, and penal systems. We cannot therefore attribute solely to the nature of the law the success or failure of the campaign against crime.

Yet law is an important element in this whole. The task of determining the scope of law and the particular kind of acts which should be made punishable by the state is one of the most exacting problems of political science. The need for balance between liberty and social protection is still with us. The very weaknesses of our law and its enforcement are partly inherent in just those liberties which we cherish in a democracy.

If the analysis in this book is at all sound, it is significant that law itself is moving toward acceptance of the findings of criminology as the basis for a rational code of treatment of the crime problem. Specific aspects of this need and its partial recognition in many areas will appear, as we describe in later chapters various effects of our system of justice and of our delinquency prevention programs.

Suggested Readings

American Law Institute. *Model Penal Code*. Philadelphia: The Institute, various years. The student should study, under this general heading, the many drafts of a proposed revised penal code upon which the A.L.I. has long been working. Of particular interest are the commentary sections, which discuss the legal, scientific, and social bases for specific proposals.

Nice, Richard W., editor. *Crime and Insanity*. New York: Philosophical Library, Incorporated, 1958. Eight essays on problems of justice for mentally disturbed defendants. Six of the authors are psychiatrists or psychologists, so the book generally pleads for liberalizing the law of insanity.

Radzinowicz, Leon. *A History of English Criminal Law and Its Administration from 1750*. 3 volumes. New York: The Macmillan Company, 1948–1957. An exhaustive, scholarly, and fascinating account.

CHAPTER 19

Police

For most people public authority is perceived most concretely in the form of local uniformed law-enforcement officers. In all communities except the tiniest hamlets can be found one or more of these public employees who are specifically charged with the daily responsibility for protecting their communities from a variety of more or less clearly specified persons, acts, and circumstances deemed harmful to the public well-being, ranging from berserk killers to overtime parking. In addition, the police may be called upon to perform certain routine and prosaic tasks only incidentally related to law enforcement: administering drivers' tests, reporting breaks in streets and sidewalks, censoring movies, helping firemen, guarding school crossings, and keeping traffic flowing smoothly in city streets.

And for most persons who break the law, contact with the police in their arresting capacity represents the initial experience such persons have with the several echelons in the state's machinery of justice. To the persisting offender the arrest experience is often significant as the most dramatic element in his relations with "the law." Unnecessary harsh treatment by police may be injurious not only to the body of the offender but also to his attitudes toward the state and society generally, for it may be at this point that he begins to define himself as one who is in conflict with society.

Commentators on the police in modern American society have

317

for many years complained with drum-beat regularity that the police are inefficient, brutal, corrupt, and lawless. The present authors are aware of few criminology texts in which these complaints are not repeated, and the readers can probably recall hearing them voiced from time to time by civil rights and race relations groups and by clergymen, social workers, and other individuals working in human relations. There can be no doubt that *some* police are inefficient, brutal, corrupt, and lawless, but to tar entire police establishments with this brush, particularly in the absence of quantitative measures of these undesired characteristics, seems to us to engage in loose and quite unscientific thinking. The complainants, moreover, seem indifferent to the gains made in the quality of police work over what existed in the past. Contrasted with the "watch" of the eighteenth century and before, and with the police of the nineteenth century, today's officers are paragons of virtue and efficiency. To contrast the present with the actual past rather than with an ideal future can often be instructive.

History of the Police

Two disparate traditions of the police have existed in post-medieval Western cultures: the "continental" and the "Anglo-Saxon." Under the former, law enforcement developed as an arm of centralized authority attendant upon the growth of national governments and sometimes, as in Czarist Russia and in France of the *ancien régime,* functioned principally as an instrument of despotic monarchs. Police bodies were often branches of national military establishments, and in terms of training, discipline, regular pay, centralized administration, and uniform clothing they became, at an early date, "efficient" keepers of law and order. To this day continental European countries benefit from this tradition not alone in efficiency of law enforcement but also from the fact that career police officers enjoy a social status akin to that of career military personnel.

The Anglo-Saxon police tradition, on the other hand, springs from a configuration of attitudes which were profoundly suspicious of central authority and hostile to the idea of guarding the local peace with militia. For an astonishing length of time English-speaking cultures preferred to put up with disorder and crime rather than take the risk of strengthening those who might oppress them. From the eleventh century on, with the decay of feudal authority and the growth of urban communities, the problem of social control, minimal under essentially rural patterns of social organization, became increasingly acute as the capacity of family, manor, and church to give order to social relationships declined. Economic and social survival in the growing commercial towns were based upon individualized struggle, rather than upon the older sense of responsibility to kin and commune. The problem was further complicated as the new towns—and the trade routes connecting them—fell prey to a class of brigands known as *outlaws:* rootless persons, shunned and friendless, who had been placed outside the protection of civil law as punishment for certain judicial offences. With few means of surviving other than by grubbing a precarious living in isolated regions or by pillage, outlaws had been a problem for centuries. Now, with material wealth increasing as trading contacts grew between Europe and the Near East, and with the concentration of this wealth in towns instead of castle keeps, brigandage in the forms of robbery, burglary, pocketpicking, and the like arose to plague the peaceful burghers, who wished only to enjoy the benefits of trade.

The beginnings of civil protection against crime and disorder in the towns of England came with the promulgation in 1285 by Edward I of the famous Edict of Winchester. Among the several provisions of this act was one requiring local groups of property owners, numbering 100 each, to be responsible for keeping the peace in their district, an attempted revival of a much earlier Saxon custom. In this way the Edict laid down the principle of local rather than central responsibility for law enforcement. This principle was followed for centuries in Great Britain and is still followed throughout the United States, where it is the source of certain difficulties of police administration and law enforcement. The machinery of protection within each "hundred" was to consist of members patrolling in turn their districts each night, constituting thereby a citizens' *watch.* By the same Edict was created for each hundred a *conservator of the peace* charged, along with certain minor judicial duties, with responsibility for overseeing the watch. From these simple beginnings came the basic structure of town and city protection which endured in Great Britain until early in the nineteenth century and in the United States until the middle of that century.

Those who drew up the Edict of Winchester, however, failed to reckon with the growing spirit of individualism among the burgeoning bourgeois class. The sense of communal responsibility prevailing in Saxon culture could not be revived by fiat. However reasonable it might have seemed that property owners would have a vested interest in protecting their holdings, the fact was that the onerous chore of night patrolling was soon handed on to hirelings drawn often from the communities' least employable members: elderly men, boys without apprenticeships, cripples, unskilled migrants. From the beginning the pay, the conditions of employment, and the physical and mental requirements of hired watchmen were inadequate for the task they faced. The propertied citizens relied for protection, meanwhile, upon heavily barred and shuttered dwellings and upon the skill with weapons of themselves and their menservants. Those without such means of protection—probably the majority of town dwellers—continued to be the prey of growing numbers of criminals.

By the early decades of the eighteenth century, city population increases, complicated by the government's deliberate fostering of gin consumption for revenue purposes,[1] produced social conditions which approached an incredible nadir of drunkenness, illegitimacy, violence, crime, and brutalizing amusements. But so strong were the sentiments against establishing regular police forces that repeated efforts to do so for London alone—already a city of half a million by 1700—came to little until passage of the Middlesex Justices Act of 1792, which set up a kind of police force of 126 constables. The inadequacy of so small a number in a London grown by then to nearly one million soon became evident. Crime and disorder went unchecked, the latter becoming particularly threatening after the turn of the nineteenth cenutry, when riots against the corn laws and against machines put the English government in fear for its very existence. Reluctantly, and only after much maneuvering by Sir Robert Peel, the famous Police Bill of 1829 was enacted by Parliament, creating a uniformed force of 3,314 men. The uniforms were pointedly unmilitary in cut and color, and the officers were allowed only truncheons as weapons.

In less dramatic form, the growing cities of the United States similarly long put up with crime and disorder, relying upon ineffective day and night watches, private police, and, in a few places, militia. New York had no regular police force until 1844; Chicago, then a city of 100,000, depended on Fort Dearborn soldiers to quell crime until 1855. The adoption of regular police in American cities did not result in an immediate increase in law-enforcement efficiency. Nor did the extremely low wages offered attract high quality recruits—brawn and a taste for violence were the main prerequisites for joining the early forces. The new police soon became pawns in the spoils system so prevalent in our post-Civil War cities and shared in the general corruption in municipal politics.

---

[1] Patrick Pringle, *Hue and Cry: The Story of Henry and John Fielding and Their Bow Street Runners* (New York: William Morrow, 1955), pp. 26–27. For a graphic picture of London conditions, see chap. 1.

Town and Small-City Police [2]

The closest remaining counterparts to the ancient watch are the police departments in small, non-satellite towns and cities within which, considered in descending population rankings, crime and traffic problems diminish and other kinds of police responsibilities increase. The wages of small-town police are ludicrous. The median *maximum* salary for patrolmen in towns of 10,000 to 25,000 population in 1962 was only $4,800; in towns of 25,000 to 50,000 it was but $5,103.[3] Since the median salaries of new policemen in these cities were $4,248 and $4,551 [4] respectively, patrolmen can look forward to very little salary increase even after years of service.

The result is, of course, that serious, career-minded men are seldom found on the smallest police forces, those in towns under 10,000 population. These forces are manned instead by *time-servers,*[5] men to whom one job is pretty much like another, who complete their tours of duty with a minimum expenditure of energy, and who have no desire to improve their skills as policemen. In somewhat larger communities with better pay scales there are found, along with the time-servers, *law enforcers,* men impressed with the authority of their office, with their uniforms, clubs, and guns, and with their presumed public image as upholders of law and order. These men participate eagerly in police training conferences and related activities (academy training is seldom available) and seem particularly intrigued by instruction in judo, weapons, personal searches, and the like. In still larger forces are found, in addition to the other two types, *conciliators.* These are better-educated, articulate men for whom the courteous settling of disputes between citizens and between citizens and police is a main criterion of good police work. Like the law enforcers, they seek to improve their skills but lean toward scientific police work, legal learning, and the use of manipulation rather than authority in enforcing the law.

Non-satellite cities of fewer than 50,000 population seldom have pressing crime problems, nor, except on shopping days or high-school game

[2] The observations in this section are based on interviews with downstate Illinois policemen carried out in 1959 by the junior author. Gratitude is here expressed to the University of Illinois Faculty Research Board for its financial support of this project.

[3] *Municipal Year Book: 1962* (Chicago: International City Managers' Association, 1962), p. 432.

[4] *Ibid.*

[5] This and the two other type-designations used below were adduced from police interviews.

days, does traffic constitute particular difficulties. Police work of the storied variety—tracking down dangerous felons, doing intricate detective work, fighting gun battles, quelling public disturbances—is nearly nonexistent. What, then, do small-town officers do? At the request of the junior author a patrolman on a 14-man force in a mid-Illinois town of 12,000 carefully kept a log for three weeks in which he recorded every action taken during his tours of duty. Quoted below are his entries for a 7:00 p.m. to 3:00 a.m. tour on a Saturday night in July:

P.M.

7:00	Began tour of duty at station.
7:15	On duty in patrol car.
8:05	Received a complaint to pick up a man for beating his wife. A warrant was signed.
9:40	Received call on a prowler. Answered call. Could not find anyone in the area.
10:40	Provided an escort for a businessman transferring a large sum of money.
11:27	Had owner move an illegally parked car.

A.M.

12:20	Provided escort for businessman making night deposit.
12:42	Received call that there was a man at police station with a car on fire. Answered call. Helped extinguish fire in back seat of auto.
1:25	Found door of business place standing open. Checked building. Not a break in. Nothing disturbed.
3:00	Ended tour of duty.

During daylight hours the town fathers require of the officers numerous quasi-police duties, most of which the police feel should not be their responsibilities.[6] Some of them are: being present when banks open and close; distributing mail to town offices; carrying messages for town officials; driving officials to and from work; putting out brush fires; desk officer driving pumpers to fire for volunteers; reading water meters; helping count parking-meter receipts and other cash receipts; directing traffic on shopping-center parking lots; reporting burned-out street lights and broken pavement; catching stray animals; picking up and disposing of dead animals. Small-town officers are thus expected to "help out" around towns in ways which do little to strengthen their self-images as policemen.

---

[6] The *time-servers* seem not to mind ancillary duties: a job is a job. The *law enforcers* and *conciliators* prefer police work exclusively; traffic patrol and criminal investigation appear, respectively, to be favored by these two officer-types.

The State Police Movement

The response to the inadequacy of the sheriff-constable system of law enforcement in rural and rural non-farm areas has been the development of state police, some form of which is found in all states. That movement began with the establishment of the famous Texas Rangers in 1835. But the first permanent state police organization intended to enforce all state laws and organized on a semi-military basis was the Pennsylvania State Constabulary. As in some other states, that force originated partly because of desire to control violence connected with industrial unrest. Yet it has been precisely in that field that the opposition of organized labor has most restricted state police activities. In some states the force may not enter cities where there is industrial unrest except on request of the mayor or chief of police or on the explicit orders of the governor. There is no doubt that in the earlier days, at least, the unions had some reason for their objection that state police seemed more interested in protecting the employer's property than in protecting labor's personal rights. Such a bias is especially evident when the police are quartered on the property of the industrial plants, and improvement is reported when a place is provided for them elsewhere. The opposition of organized labor has declined, but both sides in a labor dispute may at times exert pressure making impartial law enforcement more difficult.

In spite of the universal spread of the state police movement, only in about 25 of the states do they have power to enforce the law against all kinds of crime. Elsewhere they are often concerned with the control of traffic chiefly. But the state police have sold themselves to the public. They are generally held to be more efficient and less often involved in politics than the average city police, and much more effective than the old sheriff-constable system. Illinois is a recent example of how a state police force, previously ineffective and politics-ridden, may have political influence almost completely eliminated in the selection of its personnel. On the initiative of the then Governor Adlai Stevenson, the state police were chosen on a competitive merit basis by a nonpartisan commission appointed by the governor for staggered 6-year terms. The board brought about substantially equal balance in the force between affiliates of the two major parties through discharge of large numbers of men belonging to the party which then had more than its "share" of police officers. That achieved, inquiries as to political affiliation of new candidates ceased, so that a nonpartisan, rather than a bipartisan, force should eventuate. Since participation in political activities of any kind by members of the state police constitutes grounds for removal, there is no more of the former almost universal spectacle of officers compelled to electioneer and do political favors for party leaders to whom they owed their jobs.

Besides partly making up for the inadequacies of the sheriff-constable system in rural areas, the state police in a number of jurisdictions render valuable services to smaller urban and town police by providing laboratory and other investigatory services in felony cases, operating limited police training programs, acting as radio links in communication between distant local points, and keeping state-wide criminal identification files.

City Police

NUMBERS AND SALARIES

There are over 200,000 policemen in the United States. The number of police needed in cities varies considerably not only with their size but also with the composition of their population, the prevalence of conditions making for crime, the caliber of the personnel employed, and the scope of the activities in which they are expected to engage.[7] In 1962 the median number of police employees per 1,000 population ranged from 1.37 for cities of 10,000 to 25,000 population to 2.68 for cities over 500,000 population. Salaries of patrolmen have also increased and vary with community size. Median entrance salaries in cities of 100,000 to 250,000 population amounted to $4,573; the figure for cities over a half million was $5,129. Chiefs of police had widely varying salaries with medians ranging from $10,000 to $16,000.[8]

FUNCTIONS

City police have been given many functions to perform and in addition have had to develop specialized activities such as identification and laboratory technical research. It is held, however, that the function of general crime prevention through the proper management of patrolmen remains basic, with specialized work increasingly needed but auxiliary.[9]

[7] O. W. Wilson, "Police Administration Developments, 1953," in *Municipal Year Book* (Chicago: International City Manager's Association, 1954), pp. 423*ff.*

[8] *Municipal Year Book, 1962*, pp. 431, 432.

[9] V. A. Leonard, *Police Organization and Management* (Brooklyn: The Foundation Press, 1951), p. 281.

Thus patrolmen, performing their basic duty to make crime dangerous, utilize increasingly scientific methods. Automobiles with two-way radios connected with a central control room have increasingly replaced or supplemented foot patrol. Police may arrest without warrant when they observe the commission of a crime or, in the case of a felony, when they have reason to believe that a crime has been committed by the man suspected.

A second police function is to protect property; a third to protect the innocent; a fourth to protect those charged with crime, including those they know to be guilty. Police share with the prosecutor's office the function of detecting crime and often have a separate bureau of detection. Police have also special divisions for fingerprinting, photographing, and otherwise identifying criminals, and for filing records.

Police have an important role to play as witnesses in court. Officers may be efficient thief-catchers and yet make a miserable appearance under cross-examination by a capable defense attorney. More important still is the unavoidable judicial function performed when the policeman must decide under what conditions to arrest. Here there is a basic need for absolute impartiality as between individuals, classes, races, and other subgroups. Yet it is realistic to remember that no one wants all laws enforced. Hence the police probably protect society best when they know when to look the other way, when to assist instead of arresting, when to warn, when to refer to other agencies, and when to bring a child or adult to the police station. The best protection against misuse of this important power of discretion seems to be the appointment of trained, incorruptible officers.

In recent decades the great increase in urban vehicular traffic in physical settings hard put to adjust to this increase has burdened the police with the difficult, highly technical, and relatively new responsibility for maintaining orderly, fast, and safe traffic flow. Perhaps in no other area of behavior is the ordinarily law-abiding citizen more likely to jeopardize public safety and good order than in his conduct as either a driver or pedestrian, and more likely to run afoul of the law. And in no other area are good relationships between the public and the police so apt to be jeopardized. O. W. Wilson, former dean of the University of California's School of Criminology and presently (1963) Chicago's commissioner of police, consequently recommends discretion in dealing with traffic violators:

The customary police procedure, on observing a violation of a criminal law or . . . a regulatory measure, is to arrest and prosecute the offender. This procedure, however, is not so effective against the traffic violator as against the criminal because the public frequently does not favor rigid traffic enforcement, although nearly all approve the punishment of criminals. Punishment will not correct the physical defects of the motorist or his car, though it may influence the owner's attitude. Punishment by itself will not increase driving skill, and if unfairly applied, it may create or aggravate an improper driving attitude.[10]

Wilson feels that the primary purpose of police action against the erring motorist should be to improve his driving habits; over-zealous traffic enforcement creates in a community antagonism toward the police which may interfere with the successful accomplishment of the total police job. For good public relations the police should know how much enforcement their community will tolerate, and work within this limit.[11]

LAW ENFORCEMENT AND POLICE DEPARTMENT STRUCTURE

To perform its basic repressive function effectively, a police force requires a semi-military type of organization, permitting the commissioner or chief to control and be responsible for the entire program. A department of 10 men will usually consist simply of a chief and his patrolmen. The task of coordinating a force five times this size will, of course, require a more elaborate organization: each 8-hour tour will need a lieutenant-in-charge, aided by a sergeant; the three lieutenants may be responsible to a captain, who in turn reports to the chief. The 20 or so cities in the United States with forces numbering 1,000 men or more [12] are organized on a *precinct* or *district* basis with (usually) a captain in charge, aided by three or more lieutenants, to whom sergeants are responsible. In the very largest forces (5,000 or more officers), the captains report to inspectors or their equivalent, who in turn are responsible to division chiefs, deputy commissioners, or the commissioner himself.

The problem of effective operation against crime in large cities is made more difficult by the very complications in police department structure. The longer the reach from those establishing basic policy to those executing this policy at the street level, the more likely that the seemingly inevitable difficulties arising from the nature of bureaucratic structures will intrude. Problems of communication upward and downward, of coordination, of control over subordinates, and of the growth of informal structures (working outside the established chain of command) are further complicated by the tendency for cultural heterogeneity of personnel to be greater at lower echelons than higher.[13] In terms of race, nationality background, religion,

[10] O. W. Wilson, *Police Administration* (New York: McGraw-Hill Book Company, 1950), p. 158.

[11] *Ibid.,* p. 159.

[12] *Municipal Year Book: 1960,* Table XVII, pp. 398–99.

[13] The possible significance of this was first pointed out to the junior author by Professor J. P. Shalloo.

age, education, and social class, greater variety, proportionately, appears to exist at the ranks of patrolmen and sergeants, less at the ranks of lieutenants and captains, and still less above them. The reason for this distribution lies mainly in the requisites for promotion, which not only are spelled out formally (efficiency, experience, ratings on examinations, etc.) but exist informally as well (for example, reluctance to promote non-whites or officers who are rigid in their enforcement practices). Heterogeneity would be most evident at the street level, and consequently so would the likelihood of the precinct men presenting in their bailiwicks diverse value systems toward law enforcement. A religious, lower-middle-class Protestant who regards gambling as morally harmful might be paired off in a squad car with a working-class Irish Catholic who plays the horses now and then. Similar variations in values may likewise exist with reference to prostitution, traffic in bootleg liquor, and the use of such "harmless" narcotics as marihuana and the barbiturates. However enthusiastically a new city administration possessing a more or less uniform cultural front may embark upon a program of "cleaning up crime," the enthusiasm will diminish as enforcement orders proceed downward, and may have largely evaporated by the time they reach the street level.

CITY GOVERNMENT AND THE POLICE

For efficient police service there should be freedom from undue influence of political parties and the sundry other pressure groups seeking power, immunity from punishment, or other favors. To these ends various types of appointing and control systems have been used. Direct election of top officers, appointment and control by legislative bodies, and control by groups and by individuals have been tried. To meet the corruption of partisan police boards, bipartisan boards have been set up. To avoid the scattering of responsibility involved in an administrative board, single commissioners or chiefs have been substituted in most cities. To escape from demoralization resulting from corrupt local politics, state-controlled metropolitan forces have been established in a few cities, including Boston and St. Louis. A leading specialist concludes that under the city-manager or council-manager plans, professional standards have been possible, and political meddling has tended to be avoided. Two almost opposite principles seem to need consideration here. On the one hand, if the police are to be effective and avoid undue political interference, their leaders should be far removed from popular votes or political parties. On the other hand, it is all-important that the people of a community feel that the police are their representatives.

In terms of this second principle, it seems that it is not so much the form of organization as its popular acceptance which is requisite.

QUALIFICATIONS

The usual qualifications for city police service in the United States concern little more than age, weight, height, residence, and citizenship, together with some sort of character investigation and perhaps certain mental standards for admission to civil service examinations. Requirement even of high school graduation, though increasing, is still unusual. Residence requirements are usual and have been called a "truly malignant spot in our police recruitment program." [14] The period of residence required varies from three months to three years. Residents may have obligations to local friends, and the limitation prevents search for better-qualified candidates elsewhere.

The Boston Crime Survey said of qualities needed by a policeman:

> There are few vocations which, if adequately performed, require so much of a man—physical courage, tact, disciplined temper, good judgment, alertness of observation, and specialized knowledge of law and procedure. . . . He must keep a cool head and take decisive action when trouble arises.
>
> Not only physical courage but strong moral fiber is required of the policeman. He is at war with thieves, fences, and sharpers of every sort who will stop at nothing to avoid interference by the police. . . . Gamblers, prostitutes, narcotic peddlers, and bootleggers are ever on the alert to tempt him. They do not always resort to the cruder forms of bribery, for they have gained high skill in employing subterfuges and in devising ways to bring the unwary officer under obligation. . . .
>
> The handling of quarrelsome or difficult persons, delinquent children, and handicapped defectives of every sort demands sympathetic understanding and abundant common sense.[15]

O. W. Wilson [16] urges that there is far greater need that police be intelligent, emotionally stable, and have high ethical standards than that they be physically capable. The often-heard requirement concerning intelligence, however, has recently been given closer scrutiny by a New Jersey police official,[17] who suggests that specification of the kinds of intelligence needed

[14] Charles F. Sloane, "Police Professionalization," *Journal of Criminal Law, Criminology and Police Science* (May–June 1954), p. 79.

[15] Leonard V. Harrison, *Police Administration in Boston* (Cambridge, Mass.: Harvard University Press, 1934), pp. 28–29.

[16] "Toward a Better Merit System," *Annals of the American Academy of Political and Social Science* (Jan. 1954), pp. 88 and 90.

[17] John Duffy, "A Proposed Experiment in Police Selection," in Herbert A. Bloch, *Crime in America* (New York: Philosophical Library, 1961), pp. 155–68.

in police work would be useful. Many of the policeman's duties are so dull, distasteful, and routine that officers selected on the basis of general intelligence test scores either quit the force or, if they stay, become part of that "sizable quota" of embittered and perfunctory officers reluctant to quit because of their investment in retirement time.[18]

Still in dispute are the relative merits of selection of police through civil service and efforts to establish a real merit system without the handicap that civil service rules almost always mean. The trend seems to be toward giving the police head full control over hiring and firing his subordinates, toward some form of separate police-selecting board, or toward a combination of control by the chief and by the board.

Where a police chief is himself unqualified, corrupt, or primarily appointed for political reasons, he will often demoralize the police force under him and should not control the appointment and discipline of his subordinates. On the other hand, we have good examples of systems where the chief is given limited control, sufficient for him to carry out his policies, and where an effective nonpolitical police regime has resulted outside of the usual civil service organization. It has proven easy for politicians to get around many civil service requirements in various ways. Civil service cannot provide qualified men unless standards higher than usual are written into the law. As Leonard puts it,[19] civil service, though working well in spots, at its worst recruits mediocre men and then protects their tenure.

TRAINING

There has been much recent progress in the training of police personnel, but with high-school graduation as yet an unusual requirement, reliance still is chiefly placed on various forms of in-service training, in spite of a number of promising university programs usually aimed at the more responsible administrative positions. Among college-level curricula held worthy of honorable mention are the now much-expanded graduate training in police administration at the University of California and courses for undergraduates at Michigan State University, San Jose State College, and the College of the City of New York. More recent has been the establishment of the Delinquency Control Institute at the University of Louisville. A system of itinerant instructors has been set up at Oklahoma Institute of Technology, the University of Illinois, and the University of Missouri, and graduate-level courses are offered at New York University. By employing

[18] *Ibid.,* p. 159.
[19] *Op. cit.,* p. 128.

instructors acceptable to both educational and law-enforcement officials, such programs have promise for the future of adequate preparation, not only of patrolmen, but of top police administrators.[20]

In-service training is of a different sort. Many colleges and universities have brief institutes of some value. One can distinguish state and local police-training programs, systems of zone schools conducted for a limited time by state police and other organizations, zone training service furnished to local police by the Federal Bureau of Investigation, and the excellent work of the FBI National Police Academy, which provides in Washington repeated 12-week courses for policemen selected by their own organizations. Many of the trainees at the Academy have been instructors in state and local police schools. A few are given an opportunity to return to Washington for graduate-level courses.

Public Relations

Even if the sole function of the police were to make crime dangerous through arrest and threat of arrest, their relations with the general public would be important. When those functions are parts of a far broader community safety program, favorable public relations become doubly important. As Gourley tells us, "police work is no longer concerned primarily with a small outlaw group," [21] and perhaps nine-tenths of police activities are not of a strictly criminal nature. On the one hand, the police must avoid pressure from special-interest pressure groups. On the other hand, without public assistance "arrests become difficult, and convictions almost impossible." [22] Moreover, when relations with the public are cooperative, police morale is improved, while it is impossible to maintain enthusiasm for one's job if it is not appreciated. Actually, the public is described [23] as often having considered the police stupid and uneducated; rude, domineering, and "smart-alecky"; and given to the use of violent third-degree methods. The police are also held to be under the dominance of politicians and amenable to the use of "pull" by the rich or even by the gangster element. Such generalizations are clearly unfair, yet at certain times and

---

[20] Sixteen colleges and universities by 1960 were offering four-year undergraduate degree programs in law-enforcement. Among the largest is that of City College, all of whose 13-man police training faculty are regular members of the New York Police Department. See "More on Four-Year Programs," *Police* (Jan.–Feb., 1962), pp. 76–77.

[21] G. Douglas Gourley, "Police Public Relations," *Annals, loc. cit.,* pp. 135–42. Cf. also his book, *Public Relations and the Police* (Springfield, Ill.: Charles C. Thomas, 1953).

[22] *Ibid.,* p. 137.

[23] *Ibid.,* p. 136.

places, every one of them has had some basis in fact. Police especially need to develop a reputation for fairness and understanding when they deal with sensitive minority groups.

Because race riots are one of our most serious types of public violence, and because police on occasion have themselves aggravated interracial tensions, every police force needs training in the proper handling of racial tensions both at their incipient stages and after actual riots have begun. It is held that trained police can prevent rioting and can keep violence to a minimum after it has begun.[24] During World War II, there were fine examples of preventive work on the part of the police in such cities as Washington, D. C.; Flint, Michigan; Houston, Texas; and Passaic, New Jersey. On the other hand, the Detroit riots of 1943 cost 35 lives, and the Harlem riots in August of that year destroyed $5 million worth of property. The latter, though not prevented, was an example of effective mobilization of police, and police behavior brought almost universal praise. The general policy which seems to have justified itself has been absolute impartiality both in allowing meetings, parades, and other legal activities and in the arrest and fair treatment of members of both races engaged in unlawful activities. Police can thus set examples of coolheadedness and avoidance of violence. They can tactfully disperse threatening crowds; patch up clashes between school children; make personal appeals to rioters; employ a fair share of Negro policemen; use no discrimination in their promotional policies; train members in nondiscrimination; encourage patrolmen to report on danger areas and incidents ahead of real trouble; watch out for the beginnings of provocative false rumors; set up social race relations units, including a juvenile division; develop press relations which will discourage sensational, provocative newspaper reporting; and cooperate with scores of social agencies concerned with prevention of discrimination and interracial strife.

Police Brutality and Civil Rights

The need to protect the civil rights of minority groups suggests the question of the protection of the rights of the accused.

Police are at war with dangerous men. Their reputations depend upon

[24] On this subject, see J. E. Weckler and Theo E. Hall, *The Police and Minority Groups* (Chicago: International City Managers' Association, 1944); William M. Kephart, *Racial Factors and Urban Law Enforcement* (Philadelphia: University of Pennsylvania Press, 1957); Joseph D. Lohman and Dietrich C. Rietzes, "Note on Race Relations in Mass Society," *American Journal of Sociology* (Nov. 1952), pp. 240–46.

their arrest and conviction records. Being at war, they tend to use the weapons of war. Hence it is not surprising that our police have been charged with wire-tapping, illegal detention of suspects, and unnecessary brutality in the handling of criminals, especially when securing confessions.

Thirty years ago, the National Commission on Law Observance and Enforcement concluded that "confessions of guilt frequently are unlawfully extorted by the police from prisoners by means of cruel treatment, colloquially known as the third degree." [25] Apparently the evils to which the commission called attention persist today. Yet many authorities feel that legal restrictions on police methods often aid the escape of the guilty. Third-degree methods thus sometimes appear as understandable, if mistaken, reactions of the police to the activities of lawyer-fixers engaged in protecting gangsters.[26] However, there is agreement among specialists that third-degree methods are not only illegal and repugnant to our basic traditions of freedom, but actually reduce police efficiency. Brutality often seems to untrained police officers the easy way to get results. The third degree seems to them to make the laborious collecting of scientific evidence unnecessary. Use of force leads, however, to court reversals of convictions and so defeats the ends of justice. Some years ago Beyle and Parratt [27] showed that a considerable section of the public approved the use of the milder forms of the third degree. A more recent sociological analysis [28] of the third degree showed how the occupational status of the police, and their feeling that in some kinds of cases the public desired "roughing up of prisoners," has led to the frequent use of the third degree in the case of felons. They have found the control of sex offenders, especially, so difficult, and the public demand for it so incessant, that violence on their part was the natural result.

The third degree conflicts with the principle that a man shall not be compelled to furnish evidence against himself. Many states have laws penalizing the practice. Protracted questioning, often accompanied by being kept standing for hours, deprivation of food or sleep, threats of physical injury, violations of legal right to consult counsel, and sometimes blows are the most common forms of the third degree.

[25] *Lawlessness in Law Enforcement,* Report No. 11 (Washington, D. C.: The Commission, 1931), p. 3.

[26] Audrey M. Davies, "Police, the Law, and the Individual," *Annals, loc. cit.,* p. 143.

[27] Herman C. Beyle and Spencer D. Parratt, "Approval and Disapproval of Specific Third-Degree Practices," *Journal of Criminal Law and Criminology* (Nov.–Dec. 1937), pp. 526–50.

[28] William A. Westley, "Violence and the Police," *American Journal of Sociology* (July 1953), pp. 34–41.

The above-mentioned early report found Negroes and people without influence more often but not exclusively the victims; and first offenders as well as old-timers or professionals or gangsters were involved.[29] While a majority of those subjected to the third degree were probably guilty, not a few innocent persons were apparently included. The third degree enables the criminal to charge the guardians of the law with violation of the law they guard.

The various forms of police violence are often illegal under the laws of the several states. They have been declared unconstitutional by the United States Supreme Court,[30] and federal action against police using them has been instituted by the Civil Rights Section of the Department of Justice. Wire-tapping was also finally outlawed, though the Department of Justice has at times banned and at times condoned its use. Some seem to feel that when restricted to cases of alleged subversive activities, its use should be permitted, and legislation to that effect has been introduced into Congress. Both legal prosecution and rehabilitation of criminals are impaired by police violence and violation of civil liberties.[31]

Women Police

Beginning in Chicago in 1893, not a few police departments organized bureaus of women police either as separate units or attached to precincts of other organizations. There was at first opposition to their employment on the part of the male force, but in larger cities especially they seem to have made a place for themselves. Such women police have rarely been professionally trained. Mature judgment, emotional stability, youthful viewpoint, and absence of both sentimentality and callousness have been among the traits desired for them. They have acted as matrons; searched for missing persons and runaways; dealt with women and girls brought to the police station; patrolled parks and other public places chiefly for the protection of women and children; aided attendance officers and supervised probationers; censored motion pictures; supervised dance halls, burlesque shows, and other places of amusement; cared for wayward girls and vagrant women; and had other special dealing with sex delinquents. In addition

[29] *Lawlessness in Law Enforcement,* pp. 156–61.
[30] In *McNabb* v. *United States* (1943) for federal jurisdictions, and in *Ashcraft* v. *Tennessee* for the states. Cited in Davies, *loc. cit.,* p. 145.
[31] For a set of principles to govern police practices in this area, see Davies, *loc. cit.,* pp. 150–51.

some of them have done important case investigation, especially with children and women first offenders. The Juvenile Aid Bureau of the New York City police has been an example of such preventive activities.[32] At one time the New York women police were headed by a professional social worker and engaged in case work. Later that leadership was changed and the scope of activities limited. Because two-thirds of missing persons are females, and because the roots of their problems so often are in family relations, women have been very active in that field. Their special usefulness in developing favorable relations with the press and with the public generally has been recognized.[33] However, it is the relationship of the employment of women as police to work with juvenile delinquents and to the larger question of the constructive preventive activities of police which are the most important considerations.

Federal Police Activities

Our historical tradition has been against a centralized national police force, and the American police system is decentralized. With the great expansion of federal criminal law since the turn of the present century, however, has naturally gone a great increase in the functions of federal police agencies. The growing complexity of social relations, vast improvements in transportation, increased interdependence of the several regions of the country, and increased organization and scope of criminal activities have called for great expansion of federal police work. This expansion has had the hearty approval of the people generally.

Several thousand federal police of all kinds are employed by about 40 agencies, of which the Federal Bureau of Investigation, the Immigration and Naturalization Service, the Bureau of Narcotics, and the Secret Service employ a total of 22,000 in police capacities.[34] The specialized and often highly technical nature of their work, plus salaries, prestige, and working conditions superior to those of most state and local police, mean that federally employed police officers have little similarity to their non-federal counterparts.

[32] Henrietta Additon, "The Crime Prevention Bureau of the New York City Police Department," in Sheldon and Eleanor T. Glueck, *Preventing Crime* (New York: McGraw-Hill Book Company, 1936), chap. 12.

[33] Cf. Evabel Tenny, "Women's Work in Law Enforcement," *Journal of Criminal Law, Criminology and Police Science* (July–Aug. 1953), pp. 239–46.

[34] *Statistical Abstract of the United States: 1962* (Washington, D. C.: U. S. Bureau of the Census, 1962), p. 154.

Suggested Readings

Annals of the American Academy of Political and Social Science (Jan. 1954). This issue is concerned with police management. Most of the 19 articles were written by practicing police officials.

Costello, A. E. *Our Police Protectors.* New York: Charles F. Roper and Company, 1884. The first six chapters of this book describe New York's early efforts at crime suppression before a day-and-night police existed. The rest of the book is concerned mainly with personalities and police heroism.

Goddard, Henry. *Memoirs of a Bow Street Runner.* New York: William Morrow and Company, 1957. The Bow Street runners were early London police detectives attached initially to the court of Magistrates Henry and John Fielding. This book is an apparently authentic account of the Runners in the early ninenteenth century. Interesting details on crime and justice in that day.

Kantor, Mackinlay. *Signal Thirty-Two.* New York: Random House, 1950. The first portion of this novel about a New York City police precinct contains a graphic description of a patrolman's daily chores.

Kephart, William M. *Racial Factors and Urban Law Enforcement.* Philadelphia: University of Pennsylvania Press, 1957. Based on interviews with policemen and officials, the place of Negroes in the Philadelphia Police Department is explored.

CHAPTER 20

The Jail

Importance of the Detention Experience

Whether criminals are to be punished or dealt with constructively, the accused must not escape before his guilt or innocence has been established. His appearance for trial may be secured through an acceptance of his own promise to present himself. Usually however, he must either provide bail as a guarantee of appearance or be committed to jail to await trial.

The waiting or detention period is an important part of the experience of the accused, whether guilty or innocent. If he is innocent, it is important to society that he be impressed with the fairness of our machinery of justice in assuming his innocence until his guilt is proved. If he is guilty, it is even more important that he, who has acted "unjustly," be impressed with the contrast between his own behavior and that of the state, which is theoretically the embodiment of justice. Yet sometimes the impression of the detained is rather one of injustice. Sometimes he is detained in jail when others whom he knows to have arranged a fix are released; his bail is high, while another man's is low; he is offered assistance in return for a bribe he cannot pay; the well-to-do returns home, while he languishes in jail; the jail is foul and full of vice and corruption at which the jailer connives or in which he participates; he endures more hardship in jail before he is proved guilty than many endure in prison afterwards.

If public services can, like people, be said to have varying degrees of prestige, jails would rank in the public eye with such regrettable but necessary establishments as almshouses, morgues, and dog pounds. For centuries the jail in Anglo-American countries has been a neglected and bedraggled stepchild within the family of agencies of justice. Fathered by Henry II at the famous Assiz of Clarendon in 1166 to hold persons awaiting trial or punishment, the English jail [1] was combined with the house of correction in the late eighteenth century to save expenses and thereafter served the dual functions of short-term punishment *and* detention. In the United States the jail is typically under the authority of county sheriffs, who typically use it as a time-honored source of patronage jobs for their political supporters. Nestled snugly within county politics, having as clients the poor and powerless, called upon to perform tasks for which it is seldom equipped, operated by unqualified individuals, insulated from the main currents of correctional reform by its relative obscurity, it has understandably remained a sorry institution.

A well-known authority in correctional administration has recently stated:

It is an unhappy but well-established fact that far too many jails—hundreds of them—while presumed to be the bulwark of community social protection, actually are little more than the enforced common meeting places for social derelicts who find there the greatest opportunity to infect the casual offender, the weak, the unsophisticated, the morally retarded, and the socially inadequate. Moreover, such jails are often unsuccessful in performing their basic mission of secure detention. In them, jailers' responsibilities are delegated to the most sophisticated and experienced criminals who proceed to prey upon the majority of other prisoners through tacitly approved kangaroo courts, "sanitary" courts, and other devices and insidious methods concocted by those morally corrupt criminals schooled in the slimy culture of mankind's social backwash. [2]

The jail is important because, though it holds men for relatively short periods, it is an institutional experience of hundreds of thousands of Americans each year. The proportion of repeaters in jail is high, but for all of them there was once a first experience. The jail is important because it tests the sincerity of our theory of equal treatment regardless of status. The jail problem is important because the jail is recognized as perhaps the worst of our social institutions. Nonetheless, not before well into the twentieth

---

[1] The English spelling is "gaol" but has the same pronunciation.

[2] Myrl E. Alexander, *Jail Administration* (Springfield, Ill.: Charles C. Thomas, 1957), pp. 5–6.

century was much attention paid to the American jail problem. The jail is still too often forgotten, and jail inmates have not inappropriately been called "forgotten men."

The Population of Jails

There are some 10,000 local police lockups and perhaps 3,100 county and city jails in the United States. In addition some states have workhouses or county penitentiaries intended for convicted misdemeanants, as distinguished from persons awaiting trial. At a given time something like 50,000 inmates may be found in our jails, and not far short of 2,000,000 are committed there annually. Of these three-fifths are sentenced prisoners and two-fifths are awaiting trial. Commitments to jails exceed those to the better-known prisons and reformatories by about 10 to one. Women in jail comprise about one inmate in seven. If one considers as children all under 18, then tens of thousands are annually sent to this demoralizing institution. The proportion of the population going to jail varies. At one time it was 10 times as great in Delaware as in New Hampshire.[3] An early study showed that about three out of 10 prisoners sent to jail were sent because of failure to pay a fine. The population of some jails is exceedingly small. At one time no fewer than 390 jails reported no prisoners at all, and no doubt a large proportion of the 1,000 which made no report were also empty at the time. Jails, then, vary all the way from "four-bunk hoosegows" to one which houses 3,000 inmates.[4] When the number of inmates is small, there is little opportunity for classification and isolation of types which should be separated.

Our jails house a motley crowd. Strictly defined, the majority of jail inmates are recidivists, the usual report being that former crimes are known in over three-fifths of the cases, and such statements are always understatements. The Connecticut jail survey reported only 19 per cent as first offenders.[5] At any rate, there is much weight to the contention that the typical man committed to jail for punishment is not a true criminal but a

---

[3] *County and City Jails, 1933* (Washington, D. C.: U. S. Bureau of the Census, 1935), p. 2; Roy Casey, "Children in Jail," *National Probation Association Yearbook, 1943,* pp. 175–82.

[4] Cf. Roy Casey, "Catch-all Jails," *Annals of the American Academy of Political and Social Science* (May 1954), pp. 28–34.

[5] Jerome Davis, "The Jail Population of Connecticut," in *Report of the Legislative Commission on Jails* (Hartford, Conn.: Dec. 3, 1934), p. 3; cf. also Leon T. Stern, "A House of Detention for Philadelphia," *Proceedings of the American Prison Association, 1937,* pp. 334–35.

victim of demoralization. Some sheriffs even report that their jails are more frequently used for sheltering transient hoboes, tramps, and drunks than for detaining law violators.[6] Our jail population includes the young and old, sick and well, hardened violators and first offenders. They are life's misfits, disproportionately uneducated, illiterate, addicted to drink and drugs, diseased, crippled, and without friends.

Descriptions of Jails

Many picturesque descriptions of jails have been written.[7] Said an English visitor some 26 years ago:

Young and old, virtuous and depraved, innocent and double-dyed, are thrown into the closest association by night and day. For the most part, they spend the whole day in idleness, reading tattered newspapers or playing cards, herded in cages, devoid of proper sanitation, with little chance of exercise or occupation. The smell of these places is foul, their whole suggestion is infamous; their effect on the young or innocent can only be deplorable. There they sit and lounge and lie this day, rotting in the foetid air, and though all agree that these things are unspeakably evil, yet they continue from year to year, and the public conscience is not sufficiently aroused to demand a cleansing of the stable.[8]

The following from one who perhaps knows as much about jail conditions as anyone in the country is eloquent of the leadership provided in our jails:

Over three thousand small county units, each jealous of its powers and with few exceptions indifferent with regard to its responsibilities, are intrusted with the care and custody of the largest number of offenders taken into custody in the country. . . . There are just as many systems as there are jails—in fact most of them lack any semblance of a system. . . . It is futile to argue that hundreds of untrained persons in these small distinct units will ever accomplish successfully the task that has been imposed upon them. One of the greatest evils of the jail is the fee system, assuring the sheriff of a per diem fee for every prisoner held in his jail. This remuneration is a stronghold among the county sheriffs and jailers, and is probably the most difficult obstacle to overcome. . . . In many instances, [sheriffs] having numerous other profitable interests and responsibilities, give little of their time to the management and control of the jail, and have no qualms about delegating authority to inefficient and wholly unqualified

[6] Editorial in the *Jail Association Journal* (March–April 1939), p. 4.

[7] Cf. especially Joseph F. Fishman's incomparable *Crucibles of Crime* (New York: Cosmopolis Press, 1923).

[8] Honorable Alexander Patterson, quoted in Sanford Bates, *Prisons and Beyond* (New York: Macmillan, 1936), p. 39.

guards, who in turn often leave the actual management of the jail to the "kangaroo court." A typical example of a sheriff's interest in the prisoners in his county jail, for whom he was drawing a fee each day, is expressed in a letter to the Federal Bureau of Prisons, which had called his attention to the necessity for correcting deplorable conditions which existed in his jail:

"My failure to reply to these letters is due to the fact, as you know, that this state during the months from September to April was involved in a campaign. For your information I was also in that campaign which campaign I started the later part of September and did not finish until about the 3rd of April. We were re-elected by a very handsome majority. . . . I am out of the campaign now and can give these matters my personal attention." [9]

Guilty or not guilty of crime, a jail inmate has usually a nauseating experience. He cannot avoid contact with every type of depravity. He must witness obscenity and hear endless profanity. Rarely may he work, even if he so desires. He is without any educational facilities and is fortunate if the jail "library" affords a few tattered, filthy old books. His very presence in jail labels him usually either as a suspect of serious crime or more generally as a member of a despised derelict class who cannot afford bail or have not the means to pay their fines. Far more even than inmates of our prisons do such jailbirds deserve Sanford Bates' appellation "forgotten men."

Jail Evils and Problems

POPULAR ATTITUDES

The most basic jail evil is a popular mind set. If the jail is to protect against crime, it is essential that the people look upon the drunks, disorderly persons, vagrants, and other petty offenders which it houses as *products*. They must be recognized for what they are—the natural waste products of the social system. Just as to deal adequately with the slum we must see it as a receptacle in which life's failures are collected, so to provide a more adequate jail we must see it as a receptacle into which are thrust the most degraded of these failures. Only with such an attitude will there be desire to provide in the jail an experience of justice and constructive aid.

Yet actually the basic public attitude seems rather to be that the denizens of the jail wilfully have failed. Along with this attitude goes the conviction that disturbers of the public peace should pay a penalty for their misconduct. The public generally also feels that as little expense as possible

[9] Nina Kinsella in *Proceedings of the National Conference of Social Work, 1937*, pp. 585–86.

should be incurred even in the punishment process; that any building which will house petty offenders with reasonable security will answer; that almost any local man can be a satisfactory jailer, since no great skill is required of those who act as mere custodians of the jailed; that whatever political advantage can be obtained out of the process of safekeeping this local and transient riffraff must be expected and tolerated if not actually approved; and finally that the whole matter is of purely local concern, requiring no interference by the state.

UNTRAINED AND SOMETIMES UNSCRUPULOUS PERSONNEL

Given such attitudes, it follows that sheriffs, jailers, and others responsible for the upkeep of the jail will usually be untrained and inefficient, that they will be local men in no way prepared for the exacting task of dealing with their difficult wards. Managing the jail is but one of the sheriff's duties. The jailer's job is often part-time in another sense, since he knows that with the next turn of the political wheel, he will be out and another equally ill-prepared man, differing chiefly in that he owes political debts to a different party, will be in his place. Such statements are, of course, not true of our most conscientious jailers.

INJUSTICES IN JAIL SYSTEM

Even under capable leadership the jail system does not permit justice. The most serious exploiters have escaped this institution. Seldom does it house a white-collar criminal. A few dollars will permit the man of means to await his trial in the comfort of his home or pay for his inebriate indiscretion with a small fine instead of "working it out" in idleness within the iron cage of the jail. If the law itself commands such inequalities in treatment, it is not surprising if the jailer finds his charges also looking for a fix. There occurs not infrequently the exploitation of prisoners by the sheriff or jailer who is allowed a moderate fee for feeding them but may save as much of this as possible for himself by providing inferior food. Yet the cost per inmate of maintaining especially the smallest jails is very high, and judged as a whole on a per capita inmate basis, they are our most costly institutions to maintain. County and state officials may inspect jails, but only rarely have the latter any power to demand improvements. In addition to abuse of the fee system, the unscrupulous jailer may also profit through the sale of commodities to prisoners or even through the sale of forbidden privileges. Some jailers are honest, but it is clear that the jail system often makes exploitation possible.

MORE SPECIFIC EVILS

The attitudes listed above, and the nature of our political and economic system, account for a long list of jail evils. These include problems of security, sanitation, idleness, discipline, criminogenic association, and juvenile detention.

Jails often insecure. Sanford Bates says, "It is doubtful if one-fourth of the county jails in the country today are capable of restraining desperate resourceful men." [10] Stories of jail breaks, of jailers disarmed, or of escapes with wooden guns are not infrequent. Some years ago:

Two prisoners in the Warren County, New York, Jail, removed bricks from the wall, escaped, committed two robberies, returned their loot to the jail, and replaced the bricks. . . . Some time ago, 16 prisoners escaped from the Sullivan County [Virginia] Jail. Three weeks later bars were pried with a broomstick permitting the escape of six more.[11]

Jails often unsanitary. Jails are very frequently unsanitary and unhealthful, with vermin and filth abounding. The federal government reports over 2,000 jails as never visited by any health organization. One of its inspectors tells of an extreme case where jail inmates were held inside for quarantine for smallpox, but new commitments, including children, nevertheless continued to be admitted. Writing in 1954, Roy Casey said:

In the vast majority of catch-all city and county jails prisoners are compelled to wear their own clothes regardless of how filthy or vermin-infested they may be; facilities for delousing drunks, vagrants, and bums are totally lacking; and too frequently . . . any sort of provision for washing face and hands is nonexistent.[12]

Idleness general in jails. It is impossible, under the law, to compel untried inmates to work, though some of them will do so voluntarily if opportunity is offered. But to provide work for a few misfits costs money, and really efficient production may compete with free industry. Idleness is the rule, work the exception. Idleness spells deterioration. As Bates puts it:

The idle mind is the devil's workshop, and the devil has plenty of work in the average county jail. In fact, he is about the only one who does any work. . . . What do people do when they have nothing to do? They nurse grievances. . . . They plot revenge. . . . And thus a jail becomes . . . a veritable source and inspiration of moral degradation.

[10] Bates, *op. cit.,* pp. 44–48.
[11] *Jail Association Journal* (May–June 1939), p. 24.
[12] *Loc. cit.*

Disciplinary problems in jail. Idleness and poor personnel and moral degradation mean disorder and lack of discipline. The inability of the jailer to enforce discipline has produced that vicious if picturesque jail institution —the kangaroo court. This is the prisoners' effort to provide some needed degree of order, but like other extra-legal racketeering it is also an agency of exploitation. The kangaroo court often functions with the approval of the sheriff or jailer, since it solves after a fashion one of his problems. In a Virginia jail the kangaroo court once formulated the following rules and penalties:

1. Entering jail without consent of inmates, $1.00 or 100 licks with the strap.
2. Spitting without cleaning it up, 10 licks.
3. Stealing from another prisoner, 100 licks without mercy.
4. Not taking bath and not spraying bed, 25 licks.
5. Not keeping back five feet from the door when the jailer puts one in or takes one out, 10 licks.
6. Disturbing court when in session, 25 licks.
7. Making noise after lights go out, 25 licks.
8. Failing to keep out of front cells when another prisoner has a visitor, 100 licks without mercy.

Occasionally the kangaroo court is defended on the ground that it is a lesson in self-government. But under proper leadership more effective social control is possible. The federal government will not place its prisoners in a jail with a kangaroo court.

Criminogenic association. One of the most serious defects in the jail system is the lack of segregation of different types of prisoners. A medium more effective than the jail for the spread of criminal patterns could hardly be devised. The contagion is serious enough when only adults are involved. It is far more disturbing when we learn that large numbers of children are still sent to jail. The young boy, shocked and possibly repentant over his first offense, is encouraged to change remorse into hostility by the sympathetic attention of hardened inmates who recount their delinquent exploits and tell the newcomer he is now one of them for life.

Classification with isolation of types is feasible in our larger jails. Yet so little can be known of many of them when they are first admitted that the jailer can hardly take into consideration detailed facts about personalities, social relations, and so on, which would be needed for scientific classification. Hence separation of inmates, when provided, is apt to be based on routine criteria such as sex, age, physical condition, and what is known of the nature of the offenses with which they are charged.

Federal Inspection of Jails

Such improvements as have been made in the American jail system may largely be attributed to two agencies: the National Jail Association and the Jail Inspection Service of the United States Bureau of Prisons.

The National Jail Association offers a consultation service on jail training, conducts regional jail meetings, and publishes, together with the American Correctional Association, a bi-monthly magazine, *The American Journal of Correction.*

It has long been necessary for the federal government to house a large proportion of its prisoners awaiting trial, or detained for other reasons, in local jails. Desirous of providing decent jail conditions for its own prisoners, the Bureau of Prisons has established an inspection service and set up minimum standards qualifying jails to receive federal commitments. Since the rate paid varies with the rating of the jail in question, federal inspection furnishes a motive for improvement. Despite the fact that the federal government has no authority over local jails, it exercises indirect influence for jail improvement. Under a new system installed in 1953, 11 jails were rated "good," 287 "fair," 143 "poor," and 33 "bad" in 1954.[13] Physical conditions, food, and discipline, though leaving much to be desired, were relatively satisfactory, while medical facilities and provision for employment of prisoners rated very low indeed.

Suggested Remedies

Suggestions for improving the jail vary all the way from mere tinkering to demands that the whole system must go. The first requisite, whatever is to be done, is that the public be informed as to the jail problem. And the most effective first step would undoubtedly be to set higher standards for personnel in charge of jails, pay them adequately, provide for their in-service training, make longer terms and reappointment possible for them, and insulate them from all political pressures.

While an interested community and an alert state inspection service may often compel officials to improve conditions, the public is generally apt to stop short with condemnation of individuals for evils which really are due to the law and the vicious system which the public has tolerated. Even the occasional corruptibility and the more infrequent inefficiency of per-

[13] For ratings under the previous system, see Federal Bureau of Prisons, *Federal Prisoners* (Washington, D. C.: The Bureau, 1952), p. 41.

sonnel often reflect the nature of that system. The Federal Bureau of Prisons [14] has given us not only a challenging analysis of the historical development of jails, but a series of plans to relate jail structure to jail functions. They picture in detail plans for jails to house variously from 25 to 250 inmates.

The number of accused awaiting trial can be generally reduced (1) by providing facilities for determining the reliability of the accused, so that many may be released on their own recognizance without bail; (2) by reducing bail to a safe minimum, so that more can afford to pay it; (3) by speeding trials and thus reducing the time which needs to be spent in jail.

Similarly, minor changes in court policy, such as wider use of probation, will reduce the number of the convicted sent to jail. Experiments already made in permitting convicted misdemeanants to pay their fines in installments might well be greatly extended, though such a plan is not without its administrative difficulties. Even if poor men released to pay their fines were occasionally to escape payment, the danger of their repeating crimes would hardly be greater than in the case of the man who pays the fine. In addition, the community saves both the cost of keeping such men in jail and the demoralizing effect of the experience upon them.

Better inspection of jails is also plausibly urged. State inspection is ineffective today when there is inadequate power to compel local authorities to make needed changes or when inspectors are unwilling to offend local officials who are politically influential. It has been suggested that the federal government might offer to pay part of the expense of an improved jail system, provided the states assisted met federal standards of excellence. A recent trend toward building jails above courthouses has not been generally approved by criminologists. The Federal Bureau of Prisons has published its *Manual for Jail Management,* filled with useful suggestions and standards and a model set of rules for inmates. The Bureau is also performing a service by holding free institutes for sheriffs and jailers of certain states.

More thoroughgoing would be the substitution of state-owned central or regional jails for the local county and city jail. Such a plan implies some expense for transportation. This expense, however, has the virtue of keeping to a minimum those detained in jail. The more basic difficulty is to overcome local jealousies and fear of the loss of petty political prerogatives rooted in the county system.

Whether detention quarters be state or locally owned, they should logically be very different from institutions planned, like our typical jails, also as places of punishment. Secure individual rooms in buildings equipped

[14] See their beautifully illustrated *Handbook of Correctional Institutions Design and Construction* (Washington, D. C.: The Bureau, 1949).

much like a clean third-class hotel would answer. The sense of just treatment would also be enhanced if bail could be abolished and the quarters and treatment of the rich and the poor awaiting trial be absolutely alike.

Special Programs for Petty Offenders

Despite the apparent hopelessness of the jail situation, a number of encouraging programs, both experimental and established, have been developed within jails and other short-term institutions. No one of these is a panacea for the jail's problems, of course, but they are evidence that earnest rehabilitation efforts *can* be made to salvage the social derelicts whose "crimes" warrant only short sentences.

Wisconsin's Huber Law. Since 1913 the county sheriffs of Wisconsin have been authorized to allow prisoners serving misdemeanant sentences to work at regular jobs in the free community, returning nightly to their institutions. Their earnings, collected by the sheriffs, are used to reimburse the county for their board and personal expenses, support dependents, and repay pre-existing debts. A 1960 survey of the Huber Law's operation revealed that the 2,281 prisoners employed in that year earned over $633,000, of which sum $229,000 went to their dependents. Only 182 absconded.[15]

Half-way houses for problem drinkers. A sizable proportion of jail prisoners are serving terms for public drunkenness. Upon release, most return to their Skid Road environments sobered up but helped not at all in dealing with their problems. To help counter the jail's inability to treat such men, there have been organized in recent years about 30 so-called "half-way houses" under both private and public sponsorship. Through cooperation with short-term institutions, selected inmates upon release are sent, not to Skid Road, but to a facility intended to bridge the gap between the jail and the community. The houses average 26 beds and are staffed by paid and unpaid professional and other workers; inmates receive employment help and therapy intended to change their drinking habits. As in any penological program, the success rate is difficult to determine. Blacker and Kantor state that perhaps one-third of those treated do not continue as problem drinkers—not too low a figure considering the "hopeless and unreachable" condition of the men prior to treatment.[16]

[15] *1960 Survey of Wisconsin's Huber Law* (Madison, Wis.: State Department of Public Welfare, 1962), pp. 1, 7, 9. See also Sanger B. Powers, "Day-Parole of Misdemeanants," *Federal Probation* (Dec. 1958), pp. 42–46.

[16] Edward Blacker and David Kantor, "Half-way Houses for Problem Drinkers," *Federal Probation* (June 1960), p. 21.

Treatment programs. Jails and houses of correction are far from ideal settings for treatment programs. Some experimental departures, however, which take frank cognizance of jail limitations, have been made in recent years. In a new approach to rehabilitating short-termers, the Cleveland House of Correction sponsored an attempt to reach its down-and-out inmates by disguising group therapy as "courses" in psychology, family relations, music, current events, arithmetic, and creative writing. The "instructor" obtained his "students" through non-directive techniques; the prisoners themselves built a classroom and office within an existing building.[17] While no evaluation of the experiment has been made, the therapist was reportedly successful in maintaining the active interest of his subjects.

Both group and individual therapy for short-term female derelicts was instituted in a minimum-security clinic operated as a unit within Ontario's Department of Reform Institution. A unique feature was the use of follow-ups in the form of continued unofficial, friendly, supportive contacts between clinicians and released women who might otherwise return at once to their drifting existence. Some 25 of the 44 women treated reportedly were not re-convicted.[18]

The Seattle Police Department operates a rehabilitation project for selected chronic alcoholics sentenced to the city jail. Something like shotgun therapy is used, including documentary films, A.A. meetings, high-protein diets, and discussion sessions. A 1956 study revealed that the arrest rates of 95 men so treated were significantly lower than before treatment; 37.5 per cent experienced no arrest during a 6-month post-treatment period.[19]

Suggested Readings

Alexander, Myrl E. *Jail Administration.* Springfield, Ill.: Charles C. Thomas, 1957. Contains interesting information on the problems peculiar to the operation of short-term institutions. The author is a former deputy director of the Federal Bureau of Prisons.

Fishman, Joseph F. *Crucibles of Crime.* New York: Cosmopolis Press, 1923. The incredible jail conditions described here have been somewhat improved since Fishman's day, but since the jail remains politically where it was then, the basic corrupting forces are still at work.

[17] W. Marlin Butts, "An Education Program in a Short-Term Correctional Institution," *Federal Probation* (Dec. 1957), pp. 39–43.

[18] Lorraine O. Williams, "Short-term Treatment of Women: An Experiment," *Federal Probation* (Sept. 1957), pp. 42–51.

[19] Joan K. Jackson, Ronald J. Fagan, and Roscoe C. Burr, "The Seattle Police Department Rehabilitation Project for Chronic Alcoholics," *Federal Probation* (June 1958), pp. 36–41.

Lunden, Walter A. "The Rotary Jail, or Human Squirrel Cage," *Journal of the Society of Architectural Historians* (Dec. 1959), pp. 149–157. In the 1880's six midwestern counties built jails which "locked" by literally rotating them within an encasing cylinder.

Robinson, Louis N. *Jails: Care and Treatment of Misdemeanant Prisoners in the United States.* Philadelphia: John C. Winston Company, 1944. Still the only full-scale study of this institution.

Steiner, Jesse F., and Brown, Roy M. *The North Carolina Chain Gang.* Chapel Hill, N. C.: University of North Carolina Press, 1927. County convict road work several decades ago. Merely by dispassionately reporting the facts, the inhumanity of chain gangs is depicted.

CHAPTER 21

Criminal and Juvenile Courts

American law, police, courts, and penal practices have been seen as parts and products of social processes involving conflict between law-makers and law-breakers.[1] The American system of justice is then a more or less structured continuance of the conflict into the trial process. Courts are generally thought of as engaged in coldly dispensing an abstract and even-handed justice in terms of principles set forth in an absolute law. Actually, the personnel of courts and related agencies are groups of human beings engaged in selecting within the limits of the law those whom they deem it appropriate to punish. Judge, prosecutor, jury, lawyer, accused, and witnesses play in the very human court drama roles which express in part their interests and roles in the larger drama of life. Traditionally, the *dramatis personae* of the court scene are marionettes manipulated from above by the blind goddess of abstract justice. To the student of reality, the marionettes come to life to strut their eager parts or themselves attempt to pull the strings of the show.

The court really exerts a more or less personal discretion in

[1] Cf. *supra,* Chapter 2. For a challenging emphasis on the human influences which are brought to bear on the trial process, see Jerome Frank, *Courts on Trial* (Princeton, N. J.: Princeton University Press, 1949). Cf. also Benjamin N. Cardozo, *The Nature of the Judicial Process* (New Haven, Conn.: Yale University Press, 1921); Roscoe Pound, *Justice According to Law* (New Haven, Conn.: Yale University Press, 1951).

various ways. Thus judges are meticulous or liberal in the interpretation of the law, and tender or tough in passing sentence. Prosecuting attorneys may be hard-boiled, considerate, or politically diplomatic in pressing an advantage, and juries sentimental or callous. Judgments are swayed by factors varying from the quality of the judge's philosophy of life to the digestibility of his breakfast. All concerned are subject to the influence of public opinion in important cases, and public opinion is fanned or quieted by news media. The most intense combats in our courts are good copy for newspapers, though the typical trial is not. Where the victim or the accused has moved in high society, or where the crime itself arouses sex or other sensational interest, the flash-bulb will be used as much as is permitted. Moreover, as we saw when dealing with the influence of newspapers on crime, some judges, jury members, and prosecuting and defense attorneys welcome the personal "build-up" which the story in the papers affords. If most judges insist on decorum in the courtroom, the public is apt to derive its impression of the machinery of justice from cases most widely publicized. Judge Leibowitz once said that the court is like an iceberg: four-fifths of it remain hidden, and the hidden part may be the most important.[2]

Yet courts must operate within the limits of the law, and in addition they follow traditions of their own. These laws and traditions give a certain degree of uniformity to the exercise of discretion by the judge or the prosecuting attorney or even the lawyer for the defense. In the past, courts have operated in partial isolation from the rest of society and hence from reality. In order to prevent star-chamber procedures behind closed doors, democracies require that trials be public. This requirement both permits and prevents impartial consideration of facts, which is essential to accurate decisions as to guilt and treatment. Together with the requirement of jury trial, it brings the court into touch with social reality, but it also brings into the court's contentious system of justice the emotions and contentiousness of the outside society. Yet, in spite of some knowledge of such external influences upon justice, court pronouncements are looked upon with a considerable measure of respect by society generally, and its top staff are given corresponding social prestige, at least at the higher levels. A product of precedent, the court's orientation has been toward the past, hence its conservatism. Dependent upon formal law, its philosophy has been legalistic. Yet contact with the grass roots of the real social world has meant a certain seeping into the formalism of justice of both the "humanness" and the humaneness of man. Thus court personnel enter into personal relationships with the criminal and the public generally. For the most part in the past, the

[2] See Quentin Reynolds, *Courtroom* (New York: Farrar, Straus and Company, 1950).

influence of personal relations on the court has been at the sentimental rather than the scientific level. Only rather recently, as objective evidence and the specialist have increasingly been brought into court, has the influence of men of scientific viewpoint been evident. This trend may eventually revolutionize the functions of courts and deprive them of some of their traditional duties in the treatment of criminals, if not in the determination of their guilt. Social science has begun to permeate the thinking of some lawyers.

Finally, the court is an experience of the accused. The impression of justice or injustice which it makes upon him, whether acquitted or convicted, is significant for his future behavior. Just as the behavior of the average citizen is influenced by his reaction to what he conceives to be the court process, so the behavior of the criminal, who has experienced court "justice" first-hand, is influenced toward reform or toward continuance in a life of crime by that experience.

History of Our Courts [3]

The nature of the judicial process has always reflected the conditions of the time. Primitive justice was not so much concerned with determining guilt as with seeing that the proper religious ritual was observed by private parties in settling private disputes. Only when the judicial function had become differentiated from the priestly and political and had developed a body of formal law and procedure did courts as distinct public institutions come into being. These acted as arbitrators in private disputes and in determining the punishment for acts against the state. Criminal courts distinct from civil courts and separated from the administration of government had their origin in the Roman Republic some two centuries before Christ and became firmly established under the Empire.

In the early Christian era the church forbade its adherents to resort to the state's courts, and later in the medieval period, as the power of the state courts declined, that of the canonical courts increased. Later English history involved a sort of three-cornered struggle between the manorial and church courts and the growing power of the King's Bench. Along with this came the hit-or-miss development of a wide variety of new courts, resulting in the disorganized judicial system America inherited from England.[4]

The American court system, however, is also the product of American

---

[3] Cf. Max Radin, "Courts," *Encyclopaedia of the Social Sciences,* IV, pp. 515–28.
[4] Roscoe Pound, *Organization of Courts* (Boston: Little, Brown, 1940), p. 4.

influences. The development of trade and commerce created need for new and complex laws and for a professional class of lawyers. Moreover, Americans lacked confidence in authority and preferred that juries representative of the people, rather than single justices, control the judicial process.

The period between 1789 and the Civil War was characterized by the passing of lay judges, the development of appellate courts, and the tendency to abandon the fee system for others than justices of the peace. In this period the general outlines of our present court system developed. The more recent trend has been to increase somewhat the influence of the judge in court and to permit jury trials to be waived by the accused. But it has also been to exclude part of the determination of punishment or treatment from the court, and give it to nonjudicial bodies, including our modern tribunals for the treatment of youthful criminals to be described later.[5]

For the great mass of people who become litigants, the court experience is confined to courts of original jurisdiction, since not more than 3 to 5 per cent of cases are appealed to the higher courts.[6] A considerable part of the problems connected with our courts is rooted in procedures in these lower courts. Hence it is held unfortunate that there is relatively little interest in them. The general public knows the court experience in connection with traffic cases, which, in New York City in 1951, for example, made up four-fifths of all cases tried, while the majority of other cases are those of drunkards and other petty offenders. From among the mass of petty cases, those of alcoholics should be screened for special attention, but this procedure is still most unusual and alcoholics crowd our jails or are released to populate our "skid roads." Among other steady customers in the lower courts are family cases, policy runners, bookmakers, drug addicts, prostitutes, and wayward youth generally.[7] For some of these cases special courts have been provided in our larger cities, but many of them need rather the attention of social agencies, psychiatrists, and other specialists, who sometimes are, but more often are not, available.

The American Court System

In spite of considerable local differences, one may roughly classify types of courts in the American court system as follows: (1) local magistrates and inferior courts, including justices of the peace, for summary

[5] Cf. *infra*, pp. 366*ff*.

[6] Cf. Council of State Governments, *Trial Courts of General Jurisdiction in the Forty-eight States* (Chicago: The Council, 1951).

[7] Cf. Morris Ploscowe, "The Inferior Courts in Action," *Annals of the American Academy of Political and Social Science* (May 1953), pp. 8–12.

offenses; (2) county and municipal courts trying misdemeanors; (3) superior, district, or circuit courts trying felonies and indictable misdemeanors and hearing appeals from the court trying misdemeanors; (4) one or more appellate courts with little or no original jurisdiction. In addition there has been a great flowering of special courts added with little plan. The lower courts have, in addition to their trial function, the duty to conduct preliminary hearings to determine whether a case is to be tried in the higher courts. The federal system of courts corresponds roughly with this state system, with original jurisdiction vested in District Courts and appellate jurisdiction divided between Circuit Courts of Appeal and the Supreme Court.

Such organization or lack of organization of our judicial system has brought about sundry problems.[8] It has meant some dockets overloaded with cases with consequent delay of justice, while other judges may be idle. Delay defeats justice. It has also meant lack of central administration to plan and coordinate the work of the courts, and piecemeal handling of different aspects of cases by different courts. Similarly, difficulties have arisen out of the separateness of state and federal courts and out of lack of cooperation between courts and other parts of the penal system. Another problem has been the lack of continuity of personnel. A number of different judges may each sit for short terms in the same court. A defense attorney can often select among a panel of judges the one he deems most likely to favor his client.

A special type of miscarriage of justice grows out of the place of the justice of the peace in the court system. This official is still usually paid by fees and not by salary. It is therefore charged that he has a personal interest in handling as many cases as possible, and that the justice of the peace in some localities is occasionally little more than a racketeer engaged in administering "injustice" in the interest of his own pocketbook. Such a charge, of course, cannot be laid against salaried judges or against most justices of the peace. The typical justice of the peace often lacks legal training.

The Process of Trying a Criminal Case [9]

Disregarding local differences, the process of bringing a case to trial may be generally described as follows:

[8] Cf. Pound, *Organization of Courts, loc. cit.,* pp. 247–60.

[9] The following account is based chiefly on Clarence N. Callendar, *American Courts* (New York: McGraw-Hill Book Company, 1927), chaps. 12, 13. For an account emphasizing the legal and procedural problems encountered, see Roy Moreland, *Modern Criminal Procedure* (Indianapolis, Ind.: Bobbs-Merrill Co., 1959), parts III and IV.

Following arrest and arraignment at a police station, an offender will either be released on bail or placed in the lockup or jail to await trial. He has the right of access to an attorney. In the large number of cases where the offense is not observed by the police, the victim or some interested party makes a complaint to the prosecuting attorney. This official may confer with the complainant and perhaps also, the accused and may decide not to prosecute the case but to secure a settlement between the parties out of court. Otherwise a warrant for the arrest of the accused is issued. If the case is a misdemeanor, a summary trial will be held before either a justice of the peace or a municipal or other local court. This trial will ordinarily be without jury. If conviction follows, the court may impose a small fine or commit for a short period to a jail or house of correction. From such a sentence there is usually a right of appeal to a higher court.

If the charge is a felony, on the other hand, the justice of the peace or municipal court merely conducts a preliminary hearing which, in many jurisdictions, the accused may waive if he wishes. At the preliminary hearing, the court normally hears only evidence against the accused, though he must be given an opportunity to make a statement if he desires. Then court decides whether there is sufficient evidence to warrant trial, and if so, the accused is bound over to the grand jury. At the preliminary hearing, the prosecuting attorney may move to *nolle pros* or "no paper" the case, meaning that he feels prosecution is not warranted; or the accused may be discharged by the court for "no probable cause." If bound over, the accused is again entitled to bail except in some murder cases. Among other rights is that of using the court's processes for subpoenaing witnesses in his behalf. The magistrate sitting in the lower court makes a return of the case to the trial court, sending a transcript of the record, a copy of the complaint or information, and a copy of the bail bond if the man has been released. These documents become the basis for a bill of indictment prepared by the prosecuting attorney. If the accused is confined, he may at various stages in this process obtain a writ of habeas corpus, which secures for him a prompt hearing in court to determine whether he is being unjustly held.

The prosecuting attorney presents the bill of indictment at the next meeting of the grand jury, a body of men traditionally 23 in number who have been drawn by lot from a list of qualified voters. Unlike the petit jury, the grand jury decides issues by majority vote. They are brought into court by summons and usually serve for the entire term of court. Formerly very minute defects in the wording of the bill of indictment were sufficient to render it unacceptable, though the tendency now is to permit minor corrections. The judge charges the grand jury, explaining their duties and powers, and he may assist them later on their request. The defendant and his counsel are not permitted to attend the meeting of the grand jury. Grand juries are often subject to the influence of the prosecuting attorney, for they are often ill-informed and easily influenced. Nevertheless, they have much potential power and popular prestige, and their independence is relative to their personnel and the personality of the prosecuting attorney. Their deliberations may result in finding a "true bill" or "no bill." This may be with reference to some or all of the counts set forth in the bill of indictment. In the process of their investigation, the grand jury may discover additional evidence and may on their own initiative make a presentment of this evidence. In some jurisdictions, cases may be brought before the trial court by information from the prosecuting attorney without indictment, and there is increasing demand for such simplification of procedure. When a "true bill" has been found, its legality may be attacked by the attorney for the defense through the process of demurrer, which must be argued at a sepcial court session. If the indictment is found defective, the accused will be released, and though he may be rearrested, he often is not.

On the date of the trial, the defendant, if in jail, is produced in court by the sheriff; if on bail, his sureties are notified to produce him. If he fails to appear, a bench warrant for his arrest will be issued, and if this is unsuccessful, the judge will direct the district attorney to sue out the bail bond. There is much criticism of failure to prosecute bail-bond cases effectively. If the defendant appears in court, the court crier or other official reads the charge and demands a plea of guilty or not guilty. If the defendant pleads guilty, the court may impose sentence on the spot, or may delay sentence to a later date. A plea of *nolo contendere* is tantamount to a guilty plea but differs from the latter in that it eliminates a basis for damage suits against the accused.[10] Standing mute or entering a plea of not guilty makes necessary a trial. In some jurisdictions, as many as 90 per cent of the cases are disposed of by guilty pleas, and most of the remaining 10 per cent are tried without juries.[11]

At the court trial again, the prosecuting attorney may move to *nolle pros* the case. Possibly the accused will oppose the motion if he thinks he has a good chance of acquittal. Either side may request a continuance to postpone the trial, and this is a favorite device of the defense to attempt to tire out the witnesses for the prosecution.

The trial next proceeds to the drawing of the petit or trial jury. The

[10] Robert E. Knowlton, "The Trial of Offenders," *Annals of the American Academy of Political and Social Science* (Jan. 1962), p. 126.

[11] Frank W. Miller and Frank J. Remington, "Procedures Before Trial," *Annals of the American Academy of Political and Social Science* (Jan. 1962), p. 117.

prosecuting attorney and the attorney for the defense may challenge any juror drawn. Any number may be challenged if reasons acceptable to the judge are given, and each side has a limited number of peremptory challenges for which no reasons need be given. The petit jury normally consists of 12 members, though in some states a smaller number may try minor cases. Unanimous vote is usually necessary to convict.

The jury drawn and sworn, the prosecuting attorney, in his opening address, outlines the case he expects to prove. The prosecution has the burden of proof. The state's witnesses are then examined by him and cross-examined by the attorney for the defense. The prosecution then rests its case, although it will later cross-examine defense witnesses.

The defense may then, if it desires, ask the court to dismiss the case without hearing further evidence on the ground that the evidence against the accused does not warrant its submission to the jury. The defense may also ask for a directed verdict.

The defense may next call its witnesses. However, in rare cases the attorney may wish to try a finesse. If so, he tells the court the defendant offers no evidence, hoping thus to impress the jury with his belief that the state's case is so weak that no reply is needed. The defense may or may not put the defendant on the stand. As a rule, no comments are allowed on its failure to do so, though there is demand for allowing such comments, and in any case the jury no doubt often draw their own conclusions, even though instructed to disregard the fact. Evidence of the good character of the accused may be introduced, and only then may the state present evidence that he has been previously convicted. Thus a trial does not permit consideration of all the facts. Each side raises objections to questions asked by the other. Objections by the defense, if overruled by the judge, may become the basis for an appeal to a higher court.

Addresses of counsel follow the conclusion of testimony, the first speech usually being that of the prosecuting attorney. He should confine his remarks to the evidence, but he often does not. At the close of these addresses the judge charges the jury, explaining the evidence necessary to convict. He tells them they must be convinced of the guilt of the accused "beyond a reasonable doubt," the presumption being in favor of innocence. Yet, he adds, the jury need not establish guilt "beyond any possibility of doubt." "Assuming," says Callendar,[12] "that the jury understands what he means, it is not unlikely that they will have some difficulty in applying the doctrine." In most states the judge must not comment on the evidence in a way to indicate his opinion, and it is reversible error if he does so. Either

[12] *Op. cit.*, p. 194.

side may suggest errors in the charge and request that it be modified. The jury announce their verdict through their foreman, but the accused may have the jury polled if he desires. A verdict is reached on each count in the indictment.

If the accused is found guilty, his counsel may make a motion for an arrest of judgment or for a new trial. The former means discharge if granted, but does not debar further prosecution for the same offense. A motion for a new trial is based on some alleged error in the course of the trial, such as that improper evidence was admitted or that the conduct of the jurors was prejudicial to the interests of the defendant. Exceptions to adverse rulings must usually have been made at the time they occurred, though this technical requirement is not infrequently criticized in cases where manifest injustice has resulted.

Following the verdict, the judge sets a date for sentence. On that occasion final pleas for mercy may be made before sentence is pronounced. In cases where the law permits, sentence may be suspended by the court, and probation may be granted. At the court level, the last hope of a convicted man is an appeal to a higher court. Application for such an appeal must usually be made within a few weeks after the judgment. Appeal is usually possible when the judgment has gone against the accused. In certain instances the state may appeal, but never against a verdict of acquittal. In a new trial the whole criminal process is repeated.

THE ROLE OF THE PROSECUTING ATTORNEY

The prosecuting attorney decidedly plays the "lead" in the criminal court drama. Indeed, the show does not go on at all unless the state's attorney so decides. Even judge and jury are dependent on the prosecuting attorney. Illinois research of an earlier date,[13] at least, showed that only from two- to three-fifths of felonies prosecuted reached the trial court. In very many other cases the state's attorney arranged settlement out of court. This indicates the significance of the stage in judicial proceedings prior to jury trial and during which the possible influence of the prosecutor is greatest.

History and place in the traditional penology. Prosecution of crime was originally a private function. In the United States the public prosecutor had become an established American institution by the end of the eighteenth century.[41]

13 John J. Healy, "Prosecution in Chicago," *Illinois Crime Survey*, p. 287.

14 National Commission on Law Observance and Enforcement, *Report on Prosecution*, No. 4, 1931, by Alfred Bettman *et al.*, p. 7.

Theoretically the government is equally interested in justice to the complainant and justice to the accused. Actually the function of defense is generally private, though public defenders have been established in some cities. The popular interest in defense is undoubtedly weaker than that in prosecution, except where the enforcement of unpopular laws or the defense of popular defendants are concerned. On the whole, and quite logically in a democracy, our court system probably acquits far more of the guilty than it convicts of the innocent. Yet Borchard's collection [15] of 65 cases of the latter type must be a mere sampling of such miscarriage of justice.

Nature and function of prosecuting attorneys. Prosecuting attorneys have four general functions or roles: [16] they are criminal investigators; magistrates determining who shall be prosecuted; solicitors preparing cases for trial; and advocates trying them.[17] Their roles as investigators have involved some rivalry with the corresponding role of the police.

The usual qualifications for the office of prosecuting attorney are not exacting. Generally such officials must be old enough to vote, residents of the area of jurisdiction, and members of the bar. In both rural and urban areas, the position is eagerly sought as a possible stepping stone to higher political office.

The social role of the prosecuting attorney.[18] A prosecuting attorney in the less populous counties or judicial districts works under many handicaps. He usually lacks needed assistants and secretarial help; his library facilities are limited; and his many civil duties interfere with his prosecution of crime. He is further handicapped as a local man by personal obligations which a neighbor feels toward his friends, complicated by a sense of obligation toward those who have promoted his election and whose assistance may seem essential to any further political advancement to which he may aspire. He must be a joiner. He is looked upon as the "people's attorney" and is asked to perform services which rightly belong to a private attorney.

The prosecuting attorney acts as a sort of father confessor and counselor to the community. His investigation, personal advice, and discretionary

[15] Edwin M. Borchard, *Convicting the Innocent* (New Haven, Conn.: Yale University Press, 1932). Cf. also Robert S. Morris, "Convicting the Innocent," *Journal of Criminal Law and Criminology* (Jan.–Feb. 1947), pp. 408–12.

[16] National Commission on Law Observance and Enforcement, *op. cit.*, pp. 16ff.

[17] Newman F. Baker and Earl H. Delong, "The Prosecuting Attorney: Provisions of Law Organizing the Office," *Journal of Criminal Law and Criminology* (March–April 1933), p. 934.

[18] Cf. Newman F. Baker, "The Prosecutor: Initiation of Prosecution," *Journal of Criminal Law and Criminology* (Jan.–Feb. 1933), pp. 770–96.

activities constitute an important type of social case work, albeit usually performed by a man untrained for it. It is impossible and unwise to prosecute all cases. Yet the prosecuting attorney must make a record for convictions if he is to be considered a success, but he must also use wise judgment as to when to prosecute vigorously, when to refuse to act, when to bring accused and complainant together for friendly settlement, when to change the nature of the charge, and when to secure a plea of guilty to a lesser offense than that committed. All these discretionary powers make corruption and miscarriage of justice possible, it is true, and certain restrictions are called for; but granting our present system of justice, none of these restrictions will remove the necessity that someone do an intelligent piece of case work.

Being human, prosecuting attorneys have their pet peeves and prejudices. One abhors the prosecution of bootleggers and lets them alone; another pursues them with missionary zeal. A third shows wisdom by skillfully convincing many deserted wives that since they are better off without their erring husbands, prosecution for desertion would be foolish. Still another effectively uses peace bonds as a substitute for prosecution as protection against those who threaten violence. One prosecutor told Professor Baker he did not take one case of rape out of ten to court. Local attitudes determine policies of prosecution. Thus, in a community generally opposed to gambling, but with a considerable minority eager to gamble, the "heat" may be turned diplomatically off and on with changes in a fickle public sentiment, and with or without any real corrupt practices.

Bargaining between prosecution and defense, resulting in pleas of guilty to a lesser offense than that charged, is prevalent, and its desirability from the social viewpoint is often questionable. At one time in Chicago three-quarters of convictions where the original charge was a felony had involved such reduction of charge. A special problem is the assumed necessity of granting immunity to informers. When such bargains are made, it is possible in some cases for the informer to compel states' attorneys to live up to them, but the bargain is usually kept without compulsion. Peter Kihss, writing in the *New York Times*,[19] reported on several important cases of this sort. In one case three men who hired a murderer for a public official thus escaped punishment. A district attorney in the New York area has indicated an average of some five letters a week from prisoners offering thus to turn state's evidence. The notorious gambler, Harry Gross, at first refused to take advantage of such an offer, but later received a 4-year reduction in

[19] Dec. 16, 1954.

his prison sentence for testifying against certain policemen. As Baker and Delong once wrote, "We pay a high price for such squealing," [20] for we encourage false testimony and release dangerous men thereby. Yet there seems to be a far from unanimous outcry against the practice, and it must be admitted that its immediate effect has often been to secure convictions which would perhaps have been impossible otherwise.

In our largest cities, prosecution presents complications. Sheer numbers mean neglect of the careful attention required in the social interest. While large cities may usually secure better-qualified prosecutors, the baneful influence of politics is even more evident there, and the complexity of the situation makes it more difficult for the citizen to trace responsibility. The prosecution of misdemeanors is especially apt to be neglected, and such often make up over 85 per cent of total cases tried. The youngest, least experienced, poorest paid, and politically chosen assistants are apt to handle these cases. This is because of the vast number of cases and because they have no publicity value and therefore no political value. Settlements of petty cases are often made without court activity, but using the court as a threat. In such cases prosecution is often dropped because the complainant has received restitution or has been satisfied with the imposition of a lighter punishment than that called for under the law.

Federal prosecution has been so extended, improved, and partially socialized as to set an example for local authorities. The United States Attorney General's Office was established in 1789 and the Department of Justice set up in 1870, but not until 1909 was central control over prosecution fully established. Though the appointment of district attorneys has at times furnished an opportunity for patronage, the federal organization has meant more efficient prosecution than that usual in state courts. Within the federal system, waiver of indictment is expressly permitted, and a case may be dismissed only by leave of court. The Civil Rights Division of the Department of Justice evidences an important government interest in protecting personal freedom. It is responsible not only for the enforcement of all federal statutes relating to civil rights, but also handles all legal and administrative questions and problems arising with respect to federal prisoners from arrest to release. Important at all times, this protection has become increasingly needed in times of interracial friction and in times of cold war tension, such as the present.

Baker and Delong recommended relieving prosecuting attorneys of

[20] Newman F. Baker and Earl H. Delong, "The Prosecuting Attorney: The Process of Prosecution," *Journal of Criminal Law and Criminology* (May 1935), pp. 3–21, and "The Process of Prosecution," *ibid.* (July 1935), pp. 185–201.

their civil duties and consolidating counties to make needed changes possible in small communities. However, they would not follow the usual suggestion of restricting the discretionary powers of prosecuting attorneys. They urged the development of more private organizations like the Chicago Crime Commission to watch and publicize the process of justice, including the work of the prosecutors. The extension of the power of state attorneys general over both police and prosecution is a possibility.

THE ROLE OF THE DEFENSE ATTORNEY [21]

A study by Professor Arthur Wood based on interviews with 205 criminal and civil lawyers provides some glimpses into the sociological factors accounting for certain features in the practice of criminal law. Criminal lawyers, more often than other members of the bar, tend to be champions of the underdog, as suggested not only by their interest in defending accused persons, but by their greater interest in charitable activities, their more frequent voting for Democratic candidates, and a greater tendency to be dissociated from the business community and to associate and identify with persons at less elevated positions on the social and professional scale.

"Informal relations," i.e., working ties with politicians, court attachés, the prosecutor's office, and the like, which are not called for by formal systems of professional norms, are more or less built into the practice of criminal law for three reasons: (1) The problem of building a practice, difficult at best, is even harder for the poorly-connected beginner interested in this branch of the law; he must, therefore, seek friendly ties with law-enforcement officials and politicians to obtain clients. (2) The adversary system of criminal justice, with opposing litigants doing public battle, runs counter to the norms of friendliness and professional courtesy and creates anxiety among the participants. (3) Since "the majority of clients are guilty of something," and since the lawyer wishes to render *some* service to his client without having grounds for a successful defense, the lawyer finds himself in an awkward position. The role strains resulting from these three sets of factors are minimized by such devices as bail reduction, bargaining and pleading guilty to reduced charges, and recommendation for leniency in sentencing. Thus, "deals" between criminal lawyers and prosecuting officials tend to be inevitable features of criminal jurisprudence and do not necessarily bespeak ignoble motives on either side.

[21] Arthur Lewis Wood, "Informal Relations in the Practice of Criminal Law," *American Journal of Sociology* (July 1956), pp. 48–55. This section is based on Professor Wood's findings.

PUBLIC AND PRIVATE DEFENDERS

The injustice done the indigent or ignorant litigant is obvious. It is not universally obligatory to tell a defendant of his right to counsel. The poor defendant is easily exploited by unscrupulous attorneys for either the prosecution or the defense. The traditional and still the most prevalent solution of this problem is the assignment by the court of unpaid or sometimes of paid counsel. Brownell's study [22] about 1951 showed that in only 23 states was compensation paid in other than capital cases. Such assignment is mandatory in 18 states only. The assignment system works relatively well in small communities, where people know one another and where the young, inexperienced attorney, of the type usually called upon by the court, is carefully watched. But even in such communities the poor man is handicapped. In the large city such inexperienced lawyers are utterly incapable of competing with highly paid and well-trained prosecuting attorneys.

The obvious injustice involved has led to the establishment of voluntary defender offices connected either with a Legal Aid Society or an independent local organization. Legal aid officers of this type were recently handling without cost to defendants over 300,000 persons every year, including both civil and criminal cases. The movement is sponsored by the National Legal Aid Association. It is preferred by some who consider the public defender an unwarranted extension of government activity threatening the independent bar and smacking of socialism. It is perhaps preferred by a few others who think the public defender less effective than the legal aid lawyer.

Nevertheless, a strong movement to parallel public prosecution with a public defender system has sprung up, beginning in Los Angeles in 1913. Only in Colorado, Connecticut, and Rhode Island was there by 1956 a state-wide effective public defender system. Usually the expense is borne by the local government. Brownell considers the quality of the service rendered uniformly good except where politics rather than merit has governed appointments. Without the aid of a public defender or the best type of legal aid lawyers, the indigent accused is said to receive his assigned attorney too late; to be left incommunicado too long; to have less protection against the third degree; and either to be led too readily to plead guilty when innocent, or to receive less efficient protection when guilty than the man who can hire an attorney of his own. The public defender system secures a more competent lawyer; is open to all of the indigent and not just

[22] Emery A. Brownell, *Legal Aid in the United States* (Rochester, N. Y.: The Lawyer's Cooperative Publishing Company, 1951), chap. VI.

a part of them; saves valuable time; avoids unnecessary trials; and raises the general tone of the courts. In some places it is provided that the accused may ask for an assigned attorney if he prefers. The chief objection has been the intrusion of politics. Apparently only rarely has it been charged that the public defender injures his client by securing too ready pleas of guilty. In our larger cities, at least, the public defender seems to have become a necessity. It is not easy to show just why prosecution should be a public function and defense a private one. There is little likelihood that all criminal defense will become public, but if it were we should at least be rid of the unscrupulous lawyer who, on the one hand, exploits the needy and, on the other, aids the guilty rich gangster to avoid the punishment which the poor man receives under precisely similar circumstances. Our most reputable lawyers will refuse the cases of clients they know to be guilty.

THE ROLE OF THE JUDGE

Judge Cardozo [23] has held that the personality of the judge is, in practice, the only real guarantee of justice. Yet in 1951 [24] 38 states elected their judges by popular vote, in four they were elected by the legislature, and only in six were they appointed by the governor. The judge settles questions of law, determines probation or form of punishment, issues bench warrants, determines the admission and rejection of evidence, exercises discretion in control of witnesses, sets the level of decorum of the courtroom, sometimes examines witnesses himself, orders new trials, charges the jury, and so forth. We give his role less space because much we have already said applies also to him.

The judge is not all-powerful in theory, and numerous forces restrict his power in fact. He cannot compel the jury to convict. He may not usually comment on the evidence, though federal judges have more power here, and in some states such comment is permitted. He must act within the laws. Moreover, in most states outside of New England and New Jersey the judge is elected, and this fact often binds his hands more effectively than the law. He dares not offend lawyers, whose political support he needs. He probably seeks re-election, and he may have political debts left over from the last election. The newspapers have him partly in their power, for he cannot disregard the omnipotence of the publicity he both fears and needs. Most students of the judiciary favor appointment of judges,[25] as,

[23] Cardozo, *op. cit.*
[24] Council of State Governments, *op. cit.*
[25] Cf. Harold J. Laski, "Judiciary," *Encyclopaedia of the Social Sciences,* VIII, p. 468.

for example, in Massachusetts. The picture of his honor appealing for votes and mayhap making promises in every cheap barroom is not wholly unreal and is not conducive to reverence for justice. Yet we do elect some good judges. Missouri has pioneered in using a system which combines some of the good features of election and appointment.[26] Judges are appointed by the governor from a list approved by a selection committee of the legal profession and laymen. When these judges have served a year, they are voted upon by the people. The system is said to have eliminated partisan influences in the selection.

THE JURY SYSTEM

The most democratic element in the trial scene is the petit or trial jury, and it has some of the strength and much of the weakness of democratic institutions. Originating in France in the ninth century, trial by jury by the thirteenth century had replaced the various ordeals and other medieval forms of trial. The institution of the jury was given increased powers in America because the colonists preferred to preserve liberty rather than to create an efficient tribunal. In a few jurisdictions the jury have even been made judges of law as well as of fact, and they often participate, at least in serious cases, in determining the punishment. A recent feeling that this process has gone too far has led to a steady growth of laws permitting waiver of jury trial.

The jury are selected by lot from a panel of electors. One study showed that no fewer than 68 classes of persons are exempted from jury service in different states. Such exemptions are said to result in the selection of the relatively unintelligent and uneducated for this important service. Some critics urge that the number of possible bases for exemption be reduced. Others would give the judge greater discretion in making exemptions, and urge interviews to determine fitness. There is much force in Moley's contention[27] that, after all, selection from among the educated and privileged classes would weaken the value of the jury as an indication of the popular will.[28]

Judge Frank [29] has characterized and criticized the jury system somewhat as follows: Juries are biased, and prejudice has been called the thir-

[26] Laurence M. Hyde, "The Missouri Plan for Selection and Tenure of Judges," *Journal of Criminal Law and Criminology* (Sept.–Oct. 1948), pp. 277–87.

[27] Cf. Raymond Moley, *Our Criminal Courts* (New York: Milton, Balch & Company, 1930), pp. 116–17.

[28] Recent experiments suggest that jury-room deliberations produce a drift of authority toward jurymen who are articulately assertive, these usually being representative of upper socio-economic levels. See Fred L. Strodtbeck, Rita M. James, and Charles Hawkins, "Social Status in Jury Deliberations," *American Sociological Review* (Dec. 1957), pp. 713–19.

[29] Frank, *op. cit.*, pp. 110ff.

teenth juror. Lawyers select jurors not to get the facts but to win a case. The jury is able to disregared rules of evidence and the instructions of the judge. In effect its decisions make law. It becomes an unelected legislature and thus is an even worse enemy of the supremacy of law than a judge unbound by law would be. The jury does not ordinarily report the facts upon which its decisions are based. Indeed, its existence blocks the way to increased use of scientific data, which is the best guarantee of real justice.[30]

On the other hand, a powerful argument may be made for the merits of the jury system in a democracy. The jury brings the interpretation and administration of the law into line with the attitudes of the people in whose interest the law exists. The jury is a sort of dictionary which defines indefinable terms such as "negligence" or "responsibility" as they are defined, not in law books, but on the streets.[31] The jury can be cruel, but more often it humanizes justice. Moreover, it is argued that some of the weaknesses of the jury mentioned above may be eliminated or greatly reduced through available means. Judge Frank himself recognizes this possibility when he urges that special juries of fact are a great help, and that juries might be required to state the facts upon which their decisions are made. Clever devices for bringing factual data into the courtroom are increasingly used, and it has been found possible to interpret even rather technical evidence. Suggestions have been made that the power of the judge over the jury be increased by permitting him to comment on the evidence and to make more definite charges to the jury; that educational qualifications be introduced; that less than unanimous decisions be required for conviction; and that waiver of jury trial be further encouraged. Some of these suggestions have been put into effect in certain jurisdictions. Such suggestions reflect growing dissatisfaction with jury acquittals on technical grounds and growing fear of crime. Yet many who recognize the evils urge that some of the changes suggested threaten important popular liberties. Some states and the federal courts have endeavored to educate jurors by distributing a primer informing them of the law and of the nature of their duties. Curtis Bok [32] writes that the jury system cannot be abolished, but is slowly disintegrating. There is a greater urge to use majority instead of unanimous verdicts in certain types of cases and to reduce restrictions in rules of evidence to permit "the full story." Bok even considers it odd to keep hearsay evidence from the jury when so much of our opinion is based

[30] At any rate the typical jury is just such a collection of average citizens whom the trained spellbinder can manipulate through knowledge of local prejudices.

[31] Curiously enough, this popularization of law, which is a major function of the jury, is precisely a duty which they are supposedly forbidden to perform.

[32] "The Jury System in America," *Annals of the American Academy of Political and Social Science* (May, 1953), pp. 92–96.

on hearsay and when the jury is compelled to struggle with the complexities of law. The problem is complex and controversial. Meantime we lack scientific evidence as to how juries actually make up their minds, though research in that area seems currently to be under way.[33]

It has been said that the grand jury, which prepares indictments, and the coroner's jury, which assists in the determination of probable cause of death, are even more obviously nearing the end of their usefulness than is the trial jury.[34] Yet the investigative function of the grand jury is widely held to be essential, even among many who would abolish the requirement that a felony case must pass through the process of grand jury indictment before coming to trial. That requirement has already been eliminated in less serious cases, and the accused with increasing frequency is permitted to waive it. The grand jury has at times been most useful in making general crime investigations and in looking into the conduct of public officials. Its powers to do these things are not clearly defined [35] and seem to be inadequate. The public has greater confidence in grand jury indictments and investigations than in police charges and the findings of scientific research. Since the legislature cannot commit a crime, it has been said that grand juries should not inquire whether they have done so. Grand juries have performed services by investigating situations where crime seemed to be imminent, but their right to do so has been questioned. When they deal with conditions rather than name individuals, their rights are clearer, for in the latter case they may be subject to suit by those held to be wrongfully accused. The court supports its grand juries by giving them the right to subpoena witnesses and by procedure for contempt of court against those who refuse to testify. On the other hand, the court may control the grand jury by not accepting its report for filing. Usually no action is taken unless a case for indictment is found.

The Juvenile Court

The juvenile court movement originated in part as a protest against severity in the treatment of children by the courts. During medieval times and in the seventeenth and eighteenth centuries, much cruelty characterized

[33] Cf. Strodtbeck *et al., loc. cit.*

[34] Bok, *loc. cit.*

[35] "The Grand Jury: Its Investigatory Powers and Limitations," *Minnesota Law Review* (June 1953), pp. 586–607. Cf. also William G. Morgan, "The Grand Jury," *Journal of Criminal Law, Criminology and Police Science* (May–June 1953), pp. 49–72.

this treatment. For example, "a child of eight years who had 'with malice, revenge, craft and cunning' set fire to a barn was convicted and duly hanged." [36] Popular reaction against such severities awaited the influence of the modern liberal and humanitarian movement, and not until the nineteenth century did this reaction show itself in legislation favorable to children. In Illinois before 1840, penalties could legally be different for children than for adults. The English Juvenile Offenders' Act of 1847, as amended in 1879, gave justices power to try summarily children under 14 for all offenses except homicide. Illinois earlier provided for hearing certain types of children's cases out of court. In a few other states, during the last third of the nineteenth century, laws "embodied some of the essential features of the present-day juvenile court, including trials separate from those of adults, investigation of cases, and the use of probation." [37]

The juvenile court itself originated almost simultaneously in Cook County (Chicago) and in Denver in 1899, a school law in the latter city having been adopted two months earlier than the Illinois law, which was the first true state juvenile court act.

Based on principles different from those of the criminal courts, juvenile court laws nevertheless have roots in the development of certain legal traditions. During the reign of Edward the Confessor in the eleventh century, the crown, through the office of the chancellor, began assuming supervision over the feudal estates of minors in order to protect their property from appropriation by covetous neighboring nobles. The rationale evolved for this chancellory function (later extended to include neglected and dependent children) was that the crown is every child's ultimate parent, and that the state therefore can act *in loco parentis*—in place of the parent —if a child's welfare requires this. The juvenile courts extended the doctrine of this wardship principle to delinquent children.

A second root of the juvenile court is found in the common-law notion that the capacity to possess evil intent does not exist prior to one's seventh birthday but develops between then and one's fourteenth birthday and exists fully thereafter. The presumption of partial responsibility on the part of youngsters between seven and fourteen, therefore, was believed to justify less harsh prosecution and punishment for wrong-doers of those ages. Juvenile court legislation pushed up the age range of partial responsibility, in some states to the age of 21.

Apart from these legal bases, nineteenth-century humanitarianism and

[36] H. H. Low, *Juvenile Courts in the United States* (Chapel Hill, N. C.: University of North Carolina Press, 1927), p. 13.
[37] Gilbert Cosulich, *Juvenile Court Laws of the United States* (New York: National Probation Association, 1939), p. 7.

the development of scientific thinking about the causes of criminal behavior constitute other roots of the juvenile court.

From its early beginnings in Illinois and Colorado, the juvenile court movement has spread rather rapidly. At present all states have either separate juvenile courts or essentially juvenile court procedure in other courts.

JUVENILE COURTS IN THEORY AND PRACTICE

The purpose of the juvenile court movement to apply scientific principles to the treatment of child delinquents was revolutionary. Their partial application has not only altered the treatment of children but that of the supposedly potential delinquent in and out of court. It is also influencing the treatment of the adult criminal. Changes actually made have brought problems as well as benefits. These underlie certain controversies among members of the legal profession, psychological and social scientists, practitioners, and social workers. A number of these were discussed in the chapter on criminal law. Dealing with some of these problems, Professor Paul W. Tappan,[38] in a very scholarly book, has also shown how far many juvenile courts depart in practice from the theory of the movement and how their wide variety makes characterization almost impossible. In spite of general agreement as to what should distinguish juvenile from adult court procedures, this variety reflects lack of agreement on some general principles. Tappan [39] indicates that many juvenile courts are distinguishable in little more than the fact that they have separate hearings for children. On the one hand, many children are still treated much like adults in juvenile courts; on the other hand, certain progressive adult courts increasingly apply some of the principles of the juvenile court movement so far as the law permits. The following contrasts are therefore to be taken as existing between traditional criminal court practices and what juvenile courts are supposed to be like, or what they approximate in our best examples.

In theory, then, though as we note below, not by any means fully in practice, general differences between juvenile courts and adult courts in procedure and methods include separate hearings for children's cases, informal chancery procedure, regular probation service, detention separate from adults, special records, and provision for mental and physical examinations. All these matters are important, but all are subsidiary to the basic difference in philosophy which supposedly distinguishes the two systems. The

[38] *Juvenile Delinquency* (New York: McGraw-Hill Book Company, 1949).
[39] *Ibid.*, p. 180.

delinquent is conceived of as a child with a problem; his misbehavior as a symptom of that problem. Society is to be protected through constructive treatment. Even punishment when found necessary, is called and is intended to be "rehabilitation." The misleading use of that word is part of the language which Judge Edwards [40] calls "socialworkese." It is criticized by candid juvenile court judges, conscious of how far their courts fall short in practice of fully nonpunitive treatment.

Juvenile court theory and in part juvenile court practice differ, then, from *traditional* adult court theory and practice in the following respects. [41]

1. An adult court makes charges *against* the accused and stages a *battle* of wits before a jury or judge to determine his guilt or innocence. A juvenile court acts theoretically *in behalf* of a delinquent child and conducts an *investigation,* not only of the offense and his guilt, but also of the conditions which explain it.

    The theory that the court acts in the interest of the child permits the complete or partial elimination of many devices used in a criminal court to protect the accused, such as lawyers, jury, and meticulous rules of evidence and procedure. On the other hand, this very theory also gives power to the court to hear types of evidence not permitted in criminal courts and to adopt policies and a degree of control over the child and his family which is not permitted as a result of criminal court action. Assuming this power to be well-used in most cases, it may nevertheless be abused.

2. In a criminal court the traditional aim is to determine guilt and fix punishment primarily in proportion to the offense. In a juvenile court the purpose is to understand causes and treat persons or conditions.

3. Criminal trials are public; juvenile trials are private except for the admission of interested parties.

4. Adult courts examine intent as a measure of guilt; juvenile courts supposedly examine intent as an indication of the causes of behavior and of the likelihood that it may be repeated.

5. Criminal courts traditionally are solely concerned with a particular act so far as the determination of guilt is concerned, while juvenile courts consider a particular act only in relation to other acts and to the total personality and situation of the child.

[40] Judge George Edwards, "Meeting the Challenge of a Juvenile Code," *National Probation and Parole Association Yearbook, 1953,* pp. 93–105.

[41] To a considerable extent these are taken or suggested by the discussion in Pauline V. Young, *Social Treatment in Probation and Delinquency,* 2d ed. (New York: McGraw-Hill Book Company, 1952), chap. 10.

6. In a good juvenile court a careful case study with collateral reports of social agencies precedes the court hearing. Adult courts passively await evidence to be brought to them by attorneys interested in "making a case."

7. In the criminal courts, jury trials are used unless waived, while in a juvenile court they are "waived" unless demanded.

8. Criminal court judges are not usually specialized, while juvenile court judges *may* have had special training and give full time to cases involving children.

9. Accused adults are either jailed or bailed; juvenile delinquents are supposedly never bailed and may be detained in their own homes, except where greater security requires their detention separately from adults elsewhere.

10. Children's courts are more concerned with the treatment and its outcome after the court has acted than are criminal courts.

JUVENILE COURT LAW

In all states where juvenile courts exist, the law gives them jurisdiction over cases of delinquency, but the term is not uniformly defined.

In addition to violations of laws and ordinances, delinquency is defined more or less broadly in practically all juvenile court laws to include certain other acts and conditions, such as incorrigibility, association with immoral or vicious persons, truancy, using obscene language, engaging in immoral conduct, growing up in idleness or crime, begging, wandering about the streets at night, trespassing on railroad property, running away from home, endangering morals or safety.

It is clear that such a list defines as delinquent in the case of children much behavior which is not defined as crime in the case of adults. This has been justified on the ground that certain juvenile behavior may so obviously lead in the direction of later behavior dangerous to the community as to be in itself dangerous and hence appropriate for the consideration of a court acting *in loco parentis*. The most frequent offenses for which boys are actually brought before children's courts are stealing (about half of all cases) and acts of carelessness and mischief. For girls sex and "ungovernable" offenses are about half the total, and running away from home comes third. It appears that a little under one-half of boys' cases are dismissed, adjusted, or held open for further action. About one-third of girls' cases are similarly disposed of. About three cases out of ten of both sexes are supervised by a probation officer. About 10 per cent of boys and nearly one girl in five are committed to an institution. One per cent only of boys and less than 0.5 per cent of girls are required to pay fines or cost. These statistics are much affected, however, by policies of dealing with delinquents informally without making a record, and by the increased activities of public welfare and other agencies.

Nearly all states give juvenile courts jurisdiction over dependent and neglected children in addition to delinquent children. Other problems sometimes dealt with by juvenile courts independently or jointly with other courts include adoption and guardianship, consent to marry and annulments of marriage where one party is a juvenile, nonsupport and related cases, domestic relations cases, custody of children in divorce cases, and "mothers' aid" cases. In addition, in a majority of states adults charged with contributing to the delinquency or dependency of children are tried in juvenile courts.

THE JUVENILE COURT IN ACTION

Founded on a law permitting great flexibility in treatment, the juvenile court may punish a child in order to show him that crime does not pay. At the other extreme it may largely disregard his role as a law-breaker and offer him, perhaps for the first time in his life, sympathetic understanding. Through its relationships with kindly individuals and constructive agencies, it may meet his needs and satisfy his thwarted desires.

To appreciate the appropriateness of a wide range of treatment possibilities, one need only visualize the motley crowd of complaining, puzzled, or angry parents, and mischievous, abnormal, frustrated, spoiled, sophisticated, exploited, discouraged, self-satisfied, yet sometimes truly dangerous children who jam the waiting room of the court. The distinctive characteristic of the juvenile court *among courts* is its opportunity to deal constructively with delinquents. Yet the distinctive characteristic of a court *among social agencies* is its power to threaten and control. Ideally, cases which do not require this degree of possible compulsion should not be brought to the court. The public welfare agency, clinic, hospital, school, character-building agency, and the like, are indispensable adjuncts to the court. Where they do not exist, the court itself must perform some of their functions. It seems to us that critics of the courts sometimes overlook the very real need, in many communities without such facilities, that the court itself become in some degree a welfare agency.

Formal disposition of cases in a children's court may include dismissal, continuance, probation, or commitment. Fines are usually discouraged.

The delinquent may be required to make restitution for injury inflicted upon others if his or his family's resources permit. When a case is continued, a minimum of court interference is usually implied, the family being left to deal with the problem itself according to court instructions and advice. Probation is widely used. Institutional commitment is naturally reserved for more serious cases where greater control is desired than is involved in probation, where training provided in the institution is specifically called for, or where probation at home or elsewhere is impossible.

A fair number of states authorize the appointment of referees, especially of women to hear girls' cases, and in many other courts the functions of probation officers include investigation duties amounting to a referee system. As a rule, referees may not make final decisions.

Problems of juvenile delinquency are intimately related to sundry other social problems. Hence a juvenile court has relationships with adult criminal courts, courts of domestic relations, clinics, and a host of social agencies. Ideally, there should also be follow-through in treatment from the time a child first comes to the attention of a preschool clinic to the time when, as an adult, he is finally released from the supervision of a parole officer. The court should participate actively in any coordinating council or other device to secure community cooperation in the prevention and treatment of delinquency. The court should visit and inspect institutions to which it commits cases and the parole organizations of the state.

CRITICISMS AND SUGGESTED CHANGES

Some critics have held that juvenile courts are conducive to crime because they are not sufficiently punitive to turn wayward boys away from delinquency or make them examples to potential delinquents. Sometimes boys who need to be shocked into a realization of the seriousness of their conduct have been given probation and have gleefully ridiculed the softness of the court. But the *generalization* that juvenile courts have lacked success because they are too lenient is debatable. The contrary generalization that juvenile courts in practice often apply the same old penal methods of deterrence which have been proven ineffective has a greater basis in fact. More pertinent are the criticisms of careful scholars such as Paul W. Tappan, who, accepting the basic goals of the juvenile court movement, point to reasons why they have not been reached, and stress collateral dangers to basic human liberties involved. Neither undiscriminating leniency nor undiscriminating severity but discriminating individualization of treatment is needed.

Tappan objects to the vagueness of the definitions of offenses for which juvenile courts may try children. Since in practice the court may commit children to institutions which often are very much like prisons for adults, this vagueness makes possible serious interference with their liberties without the due process of law which is guaranteed to the adult criminal. Of course it is precisely this vagueness which is relied upon by many very high-minded judges, probation officers, and social workers to permit the court to deal with children needing attention but who have not been guilty of technical crimes. Tappan holds, in spite of the efforts of probation officers to protect them, that children should have oportunity for legal protection.

Another critic of the juvenile court [42] has stated:

> The danger in not utilizing more detailed and precise norms lies in the retention of court jurisdiction over children who have committed no violation of law. It is a fundamental American belief that in order to protect individual rights there is a presumption of innocence until or unless the reverse is proved beyond a doubt. Juvenile court philosophy, taking its cue from social work ideology, does not speak in terms of innocence or guilt. On the other hand, though there may be no presumption of guilt, there is sometimes the assumption that any child referred to the court needs the court's "attention." The problem of delinquency is often taken for granted or ignored.

In commenting on the presumed irrelevance of civil rights guarantees in juvenile proceedings, a third critic has put his case strongly: [43]

> It seems to be a most pernicious doctrine to eliminate constitutional guarantees en masse under the cover of a paternalistic nostrum that juvenile court proceedings are merely for the good of the child and do not injure him. Juvenile court proceedings, *in fact,* as contrasted to theory, closely parallel criminal proceedings in terms of the subjective reactions they can produce in the child, in terms of the reactions of persons close to him . . . , and obviously in terms of "treatment" that may be undertaken, particularly if this treatment is punitive.

Recognition of some of the above weaknesses has led to the demand that juvenile courts cease combining legal and social functions and concentrate on the determination of guilt. The treatment function would then be transferred to other agencies, either public or voluntary.[44] Defense of the system which gives the court both legal and social functions may be based on the assumption that personal rights are adequately protected because the court acts *in loco parentis,* in the best interest of the child, and because

[42] Lewis Diana, "The Rights of Juvenile Delinquents: An Appraisal of Juvenile Court Procedures," *Journal of Criminal Law, Criminology and Police Science* (Jan.–Feb. 1957), p. 562.

[43] Gilbert Geis, "Publicity and Juvenile Court Proceedings," *Rocky Mountain Law Review* (Feb. 1958), p. 23.

[44] *Standards for Specialized Courts Dealing with Children,* Children's Bureau Publication No. 346 (Washington, D. C.: The Bureau, 1954), p. 97.

wide power of discretion is necessary to serve those interests. It is also replied that courts must have wide jurisdiction over acts not specifically listed as violations of the law, in order to deal with the beginnings of delinquency and to meet problems of which that delinquency is only a later symptom. When the despotic power of courts is pointed out, it is replied that the court acts as a "benevolent" despot. The benevolence of judges and probation officers is said to be guaranteed by their interest in children.

The present writers feel that the criticisms by Tappan, Diana, and Geis carry great weight. They underline the need to separate determination of guilt from decision as to treatment. Where behavior is so mild that guilt need not be determined, because the restraints of commitment or even probation will not be needed, it would seem that welfare agencies should handle behavior problems. However, it cannot be assumed that all communities will quickly acquire adequate welfare facilities. Until they do, juvenile courts must retain social functions.

There is need for a thorough examination of juvenile courts in action and even for a rethinking of some of the philosophy of this important movement. However, the present writers must fall back on the undoubted fact that there is a great variety in the practices of our children's courts. Certainly we owe much to the movement, and certainly there are courts where a judge with almost dictatorial power uses that power to the best of his ability in the best interests of the children, their parents, and society generally. The juvenile court movement must not be scrapped; but its faults must be known and corrected. Some of them grow out of the sheer impossibility in a number of our cities of dealing adequately with the pressure of an increasing load of work, and the basic difficulties involved in attempting to solve a problem which has roots beyond the reach of any court acting alone with an inadequate staff. The problem of juvenile delinquency is not an easy one at any level, and our courts deal with delinquents at a late stage in their careers.

Suggested Readings

Annals of the American Academy of Political and Social Science (Jan. 1962). Symposium on crime and the American penal system, including criminal conduct, justice, and sentencing and treatment.

Law and Contemporary Problems (Summer, 1958). A symposium of nine outstanding articles on sentencing, including two important evaluations of sentencing provisions in the Model Penal Code.

Moreland, Roy. *Modern Criminal Procedure.* Indianapolis, Ind.: Bobbs-Merrill Company, Incorporated, 1959. A clear, detailed description of the machinery of justice in the United States.

CHAPTER 22

Probation

"Probation is a process of treatment, prescribed by the court for persons convicted of offenses against the law, during which the individual on probation lives in the community and regulates his own life under conditions imposed by the court (or other constituted authority) and is subject to supervision by a probation officer." [1] Juvenile probation in a children's court is similar except that less formal and noncriminal procedures are involved. In this chapter we shall discuss principles common to both types, noting differences in law or practice when appropriate.

It is sometimes said that probation is neither punishment nor giving offenders another chance. Good probation is never *intended* as an easy way out for the criminal or delinquent, but it is often *received* by them and by their parents and friends as such. The statement that probation is not punishment is misleading. However much preferred by the delinquent, good probation may involve restrictions upon freedom and requirements to refrain from disapproved behavior or to perform required acts which may be irksome and even painful to the probationer.

More specifically, probation, whether juvenile or adult, permits a more normal social experience than institutionalization, but

[1] *Probation and Related Measures* (New York: United Nations, Department of Social Affairs, 1951), p. 287.

makes possible varying degrees of control over the delinquent, together with the possibility of sentencing him to an instituiton if probation proves ineffective. Probation permits contacts with the other sex, with family, with constructive social agencies of all kinds. It means a less routinized and more self-directed existence. It does not, like imprisonment, make the offender a dependent but leaves him responsibility for self-support. Probation leaves less stigma than incarceration. The probationer avoids the criminogenic associations of prison. The probationer can earn his living rather than be idle. His family will not accumulate a burden of debt as the prison inmate's family often does. The taxpayer should prefer probation, for its annual cost has been estimated as only one-tenth or less than that of prison expense. Moreover, even when there are social dangers in the probation community, probation furnishes for that very reason a better test of ability to adjust than does life in the socially isolated prison or institution for juvenile delinquents.

History of Probation

Probation in part has its historical roots in suspension of sentence without supervision and also in benefit of clergy and reprieve. Benefit of clergy—dating from medieval times but surviving in England and America into the nineteenth century—permitted clergy and other literates to escape the severity of the criminal law. Reprieve differs from probation in being a withdrawing of sentence for an interval of time only, thus suspending the execution of sentence.

Under the common law, English courts had developed a policy of suspending sentence for an indefinite time or during good behavior. American courts copied this policy in order to avoid inflicting the severe punishment called for under Colonial law.

Before the first probation law was passed in Massachusetts in 1878, voluntary supervision had sometimes been provided. Among these volunteer probation officers the name of John Augustus, a Boston shoemaker, became famous. His pioneer work with several hundred offenders was said to have been markedly successful, and many other volunteers followed his lead.

Other states were rather slow to follow the Massachusetts example. Illinois provided for juvenile probation in 1899. Rhode Island was the first state to have a state-controlled probation system. By 1956 every state had some kind of probation statute. Some 7,000 probation and parole officers serve our courts and parole boards, though the actual need has been put at

40,000.[2] About 700,000 individuals are placed on probation each year. The use of adult probation varies greatly, from about one case in eight tried to seven cases out of ten, while the average in federal courts has been put at two out of five.[3] Opportunity for probation is open to misdemeanants far less than to felons, less than 10 per cent of the former having been so dealt with. Yet where services of a high order are available, use of probation may run as high as 65 per cent. Finally, wardens tell us that from 25 to 40 per cent of their inmates could safely have been given probation.[4] The federal courts had no probation law until 1925, although for 50 or 60 years they had exercised probationary powers without statutory authority. Many statutes narrowly restrict the application of probation or curtail its administration in ways inconsistent with good results.

Functions of a Court Probation Department

In spite of its lower cost and many attractions to the offender, probation can, of course, only justify itself if the probation department and others concerned perform their many functions efficiently. Types of offenders who shall be eligible for probation must be defined. Pre-sentence investigations of a very thorough nature must furnish the factual basis for granting or refusing probation and for the types of specific treatment to be accorded in each case. The conditions under which probation shall be granted must be wisely determined. The all-important supervision and assistance to the man, woman, or child on probation must employ approved methods. Staff for this exacting task must be qualified, selected on a merit basis, and properly trained before and after appointment. Probation must be sold to the citizens of the community, and their aid solicited through a good public relations policy. The probation function must be integrated with that of all other public and private agencies concerned with crime and delinquency prevention. Research as the basis for improved standards of work must be undertaken. Research cannot be the primary activity of our probation officers, already overloaded with work. Nevertheless, carefully kept probation records and full case investigations form part of the basis for more thorough studies made by universities or other research organizations. Moreover, every probation officer ideally should have engaged in research, and all may

[2] Will C. Turnbladh, "Review April, 1952, to March, 1954," *National Probation and Parole Association Yearbook, 1953*, p. 241.

[3] Ben S. Meeker, *op. cit.*, p. 170.

[4] Will C. Turnbladh, "Substitutes for Imprisonment," *Annals of the American Academy of Political and Social Science* (May 1954), p. 114.

cooperate with specialists in that field. Such research activities are not only important in themselves but assist in self-evaluation by the department and help to interpret probation to the community, to elicit its interest, and to advance probation to the status of a profession.[5] We consider other functions below.

Eligibility for Probation

Eligibility for probation may be limited by law or may be left to the court for determination. In any case, if the court grants probation, it is on the basis of the investigation of the individual case. Many children's courts use informal probation following investigations by probation officers without bringing the case officially to the attention of the court at all. This practice, designed to save the child from whatever stigma may be attached to appearance in juvenile court, is now frowned upon by some critics as lending itself either to sentimental leniency or to unrecorded, uncontrolled, and arbitrary severity in decisions, as well as to sloppy treatment policies. Speaking generally, the steps usually followed by a progressive juvenile court are: several continuances, probation at home, foster-home care, commitment to intermediate private or public institutions, and finally commitment to a state institution, with discharge from court supervision possible at any one of these stages where successful adjustment seems to have been achieved. However, the needs of the individual cases, and not any fixed order of procedure, should determine what is to be done. There usually are fewer alternatives in the treatment of adults.

Eligibility for probation in adult cases varies greatly among states. Many states deny probation to those convicted of specified crimes, especially certain crimes of violence, certain sexual crimes, and political crimes, such as treason and even violation of election laws. In a few states, those who have been previously convicted of any crime, including a misdemeanor, are denied probation, but more often it is previous conviction of a felony which disbars the criminal. There "is no clear indication that offenders who have committed the so-called more vicious crimes are poorer probation risks than others." [6] Though studies show that recidivists in general succeed less frequently than so-called first offenders, "many recidivists have

---

[5] John O. Reinemann, "Research Activities in the Probation Department," *National Probation Association Yearbook, 1946,* pp. 196–217.

[6] Herbert H. Lou, *Juvenile Courts in the United States* (Chapel Hill, N. C.: University of North Carolina Press, 1927), p. 122.

good behavior records while on probation." [7] Through insisting on trained and nonpolitical personnel, adequate facilities for investigating and supervising cases, full records, and so forth, the public will be better protected against the possible abuse of probation than through legislative restrictions on its use.

Defendants have no absolute right to probation. Nor may a defendant in all courts be forced to accept probation. Nevertheless, the probation agreement between court and probationer appears to be somewhat analogous to a voluntary contract not to be lightly violated by either party. A federal statute of 1958 allows judges in certain instances to precede a probationary term with a maximum sentence of six months in a short-term institution.[8] This practice, unfortunately found in a number of states as well, has been condemned as inconsistent with the purpose of probation.[9]

Pre-sentence Investigations and Intake Control

The process of determining which individuals shall be "screened" for special attention because of their misbehavior begins long before any case gets to court. It involves what we have previously called the discretion of police, but earlier it is within the discretion of parents, school teachers, clinics, and many social agencies to decide how serious behavior is and what steps shall be taken to repress or help children. In juvenile cases in particular, and perhaps ideally in all cases, a community may be organized to make such decisions in an orderly way with definite goals both of social protection and individual and social welfare in mind. Where there is a co-ordinating council, a council of social agencies, and a confidential exchange supplemented, perhaps, by a special group concerned with behavior problems, screening of cases needing court reference can be made through these agencies. Even when the police have to make immediate arrests or where official complaints are lodged with states' attorneys or probation officers, many cases may sometimes first be referred to such private and public clearing houses before they are brought to court. Such complete organization is rare but is being approximated here and there. With or without such community organization, cases brought to court must be investigated to see which need official court attention and which do not.

Adequate investigation is vital to effective court action and effective

[7] *Ibid.*, p. 123.
[8] Public Law 85–741, 85th Congress, August 23, 1958.
[9] Kenyon J. Scudder, "In Opposition to Probation with a Jail Sentence," *Federal Probation* (June 1959), pp. 12–17.

probation work. The decision to grant or to deny probation should be based upon facts peculiar to each case. It is necessary to know "the probable causes of the situation, the resources of the offender—physical, mental, moral, economic, and social—and the resources of society applicable to the offender's particular case." [10] Although preprobation investigation is mentioned in the laws of at least two-thirds of the states, in only a few is it absolutely mandatory, and it is still far from general, especially in adult cases. Most specialists prefer that the officer who would later supervise a case also make the investigation. One writer, however, has made a strong argument for separating these functions on the grounds that pre-sentence investigation serves purposes other than probation alone and is not in itself part of the probationary process of constructive and rehabilitative treatment.[11]

Investigation follows various procedures.[12] In at least one federal district, the candidate for adult probation is asked to fill out a questionnaire and invited to write his own history. This procedure makes him feel that the plan is based upon his own statement and that he has some part in it. Local and out-of-town police records must be examined, and state bureaus of identification and the FBI should be utilized. Contacts or correspondence must be had with each agency which has had any member of the delinquent's family as a client. Interviews with parents and other members of the family, school teachers, employers, clergymen, neighbors, and all others who have known the offender are important. Special caution is required in contacting employers and neighbors lest unnecessary injury be done to employment opportunities or neighborhood status. Ideally, the investigating probation officer should obtain facts as complete as in a thorough research investigation. Practically, however, heavy case loads preclude such thoroughness. Practical considerations will help determine the facts to be uncovered. The circumstances immediately surrounding the offense must be known. If possible, the circumstances and causes of the first offense should be discovered. When necessary, the investigation is shortened by an attempt to know the delinquent's current personality and social relations, without an extended inquiry into earliest beginnings such as a research investigation would imply.

In any case it is all-important to include definite study of the probationer's attitudes, interests, and ambitions, in terms of which the probation

---

[10] Ralph Hall Ferris, "The Case History in Probation Service," in Sheldon Glueck, ed., *Probation and Criminal Justice* (New York: Macmillan, 1933), p. 151.

[11] Thorsten Sellin, "Adult Probation and the Conditional Sentence," *Journal of Criminal Law, Criminology and Police Science* (March–April 1959), p. 554.

[12] The facts ideally included in an adequate pre-sentence investigation are outlined in *Manual of Correctional Standards* (New York: American Correctional Association, 1959), pp. 520–21.

plan may often be "sold" to him.[13] Ziegler [14] rightly warns of the danger of assuming that a mere investigation of the family is enough. The influence of group patterns upon the potential probationer's behavior; his social situation relative to that of others with whom he habitually compares himself; the constructive or harmful groups he belongs to, the behavior patterns which characterize them, and the basis for status in each—all these must be known, together with his attitude toward these groups, their attitude toward him, and the effect of loss of status in any group.

In assessing an offender's character, the investigator must be acquainted sufficiently with the varieties of subcultures in his community to enable him to distinguish between traits peculiar to the offender and traits the latter possesses by virtue of his membership in one or another subculture. Psychiatrically-oriented investigators are sometimes prone to view *cultural* traits as clues to an individual's psychodynamics; even such presumably idiosyncratic characteristics as aggressiveness, passivity, degree of emotional maturity, and self-confidence vary with the segment of the social structure from which an offender comes. A particular constellation of traits might be entirely "appropriate" within one cultural context but, when evaluated against a set of theoretically "normal" traits, stand out as apparent signs of personality maladjustment.[15]

The tendency in case work is increasingly to dispense with formal outlines and to permit the nature of the case to determine actual questions to be asked. Too complete reliance on this source is a mistake, however, and every investigator needs a very complete outline, even though he should not use it mechanically, or he is apt to neglect facts, including those concerned with social protection.

On the basis of the investigation a report and usually a recommendation to the court is made. A concise, clear summary is necessary.

Conditions of Probation and Their Violations

A particularly difficult aspect of probation and parole work is the problem of dealing with the offender *vis-à-vis* the general conditions by which he agrees to abide, usually by signing a document containing certain

---

[13] Cf. Ethel N. Cherry, "The Probation Officer on the Job," *National Probation Association Yearbook, 1945*, p. 198.

[14] Edwin B. Ziegler, "Presentence and Preparole Investigation," *ibid.*, 1942, pp. 165–76.

[15] Cf. Otto Pollak and collaborators, *Social Science and Psychotherapy for Children* (New York: Russell Sage Foundation, 1952), chap. 5.

stipulations. An examination of the conditions currently in effect in various jurisdictions indicates that they are products of a union between the Puritan ethic and the middle-class value system, with their emphases upon temperance, hard work, wholesome avocations and companions, moderate hours, and concern over financial obligations. Their establishment early in the history of parole and probation was probably partly motivated by the mistaken notion that wrong conduct results from wrong habits. But adopting the outward forms of the "respectable" middle-class citizen will not convert the offender into such a citizen: the tail cannot wag the dog.

Demanding that an offender adhere to rules appropriate to a class or subculture other than his own can have at least two deleterious effects on the correction process. First, anxiety can emerge to plague an officer-probationer relationship if the latter becomes fearful that his "violations" (drinking excessively, ignoring debts) will be discovered, while at the same time he can see nothing wrong with such actions if they conform to the norms of his membership or reference groups. The officer in turn worries about the significance of known "violations" and about the advisability of taking firm action with respect to them. Secondly, because heavy case loads in busy jurisdictions make close supervision difficult, many violations can occur with impunity, producing a feeling on the part of some clients that they are putting something over on their officers. Contempt for the officer and for the purposes he represents might result.

Conditions of probation suggest what must not be done and threaten possible commitment to an institution if they are done. They emphasize the authoritative element in probation. But as Irene Kawin has written,[16] probationers can be helped by authority only when administered by those who are dispassionate, warm, and understanding, and who respect personality. Moreover, probationers need assurance that acceptable behavior will reap the reward of increasing self-direction. Ultimately, in probation as in life, rewards are more effective than punishments, and the task is not only to demonstrate that it hurts to be bad, but that it is fun to be good.

Quoting Charles S. Boswell, Doyle writes:

> Any judge who believes that delinquent children in their middle teens should remain home after dark has forgotten his own adolescent years. . . . It is also unrealistic to expect to separate two boys who live next door to each other or to expect a 17-year-old boy to give up smoking when he has had the habit for two years. The condition of requiring youngsters to attend church . . . tends to associate the church with punitive action.[17]

[16] "Therapeutic Use of Authority," *Federal Probation* (Sept. 1953), pp. 22–26.

[17] Richard F. Doyle, "Conditions of Probation: Their Imposition and Application," *Federal Probation* (Sept. 1953), p. 20.

Meacham [18] has shown the bad effect of making conditions well-nigh impossible to fulfill. Thus if a probationer has habitually used alcohol and must associate with others in groups where at least beer-drinking is expected, he is often nevertheless forbidden to drink and hence drinks furtively. The introduction of positive rewards and satisfying associations into probation is basically important and leads us to the discussion of supervision.

Supervision of Probationers and Parolees

Probation utilizes a balance of watchful control and constructive aid, adapted to the individual case. Probation supervision is case work in an authoritative setting. Delinquents who do not need restraint do not need probation, and probationers who have achieved full self-control should be discharged, though they may still need assistance. To say this is not to deny that the restraint element makes constructive aid more difficult in some cases. Successful case work requires rapport. One does not easily confide in a helper who packs a potentially effective, if gloved, punch. Yet it is contended that sometimes the very authority of the probation officer makes him more respected by the probationer and gives to the latter a needed sense of security in seeking advice. The main purpose of supervision is to restore "self-control" and self-respect. Bettleheim has said [19] that self-respect comes through discovery that one can control himself. But rarely can a man control himself without group support. Having been accepted in a constructive group, the offender discovers that social behavior is more satisfying than antisocial behavior. It is more satisfying because it brings him social status in the group. Without such group support the best efforts of the probation officer may be ineffective.

Probation officers realize the seriousness of crime and never condone it. But they also see their clients as products of their life experiences. Rapport is thus possible because of understanding and because of absence of any attitude of blame. This is not inconsistent with the use of restraint or even of a sharp scolding. Threats of commitment are probably most appropriate where there is evidence that the probationer looks upon his "easier treatment" as indicating the soft-heartedness of the court. Restrictions on freedom are necessary, but their reasonableness must always be

[18] William S. Meacham, "Conditions of Probation and Parole, Do They Help or Hinder?" *National Probation and Parole Association Yearbook, 1947*, pp. 50–59.
[19] Bruno Bettleheim, "On the Rehabilitation of Offenders," *Federal Probation* (Dec. 1949), pp. 5–15.

evident. The probationer may well be told that such restrictions are for the childish, and that as he shows he is a man they will be removed.

As the United Nations Department of Social Affairs emphasizes,[20] a probation officer may strive to relieve emotional tensions by developing appropriate emotional and interpersonal relations with the client. He seeks the client's own interpretations of his experiences and their meanings for him, regardless of how illogical those interpretations may seem. Through a sympathetic and understanding attitude, the case worker creates on the part of the client a readiness to be helped. Emotional tension is reduced through the realization that someone understands and sympathizes. Comfort is also derived from realization that problems and tensions and even "shameful acts" are not unique to the individual but common to many others.

A probation officer using this approach must, of course, guard against forgetting the seriousness of the offense because he sees it through the probationer's eyes. This the officer will do by seeing the offense also from the point of view of the injured party and of society generally. He will hope and strive that the probationer will ultimately gain this larger perspective.

Sometimes social relations which have led to crime cannot immediately be changed. Jim's behavior might improve if he had a better father; Mrs. Jones's if she had a better husband; Fred's if for his gang more wholesome associations could be substituted. But fathers are not easily remade; Mrs. Jones has about as good a husband as she "deserves"; and Fred finds his gang far more fascinating than his home, the Y, or the Sunday-school class. Sometimes the probationer must return to the same dull job, the same cranky wife, the same rebellious children, the same relative defeat in the struggle with better-equipped competitors in work, school, recreational, affectional, or other relationships. But following the efforts of the case worker, these experiences can have less emotional significance and somewhat different meanings. New and more socially approved outlets for the emotions produced by irritations have perhaps been made possible. In such cases interpersonal relations between probation officer and client sometimes help.

But often this is not enough. Social situations must be and can be changed. Case work with families must be done if the family situation is not to keep tending toward continued crime. New constructive neighborhood, spare-time, and work experiences must be obtained for the probationer. The probation officer will use other agencies. He will interpret the difficulties of probationers to the institution whose failure partly accounts for the difficulties. He will, when necessary, bodily remove his charges from the most deleterious influences. He will even realize the deeper levels

[20] *Probation and Related Measures.*

of the crime problem, which cannot be reached save through more basic social changes.

The most important task of probation, however, seems clearly to be to change the group life of probationers. If social behavior is to replace unsocial, the social status of the individual must be derived from a group which approves such social behavior. From this viewpoint one might almost define a successfully adjusted probationer as one who enjoys status in one or more groups where prestige depends upon socially desirable behavior. It is doubtful if any amount of sympathetic understanding between probation officer and probationer will be effective in improving behavior as long as the probationer continues to enjoy status in a quasi-delinquent group.

There must also be a systematic inventory of the resources of the probationer and of his associates, present and potential, as well as those afforded by the neighborhood and community. Here is where a neighborhood committee such as we shall note when discussing the Chicago Area Project is so extremely useful; and where special citizens' councils set up in New Jersey may also cooperate effectively. Hospital and clinic service must be available. In the case of adults, few problems are more immediately important than provision for suitable employment. This must keep the probationer off the streets, bring tangible financial returns in accordance with his standard of living, elicit if possible his genuine interest, and contribute to his self-respect and the esteem in which socially desirable groups hold him. If the employer is to know of the delinquency of the probationer, his proper attitude toward that situation is all-important.

The officer must establish friendly relations with the probationer's family, and it may well be that the task is the adjustment of the family rather than that of a single member.

The probationer's spare-time activities may be of more significance for his behavior than even his family or conditions of employment. To wean him away from demoralizing and dangerous associates is a process of positive attraction rather than of mere negative forbidding.

Success in probation supervision requires a case load light enough to permit individual consideration; the National Probation and Parole Association has set the standards at 50 "units" per officer, counting a supervised probationer as one unit and a pre-sentence investigation as five units.[21] But like the railroad porter's hoped-for average tip, this is a standard seldom achieved in urban probation settings, where case loads range typically between 100 and 200 units.

Clearly we cannot expect the quality of work we need until case loads

[21] *Manual of Correctional Standards*, p. 525.

are more reasonable. Since judges are increasingly calling upon probation officers to make pre-sentence investigations in all types of cases, and since these are very important, the case load has been substantially increased thereby. The result is that officers are compelled to select for more careful attention those seeming most to need it, and to neglect others.

At the adult level, there has been a sad neglect of the important field of probation for the misdemeanant, who has been called the forgotten man of the criminal courts. Obstacles here have been public ignorance and apathy,[22] the large numbers and consequent expense involved, lack of facilities, and even political and other vested interests. The public somehow seems convinced, says Oldigs, that "anybody is competent to handle these drunks, bums, and jailbirds on probation." Wisconsin, however, is an example of a state where the law provides for probation for misdemeanants for a maximum of two years. Milwaukee's municipal and district courts have a joint probation department engaged in such work. Courts elsewhere in the state have not made extensive use of the opportunity provided in a law of 1947 to place misdemeanants on probation to the Bureau of Probation and Parole of the State Department of Public Welfare. Apparent success has varied in Wisconsin with the type of case: drunken drivers who have not been chiefly chronic alcoholics showed a success ratio of 92 per cent; "wife-beaters" of 97 per cent; minor sex offenders of 85 per cent; vagrants of only 52 per cent. Speaking of the use of fines, and jailing because the fine cannot be paid, Oldigs, properly comments:

> When we commit in default of a fine we are saying: "You owe the state a debt; you can't pay it; therefore the state will provide you with room and board at roughly a dollar a day until your debt is doubled; then the state will forgive you both debts, wipe the slate clean and release you." [23]

As the public comes to realize the costliness of alternative methods of dealing with petty offenders, they may be increasingly willing that probation, which is possible in such cases in most states, shall actually be used.

Personnel and Personnel Training

Effectively to perform all the functions indicated above, probation officers clearly need not only to possess unusual personal qualities but to have had rather definite types of training. We have already mentioned

---

[22] For an effective discussion of this question, see William Oldigs, "Probation in Misdemeanant Cases," *National Probation and Parole Association Yearbook, 1952,* pp, 76–84.

[23] *Ibid.,* p. 83.

the handicap implied in the very general requirement that probation officers be residents of the state where they are appointed. Wisconsin is an example of a state without this handicap which has consequently been able to attract capable social workers from as far away as Oregon and Massachusetts,[24] thus contributing to the state's progressive plan to professionalize probation service. Personnel standards urged in the best-organized probation departments include graduation from a college or from a school of social work, and from one to five years' field case-work experience. Typical courses in family case-work principles and practices seem, however, to be inadequate. Or rather they need to be supplemented by specialized training in criminology, penology, and crime prevention. Experience in dealing with juvenile delinquents and criminals is imperative. The mental hygiene slant which characterizes so much case-work training is certainly not to be decried as one element in preparation for work with the offender. But we hope it is not just the bias of the sociologist but actual facts and experiences which lead us to emphasize its limitation. The frequent absence of search for peer-group patterning in studies of delinquency made from the psychiatric angle is shocking in the face of unquestioned evidence of the importance of these and other group relations in the genesis of criminal behavior. This defect is paralleled by a similar absence of training in the manipulation of group relations and the use of natural groups in the treatment of both juveniles and adults.[25] In addition there seems to be a certain static philosophy associated with the psychiatric emphasis, which assumes that only minor changes in social situations are to be attempted. The success of movements like Alcoholics Anonymous, the use of natural groups in the Chicago Area Project and elsewhere, and the promise associated with community preventive programs such as those of the New York City Youth Board [26] argue strongly that the potential probation officer should know of such success and be prepared to include in his own work the use of constructive groups as "natural" as possible, to assist in affording his clients the social status without which their rehabilitation would seem to be uncertain.

Apart from this matter of the kind of training needed, it must be said that in practice only a few of the large city departments of probation have

[24] Russell G. Oswald, "Professionalizing Services," *National Probation and Parole Association Yearbook, 1951,* p. 140.

[25] Cf. Donald R. Cressey, "Changing Criminals: The Application of the Theory of Differential Association," *American Journal of Sociology* (Sept. 1955), pp. 116–20.

[26] Juvenile Delinquency Evaluation Project of the City of New York, *The Planning of Delinquency Prevention and Control,* Final Report No. 1, (Feb. 1961, mimeographed), pp. 23–25.

personnel qualifications as high as the above-mentioned standards. The following quotation indicates the wide variety of tasks the probation officer is called upon to perform. That variety, together with the complex and delicate nature of the task of remaking men, underlines the need for broad as well as technical training.

The probation officer must know how to analyze the occupational abilities, skill and aptitudes of his probationers, and . . . [have] a comprehensive knowledge of the industrial and economic conditions of the areas in which he serves. . . . [He] should have a knowledge of housing conditions, rental standards, the proximity of certain areas to vice and gambling resorts, and other establishments of questionable moral character, availability of play space, adequacy of educational facilities, attitudes, customs, habits, cultural and racial conflicts and other factors which affect conduct. . . . [He must] have information regarding public health laws, child protection laws, the location and capacity of various hospitals, clinics, sanatoria, dispensaries, health stations, and the types of persons whom institutions will accept, and the personalities in charge. . . . [Moreover] probation officers must in a sense be spare-time architects. They should have a working knowledge of the recreational resources of the community, both for children and adults. . . . Probation officers should have at least an elementary grasp of statutes. . . .[27]

Probation officers are usually appointed by judges, though the trend is away from this in the direction of appointment by a state administrative agency where probation is organized on a state-wide basis. In a few states, all or a majority of probation officers are under civil service.

Since judges direct probation officers, it is logical that they appoint them, but some judges are not interested in adequate qualifications. Also the tenure of judges is often short, and they may be involved in politics. Appointment by state agencies tends toward more standardized qualifications and methods. Civil service usually errs in requiring candidates to be residents and emphasizing formal qualifications over against more important personal qualities. Moreover, it has not proved impossible for politicians to get around a civil service law.

After appointment, probation officers may be given a period of apprenticeship and only gradually be allowed to assume full responsibility for either investigation or supervision of cases. More formal in-service training should not be thought of as a substitute for needed pre-service education and experience. Rather it is a continuance of that training. However, since the actual situation in most jurisdictions is that officers have lacked part of this previous education, in-service training becomes even more important

[27] Joseph P. Murphy, "Training for and on the Job," *The Offender in the Community, National Probation Association Yearbook, 1938,* pp. 98–102.

for them. Requirement that appointees take formal courses outside of the court is still very unusual, though most judges encourage officers to attend conferences and get such informal help as they can. Since the federal organization is an example of unusual development of in-service training, we follow the account of one of its leaders in what follows.

The vast majority of probation officers in the federal and some state organizations are men. Where women are employed, there is a strong tendency to confine their duties to work with girls or pre-adolescent boys. At least one experienced officer [28] has challenged the need for such division along sex lines. No doubt many without professional experience would at least support careful experimentation with the use of women without observing rigid sex lines of assignment. Some would also contend that in spite of the general desirability that male officers have assistance from women in dealing with girls, there are types of offenders, including perhaps prostitutes, with whom the use of male officers is preferable.

Organization and Administration of Probation Systems

The administration of probation is still primarily a local responsibility. Yet more than half of the states have established state aid or administration in some degree. For the most part, state organizations lack adequate control over the qualities of personnel, although in a fair number of states a state board appoints state-paid probation officers. Occasionally state funds may be used to provide a subsidy to counties to develop probation in localities unable to support adequate facilities. In the North Carolina system, local records are centrally filed, cases may be transferred from one district to another, and probation officers are trained at the central office for service anywhere. Since the courts enforce a state law, it is logical to have state-controlled and state-administered systems of probation. However, local sentiment tends to prevent this development, and it is true that probation will be ineffective unless it is supported by strong local opinion. It appears, however, that in a well-organized state system the advantage of local support need not be wholly sacrificed. The need for a state-wide system is especially evident in rural states. Smith reports,[29] for example, how in New Hampshire, by means of a state-wide probation service,

---

[28] Cf. Blanca J. Arce, "Caseload Segregation by Sex," *Focus* (Sept. 1953), pp. 140–44.

[29] Richard T. Smith, "Statewide Organization of Probation Services," *National Probation and Parole Association Yearbook, 1950*, pp. 131–38.

the work reaches into the smallest hamlet. Two other New England states, in spite of a strong home rule tradition, have found it wise to organize on a state-wide basis. The aspiration of states,[30] including some in the South which have adopted the NPPA Standard Act, is thus to extend probation to all communities. The advantage is obviously that common standards may thus be developed and basic services may be provided independently of the financial capacity of the community. There is perhaps some danger that a state system may inhibit the development of county services in urban centers where state services may be inadequate and where the development of local services should be encouraged. Legislative councils and various state commissions have developed new probation legislation. The Council of State Governments encourages and reports progress in this area, while local community planning councils are similarly working for lay-citizen participation in probation work.

In addition to the desirability of state-wide coverage, there is the general agreement that probation and parole administration may advantageously be combined.[31] The federal system has long utilized probation officers for supervision of parolees to advantage, and the similarities of the two functions outweigh the rather slight differences. A good number of states have combined these two functions in one organization. Meanwhile the Administrative Office of United States Courts has taken over the administration of probation in the federal field and has done an admirable piece of work which is a model for the states. Among the improvements which have been brought about under the leadership of Henry P. Chandler have been increased use of pre-sentence investigations and the constantly improving caliber of federal probation officers, together with an admirable system of in-service training.

How Successful Is Probation?

The acid test of the value of probation is, of course, its effect on recidivism. Yet that test can never be fully accurately carried out, chiefly because so many other factors influence abstention from crime and because the quality of probation changes with time and varies among different jurisdictions. All penologists seem to look upon probation as one of the

[30] Cf. Frederick Ward, "Extending Adult Probation Services to All Communities," *National Probation and Parole Association Yearbook, 1951*, pp. 31–38.

[31] For experience in Minnesota, see Gordon S. Jaeck, "Separate or Combined Probation and Parole Caseload—Must There be a Conflict?" *National Probation and Parole Association Yearbook, 1950*, pp. 146–57.

most promising methods of protecting society against crime. Some years ago the *Attorney General's Survey of Release Procedures* [32] concluded that the advantages of probation far exceeded its weaknesses. The usual court reports are concerned with the proportion of probationers not known to have committed crimes or violated the terms of their probation during a limited period of supervision. Such reports have often shown that proportion to be as high as 75 to 85 per cent. Such statements probably somewhat overstate the success of probation even in our best systems, although those doing the best work will sometimes show a higher proportion of failures just because reporting is more accurate. These figures would seem to understate, however, the potential success of probation under improved conditions which could rather easily be created. Chandler [33] tells us that during the fiscal year of 1954 only about 16 per cent of federal cases on probation were reported as violators.

Few studies have followed cases beyond the period of active supervision. An attempt to do so was made about 1951 by Dr. Morris G. Caldwell,[34] who followed 403 federal cases for periods of from five and one-half to eleven and one-half years after the end of their probation. Of these, he found all but 2 per cent free from convictions for felonies, and five out of six free of any criminal record. The results of a companion study of federal probationers in eastern Pennsylvania produced findings closely paralleling those of Caldwell.[35] Using the criterion of postprobation re-conviction, Caldwell found a failure rate of 16.4 per cent in a sample differing markedly in socio-economic characteristics from that of Pennsylvania, whose failure rate was 17.7 per cent.[36] Dr. Caldwell found that among more than 1,800 cases which he studied during the period of probation supervision, a total of only 23.1 per cent either violated probation or absconded. This proportion corresponds fairly well with the percentages given in other studies of state offenders.

[32] (Washington, D. C.: Department of Justice, 1939), II, p. 471.

[33] *Annual Report of the Director of the Administrative Office of U. S. Courts for 1954* (Washington, D. C.: The Office, 1955), p. 73.

[34] "Review of a New Type of Probation Study Made in Alabama," *Federal Probation* (June 1951), pp. 3–11. Among several other studies which have attempted to measure the success of probation should be mentioned Elio D. Monachesi, *Prediction Factors in Probation* (Hanover, N. H.: Dartmouth University Press, 1932), and Jay Rumney and Joseph P. Murphy, *Probation and Social Adjustment* (New Brunswick, N. J.: Rutgers University Press, 1952).

[35] Ralph W. England, "A Study of Postprobation Recidivism Among 500 Federal Offenders," *Federal Probation* (Sept. 1955), pp. 10–16.

[36] The fact that success rates in these and similar studies show a curious tendency to cluster between 70 and 90 per cent has prompted some theoretical speculation as to its significance. See R. W. England, "What Is Responsible for Probation and Postprobation Outcome?" *Journal of Criminal Law, Criminology and Police Science* (March–April 1957), pp. 667–76.

At any rate, while much more study is called for, we see no reason to doubt the truth of the widespread opinion that with proper selection of cases and with proper personnel and methods, probation has proven itself a highly desirable method of dealing with large numbers of offenders, including many types now habitually sent to penal or correctional institutions. The *Attorney General's Survey* referred to above found that regular employment and absence of previous criminal record were the two factors most highly related to success on probation. Nevertheless, it is important to record that the *Survey* also found that some second and third offenders likewise succeeded. Sutherland lists as other factors unfavorable to probation success: low occupational and economic level, residence in deteriorated neighborhoods, families with records of crime and vice, great mobility of residence, and few or irregular contacts with schools and churches. Some of these are factors of social relationship, and it seems probable that peer-group relations, which have too rarely been studied in the research, are highly important.

Suggested Readings

Chute, Charles Lionel, and Bell, Marjorie. *Crime, Courts and Probation.* New York: The Macmillan Company, 1956. The origins and development of probation in the United States are described in half the chapters, and modern probation theory and practice in the other half. Not much is said about crime or courts.

Dressler, David. *Practice and Theory of Probation and Parole.* New York: Columbia University Press, 1959. An authoritative book intended for both academic students and field trainees. It reflects the eclecticism which most practitioners are obliged to adopt because of practical difficulties and contradictory ideas about treatment.

Pigeon, Helen D. *Probation and Parole in Theory and Practice.* New York: National Probation Association, 1942. A standard manual on the subject. The six chapters on treating the individual case contain a good exposition of correctional case-work procedures and problems.

CHAPTER 23

History of Prisons

The significance of imprisonment among reactions to crime lies in the preservation of the criminal under control in an artificial community isolated from the general public. Imprisonment may be motivated by vengeance attitudes; it may be designed to deter past and potential offenders; it may simply have a custodial aim—to put criminals temporarily or permanently out of action. It may be based upon some notion of "justice" such as the view that punishment must nicely balance accounts with wrongdoers: a debt is to be paid by "doing time." Yet the very preservation and control of the prisoner suggest the possibility of experimentation in reforming him. Imprisonment under the new penology raises this question: Can the attitudes and behavior of those who have committed antisocial acts be changed in desired directions through compulsory confinement in an artificial community composed of other criminals?

The Origin of Imprisonment

Like any crescive social institution, the prison is a melange of cultural elements accumulated from divers times and places. Unlike many institutions, however, the contemporary prison embodies   393 an inchoate variety of values, procedures, and ends. No single penological doctrine can be identified as ever having guided the evolution of the prison. Today's prison administrator is the unhappy inheritor of a penological crazy-quilt whose pieces originated in religious beliefs, popular dogmas, humanitarian sentiments, military traditions, "scientific" theories, and administrative expediency. Now one, now the other of these sources achieved pre-eminence in the past as particular groups won the ear of legislatures and policy-makers.

Imprisonment as the conventional punishment or treatment of major criminals is largely a development of the nineteenth century and later. Commitment to institutions for detention while awaiting trial, for torture and the extortion of confessions, as a punishment for political offenses or for prisoners of war, to secure the payment of debts or fines, or as part of ecclesiastical penitential treatment of offenders has a much longer history. Dungeons and other places of safekeeping are to be found in primitive, ancient, and medieval times. Medieval Anglo-Saxon society, with its wide use of capital and corporal punishment, had little use for imprisonment, however. "The freemen atoned for their transgressions with fines when possible, and by slavery, mutilation, outlawry, or death when they could not pay. . . . Up to the middle of the twelfth century some counties [in England] were without public gaols or prisoners' cages, and Henry II commanded their construction at the Assize of Clarendon, 1166. . . ." [1] In such places prisoners and their families were kept at their own expense for months or years awaiting the time of trial, well fed if they had means, but perhaps starved to death if they were poor. At a later date, the prisoners hung collecting bags out of their windows on Sunday mornings. Sentences of imprisonment began about the time of Edward I, and in the prisons of the day the convicted were "squeezed" to secure payment of their fines. A monk's observations are quoted by Ives: [2] "I see also a pytyful abuse of presoners. Oh Lord God, their lodging is too bad for hoggys, and as for their meat it is euil enough for doggys, and yet, the Lord knoweth, thei haue not enough thereof." Yet at all times life in English penal institutions depended also upon the nature of the jailers, some of whom were friendly, others brutal.

In the middle of the sixteenth century a former palace at Bridewell was selected as a place for locking up, employing, and whipping beggars and prostitutes. This was the origin of the English houses of correction,

[1] George Ives, *A History of Penal Methods* (Philadelphia: Frederick A. Stokes Company, 1914), pp. 7, 10.
[2] *Ibid.*, p. 15.

which became mandatory in every county in 1609. They were at first connected with the administration of poor relief. Later assimilated with the jails, these institutions lasted in name until 1865. With the diminution of capital punishment and corporal punishment these local institutions were increasingly used for imprisoning misdemeanants. Yet as late as the beginning of the nineteenth century, imprisonment was an unusual punishment in England except as applied to political and religious offenders and debtors.

The practical beginning of imprisonment as the normal method of punishing criminals came in the last quarter of the eighteenth century, the way having been prepared by the moral revival led by Wesley and Whitfield, the humanitarianism of the French *philosophes,* and the English and American Quakers, and the progress of rational jurisprudence in the works of Montesquieu, Beccaria, Romilly, and Bentham.[3]

The condition of "prisons" in England in the eighteenth century, little changed from the past, became well advertised through the work of John Howard, whose book, *The State of Prisons,* aroused the public with its description of the filth, corruption, sexual license, and other evils disclosed. A few quotations will suffice:

There are prisons, into which whoever looks will, at first sight of the people confined there, be convinced, that there is some great error in the management of them. . . . Some [inmates] are seen pining under diseases, "sick, and in prison;" expiring on the floors, in loathsome cells, of pestilential fevers, and the confluent small-pox; victims, I will not say to the cruelty, but I must say to the inattention, of sheriffs, and gentlemen in the commission of the peace. . . . The prisoners have neither tools, nor materials of any kind; but spend their time in sloth, profaneness and debauchery, to a degree which, in some of those houses that I have seen, is extremely shocking. . . . I have now to complain of what is pernicious to their *morals;* and that is the confining of all sorts of prisoners together; debtors and felons; men and women; the young beginner and the old offender. . . . Few prisons separate men and women in the day-time. . . . In some goals you see (and who can see it without pain?) boys of 12 or 14 eagerly listening to the stories told by practiced and experienced villains, of their adventures, successes, stratagems, and escapes. I must add, that in some few goals are confined idiots and lunatics. These serve for sport to idle visitants at assizes. . . . The insane, where they are not kept separate, disturb and terrify other prisoners. No care is taken of them. . . .[4]

In the extraction of fees and charges,

[3] Harry E. Barnes, *Society in Transition* (New York: Prentice-Hall, 1939), p. 724.
[4] John Howard, *The State of Prisons,* 2d ed., (London: Cadell and Conant, 1780), pp. 5–11, *passim.*

thumb-screws and iron skull-caps were sometimes used. . . . Prisoners might be loaded with heavy irons unless they would pay to be allowed lighter ones. . . . They might be kept in damp dungeons and darkness; the living were sometimes locked with the dead. They could be set apart and purposely exposed to utter starvation, gaol fever, and small-pox, or actually done to death by their keepers' violence. Lastly, the new arrivals at a prison were fleeced and pillaged by their fellow gaolbirds. . . .[5]

Apart from punishment by public authorities, there was the penitential discipline of the church. In addition to all sorts of tasks required of penitants, the church used solitary confinement in order that the offender might ponder his sins and not be contaminated by contact with other sinners. Generally speaking, the church prisoners were treated better than the lay convicts in the jails. Their sentences were shorter, and they might hope for pardon on special occasions.

Transportation and Penal Colonies

EARLY OUTLAWRY AND ABJURATION

Outlawry was a medieval institution under which criminals and others banished from organized society took refuge in the forests of England. It has been said that more criminals were outlawed than hanged. In Elizabethan England, Catholics and dissenting Protestants were permitted to abjure the realm, and a similar privilege was later accorded certain types of criminals.[6] Such practices were precedents for more organized transportation to colonies which came in later centuries.

CONSIGNMENT TO GALLEYS

Captured enemies and maritime prisoners in many countries were set to work in galleys. France in the seventeenth century and England under Queen Elizabeth used many prisoners to row ships. The hardships of these prisoners make up a chapter of horrors. When sailing ships replaced the galleys, convicts were worked in gangs ashore.

A recent book describes in chilling detail the plight of those condemned to French galleys during the sixteenth, seventeenth, and eight-

[5] *Ibid.*, pp. 20–21.
[6] Frederick H. Wines, *Punishment and Reformation,* new enlarged ed. (New York: Thomas Y. Crowell Company, 1910), p. 168.

eenth centuries. Far from seaworthy, these vessels performed coastal duties and then only in good weather. Three classes of rowers made up the rosters of the 250 to 275 men per ship: paid volunteers, slaves (captured Muslims), and convicts, many of whom were victims of anti-Protestant laws. French ideas of justice at the time were such that men sentenced to definite terms usually served far beyond their sentences unless they could afford to purchase, at 400 *livres* each, a slave substitute. Life was wretched, even for those hardy enough to survive the first three mortal years of servitude:

In the galleys that were kept in a state of readiness for action the convicts, chained night and day to the thwart—a hefty piece of wood covered with padded calfskin on which the five men banged their bottoms each time they lifted the sweep out of the water—ate their poor meals at their posts, slept even more badly and, as they were never released from their chains, relieved themselves as best they could . . . The smell was bad enough by day, but it paled into insignificance compared with the stench that reigned in the morning before the tent was folded. Each evening a gigantic canvas envelope was put up over the whole length of the vessel and duplicated, in cold weather, by a second tent of calico. Even those used to it averred that to enter it in the morning was a hard task to carry out; purely and simply, there was a risk of falling suffocated. The officers vainly drenched themselves with musk and stuffed up their nostrils with snuff; they could not grow inured to it.[7]

TRANSPORTATION TO AMERICAN COLONIES

Early in the seventeenth century, the colonies in America needed labor, and the policy of transporting criminals, authorized in 1597, became regular about 1618. Eventually contracts for their transportation were made with private individuals, who could sell the convicts into periods of servitude of from three to 14 years. The number brought has been estimated at 50,000.[8] It appears that this criminal element was eventually successfully absorbed into the citizen population of the American colonies. However, these transportees were hardly typical felons, including, as they did, many political criminals, debtors, and others not found in our prisons today. The Revolutionary War closed this outlet for English criminals.

[7] Michel Bourdet-Pléville, *Justice in Chains: From the Galleys to Devil's Island* (London: Robert Hale, 1960), pp. 28–29.

[8] Barnes, *op. cit.*, p. 261.

PRISON HULKS

After the loss of the American colonies, the first resort was to the use of retired warships and merchantmen, a "temporary expedient" used until 1857. These once-noble vessels, cannon removed and truncated masts holding washlines, were moored in the Thames and other waterways, their chained prisoners employed at such hard and hazardous tasks as building quays and seawalls and draining estuary marshes. The miasmic and verminous living conditions aboard these ships—bad enough in sea-going vessels of the day—were "corrected" from time to time following sensational exposés, but the policy of crowding numbers of men into damp and rotting hulks made their return inevitable.[9]

TRANSPORTATION TO AUSTRALIA

Meanwhile Captain Cook had claimed part of Australia for Britain, and in 1787 some 759 prisoners, of whom 190 were women, were shipped there. Other shiploads followed. In 1791 Governor Philip began making grants of land to the convicts who had served their time, together with tools, seed, and government rations for the first 18 months.[10] With the arrival of free settlers, convicts were assigned to them and came completely under their power. Though there were exploitation and hardships and many failures, it is reported that "many convicts were really reclaimed through the new life transportation afforded them, and . . . occasionally they earned such good reputations as to be placed on the magisterial Bench." [11] In its early stages the experiment seemed a success.

However, the two elements—ex-convicts and free settlers—soon came into conflict. In 1837 the government stopped the assignment of convicts to private persons. Opposition continued, and after 1867 no more shipments were made.

At its height the Australian transportation system included five stages: [12] (1) Life transports and most of the "fifteen-yearers" were sent to Norfolk Island, east of Australia, for a minimum of two years of abject slavery. (2) Thence they and men with shorter sentences were transferred in "probation gangs" to Van Dieman's Land. Here the men performed

9 W. Branch-Johnson, *The English Prison Hulks* (London: Christopher Johnson, 1957).

10 Ives, *op. cit.*, p. 133.

11 *Ibid.*, p. 140.

12 W. L. Clay, *Our Convict System* (London: 1862), cited in Helen Leland Witmer, "The History, Theory and Results of Parole," *Journal of Criminal Law and Criminology* (May 1927), pp. 24–64.

hard labor under government auspices, building roads, felling timber, and so on. (3) After perhaps a year in such a probation gang, the convict might obtain a probation pass permitting him to enter into private service and receive wages, which, however, he was not permitted to spend freely. (4) After a time a passholder was entitled to a ticket-of-leave corresponding to our parole. (5) Finally, he might expect a conditional or complete pardon.

Conditions in the several penal settlements in which the convicts spent the first part of their sentences were often most cruel and revolting. A clergyman visiting Norfolk Island reported:

And now I have to record the most heart-breaking scene that I ever witnessed. The prison was in the form of a square, on one side of which stood a row of low cells covered with a roof of shingles. The turnkey unlocked the first door and said, "Stand aside, sir." Then came forth a yellow exhalation, the product of the bodies of the men confined therein. The exhalation cleared off, and I entered and found five men chained to a traversing bar. . . . I announced to them who were reprieved from death, and which of them were to die after five days had passed. I thus went from cell to cell until I had seen them all. It is a literal fact that each man who learned his reprieve wept bitterly, and that each man who heard of his condemnation to death went down on his knees with dry eyes and thanked God.[13]

Into this settlement there came in 1840 a new governor, Captain Alexander Maconochie. The mark system which he introduced brought order out of chaotic turbulence. In place of definite time sentences the men were required to serve out units of labor. Marks were paid for work performed and deducted for expenses incurred and as punishment for misbehavior. Combined with the ticket-of-leave system already mentioned, we have here some of the elements of the indeterminate sentence and parole and of our "good time" laws.[14]

Transportation to Australia was abandoned chiefly because of the opposition of the free settlers. Other contributing factors were the great expense involved, the crime problem created in Australia, and the fact that criminals were not considered desirable elements in the building up of a colonial empire. It was also held that this method of punishment did not deter, since some returned to crime in England and since the sufferings of the transported were not open to public view. The use of transportation by France, Russia, and other countries in the past and its continued use today has not been encouraging.

[13] Quoted in Ives, *op. cit.*, pp. 164–65.
[14] See J. V. Barry, *Alexander Maconochie of Norfolk Island* (Melbourne: Oxford University Press, 1958), for a detailed description of the mark system.

HAS TRANSPORTATION A PLACE IN THE NEW PENOLOGY?

At first sight, at least, transportation offers apparent advantages. Men believed dangerous are removed from populous centers. This removal is supposed to make possible a more normal life where they can, under supervision, learn to adjust themselves through self-support. Their capacity for possible return home can thus be tested under conditions less dangerous to the community than under probation.

On the other hand, the device bristles with difficulties. It is not normal to live in a distant land with other convicts as one's chief associates. Since convicts are predominantly males, the resulting community will be almost womanless. The alternative of permitting families to accompany the men or of attracting girls as potential wives seems a bit hard on the families and potential wives. With the passing of the frontier it is not easy to find suitable locations for penal colonies. If they are reasonably attractive, free settlers will come and there will be conflict between the two classes. Even with reasonably responsible leadership, the exigencies of unquestioned power over men difficult to control have often led to gross cruelties.

If penal colonies have a place in the new penology, it would seem to be in connection with a classification system which would transport only individuals or families selected on the basis of their adaptability to it. Certain types of men who have committed dangerous acts but who seem otherwise capable of making good in a frontier region might perhaps be sent away. The most effective argument for transportation is the sight in prison of drab lines of long-term men shuffling aimlessly from cell block to shop, to mess hall, to cell block. Yet prisons themselves may be, and here and there have been, improved.

ORIGIN OF ENGLISH NATIONAL PRISONS

The failure of the penal colonies called for a substitute. As a result of John Howard's earlier criticisms, local cellular prisons had begun to be built where it was thought corruption through association could be avoided. The earliest example of cellular structure seems, however, to have been Pope Clement XI's boys' prison of San Michele in Rome, built in 1704. The structure of this institution and that of Vilain's prison of Ghent in Belgium, designed for the reformation of disorderly paupers who were then overrunning the land, suggested that of the later dominant prison system in America. The organization at Ghent also illustrates early classification, for it contained a varied population separated into departments.

Unlike the treadmill of English prisons, occupations at Ghent were productive. Another plan never carried out was that of Jeremy Bentham for a prison, circular in shape and called the Panopticon, so designed that guards could look into all cells from the center of the building. This idea influenced the construction of cell houses at Pittsburgh, Pennsylvania, Joliet, Illinois, and Richmond, Virginia.

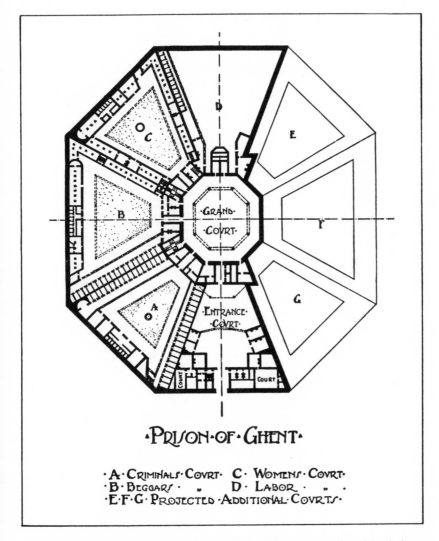

·PRISON·OF·GHENT·

·A· CRIMINALS·COVRT· C· WOMENS·COVRT·
·B· BEGGARS·   „   D· LABOR·   „   ·
·E·F·G· PROJECTED ·ADDITIONAL· COVRTS·

FIGURE 4   The Prison at Ghent, 1775. The courtyards with their surrounding living quarters were ingenious solutions to the problem of indiscriminate mingling of prisoners.

Following the failure of transportation, national prisons were built in England, of which Millbank and Pentonville were early examples. English prisons were, however, greatly influenced by new prison systems developing in the United States, and interest in prison history therefore shifts across the Atlantic.

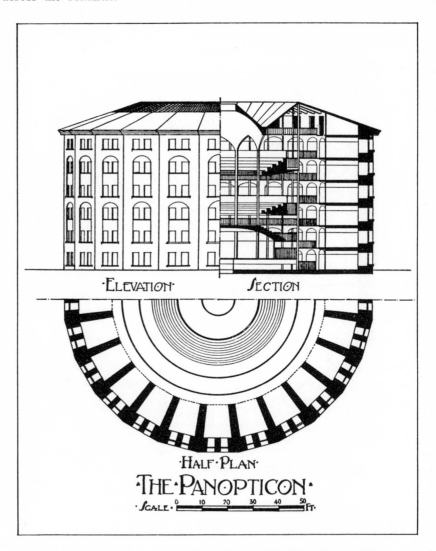

FIGURE 5   Bentham's Panopticon Plan, 1791. King George III's personal hostility toward Bentham helped block the adoption of his "fanatical scheme."

Penal Institutions in America Before 1820

There had been free employment of capital punishment in the American colonies even for minor offenses, though the number of crimes actually punished by death was never so great as in England. Imprisonment was unusual except for political and religious offenders and debtors.[15] In addition to death, colonial punishments included stocks and pillory, where the culprit was subjected to the taunts, ridicule, and missiles of the populace; the whipping post; and the branding iron. The colonies had local jails, and the English house of correction was later copied, but these local institutions were long not true penal institutions but places of detention or for the housing of paupers.

Reaction against these conditions came first in Pennsylvania. In 1682 William Penn's charter retained the death penalty for homicide only and allowed the substitution of imprisonment at hard labor for the former bloody punishments. Penn's aim was clemency, and, if possible, rehabilitation. He would have made all prisons workhouses and would have taught all children trades in order to prevent idleness and crime. Moreover, his code provided that:

1. All prisoners were to be bailable.
2. Those wrongfully imprisoned could recover double damages.
3. Prisons were to be free as to fees, food, and lodging.
4. The lands and goods of felons were to be liable for double restitution to injured parties.
5. All counties were to provide houses to replace the stocks, pillory, and the like.

This Quaker code also was without the long list of religious offenses which appeared in most of the other colonial codes. Such liberal laws and measures were too advanced for the home country, and after Penn's death in 1718 the old sanguinary laws were restored, to remain in force until after the Revolutionary War.

But Pennsylvania was again to take the lead in penal reform. Such men as Benjamin Franklin and Dr. Benjamin Rush supplemented the

[15] Cf. Harry E. Barnes, *The Repression of Crime* (New York: Doubleday, Doran & Company, 1926), chaps. 2 and 3, *passim;* O. F. Lewis, *The Development of American Prisons and Prison Customs* (Albany, N. Y.: The Prison Association of New York, 1922), chap. 1; Blake McKelvey, *American Prisons* (Chicago: University of Chicago Press, 1936), chap. 1.

influence of English reformers. Dr. Rush's penal program [16] was amazingly advanced and in some respects more liberal than is usual today. The influence of the prison relief societies founded in Philadelphia about this time was exceedingly important. As an alternative to jail evils, Pennsylvania first tried employment on public roads. The wretched men were loaded with collars and chains, with heads shaved and garbed in an "infamous" dress. The result was drunkenness, profanity, and indecency on the street—a public exhibition of the human animal in disgrace.

In 1790 the Walnut Street jail in Philadelphia was remodeled along revolutionary lines. The most serious and the lesser offenders were separated, the former being housed in solitary cells without labor, the latter living together in rooms and working in shops. The cells, 16 in number, were housed in a small brick structure added to one wing of the original building. Professor Negley Teeters contends that this structure was the world's first penitentiary; [17] some Britons have claimed otherwise. In the congregate section for lesser offenders, separate quarters were provided for women, debtors, and vagrants, the enclosures for each being fenced off. Inmates not in solitary worked from eight to 10 hours a day according to the season of the year and received wages. Moral and religious instruction was provided them.

There was at first great enthusiasm for this institution, which reported improved behavior and fewer arrests and escapes. The general plan was copied in 10 states.[18] Labor and humane treatment were the basic principles. Corporal punishment was unknown.

In spite of this fine beginning, the Walnut Street Prison deteriorated due to overcrowding and to ildeness following a disastrous fire in the shops.[19] Discipline relaxed, production declined, the pardon power was abused by the governor, vice entered. A demand consequently arose for a a new prison.

The Pennsylvania System

There were a number of interesting early American prisons, but we confine our attention to the development of the more influential Pennsylvania and Auburn, New York, systems.

[16] Cf. Lewis, op. cit., pp. 21–22.

[17] Negley K. Teeters, The Cradle of the Penitentiary: The Walnut Street Jail at Philadelphia, 1773–1835 (Philadelphia: 1955), p. 39.

[18] The Attorney General's Survey of Release Procedures, Vol. V, "Prisons" (Washington, D. C.: Dept. of Justice, 1940), p. 2.

[19] Teeters, ibid., p. 90.

Though their relative merits were hotly debated they were alike in (1) opposition to communication between prisoners and (2) separation at night. Because the Pennsylvania system called for isolation in individual cells day and night, while the Auburn provided congregate work in shops with communication forbidden, the former is called the separate system, the latter the silent system.

The Eastern Penitentiary of Philadelphia, exemplifying the Pennsylvania system, was at first planned to provide solitary confinement without work. It was argued that without work men must reflect; that terms spent in solitary confinement without work would be shorter since they would result in quicker reformation. It was also felt that solitary confinement itself would be unusually deterrent, since men crave above all else association with their fellows. But the experience at Auburn to be described below was showing the terrible results of complete isolation and the economic value of work. Hence work was introduced, but it was done in isolation in the cells and not in congregate shops as at Auburn. The cell-houses at the Eastern Penitentiary radiated from a central guardroom like the spokes of a wheel. Relatively large cells, 7 feet 6 inches wide, 11 feet 9 inches long, and 12 feet at their highest point, had, if on the ground floor, an exercise yard 8 by 20 feet with an individual wall 11 feet 6 inches high. Communication between these cells was possible only when the pipes were being flushed for 10 or 15 minutes each day. Spying guards and severe penalties were intended to prevent such communication.

There was a toilet and water spigot in every cell. . . . The prisoners were fed in their cells. Every part of the building was so constructed that it should never be necessary to remove the prisoner from his cell and exercising yard, except when sick. No chapel and no schoolrooms were provided, and no places for labor except the cells.[20]

With rare exception this method meant complete permanent isolation. The inmate was led in hooded so that he might not recognize his fellow prisoners. He was given a physical examination and bath, but no humiliating dress. Unlike practice at Auburn, work was considered a privilege, and Sunday without it was an especially long day. After 1840 an overstint of work was paid for. Since no other reading was provided, the Bible become a book eagerly sought for. A butterfly or cricket became an object of much interest. The reality of the isolation is shown by the fact that cholera, scourging the city in 1832, did not attack the prisoners. Though there were contacts with certain designated officials there were no contacts with friends, relatives, or other inmates. No tobacco or wine was allowed.

[20] Lewis, *op. cit.,* pp. 124–25.

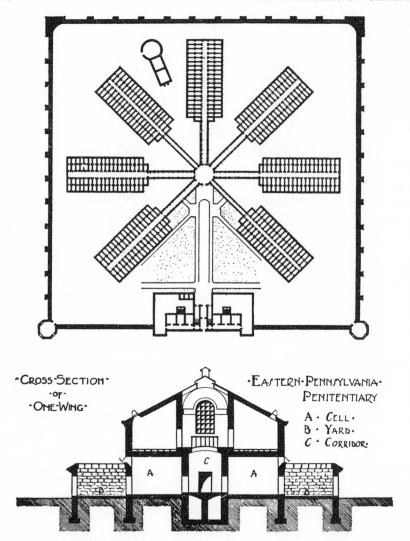

FIGURE 6   Eastern State Penitentiary at Philadelphia, 1829. With added cell-houses and other structures, this prison is still in operation, although separate confinement was abandoned long ago.

The stimulus to good behavior and industry was during the first 11 years (1829–1840) based on the fear of deprivation of the privileges of labor, on moral literature, and on fear of positive punishments, ranging from reduction in diet to the extremes of the strait jacket, the shower-bath and the gag. The general behavior of the convicts was undoubtedly very satisfactory. The majority of the inmates seemed "resigned, if not happy" after the first horror of separate confinement had diminished or departed.[21]

21 *Ibid.* p. 220.

The originators of this system of solitary confinement alleged that it possessed the following virtues: protection against possible moral contamination through evil association; an unusual invitation to self-examination and self-reproach in solitude; impossibility of the convict being visited by anyone except an officer, a clergyman, or a reformer; great ease of administration; an unusual degree of individuality in treatment; little need for disciplinary measures; the absence of any possibility of mutual recognition of each other by prisoners after discharge; and the fact that the horrors of loneliness made the prisoners usually eager to engage in productive labor, during which they might be taught a useful trade, preparatory to their attaining freedom. But, whatever its incidental advantages, the item most uniformly and vigorously emphasized by the founders of the Pennsylvania system was that solitude was most certain to be productive of earnest self-examination and a consequent determination to reform.[22]

The Pennsylvania system was widely imitated in Europe, but only three states in America maintained a genuine solitary system and they only temporarily. Even in Philadelphia the system was completely given up in 1913, and practically abandoned half a century earlier. The chief reasons for the triumph of the rival Auburn system were, however, the zeal of Louis Dwight and his Boston Society in propagating it, and still more the fact that its congregate labor proved profitable, the Pennsylvania system being too expensive for the permanent approval of taxpayers. When penology and economics clash in a materialistic culture, economics generally wins. American prisons became industrial enterprises until—much later—fear of competition with free industry made them houses of idleness.

The Pennsylvania system lacked a sound criminological basis. By stressing sin and inducing remorse it was supposed to reform. But remorse without understanding cannot bring rehabilitation. To this the sociologist would add that even understanding without status in a constructive group may prove inadequate. The Pennsylvania system provided neither understanding nor association. At any rate, we know today that attitudes and behavior patterns are changed, if at all, through satisfying group association rather than through enforced isolation of basically social human beings. Nevertheless, it should be said in fairness to the founders of the Pennsylvania system that they were much more concerned with the rehabilitative possibilities of imprisonment than with its deterrent and punitive aspects. Their humanitarian vision, moreover, prompted them to subordinate to a loftier motive considerations of efficiency, productivity, and economy of operation. Not for them were the criteria of capitalistic enterprise to be applied to the reformation of errant human beings.

[22] Barnes, *Society in Transition,* p. 725.

The Auburn System

Meantime, in New York State, Newgate, the first state prison, had become so overcrowded that by 1810 the governor was pardoning as many each year as were committed.[23] As a result of such conditions, a new prison modelled after Pennsylvania thinking was built at Auburn between 1816 and 1819. The most hardened prisoners were at first in solitary confinement without work. Within 18 months a number of these were insane, and by 1823 the governor ordered the abandonment of the solitary system and pardoned most of the survivors. By 1823 the true Auburn system was in operation. Its keynotes were enforced silence and separation at night but congregate work in shops during the day. The north wing was five stories high, with 550 tiny cells 3.8 feet wide, 7.5 feet long, and 7 feet high, and thick walls. The ventilation was defective, and conversation was possible through the pipes. Heat was imperfectly furnished by stoves in the corridors. Around the workshops was a corridor from which visitors who had paid 12½ cents (one bit) could see the convicts at work, unseen by them. The system involved absolute separation from the world, with visits even by members of the man's family forbidden. The rule of silence meant constantly impending punishment with a rawhide whip or in extreme cases the cat. Sometimes groups were flogged to be certain to get the guilty party. Even the insane and feeble-minded were flogged.

The system as a whole provided no exercise, play, or sociability. Church attendance was optional, but conversation except about the lesson was forbidden at Sunday School. In addition there was some teaching of reading, writing, and arithmetic. The warden himself had no conversation with the prisoners until just before release, when each man was given three dollars and advice. Warden Powers reported that most released convicts ceased crime, but this statement should not be taken at face value any more than similar more modern reports.

Claims for the Auburn system included: [24]

1. Economy of construction.
2. Reduced expense through associated labor.
3. Avoidance of ill effects of complete isolation.
4. Avoidance of moral contamination through rule of silence.

[23] Lewis, *op. cit.*, pp. 60*ff.*
[24] Barnes, *Society in Transition*, pp. 726–27.

Such was the prison which set the fashion for prison building and prison programs for 50 years in 23 states prior to the reformatory movement in 1870. The majority of our modern prisons have the general style of structure and the remains of the discipline of Auburn.

Later Developments

The major changes in the Auburn system have been connected with the reformatory movement, which developed first in the seventies, the more recent rise of the social and psychological sciences, and the emphasis on individualization of treatment. None of these influences has revolutionized most American prisons, though they have been of importance in a few institutions. The school and the psychiatrist have here and there been admitted to prison, but major reliance is still upon walls, and guards, and tool proof steel, and the solitary cell for those not amenable to discipline.

The supporters of the Auburn system looked upon crime as an uncaused event and upon the criminal as self-generating and designedly evil. They hoped to see him renounce crime. They relied chiefly upon a prison experience which should be painful to him and exemplary to others. They advocated stern discipline and even-handed justice rather than cruelty, but their methods almost necessitated at least occasional cruelty. They saw the chief source of evil in association with other wrongdoers, but they did not rely upon association but upon religious experience to reverse the process—to socialize the antisocial.

Yet the visitor to the typical prison today would be impressed with changes. The men would march, but not in lock step. The cell block, if of recent construction, would have larger windows, better light, improved sanitation. The men would be seen eating in dining rooms instead of in their cells, though still perhaps in silence. Most would shuffle about in monotonous gray uniforms instead of stripes, and minor differences in clothing would indicate the results of a grading system. The more obviously insane would have been removed to still more dismal oubliettes. There would be a school, and recently great advances have been made in formal education in both prison and reformatory. There would be a library, but if the institution were typical, the men would have little if any direct access to it. Instead of a visitors' corridor where wives or sisters might peek unseen at their prisoner relatives, there would be a visiting room, probably with a mesh screen to prevent the passage of drugs or other contraband and a guard perched on a high platform to observe and if necessary to listen in, though possibly tolerating one quick embrace on entering and departure. The daily routine would be cheered quite a bit by a few hours a week devoted to exercise and recreation, and there would be a movie perhaps once a week. The mess, though still cheap and unattractively served, would be adequate in calorie count, if occasionally excessive in maggot count. The warden and guards would probably be mere untrained political appointees, though to this there are important exceptions. Today civil service often either provides a somewhat higher type of guard or serves to camouflage actual political appointment under the form of a merit system.

The evil of politics, evident in 1842, is still evident. New staff members, including psychiatrists and psychologists, have appeared in a number of institutions. Their presence has modified, but not basically changed, the system. Perhaps the most notable change would be seen in a partially indeterminate sentence for some of the men, with parole decisions and supervision of varying quality. Yet with all these changes the atmosphere of the place would not have altered greatly during the century. Men marching but not going any place new. Men listless or rebellious or cowed. Men looking forward to a future of crime or to a struggle to get a job and social recognition. Men who "can take it," but who get less than nothing out of it. Such a picture is not fair to a few prisons and some reformatories.

The above discussion has perhaps too much minimized changes in the American prison system since 1830. A government report [25] subdivides this period into: (1) 1830–70, the Pennsylvania and Auburn systems; (2) 1870–1900, the reformatory system; (3) 1900–35, the industrial prison. To this one might add (4) 1935–41, the state-use system of prison industry and trends toward individualization; (5) 1941–a date when somewhat favorable influences of World War II upon American prisons, a considerably greater use of classification of inmates, and the very occasional use of group methods are to be noted. The first period is characterized by enforced isolation, the development of a prison industries program, and some emphasis on religious reformation. The second differentiated between adult and hardened criminals and younger first offenders, introduced the indeterminate sentence and parole, and applied to first offenders mass education and a somewhat more constructive program in reformatories. Later, though the reformatory had largely failed, some of its methods were introduced into the prison. With the founding of the National Prison Association in 1870, there began a movement toward the improvement of every aspect of our prisons which has continued to this time. The

[25] *Attorney General's Survey of Release Procedure,* pp. 2*ff.*

story of those changes will be told later in this book more or less piece-meal, as we speak of each of these aspects in turn. The third period continued mass treatment with emphasis upon industries, but witnessed a struggle against these very industries which compelled some change in emphasis in the fourth period. Loss of prison industries compelled attention to education and other methods of keeping prisoners occupied, and the influence of psychiatry showed itself in at least a paper interest in the individual. The last two periods will be further described in later chapters. Prisons are still primarily custodial. However, in the institutions of the Federal Bureau of Prisons and in a number of states, some genuinely constructive work is undertaken. The hope, we feel, is now slow experimentation with group methods. It is not certain how large a proportion of criminals may be led to develop social attitudes instead of exploitative attitudes. But if the trick is to be turned, it seems certain it must be through development of constructive social relations.

The Reformatory

There presently exist in this country about 50 institutions known as "reformatories," including five operated by the federal government. The first reformatory was opened at Elmira, New York, in 1876 in a new structure intended originally as a maximum-security prison. The product of correctional theories conjoining from such diverse sources as Spain, Bavaria, Australia, and Ireland, the reformatory marked a distinct change of emphasis in our penal methods and at the time was hailed by progressive penologists as the final answer to the problem of correcting offenders.

Prison theory, such as it was, had become by the 1870's an inchoate amalgam of doctrines of repression, penitence, deterrence, and reform-through-hard-work, structured within an inflexible scheme of specified time sentences for specified crimes. Reformatory theory, although developed in strict accordance with the classical conception of man as a rational being possessing free will, was a curious mixture of humanitarian sentiment and an optimistic regard for the constructive possibilities of man's presumed self-serving impulses. The reformatory was seen as an institution wherein prisoners are motivated to "reform" by giving them an opportunity to earn an earlier release. To accomplish this, the inmate must subordinate himself to an institutional regimen designed to retrain him through the inculcation of habits of honesty and industry. As certain wire products are formed by drawing strips of hot metal through dies, so the prisoner, attracted by the irresistible carrot of freedom, squeezes himself through the behavioral dies of the reformatory. He emerges truly "reformed."

Basic reformatory theory was first explicated by one Alexander Maconochie (1787–1860),[26] a Scottish-born ex-naval officer and civil servant who, for four tumultuous years, headed a penal colony on tiny Norfolk Island, some 900 miles east of the Australian mainland. Denying the utility of vindictive or vengeful punishment, Maconochie held that the creation of self-discipline should be the aim of imprisonment, and, because the time required for this would vary from individual to individual, terms of imprisonment should be indefinite. Instead of time sentences, prisoners should serve "task" sentences, the fulfillment of one's task being measured by "marks of commendation" (hence, Mark System) earned through labor and good conduct. Imprisonment should be in stages, beginning with a short period of stern deprivation, accompanied by moral and religious instruction to induce penitence and humility. In the second stage the prisoner begins earning marks, a fixed number of which "pay" for his keep, while excess amounts earned by "frugal living, constant industry beyond the allotted tasks, and exemplary behavior and demeanor" pay his way to the third, or social, stage. Here, he is not only allowed more comforts, but earns marks in cooperative effort with a working party of five or six other prisoners. The final stage approximates the conditions he will likely encounter upon release.

Maconochie's experiments with his scheme on Norfolk Island so disturbed his tradition-minded superiors that he was removed from his post in 1844. Although he met with little success in selling his ideas to English prison authorities after his return to England in that year, his doctrines became the basis of the "Irish" or "Progressive Stage" system, initiated by Sir Walter Crofton after 1854. Enthusiasm for the Irish scheme came to be shared by American correction leaders, and, somewhat modified, it served as the model for the American reformatory. Only with considerable difficulty did its supporters win legislative approval from New York State. The compromises made necessary by conservative opposition helped shape its main features, which were closely copied in many other states. Its main elements were as follows:

1. Limited to first offenders between 16 and 30 years of age.
2. A minimum of 12 months imprisonment, divided into two 6-month progressive stages.

[26] Barry, *op. cit.* This paragraph is adapted from pp. 74–75.

3. A mark or grading system.
4. A parole period after release, with imprisonment plus parole not to exceed four years. Intractable inmates could be transferred to a prison, there to serve out the fixed sentence called for by their particular offenses.

Under the gifted and energetic leadership of its first superintendent, Zebulon R. Brockway, Elmira came to embody a number of features which, at that time, were viewed by many as radically dangerous departures but which subsequently were adopted in most prisons and penitentiaries. A partial list of Brockway's innovations include: uniform but not degrading clothing; a liberal dietary; gymnasium and appliances for physical culture and athletics; instruction in trades; military band; school of letters with classes from kindergarten through high school; library; weekly institutional paper; entertainments in the auditorium; optional religious attendance.[27]

Originally, the reformatory regime meant a relatively friendly constructive aim, with much emphasis upon education. The reformatory as a distinctive institution for the mass education of younger offenders has come to an end with the newer emphasis on individualized programs in all progressive correctional institutions.

Suggested Readings

Barry, John V. *Alexander Maconochie of Norfolk Island*. Melbourne: Oxford University Press, 1958. Maconochie laid the foundations of the reformatory on his tiny island colony, despite ceaseless official and popular criticism from mainlanders.

Bateson, Charles. *The Convict Ships, 1787–1868*. Glascow: Brown, Son and Ferguson, Limited, 1959. The complexities of safely transporting prisoners in the four-month voyages to Australia are recounted.

Bourdet-Pléville, Michel. *Justice in Chains: From the Galleys to Devil's Island*. London: Robert Hale Limited, 1960. French galley and *bagne* life in all its horrific detail. Particular attention given to technical aspects of operation.

Branch-Johnson, W. *The English Prison Hulks*. London: Christopher Johnson, 1957. The futilities—and fatuities—of a bizarre penological stop-gap are given scholarly examination.

Howard, John. *The State of the Prisons*. New York: E. P. Dutton and Company, 1929. In his middle years, this eccentric and altogether remarkable English

[27] See his autobiography, *50 Years of Prison Service* (New York: Charities Publications Committee, 1912).

gentleman became an avid penal reformer. This book contains his eye-witness descriptions of eighteenth-century British gaols and prisons.

Sellin, Thorsten. *Pioneering in Penology*. Philadelphia: University of Pennsylvania Press, 1944. Description of the Amsterdam houses of correction in the sixteenth and seventeenth centuries, based on the author's study of Dutch records. The prisoners rasped dye-woods and spun cloth under paternalistic but not unkindly supervision.

Tannenbaum, Frank. *Osborne of Sing Sing*. Chapel Hill, N. C.: University of North Carolina Press, 1933. A highly sympathetic study of an important penological innovator whose charismatic qualities probably accounted for his unusual success as a warden.

Teeters, Negley K. *The Cradle of the Penitentiary: The Walnut Street Jail, 1773–1835*. Philadelphia: University of Pennsylvania Press, 1955.

Teeters, Negley K., and Shearer, John D. *The Prison at Philadelphia: The Separate System of Penal Discipline, 1829–1913*. New York: Columbia University Press, 1957. Together these books constitute a definitive study of the American beginnings of the penitentiary.

CHAPTER 24

The General Nature of the Prison Community

The popular view that to reduce crime we should send more men to prison is in contrast with the view of penologists that we should keep as many as possible out of prison. Yet imprisonment at least incapacitates the inmate for crime for a time. When we have increased greatly the number put on probation, there will still be a need for confinement. Use of other methods has left prison inmates a selected, if still inadequately selected, group and a more difficult type to rehabilitate. The American Correctional Association [1] has adopted the view that a prison operated on the basis of a purely punitive philosophy would produce more criminals than it would prevent; that while imprisoning more might deter a few from crime, punitive imprisonment is not an effective deterrent for most inmates today. This does not mean that penologists have dismissed the whole idea of punishment. It does mean agreement that prisons protect society best when their major emphasis is on rehabilitation.

The historical development described in the last chapter has left us with a variety of penal institutions. To these are committed

[1] American Correctional Association, *Manual of Correctional Standards* (New York: American Correctional Association, 1959), pp. 6–10. This manual will be referred to from time to time in this and following chapters. It should be taken as a statement of standards approved by progressive leaders of the American Correctional Association, which for over 90 years has annually brought together wardens and other leaders in prison work.

415

a greater variety of convicted men and women. In the present chapter we disregard this variety and characterize the general nature of the prison system.

The Nature of a "Normal" Community

The free community is in part an unplanned natural growth, in part the product of a plan designed to meet the interests and wishes of its members. If men on the outside eat poorly, they at least eat what they wish, given their meager incomes. If they dress somewhat shabbily, their clothing is not standardized and a mark of despised status. On the outside there are women, and this means not only a normal physical relationship but the genesis of emotions which at times soften and compensate for life's hardships. When a man goes to prison, he usually leaves behind in the free community some intimate primary group which cares for him in spite of, if not because of, his personal worth or worthlessness.

In the normal community also there is at least the form of democracy. Laws and rules there are, but theoretically every citizen participated in their making. There, too, life is competitive, there is incentive to effort, and men are supposed to be economically independent. If this fact brings some of life's chief problems, it also brings some of life's chief satisfactions. Men may live in undesirable neighborhoods on the outside, but they are confined there by low incomes rather than by walls and bars. Outside one is indeed a part of a regime which perhaps represses as many desires as it satisfies, but at least one has the very fond, if misleading, illusion of self-direction and self-control and often of self-respect.

The nature of a prison community, however, is in sharp contrast.

First, all aspects of life are conducted in the same place and under the same single authority. Second, each phase of the member's daily activity is carried on in the immediate company of a large batch of others, all of whom are treated alike and required to do the same thing together. Third, all phases of the day's activities are tightly scheduled . . . , the whole sequence of activities being imposed from above by a system of explicit formal rulings and a body of officials. Finally, the various enforced activities are brought together into a single rational plan purportedly designed to fulfill the official aims of the institution.[2]

2 Erving Goffman, *Asylums* (New York: Anchor Books, 1961), p. 6.

The Structure of Prisons

SIGNIFICANCE AND HISTORY

The structure of any building reflects the purpose for which it was intended at the time it was constructed. Only a handful of our 150-odd state penal institutions have been built during the last 25 years, and a few are over 100 years old. The majority of our prisons, therefore, do not physically reflect modern treatment policies aimed at rehabilitation, but rather penal policies of older days when safekeeping and deterrent punishment were the primary considerations. With notable exceptions, our prison structures remain out-of-date partly because the secure fortress type of institution costs too much money to be abandoned and also because the general public still thinks of all prisoners as being high escape risks. Actually there are thousands of inmates who would not take advantage of an "open-door" policy, and a very few who will risk death to tunnel or blast their way out of the most secure prison. In addition a variety of structures are needed to provide a variety of institutional programs. Every student of criminology might well read carefully the United States Bureau of Prisons' significant and artistic publication, *Handbook of Correctional Institution Design and Construction,*[3] a book which contends that a structure which is designed to deal constructively with the type of inmates for which it is built can be made as secure as need be against escapes. This possibility depends, of course, upon a classification system which will give information for each offender concerning his degree of dangerousness and likelihood of escape as well as his special program needs.

The types and needs are so varied that not even a 32-institution system as that of the United States Bureau of Prisons nor a system of a populous and largely urbanized state like New York or California can have a separate institution for each type. Medium-sized states can have several institutions, including one designed to separate within itself several degrees of escape risk with corresponding degrees of secure construction, and several types of programs, some to be shared by all inmates, some intended for subgroups among them. This has been the aim of one of our most modern institutions, that at Angola, Louisiana, where publicity given to some of the most shocking conditions in the country has led to this radical improvement.

In the present chapter we speak only of the most general, over-all

---

[3] Washington, D. C., 1949. A valuable updating of this subject will be found in *Recent Prison Construction: 1950–1960* (Leavenworth, Kansas: Federal Prison Industries, Inc., 1960).

types of structure and of the relationship of structure to questions of general organization, inmate control, and discipline.

The history of prison structure reflects changes in the function of prisons. Among the Jews and Romans, where imprisonment was for purposes of detention or torture or slow death, we find prisons built like the Mamertine at Rome, consisting of an upper rectangular room with a dome-like dungeon below, where men were strangled or left to die of starvation.[4] Medieval keeps were damp, dark cells with stone floors and little or no light. The idea of cellular construction probably came from the monastery cell. In spite of improvements, the Auburn type of prison structure still handicaps the warden who desires to introduce modern classification methods and to deal with his charges as individuals or in small groups.

THE STRUCTURE OF MODERN PRISONS

The earliest Auburn-type structures, such as those in Boston, Auburn, Ossining, and Columbus, are either still in use or have just been abandoned. That type has been modified by use of modern devices to make escape more difficult and by other improvements. Thus tool-proof steel bars, underground passages, machine guns, walls more difficult to scale, gun detectors, electric eyes which will discover the presence of steel or other contraband on the person of prisoners or visitors, and devices to prevent the passing of contraband between visitors and prisoners have been added. On the other hand, windows in newly constructed prisons are generally far wider, cell doors no longer are nearly solid but are barred, sanitation is improved, dining room and chapels have been constructed and so on.

The Federal Bureau of Prisons distinguishes general types of penal institutions for adult males, which may roughly be grouped into penitentiaries of different degrees of security, correctional institutions, reformatories, and open road or forestry camps; though the restrictive or liberal nature of the life within them may not always follow these lines exactly. In addition there are various specialized institutions, including detention or classification quarters, medical centers for both the physically and mentally ill, and institutions for drug addicts or special types of inmates.

In terms of security we have special supersecurity institutions, such as Alcatraz in the federal system in San Francisco Harbor,[5] general maximum security institutions such as Atlanta and Leavenworth in the federal system,

---

[4] Rexford Newcomb, "The Evolution of the Prison Plan," *American Architect* (Oct. 18, 1916), p. 243.

[5] At the present writing (1962) the Federal Bureau of Prisons is planning to close Alcatraz because of the expense of operating it.

and a large number of state prisons. Mixed types of institutions with provision for different degrees of security within are increasingly advocated for the smaller states. The new Louisiana prison is an example of these, although the number provided for there (2,500) is about double that considered most desirable. Our largest prisons, which could accommodate up to 6,000, are universally considered far too large.

Alfred Hopkins, a pioneer in the development of modern prison architecture, once wrote: "Why spend a million dollars on a wall to retain 2,000 men when 1,800 would stay in prison without a wall?" [6] The old fortress-like cell-blocks cost up to $7,500 per inmate to build and would cost much more today. A large state with a classification system can house a quarter of its inmates in rooms costing not over $1,500, a half in medium security quarters at $2,500, and the rest in sufficiently secure inside cells at say $3,500. Special supersecurity prisons for desperate, dangerous men are no longer considered necessary. Alcatraz has made the public think mistakenly of the federal regime as extremely tough, which it certainly is not. Even on "the rock" there is more freedom than is supposed, and there is not complete absence of hope for "graduation" elsewhere. The excessively dangerous inmate, or more often the man whose violent career has received wide publicity, is real; but such men are few in number and can be housed in a special section of a general maximum security institution.

Beyond the needs of this small group, three degrees of prison security have been distinguished. Although the criteria for these are based on structural attributes, their penological significance relates principally to the varying degrees of freedom of movement accorded prisoners within them. Most states still have *maximum security* prisons with floodlighted walls 13 to 50 feet high and rows of secure inside cells with no cell windows overlooking the yard. However, the American Correctional Association [7] is skeptical about the need for masonry walls, since properly constructed, supersecure fences will answer as well. The federal penitentiary at Terre Haute, Indiana, was the first American institution for adult male felons to be built without a wall. It has been estimated that no more than 15 per cent of an unselected prison population needs to be housed within maximum securities facilities.[8] *Medium security* prisons cannot be simply defined. Such institutions are often fenced, rather than walled, or the cell-houses themselves constitute the wall; dormitories as well as cells might be used; ordinary wooden doors may be used on the cells instead of steel gates. The federal institution at

[6] Alfred Hopkins, *Prisons and Prison Building* (New York: Architectural Book Publishing Company, 1930), p. 8.
[7] Cf. *Manual of Correctional Standards*, p. 192.
[8] *Ibid.*, p. 192.

Danbury, Connecticut, and Wallkill Prison in New York State are examples of this security grade. *Minimum security* for adults is seen in cottage-type institutions, without walls, fences, or other elaborate safety devices, and is illustrated by the federal institution at Seagoville, Texas, the California Institution for Men at Chino, and an increasing number of road and forestry camps.

The typical modern prison or reformatory will have enclosed within its wall a variety of buildings: an Auburn-type cell block, administration building, power plant, workshops, dining room, and kitchen plant. In addition, chapel, hospital, school, library, and gymnasium, if provided, may or may not be separate buildings. Space available for parading and recreation will vary greatly as between prisons. Quite different from the Auburn type of prison is the telegraph-pole type. Here the cell blocks, shops, and other buildings lead off a central corridor which connects substantially all of them. Glass doors separating sections of this corridor may provide recreational rooms and isolate men when they most need isolation, and yet all may be under constant observation. At any rate separate day rooms must be provided in almost all types of institutions.

The typical inside cell block of today is an oblong building enclosing what amounts to another building composed of four or five double rows of cells backing up to a service corridor in the center. While the distance from windows to cells is considerable, prisons of recent construction may have fairly ample daylight and 15- or 25-watt electric lights in the cells. Narrow passageways lead past the upper cells, and a catwalk permits a guard to shuffle along and peer into any cell. Each cell has an individual lock, but all cells in a gallery may also be locked or unlocked from a central switch. Today modern plumbing is provided in each cell in nearly all prisons. The cells are wider than the old Auburn cell, but two hinged cots which fold up to the wall when not in use serve as beds for two occupants, while when the institution is crowded a third sleeps on a mattress on the concrete floor. Each cell also has a wash bowl, but full baths are supplied in a shower room under the eye of a guard watchful for fights or homosexuality.

Newer than the telephone type of structure is the prison with separate housing units, as at Seagoville, or with a combination of both types. At Angola, Louisiana, there are solitary outside and inside cells for only 10 per cent of the population. All the rest are housed in no fewer than 40 separate units of 60 men each sleeping in dormitories. Dormitories require supervision but are cheap to construct and can be partitioned off into cubicles for smaller groups. At Angola the warden thus has opportunity to separate 40 types on the basis of most desirable or least undesirable

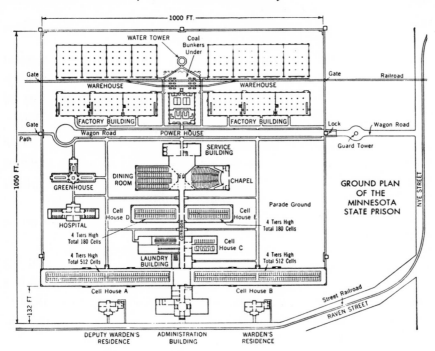

FIGURE 7 Minnesota State Prison. The drawing illustrates, in part, the telegraph-pole plan. Note the back-to-back cellular arrangement, characteristic of Auburn-type maximum-security prisons.

association, or some other principle found wise as a result of study of the men by his classification unit.

Prison construction costs money. States are often poor. Taxpayers hate to spend money. People tend to worry little over the living conditions of prisoners. In addition the public fails to realize the effect of overcrowding upon prison discipline. For all of these reasons our prisons have often been overcrowded even in terms of the close living for which they were designed. With the same appropriations most states might have housed many more prisoners without overcrowding had they set up adequate classification bureaus and built more of the less expensive medium and minimum security institutions. Overcrowding, together with poor food and idleness, has frequently characterized institutions where riots have occurred.

One of the most important needs is that, regardless of the type of inmate housed, prisons be so constructed that at night inmates may safely be given access to all kinds of educational, recreational, or other activities. Today most prisons have congregate dining rooms, which are usually considered danger spots because of the large number of men brought together with eating utensils as possible weapons. Most prisons and many reformatories seat the men in one direction, though the trend is toward tables for small groups, which are soon to be state-wide, for example, in California. At one end of the dining room may be a raised platform behind a screen where guards armed with machine guns stand ready for trouble. Cafeteria service is growing in popularity but is not universal. Most European prisons still feed the inmates in their cells.

Save for generally poor equipment and overcrowding, typical prison shops are not unlike those on the outside. Prison hospital buildings vary from some which are a disgrace to model institutions equal to almost any civil hospital in structure and equipment. Punishment cells, sometimes in a separate building, are almost always provided for the isolation of troublemakers. Many prisons, of course, also have a death house with large cells where the condemned await their end.

The reader may well ask what such community housing does to human personality. What do constantly jangling cell doors and snapping locks do to the nerves? What are the implications of the replacement of home life by a cubicle existence in a cell block? What does it mean to the human spirit, however depraved, to see for many years practically no material object which is designedly beautiful? What do guard towers, bleak, gray surrounding walls, the whole stench and monotony of the prison, and the feel of its massive structure pressing down on the person—what do all these do to a man? These questions cannot be fully answered. But modern prison architects have proven that prisons may keep men securely and yet be humanly livable and even beautiful in some of their features.

Prison Systems and Prison Administration

A prison system, whether national, state, or local, is the public aspect of the process of protecting against crime. The process may begin in community preventive programs and school or other planned relations with little children. Failures at the earlier stages of the process are recognized by the commitment of a considerable number of adults to correctional institutions. Ideally, then, a state correctional system will be organized as one element in an integration of a many-sided program of both public and private agencies. Actually such complete integration of protective activities is almost nonexistent. We shall characterize an approximation to it in California in a later chapter. Most prevalent are segmented and largely disconnected prison organizations,[9] with inadequate relationships to police, courts, probation, and parole administration, to say nothing of almost complete separation from work with juveniles in preventive activities. Facts about the reasons for delinquency and crime and the reasons for failure to deal adequately with specific cases should be carefully accumulated all the way along the line, and full records should accompany the adult to prison or parole. These facts would include characterization of communities, group value systems, and social relations, as well as facts about the individual criminal.

Even if such a complete integration were achieved, there would still, of course, be a somewhat distinct task of organizing a system of institutions for adult criminals. Administrators seem in fair agreement [10] on certain principles involved in such an organization. Dealing with dangerous men, the prison administrator, like the police executive, requires some elements of a semi-military line and staff organization, varying in degree in different institutions, with as much of more democratic elements introduced as possible, but with clear-cut lines of responsibility and command. A separate state department of corrections dealing with adult felons is generally preferred. Something might be said in favor of combining over-all direction of juvenile institutions and parole with that of adult prisons, *provided* a common ultimate constructive aim can dominate. At any rate, coordination of adult and juvenile programs is needed. A common correctional philosophy is all-important but rarely achieved. The states have many types of control by boards and commissioners with varying labels, but a single director appointed by the governor with a small but active advisory board seems preferable to wider dissipation of authority. Freedom from political interference at the top and a personnel appointed on a strictly merit basis is imperative, but unusual. A legal basis making a flexible policy possible, organized planning and research, and adequate financial support are obviously important.

Within the central state department, various deputies assume subordinate direction of different aspects of the prison program, their number necessarily varying with the size of the state, though even in small states their basic functions must be performed. Separate deputies in the larger organizations may each deal wtih central office personnel and general administration, fiscal matters, classification, education and related programs, prison industries and farms. A variety of other functions may be grouped under a fifth deputy director. So extremely important are public relations

[9] Need for and lack of such coordination has been commented upon by visitors from other countries. Cf. Elmer K. Nelson, "The Gulf Between Theory and Practice in Corrections," *Federal Probation* (Sept. 1954), pp. 48–50.

[10] Cf. *Manual of Correctional Standards*, chaps. 3 and 4.

of the system and its constituent institutions, and the deliberate organization of cooperation between institution and community, that a separate deputy director in charge of such matters would seem to be appropriate.

Similarly, the internal administration of each correctional institution must express its agreed-upon functions.[11] It is important that there shall be suitable channels of command and control not only from top to bottom but horizontally. This means that custodial, educational, and all other staff and subordinate personnel must see their work as part of the total program of the institution. It is appropriate that under the warden there be staff heads concerned with each of the following functions: custody and discipline, classification, inmate education, in-service training of personnel, business management, industrial and agricultural enterprises, medical and psychiatric services, public and community relationships, and the organization of inmate groups. More than one visitor from abroad has recently commented upon the general absence of the group approach in American prisons and upon its great importance where tried both here and abroad. So-called group therapy can be set up under the educational director, the psychiatrist, or even the chaplain. It is arguable, however, that the constructive possibilities of group organization of inmates are so promising that they might well be the major concern of a deputy warden.

Leadership and Personnel in the Prison Community

Closer to the prisoner than the stone walls is the human wall of guards [12] with peering eyes, watching, always watching. Human communication in the form of cries, curses, commands, laughter, jibes, furtive signals— these give to the material prison its effective meaning.

IMPORTANCE OF PERSONNEL

The usual prison is an autocracy within a democracy. Someone has extravagantly said that a prison is but a shadow of a man—the warden. Occasionally the real leader is the deputy warden, and too often certain

---

[11] *Ibid.*, chap. 9.

[12] We shall use the terms "guard," "custodial officer," and "correctional officer" almost interchangeably in this discussion. The first term was long used in the traditional prison of the past; the second has been employed for some time in the federal prison service; while change to "correctional officer" is intended to imply de-emphasis on purely watchful and repressive functions and emphasis on constructive activities. Most important, perhaps, is the label attached by the inmate and the hope that the correctional officer will cease to be named the "screw."

"big shots" among the inmates "run" the institution. Increasingly, counselors, psychiatrists, and other specialists deal with a part of the prison population. But always in theory and often in practice the ultimate power in prison is the warden. So far as influence on the character of prisoners is concerned, however, the subordinate staff are a more immediate, constant, and therefore effective force. The quality of prison guards is therefore all-important.[13] A New York State prisoner once testified that one custodial officer had "completely reformed" his life. Such testimony is far from general, and cases are known of guards who themselves have criminal records and of others who supply anything but admirable patterns for their charges.

TYPES OF PERSONNEL AND THEIR FUNCTIONS

In the old-line prison, and probably in most prisons today, the custodial staff tends to control. The rehabilitative staff either is isolated and to a degree in conflict with those concerned with discipline or are "institutionalized" themselves. Yet the trend is toward a personnel including guards and officers of all ranks working cooperatively on a constructive task, of which necessary discipline is a consistent part.

In the typical prison, the warden carries out centrally determined policies with varying degrees of freedom to run his own institution as he pleases. Much is expected of him. He must keep large numbers of men in, whose common attitude is that they "want out." He must keep the cost of operation down when, if he is to do a decent piece of work, it should go up. He must employ as many as possible of his inefficient and unenthusiastic charges in ways which shall at the same time be productive and yet produce nothing to endanger the profits of private industry or threaten its wage scale. He must, even so, keep aggrieved men reasonably satisfied and orderly. He must satisfy somewhat the desires of sections of the public who ask him to socialize antisocial prisoners in spite of a prison structure, organization, and program designed to deter from crime and actually creating embitterment. Above all, in most prisons, he must so conduct his institution as to bring credit to and avoid criticism of a political party primarily interested in preserving a spoils system. Being in charge of a miniature community, he should ideally know something of every aspect of community life. Educational, religious, medical, political, and above all disciplinary problems crowd upon him, each complicated by the nature of the population concerned. A past achievement in acquiring the good will

[13] Walter M. Wallack, *The Training of Prison Guards* (New York: Bureau of Publications, Teachers' College, Columbia University, 1938), p. 19.

of a political machine often has imperfectly prepared many wardens for so exacting a task.

A deputy warden usually has special charge of discipline. In the federal system, a second deputy warden may similarly direct the treatment program. The captain of the guards supervises this work and is still more immediately responsible for discipline. The superintendent of industries is of major importance in industrial prisons. The dietitian and cook can disrupt an otherwise orderly prison by failing to provide at a cost of a few cents per day the acceptable food which is a first essential to a tractable body of inmates.

In the old-line prison, the function of the guard is to watch, to report violations of rules, to inflict punishment if occasion requires, to act in crises such as escapes and riots—and little more. Physically closer to the prisoner than any other prison officer, the "good" guard in such a prison maintains a social gulf between himself and the inmate which he supposedly never crosses. Yet even in the old-line institution, guards do on occasion cross the social gulf and show consideration and even friendliness for inmates. The old prison system, however, discourages such gestures. Even the progressive prison, fearing the temptation to do favors for inmates and so bring the guard under obligations to them, may still frown on too much fraternization.

In the opinion of some observers there exists within maximum-security settings a chronic control problem whose solution is unlikely, short of returning to the individual isolation of the defunct Pennsylvania system. The problem is that of maintaining control of a firmness sufficient to minimize the perpetuation of inmate values and attitudes which tend to impede resocialization in conformity with conventional values and attitudes. Firm control is undermined in at least three ways. (1) The individual guard's wish to "get along," to "be a good Joe," may lead him to avoid actions which would make him an object of hatred, contempt, or ridicule by the inmates. Since some of these actions include keeping a firm hand over his charges, their avoidance reduces the guard's needed exercise of authority. (2) To maintain a modicum of order in his bailiwick the individual guard must rely not upon force or a blizzard of disciplinary tickets sent to higher echelons, but upon "purchasing" good behavior from his charges by ignoring minor rule infractions. (3) The need to trust minor chores to runners and other inmates may lead to an "established pattern of abdication" in which the guard's power is transferred to certain prisoners.[14]

[14] Lloyd W. McCorkle, "Guard-Inmate Relationships in Prison," reprinted in Norman Johnston, Leonard Savitz, and Marvin E. Wolfgang, *The Sociology of Punishment and Correction* (New York: John Wiley and Sons, 1962), pp. 108–110.

Given the old penal philosophy and political system, the existing personnel are just what one would expect. In 70 years' time one prison showed an average tenure of less than two years per warden. Guards are still often political appointees. Often politicians can circumvent civil service requirements through such devices as delayed examinations and the abuse of the privilege of making temporary appointments. It is important to note also that civil service does not of itself guarantee even approximately adequate standards.[15] Careful job analysis studies are requisite, with standards set up which recognize the social as well as the disciplinary functions of prison personnel. Probably in a majority of states there are practically no standards for the position of guard. A few years ago about half our prisons had the 48-hour week for guards, but in some the hours were still between 70 and 84. Today the 40-hour week is the approved standard. Rarely do the salaries paid attract high-grade- men.

Control of Inmates and Prison Discipline

Even under the very best conditions involving the most tractable men, inmates are a group of mature men held against their will. Prisoners want out. The purposes of custody, control, and discipline are (1) to prevent escapes, (2) to provide an orderly institution, and (3) to deal adequately with inmate misbehavior. Proper treatment of inmate offenses may improve inmates' capacity for voluntary self-control within the prison community. More importantly, it is hoped that patterns of behavior acquired on the inside will carry over into community life after release. In its broadest sense, discipline is, then, not something separate from the constructive program of the institution, but an integral part of it. The public generally demands safe custody and deterrent punishment but without "inhuman" cruelty. Beyond that, the public is usually indifferent except as dramatic escapes, riots, or exposure of extreme conditions dramatize what goes on in prison. All three of these aspects of discipline will depend in different degrees upon the structure of the institution, the leadership provided, the

---

[15] In fact, conventional civil service standards for guards may be unexpectedly inadequate. Korn and McCorkle found that "a surprisingly high number of the guards and higher officers who had generally distinguished themselves in routine and emergency situations had *failed* to distinguish themselves on civil service examinations." Non-talkativeness, reserve, and personal coldness, usually seen as social liabilities, characterized the better custodians. Richard R. Korn and Lloyd W. McCorkle, *Criminology and Penology* (New York: Henry Holt and Company, 1959), p. 503.

nature of the inmates cared for, and the capacity of the program to bring reasonable contentment to men chronically discontented by the very fact of their incarceration.

It is necessary that the conflict be resolved between the aims of custody and "reformation" and between the staffs performing these related functions.[16] Among the more technical requirements of custody and control are: continuous control of keys, firearms, records, drugs, tools useful as weapons, contraband, channels of possible egress, and so on. The movement of inmates about the institution during idle and recreational periods and in the dining room and kitchens and, when permitted transportation, outside the prison calls for special supervision. There should be a supply of tear gas and access to additional quantities outside the prison. There should be a minimum of necessary occasions for inmates leaving their cells after lockup. Among the immediate means to accomplish this are at least four official regular daily counts of inmates and other irregular counts. Firearms should be stored outside the main institution, and no one should be armed on the inside, because the danger of a guard being disarmed is greater than the danger that he will be unable to control a situation because unarmed. Training in the use of arms is obviously needed. In spite of all we shall later say about the constructive use of visits and correspondence, both need supervision for the sake of security, though that need naturally varies with the type of institutions and the type of inmates housed. In all institutions there should be frequent inspections and careful reports on findings. A central office should know the whereabouts of all inmates and employees at every moment. The frequency with which men have to be disciplined varies within the same institution, not only as between inmates but as between the guards or foremen under whom they are working.

It is generally agreed that penal institutions need rules but that these should not be long lists of specific "thou-shalt-nots," but general rules of decorum set forth in booklets for the prisoners and annotated ones for custodial officers. It is imperative that inmates know the reasons for all rules and that these seem reasonable to them in the prison situation. The following contrasting excerpts from rule books in use in two institutions some years ago speak for themselves:

"Strict silence and decorum must be observed during the meal. Talking, laughing, grimacing or gazing about the room is strictly forbidden." Rule 51 reads: "If

---

[16] The following brief characterization of the custodial aspects of prison discipline is based in part on two sources: The APA *Manual* already referred to, pp. 197–214; and Charles McKendrick, "Custody and Discipline," in Paul W. Tappan, *Contemporary Correction* (New York: McGraw-Hill Book Company, 1951), pp. 157–71.

you want bread, hold up your right hand; coffee or water, hold up your cup; meat, hold up your fork; soup, hold up your spoon; vegetables, hold up your knife." (There follows a list of no fewer than 55 forbidden acts including: hair not combed, insolence to officers, laughing and fooling, staring at visitors, talking in corridor, and so on.)

The following is an example of an attempt to create cooperative attitudes in the minds of inmates in a different prison:

To you who are perhaps coming into a prison for the first time in your life, we offer the following advice and suggestions which we believe will be helpful to you for whatever period it may be necessary for you to remain here:
    . . . Upon leaving the dining room at 5:30 you have the option, weather permitting, of going to the yard, or to your cell, where you may read or write, as you see fit, but we earnestly urge that you spend at least part of your evening in the yard at some sport or recreation in order to get the benefit of the fresh air. . . . We have arranged a series of activities in which we cordially invite you to join . . . assuring you of a splendid chance to increase your earning ability through educational improvement.
    With the thought of having the men live a perfectly normal life here, no rules are in force except those absolutely necessary for the welfare of the men and the institution. No restriction is placed on your talking to your fellow men at any time as long as it is done in a quiet, orderly tone, except after 10 o'clock p.m.

Based on his observations at Michigan's huge Jackson Prison, Vernon Fox found the following to be the offenses most frequently reported in custodial summary courts: [17] fighting, gambling, homosexual practices, stealing, smuggling or possessing contraband, being in unauthorized areas, disobedience, refusal to work, making alcoholic beverages, bartering with other inmates without permission, and conniving at escapes. Gambling, sex, and fighting are the most common major disciplinary problems; the fighting frequently results from the gambling and sex problems.[18]

Prison offenses such as serious assaults and murders will bring the inmate before the courts. Most misbehavior is dealt with inside the institution. Penalties range from reprimands, through loss of privileges, to isolation of different degrees, varying from being locked in the inmate's own cell to solitary confinement in totally dark cells without furniture. Usually most dreaded of all is the power to take away good time and thus to add to the inmate's actual time spent in prison. On entering the prison, inmates are usually credited with full deduction in their sentences for good behavior. The inmate tends to think of the sentence thus reduced as his right. Then

[17] Vernon Fox, "Analysis of Prison Disciplinary Problems," *Journal of Criminal Law, Criminology and Police Science* (Nov.–Dec. 1958), p. 324.
[18] *Ibid.*, p. 324.

additions to the expected sentence are made in the form of loss of "good time." Thus good time is not used as a positive inducement to be cooperative beyond the general degree tolerated, but as something which may be taken away as negative punishment. The amount of good time it is possible to earn varies, but has often been one month during the first year, rising to six months for each year exceeding the sixth. Sentences imposed by the institution may be suspended and held over the inmate as inducement to good conduct. In addition rewards are also effectively used in progressive institutions. Physical punishments are generally forbidden and ineffective, but are still used in many institutions. When inmates are sent to solitary, they may be kept on bread and water, usually for a limited period. Some institutions give a 2,300-calorie diet, and some make it adequate but monotonous and unappetizing.

In 1952 Negley K. Teeters [19] reported an APA study of punishment practices in 58 American penal institutions. Nearly all used deprivation of privileges, 42 some form of solitary confinement, and 47 loss of good time. Bread and water diet used in 20 prisons was always broken by one full meal every two or three days. In a few there was no bread and water diet but just one full meal a day. A single administrator admitted flogging. About half of the institutions still were without disciplinary boards.

Prison Riots

Prison riots have a long history. Between 1951 and January of 1954, about 30 occurred, especially in 1952. In a sense almost every penal institution by its very nature has the potentialities of such revolt. For this reason there probably was an element of epidemic in 1952, as the grapevine and the newspapers spread news both of some success and much failure in the achievement of the inmates' aims. Some lives were lost and there was heavy damage to property. Property losses from fire and destruction were estimated at $1,000,000 at Columbus, $2,000,000 at Jackson, Michigan.[20] A serious aspect of most of these riots has been the holding of guards as hostages, sometimes with threats to kill them unless demands were met. The fact that in 1952 only about 8,000 inmates, or one in 20 in the total population, were involved, and that some of these acted against their will, by no means proves that the other 95 per cent were satisfied, but it does

[19] "A Limited Survey of Some Prison Practices and Policies," *Prison World* (May–June 1952).

[20] Frank T. Flynn, "Behind the Prison Riots," *Social Service Review* (March 1953), 73–86.

underline the influence of leadership and group pressures in certain cell blocks. The leaders were naturally often the most desperate and unstable men. Such men are numerous in prison, and, in our judgment, it does not explain the problem or assist in its solution to follow some of our leading penologists and label them "psychopaths." [21] Our eyes should be centered, not on meaningless labels, but on the earlier process which produces such unsocialized personalities and on the prison conditions which produce riots under their leadership. Nor is self-mutilation, as by cutting the tendons of the feet, to be adequately explained as due to inherent masochistic tendencies of those who have protested intolerable conditions in this painful manner in Louisiana and elsewhere.[22]

In spite of improvements, American prisons generally continue to be characterized by avoidable conditions tending to lead certain inmates to revolt in the face of possible death and almost certain severe additional punishment. The generalization that riots do not occur when the most advanced and constructive penal programs are in effect is not quite true, because the Federal Reformatory at Chillicothe had a riot in 1952, but is far more nearly true than the opposite claim that humane treatment just gives convicts the opportunity to escape or revolt. The federal system is liberal and has been relatively free of revolts, but includes "the rock" of Alcatraz, where serious trouble occurred at an earlier date. New Jersey, with highly enlightened leadership, repeatedly has had very serious trouble at its more-than-a-century-old prison at Trenton.

Schrag's study of the prison riots which occurred in the early 1950's suggests that these riots had "natural histories" in which four stages were discernible: (1) a brief period of expressive behavior and destruction; (2) small bands of inmate leaders emerged from the turmoil; (3) grievances were presented against the administration and appeals were made for public sympathy and support; (4) power gradually reverted to the prison authorities.[23] In attempting to explain the temporal clustering of these particular riots, Schrag rejects as untenable the allegations that they were caused by bad food, repressive treatment, idleness, and inadequate administration, since these features have long characterized prisons. Rather, he thinks, the riots were responses to administrative adjustments to a gap which had opened between correctional precept and practice:

[21] Cf. Austin H. MacCormick, "Behind the Prison Riots," *Annals of the American Academy of Political and Social Science* (May 1954), pp. 17–27.

[22] For a discussion of this problem, see Rupert C. Koeniger, "What About Self-Mutilation?" *The Prison World* (March–April 1951), pp. 3*ff*.

[23] Clarence Schrag, "The Sociology of Prison Riots," American Correctional Association *Proceedings* (1960), p. 139.

What apparently happened is that a severe breach had developed between public precept and institutional practice in the field of correction. This breach was fostered by the popularization of a new treatment philosophy at a time when prison staffs and programs were sufficient only for routine custodial care and were hopelessly unable to keep pace with rapidly changing public conceptions of treatment methods and objectives. . . .

However, the riots did not occur when the discrepancy . . . became evident, but when program changes aimed at reducing this discrepancy were initiated. Again, institutions that had static programs and a well-established tradition of indifference to the new philosophy were less vulnerable than institutions in the process of change.[24]

. . . [M]any of the riots seemed to occur at precisely that point in time when correctional authorities were initiating program improvements, tightening controls, and developing staff training measures. The evidence is that administrative changes, even though they were viewed as beneficial and necessary, were frequently associated with tension and anxiety among both staff members and inmates.[25]

The *Prison Journal* [26] attempted to answer the question: What lessons have the states learned and what have they done as a result of the epidemic of prison riots? As of that date, the answer was mixed and perhaps unfair because sufficient time may not have elapsed for improvements to be made. To cite a few specific examples: at the Illinois Penitentiary at Menard, and in Pennsylvania, Washington, and Louisiana, definite progress followed the riots. In some states like California where the riot was small and exceptional, there was simply a continuance of marked improvement which had long been under way. At least at the date of the report, Ohio and Michigan seemed to have learned little from their serious experiences. Some progress was noted in Massachusetts but was followed by serious trouble in January, 1955; while New Jersey, under a new governor, retracted her plan to abolish at long last her over-a-century-old state prison and thereby to enable her really excellent top leadership to carry on effectively. The view held by some that the demands of convicts in revolt should never be met and that unconditional surrender with severe penalties is the only appropriate answer to riots seems unfair and very shortsighted. On the whole, the regrettable riots may well have furthered real prison reform.

[24] *Ibid.,* p. 145.

[25] *Ibid.,* p. 138. Whether or not Schrag's hypothesis is correct, its superiority over the "reasons" for the riots given by inmates, prison employees, investigative bodies, and the press lies in the fact that it takes cognizance of the role of social structures in ordering human relationships.

[26] April, 1954.

Classification, Reception, and Case Work

For a long period, prison programs meant undifferentiated mass treatment. Even today the majority of inmates probably have little feeling that their widely varying individual characteristics and needs are given much attention in our correctional institutions. For several decades, however, the distinctive trend in our more progressive institutions has been toward individualization. A still-more-recent slight tendency to use groups of inmates in the program may well prove to be still more significant. Classification of inmates into types for differential treatment is the first step toward individualization.

Individualization in social service is called case work. Case work implies effort to aid the individual even though the welfare of society be the ultimate goal. Yet to most people there seems to be an antithesis between case work and prisons. Case work breathes friendliness, prisons imply enmity. Case work strives to meet needs and grant reasonable desires. Prisons traditionally disregard all but the most primary needs and seem to exist to block men's desires. Progressive correctional institutions understandably give attention to the individual case, not because of first concern for the criminal, but because first concern for the protection of society demands treatment adjusted to the needs of a vast variety of individual offenders. Separation of inmates according to their treatment and security requirements, as well as on the basis of their behavior towards each other, permits maximum specialization and efficiency in the use of prison resources.

HISTORY OF CLASSIFICATION

Some common-sense distinction between types of criminals existed, of course, from an early date. The canonical courts distinguished between clergy and laity. We have seen that separation by sex, age, and nature of offense was imperfectly carried out in some early European and American institutions. Baltimore segregated women in its prison system in the early nineteenth century. The three juvenile institutions built about 1825 dealt separately with children. The isolation of the insane seems first to have been proposed in 1844. Later a few states permitted the transfer of criminals to these asylums, and in 1859 New York opened the first hospital for the criminally insane. Early in the eighteenth century the development of American houses of correction separated misdemeanants from felons. The building of Indiana's separate prison for women in 1873 is usually regarded as the beginning of the women's reformatory movement. The pioneer men's reformatory at Elmira dates from 1876. Modern classification at the institutional level implies the organization of special centers for this purpose, and that movement is about 35 years old.

Classification has been defined as a process of "organized procedures by which diagnosis, treatment planning and the carrying out of the component parts of the general program of treatment are coordinated and focused on the individual in prison and on parole." [27] Its introduction in prisons was revolutionary, for it meant not only a commitment to the principle of individualized treatment but also a break in the classic pattern of authority in which the deputy warden was exclusively responsible for work, training, and quarters assignment, as well as enforcement of discipline. This is not to say that treatment personnel now hold the balance of power in prisons, for the opposite is the case, but classification pushed wide the door to the sanctum of prison policy-making, into which trooped an increasing number of prison functionaries whose occupational values centered around treatment rather than custody.

CLASSIFICATION BODIES [28]

The law itself may define the type of penal institution in which a convicted felon not granted probation shall be incarcerated. Or discretion to determine this may be given to the courts. For various reasons neither of these practices is satisfactory as preparation for intelligent treatment programs. For such preparation the collection of a vast amount of information is needed. Such fact-gathering requires a considerable period of time, trained personnel, adequate funds, and freedom from local prejudices and politics, such as few courts possess. Classification as carried out by some courts has been aptly characterized as follows:

> In some way judges have convinced themselves . . . that they can look into the eye of an offender and say: "Young man, in 10 years you will be ready to go back into the community." It is a good deal like trying to buy a watermelon by its feel. The judge does not even thump to find out what is inside.[29]

Our best pre-sentence investigations are much more thorough but can hardly be planned with a prison program in mind. Hence it has become advisable to set up special administrative agencies within the correctional

[27] *Manual of Correctional Standards,* pp. 283–84.

[28] Though we distinguish certain types of organization below, we shall use the terms "classification organization," "committee," "board," and "center" somewhat interchangeably. It is believed the context will indicate when the terms are used in a general or specific sense.

[29] V. C. Branham, "A Practical Discussion of Case Work and Classification in the Adult Prison," American Prison Association *Proceedings* (1934), pp. 156–57.

system of a state. These are of three general types: central classification centers, to which all convicts who are to be imprisoned are sent for study and determination of their future disposition; classification committees located within each institution, which decide upon the treatment program there; and reception centers, which house and have more or less control over the new inmates for a month or more, including or after their quarantine period, and prepare them for the subsequent stages of their life in the institution. Frank Loveland [30] has said that in 1951 not over one-third of our state penal systems had a classification committee or center, and that many of these existed hardly more than in name. Yet when prison administrators gather at their annual Correctional Congress today, absence of a classification system is looked upon as an indication of backwardness. The classification movement is extremely important but still in process of extension and improvement. Even in our most progressive state systems, where classification means relating the institutional program of each inmate to his needs, it is still rare that that program can plan for his adjustment to known specific conditions and social relationships in his home community after his release. Ideally, classification will include this long look ahead.

In a populous state, such as California or New York, with many alternative types of institutions, the first type of state classification center seems desirable, though the federal correctional system, with about 30 institutions scattered over the entire country, gets along well with only local institutional committees. These local committees are directed, however, by classification specialists at the central office of the Bureau in Washington. When their investigation shows that the federal court might better have sent an inmate elsewhere, he may readily be transferred. In large states like Illinois, more than one general classification center has been found advisable. Where commitments are to such a central classification agency, further study of the individual would seem to be needed after he reaches the institution in order to prepare him for his program. Here the third type—the reception center —performs an important and more continuing function of investigation and orientation. They not only aid the study of inmates, but they facilitate the inmate's acquaintance with prison opportunities.

CLASSIFICATION CENTERS AND COMMITTEES

A classification center of any type must first gather appropriate information about each prisoner. This information will come in part from records of various degrees of fullness derived from public and private agencies which have had previous contact with the man or his family.

30 "Classification and the Prison System," in Tappan, *op. cit.*, chap. 7.

More important are facts based upon interviews with the prisoner after his arrival at the classification depot. Information is also gained through correspondence with his family, friends, and associates. No decision can be considered adequately founded in fact which does not include a recent field study of the family and community or communities from which the inmate came. Such studies made by the classification committee itself are costly and rare. The assistance of probation or parole officers may be solicited, or the adequacy of field information must depend on the fullness of reports routinely sent from the courts.

On the basis of facts thus obtained, a central state classification board recommends or itself determines to which of available institutions the prisoner shall be sent. Even classification between institutions is not properly final, and frequent re-study, with transfer elsewhere when indicated, is essential. Beyond this the classification board may recommend or determine what treatment shall be given the man in the institution, seeking aid from outside agencies and specialists when needed. It may be provided that important changes in inmate programs must be referred to the classification board, while minor ones may be made by the staff member in charge of education, work assignment, or any particular aspect of the institution's activities. The board may also recommend concerning the prisoner's potentialities for parole, and changes needed in the home or in associates in the interest of his later community adjustment. Where there is a central state classification center, facts obtained there will, of course, be handed on to the institutional reception center, where further study will be required for the detailed planning of the man's institutional program. The institutional classification committee or reception center provides for regular periodical reviews of each case and for special reconsideration when new needs occur. When a man first becomes eligible for parole, re-study should be routinely provided for even without his request. Ideally, classification is a continuous process rather than a periodic gesture.

The above functions with respect to the inmate by no means comprise all the duties and advantages of a good classification system. These include the following considerations: (1) Classification provides facts needed by the prison staff. (2) It prevents their overdepartmentalization by integrating the views and programs of the many specialists and administrative heads involved. (3) It prevents the warden's control from being a dictatorship by requiring him to share control with the classification committee. (4) It tends to reduce escapes and results in better discipline through basing treatment in each case partly on facts concerning the inmate which have been recorded by the committee. (5) Deliberations of the committee have meant better utilization of inmates for industrial output. (6) Inmate morale is improved because inmates know that individual attention is given to personal needs, and the barrier between inmates and staff is reduced. (7) Staff morale is increased through mutual appreciation of the roles and problems of each member. (8) Classification gives the parole board facts essential to their decisions. (9) Classification reports aid other institutions to which the inmate may later be committed. (10) The research value of facts obtained is important both in the study of causes and in the evaluation of the effects of specific institutional programs. (11) A well-staffed institutional committee brings together the professional specialist and the administrative specialist, who thus acquire respect for each other. (12) Indeed, the fully functioning classification committee becomes the very heart of the entire institutional program and may appropriately be chaired by the warden, since decisions reached by the committee must have behind them the force of authority.

But however pious our expectations may be for the functions and advantages of classification, this device is in constant danger of being used to serve lesser ends than those of treatment. A deputy assistant director of the federal prison system has made this point well:[31]

> In all too many instances classification contents itself largely with being an administrative device through which we identify potential "problem" inmates— the escape risk, the homosexual and the strong-arm leader—and solve the problems of managing inmate work details. In the measurement of inmate response to programs we are forced to fall back upon a statistical recapitulation of the number of disciplinary violations reported, the number of work changes which have taken place, the number of courses completed, the frequency of attendance at religious service, the number of counseling sessions in which he participated and the extent of his generosity in donating blood.

TYPES OF INSTITUTIONS AVAILABLE

Our larger and more progressive states have available for disposition of inmates such different institutions as the following: (1) receiving and detention prisons; (2) prisons and subdivisions of prisons of maximum, medium, and minimum security for adult male offenders considered relatively normal; (3) reformatories for young males capable of making use of educational opportunity; (4) similar reformatories for women, which

[31] H. G. Moeller, "Changing Trends in Classification," *American Correctional Association Proceedings* (1960), p. 215.

in many states take the place of women's prisons; (5) prison farms; (6) road-building, soil-conservation, or forestry camps in some states; (7) institutions for the criminally insane; (8) institutions for mentally defective criminals; (9) farms or other state institutions for misdemeanants; (10) in addition separate institutions or more usually departments for drug addicts, tubercular inmates, the venereally diseased, homosexuals, and so forth.

Classification between institutions thus may be based upon age, sex, likelihood of escape, nature of offense, likelihood of reform, need for education, physical or mental condition, capability of work, or race. Its purpose may be mere administrative convenience or provision for the special needs of the group in question. Many have claimed there is virtue in the mere collection in one institution of homogeneous groups, thus preventing contamination and permitting a program adapted to a group with similar needs. Undoubtedly there is much to be said for this grouping on the basis of likeness, but it seems to date to have been too slavishly followed. As we come to plan a prison as a community, we shall find more significant bases for association and realize also that a certain degree of heterogeneity of population is normal in prison as elsewhere, provided that it does not disrupt organization.

Classification based upon the nature of the crime is almost useless. The practical prison warden, however, will insist that the interest of order in his institution must come first. Though mere separation of troublemakers does not imply their proper treatment, it does permit more constructive programs for the average inmate, as well as for the most tractable inmates. Within the institution a warden may also find it convenient to house men who work in the same shop together or to separate those who have achieved different levels in a conduct grading system. He will also appreciate the value of segregating the syphilitics, and his disciplinary problems will be less if he is rid of drug addicts and so-called "sex perverts." Since apparently hopeless recidivists have occasionally been resocialized, there is great danger in utilizing at a classification center such labels as "unimprovable" or "psychopath."

Even the most liberal penologist must admit that in classification certain administrative considerations must take precedence. Reasonable safety from escape and the health of the prison population are primary. Moreover, at any given time the nature and structure of the institutions available will limit the possible bases for classification. Granting the primacy of such considerations, the sociologist insists that major consideration be given in assignments to the basic need of grouping together, especially in informal activities, those who will profit most or suffer least through association. Awareness of ties and conflicts between inmates is essential to sociologically sound assignment.

THE PERSONNEL OF CLASSIFICATION BOARDS

Classification calls for participation in its discussions and decisions of two kinds of specialists, professional and administrative. Indeed, we have noted among the advantages of classification, not only the cooperation necessitated but also the mutual education involved in the association of these specialists and of the different subdivisions within each group. The psychologist, psychiatrist, and sociologist need to learn from one another. Similarly, the warden and his deputies, the industrial superintendent, the physician, and the recreational director need to learn to respect the importance of each other's contribution to the total task of rehabilitation. Even the custodial staff of a prison should visit meetings of the classification committee and thus not only learn about particular inmates in its charge but absorb the philosophy of the institution and the larger meaning of its total program. Where the staff is primarily professional, it is traditional that the director be a psychiatrist, although there seems to be no logical reason why the psychologist or the sociologist should not occupy this position, since it is by no means clear that the treatment of criminals is primarily a medical problem.

Personal Case Work in Penal Institutions

Personal prison case work includes promoting the individual's adjustment first within the prison community and then in preparation for the post-prison community. The man must be assigned to a cell block or dormitory; he must be given a job; he may need assignment to a class in the academic school or to a shop in the program of vocational training. If he has individual physical or health needs, they must be attended to. Knowledge of his case may and should affect the disciplinary policy used if he violates prison rules. The individual case record will assist in determining the use of leisure time allowed the individual.

Beyond all this, however, each man has personal problems. His mental state, including his fears and worries and general emotional instability, calls for individual attention from psychiatrist, social worker, or other counselor. It is most important here that the prison administration realize the need for confidential relationships between prisoners and counselors and leave to its professional staff a high degree of discretion in protecting the confidences of the men. Prisoners can be frankly told that information pertinent to the safety of the institution will be reported.

It is sometimes implied that an emotional relationship between the social worker and the prisoner is the chief dynamic influence. Undoubtedly this influence is important, but unless the number of case workers is greatly increased, its possibilities are limited. Moreover, inmate relations with case workers are external to the inmate's social experience in prison, are applied to him, and are not consistent with his role as a member of subgroups in the prison community. The introduction of increasing numbers of interns and the socialization of guards, together with experiments in utilizing natural leadership and natural groups among the prisoners themselves, probably hold out more promise than the influence of a few trained psychiatrists or case workers. Both approaches are needed, however.

The development of pleasant relations between the prison case worker and the inmate's home and community goes far to overcome antagonism. It promotes contacts with every constructive force in the community, tends to prevent that suspicion and hostility toward the prisoner in the home community which too often drive the parolee back to his gang, and reacts favorably upon the attitudes of the man on the inside.

RECEPTION CENTERS AND INMATE ORIENTATION [32]

When an inmate is received at a correctional institution, he must first pass through quarantine. Following this he may be kept separate from the rest of the institution's population for a period which may extend to 60 days and more in special cases. If there is no state classification depot, the reception center may itself do classification work similar to that of the classification committee already described. But the major function of the reception center is inmate orientation. The center does not partake of the

[32] Cf. Norman Fenton, "The Process of Reception in the Adult Correctional System," *Annals, loc. cit.,* pp. 51–58; Glenn Kendall, "Reception Center," in Tappan, *op. cit.,* chap. 10.

repressive atmosphere which may characterize the institution as a whole, and its staff often radiates a friendly attitude as they try to prepare the newcomer for success in the institutional program. He may be introduced to the institution by means of a booklet, group meetings where the program as a whole is discussed, a trip about the institution, the use of pictures, and so on. According to Kendall, the center should be administered wholly separately from the prison administration, though the desirability of such separation may be questioned. The center itself will give tests, provide interviews with members of the prison staff, evaluate the inmate's attitudes, require him to write a letter to his family or other close relatives and study his correspondence, and write itself to his family. It will have its own separate educational, vocation guidance, and recreational program. When all information is gathered, there will be a staff conference much like that already described. The cooperation of the new inmate in formulating his own program is solicited. The program arrived at will be carefully explained to him. The plan will then be presented to the administration of the institution.

Walter M. Wallack,[33] a leading penologist of New York State, has developed for Wallkill prison an organization known as the Service Unit, which has been copied in other New York institutions and which seems adaptable to all types of penal institutions. Its distinctive characteristics are its coordinating and follow-through functions. The staff of the Service Unit aims to coordinate all the activities of the institution and follows up each inmate's progress there. It counsels inmates and acts as consultant to the prison staff when problems arise in any case. The Service Unit is especially concerned to coordinate the institutional program with parole, and representatives of the Division of Parole take active part in its work. One of the first interviews of the inmate is with the parole representative, so that he is early oriented toward a program in which success will favor his early parole. The parole representative assists with the solution of family problems which may affect his success on parole and with which the parole representative is familiar through his field investigation. Initial interviews are also arranged by the Service Unit with the vocational guidance director, the warden, the educational and recreational directors, and many others. After his admission to the prison itself, reports on the man's progress are submitted to the Service Center periodically by the head of various institutional activities. Discussion of reception centers and the Service Unit indicate how classification, reception and

[33] "The Service Unit," in Tappan, *op. cit.,* pp. 141–53.

orientation, institutional programming, and parole planning may be made to merge into one another in a continuous process.

CASE WORKER IN PROGRESSIVE CORRECTIONAL PRACTICE

Existing classification and case-work programs have developed in a promising way. Yet case work is still handicapped even in the best systems. Often the work is cramped because its spirit is inconsistent with much of the rest of the prison program. Rarely indeed would a case worker, if concerned solely with improving the attitudes of the individual, send him to prison at all. Never would he subject him to the demoralizing influences which still characterize most prisons. Prisoners need to learn self-reliance; prisons make them dependent. Prisoners need to have their self-respect restored; prisons often further degrade them. Prisoners need to be associated with constructive outside influences; imprisonment isolates them from all such influences, although the best prison case work rebuilds selected outside contacts wherever it is permitted to do so. Most case work in prisons is individualistic in spite of some recent development of group therapy, while character is formed and "reformed" in primary groups, which originate naturally without external pressure. In the more natural prison community suggested in a later chapter, case work should find its proper setting.

Until very recently the most ambitious effort to combine a degree of community organization in prison with social case work was probably Norfolk Prison Colony in Massachusetts, especially under the leadership of Warden Howard Gill. A brilliant analysis of the work of this institution was published in 1940.[34]

Case work at Norfolk was by no means wholly a failure. The Norfolk experiment was terminated for reasons independent of the validity of either of its two methods. Yet the considerable degree of success Mr. Gill had during its early stages seems to have validated the small-group and community approach more than that of individual case work. At least the Norfolk experience showed that case work in prison to be effective must be coordinated with group work and the organization of the prison as a community and must be related to the free community.

---

[34] Edwin Powers, "Individualization of Treatment as Illustrated by Studies of 50 Cases," in *A Report on the Development of Penological Treatment at Norfolk Prison Colony in Massachusetts* (New York: Bureau of Social Hygiene, Inc., 1940), pp. 240–51.

Institutions for Juvenile Delinquents

HISTORICAL BACKGROUND

Early in the eighteenth century, delinquent children were separated from adults for special training in Pope Clement XI's hospital of St. Michael at Rome. Boys sentenced to transportation or imprisonment in the latter part of the same century in England were often cared for by private philanthropic societies. In America a report that 75 boys a year had been sent to prison from New York led to the formation of a society which collected funds for the establishment in 1825 of the first juvenile reformatory in the United States, the New York House of Refuge. Somewhat similar institutions were established about the same time in Boston and Philadelphia. These introduced emphasis on training rather than mere punishment, and some included such progressive features as the indefinite sentence and grading system which were later adopted in adult reformatories. These early institutions did not have a distinctive structure, however, but were characterized by walls, cells, and the contracting of the children's labor to private individuals. However much they resembled adult prisons, these institutions had the advantage of being privately maintained and administered under the innocent and warm-hearted philanthropy of preindustrial American culture. They were run by dedicated and zealous individuals, often clergymen, and their staffs were, for those times, well-qualified and well-paid. The first tax-supported reform school opened in Westboro, Massachusetts in 1847 and is now the Lyman School for Boys. The structural pattern predominating in most reform schools today is the so-called cottage system, first used in France and brought to this country in the 1850's.

PRESENT PICTURE

There now exist 129 state training schools for juveniles harboring, at the last available census (1956), 33,000 children,[35] three-quarters of whom were boys. The average stays are short: 8.6 months for boys and 12.2 months for girls. Median per capita operating expenditures approximate the yearly cost to a parent of sending his child to a state university, $1,796. Unlike prisons, most of whose staffs are custodial personnel,

---

[35] *Statistics on Public Institutions for Delinquent Children: 1956* (Washington, D. C.: U. S. Children's Bureau, 1958), p. 3.

juvenile institutions report that nearly 60 per cent of their personnel are engaged in treatment and educational work.

The existing wide variety of state training schools in terms of physical plant, quality of personnel and programs, size, admission policies, nature of inmate population, and other factors make it risky to generalize about the schools. Practically all are organized on the cottage system, in which the youngsters live in housing units designated for particular categories of inmates. Far from being "cottages," the units at many schools are large, substantially-built structures providing dormitory, recreational, and some-times dining facilities for as many as 70 children. Some cottages contain individual occupancy rooms whose size and security features make them virtually cells. Cottages are customarily in the charge of "cottage parents," married couples whose responsibilities include attempts to create a home-like atmosphere. One element which interferes with this desired atmosphere is the inevitable institutional routine.

With slight variations in time the routines established at the various schools were quite similar. In each all the boys rose at the same time, dressed, break-fasted, performed such chores around their cottage as were assigned to them, and then reported to the classroom, the shops, or work assignments. Some boys belonging to squads that worked in the dairy, in the kitchens, and on other assignments requiring early rising had to go to work earlier than the rest of the group. At noon there was usually a recreation period following the noon meal, then all boys reported back to school, shop, or work. Most schools released the boys from shop and school and work assignments early enough to allow a short period of free time before the supper hour. Supper was fairly early in most of these institutions and was followed by the longest recreation period of the day. The retiring hour varied somewhat, being usually around 8, 8:30, or 9 o'clock.[36]

AIMS AND PHILOSOPHIES OF STATE TRAINING SCHOOLS

As increased use of child welfare procedures has reduced resort to juvenile courts and probation, so increased use of probation and home placement has reduced the proportion, if not the number, of delinquents committed to state training schools. This reduction has not been so great as in the case of dependent children, because it is more difficult to find homes for delinquents. But one result of the trend has been to bring to the institutions increasingly difficult types of rebellious youngsters and adoles-cents. These rebels are probably more difficult to control than the *average* adult prisoner.

Juvenile institutions have expressed various views.[37] Some people have

[36] U. S. Children's Bureau, "Institutional Treatment of Delinquent Boys," *Publication No. 288,* pp. 1–4.
[37] *Ibid.*

believed that rigid discipline of a military character will wipe out bad habits. Others have urged the beneficial effects of a rural setting and contact with cows and "God's open spaces" on the theory that there is something regenerating about getting close to nature. Still others have wished to indoctrinate naughty children with virtues through a mass program of academic education or through the inculcation of "habits of industry" by way of vocational training or productive work. Hence the prevalent name—"industrial schools."

Mass handling of delinquent boys has partially given way to more individualized programs dominated in theory by the philosophy of psychiatric social work. The individual-centeredness of institutional programs approved by case workers is evident in a Children's Bureau *Bulletin* [38] which defines the therapeutic aim of the training school as "to alter the delinquent's concept of the world around him." In this view the delinquent is conceived of as aggressive, destructive, and primitive because he was rejected and punished by his parents. Deriving attitudes of hostility from them, he now misinterprets the world as hostile to him when in reality it is not. The institution is not to punish but to give the child protection, understanding, and then insight into his own mistaken view of life. All agree on the need to understand and protect the child. But setting aside the point that delinquents have often *actually* faced hostile elements in society, the above view of the purpose of training schools seems exceedingly narrow and inadequate even as an example of the psychiatric casework conception of the task. It is to be contrasted with the far broader and wholly satisfactory view expressed in the Children's Bureau *Bulletin* which immediately preceded the one just referred to.[39] The latter, attributing some success to preventive programs applying many disciplinary approaches, implies, at least, not one but many-sided institutional programs, using group approaches among others. But the psychiatric approach is accepted in principle and partly in practice in a good many institutional programs. It usually implies the provision of a key, professional, psychiatrically trained staff working under the superintendent. They strive to sell their philosophy to the subordinate staff, especially to the cottage parents. The latter are not deemed capable of doing real remedial case work, however. Yet the contacts of cottage parents with the children are by far the most intimate, numerous, and influential of those of any staff members unless they be some recreational leaders. The psychiatrist's quite correct

[38] "Tentative Standards for Training Schools," *Bulletin No. 351* (Washington, D. C.: U. S. Children's Bureau, 1954), pp. 4–7.
[39] Helen L. Witmer and Edith Tufts, "The Effectiveness of Delinquency Prevention Programs," *Bulletin No. 350* (Washington, D. C.: U. S. Children's Bureau, 1954).

view that delinquency originates in part in parent-child relations is thus imposed from the top and without adequate cottage staff to play the role of substitute parents and to provide the desired new parent-child relations.

No sociologist will deny the great importance of parent-child relations. But all sociologists will add emphasis upon the importance of peer-group and prestige-group patterning and influence and upon the influence of community relations outside the home, which they will hope to change as a result of the institutional experience. In addition, therefore, to mass programs and the psychiatric case-work type of individual programs, we have a third type of philosophy and program which is built on this last emphasis. Seeing delinquency as a group product, this program will use groups in the training school formed as naturally as possible. The institution itself will be conceived of, as a whole, as a sort of community, related to and planning for the return of the delinquents to their own communities. Perhaps institutions desiring or compelled to use chiefly mass treatment programs are still the most numerous. Among the rest the individual approach has come in and is widely approved. The sociological group approach is increasingly recognized in institutions for adults and youths—less in training schools for children.

SELECTION OF INMATES

Most state institutions have to deal with far too heterogeneous a population. Local communities without facilities for dependents tend to use the state institution, while larger cities, better provided, send only the tougher delinquents, who have failed under probationary or other constructive efforts. Thus the program must be adapted to the needs of the most troublesome children, except where a number of alternative institutions are available. Children may be kept in the institution until their majority, although the actual period of confinement averages far less. In addition, parole violators may be returned even after they have reached the legal maximum for original commitment. One means of promoting the exclusion of mentally deficient or other children who should not go to the training school is to provide for commitment to a state department of public welfare with power to determine where they shall be sent. A law like that in Illinois, under which managing officers may place in foster homes children who they feel do not belong in the institution, aids in correcting court mistakes.[40]

[40] Harrison A. Dobbs, "Correctional-School Training for Delinquent Children from Community Standpoint," *Proceedings of the National Conference of Social Work*, Atlantic City, 1936, pp. 484–86.

The nature of the offenses committed by institutionalized delinquents varies. Institutions drawing children from industrial cities will usually have a larger proportion of juvenile gang members and of serious offenders. Among 668 offenses committed by state industrial school boys in Illinois, there were no fewer than 172 burglaries, 84 automobile larcenies, 22 grand larcenies, and 47 robberies, together with smaller numbers of assaults with deadly weapons, and cases of arson, rape, forgeries, and so on. Such offenses lead the public to demand greater security than is desirable in the interest of constructive rehabilitation. Research has shown repeatedly that the nature of the offense, though of some significance as indicating maturity in crime, should be given little consideration in determining a treatment program.

As favorable aspects of institutional treatment, the controlled environment provides, its more organized and active programs, and the varied group motivations it stimulates have been listed. It is held generally desirable to send to institutions the mentally defective, children who have been consistently spoiled at home, those who are too old to profit by family placement, and those who have failed when placed in homes previously. Not all of these characteristics should necessarily exclude children from probation, of course. It may be said that the typical training school at best provides but a short-term protection to society through the immediate isolation of those who injure her. The training school does, however, provide close observation for boys who need it, but at the cost of subjecting many who do not need it to a similar close custody.

Among the unfavorable aspects are the following: (1) There is persistence of punitive motives, made evident, for example, by harsh, vindictive punishment. (2) Institutions tend to create habits of dependence in the boys when they need to learn to take initiative. (3) Routinized quasi-military programs can still be found. (4) With such mass programs the institution fails to prepare the boy for life in his home community. (5) Many institutions give the boy inadequate preparation for the difficult adjustment to its restrictions and program. (6) More important is lack of specific preparation for discharge. (7) Except so far as there is provision for more than one type of institution to which transfer may be effected, the training school inevitably involves association of the novice with the more sophisticated delinquent, with resulting criminalistic contagion. (8) The institution which houses large numbers of boys usually lacks opportunity to deal individually with the specific needs of each boy. (9) If individualization in treatment is effected, the boys often do not understand it and think it unjust that one boy be treated differently from another boy. (10) Possibly the major hindrance to success has been the quality of personnel hired in most state institutions. The most important position is that of cottage parent, but almost always these intimate associates are political employees, ill-paid, without any attractive opportunity to advance, untrained, easily discouraged, and out of sympathy with the philosophy of a truly constructive institution, which views crime as a symptom and product. They are apt to be jealous of the better-paid, professionally trained social workers, who set up the program and with whose methods they are out of sympathy. Not only is this the case, but some top professional case-work leaders never expect that these key cottage-parent positions can be made attractive to professionally trained men and women or even to the typical college graduate.

SUCCESS AND FAILURE RATES

The problems encountered in measuring adult recidivism apply likewise in assessing juvenile institutions and will not be repeated here. If anything, an even larger number of criteria of success-failure has been used in studies of juvenile institutional results than in adult studies, including such essentially undefinable ones as "satisfactory adjustment" and "temporary success."

Numerous post-institutional recidivism studies have been made since the 1930's, with results showing a range of success rates between 6 and 80 per cent. One large group of reports, however, clusters in the 60 to 70 per cent range, and another around 50 per cent.[41] The multitude of uncontrolled variables present in these studies make comparisons between institutions and over periods of time meaningless. It is likewise unreasonable to expect training schools to "achieve" success with their charges at some preconceived rate, because so many factors intimately bound up with success-failure are largely beyond their control, including such basic ones as nature of inmate population and quality of parole and of community influences encountered upon release.

Only a small fraction of society's delinquent children are ever institutionalized. Increasingly, this fraction consists of youngsters for whom treatment by other means has proved unsuccessful; it constitutes our "hopeless," hard-core cases. In view of the relatively few delinquents who pass through their doors, and in view of the dubious quality of treatment available within the 129 training schools, we cannot reasonably expect the

[41] "How Effective Are Services for the Treatment of Delinquents?" (Washington, D. C.: U. S. Children's Bureau, 1960), p. 9.

schools to play more than a very minor role in the rehabilitation of individual delinquents. Their real value, however, may lie in their role as instruments by which society from time to time underscores norms, persistent departure from which cannot be tolerated.

Suggested Readings

Cloward, Richard A., *et al. Theoretical Studies in Social Organization of the Prison.* New York: Social Science Research Council, 1960. The melancholy burden of these essays is that prisoner rehabilitation programs are probably fatally impeded by inmate social structures. The pieces contribute, however, to an understanding of the custody-treatment impasse of contemporary corrections.

Cressey, Donald R., editor. *The Prison: Studies in Institutional Organization and Change.* New York: Holt, Rinehart and Winston, Incorporated, 1961. The quality of the insights, research leads, and above all the *sociological* emphases of the 10 essays comprising this book make it of first-rate importance.

Hassler, Alfred. *Diary of a Self-Made Convict.* Chicago: Henry Regnery Company, 1954. Account of life in a federal prison, 1944–45, by a conscientious objector. He found both the food and company dull and the housing depressing, but then, he'd never been in the Army.

McCleery, Richard H. *Policy Change in Prison Management.* East Lansing, Mich.: Michigan State University Governmental Research Bureau, 1957. A study of the sociological forces set loose in a prison when a "better" administration takes over, upsetting the existing inmate system.

Nelson, Victor F. *Prison Days and Nights.* Boston: Little, Brown and Company, 1933. Probably our best account of the moral and spiritual erosion some prisoners experience in their drearily monotonous confinement.

Skyes, Gresham M. *The Society of Captives.* Princeton, N. J.: Princeton University Press, 1958. A study of New Jersey's maximum security prison at Trenton, focussing on prisoner social structures and their influences on behavior and rehabilitation.

Teeters, Negley K. *Penology from Panama to Cape Horn.* Philadelphia: University of Pennsylvania Press, 1946. Report of a personal survey of Latin American prisons. Impressionistic, but the unique flavor of Latin penology comes through.

CHAPTER 25

Prison Labor

The public image of state prisons as beehives of productive activity, with "cons" working long hours manufacturing auto tags, road signs, brooms, and clothing, is largely false. Even the few so employed seldom work more than six hours a day; three or four hours a day is more likely. The other prisoners are subjected to the demoralizing and wasteful assignment of trying to appear busy at housekeeping tasks, most of which can be completed easily in the first hour or two of the work period. Many penologists are convinced that idleness in prisons is a contributing cause of riots and other disturbances, homosexuality, and feelings of bitterness and hostility toward society. At the very least, such idleness does nothing for inmate rehabilitation and is a wasteful drain on a state's resources.

Until 30 years ago American prisons were, however, busy places, with idleness no problem except among the few prisoners unable to work. In the late '20's and early '30's a series of federal and state laws, designed to protect "free" labor and industry from alleged unfair competition arising from the public sale of prison-made goods, dealt blows to prison industries from which they have not yet recovered. However, the problem of how best to organize prison labor is one which has not been solved even after two centuries of experience with prisons. Frequent changes in theories of correction, along with shifts in the social, economic, and political milieus in which prisons have existed, not only militated against agreement on a final "solution," but virtually guaranteed that any such solution, even if reached, would soon become outmoded.[1]

A basic factor contributing to the difficulties of solving the prison labor problem has been the presence in correctional theory of divergent—and in some degree inconsistent—ideas as to the purposes of prison work:

(1) Work has often been *penal* in nature. The crank and the treadmill served this purpose, and if these are gone, the same punitive motive is seen here and there today in the use of the quarry or rockpile whether a marketable product is obtained or not. The criminal law still frequently provides "imprisonment at hard labor" as the penalty for crime, though there are instances when the "hard labor" in "workhouses" has meant almost complete idleness in the cell.

(2) Similarly, the purpose of prison labor may be to *promote discipline* in prison. Any sort of make-work is resorted to by wardens as a substitute for demoralizing idleness. At one time in Joliet prison in Illinois, for example, men were extensively set at "boon-doggling" in the form of carrying rocks in baskets across the prison yard. "Boon-doggling" keeps men occupied but probably creates attitudes almost as antisocial as idleness.

(3) Again, prison labor may aim at *maximum production* and maximum profit in order to keep within an inadequate budget. Work somewhat reduces expense, and a few prisons in the North and a good many farms and road camps in the South have been sources of income.

(4) A fourth aim of prison labor is to teach the men so-called *habits of industry*. However, such habits do not develop through the mere forced repetition of undesired and uninteresting work. Habits of industry develop when work, or at least the rewards of labor, are satisfying to the worker.

(5) More psychologically sound are the efforts to use prison labor to *teach trades* chosen by the inmate which he may follow after prison. But inmates should know the use of as many tools as possible. More importantly, they need to acquire initiative and a sense of responsibility in their work.[2] However, inmates rarely use their half-learned prison trades after release. The Gluecks [3] found that about two-thirds of reformatory men after release did not use the trades which they had been taught in the

---

[1] The above paragraphs are adapted from R. W. England, "New Departures in Prison Labor, *The Prison Journal* (Spring, 1961), p. 21.

[2] Allan L. Robbins, "Relation of Industries to Rehabilitation and Prison Administration," American Prison Association *Proceedings* (1953), pp. 61–66.

[3] *500 Criminal Careers* (New York: Alfred A. Knopf, 1930), pp. 198–99, 272.

institution, and that of the one-third who did use them, over half had worked at the same trades before imprisonment.

(6) Finally, prison labor may have as its object *the accumulation of wages by the inmates*. As a means of securing the favorable attitudes of the men, and of enabling them partially to support their families on the outside or to accumulate savings to assist them in the difficult task of adjustment after prison, prison labor might be of the greatest significance as one element in rehabilitation.

Actually the policies have been designed to provide some work which will interfere as little as possible with free industry. Today legislation almost demands that this last aim be the sole determinant of prison labor policy.

Systems of Prison Labor

Whatever their aim, prison labor systems vary in their effectiveness. Yet more important than the nature of the system in its effect on prisoner attitudes are the extent to which individual needs and preferences are considered, and the relationship of employment to life after prison.

THE LEASE SYSTEM [4]

Under the lease system, the state turns the convicts over to a private lessee who not only works them but feeds, clothes, guards, houses, and disciplines them. Authorized by law in some states before the beginning of the eighteenth century, this system flourished in the South in Reconstruction days and after. Health, morality, and every other consideration of the convicts' welfare tend to be neglected under this system, which has involved much cruelty. Scandals growing out of its abuse led to the virtual abandonment of the system in the United States, although it is still operating in at least nine countries throughout the world, in some of which restrictions surrounding its use have removed its older semi-slavery characteristics.[5]

[4] "Convict Labor in 1923," *Bulletin 372* (Washington, D. C.: *U. S. Bureau of Labor Statistics*, 1925), pp. 3–4.

[5] Department of Economic and Social Affairs, United Nations, *Prison Labour* (New York, 1955), Table 1, p. 13, and pp. 17–19.

THE CONTRACT SYSTEM

Under this system, the state feeds, clothes, houses, and guards the convict. A contractor engages with the state for the labor of the convicts, which is performed within or near the institution. The contractor pays the state a stipulated amount per capita for the services of the convicts, supplies his own raw material, and superintends the work.

The history of the contract system is one of grave abuse. Not only is there the tendency for the prison administration to be more interested in profits than in rehabilitation, but at times foremen have been ill-paid and allowed bonuses for all the work they could extract from the "slave" labor. On the other hand, prisoners may also be paid bonuses to their great advantage. "Conducted under proper supervision, a contract shop need not be any worse for the worker than a shop run by the prison." [6] Yet it is difficult for states to secure contracts which provide reasonably adequate wages and proper conditions for convicts and which will also attract the bids of contractors, whose profits tend to depend on labor exploitation. The contract system was extensively used in the early state prisons and frequently made profits above all expenses both for the state and the private contractor. Contract labor is now practically nonexistent in this country but is used abroad.[7]

THE PIECE-PRICE SYSTEM

Under the piece-price system, the contractor supplies the raw materials and pays the state a determined amount for the work done on each piece or article manufactured by the convicts. For the prisoner this system has sometimes meant the advantage of tutoring from civilian instructors hired by the state to minimize losses from poor work, but it has likewise often meant being forced to work under pressure to produce as many finished items as possible.[8] Though this system eliminates the objections to private control of convicts, it does not eliminate the difficulties associated with marketing the product. It therefore came to be as vigorously objected to by free labor as was the contract system.

[6] Louis N. Robinson, *Should Prisoners Work?* (Philadelphia: John C. Winston Co., 1931), p. 91.

[7] *Prison Labour, loc. cit.*, p. 13.

[8] *Ibid.*, p. 11.

THE PUBLIC-ACCOUNT SYSTEM

Unlike the three systems thus far discussed, five others call for public control only. "In the public-account system the State . . . buys the raw material, manufactures and puts the product on the market, and assumes all the risk of conducting a manufacturing business." [9] This system would perhaps prove the best under proper restrictions, but business and labor interests do not permit it.

THE STATE-USE SYSTEM

The most prevalent and most generally approved system of prison industries today is the state-use system.

Under this system the State conducts a business of manufacture of production, as in the public-account system, but the use or sale of the goods produced is limited to the same institution or to other State institutions. The principle of the system is that the State shall produce articles of merchandise for its own consumption alone and shall not compete directly with the business of manufacturers employing free labor. [10]

The chief purpose of the state-use system has been to avoid competition with free industry. This purpose it only partially accomplishes. Clearly, the goods made by prisoners and sold to public institutions might be made by outside industry. Yet under this system, prison-made and "free" goods do not come into direct price competition. Moreover, the state-use system requires a diversification of industries if the needs of institution and government bureaus in a single state are to be met. This diversification prevents competition from being concentrated in a few industries. Organized labor has advocated the state-use system but has been unable to prevent its constituent members from opposing prison-made goods in their particular fields. An additional difficulty is the fact that public institutions and bureaus often do not wish to purchase prison-made goods, preferring to buy the quality they wish in the cheapest market. New York prisons at one time utilized but 10 per cent of a potential $20 million market. [11] To meet this difficulty the laws of some states make the purchase of prison-made goods compulsory upon such agencies, but

[9] "Convict Labor in 1923," pp. 3–4.

[10] *Ibid.,* p. 4. Recently, however, the state-use system has been considered to have the purchases of any public authorities, whether state, national, or local, as its potential market.

[11] *Attorney General's Survey of Release Procedures,* Vol. V, "Prisons" (Washington, D. C.: Department of Justice, 1940), p. 220.

such laws have been difficult to enforce. An additional difficulty with the state-use system is its inefficiency. The atmosphere of many a state-use industry has been anything but industrious. Its administrators tend to be less willing to spend money for improved machinery, to overstaff the shops rather than to expand, and to produce inferior goods at excessive cost. Yet at the moment the state-use system is tolerated even by its critics as the only program possible because of the attitude of free labor and industrialists.

PRISON FARM WORK

Prison farms may be only small units where a few trusties or men soon to be released care for cattle and raise vegetables. Climatic conditions prevent the year-round use of convicts on any large scale in the North. In the South, however, large and sometimes profitable penal plantations have been developed, as in Texas, Louisiana, Arkansas, and Mississippi, but the plantation system is aimed at profits rather than rehabilitation of convicts. However, farm work for selected prisoners is universally advocated as an aid to the health of convicts, as a prelude to release from prison, and for its vocational value for men intending to go back to farm work.

Farmers are less well organized than industrialists and farm laborers less than factory workers. Moreover, diversification is easier in farming than in factory work. Hence there has been less opposition to the agricultural employment of inmates.

PUBLIC-WORKS-AND-WAYS SYSTEM

This system is really a form of the state-use system. We include here not only road and building construction for the state or local government, but also reforestation, prevention of soil erosion, or other forms of outdoor work. This system partly avoids competition with free industry, since it is possible to select work which is not commercially profitable and yet which may be very useful. Road-camp work has not wholly escaped opposition from construction companies.

Some of the worst examples of the abuses of the lease system were found in the chain-gang camps long maintained by lessees in the South. Often no permanent structures were built. Earlier wooden boxcar bunkhouses were replaced by crowded iron cages with two layers of bunks so low that the man could not sit up on his bed. At night, on days when the weather did not permit work, and generally from Saturday noon to Monday morning the convicts would be housed in these tight quarters.[12] The men put in charge of such road gangs were frequently not very different from the convicts themselves. The chain gang is a dying institution, and its death is to be welcomed.

At the other extreme are the best of honor conservation camps, of which those in California may be taken as an example. Prisoners in some of these camps have already served part of their sentences in prison. The program operates in conjunction with the State Highway and State Forestry Divisions and the United States Forestry Service. There are no restrictions as to the type of crime the man may have committed, although only non-violent men are eligible for the camps. Inmates receive a small wage, 20 per cent of which is set aside against their day of release; if their families are on public relief, two-thirds of the wage is applied to this support.[13] So successful has been the conservation camp program that expansion from its present population of 2,000 to more than 5,000 by 1965 is planned.[14]

Wage Payment and Other Incentives

Wage payment to prisoners may be intended merely to give incentive to production, to benefit the dependents of the men, or as a major element in a program of rehabilitation. Wage payment allegedly creates friendly attitudes, develops the feeling that one is a useful worker, and permits the accumulation of savings for the future. A 1955 survey revealed that 34 states pay wages, ranging from 4 cents a day (Kansas) to one dollar a day (Oregon). The most frequently reported range, however, was 10 to 50 cents.[15] As little as a cent and a half a day has been paid, while under a piece-rate system inmates have earned up to $25 a month. Under wartime contracts, inmates were paid from 25 to 50 cents a day.

Under the aegis of the Department of Economic and Social Affairs of the United Nations, an interesting move is afoot with respect to prisoners' wages. Contending that a sentence to imprisonment does not cancel

[12] Jesse F. Steiner and Roy M. Brown, *The North Carolina Chain Gang* (Chapel Hill, D. C.: University of North Carolina Press, 1927), pp. 16–17, *passim*.
[13] State of California Department of Corrections, *Biennial Report 1959–1960* (Sacramento, Calif., 1961), p. 16.
[14] *Ibid.*, p. 14.
[15] "What's New In Prison Industries," *Correctional Research*, Bulletin No. 6 (April 1955), Table 2, p. 12.

an individual's basic human rights to work and to payment at the customary rate, the Department is advocating an integration of prison labor with the free economy of such a nature as to allow, among other things, paying employed prisoners at the going outside rates.[16] Under certain European pre-release work schemes some promising steps in this direction are being made (see below, pp. 461–63).

Yet the prison has to rely largely upon nonmonetary incentives. In not a few states employed prisoners are paid in "good time" (reduction of sentences). Rhode Island permits an additional deduction of two days per month for satisfactory work.[17] Various other devices have been used. Assurance of assistance in securing a job after release, diplomas indicating accomplishments, and bringing inmates' skills to the attention of industrialists are among these.[18] Inmates' incentive is greatly increased when they have as much opportunity as possible to choose their type of employment in prison. To avoid jealousy and as a matter of justice, maintenance men should be paid out of profits of industry. Inmates react favorably to opportunity to assist in planning improvements.[19] Other methods of stimulating incentive have been listed as follows: fair promotion practices, emphasis on the contribution each man makes to the total product, showing the value of the work for outside employment, a sound accident program, attractive shop surroundings, care in adapting assignments to individual capacities and needs, strict avoidance of all favoritism, and provision of capable foremen who will understand and inspire their charges.[20] In the interest both of production and morale, job analyses are important. As we shall note in a later chapter, industries are essential to any program of vocational education, and the two should be coordinated.

Not all prisoners should be employed at productive labor. Some 15 per cent or more are required for maintenance; perhaps 10 per cent properly require medical care; 30 per cent are capable of trade training and may be kept in school at least half the time; while some personality deviates will do better if given special nonproductive tasks to do. Those in quarantine or reception centers or in solitary confinement are not available for

[16] United Nations, Department of Economic and Social Affairs, *The Integration of Prison Labour with the National Economy, Including the Remuneration of Prisoners* (New York, 1960).

[17] Joseph G. Ianelli, "Prison Industry Activity in Rhode Island," American Prison Association *Proceedings* (1953), pp. 71–76.

[18] Robert R. Anderson, "Employment Incentives in Prison Management," *ibid.,* (1952), pp. 192–97.

[19] J. A. McLaughlin, "Employment Incentives in Prison Management," *ibid.,* pp. 186–91.

[20] Albert C. Wagner, "Incentives in Penal Institutions," *ibid.,* pp. 179–85.

productive employment. This would leave something like two-fifths, or double the usual actual proportion, for whom productive labor would be possible.

Legal Restrictions

A series of federal laws, including the Hawes-Cooper Act of 1929 and the Ashhurst-Summers Act of 1934, designed to limit the sale of prison-made goods in the open market, culminated in the act of 1941 which forbade their shipment in interstate commerce. These laws were disastrous to prison industries. Their immediate effect was to create such idleness as never before had existed in American penal institutions. In 1935 President Roosevelt had set up the Prison Industries Reorganization Administration, which conducted surveys in nearly half the states. These investigations led to somewhat better general penal methods but did not challenge the state-use system of employment. Earlier NRA compacts with prison administrations had been drawn up and seemingly proved that industries could be organized under a system of agreed prices without serious injury to private enterprises, but these had to be given up because of violent opposition.

World War II was a temporary boon to prison industries. The idle manpower behind the walls was discovered when it was realized that maximum total production was necessary. Huge profits for many employers and full employment for workers made less insistent the traditional fear of competition from inmates. Army and Navy contracts for the production of some $138 million worth of goods by prison industries were successfully carried out.[21] Women prisoners rolled bandages and sewed for the soldiers. Men retrieved valuable copper from ship cables of the wreckage at Pearl Harbor and made army motorboats, shell cases, and so on. Hours of work in prison were increased. The war also led to experiments with the employment of inmates outside the walls, with generally favorable results.

Wardens testified to the vastly improved morale among inmates when they could share in the common war effort. A representative of Federal

[21] *American Prison Association Manual*, p. 28; Arthur G. Eaton and William H. Burke, *Prisons in Wartime* (prepared by Harry E. Barnes) (Washington, D. C.: Government Division, War Production Board, 1944); Joseph D. Lohman, "Convicted Felons as a Manpower Resource in the Present Emergency," American Prison Association *Proceedings* (1951), pp. 59–66; Charles V. Jenkinson, "Prison Labor in National Defense," *ibid.*, pp. 37–42.

Prison Industries Inc. attributed a 300 per cent increase in prison production primarily to the war incentive. With the end of the war contracts, prison idleness returned. In 1946, 30 per cent of Michigan's prison population were reported idle.

With the defense preparation of the cold war, strenuous efforts were made to secure a share in them for the forgotten men in our prisons, but largely without success. Studies made by the American Prison Association and the Penal Industries Association brought to the attention of the National Production Authority the manpower available in penal institutions and the definite types of goods and services they could provide for postwar national defense needs.[22] There was recognition by leaders in the armed services of the need to utilize this inmate manpower. A certain amount of progress was made. But the current situation is not too promising because of continuing legal restrictions.[23] Early federal laws or administrative orders of 1887 and 1905, forbidding federal employment of prisoners, were designed to prevent the national government from participating in the exploitation of convicts under the then-prevailing contract or piece-price systems, and not to restrict the use of prison labor as such. Later the restriction was changed so as not to apply to federal institutions. During both world wars the restrictions were specifically suspended as they applied to state institutions. Some recent administrative interpretations of the regulations, however, have been rather literal, so that strict conformity to them would preclude any considerable use of prison labor by the armed services. The situation is not quite clear-cut, for there seems to be some loose enforcement of the rules in terms of their original intent rather than their exact words, and the Navy has long utilized San Quentin for extensive salvage operations, difficult to provide for through the use of free labor. While other exceptions may be possible, and while in any future war the manpower resources of the prisons would undoubtedly be rediscovered and used, it appears that, as of the beginning of 1964, the problem of idleness in prisons cannot be solved through reliance on the armed services market. Hence, again, chief reliance continues to be upon the state-use system and market.

22 Cf. James W. Curran, "Prison Industries in National Defense," *ibid.,* pp. 43–47; John C. Burk, "The Use of Prison Labor in National Defense," *ibid.,* pp. 48–53; Brunswick A. Bagdon, "The Use of Prison Labor in National Defense," *ibid.,* pp. 54–58.

23 Cf. Lt. Col. Van H. Tanner, "Inmate Labor; Its Use on Projects of the Armed Forces," *Prison World* (May–June 1954), pp. 5 *ff.*

Attempts to Improve the State-Use System

Saddled, perhaps permanently, with a faulty state-use system of prison industry, administrators have striven mightily to make it serve. Such steps as the following are recommended [24] and have been made in some states: (1) survey of the needs of the prison population, (2) evaluation of the potential market in the state, (3) selection of suitable diversified activities, (4) adequate methods of assignment and realistic employment practices, (5) quality production so that state institutions will not object to purchases which are required of them, and (6) employment integrated with all the other phases of the prison program.

The basic hindrance remains the opposition of free labor and industry, but significant developments have taken place in that area, for example in California.[25] Progress in that state has come through bringing representatives of organized labor, industry, agriculture and the general public into conference, informing them of the need, and securing their cooperation. A Correctional Industries Commission made up of two representatives of each of these three interest groups has been set up, with the Director of Corrections as its chairman and seventh member. In addition it has been possible to secure the continuing cooperation of a long list of specific organizations. In this way a substantial productive enterprise was made possible in California "without opposition from any source." California public schools are expected to cooperate not only by purchasing prison goods now manufactured, but by suggesting new articles the institutions could make. On the other side, a State Coordinating Committee integrates the activities of state departments in the fields of industries, corrections, and parole. Advisory committees represent specific trades. More fundamental still is the work of a full-time public relations man employed by the Correctional Industries Commission, who heads the effort to develop among the population generally an understanding attitude toward the needs of prisoners. Even in California, however, there is still opposition from particular local business concerns and labor unions. A significant aspect of the California system has been the setting-up of small pilot experiments to do research and propose schemes for the better employment of prison inmates. As penologically advanced as it is, however,

---

[24] Cf. Frank T. Flynn, "Employment and Labor," in Tappan, *op. cit.*, pp. 245–50.

[25] For a challenging characterization of the California prison industry system, see Richard A. McGee, "Saving Prison Waste," *Annals of the American Academy of Political and Social Science* (May 1954), pp. 59–69.

California employs less than 15 per cent of its inmates in industry.[26] A few other states have had some success with efforts to work hand in hand with representatives of labor and industry. Space does not permit further detailed discussion of specific programs. For the country as a whole, the organization of the Penal Industries Association and the Correctional Educational Association has furnished leadership and publicity in this difficult aspect of the prison problem.

A Prison Labor Policy

It is an unhappy fact that the state-use system has not achieved the goals of full, diversified, and meaningful employment envisioned by its early advocates. State use was not, in its origins, a "better" system than those it replaced: it was a retreat to which prison administrations were driven by dogged opposition from labor and management groups. The administrations have had to make their peace with reality, however, by becoming spokesmen for the only system left to them. The present thinking of the American Correctional Association is to stay in the retreat, make it as comfortable as possible (with second-hand furniture), and pretend to like it. It is our contention that the problem of prison idleness cannot be solved, however, as long as we persist in trying to put the square peg of prisoner employment in the round hole of state use. At the very least, state use must be supplemented by other systems.

The utilization of prisoners by private interests was an unsavory chapter in penological history, *but the use of free workers by private interests* was nearly as unsavory. Low wages, long hours under dreary conditions, and harsh supervision characterized workingmen's lives during most of the early and middle stages of the industrial revolution. The conscienceless exploitation of prisoners in the nineteenth century under the contract, lease, and piece-price systems was a reflection of general values of the time. The determination of American prison administrators to repudiate any suggestion that private interests again play a role in prisoner employment [27] needs re-examination in the light of present economic and social realities. The increasing democratization of industry, higher living standards for the masses, legislative safeguards against exploitation, and the

[26] *Biennial Report 1959–1960*, p. 24.

[27] This attitude was reasserted at an international correctional congress in 1955; see United Nations, Department of Economic and Social Affairs, *First United Nations Congress on the Prevention of Crime and the Treatment of Offenders* (New York, 1956), p. 33.

general trend toward welfare statism reflect basic value changes in Western cultures. Granting that all of our social problems have by no means been solved, the deplorable industrial conditions of the past are vastly improved in the present, and the fear that the reintroduction of private interests in prison labor would revive past abuses seems to us to lack reasonable foundation.

Three possible lines of development for the rejuvenation of prison employment deserve exploration:

(1) Modifying of federal and local laws regulating the public sale of prison-made goods, together with measures taken to equalize production expenses with those in private enterprise—including, perhaps, the payment of standard wages to prisoners. The production and marketing of such goods under the *expertise* of private entrepreneurial interests might be desirable.

(2) The production and marketing of prison goods for state use under private auspices. Poor quality control and the absence of vigorous marketing practices partly account for the paucity of state-use output. Prison industrial managers, unlike those in private industry, no longer stand or fall on their capacity to show a profit, and it might be useful to reinstitute this "capitalistic" test of efficiency. It seems to us unfortunate that prisons should be so insulated from the values of private industry that the powerful drive imparted by those values is inoperable.

(3) Extra-mural private employment of prisoners. The practice of allowing unguarded prisoners to go forth daily to work for private employers is not new. Jessie Hodder and her successor, Miriam Van Waters, used such a system for many years after 1910 at the Massachusetts Reformatory for Women; under Wisconsin's Huber Law of 1913, hundreds of jailed misdemeanants annually work for private employers, returning to their cells each night. It is in Europe, however, that this system finds most of its champions. Beginning in Sweden in 1945, selected felony prisoners in seven countries may now work privately away from their prisons during the day under conditions approximating those of free men, even to the extent of benefiting from social security protection. Their wages, paid at the going free rates, are budgeted by the prison administrations for dependents, savings, debts, and room and board.[28] From experimental beginnings in 1957, North Carolina's prisons are now permitting

---

[28] *Prison Labour*, pp. 22–26. The seven countries are Sweden, Great Britain, Norway, Denmark, the Netherlands, France, and West Germany, the last-named starting its program in 1959 at a new open institution for male felons in Frankfurt am Main [see "Letters to the Editor," *Federal Probation* (March 1961), pp. 65–66].

more than 300 inmates to hold outside jobs as barbers, mechanics, cooks, secretaries, and farm laborers. All inmates serving five years or less and who are not sex offenders, alcoholics, or drug addicts are eligible for the program.[29]

Suggested Readings

Ball, Roy S. "Operations Suitable for Correctional Industries," in *Proceedings (1960) of the American Correctional Association*. New York: The Association, 1961, pp. 240–48. The problems peculiar to prison industries are briefly but cogently examined.

"Institutional Employment" in *Manual of Correctional Standards*. New York: American Correctional Association, 1959. The "official" thinking on the subject by practitioners and prison administrators.

Lopez-Rey, Manuel. "Some Considerations on the Character and Organization of Prison Labour," *Journal of Criminal Law, Criminology, and Police Science* (May–June 1958). A far-reaching essay in support of the position that only by integrating prison labor with free labor can the rehabilitative potential of prison labor be realized.

Robinson, Louis N. *Should Prisoners Work?* Philadelphia: John C. Winston Company, 1931. One of the very few full-scale studies of the subject, but of only limited value after 30 years.

[29] *Time* (Sept. 14, 1962), p. 33.

CHAPTER 26

The Prison Community as a Possible Socializing Agency

Three decades ago academic and popular writers on penology, pointing to the discouragingly high recidivism rates of conventional prisons, began promoting the idea that maximum security prisons had "outlived their usefulness," were "archaic" remnants of out-moded punitive doctrines, and should be abandoned. Overcrowded, their prisoners unable to work because of new restrictive legislation on prison products, ruled internally by big-city racketeers, and their officials subjected to brazen political interference, the dismal failure of the old-line prison called for its replacement by enlightened measures. The extensive use of probation and other measures short of imprisonment, and the increased use during the last three decades of less severe forms of incarceration, while reducing the proportion of convicted persons detained in old-line prisons, by no means signify their imminent abandonment. Substantial numbers of felons will continue to crowd their yards and cells for many years to come, as our growing American culture continues to generate offenders requiring maximum custody.

Are these prisons hopeless, except for their incapacitating function? The purpose of this chapter is to discuss two related matters: (1) the findings and the significance for treatment of recent researches into the nature of prison social structures and (2) the utilization of this knowledge for forms of treatment,

464

mainly so-called group therapy, which holds some promise that even old-line prisons can yet be of positive value. To salvage something from such prisons requires that we know the effect of the prison regime upon inmate behavior. One must also know the group relations prisoners have had before commitment; the attitudes and values they bring with them as they enter prison; and those which characterize them in the old-line institution. We must know the culture and structure of inmate society. Knowing this, cautious estimates may be made of the potentialities for socialization of types of inmate populations and types of institutional programs. Knowledge of the peer-group origins of a vast amount of our criminal patterns on the outside has strongly suggested constructive use of natural or planned inmate subgroups for the purpose of socialization. The partial success of group therapy, the greater success of groups like Alcoholics Anonymous, and the accomplishments of community organization in institutions like Chino in California, with its planned relations with the outside community, have underlined the potentialities of this rather new community and subgroup approach.

We shall tentatively suggest how a somewhat fuller use of knowledge of group values and inmate leadership might make these promising new beginnings still more successful. We shall then emphasize the need to make the entire institutional program consistent with its aspects of group therapy and community organization. Further, we shall stress the importance of relating the prison community to the outside community, as the federal institution at Seagoville, Texas, and the state institution at Chino have tried to do.

On the one hand, we need to realize that what is possible along these lines with a selected population such as that of Seagoville and Chino may not be equally possible in institutions like Jackson or Leavenworth, which house either a more dangerous or more mixed population. On the other hand, we must avoid the error of assuming that the principles of community organization and utilization of group experience are applicable only to a small selected group of inmates. The men in a maximum security institution are just as much group products and seem as amenable to use of adapted types of group organization as those in our open-type correctional institutions with inmates selected for this purpose. Finally we must not fail to note that a program of socialization ideally begins in childhood and continues all along the line to the final effort to fit the ex-prisoner into the life of the community into which he is released. It is appropriate to stress the institutional level of the program, however, because inmates at least may be more fully controlled on the inside than, for example, when on parole on the outside.

The Selected Population of the Old-Line Prison

To the selection involved in the fact that prison inmates are convicts is added that which results from the development of separate institutions for men and women, children and adults, first and habitual offenders, sick and well, mentally normal and feeble-minded or psychotic. Paradoxical though it may seem, the most distinctive characteristic of prisoners is not that they are criminals. Uncaught predatory criminals of the usual types, white-collar criminals, and noncriminal exploiters are mostly outside of prison. The *distinctive* characteristic of prisons is that their population is *looked upon* as criminal. The distinction is vast and important. Prisoners have had the common experience of court conviction; they are supposed to have the common attitude of guilt. In such a situation some inmates do feel guilty and develop defenses against guilt feelings. Others probably have little sense of guilt, because they feel the support of groups which accept values which justify crime.

One could hardly find a group less promising for social unity than that in the typical prison. For prisoners do not generally trust one another. The prison community is divided against itself. It is still less promising as a preparation for adjustment to the larger community, where cohesion is based upon the acceptance of social values opposite to some though not all which characterize the prison community. The prison community is thus abnormal in the nature of its social bonds.

As a one-sex community, the prison is abnormal. Men's personalities become strangely warped whenever they try to get along for long periods without the gentler sex. Important, yet less important here, is the physiological effect of the absence of women. Sex expression is one gratification denied the prisoner which is not denied even the slave. Put the most normally adjusted men in a womanless society and there will be increased resort to substitutes for the normal sex relationship. Autoerotic practices are prevalent in prison. Probably prisoners generally share society's disapproval of homosexual relationships. Yet there is naturally a relative tolerance of perversion by the prison community generally. Whether their marital adjustment is jeopardized or not, most prisoners do not continue homosexual practices after release. At any rate no one can comprehend the prison experience without feeling the significance of deprivation of sex.

Is it any wonder . . . that the prisoner should seek relief in any available form? . . . It is merely a matter of satisfying as best he can the hunger which besets him. I mean a hunger not only for sexual intercourse, but a hunger for the voice, the touch, the laugh, the tears of Woman; . . . Woman is, speaking generally, the civilizing, the refining, the cleansing agent of the community. Deprived of contact with her, the prisoner inevitably becomes coarsened, ill-mannered, lowered in any number of ways.[1]

In prison men are starved for the companionship of wife, children, or friends. At the least, prison spells a continuance of a significant void in the prisoner's past affectional life. At the worst, it cuts him off from conscious associations which give life a goal and meaning, and from his most social motivations. A prison without children removes from the horizon completely a primary source of human tenderness, the significance of which for socialization cannot be measured. The absence of both children and the aged in prison also prevents the development of relations of dependence and protection which are part of the socializing influence of a normal society. Relationships such as develop between cellmates and in prison cliques play an exaggerated role in the life of the prisoner because of the absence of wife and family.

Visits between prisoners and their spouses, valuable for maintaining family ties and for relieving some of the tensions generated under sexual deprivation, must be adjusted to the limitations imposed by maximum security plants and requirements. Such prisons are often remote from population centers or are difficult to get to by public transport which spouses without access to automobiles must use. Drab, ill-lighted rooms in which the visitants are separated by glass, wire mesh, or other barriers under the eyes and ears of guards are commonly found. Visits not exceeding two hours monthly are the usual pattern.[2] Conjugal visits, in which a husband and wife may be together privately, are unknown in the United States. One state—Mississippi—lets prisoners go home for 10-day periods after serving three years with good conduct.[3] No fewer than eight European countries allow periodic home leaves for selected prisoners, a privilege likewise found in some Latin-American countries.[4] Conjugal prison visiting is permitted in two Mexican prisons, and Sweden apparently allows it for minimum security men.[5]

[1] Victor Nelson, *Prison Days and Nights* (Boston: Little, Brown, 1933), pp. 143 and 149. Cf. also Robert M. Lindner, "The Inmate Tells His Story," chap. 22 of his *Stone Walls and Man* (New York: Odyssey Press, 1946).

[2] Eugene Zemans and Ruth Shonle Cavan, "Marital Relationships of Prisoners," *Journal of Criminal Law, Criminology and Police Science* (May–June 1958), p. 51.

[3] *Ibid.,* p. 52.

[4] Ruth Shonle Cavan and Eugene Zemans, "Marital Relationships of Prisoners in 28 Countries," *Journal of Criminal Law, Criminology and Police Science* (July–Aug. 1958), pp. 135, 136.

[5] *Ibid.,* pp. 134, 137. It is said that some wardens of Latin American prisons permit prostitutes to visit inmates, not as a pattern of corruption but because, in the wardens' view, prisoners have an inalienable right to heterosexual outlets.

Attitudes of Incoming Prisoners

Our picture of life in the prison community is largely derived from what is still the classic study by Donald Clemmer, *The Prison Community*. That book seems to differ from more recent studies chiefly in that it emphasizes, probably with reason, the lack of unity and mutual confidence among inmates. Says Clemmer of a prison in southern Illinois: "The great bulk of the . . . population is composed of awkward, amateurish and occasional offenders," [6] with possibly 20 per cent professionals. Popularly classed together as "crooks," these men may be first offenders entering a dreaded but unknown experience or recidivists returning to an accustomed scene. Rural and urban, dependent and self-supporting, from the suburb and from the slums, beloved and despised, lone wolves and gangsters, backed by powerful interests and quite deserted—the motley crew have had varying past experiences which imply some contrasts in the attitudes with which they enter the prison gate. Varying attitudes are also to some extent implicit in variations in the crimes they have committed. A banker caught in shady financial deals in which he and his associates have been engaged for a decade; someone who was the unlucky member of a group of men who mistook or disregarded the age of an essentially willing young girl; the real, but rare and much misunderstood "sex fiend"; a young robber whose delinquencies began with stealing bits of pipe out of vacant houses; a professional pickpocket whose usually reliable fix has at last failed him because of a change in the political complexion of the police force or the prosecuting attorney's office; a murderer whose irrational jealousy has led him to apply the unwritten law or who has killed in self-defense when committing robbery; the rare professional killer; a half-demented farm hand who stumbled into trouble not really knowing what it was all about; the less-often incarcerated racketeer and the still-more-rarely caught white-collar criminal—each of these must react to imprisonment a bit differently.

By reason of his imprisonment, the inmate has crossed the subjectively very real, but objectively very ill-defined, line supposed to separate the citizen from public enemies. Thus classed as a crooked stick amid essentially straight timber, the criminal entering prison knows that he is rather unlikely ever to be able to obtain social recognition again as a trustworthy associate, and this sometimes somewhat regardless of his own future behavior.

Unconscious of his own more subtle motivations, the inmate exag-

[6] Donald Clemmer, *The Prison Community* (Boston: Christopher Publishing House, 1940), p. 56. This book is now available in paperback (New York: Rinehart and Company, 1958).

gerates the "excuses" he finds in the immediate conditions which influenced his act. The crankiness of his wife, the stimulus of too much whisky, the "just" rage produced by ill-luck in gambling, his envy at the easy money obtained with impunity not only by other criminals but by exploiters not classified by society as criminals—such "causal factors," superficial and inadequate as they are, must be very clear in the consciousness of the criminal entering prison. Some prison administrators consider such "excuses" as unfounded in fact. Careful study shows they are a mixture of rationalization and truthful explanation.

Almost all prisoners must enter the gate with some sense of failure and defeat. They may be remorseful over their behavior or they may be regretful only that they were caught. As a believer in luck, the prisoner considers himself the victim of a "bad break" in the gamble of life. The more intelligent prisoners have rationalized upon life's experiences and often hold, as we have seen, that everyone has a racket, their own criminal careers being but one of the more open forms of rackets. On the other hand, the great mass of "scissorbills" do not philosophize but just "take it."

With such a setting, that criminals enter prison with a considerable degree of resentment is not surprising. This resentment may be directed toward family, associates, police, court officials, the world in general, or, in a measure, themselves. Whatever the dominating motive of the penal system, they feel that they are being punished. This feeling has probably been impressed upon them by their police, jail, and court experiences. They do not usually see in the prison cell, rock pile, and regimented routine, nor even in the prison's schoolrooms and shops, an opportunity to be embraced, but rather forced discipline to be endured.

Social Life and Control

In the 23 years since Clemmer's *The Prison Community* was published, the sociological literature on the subject has grown considerably.[7] Working within the general sociological premise that individual behavior is heavily,

[7] Some representative books and articles are: Clarence Schrag, "Leadership Among Prison Inmates," *American Sociological Review* (Feb. 1954), pp. 37–42; Lloyd W. McCorkle and Richard R. Korn, "Resocialization within Walls," *Annals of the American Academy of Political and Social Science* (May 1954), pp. 88–98; Richard T. McCleery, *Policy Change in Prison Management* (East Lansing, Mich.: Michigan State University Governmental Research Bureau, 1957); Gresham M. Sykes, *The Society of Captives* (Princeton, N. J.: Princeton University Press, 1958); Richard A. Cloward, Donald R. Cressey, George H. Grossner, Richard McCleery, Lloyd E. Ohlin, Gresham M. Sykes, and Sheldon Messinger, *Theoretical Studies in Social Organization of the Prison* (New York: Social Science Research Council, 1960).

if not entirely, shaped by the groups with which one identifies, and that group characteristics are produced in part by intergroup relationships, considerable light has been shed on a number of hitherto obscure aspects of prison life. Some of these features have operated to block correctional efforts; recidivating offenders, usually labeled "hardened" or "intractable," with the implication that deep-rooted personality quirks account for their repeated failure to be affected by treatment efforts, may actually be insulated from these efforts by a barrier of social forces arising naturally within any maximum security prison. Clemmer's original findings have been generally confirmed, except that most researches have implied that the inmate population is more united and homogeneous than Clemmer found it to be.

Clarence Schrag,[8] studying inmate leadership in a Washington state prison, characterized the inmates as generally choosing leaders whose behavior expressed hostility to the administration. However, he also found various minority groups with less hostile attitudes, which could be sent to smaller institutions where they might be willing to cooperate in constructive programs. McCleery,[9] investigating North Carolina's Central Prison, found it possible, though with great difficulty, to gain rapport even with incorrigible inmates and recidivists hostile to the repressive regime of the institution. He found opposition to the prison staff, hatred for the "rat," and a pervading sense of injustice. McCleery seems to consider inmate "excuses" to be in some measure based on fact and not as mere rationalizations. McCorkle and Korn,[10] basing their views on considerable experience as administrators of correctional institutions, explain inmate conflict attitudes as due to a need to rationalize painful guilt feelings rather than the result of real experiences. For an inmate to accept "treatment," he must first accept the definition of himself as a person *needing* treatment, that is, as one properly rejected and cast aside by society. As a defense against such an ego-shattering experience, the inmate is apt to deny the validity of this rejection and, in so doing, deny the need for treatment. This "rejecting of the rejectors" necessarily produces negative attitudes toward prison personnel, who are daily reminders of the inmates' outcast status. McCorkle and Korn insist, however, that a tough prison tends to confirm such erroneous inmate rationalizations by giving prisoners something real to gripe about. On the other hand, these particular writers hold that sympathetic psychiatrists and counselors also tended to confirm these

[8] *Loc. cit.,* pp. 37–42.
[9] Richard McCleery, "The Strange Journey," *University of North Carolina Extension Bulletin* (March 1953), pp. 1–63.
[10] Lloyd W. McCorkle and Richard Korn, *loc. cit.,* pp. 88–98.

rationalizations by partly justifying them and thus taking sides with the inmates against the custodial staff. The need, as McCorkle and Korn see it, is for both types of staff leaders to combine in an effort to disabuse inmates of their faulty rationalizations.

An alternative explanation of the source of anti-personnel attitudes among inmates is offered by Gresham Sykes.[11] Without intending to do more than deprive incarcerated offenders of their liberty so far as "punishment" is concerned, society inadvertently visits upon the prisoner additional deprivations: he is reduced to a state of impoverishment in which little comforts become luxuries; he is deprived of heterosexual relationships; his right of self-direction is lost; the presence of rough, aggressive fellow prisoners means the loss of security.

And however painful these frustrations or deprivations may be in the immediate terms of thwarted goals, discomfort, boredom, and loneliness, they carry a more profound hurt as a set of threats or attacks which are directed against the very foundations of the prisoner's being. The individual's picture of himself as a person of value—as a morally acceptable, adult male who can present some claim to merit in his material achievements and his inner strength—begins to waver and grow dim. Society did not plan this onslaught, it is true, and society may even "point with pride" to its humanity in the modern treatment of the criminal. But the pains of imprisonment remain and it is imperative that we recognize them, for they provide the energy for the society of captives as a system of action.[12]

Whichever explanation is correct, it appears that in an old-line prison with an unselected inmate population and repressive policy, generally hostile attitudes are to be expected; that nevertheless a proper approach by an outsider can gain rapport and partially overcome this hostility; and that types of inmates may be found from whom cooperation may be hoped for when they are housed with others of their sort and are not obliged to follow the "big-shot" leadership of the most hostile inmates in a mixed population. At any rate, knowledge of the prison community and of inmate group values, attitudes, and types of preferred leadership is requisite to an effective institutional program of socialization.

Classification and orientation procedures are not always understood by the man entering prison. He may have contempt for the "bug-doctor" and his fraternity. Not infrequently, however, the new prisoner finds in the classification staff, sometimes for the first time in his life, men of understanding who show appreciation of his problems without condemnation of his acts.

[11] Sykes, *op. cit.,* chap. 4.
[12] *Ibid.,* p. 79.

After the classification procedure, life in the typical old-line prison community becomes a matter of monotonous routine. Men have numbers rather than names. There is routine response to bells and curt orders; routine counts, marching, assignments; even routine eating and sleeping with little or no personal choice. To most people the end of the day's work brings a moderate sense of satisfaction; to prisoners in many American institutions it means only a return to the cells after perhaps a bit of exercise or ball-throwing in the yard. Lights go out in the cells at the same time, commonly at nine o'clock. Thus a prisoner may neither retire comfortably earlier than others, nor may he stay up later than others, no matter what his tiredness, the condition of his health, or his personal desire.

Such an old-line prison is impersonal. There is an inescapable atmosphere of moral contagion within which a social aspiration or a beautiful thought can scarcely be born. Human personality is there suffocated. Inhuman acts seem at home and thrive like weeds. Watching eyes, suspicious glances, numbers in place of names, doors to enter but not to leave, commands and oaths in place of requests and commendation, unwilling compliance to escape punishment, shuffling lines of men, silent meals, overlooking gun turrets, noisily clanging steel doors, uncertain day of escape, blank futures—these are among the elements which symbolize the curse society has uttered upon those who have broken her laws.

The curse of the prison is relative, and many of the above elements are relatively lacking in our better institutions. But the psychological impact of being imprisoned is universal.[13]

The new prisoner enters not only as an individual but as a person— as a member of social groups on the outside. He may have been a family man, a gang member, a neighbor, a member of a labor group in a shop, an habitué of sundry "hangouts" where, with others, he has shared a common group experience. This socially determined person enters prison, however, as an individual with reference to fellow prisoners and the prison world.

Of course life becomes social for him in a sense during the first night, as he identifies himself to his cell partner or partners. His offense, his attitude toward it, his degree of sophistication—such characteristics place the "fish," or new man, tentatively in the hierarchy of the esteem or disesteem of prison society. Moreover, it gradually dawns on the "fish" that it is to this new prison world—this new hierarchy of social values—to which he *must* adjust himself. Its praise or blame, its applause or ridicule, will come largely to dominate his judgment and behavior. Inmate society de-

[13] Cf. Tom Runyan, *In for Life* (New York: W. W. Norton & Company, 1953).

velops its own notions of how fast a man should work, what nicknames to apply to guards, what type of behavior is to be approved or condemned, and so on. These notions may conflict with the imposed rules. Individuals may differentiate themselves from the mass of prisoners in some of their private thoughts. But their overt behavior cannot disregard prison opinion.

All this implies the development and enforcement of the inmate prison code.[14] This code "runs" the prison in some types of social relationships as completely as does the will of the most dictatorial of wardens. Indeed, the warden himself is in a measure subject to it. It is nevertheless not easy to define clearly, a consistent, definite code covering all situations and common to the prison community as a whole. Prisoners have all been in a sense enemies of society, but that does not imply that they have all been friends of one another. Criminals in reality have been not only antisocial but also anticriminal, except where they have been united in a loyalty to a particular gang. The prison situation serves imperfectly to unite this army divided against itself, not because its members are all criminals, but because they are all under punishment. This prison code is a conflict code. Even as such, it is a rather weak code, since there is always the possibility that it will be broken when its violation means the favor of the deputy warden. Prisoners are suspicious of the prison administration; but they are often equally suspicious of one another. Very often values in the prison code include no unnecessary converse with the guards and fierce condemnation of informers or "rats."

An interesting evidence of the lack of traditional American loyalty for the institution of which one is a member is the fact that prisoners usually "root" for the opposing side when the prison team plays football or baseball. Prisoners feel regret that they are at Sing Sing or Joliet, whereas students are proud of their identification with Notre Dame or Old Nassau.

Inmates for the most part have had a very poor education in cooperation and loyalty except that developed in the gang. Moreover, the temptation to disloyalty is tremendous. A hated warden may walk in safety across a prison yard partly because the man who would attack him knows that another prisoner would come to the warden's rescue, not because he loves the warden, but because such an act might bring a reward which would mean earlier partial or complete escape from the hell of prison. Thus the code of loyalty has almost universal lip approval, but is daily violated.

Within the limits of the situation, small groups of twos and threes are found with affiliations based upon such factors as "mutual home background, association in crime, expressed or unexpressed homosexual attrac-

[14] Cf. Clemmer, *op. cit.,* chap. 7, *passim.*

tion, mutual toleration by a forced propinquity, the wish of a submissive personality to share in the prestige of a notorious and dominant one, and groups who plot and plan for future crimes." [15] Prisoners distinguish different types of inmates who tend to gravitate together or who are isolated by the authorities: such as the "fish," newcomers; the "hoosiers," the general run of relatively stupid, colorless inmates; the "stools," those who will inform upon other prisoners; and the "right guys," who are both more loyal and more stable than the majority. Such groups are the basis for somewhat conflicting attitudes in spite of the common punishment situation.

Leaders in the old-line prison are those whose previous crimes and prison behavior symbolize the conflict between inmates and administration. Clemmer [16] found other approved qualities in leaders to include: courage; generosity; modesty; education; an interesting vocabulary; personal cleanliness; clever gambling; the ability to "con" (fool) officials; a reputation for holding liquor; possession of money with which luxuries could be dispensed; a large body of knowledge about a particular technique of crime; a fund of vulgar jokes; the possession of attitudes against the judiciary, the prison administration, the parole board, and God; demonstrable sophistication in female companionship as evidenced by suggestive letters; the dignity and poise which come to some men after long years of prison life; participation in a spectacular crime, riot, or escape; a great capacity for eating; the ability to turn handsprings, seduce younger men, and play a guitar!

Certain general moods result from life in prison. There is first the pervasive prison stupor, listlessness, and failing power of attention. The experienced visitor can sense it in the slouching gait of the marching lines of men, the dull make-time demeanor of shop workers and maintenance men, the extraordinary effort required to arouse any interest in the classroom. The prison stupor is far more general than any definite mental breakdown, which is partly prevented by the protective shield of the other convicts.

The inmate finds in prison a "new morality"—a new concept of respectability in terms of which he has a place. The discovery of relativity in the moral realm is a bit comforting to the immoral. Yet the prisoner never quite loses his sense of being a condemned man. By the same token, any sense of contrition which the inmate may have felt on entering is dulled as a result of life in the prison community. The prison experience does, no

---

[15] Donald Clemmer, "Leadership Phenomena in a Prison Community," *Journal of Criminal Law and Criminology* (March–April 1938), p. 863.

[16] *Ibid.*, p. 867.

doubt, intensify the feeling that it was a great mistake to get caught. But neither this realization nor mere remorse implies reformation. Reformation implies socialization—a positive desire to cooperate, rather than to exploit others. Moreover—and this would seem to be important—reformation requires support of a group, like Alcoholics Anonymous, made up of men who will give status to members who want to overcome a pattern of behavior which the group agrees is undesirable. It seems to be this fact which psychotherapy often misses. After a number of prison experiences, inmates know that "crime does not pay," but by that time, for many, there is little alternative to crime.

Of all prisoner attitudes, none is more significant, it seems, than the view of the more intelligent inmate that every man has a racket. Even authorities administering our penal institutions are included in the prisoner's definition of racketeer. Thus Nelson quotes an old-timer:

What I say is, everything's a racket nowadays—lawyers, judges, district attorneys, welfare workers, ministers, mayors, and governors. . . . They're all out for the dough just like we are.[17]

The reader will recognize the gross exaggeration in such a statement as the above. He will also see a large element of truth in it. Some convicts recognize that not all "respectable" citizens are "racketeers." Moreover, Clemmer feels that the typical criminal of the underprivileged class does not know enough to believe that everyone has a racket.

Use of Knowledge for Socialization

If both crime and the avoidance of crime are group products, it is logical that correctional programs use inmate groups for the purpose of socialization. The group therapy movement in its various forms is a promising effort to do this. Similarly, if life in the abnormal, old-line prison community "prisonizes"[18] and further desocializes its inmate body, an attempt should be made to provide a normal and better-than-normal "new-line" prison community designed to have an opposite effect. Approximations to normal community life are being attempted for selected inmates in our most progressive correctional institutions. Moreover, here and there, the necessarily abnormal institution is being made less so by the

[17] Nelson, *op. cit.*, chap. 2, *passim.*
[18] Clemmer's term for the process through which inmates in the old-line institution perforce become adjusted to the abnormal prison community and hence ill-prepared for adjustment to the normal outside community.

developing relations between its members and citizens of outside communities.

Group therapy, or "guided group interaction," [19] as it is called in New Jersey, has been defined as the use of free discussion to re-educate the delinquent to accept the restrictions of society and to find satisfaction in conforming to "social norms." Conformity in the sense of obedience to law is, of course, the opposite of crime and as such is a logically desirable institutional goal. As we note elsewhere, however, conformity is not synonymous with socialization, which implies that satisfaction comes only when the individual cooperates with rather than exploits his associates. Criminals have often conformed too well to the values their gangs have taught them. Hence group therapy which socializes is an even more basic protection against crime than that which teaches conformity to mores and obedience to the law.

Types of group therapy may usefully be classified according to the degree to which treatment is individual-centered and psychiatric, or group-centered and sociological. Though psychiatrists increasingly have acknowledged the group, they still have a tendency to look for the cure of behavior problems in the interpersonal relations established between the therapist and each inmate in the group. In previous chapters we have indicated that modern psychiatry has discovered the group and utilizes group therapy. Psychiatric group therapy is not synonymous, however, with the community and group approach suggested above.

A 1959 survey found that about half of 220 correctional institutions in the United States responding to a questionnaire use group therapy in one form or another,[20] a considerable increase since a previous survey in 1950. A shift was observed toward greater use ("almost half") of the psychoanalytical approach, despite the fact that only 19 per cent of those conducting group therapy sessions are psychologists or psychiatrists.

Group therapy is usually an adjunct to individual therapy. The therapist, still relying primarily upon his own expert knowledge and his emotional relationship with a patient, seeks to supplement his own influence with that of a group. The group he utilizes is an artificial creation of his own. It is not a natural group; it is not only composed of other inmates, but of inmates with personality problems. The therapist recognizes that to use this method he must not only have rapport with the individual but ideally must be accepted by the prison groups to which the inmate

[19] Cf. Lloyd McCorkle, "Group Therapy," in Paul W. Tappan, *Contemporary Correction* (New York: McGraw-Hill Book Company, 1951), chap. 14.

[20] Lloyd W. McCorkle and Albert Elias, "Group Therapy in Correctional Institutions," *Federal Probation* (June 1960), p. 58.

belongs. The therapist may or may not know much about the previous group life of the inmate, but he does not rely primarily on the use of that knowledge, nor on the use of quasi-natural groups in prison, nor upon planning for known specific group relations in the free community. He hopes that the patient will transfer his attachment to the therapist, who acts as a sort of father substitute. Thus he hopes the inmate will come to adopt the therapist's ideals in place of his own. The therapist may also recognize that the group benefits the inmate by reducing his isolation and affording him a permissive atmosphere where he may relieve his tensions. The inmate talks out his personal problems and discovers that his are not unique. He loses some of his resentment when the therapist does not condemn him. If his fellow inmates condemn him, he may pass the same moral judgments on them.

Sometimes the inmate is even permitted to act somewhat violently in ways not tolerated in the institution generally or in the outside community. Yet McCorkle and Korn [21] hold that such a method may confirm inmate tendencies to make rational excuses for their crimes and their institutional misbehavior and tends toward conflict between the custodial staff and the therapists. They hold that the purpose of therapy is to make the inmate dispense with his rationalizations and realize the trouble is in himself. Such a view is individual-centered in another and more basic sense. It appears to overlook the fact that *some,* though not all, inmate excuses may be based on real grievances. Psychiatric group therapy is a modification of individual therapy. It deals with artificial, not natural, groups except, perhaps, when voluntary membership implies an element of naturalness.

The sociologist deals with existing natural groups, though he may also attempt to stimulate the organization of new natural groups. He recognizes that at best the prison is a very abnormal and artificial community. He sees that the subgroups which form temporarily in prison are quasi-natural rather than truly natural groups. He tries to make the prison community as much like a free community as conditions will permit. He utilizes knowledge of pre-prison group life. He utilizes, when appropriate, some of the quasi-natural subgroups which form in prison. He tries to plan the prison program with reference to the adjustment of inmates after release to the natural communities to which they will return.

Complete organization of the prison as a community such as we have imagined has nowhere been fully achieved. The sociologist feels that the criminal is largely the product of past association in groups. He therefore feels that the best hope for rehabilitation lies in resocialization through

[21] *Op. cit.*

improved association. The ideal place for such resocialization is certainly not in prison but in a free community before the prison has been reached. Nevertheless, if the prison is not to give up all effort at constructive aid, it logically should create such desirable association. Psychiatric group therapy perhaps has the advantage of calling for less of a break with penal traditions; but in every other respect sociological group organization seems more in line with what we know about the causes of crime.

Examples of Group Therapy in Correctional Institutions

The potentialities of treatment related to the group life of inmates would seem to be great, but this by no means should lead us to minimize the favorable results of more individual-centered group therapy. An example of an intermediate type is that at the Iowa State Prison at Ft. Madison.[22] Small groups of inmates who have voluntarily joined sit in an intimate circle where each may observe the rest. Starting with the "what" of some inmate's personal or behavior problem, the group progresses to the "why" of it. The problem is often that of violent behavior. Encouraged to write their life histories in their cells, the members of the group discover, through discussion, ways to avoid "running their motors" (hasty emotional reactions). They find they have often reacted angrily to mere words rather than to objective reality. They learn to avoid tension through physical exercises in their cells which relax their muscles. The group thus experiences the cathartic effect of talking problems out, the esprit de corps which comes from intimate group association, and some knowledge of the causes of their problems. Unlike the New Jersey groups, Iowa inmates never discuss the problems of others unless requested to do so.

In New Jersey institutions group therapy has been widely used for some years. It is most thoroughly applied at Highfields, an isolated former private estate to which selected teenage delinquents are sent for short stays as a condition of their probation. Every inmate must attend one of two 90-minute therapy sessions held each weekday evening, following a day's work at a nearby institution. The treatment philosophy guiding the therapy efforts has been described in *The Highfields Story,*[23] written by

[22] Cf. Walter A. Lunden, "Antagonism and Altruism Among Prisoners: From Antagonism to Altruism Through Group Therapy," in Pitirim A. Sorokin, *Forms and Techniques of Altruistic and Spiritual Growth* (Boston: Beacon Press, 1954). See also Charles C. Graves, "Group Therapy: Principles and Practice," paper read before the Gamma Chapter of Alpha Kappa Delta, Jan., 24, 1951.

[23] Lloyd W. McCorkle, Albert Elias, and F. Lovell Bixby, *The Highfields Story,* (New York: Henry Holt, 1958).

three New Jersey correctional officials under whom the program developed. The kinds of problems presented by the Highfields boys, they point out, "seems to stem from the boys' conception of self and others as hostile, aggressive, inadequate persons, and as 'hipsters,' 'wise guys,' 'squares,' and 'suckers.' The Highfields program is organized to change and modify these distorted images of self and other people." [24] Through a process of "guided group interaction" each boy is exposed to a social experience "where, in concert with his peers and the leader, he can freely discuss, examine, and understand his problems of living, without the threats that had been so common in his previous learning experiences." [25] After several stumbling and unsatisfactory initial sessions—a necessary prelude to the development of a socio-psychological atmosphere favorable to attitude change—the boys begin a shrewd examination of each others' self-images and ego defenses, which, combined with the group dynamics peculiar to the institution, leads in many cases to modifications of images and defenses in more realistic and socially acceptable directions.

Does the system work? Although the results are not entirely conclusive, they show that 83 per cent of 240 boys who completed retraining periods at Highfields between 1950 and 1955 made successful community adjustments. A study of matched groups of boys sent respectively to Highfields and to Annandale Farms Reformatory indicated a recidivism rate among the latter which was approximately double that among the former.[26]

The sociologist [27] feels that the full potentiality of the group approach has by no means been realized. As it exists in our penal institutions, group therapy has rarely taken account of the group origin of crime. It has not been preceded, apparently, by a systematic survey of the past group relations of inmates. Nor has there been careful study of their attitudes, beliefs, codes, and leadership preferences in prison, such as Clemmer, Sykes, McCleery, and others have furnished. Little attempt has been made to use natural groups, or groups as nearly natural as possible. Leaders have not seemed to realize that inmates accept values they learned in their gangs, and develop new group values in prison.

If group therapy is to achieve its maximum potentialities, the nature of the past society from which inmates have come and of the institutional society they have created on the inside should be its foundation. The

[24] *Ibid.,* p. 68.
[25] *Ibid.,* p. 74.
[26] *Ibid.,* pp. 76–77, 144.
[27] Cf. Donald R. Cressey, "Contradictory Theories in Correctional Group Therapy Programs," *Federal Probation* (Jan. 1954), pp. 20–26. This article presents an excellent critique of current correctional use of group therapy from the sociological viewpoint. Cf. also Lloyd W. McCorkle and Richard R. Korn, *loc. cit.*

general institutional program must be consistent with it. Ascertained inmate attitudes and inmates' explanations of their behavior should not be treated wholly as rationalizations. The real causes of crime in inmate group experiences of the past must be ascertained and discussed. The criminogenic imperfections of our imperfect society must be admitted. The values inmate groups accept can only be changed when new voluntary group relations permit new values to be accepted. As we point out in the following section, group therapy and the whole institutional program will be most successful when it is related to the community in the neighborhood of the institution and the communities elsewhere to which the inmates will return. At Seagoville in the federal system, Chino in California, perhaps at Wallkill in New York, and elsewhere, the principles of group therapy of the sociological type have come to characterize entire institutional programs. Since these institutions have the advantage of a selected population, the achievements of group therapy in institutions like Fort Madison and in some New Jersey institutions have a special significance because it was necessary to sell the program in considerable measure to an unselected prison population. Ideally, the group approach should have been begun before commitment and continued after release.

Linking the Prison to the World Outside

The prison community stands midway between the communities from which its inmates come and those for which it prepares them. Its public relations in both directions are important. Nor can it afford to have the region surrounding its location out of sympathy with it. The public must not only feel that prisoners will not escape, but come to realize that its best protection will come from a constructive program aimed at their socialization. Space does not permit us to detail all the media through which good public relations may be achieved. Not only newspapers, radio, and television, but planned visits by all really concerned and all who can be helpful in the prison program are called for. The inmates' institutional paper may be used toward understanding and socialization.

At the Federal Bureau of Prisons' institution at Seagoville, Texas, visits of especial concern to the inmates include those of probation officers who will supervise them after release, of the Texas Employment Commission, of business executives, of labor leaders, and of well-known local citizens. Seagoville may also be used as one example of an institution organized somewhat as a community aiming to give a maximum of constructive aid with a minimum of restraint and with as much tie-in with the community on the outside as possible.

It must be remembered that Seagoville receives inmates who the federal courts think may safely and profitably be sent to an unwalled, liberal institution. Yet men who have committed serious crimes are included. Indeed, the Bureau states that Seagoville has proven that most federal inmates could be so housed and treated. The new inmate is received with a smile to what appears to be a sort of college campus. He is housed in a single room which is not a cell. He is told of all the opportunities for self-improvement available. His room door is never locked and he may freely visit in other rooms. His program is planned with his assistance and periodically reviewed. Links with the outer world are deliberately provided. Among these is included visiting with family and friends in a pleasant room and opportunity to eat with them at tables seating four in the cafeteria. He gains confidence through education, is taught work as a substitute for crime, and given on-the-job vocational training. Social education and discussion groups are stressed, and the whole experience is socializing. Clubs and "great-books" and "current-events" programs are available. There is a hobby shop. Discipline is flexible, and the staff are intent on understanding rather than punishing those who break rules. The Bureau recognizes the need for something like Alcatraz, but it would like to have many more Seagovilles. Even maximum security institutions may effectively utilize real group therapy and may in different degrees approximate organization as a constructive community such as institutions like Seagoville and Chino largely achieve.

Suggested Readings

Fenton, Norman. *An Introduction to Group Counseling in Correctional Service*. New York: American Correctional Association, 1960. Probably the best practical guide to the subject: complete, clear, authoritative.

McCorkle, Lloyd W., Elias, Albert, and Bixby, F. Lovell. *The Highfields Story*. New York: Henry Holt and Company, 1958. Well-written and exceedingly interesting description of the unique work and guided group-interaction program in New Jersey's institution for selected youthful probationers.

Weeks, H. Ashley. *Youthful Offenders at Highfields*. Ann Arbor, Mich.: University of Michigan Press, 1959. Concerned with evaluating the effectiveness of the Highfields program.

CHAPTER 27

Release from Prison

Methods of Release

The least complicated means of being released from prison is to go out upon *expiration of sentence.* Ironically, this is the means least satisfactory from the standpoint of good correctional practice. In 1961 about 27 per cent of state prisoners obtained their freedom in this manner (see Table 7). The hold of public authorities over the 28,000 prisoners thus released ended at the prison gates, however much prison officials may have felt it desirable that further correctional efforts on behalf of the departing offenders be continued. Such releases, moreover, perpetuate the archaic notion that convicts serving their full sentences thus "pay their debt" to society, that they have wiped clean the slate and can start life anew.

Release by *amnesty,* a kind of general pardon, is granted usually only to political prisoners as a benign gesture by a head of state following a war, revolution, palace rebellion, or similar event. Visiting heads of state are sometimes invited in some countries to exercise the amnesty power on behalf of petty military prisoners or jail inmates as part of the hospitality being extended by the host authorities. Amnesty has no relationship to correction.

A man may secure *temporary release* from prison through being permitted at large under the honor system or on furlough.

Usually this is to enable him to help with the crops, secure medical care, attend a funeral, or, as in Alabama, go home for Christmas. Condemned when used for political purposes or to obtain graft, such practices may properly be used to develop trustworthiness and favorable social attitudes in carefully selected men. There was some increase of such temporary releases during World War II, and the practice has justified itself.

Table 7 MEANS OF RELEASING STATE PRISONERS, 1961

	Number	Per Cent
Parole	51,445	50.4
Expiration of sentence	27,859	27.3
Commutation	3,484	3.4
Other conditional release	3,371	3.3
Death other than by execution	710	0.7
Execution	42	a
Pardon	14	a
Conditional pardon	32	a
Other discharges	15,165	14.8
Total releases	102,122	99.9

a Less than one-tenth of one per cent.
Adapted from Federal Bureau of Prisons, "Prisoners in State and Federal Institutions, 1961," *National Prisoner Statistics,* No. 30 (Aug. 1962).

Escaping from prison is, in itself, a criminal offense. Few escapes are made by such dramatic means as scaling walls amid gunfire or crashing the main gate in a truck. Mostly they involve walking away from work posts outside the prison or sneaking off at night from a minimum security prison farm. One state alone, North Carolina, accounted for 457 of the reported 2,512 escapes during 1960. This disproportion does not necessarily indicate lax security measures in that state but reflects in part the fact that many of its 5,600 prisoners are distributed among 83 prison camps throughout the state.[1]

Three other methods of release—pardon, commutation, and parole —deserve more extended treatment.

PARDON

"Most societies have felt a need to provide a broad discretionary executive power to temper retribution with mercy, to correct error, to do justice where the rigorous inflexibility of a judicial system has not adjusted

[1] Federal Bureau of Prisons, "Prisoners in State and Federal Institutions, 1960," *National Prisoner Statistics,* No. 27 (Sept. 1961), p. 2.

to compelling social needs." [2] The American constitutional separation of powers notwithstanding, the ancient custom of executive pardon as a corrective measure for judicial miscarriages or errors is fully recognized among the United States, as it is in most civilized countries. Individuals are sometimes erroneously convicted, or tried under improper conditions, or given excessively severe sentences, or deserve restoration of their civil rights after release.[3] Under English legal theory pardons expressed royal forgiveness for breaches of the crown's peace and in simpler days was a boon personally asked and personally granted. Growth of population plus the complexities of modern government have routinized the administration of pardon so that executives usually exercise the power at a distance, seldom seeing in person the recipient of their boon. In 34 states pardon boards (or pardon-parole boards) process all pardon requests; in eight other states the governors are assisted by pardon attorneys, advisory officers, or parole commissioners; the remaining governors handle pardons directly.

Under ancient common law a declared felon was considered civilly "dead," his property was forfeited, and various disabilities were visited upon him as a citizen. Under present legal provisions, forfeiture no longer takes place, but conviction for felony usually entails other automatic disabilities which can seriously impede one's role as a member of society. The rights to vote, hold public office, invoke the constitutional privilege against self-incrimination, be a credible witness, institute lawsuits, and serve on juries are variously abrogated. *Full pardon,* which may at the same time release a prisoner, restores these rights. Prisoners released by completion of sentence or by parole must, in most states, later petition the governor for a full pardon to obtain such restoration. *Conditional pardon,* used almost exclusively as a release measure, not only does not restore civil rights, but, as its name implies, imposes obligations upon the pardonee, who may variously be required to report periodically to state authorities, remain in the state, meet financial obligations, reimburse the state for trial cost, submit to confinement in a state asylum, or meet any other legitimate requirement deemed in the public interest.

Full pardon can be of value in rehabilitating an offender seeking to re-establish his role in society, although sound practice would dictate the automatic restoration of civil rights at some point in the correctional process.

[2] Caleb Foote, "Pardon Policy in a Modern State," *Prison Journal* (April 1959), p. 3.
[3] *Ibid.,* pp. 4–5.

The correctional value of conditional pardon is doubtful if no supervision of the released person is provided; without supervision, such pardon is tantamount to absolute release without restoration of civil rights. In Texas and a few other states without parole laws, supervised conditional release functions as parole.[4]

COMMUTATION

Commutation, usually regarded as one of the minor and less regal forms of executive clemency, is used to a much greater extent than full or conditional pardon combined (see Table 7). Commutation is essentially the substitution of a greater by a lesser penalty; its use in the United States arose to alleviate hardships imposed by long, fixed sentences and soon was used to shorten sentences where new evidence reduced the degree of guilt or where unduly heavy sentences had been passed in response to public or judicial passion.

While the use of commutation in its most dramatic form involves reducing a death sentence, it is most often used to reduce a fixed sentence to time already served, permitting immediate release without parole—an undesirable type of release in the case of hardened systematic offenders. Commutation may also reduce a minimum sentence sufficiently to allow immediate parole consideration, or reduce a maximum sentence to a degree requiring the immediate discharge of a parolee, ready or not. Such uses of commutation can constitute serious and unwarranted abrogation by the executive of functions properly belonging to a parole board.

PAROLE

Parole is release from prison after part of the sentence has been served, the prisoner, still in custody and under supervision, being permitted at large in the community under stated conditions until discharged and liable to return to the institution for violation of any of these conditions. Parole differs from probation in that the parolee has already served time in prison or reformatory. Probation is normally granted by the court, while parole is granted and administered by an executive board or the institution itself.

Parole is significant to society as a release method which retains some control over prisoners, yet permits them more normal social relationships

4 R. W. England, Jr., "Pardon, Commutation, and Their Improvement," *Prison Journal* (April 1959), p. 24.

in the community and provides constructive aid at the time they most need it. It protects them against unjust arrest or exploitation. Parole is the last and in many ways most difficult stage in correctional treatment. It was estimated that in the fiscal year 1960–1961 it cost the state of Pennsylvania $1,818 to keep a man in prison, while parole cost only $206.[5]

To all prisoners, parole means relative freedom from walls, and commands, and isolation, and monotonous routine, and association almost exclusively with a horde of other moral outcasts. Parolees can live a somewhat more normal life than they have lived in prison. They reachieve names in place of numbers. There are women again, if not always woman's affection. There is some sort of home without bars, and a family or restaurant meal which may be something of a social as well as gastronomical event. Men walk as individuals instead of marching ploddingly like automata of a cell-house squad. The geographical horizon is no longer hemmed in by walls with armed guards and the outlines of cell blocks. The parolee may see a somewhat different scene every day. There are probably better beds, fewer unpleasant odors, food—less nutritious perhaps, but what the man likes within the restrictions of his purse—free access to newspapers, and clothing which somewhat expresses the personality, instead of slouchy uniforms and caps. The ex-prisoner is free, and that freedom is intoxicating.

Yet that very freedom involves the old responsibilities with new ones added. Parolees must make their own decisions instead of following simple if galling rules. They may be drunk or sober, quarrelsome or cooperative, spendthrift or saving, sexually loose or continent, obedient or disobedient to the law and parole regulations. The prison whistle no longer summons them to work in institutional shop or quarry or maintenance job, where there is no point in efficiency and no incentive to effort. Rather the factory whistle calls them to work, where advancement and even retention of the job depend upon initiative, industry, cooperation—the very traits or achievements which are discouraged by most penal institutions.

The parolee must also face the hatred and fear of the general public, the frequent hounding of the police, and the exploitation of employer or others who know his past record. Put as high as you like the proportion of parolees who have no intention of going straight on leaving prison, the problem of those who do so intend is one of extraordinary difficulty. The protection of society against repetition of crimes by ex-prisoners de-

[5] *Eighteenth Annual Report: 1960–1961*, Pennsylvania Board of Parole (Harrisburg, Pa., 1961), p. 30.

pends upon the solution of such adjustment problems for parolees.[6] Parole is primarily a protective device for society, secondarily an assistance to ex-prisoners.

The indeterminate sentence and parole. The idea of parole is usually associated with an indeterminate-sentence law where, instead of being committed to serve a definite number of years, the inmate is sentenced to a minimum and a maximum period, parole being possible any time after the minimum has been completed. Actually, in most states where the criminal code prescribes sentences to a definite number of years rather than a minimum and a maximum, the parole legislation authorizes parole after a given fraction—frequently one-third—of the definite terms has been served. These sentences are in fact indeterminate, even though they usually are called "definite." [7]

Two main forms of the indeterminate sentence are in use. In one, statutes fix the minima and maxima for particular offenses, within which the judge in turn imposes a minimum and maximum. In the other, the judge can impose only statutory maxima, the minima being determined by the court or by a paroling authority.[8]

Under an ideal state of affairs the sentencing and release of offenders would be determined by striking a nice balance between the need to protect society and the rehabilitative needs of the individual offenders. The unique aspects of each case would be fully recognized in accordance with the correctional doctrine of individualization of treatment. Prisoners would be incarcerated for necessarily undetermined periods, since uncertainty as to the progress of their rehabilitation would have to be allowed for. Because an ideal state of affairs does not prevail, the handling of offenders falls short of these standards. Public sentiment demands some bowing to the norm of "punishing" wrongdoers by applying minimum incarceration periods proportionate to the presumed harm to society of various offenses.[9] Judges occasionally allow personal feelings to influence their

[6] For a parolee's view of the degree to which those problems are met, see Richard A. Jordan, "Parole Has Never Been Tried," *Federal Probation* (Jan.–March 1942), pp. 20–23.

[7] Evidence that in most jurisdictions having "definite" sentences parole is granted earlier than in the jurisdictions having "indeterminate" sentences is presented in Sol Rubin, *Crime and Juvenile Delinquency* (New York: Oceana Publications, 1958), pp. 128–34.

[8] In 1958 Congress authorized the use of the second form by federal judges sentencing offenders to terms exceeding one year. See George J. Reed, "Federal Parole and the Indeterminate Sentence," *Federal Probation* (Dec. 1959), pp. 12–15.

[9] The influential American Law Institute's *Model Penal Code* provides minimum-sentence ranges for each of three felony categories constructed on the basis of seriousness of offense. First-degree felonies (the most serious), for example, would

sentencing decisions and parole authorities sometimes bend to pressures extraneous to the aim of rehabilitation or base their release decisions upon inadequate information.

Preparation for parole. Every experience preceding parole is preparation for it. Most of the prison experience is poor preparation. Nevertheless, it is well that efforts specifically to prepare for parole are being made in many institutions. Important to parole preparation on the inside are the general atmosphere, philosophy, and social relations of the prison community, as well as opportunities for vocational training and for contact with noncriminals outside the prison, preferably in the community to which the inmate will go on parole. Too often pre-parole orientation programs have consisted almost entirely in stressing the negative restrictions involved in parole. Parolees must, of course, know the rules, but the great needs would seem to be: (1) to assure a satisfactory job commensurate with the parolee's abilities or with a real basis for his hoping to earn advancement to a job which will be fully satisfactory; (2) to assure a satisfactory home where the parolee will feel "at home" and welcome; (3) to assure satisfactory leisure-time contacts where the parolee may develop noncriminal friendships and interests; (4) to prepare the parolee to bear and deal with the many consequences of his being an ex-convict, including the prospect that he may frequently feel very much ostracized and unwanted when with noncriminal associates; (5) to sell the parole system to the prospective parolee as a real asset to him by giving him hope that it can be his salvation, and at the same time to avoid unrealistically over-idealizing the prospects before him. For an ex-convict to find he has fewer difficulties on parole than he anticipated is better than to have him be overwhelmed by the discovery that life on parole is much harder than he expected it to be. Most inmates over-idealize conditions on the outside while they are brooding in prison, and their disillusionment on release may contribute to their recidivism. Open-ended questionnaires administered to 53 District of Columbia prisoners elicited four main areas of concern regarding parole adjustment: community acceptance, employment, family relationships, and relationships with police and parole officers.[10] Should larger-scale studies substantiate these findings (or reveal other, more pre-

---

call for court-fixed minimum sentences of between one and 10 years, and a statutory maximum of life [*see Model Penal Code*, Proposed Final Draft No. 1 (April 24, 1961), Sec. 6.06]. This section would probably be an improvement over most present sentencing laws, but it still embraces the old notion that offenders should be handled with a severity proportionate to the harmfulness of their offenses.

[10] Reuben S. Horlick, "Inmate Perception of Obstacles to Readjustment in the Community," American Correctional Association *Proceedings* (1961), pp. 200–05.

dominant areas of concern), preparation for parole could well include focussing on these areas to promote realistic expectations.

Parole orientation classes, now widespread in prisons, should acquaint the inmates with the constructive aids and agencies available to them even more than the dangers and difficulties to be avoided or overcome. This teaching must be in terms of the particular family, the neighborhood, and the detailed social situation which each individual will face. In progressive institutions, the cooperation of social agencies in the communities to which inmates are to return is secured in arranging assistance to families of inmates, recommendation of parole jobs and advisers, and preparing parole plans. In parole orientation classes, inmates often meet their future parole officer, get to know him personally and not think of him as "a copper," and discuss their parole plans with him. In a few institutions, they even meet law-enforcement officers: this serves for mutual education in so far as prospective parolees learn to anticipate how to deal with the police should they be stopped while on legitimate business on parole, while law-enforcement officers are reminded of the problems of parolees who desire to make good. Thus the inmates, in all phases of pre-parole education, should participate in group thinking concerning the type of problems they will meet in the home community after release. They evaluate their assets and liabilities, thus planning to take advantage of the former and avoid the consequences of the latter. Finally, it is important that they air their opinions in free-for-all discussion rather than nurse private fears or grudges.[11]

Recognizing that the adjustment strains experienced by the average parolee when he goes from the confined prison routine to freedom may contribute to parole violation, the Michigan Department of Corrections constructed in 1953 an open, pre-parole camp near Jackson Prison to ease these strains. The inmates spend an average of three weeks participating in a combination work and parole lecture-study curriculum; living conditions approximate as closely as possible those on the outside. Among the nine topics taken up in the study portion of the program are budgeting, drinking, family responsibilities, employment hints, and community agencies able to assist released men.[12]

In addition to transitional facilities on prison grounds (the practice of segregating men about to be released is not particularly new), there

[11] Cf. American Prison Association, *Handbook on Pre-Release Preparation in Correctional Institutions,* 1950; George G. Killinger, "The Probation Officer as the Field Agent for the U.S. Board of Parole," *Federal Probation* (Dec. 1948), pp. 9–12.

[12] H. E. Kachelski, "An Approach to Parole Preparation," *Federal Probation* (June 1956), pp. 29–32.

exist throughout the United States private and tax-supported "half-way houses" serving both parolees and prisoners released without parole. At their worst, these houses are manned by well-meaning clergymen and friendly but untrained "older couples" who presumably create a home-like atmosphere. At their best, they are staffed by qualified workers who can provide professional guidance and counselling. In 1961 the Federal Bureau of Prisons opened half-way houses in Chicago, Los Angeles, and New York City for younger offenders released from federal institutions.

The administration of parole. Parole administration includes two major functions: it must determine when inmates are to be paroled; it must provide supervision and assistance after release. In some states these two functions are administered by the same agency.

Governors and other elective officials are not fitted to be parole administrators, because they are busy with other duties and under political pressure. Parole policies often change with the political complexion of the state. In a number of states prison officials participate to some extent in parole decisions. This practice may result in lack of uniformity in policies among institutions, undue weight given to behavior in prison or to the need to reduce overcrowding, and so on. However, institutional control makes possible a desirable follow-through in treatment from the institutional to the parole experience.

Parole boards are usually appointed by the governor. In most states no qualifications of any kind are required of appointees. In view of the crucial decisions parole boards must constantly make, boding good or ill for the prisoners concerned and for the communities to which they return, the need for appointing properly qualified parole boards cannot be overemphasized. The American Correctional Association recommends that board members be professionals in the behavioral sciences, with an "intimate knowledge" of offenders' problems gained from actual experience in correctional or related work. Their salaries should be comparable with those of of criminal court judges.[13] Salaries have varied from $17,000 a year down to no compensation at all. Minimum salaries of parole agents about 1957 varied from $2,880 in Kentucky to $5,040 in Michigan.[14] In the federal system and increasingly elsewhere, the administration of adult probation and parole are combined. Sometimes law-enforcement officers act as parole agents, but this is most unwise.

Until the decade of the 1950's, few parole jurisdictions stipulated more

---

[13] American Correctional Association, *Manual of Correctional Standards* (New York: The Association, 1959), pp. 537–38.
[14] Charles L. Newman, *Sourcebook on Probation, Parole and Pardons* (Springfield, Ill.: Charles E. Thomas, 1958), p. 213.

than minimal collegiate training for prospective parole agents. During that decade, however, increasing numbers of jurisdictions began giving preference to applicants with master's degrees in social work or to applicants with graduate training in the behavioral sciences, plus specified kinds of practical experiences. There exists no unequivocal evidence that parole (and probation) officers trained in social work produce results superior to those having other kinds of professional backgrounds. Many, if not most, of the nation's 50-odd graduate schools of social work present curricula heavily influenced by psychological doctrines of the Freudian or neo-Freudian varieties. Crime is viewed from these doctrinal positions as basically psychopathological in origin; in consequence of this the treating of offenders is necessarily perceived as the ironing out of allegedly criminogenic personality wrinkles. If the burden of this text is sound, namely, that our crime is an expression of American culture and that most offenders are individuals making responses "appropriate" to the cultural forces variously impinging upon them, it follows that to advocate the manning of parole and probation agencies exclusively with psychopathologically-oriented personnel would be contradictory. Future research on this presently unexplored matter of qualifications may well show that *self-images as professionals* of whatever behavioral approach are a prime requisite to effective parole work. Persons so viewing themselves are much less likely to fall into the comfortable ruts which become the bane of parole agencies without professional qualifications: a "nine-to-five" outlook towards the job; mechanical procedures; indifferent, slip-shod work.

The Determination of the Time for Release

RESTRICTIONS ON ELIGIBILITY

A prison inmate has no enforceable legal right to parole, even though he meets all eligibility requirements.[15] Too great readiness to release prisoners on parole has rightly been much criticized. Equally serious, however, has been the denial of parole to those fit for it. This latter weakness is not merely a hardship to prisoners; it fails to provide the public with a needed protection against crime, especially when it means eventual release without either supervision or assistance. The habit of holding a man in prison until the end of his sentence just because another state is holding a detainer over him obviously interferes with the effective use of parole. This problem of

[15] Carter H. White, "Legal Aspects of Parole," *Journal of Criminal Law and Criminology* (March–April 1952), p. 621.

detainers is serious for other reasons and too complex for adequate discussion here.[16] Perhaps there is special merit in Judge Hincks' recommendation that the Interstate Commission on the Control of Crime establish a service which any judge could call on for a study of each case having interstate features.

Restrictions on parole may be brought about by statute, by court practice, or by administrative rule or custom. Courts restrict the use of parole when they have the power to fix minimum terms in individual cases so close to the maximum that there is little or no time left for parole. Thus sentences of "49 to 50 years," "one year and 11 months to two years," and the like have been known. A similar evil results when law or administrative practice regularly requires that a long period must always be served before a prisoner may be paroled.

Another restriction on parole is its denial to prisoners who have committed certain specified serious offenses or to recidivists. An Illinois court held in 1947 that the parole board was within its rights in refusing to consider sex offenders for parole. Clearly, some sex offenders are not fit for parole, but their routine disqualification without individual consideration probably reflects uninformed popular attitudes. It is true that good parole administration will consider both the offense and the criminal record, but the law should leave discretion with the board in such cases. The chairman of Michigan's parole board once insisted that the almost hopeless recidivist is not infrequently rehabilitated. Hence there should be no routine exclusion from parole on the basis of past record only.

A particularly difficult problem is the relationship of good-time laws or rules to the time of parole. Studies have shown that the statistical correlation between good behavior in prison and adjustment on the outside is not nearly so high as the correlation between adjustment on the outside and other factors such as schooling, vocational capacity, social type, and extent of criminal career. A prison-wise professional criminal may be a model prisoner on the inside but be in no way "reformed"; experience has taught him "how to do time." On the other hand, first offenders are often highly disturbed emotionally by the prison experience and have difficulty in adjusting to prison routines and regulations. Wardens insist they need good-time laws as a major inducement to good conduct in the institution. It is legitimate to let prisoners know that good conduct *along with other factors* will be considered by the parole board.

[16] For a series of good articles on the detainer problem, see the contributions of Judge Carroll C. Hincks, Director James V. Bennett, Judge Van Buren Perry, Dr. Garrett Heyns, and Sanford Bates in *Federal Probation* (July–Sept. 1945), pp. 3–18.

Within the limits set by law, the real restrictions on parole depend upon the varying philosophy, training, and attitudes of the paroling authority. The previous criminal record of the prisoner, the nature of the offense, and unsatisfactory chances for outside employment are in practice chief reasons for denying parole. The first two are probably too much stressed even in our best parole systems. It must be remembered that most prisoners will be released sooner or later. It is wiser to release even a confirmed repeater of serious crime today than to keep him to the end of his sentence to emerge without protective supervision.

ADMINISTRATIVE PROCEDURE

Since parole is for social protection and not clemency, cases should come before the board automatically, but many states require an application by the prisoner.

Parole investigations are often either nonexistent, cursory, or based on routine facts on the record, not most significant for future adjustment. Too often the bare criminal record, and not all of that, plus some knowledge of the individual's institutional behavior and communications from states' attorneys, relatives, and friends are the only data available. We need not repeat here the outline of information needed in a case study. In Chapter 23 we made suggestions as to data requisite for probation which are pertinent here also. The plan which the supervision division may have prepared should be part of the consideration as to parolability. Most especially is required, but usually lacking, a thorough field investigation. One of the chief criticisms which can be directed toward parole administration today is the relative disregard of the social relationships from which the prisoner came, as well as of those to which he is going. Another important lack is knowledge of the attitudes of the man on entering and leaving prison.

Parole hearings are usually held periodically at the institution. The prisoner is usually but not always heard in person. Practice as to permitting the appearance of lawyers and friends varies. Parole board members should be trained to be immune from the effect of a mother's tears or the pleadings of a wife with babe in arms, and the procedure should not be legalistic. The determination of guilt generally is not a function of the parole board, although a decided tendency has been noted for some parole boards to "retry" the case in reviewing it and to seek expressions of contrition from the parole applicant. The *Attorney General's Survey* [17] cites as relatively adequate parole-consideration hearings lasting from five to 40 minutes per

[17] *Op. cit.,* p. 160.

case. Such brevity is only justified in so far as the board has a basis for confidence in the independent reports and recommendations it receives from several sociologists, social workers, psychologists, and other professionally trained personnel. These persons should have had extended contact with the parole applicant prior to the hearing, and they should be familiar with his home and community situation and his social relationships.

Hearings may be either private or public. There are opposite dangers here, of "star chamber" proceedings in private on the one hand, or of the publication by newspapers of facts which will hinder the parolee's adjustment on the other. Perhaps a system of private hearings with public records and nothing "off the record," and with the right of judicial review for the prisoner, is the best solution.

CONDITIONS OF RELEASE

From a strictly legal viewpoint, any reasonable condition except (in some jurisdictions) restrictions which go beyond the maximum sentence may be made requisite to release on parole. Employment, a suitable home, and freedom from venereal diseases are often prerequisite to release. Some states, however, including some with progressive parole organizations, do not require employment. In a few jurisdictions the candidate must have a sponsor or adviser other than the parole officer. Research has shown the importance of employment, yet, especially during a business recession, many boards recognize the injustice of a flat requirement of a job prior to release. This requirement increases the evil of fictitious employers agreeing to employ merely to secure the release of the man, as well as the problem of the economic exploitation of parolees. A 1960 survey revealed that five states give no money to parolees on their release from prison, while others pay from $5 to $30, except for Vermont, where payment is based on a rate of $1 per month served up to $100.[18] In addition, inmates may be provided with transportation to their homes and with some civilian clothing upon their‧ release, and they may be able to accumulate savings from paid work in prison. Where the latter opportunity exists, savings of long-term inmates may be appreciable. Ten states have loan funds with which to assist parolees upon release. It is clear that without aid from friends or relatives, which many inmates lack, these forms of initial aid upon release are likely to be inadequate. A considerable sum may be necessary if the parolee is to sup-

[18] Daniel Glaser, Eugene S. Zemans, and Charles W. Dean, *Money Against Crime: A Survey of Economic Assistance to Released Prisoners* (Chicago: John Howard Association, 1961), pp. 3–4.

port himself during the two weeks or more which may elapse before he can draw his first paycheck on the outside, and partially to meet his accumulated needs for clothing and his accumulated desire for some basic pleasures. During these first crucial weeks after release from prison, the temptation to return to crime may be greatest, in spite of the enthusiasm and capacity for noncriminal life which may have been built up by a good rehabilitation program in prison. Accordingly, the contribution which an interested parole agent, sponsor, employer, and friend can make is especially great in the period immediately following release from prison.

THE USE OF PAROLE ACTUARIAL DEVICES

Except in a few jurisdictions, parole administrations must rely upon more or less routine matters of record, supplemented by correspondence, interviews, and little or no field investigation. This large dependence upon records has raised the question whether statistical predictions of probable parole success are possible as a rough guide to the board in dealing with the individual case. If one can determine the characteristics of parolees who have succeeded as compared with those who have failed on parole, future candidates with records similar to those of past successes may then be favored in parole decisions.

Over a quarter of a century ago, Professor Burgess of the University of Chicago studied the records of thousands of men released from Illinois prisons.[19] He had, it seems, no fully reliable measure of their success or failure and had to use official records of parole violation or repeated crime. Yet it is practically certain that by and large the group classified as successes were more successful than the group classified as failures. Burgess found the violation rates varying markedly among parolees with different types of records, personalities, and backgrounds. On the basis of this study and subsequent analysis and experience, Illinois has set up an actuarial service for the assistance of its parole board. Violation rates of men, falling into different categories classified in terms of some seven to 12 factors found to be consistently predictive of parole outcome, can be determined. It is possible, then, by a simple statistical computation, to figure an estimated violation rate for each prospective parolee in terms of the experience with other men of his type. Each man's success percentage thus derived is not intended for use without consideration of other factors in the case. It

---

[19] Andrew A. Bruce, Albert J. Harno, Ernest W. Burgess, and John Landesco, *The Workings of the Indeterminate-Sentence Law and the Parole System in Illinois* (Springfield, Ill.: State of Illinois, 1928), pp. 205–49.

does, however, serve as a warning or encouragement in the decision with reference to any individual. Actually in Illinois, the nature of the offense, the fact of recidivism, the state of public opinion, and newspaper publicity seem to have been major factors determining parole policy.

The use of actuarial prediction in parole decisions has been criticized on the basis of technical deficiencies not yet solved: unreliability of prison records, disparity between the social milieus of the experience-table parolees and the future milieus of the predicted parolees, the need for precise measurement of attitude and character traits, and so on.[20] If one assumes the eventual conquest of these deficiencies and the subsequent development of devices of such precision that parole boards come to rely heavily upon them without qualms, there still remain more fundamental objections to their use.

(1) The adoption of "perfected" prediction devices in jurisdictions with poor standards of parole work would enable such districts eventually to show high rates of parole success, since the accurate selection of low-risk parole prospects would be possible. A poorly trained physician's shortcomings can be ignored if he has only healthy patients.

(2) To remove problematical cases from parole rosters would tend to reduce parole supervision from the professional to the merely technical level, at which professionally trained and oriented persons would find their capacities unchallenged.

(3) With increased emphasis upon paroling "good risks" who, so far as public safety is concerned, did not require imprisonment in the first place, there would exist increased reluctance to parole prisoners accurately known to be poor risks, despite the fact that such men are in urgent need of the assistance skilled parole agents can render; instead, the poor risks would be kept in prison to the end of their terms and then released without supervision.

(4) Parole prediction promotes an image of parole as a period of "testing" an offender's capacity for conventional behavior rather than as a *continuation* of correctional measures begun during incarceration. Strengthening this erroneous image in the thinking of parole boards and their agents could produce a concomitant stress upon mere surveillance carried on in order to learn whether or not the parolee is "passing" or "failing" his test.

(5) The American Correctional Association has defined parole as "a procedure by which prisoners are selected for release *on the basis of individual response and progress within the correctional institution* and a service by which they are provided with necessary controls and guidance as they

[20] Paul W. Tappan, *Crime, Justice and Correction* (New York: McGraw-Hill Book Company, 1960), pp. 731–33.

serve the remainder of their sentences within the free community." [21] But the selection of parolees by actuarial devices need not entail measurement of such response and progress. In fact, among the 12 categories used in Illinois, *none* are related to prison experience. Moreover, the "perfection" of predictive devices does not require the inclusion of such items. It seems to us that a canon of the individual-treatment philosophy is being ignored when prediction scores can be assigned without reference to prison experience.[22]

Parole Supervision

Parole supervision has two equally important aims: (1) watchful control with the possibility of quick return to the institution if the protection of society requires it; (2) friendly and constructive aid. Good parole supervision involves a nice balance between these two aims. Parole, like probation, is social work with a potential "punch" in it. Most of what we said in Chapter 23 on probation supervision also applies to parole supervision.

The parolee needs help. To secure, to hold, and to get to like the types of jobs most frequently available to parolees is not easy. He needs a job, friendship, group affiliation, opportunities which give him hope, a new basis for self-respect. His supervising officer must help get a satisfying job and must make a prospective employer somehow feel that it is good business to employ a man with a prison record. If, in accordance with the usual policy, the record is to be known to the employer, there are three other motives which may be appealed to. Some employers may be appealed to from the standpoint of the entire community, in that property will be safer if ex-prisoners are employed than if they are unemployed. Some

[21] *Manual of Correctional Standards,* p. 532 (emphasis added).

[22] The interested student should read the 10 articles on prediction collected in Norman Johnston, Leonard Savitz, and Marvin E. Wolfgang, *The Sociology of Punishment and Correction* (New York: John Wiley and Sons, 1962). Among other things, the Illinois prediction work is described by Lloyd E. Ohlin; Norman S. Hayner, a sociologist with experience as a parole board member, discusses the reasons for parole boards' present coolness toward actuarial prediction. See also R. W. England, "Some Dangers in Parole Prediction," *Crime and Delinquency* (July 1962), pp. 265–69. With reference to point 5 above, Jerome H. Skolnick has called attention to the failure to incorporate in prediction devices recognition of the role played by prison experience in parole outcome. More important, however, is the general burden of his article, in which seven proposed hypotheses focus attention on certain prison and post-prison socio-psychological factors presumably determining parole adjustment ["Toward a Developmental Theory of Parole," *American Sociological Review* (Aug. 1960), pp. 542–49].

employers may be appealed to from purely humanitarian motives. Some employers, however, have found that it is definitely an advantageous business proposition to hire carefully selected parolees. We know of a personnel officer in a large concern who states that parolees have the distinctive quality of other handicapped workers, such as crippled persons, in that they are extremely grateful for employment opportunities and therefore make exceptionally loyal and reliable workers.

In many cases it is unnecessary to make a man's criminal record known to the employer; there is no inquiry about it. Parolees must be guarded against exploitation by employers who threaten to expose their past records or by collusion between employers and parole officers who conceivably might threaten the imprisonment of the parolee as a parole violator if he does not work for abnormally low wages. We know too little of the actual degree to which there is exploitation. In part, parolees are protected by organized labor eager to maintain its own standards.

It is very important for the reader to see the parole experience as the parolee himself sees it. Space permits only the following excerpts from Lindner's account of such a parolee experience:

. . . I've been let out before and it's always the same thing. . . . I knew first of all that people would know that I was a convict. Maybe my cheap suit and shoes and new hat wouldn't give it away but I still knew inside of me that everybody on the train and in the street would know. . . . You'll say, "What about your job?" Well, Doc, that was a lot of crap. I never had a job. . . . They still don't want ex-cons unless their business is shady or they want labor spies. . . . Personally I'm finished with telling about my record. It's better to deny it and eat for a few days than to admit it and starve. Anyway I landed a job and it's like it always was, talk behind your back all the time and you worried sick about whether the auditor will find a penny missing and they land you for it. Of course there's the cops too. Everytime someone spits in the subway you get dragged in, and you can't get away from the feeling that you're branded like a steer on a ranch. . . .[23]

Parolees often have lost their right to vote, to hold office, and to engage in certain types of occupations.[24] They have not lost their American

---

[23] Robert M. Lindner, *Stone Walls and Men* (New York: Odyssey Press, 1946), pp. 471–73. For a somewhat contrasting picture, see Anonymous, "My First Workday on Parole," *Federal Probation* (Dec. 1954), pp. 15–16.

[24] A compilation made by the Osborne Association in 1959 of occupational disabilities facing ex-felons in New York City lists the following: cook, porter, dishwasher (in restaurants holding liquor licenses); elevator operator, desk clerk, porter (in hotels selling liquor); operating taxis or other commercial vehicles; cabaret jobs; jobs in amusement centers; any job requiring civil service applications [Albert Morris, "What's New in the Employment of Ex-Prisoners," *Correctional Research* (Nov. 1959), p. 11].

citizenship unless guilty of treason or of desertion from the armed forces during wartime. The parolee is often without friends other than those who will lead him toward crime. His family may reject him, may be most difficult to get along with, or may themselves be criminal or near-criminal. Untrained or oversolicitous police may hound his footsteps and make life unbearable for him. All who know his record may look upon him with distrust and suspicion. The task of keeping his past life secret is difficult and implies a life of deception most distasteful to those most likely to seek to keep out of trouble. The old haunts attract, and the old associates—not necessarily wholly bad—invite him. To walk the straight and narrow may bring ridicule rather than appreciation and may involve disloyalty to old pals. Basic human urges—for freedom, for adventure, for drink, for women—long denied in prison impinge upon a reaction mechanism usually not too well trained in self-control. The parolee is asked not only to avoid crime, but to walk a moral path far more circumscribed than that of the average man and to forgo pleasures which those who supervise him may freely enjoy. More or less embittered by his prison experience; convinced, perhaps, that men more antisocial than he are never prosecuted for their acts; overcome with a deep sense of inferiority and hopelessness—the parolee needs help.

TYPES OF SUPERVISORY AGENCIES

Parole supervision varies greatly. In a few states many parolees are only supervised to the extent that they are required to send in written reports of their whereabouts and activities, which are not verified. Some states supplement such reports by having volunteer parole sponsors who guide the parolees and also submit written reports. Full-time, state-paid agents, with or without the aid of volunteers, are employed in a majority of the states. Trained public officers are needed. Yet every parolee needs an intimate friend who is not paid for his friendship and who can give him more time than the agent. Prisoner's Aid Associations, the Osborne Association, the Salvation Army, some religious groups, and the John Howard Association are among the private agencies which have contributed much to the assistance of parolees.

METHODS OF SUPERVISION

Fifty parolees per officer have been considered the ideal supervision workload, but most state and federal offices have much heavier case assignments. In 1957 the average case loads in 43 states surveyed ranged from 50 each in Delaware, Kentucky, and Wisconsin, to 313 in South Carolina. At mid-range was Maine, with 85.[25] But mere averages can be misleading. Also to be considered is the amount of time parole agents spend working directly on behalf of their clients, and this will be influenced by such things as size of district, available stenographic and other recording services, and kind of transportation used in the field. A recent time study of Pennsylvania's 86 agents (who average 63 cases each) found that only 34 per cent of work time was spent in personal or phone contacts with parolees and collateral persons. Travel and recording information consumed 24 per cent each, while other activities accounted for the remaining 18 per cent.[26] Even with an average case load approaching the ideal of 50, each agent worked approximately one and a half hours overtime daily to complete his duties.[27]

Friends and sponsors are especially useful when the number of parole agents is too low. Since the parolee greatly needs the understanding aid of his community, and since parole in general needs the support of public opinion, it is very important to take the community into one's confidence when a parole plan is made for one of its members, if this can be done without injury to him.[28] An organized community can appoint a committee to assist the readjustment for the parolee to his neighborhood relations and can plan new ones for him deliberately. Here, too, nonprofessional sponsors, sometimes provided by Prisoners' Aid Societies, which have a long history, may be of real assistance.[29]

THE CONDITIONS OF PAROLE

To the conditions necessary for release are added other conditions which the parolee must meet while on parole or risk return to prison without a court hearing. While there is not by any means complete uniformity of conditions, the following are often included: [30]

1. He must abstain from intoxicants.
2. He must report his address promptly after release and not change it without permission of his parole officer.
3. He may not change employment without permission.

[25] William L. Jacks, *A Comparison of Parole Agents' Salaries, Caseloads, and Supervision Duties* (Harrisburg, Pa.: Pennsylvania Board of Parole, 1957), quoted in Newman, *op. cit.,* p. 215.

[26] William L. Jacks, *A Time Study of Parole Agents* (Harrisburg, Pa.: Pennsylvania Board of Parole, 1961), p. 4.

[27] *Ibid.,* p. 5.

[28] Harvey L. Long, "What Can Be Done About the Community Attitude Toward the Parolee," American Prison Association *Proceedings* (1946), p. 92.

[29] Cf. Albert G. Fraser, "The Function and Program of a Prisoners' Aid Society," *Federal Probation* (July–Sept. 1944), pp. 25–29.

[30] Cf. *Attorney General's Survey of Release Procedures,* pp. 212–13.

4. He must make prompt written reports of his situation.
5. The parolee must not, of course, violate any law.
6. He must not marry without consent.
7. A parolee usually must not drive an automobile without permission.
8. Parolees are forbidden to associate with other parolees or ex-criminals.
9. Parolees are also denied the right to leave the state without permission. Sometimes they may not leave the county where they were paroled.
10. Parolees must not carry weapons of any kind.
11. They must not use narcotics.
12. They must be home at stated hours.
13. They must not borrow money without permission.

Of these the requirement to be in at an hour considered childishly early among his associates is probably the most objectionable to the parolee. The rule tends to prevent night life liable to result in crime and also enables the parole agent to locate his man at night. Few regulations so clearly make the parolee a dependent as this one.

With trained parole agents, reasonable case loads, and knowledge of individual parolees and their supervisors, these rules have little meaning. Actually many of these conditions are not enforced. Yet all parolees sign the same statement accepting the conditions, a fact which contradicts the principle of individualized treatment. Lack of uniform enforcement implies some degree of individualization.

Formerly out-of-state parole often meant that the parolee was free of all supervision. Often the receiving state was not even notified of his parole. Out-of-state parole is wise in certain cases: where a man's family lives outside the state of his imprisonment, or where the best chance for avoiding crime rests in getting a man away from a community where his past record is known. All 48 of the mainland states have now adopted the standard Interstate Parole Compact Law providing for reciprocal supervision of parolees.

TREATMENT OF PAROLE VIOLATORS [31]

Parole naturally becomes a farce if no attention is paid to violations. On the other hand, it may defeat its own purpose if every minor violation of the conditions of parole leads to automatic return to prison.

Violation of parole may or may not bring about formal hearings. These hearings are seldom reviewable in court.[32] In about half the states, parolees

[31] Cf. *ibid.*, IV, chap. 9.
[32] White, *loc. cit.*, p. 621.

may be returned to prison without such a hearing, although some court decisions have held such procedure a denial of due process of law.[33] Since technically parolees are still paying penalty for a crime, defense counsel need not be permitted, and the usual laws of evidence which protect the accused in court do not apply to the parole violator at an administrative hearing. Here is opportunity for grave abuse. From the social viewpoint, counsel should, it seems, always be permitted, and there should always be opportunity for appeal to the courts or other tribunals. Lack of such opportunity constitutes a great source of possible miscarriage of justice and is inconsistent with our democratic principles.

DISCHARGE FROM PAROLE

It has been determined in court decisions that a parolee may be kept on parole even after the end of the time he would have served had he remained incarcerated. Discharge from parole does not restore civil rights as in the case of a pardon, yet such restoration might in some cases promote adjustment.

Is Parole a Success?

Parole has at times been widely pronounced a failure. Newspaper attacks have disregarded the actual efficiency of parole. They have often been based upon single incidents when a parolee has killed a police officer or committed some sex or other offense the nature of which arouses public emotions. Nevertheless, there have been plenty of legitimate grounds for criticism of the administration of parole. In many states release on parole has been perfunctory, supervision practically nonexistent, and the whole system much involved in politics. In spite of criticisms, deserved and undeserved, the principle of parole has been almost unanimously endorsed by all students of penology.

DIFFICULTIES INVOLVED IN ANSWERING THE QUESTION

Many studies have demonstrated both the value of parole and the crying need for its improvement. Among difficulties encountered in research of this type the following may be noted:

[33] For an interesting discussion of the legal aspects of this question, see Henry Weihofen, "Revoking Probation, Parole and Pardon Without a Hearing," *Journal of Criminal Law and Criminology* (Jan.–Feb. 1942), pp. 531–39. Weihofen even discusses an unusual case where an inmate tried to insist on his right to refuse parole.

(1) It has been claimed that the better the supervision, the higher the violation rate, because good supervision may imply that the conditions of parole are enforced.

(2) The number of parolees used as the base upon which to figure violation rates is sometimes the number of parolees handled during a year, sometimes the total released on parole, and sometimes the number of terminations of parole in a year. Similarly, violators may be only those who have committed new crimes, or included may be those who have violated one of the many parole rules, which differ between states.

(3) The length of time during which parolees have been under supervision also varies greatly. Clearly the longer the period the greater the opportunity for violations to occur, although rates of violations reported are highest during the early part of the period of supervision.

(4) Parole success is often due to exacting selection of men for parole rather than to the effects of parole guidance and supervision. However, society might be better protected if more prisoners were released by parole rather than discharged without supervision, despite the fact that the success rate on parole will decline if standards for granting parole are lowered. We need to know more about the recidivism of comparable groups of prisoners released with and without parole, but most of the available evidence suggests that parole reduces the rate of return to crime.

STUDIES OF THE SUCCESS OF PAROLE

Typical annual reports of parole authorities seeking popular approval often indicate that "90 per cent of the boys go straight." At the other extreme is the careful research of Sheldon and Eleanor Glueck in Massachusetts.[34] This research concerned behavior of the men not only while under parole supervision but also during five and 10 years after discharge from supervision. It was found that 55 per cent of the reformatory men "were officially known to have committed serious breaches of parole conditions, including the commission of new crimes," during the parole period,[35] while "almost 80 per cent of the 422 men involved committed offenses during the 5-year period following the expiration of their parole." [36] In their study of 500 women, the Gluecks found slightly fewer repetitions of offenses during a 5-year post-parole period than in the case of the men. Some have felt that the standards of success used by the Gluecks were a bit too exacting; but

---

[34] Cf. their *500 Criminal Careers, passim,* and *Five Hundred Delinquent Women, passim.* The Gluecks' later studies of great importance for other purposes cover periods beyond that of parole supervision.

[35] *500 Criminal Careers,* p. 169.

[36] *Ibid.,* p. 184.

with full allowance for this, their findings in a state which was at least not unusually backward in its parole work are far from encouraging.

A Pennsylvania study covered some 1,400 men who had been off parole for a considerable period of time. Failure was measured in terms of FBI arrest records. Of these, 450, or 32 per cent, had violated parole during the parole supervision period and 166 subsequently (making a total of 44 per cent). What we need to know is not so much how successful parole has been under admittedly imperfect conditions, but how successful it will be when adequate selection of parolees and adequate supervision have been provided.

On the other hand, many claim it fairer to test parole in terms of violations during the period of supervision only. For this reason we do not present here the results of the Glueck research, which followed the same men for a total of 15 years after their release from parole. Burgess in Illinois has published data showing that according to official statistics, without a field follow-up such as the Gluecks used, some two-fifths of Illinois parolees had violated parole during a 3-year period of supervision. If the period on parole lengthened to three years, the violation rate for all violations may reach as high as 40 per cent. Though conditions are not identical, New York State has reported figures roughly similar to those from Illinois.[37]

CONDITIONS RELATED TO PAROLE OUTCOME

Parole prediction studies have found the following conditions fairly consistently connected with success on parole: [38]

1. First offenders are more successful than recidivists.
2. Property offenders, such as burglars, pickpockets, shoplifters, and forgers, are markedly less successful than those whose crimes were

[37] Frederick A. Moran, "Parole—An Effective Social and Law-Enforcing Agency," American Prison Association Proceedings (1937), p. 308.

[38] Cf. E. W. Burgess et al., op. cit.; J. L. Gillin, "Prediction of Parole Success in Wisconsin," Journal of Criminal Law and Criminology (Nov.–Dec. 1943), pp. 237–39, and "Predicting Outcome of Adult Probationers in Wisconsin," American Sociological Review (Aug. 1950), pp. 550–53; D. Glaser, "A Reconsideration of Some Parole Prediction Factors," American Sociological Review (June 1954), pp. 335–41; S. and E. Glueck, After Conduct of Discharged Offenders (London: Macmillan and Company, 1946); M. Hakeem, "The Validity of the Burgess Method of Parole Prediction," American Journal of Sociology (March 1948), pp. 376–86; William Hurwitz and Elizabeth Peterson, "Federal Parole Prediction," Attorney General's Survey of Release Procedures, IV, Appendix A; L. E. Ohlin, op. cit.; A. C. Schnur, "Predicting Parole Outcome," Focus (May 1949), pp. 70–75; G. B. Vold, Prediction Methods and Parole (Hanover, N. H.: The Sociological Press, 1931); Hermann Mannheim and Leslie T. Wilkins, Prediction Methods in Relation to Borstal Training (London: Her Majesty's Stationery Office, 1955).

against persons, for example, murders and sex offenses. Robbers, whose crime is against persons but for the purpose of obtaining property, are about average parole risks.

3. Those who begin their criminal careers early are poorer parole risks than those who begin their criminal careers late.
4. Married parolees and those with dependents are more successful than those who are unmarried or without dependents.
5. A regular employment record prior to imprisonment is associated with success on parole.
6. The level of educational attainment and success on parole are directly related.
7. Adequacy of parole plans at time of parole hearing is directly related to success on parole.
8. When prisoners are classified on a subjective basis in terms of the social type which they represented prior to their offense, and if these types— such as "average citizens," "fairly conventional," "ne'er-do-well," "drunkard," and "hobo"—represent marked contrasts in conventionality of behavior, those classified as of the conventional types will be markedly more successful on parole than those classified in the unconventional categories.
9. The higher the socio-economic status of the parolee's family, the more likely it is that he will succeed on parole.
10. A high degree of stability in place of residence is associated with success on parole.

The following factors have been found to have little relationship with parole outcome or have been found to be highly inconsistent in their relationship, when other factors are controlled:

1. Race and ethnic derivation of parolee.
2. Intelligence, as reflected in test scores.
3. Prison punishment record.
4. Urban versus rural background, and urban versus rural parole residence.
5. Whether the inmate was a "lone wolf" or a group offender (generally the group offenders have been the most successful on parole, but in some studies, such as that by Vold which was cited above, the "lone wolves" were most successful).
6. Height, weight, and bodily structure.

It is quite likely that factors which are more difficult to measure or appraise than those discussed above, or which are less uniformly identifiable for all members of any sample of parolees, are highly related to parole outcome. These may include such things as the attitudes of prisoners and of their associates toward them and their status in various groups. The case-study approach is useful because it may yield such subtle and unstandardized information. The significance of this information may be scientifically established in so far as it can be standardized from case-study records and then rigorously tested by parole outcome studies.

Suggested Readings

Journal of the National Probation and Parole Association (July 1958). A symposium on recidivism by 13 scholars and penologists.

Newman, Charles L. *Sourcebook on Probation, Parole and Pardons.* Springfield, Ill.: Charles C. Thomas, 1958. Compendium of previously published articles on seven aspects of these correctional measures.

Ohlin, Lloyd E. *Selection for Parole.* New York: Russell Sage Foundation, 1951. A handbook for the guidance of correctional workers who wish to apply prediction methods in dealing with offenders. Describes the construction of the 12-factor prediction table used by Illinois parole authorities, and the theory underlying its use.

CHAPTER 28

Some Progressive Prison Systems

Existing correctional systems in the United States are the products of historical development and today express past and current ideas, conditions, and processes which make them what they are. For the most part they implement the neoclassical penal philosophy, because most Americans still think of the criminal in neoclassical terms. Conceiving of the criminal as very different from the non-criminal in that he chooses to violate the law, most Americans feel that it is appropriate that he be punished in proportion to the wickedness of his act. Justice is held to consist in equal treatment, though everyone is conceded the right to try to obtain favored treatment. We saw in the chapter on criminal law that progressive leaders of the bar were unable to discard wholly views that serious and repeated crimes should be punished more severely than petty or first offenses; that punishment should be designed to deter others; and that it must appear as just to the general public. However, the progressiveness of these leaders was seen to inhere in their insistence that rehabilitation be a primary aim of correctional treatment and that future dangerousness should increasingly be a prime considera-tion in determining sentence and release from prison.

We do not claim that the soundness of the philosophy implied in this book has been fully demonstrated. It is perhaps well that we have correctional systems based upon somewhat different theories of crime and that there be considerable experimentation in the treatment of offenders. But can it not be asserted that the neoclassical basis of current correctional practices has been largely discredited? Criminals are not alike. They came to crime by different roads. The past act does not define their future dangerousness. People exaggerate the effectiveness of punishment as a deterrent. We do know some of the conditions under which it is immediately necessary, and others under which it is futile or increases the danger of crime. Beyond general agreement on most of the above statements, there is difference in emphasis as to the most effective approaches to the treatment of offenders. The major difference among criminologists today is between emphasis on dealing with the individual and emphasis on working through groups. Rightly or wrongly, the present book has agreed that each case must be considered individually, but has stressed that the individual, as a group product, can only be resocialized through group association. With some degree of exaggeration, we at one point defined the "reformed" offender as one who has achieved satisfying acceptance in a constructive, socially oriented group. There is evidence of considerable success in current efforts to resocialize through the use of natural groups and through the deliberate organization of new groups. Emphasis on the possibilities of this group approach does not seem inconsistent with recognition that its potentialities are nevertheless limited because of the difficulties involved and because the roots of crime lie still deeper in the value systems of our society.

The student of correctional work needs concrete examples of the worst, the typical, and the most effective types of local, state, and federal systems. In previous chapters we often referred to the errors of the past and their continuance into the present. In the case of the county jail, for example, emphasis seems properly to be upon its defects, since many of these remain typical. We have indicated above that American penal systems remain primarily neoclassical in their philosophy in spite of trends toward "the new penology" of both the individualized and group types. Because of their variety typical American penal policies are difficult to characterize. In the present chapter we shall speak of a few examples of what appear to be our most effective correctional systems. We shall give most space to the California and the federal systems. However, we do not imply that all of what we speak of as the more or less distinctive features in California are peculiar to that state. Particular features may be even better illustrated in some other state. California is recognized as having one of our most modern systems and also seems to have achieved an unusual degree of coordination of effort in the treatment of adult and youthful offenders. Her state system is also influential in the fields of research and delinquency prevention.

The California Correctional System [1]

California is a singular combination of a varied and stimulating physical environment, a rapidly increasing population, economic prosperity, a citizenry which is characteristically Western in its willingness to experiment with new ideas, and a collection of unusually able correctional leaders. With 21,660 prisoners in its state correctional institutions at the close of 1960, California led the other states in prisoner population, followed by New York with 17,000 and second only to the federal system with 23,218. Scattered the length and breadth of its huge territory are 10 institutions and 27 road, forestry, and mobile camps. Although the system's capacity is exceeded by more than 5,000 inmates, considerable flexibility is possible in placement and subsequent transfer of prisoners to meet their rehabilitation needs.

The California correctional system in substantially its present form has been in operation for about 18 years. Today a 21-member Board of Corrections serves as an advisory correlating council for the agencies which constitute the Department of Corrections and the Department of the Youth Authority. The Director of Corrections is chairman, and the board is composed of the seven members of the Adult Authority, the six members of the Youth Authority, five members of the Board of Trustees of the California Institution for Women, and two citizens appointed by the governor with the advice and consent of the senate. In addition to its primary advisory function to member agencies, the Board of Corrections is specifically charged by law to make a continuing study of penology, crime causation and prevention, and the apprehension of offenders. Advisory services to cities and counties on jails and detention facilities are also required. To aid in this service program, the Board has compiled and distributed pamphlets on minimum jail standards and the transportation of prisoners.

As the chief administrative officer of the system, the Director of Corrections is charged with responsibility for the custody, care, treatment, classification, and training of persons confined in state prisons as adult felons and is responsible also for their parole after release.

The Adult Authority meets periodically at each of the state prisons for a study of the cases of all prisoners whose terms of imprisonment are to be determined or parole to be considered. Thus its primary responsibility is the administration of the indeterminate-sentence and parole statutes. Additional statutory duties include the restoring of civil rights to inmates and

[1] Our account is based chiefly upon the following sources: *Biennial Report of the California Department of Corrections: 1959–1960; California Prisoners: 1958–1959;* and letters from former director Richard A. McGee and A. Lamont Smith.

parolees and serving as an advisory pardon board to the governor. The Board of Trustees of the women's institution has the same duties and responsibilities with regard to women inmates.

Through its indeterminate-sentence law, first adopted in 1917, California delegates to an unusual degree the sentencing, classification, treatment, transfer, and release of offenders to administrative authorities rather than to the courts. Within statutory minima and maxima for particular offenses, the Adult Authority fixes terms and grants parole. Clinical study and classification of new prisoners are accomplished at Reception-Guidance Centers located at the California Medical Facility at Vacaville, the Deuel Vocational Institution at Tracy, both in the north-central part of the state, and at Chino, near Los Angeles.

SOME OUTSTANDING FEATURES

(1) Cooperating closely with state conservation agencies, no fewer than 27 road, forestry, and mobile camps were in operation by the end of 1960, with plans afoot to increase the present inmate population to more than 5,000 men by 1965, living in 42 camps. Under construction is a 1,200-man conservation center in Lassen County, which will operate as an administrative, supply, and training depot for the camps.

(2) All institutional and parole personnel are selected under civil service rules. There is a progressive in-service training program for correctional officers and other subordinate staff members, with classroom courses, meetings, and use of training manuals, together with supervisory training and training for special functions. Administrators also are further trained, serve temporarily in higher category positions, and are transferred among institutions to gain a broader outlook. Discussions and anonymous questionnaires bring out the attitudes of the staff toward their work and the general program.

(3) In addition to medical work at each institution, California has a special medical facility at Vacaville which corresponds roughly to the Federal Medical Center at Springfield, Missouri. Here are diagnosed and treated a variety of both misdemeanant and felony prisoners, including alcoholics, drug addicts, sex deviates, compulsive arsonists, and others with severe personality disturbances. Some 39 group-counseling classes are in operation, and about 90 psychotherapy groups meet once or twice weekly. An important program of research in diagnostic systems and treatment evaluation began in 1958. A modest but highly stimulating *Research Newsletter* is published quarterly, in which studies and results are reported.

(4) In 1960 about 118 parole agents supervised some 8,500 men, an average caseload of 72—still above preferred levels, but considerably better than those in many states. All agents must be college graduates with majors in the social sciences and at least a year's experience in some field of correction. Psychiatric outpatient services, including individual and group psychotherapy, are available for parolees requiring them. Group parolee counseling is also practiced and has proved particularly useful in surmounting the communication barrier often existing between the parolee and his agent.

(5) Narcotics traffic and narcotics addiction have been increasing in California along with the state's growth in population. Paroled prisoners who were addicted upon commitment are now subjected to a Narcotic Treatment-Control Program, which began in 1959. Specialized parole caseloads not exceeding 30 addicts are given intensive supervision; each parolee must report weekly for injection of a drug—nalline—used to detect the presence of narcotics in the blood. Parolees for whom the tests prove positive are returned to prison for further treatment and to forestall their becoming "hooked" once again.

(6) The California Institution for Men at Chino under the able initial supervision of Kenyon J. Scudder has had worldwide recognition for its unusually progressive program for tractable first offenders. Relating the program to the outside community in various ways is a key feature, along with an almost complete de-emphasizing of security. A series of honor camps operating in connection with Chino are used as a stage preceding release for prisoners whose progress at the parent institution has been satisfactory. Along with the federal institution at Seagoville, Texas, Chino has proved that a surprisingly large percentage of adult prisoners can be handled safely and successfully under "open" conditions.

(7) The California correctional system is firmly committed to the principle that continuing research on the efficacy of treatment measures is necessary if stagnation is to be avoided. In 1957 a Departmental Research Division was authorized by the legislature. The Division presently consists of a chief, seven research technicians, and a statistical section. In addition to the mimeographed *Research Newsletter,* a printed monograph series has been established whose quality rivals that of professional society publications.

Wallkill Prison in New York State

Among other progressive aspects of the correctional system of New York State, Wallkill prison deserves special attention.[2] For, perhaps more than any other American institution, Wallkill is a cooperative "follow-through" prison. It knows much of the social situation from which its inmates have come through field studies made by parole investigators. It plans its institutional program for the inmate with a future situation and a probable future job in mind. It thinks of parole planning and parole supervision as a process which begins even before transfer of the men from other prisons to Wallkill. That process then continues through counseling and through the prison program of training planned with the participation of the inmate himself; through preparation of his family for his return; through continued counsel and assistance on parole; and through his final discharge as a free citizen. Thus prison and parole programs are not only coordinated; they are actually formulated and administered by both prison and parole staff working as a team. There are many other constructive features in the Wallkill program, but this cooperative follow-through seems to be its most distinctive characteristic.

Though Wallkill is classed as medium rather than minimum-security in structure, it is in some respects comparable with open institutions like Chino and Seagoville. At first considered a frankly experimental venture, Wallkill is said to owe some of its success to careful selection of its inmates and to the fact that its population is limited to 500 men. Like all our other best efforts, this prison also owes its success largely to its leadership by Warden Walter M. Wallack. Formerly the wardens of New York's maximum security prisons nominated men for transfer to Wallkill. Today Warden Wallack can select his own admissions.

The institutional program at Wallkill aims to give the inmate confidence in his ability to live as a good citizen on the outside. The program includes vocational and academic training, in the planning of which the men themselves voluntarily participate, with an eye on a possible future job. It includes also leisure-time activities; religious and moral training; study and planning to deal with personal, family, and social problems; institutional

---

[2] This brief account is derived chiefly from Walter M. Wallack and John J. Sheehan, *Wallkill Prison Service Unit Classification* (undated mimeographed publication); from three articles in the *Christian Science Monitor* for Nov. 8, 10, and 11, 1952; and from a letter from Warden Wallack to the senior author, dated Dec. 14, 1954.

occupations to develop habits of work and experience in probable future work; and physical and mental treatment when called for. The visitor to Wallkill gets the impression of voluntary inmate-staff cooperation. Wallkill stresses education and capitalizes on the known assets of each inmate. Without using the term "group therapy," the institution accomplishes its counseling and insight-giving aim through group efforts of the trained staff to help inmates see how they got that way. Incidentally, Wallkill is said to have been the third prison in the United States to establish a chapter of Alcoholics Anonymous. There is emphasis on social education, and there are classes in successful living, religion, and social problems.

In the Service Unit a vocational guidance supervisor and social worker cooperate with a parole representative in program planning. The facilities of the Department of Correction and the Division of Parole are closely correlated. For the formerly scattered and inadequate records of facts about the inmates are substituted an integrated whole obtained from many sources. Perhaps most important of all are facts derived from field studies made by parole investigators. On the basis of all this information, the Service Unit presents to the Program Committee a long-term plan for each inmate, and to the Board of Parole and Supervising Parole Officer a later evaluation of his institutional adjustment in the light of his total situation. Employment opportunities on the outside are found usually in trades which the inmate has actually studied on the inside. This is most unusual but is the combined result of thoroughly training carefully selected inmates and of close cooperation between the prison and the state employment service. Through a series of tests and interviews, the Service Unit has come to know the past occupational experience of each man, together with his vocational interests and potentialities. From the first week of the inmate's admission he is in contact with those who are interested in his release. Important also is the work of prison officers in dealing with personal problems of the inmate and the efforts of parole officers in attempting to remove handicaps to his future success by working with his family. It is not clear how far this work includes consideration of his past and future peer-group associates. But the parole representative initiates the program of treatment of personal, marital, and other family problems in the home community.

The challenge of Wallkill and institutions like it, then, is this: How large a proportion of inmates with no such advantage might be given a comparable opportunity? Warden Wallack has expressed the opinion that only about one prisoner in five needs the traditional prison program with its emphasis primarily on safe custody.

The Federal Correctional System

HISTORY OF THE FEDERAL BUREAU OF PRISONS

Prior to 1896 all federal offenders were incarcerated in state or territorial institutions. The first three penitentiaries of the Federal Bureau of
Prisons—an agency within the Department of Justice—were authorized by
Congress in 1889. While these were under construction, former army bar-
racks at Fort Leavenworth, Kansas, were utilized for civilian prisoners. A
small former territorial prison on McNeil Island in Puget Sound, which the
new state of Washington refused to take responsibility for, was physically
improved in 1905, becoming the McNeil Island Penitentiary. The yet un-
completed Atlanta Penitentiary received its first prisoners in 1902, as did
Leavenworth in 1906. A policy of institutional diversification led to the
opening of Chillicothe as a reformatory for young men in 1926; the federal
prison for women at Alderson, West Virginia, received its first inmates the
following year. Alcatraz, in San Francisco Bay, was converted from an
army prison to civilian use in 1933. This super-security institution, surrounded by swirling fog and treacherous currents, is the most publicized but
least representative of the federal prisons. It is soon to be abandoned. The
Federal Bureau of Prisons was without its own institution for delinquent
boys until 1937, when it occupied the already aging Training School at
Washington, D.C. There is still no corresponding institution for girls, who
must be sent to Alderson or more often turned over to some approved state
institution.

Guided to an unusual degree by progressive penological doctrines, the
FBP continued to grow, until today it comprises some 32 institutions, including six penitentiaries, three reformatories for men and one for women,
nine correctional institutions, seven prison camps, one detention facility,
four facilities for juvenile boys, and a Medical Center at Springfield, Missouri. A seventh penitentiary is under construction in southern Illinois.
Two federal hospitals for drug addicts are not strictly penal institutions and
are administered by the United States Public Health Service. Generally
speaking, the security of these institutions diminishes as one goes from Alcatraz through the penitentiaries, reformatories, correctional institutions,
and camps.

The number and variety of institutions reflects the use of a distribution scheme for long-term male offenders employing the following categories:

Hardened, intractable
Habitual, tractable
Improvable: older, younger; agricultural type; road-construction type
Narcotic addicts
Narcotic offenders
Physically and mentally maladjusted

Further classification is made once a prisoner is installed in a particular facility. Reformatories stress education for younger men; correctional institutions emphasize the care of older men or of short-term offenders or others who are not major security risks. Certain education and other functions naturally cannot be as highly developed in the camps, where forestry, road building, and the like are emphasized. The National Training School for boy delinquents in Washington is a 90-year-old institution now centered in a network of superhighways and needing replacement.

ADMINISTRATION, LEADERSHIP, AND PERSONNEL

The executive officer of the Federal Bureau of Prisons is appointed by the Attorney General and is responsible to him. Two assistant directors, a commissioner of prison industries, and a medical director complete the top echelon, which has its headquarters in Washington. In 1960 field workers, comprising the officials and staffs of the 32 institutions, totaled 5,091 persons caring for slightly more than 23,000 prisoners.

The history of prisons demonstrates the essential role played in prison progress by strong, imaginative, determined, and intelligent administrators. Difficulties peculiar to the operation of correctional systems require unusual qualities in their leaders, who must be prepared to buck inertia, public suspicion, political influence, inadequate budgets, and legislative caution. The success of the Federal Bureau of Prisons in very large degree depends upon the fine initial leadership of Sanford Bates and still more upon the remarkable abilities of James V. Bennett, who has directed the Bureau for some 29 years. Mr. Bennett is an eminently practical man, but he knows and uses criminological theory. He has been wise in calling to his staff men with somewhat varying penological views. He maintains esprit de corps by making it possible for custodial officers to rise on merit to the position of warden or higher, but he makes prison service attractive as a career to men of culture and refinement from our colleges and universities.

There would seem to be few if any prison systems where merit counts for more than in FBP. Nearly all positions are subject to civil service. Relatively satisfactory salaries, advanced standards for appointment, an excellent pre-service and in-service training program, and conditions generally favorable to morale attract relatively capable personnel. Even the task of the guard in the FBP is far more than that of a mere watchdog suspiciously guarding "bad" men. In some measure, federal custodial officers become case workers, work as part of the whole team in the task of attempted rehabilitation, and absorb some of the philosophy of the system. Beyond this capable college or university graduates can now accept positions as interns for a few months and so test their fitness for a prison service career.

THE PHILOSOPHY OF THE FBP

The federal prison system contends that convicted criminals are sent to its care *as* punishment but not *for* punishment. While inmates are certainly punished in every penal institution, including the federal, this slogan represents a significant point of view. Top leaders and most, if not all, of the rank and file look upon the criminal as a product, whether they agree upon the metaphysics of free will or not. The FBP dominantly implements the new penology.

The FBP is committed to the principle of individualization. This principle is not a mere matter of words. Within the limits of knowledge and the possibility of controlling situations, individualization is actually practiced. Recently this individual approach has been significantly supplemented by the group approach. In various ways, groups are utilized extensively. There are group orientation and pre-release programs, discussion groups, occupational information sessions, great books programs, college lectures. There are chapters of Alcoholics Anonymous in most federal institutions. In at least two of them parole officers have set up groups similar to A.A. but not confined to alcoholics. Honor dormitories utilize inmate association effectively. Of tremendous significance is the use of group discussion and counseling in the pre-release program at some institutions.

Liberalized visiting-room policies are also an aspect of group treatment. At Lewisburg, Pennsylvania, the new visiting rooms may not unfairly be compared to a hotel lobby. The experiment has been surprisingly free of anticipated untoward incidents. Taken together, these trends toward a group approach in the FBP and elsewhere are of tremendous significance and may revolutionize the prison aspect of modern penology.

DISCIPLINE; CLASSIFICATION; INDUSTRIAL WORK

Prisoners are not coddled in federal institutions. Discipline is effective and on occasion can be very stern. The very existence of Alcatraz, to which the most dangerous, most professionalized, most publicized inmates, or those deemed most likely to attempt escape, were sent, symbolized the determination of the Bureau to keep its charges behind the walls. In 1960 the ratio of escapees to all forms of departure from federal institutions was 1:128; for state institutions, 1:55.[3] Varying degrees of security among types of institutions permit isolation partly on the basis of need for maximum, close, medium, or minimum custody, and similar categories exist within particular institutions. Probably the strongest argument for the abolition of the "Rock" was that it tended to give a false notion of the varied but predominantly constructive nature of FBP penal policies.

An individualized program implies that classification shall be the heart of each institution. This is literally the case in federal institutions. It will be unnecessary to describe the functioning of this heart in detail, because the general organization has been considered in the chapter on the nature of the prison community. In the FBP, if no member of the classification personnel is called a "sociologist" as in Illinois, there are nevertheless members who are concerned with the past, institutional, and possible future social relations of inmates. In the federal system the viewpoint of the practical man and that of the theoretical man correct each other. From time to time progress reports are added to the admission summary, and any situation may bring an inmate before the committee for reconsideration. This sometimes results in the transfer of a prisoner to an institution more suited to his particular needs.

A government corporation, Federal Prison Industries, Incorporated, establishes and administers the state-use production of the FBP. Six unpaid directors appointed by the President of the United States run the corporation. Each director represents a section of the economy impinged upon by prison productivity: industry, labor, agriculture, retailers and consumers, and the Departments of Defense and Justice. A daily average of 4,438 inmates were employed full-time in FBP industrial operations during 1960.[4] A considerable number of inmates are needed for maintenance work, thousands are in school, some are unemployable. Federal prisoners employed in productive work average earnings of about $31 a month. If

[3] Computed from "Prisoners in State and Federal Institutions: 1960," *National Prisoner Statistics,* No. 27 (Sept. 1961), Table 2.

[4] Bureau of Prisons, *Federal Prisons: 1960* (Washington, D.C., 1961), p. 18.

they have dependents, they are required to send part of their earnings to them. Saving is not only encouraged but, in appropriate cases, required. The amount which inmates may purchase from the commissary is limited to a small sum, and no inmate, by reason of independent funds, may live in prison on a higher material plane than his fellow prisoners.

EDUCATION

The educational work of the Bureau is on a high level. In 1960 nearly 12,000 inmates were assigned to vocational training, with 5,200 completing vocational courses. Some 8,000 inmates attended one or more high-school-level course, a successfully completed series of which can earn a prisoner a diploma issued by the state in which his institution is located. Equivalency certificates may also be earned. Because functional illiteracy among federal prisoners is as high as 20 to 25 per cent, literacy training is an important education enterprise. About 1,200 inmates completed such training in 1960, and another 1,200 received some literacy instruction. The FBP has perhaps the best system of trade and industrial training in the country. A real effort is made to make even maintenance assignments educationally valuable. In general, academic instruction depends in large measure on inmate teachers, but they work under trained civilian supervision, and the whole program is ably directed from Washington. Some FBP libraries are attractively housed, well-stocked, widely used by inmates, and supervised by trained librarians.

THE OPEN INSTITUTION AT SEAGOVILLE

Along with California's famous Chino, the unusual federal prison at Seagoville, Texas, 15 miles east of Dallas, deserves special mention. Converted to use as a prison in 1945, it received originally only inmates considered most suitable for its extremely liberal program, but in recent years the majority have come directly from the courts. Its 500 inmates are under sentences ranging from a few months to life, and they represent ages from 18 to 80-plus years.[5] Hence the Bureau's statement[6] that *most* federal prisoners could apparently be handled under the Seagoville system becomes all the more significant.

The grounds at Seagoville resemble a college campus. The inmates live in colonial-style red brick buildings containing rooms instead of cells,

[5] James V. Bennett, "Seagoville Reconstructs a Rebel," *Federal Probation* (Dec. 1958), p. 7.
[6] Bureau of Prisons, *Seagoville, Texas,* undated booklet.

keys to which are carried by their individual occupants. Several other special-purpose buildings in architectural harmony with the housing units, the whole surrounded by a 750-acre farm, make up the rest of the institution. There are no walls, fences, or guard towers. Despite the ease of escape and the hide-out possibilities of Dallas, the rate of absconding is less than one per cent. Committed to the doctrine that nothing is gained by destroying a prisoner's self-respect or by reducing his autonomy to that of a robot, the administration gives consideration to the newcomer's preferences in living quarters and associates, and regimentation in general is kept at a minimum.

At Seagoville, as many links with the outside world are preserved and developed as are consistent with incarceration. The inmate receives visitors in a normal setting without separating partitions. He may invite them to eat lunch with him. His vocational aptitudes and accomplishments are tested, and a profile of them is sent to the Texas Employment Commission to aid in his placement. There is an active chapter of Alcoholics Anonymous. Social education is much stressed. Each man must work for eight hours before he may participate in the recreational program, and he works hard. He is taught a trade. Through formal discussions and informal group relations, he acquires better behavior patterns and comes to understand himself, the problems of others, and those of the larger world. There are current-events, great-books, camera, and X-change clubs. Useful hobbies are taught and religion is not neglected. An Adjustment Board handles minor disciplinary problems, and a Disciplinary Board the more serious ones. Punishment fits the man and the circumstance and not just the act. The custodial officers are a constructive influence and are trained to understand their charges. Before release there is informal discussion with a United States Probation Officer, representatives of the state Employment Commission, business leaders, labor leaders, and leading citizens.

RESEARCH IN THE FBP

Like the California system the FBP is now actively supporting correctional research projects. The largest to date, a 4-year study of recidivism among federal offenders, is, at the present writing, nearing completion. Not only were five federal institutions directly involved, but the two top directors of the Bureau were members of the project's advisory board. Other researches are being carried out by FBP central office and institutional research committees; graduate students in correction and criminology in increasing numbers are writing theses based on data collected in federal institutions.

CHAPTER 29

Prevention of Crime

Any program of crime or delinquency prevention [1] is based upon some notion concerning the causes of these. Advocates of boys' clubs, police athletic leagues, and directed playgrounds as preventive measures quite obviously assume that there exists a relationship between misconduct and inadequate leisure-time facilities. Supporters of psychiatric attention for pre-delinquent youngsters regard intra-psychic processes as basic in producing delinquency. The application of social case-work procedures to potential offenders presumes that the incapacity to adjust to complex social demands is a cause of crime.

There are many kinds of crime and of delinquent behavior, and since a wide variety of causal factors may be assumed to exist for each, a considerable variety of preventive programs may be necessary. The student should be aware, however, that we cannot yet state with confidence what combinations of criminogenic forces produce particular patterns of unlawful behavior, which means that

[1] In earlier chapters we have described a number of correctional measures—probation, parole, group therapy, and others—the effects of which on offenders hopefully prevent recidivism. As conventionally used, however, the term "crime prevention" denotes efforts intended to counteract criminogenic influences on the young or to keep troublesome youngsters from becoming serious offenders. This chapter therefore deals mainly with preventive programs which are carried on in other than formal correctional settings and which are aimed at children and adolescents.

prevention efforts are largely hit-and-miss. The burden of this book has been that most crime is an outgrowth of what we have regarded as criminogenic aspects of our general culture, that crime is a by-product of values, norms, and attitudes. which most of us accept as "normal" features of our way of life. Consequently, the authors necessarily must view prevention programs applied to date as efforts to counteract causative processes at relatively superficial levels, since none are designed to affect the fundamental characteristics of our culture.[2] But however superficial prevention efforts may be, responsible citizens sharing the humanitarian values of our culture cannot with equanimity remain inactive before the spectacle of hapless individuals who are or may become caught up in crime-producing forces.

Identifying Potential Delinquents

The development of techniques for identifying youngsters who may one day become delinquents is one aspect of the general growth of actuarial prediction methods in the field of criminology.[3] Drs. Sheldon and Eleanor Glueck of Harvard have been among the American pioneers in this field since 1925; their latest book on the subject was published in 1959.[4]

The actuarial identification of delinquency-prone children is a refinement of the more familiar impressionistic (or "clinical") process through which we predict many kinds of problematical outcomes by appraising a particular case against large numbers of earlier cases whose outcomes are known; we are simply guided by past experience. In the refined prediction procedures developed by the Gluecks and others, such experience is precisely tabulated in the form of "experience tables," systematic arrangements of data showing the extent to which particular characteristics are linked to particular outcomes. Any case for which a prediction is desired is then assessed against an appropriate table and a statement made (often in "chances per hundred") of the likelihood that a particular outcome can be expected for that case.

[2] Clergymen, Moral Rearmament supporters, certain political groups, and others concerned with general social "evils" advocate and work toward basic value changes, but these efforts are not *per se* crime prevention programs.

[3] We cannot here describe this growth. The student is referred to an excellent historical survey in Chapter I of *Prediction Methods in Relation to Borstal Training* by Hermann Mannheim and Leslie T. Wilkins (London: H. M. Stationery Office, 1955).

[4] *Predicting Delinquency and Crime* (Cambridge, Mass.: Harvard University Press, 1959).

The tables now most used in experimental delinquency prediction at early ages are those devised by the Gluecks after examining the characteristics of 500 institutionalized male delinquents and 500 male nondelinquents of similar ethnic, social, and intellectual backgrounds.[5] After considerable experimentation, the Gluecks selected five categories of factors which best differentiated between delinquents and nondelinquents: *discipline of boy by father, supervision of boy by mother, affection of father for boy, affection of mother for boy,* and *cohesiveness of family.* Because these were factors operating in the boys' lives prior to school entrance, early prediction is presumably possible for boys for whom predictions are desired. The Glueck table finally adopted gives the percentage of delinquents and nondelinquents within subcategories of the major categories. Thus, for example, the three subcategories of *discipline of boy by father* had the following percentages of delinquents: [6]

overstrict or erratic	71.8
lax	59.8
firm but kindly	9.3

By using the percentages as weights, a *prediction score* can be obtained for any boy by determining which of 13 subcategories he belongs in and then adding up the percentages known to characterize the original 1,000 boys. The sum thus obtained for the case we wish to predict is then compared with corresponding sums in the Gluecks' prediction table,[7] which shows the percentages of boys delinquent in given score groups. A boy's score can range from 116.7 to 414.0, with a chances-per-hundred of becoming delinquent correspondingly ranging from 8.2 to 89.2. The process of computing a prediction score for a particular boy is simple enough; the crucial process is that in which we evaluate case data in order to place the boy in the correct subcategories.

Do the Glueck tables enable the accurate identification of potential delinquents? The tables have been subjected rather extensively to two kinds of validation procedures. The first are *retrospective*, in that known delinquents are rated on the Gluecks' scale and a figure obtained giving the percentage of boys who would, at a much earlier date, have been correctly identified as future juvenile delinquents. At least seven such studies have been conducted since 1952,[8] with percentages of correct identification rang-

[5] *Unraveling Juvenile Delinquency* (New York: The Commonwealth Fund 1950).
[6] *Ibid.,* p. 261.
[7] *Ibid.,* p. 262.
[8] *Predicting Delinquency and Crime,* pp. 127–32.

ing from 82 to 91. Considerably more significant are *prospective* tests of validation, in which pre-school or first-grade boys are estimated as to their delinquency potential and then followed into their early teens, when direct comparisons can be made between predicted and actual behavior. At least one such study is under way, begun in 1952 by the New York City Youth Board. The Board selected a sample of 224 boys entering first-grade classes in two public schools located in high delinquency neighborhoods. Using a slightly modified form of the Glueck scale, 11 per cent of the boys were identified as potential delinquents. After nine years, when the boys by then ranged in age from 14½ to 15½, it was found that slightly more than one-half (19 out of 36) of those so identified had, indeed, become delinquent.[9] Of 185 boys predicted to remain nondelinquent, all but 11 did so.[10]

A prediction scale developed by Dr. William Kvaraceus (KD Proneness Scale and Check List) [11] consists of 75 multiple-choice items which purportedly distinguish between delinquency-prone children and others in terms of personal make-up, home and family background, and school experience. Still undergoing validation study, the KD scale appears not to have high predictive efficiency.[12]

Use of the Minnesota Multiphasic Personality Inventory is a third major effort to predict delinquency.[13] The Inventory, a self-administered instrument consisting of 550 statements, was applied to a sample of nearly 2,000 ninth-grade boys who were then followed up for four years. The instrument proved to be 36 per cent efficient, tending to identify incorrectly two boys for every correctly identified one.

It will be observed that the Youth Board validation study of the Glueck scale over-predicted the delinquents by nearly 100 per cent. Over-prediction is a characteristic of tables of less than perfect efficiency which are based, as were the Gluecks', on the experience of a population one-half of which was seriously delinquent—a far higher proportion than exists in the general population.[14] Consequently, use of such tables for early identification of pre-delinquents who would then be subjected to preventive measures could

[9] New York City Youth Board, *Delinquency Prediction, 1952–1960* (mimeographed, Oct. 1961), p. 19. Three cases were lost track of during the nine years.

[10] *Ibid.*

[11] William C. Kvaraceus, "Forecasting Juvenile Delinquency," *Journal of Education* (April 1956), pp. 1–43.

[12] U. S. Children's Bureau, *Identifying Potential Delinquents* (Washington, D. C., 1960), p. 4.

[13] Starke R. Hathaway and Elio D. Monachesi, *Analyzing and Predicting Juvenile Delinquency with the MMPI* (Minneapolis, Minn.: University of Minnesota Press, 1953).

[14] Albert J. Reiss, Jr., "Unraveling Juvenile Delinquency. II. An Appraisal of the Research Methods," *American Journal of Sociology* (Sept. 1951), p. 119.

result not only in wasted efforts but in a morally questionable intrusion in the lives of children who would not become delinquent anyway. A similar objection can be made about the KD and MMPI instruments, but the problem is more crucial with respect to the Glueck device because of the continuing insistence by the Gluecks that prediction based on their work should be adopted by school systems and by agencies dealing specifically with the delinquency problem.[15]

Child Guidance Clinics

Agreement that serious behavior trends should be dealt with through the cooperation of several types of specialists led to the establishment of child guidance clinics. The emphasis in these clinics has been on personality deviation, and they have traditionally been directed by psychiatrists, assisted by psychologists and psychiatric social workers. The general functions of such clinics in a delinquency prevention program may be listed as follows:

1. To participate in the discovery of "pre-delinquents."
2. To investigate cases selected for study and treatment.
3. To treat cases itself or to refer cases to other agencies for treatment.
4. To interest other agencies in the psychiatrically-oriented types of treatment of behavior disorders in children.
5. To reveal to the community unmet needs of types of children.
6. In some communities, to engage in behavior research.
7. To cooperate in the training of students intending to specialize in the treatment of behavior problems.

The clinic movement has relied on a specifically trained professional staff, and to it are referred some of the more difficult types of cases with evidence of mental difficulties. Some critics have questioned aspects of the psychiatric approach and have queried whether therapy has not in some cases been as effectively provided by sociologically trained personnel specializing in work with groups. In some clinics efforts are made to change home situations or to advise parents, teachers, courts, probation officers, or others dealing with delinquent children. After interviews and examinations by each specialist in the clinic, there will ordinarily follow a staff conference in which

[15] E.g., Eleanor T. Glueck, "Spotting Potential Delinquents: Can It Be Done?" *Federal Probation* (Sept. 1956), pp. 7–13; Sheldon Glueck, "Ten Years of Unraveling Juvenile Delinquency," *Journal of Criminal Law, Criminology and Police Science* (Sept.–Oct. 1960), pp. 301–08.

information is pooled, a tentative diagnosis arrived at, and a plan of treatment decided upon.

Clinics have not typically concerned themselves, in their diagnostic procedures, with social factors of the kinds emphasized by sociologists, since the clinics' heavy psychiatric orientation leads to a focus on person-to-person rather than person-to-group relationships in understanding behavior. Clinic diagnosticians should, in our opinion, include in their case histories answers to the following kinds of questions: Of what group patterns is this child's behavior an expression? What role does he play in constructive or deleterious groups? What behavior is required of him in such groups if he is to acquire and retain social status? To what extent is the boy adjusted not to the demands of general society but to the standards of the group with whom he habitually compares himself?

It is difficult to evaluate the child guidance clinic as a crime prevention agency. Shall we judge it in terms of its success with the juvenile recidivist, or shall we hold that its role is with relatively simple and earliest beginnings of behavior problems? Shall we measure its success as of the date when it ceased treatment, and if so shall we consider cases dealt with for the minimum or for the maximum periods? Or shall we expect the "cure" to last into the future after the clinic has ceased to function? What, again, shall be the test of success? Must angelic, or average, or only slightly improved behavior define a successful case?

At the Worcester child guidance clinic, Hartwell [16] reported it impossible to measure success. He stated, however, that the children themselves would rate their treatment as successful more often than would anyone else, followed in order by policemen, parents, teachers, and foster parents. Other evaluations have held three-quarters of the cases at least partial successes. The types of cases showing least improvement, however, were precisely those where traits dealt with were deemed significant for delinquency. [17] These least successful cases included problems of pugnacity, hyperactivity, temper tantrums, destructiveness, and disobedience.

The most elaborate effort to evaluate the combined work of a juvenile court and clinic dealing with delinquent children is found in Sheldon and Eleanor Glueck's important study, *1,000 Juvenile Delinquents*. Five years after treatment, this study found 88 per cent of the children had continued

[16] Cf. Samuel W. Hartwell, "The Worcester, Massachusetts, Child Guidance Clinic," in Sheldon and Eleanor Glueck, *Preventing Crime* (New York: McGraw-Hill Book Company, 1936), pp. 376–77.

[17] Sybil Foster and Dorothy Stebbens, "Problems Presented and Results of Treatment in 150 Cases Seen at the Habit Clinic for Children," *Mental Hygiene* (July 1939), pp. 529–41.

in delinquency. Dr. William Healy,[18] director of the clinic, and two of his associates largely accepted the findings of the study, pointing out, however, the rather exacting test of success involved—abstention from delinquency five years after the end of treatment—and noting that 47 per cent of the cases did abstain during the period of probationary supervision.

In 1940 the Gluecks published a follow-up study [19] of these same children carried to a point 15 years subsequent to the study already cited. This study showed a marked decline in criminality, so that at the age of 29 almost 40 per cent had ceased to be criminals, while the proportion of serious offenders had dropped from 75.6 per cent to 47.8 per cent. The Gluecks explain the improvement in terms of growing maturity.[20]

What are the possible explanations of this rather disappointing early showing of clinic and court? Perhaps there would have been greater success could treatment have been begun earlier, or could the clinic itself have controlled treatment. Perhaps group techniques should have been utilized more fully, as they are being successfully used today. Perhaps the clinical approach itself is inadequate, and more basic changes in social relations are needed. Perhaps a large proportion of failure is inevitable simply because it is impossible fully to control human beings. Witmer and Tufts emphasize that clinics seek cases of delinquents where some problem of parent-child relations is evident. Further, they point out that they are apt to deal with cases most often and most successfully when the parents are cooperative. Therefore these authors conclude that even the rather meager success they have reported is not concerned with typical juvenile delinquents. *"They are more likely to be children of middle-class than of lower-class status and to be reacting to adverse parental attitudes alone rather than to such attitudes combined with adverse social conditions."* [21] We put the above quotation in italics because it seems to be of major importance. It seems to imply considerable criticism of current emphasis on the psychiatric and clinical approach to the prevention of delinquency. Reliance upon those approaches continues in the face of their rather meager proven accomplishments and of the fact that they do not usually deal with typical delinquents.

[18] William Healy, Augusta Bronner, and Myra Shimberg, "The Close of Another Chapter in Criminology," *Mental Hygiene* (April 1935), pp. 208–22.

[19] Sheldon and Eleanor T. Glueck, *Juvenile Delinquents Grown Up* (New York: The Commonwealth Fund, 1940), p. 264.

[20] For a study of the success of child guidance at the Syracuse Psychopathic Outpatient Department and Hospital between 1936 and 1942, see Eugene Davidoff and Elinor S. Noetzel, *The Child Guidance Approach to Juvenile Delinquency* (New York: Child Care Publications, 1951).

[21] *Op. cit.*, p. 40. Italics ours.

Preventive Recreational Activities

To the normal child nothing is more serious than play, the "business of childhood." "Wholesome play" has long been looked upon as an adjunct to good character development. Decisions as to what is wholesome and what is not have usually been made from the perspective of middle-class values. Competitive "sportsmanlike" athletics, aesthetic pursuits, educationally useful reading, instructive field trips, hobbies, and dances and parties useful in teaching the social graces—all untainted, of course, by profanity, alcohol, or concupiscence—rank high on the approved list. The adaptation of these activities to delinquency and crime prevention is clearly based on the assumption that constructive leisure time in childhood is causally linked [22] to law-abiding habits and attitudes in adulthood, either positively through the direct building of constructive personality traits or negatively by so occupying a youngster's time that he cannot get into trouble.

ORGANIZED CLUBS AND RELATED ACTIVITIES

It is appropriate that substitute and competing groups be organized to counteract gang influences or to incorporate gangs. Boys' Clubs of America, created in 1906, organizes one widespread type of club, intended for the underprivileged boy. Organizations like the Worcester Boys' Club try more specifically to reach court cases, although the Worcester club has worked more through parents than through contacts with actual gangs. One of its studies showed that over one-third of its members became delinquent after taking out membership. Organizations like the Boy Scouts were formerly criticized because they neglected the underprivileged boy, had a too intensively competitive program to suit the needs of the handicapped child, and were too expensive. However, since 1940 the Boy and Girl Scout movements have experimented with programs intended for court cases. The experiment seems to have indicated that the movement can be partially adapted to the needs of underprivileged children. Sometimes YMCA's or other settlement or community organizations have incorporated gangs or the leaders of gangs into their organizations.

No one can say how many more delinquents there would have been without the work of our traditional recreational and character-building

[22] In the authors' opinion this presumed causal linkage could bear more examination than it has received; we do not here quarrel with it, however.

activities, whether sponsored by religious organizations or not. However, many who are closest to the problem of delinquency point out the handicap involved in all movements which come from outside the experience of the delinquents and nondelinquents who are more or less isolated in our city slums and more or less in conflict with the rest of our communities. This realization has led to movements like the Chicago Area Project, where the emphasis is on democratic organization for self-help on the part of the people of the areas where delinquency is concentrated.

In the 1930's believers in the value of boys' clubs as a delinquency countermeasure were troubled by the findings of what is probably still the most elaborate effort to measure the effectiveness of a particular club.[23] Studying a New York boys' club which definitely attempted to reach underprivileged and potentially delinquent boys during the first four years of its existence (1927–31), Thrasher rated the work of these initial years unsuccessful as a preventive of crime and came to the following adverse conclusions among others:

1. Nearly half of the neighborhood's delinquents had never been enrolled in the club.
2. A large proportion of the boys failed to remain members for a sufficiently long period of time for effective influence.
3. Delinquency rates of members were higher than those of the community in general, though this was to be expected.
4. "The Boys' Club during these four years, however, had no influence in decreasing the number of offenses committed from year to year by its own members (that is, by boys who were not delinquent before they joined the Club), although a decreasing trend would be expected if the preventive influences of the Club were having a direct effect." The great majority of members' delinquencies occurred after they had become affiliated with the Club.

This study is not necessarily a criticism of all boys' clubs. Thrasher's findings suggest that a good club program must actually reach the type of boy needing its help; that it must use trained workers; that it must use both individual and group methods; that it must satisfy the wishes of the boy more adequately than do his gangs; and so on. Even when all these needs are met, the typical boys' club is not apt to appeal to most delinquents unless it is recognized as an activity of their own neighborhood.

A 1959 report of a Louisville boys' club study is as valuable for its

[23] Frederick M. Thrasher, "The Boys' Club and Juvenile Delinquency," *American Journal of Sociology* (July 1936), pp. 66–80.

precautionary tone as for its findings.[24] Comparing three city areas—one with a boys' club—matched in income, rent, education, housing, and percentage of non-whites, a substantial decline in delinquency rates was noted in the club area compared with the other two during the years of the club's operation. The authors warn, however, that certain uncontrolled variables may account for the findings, including the differential presence of industry, church organizations, and commercial activity.

REDIRECTING CONFLICT GANGS [25]

Remedies proposed for the conflict-gang problem have ranged from outright oppression to working with gangs in an effort to redirect them into socially acceptable activities. Peeling off gang members by luring them into non-gang substitute pursuits, often related to neighborhood clubs and centers, has been found effective mainly with boys whose gang membership has been marginal or to whom the gang represents "something to do." [26] Hard-core members, many of whom reportedly suffer from personality disturbances or deep feelings of inadequacy in conventional settings, are loath to leave their gangs. Another kind of program concentrates on helping gang members find employment. The Quakers in San Francisco have developed work projects for gang members in slum clearance, park care, and other chores of direct community value.[27]

Programs which leave gangs intact while rechanneling their activities are usually carried out by so-called *detached workers* whose office is wherever gangs congregate. These workers have the considerable task of hanging around with conflict gangs, winning the confidence and respect of the leaders, and persuading them to adopt peaceful pursuits. The detached-worker movement began in Chicago in the late 1920's in accordance with suggestions made by Frederick M. Thrasher. The World-War-II period and after saw the movement spread to Los Angeles, Washington, D.C., Philadelphia, Boston, and New York City.[28]

In New York City several private agencies have supported detached workers, but the major work is being done by the city-financed Council

[24] Roscoe C. Brown, Jr., and Dan W. Dodson, "The Effectiveness of a Boys' Club in Reducing Delinquency," *Annals of the American Academy of Political and Social Science* (March 1959), pp. 47–52.

[25] Part of this section draws heavily on *Dealing with the Conflict Gang in New York City*, Interim Report No. XIV, Juvenile Delinquency Evaluation Project of the City of New York (May 1960) (mimeographed).

[26] *Ibid.*, p. 9.

[27] *Ibid.*, p. 10.

[28] *Ibid.*, p. 11.

of Social and Athletic Clubs, a body within the New York City Youth Board.

Preventing further gang violence is the first goal of the worker, and his ability to accomplish this task can be regarded as the initial measure of his success with the group. But since he is concerned with considerably more than a temporary cessation of violence, the street-club worker is necessarily drawn into attempting to channel the boys' energy and time into constructive pursuits, providing "expert" advice on a variety of subjects ranging from education and employment opportunities to marriage, and directing those needing professional care or services to the proper source. A street-club worker is not long in realizing that here is no grand design by which he can assist the group in adopting sounder goals. He needs to be pragmatic, adapting his methods of work to fit newly developing situations.

There are several different ways in which a street-club worker makes initial contact with the gang. He may be introduced by another worker or a supervisor already in contact with the gang; he may be referred by a local agency; or he may simply establish contact with a gang by "hanging around" the same place that the gang frequents—whether this be a street corner or a local candy store— and get to know some of the members this way. Through them he penetrates closer to the gang and its leaders and explains the nature of his work. Generally, the gang reacts at first with suspicion and even hostility, which are overcome only after the members have become secure in their feelings toward him. As he is able to win a place among the gang, its members start responding to his guidance by agreeing to go with him on trips in and outside the City, to the movies, or to a baseball game. The worker helps them in organizing house parties, letting the gang understand that the party cannot become a drinking bout or an unruly gathering. In this manner he tries to steer the group into socially acceptable channels, hoping to show its members that life can hold more interest than the next rumble.

As a result of his close and continuing relationship with a gang, a street-club worker can often detect early signs of unlawful gang activities and help to avert them by informing the police. Under Council regulations, a worker is required to make clear to gang members that he has no alternative but to report matters connected with rumbles, weapons, and narcotics to the Police Department.

The requirement of reporting impending gang troubles, however, often places the worker on a tightrope between his obligation to the gang and his responsibility to the police. Overheard talk of an impending rumble may be nothing more than idle conversation. If he informs the police at every turn, he runs the risk of being tagged a "stoolie," thereby undermining his position with the group. On the other hand, should he be too indulgent, out of fear of straining the ties between himself and the gang, he might easily become the cat's paw of its members. He carries a heavy responsibility for which there is no pat formula.[29]

[29] *Ibid.,* pp. 17–18.

New York's detached-worker project was instituted to counteract a dangerous gang situation existing in the city's slums. As an action program, it was designed neither to test hypotheses regarding delinquency nor to facilitate measurement of its own effectiveness. A privately-sponsored detached-worker program in Boston between 1954 and 1957 was so designed, however, and attempted to answer the specific question, "To what extent did changes occur in customary patterns of group behavior—actional, attitudinal, and perceptual—during the workers' term of service?"[30] Using four indices to behavior change, the project appeared to have a measurable impact on patterns of group behavior, including a reduction in law-violating behavior.[31]

The Chicago Area Project

Among the oldest continuing crime-prevention programs in the United States, the Chicago Area Project was begun about 1934 under the leadership of the late Clifford R. Shaw and was based on ecological and social-psychological concepts evolved by the "Chicago School" of sociology. The Project's basic purpose is to develop an interest in welfare activities and organizations on the part of residents of high-delinquency neighborhoods, concentrating particularly on enlisting the aid and support of indigenous leaders.

The use of such leaders rather than professionally trained workers is defended on several grounds.[32] Such persons have extensive knowledge of their local areas; communication between leaders and residents is facilitated; access to delinquent boys is simplified; the leaders' interest lends their prestige to the project's purposes. Perhaps the most important reason for using local leaders is to establish a basis for eventual local autonomy and local financial support in the conduct of youth welfare activities, a goal deemed unattainable without the backing of neighborhood leaders.

Beginning either with such existing neighborhood organizations as churches, P.T.A.'s, lodges, and business groups, or with newly-created organizations, three major programs are set up:[33] (1) standard recreation programs for local youngsters, including athletics, camping, and field trips;

---

[30] Walter B. Miller, "Preventive Work with Street-Corner Groups: Boston Delinquency Project," *Annals of the American Academy of Political and Social Science* (March 1959), p. 99.

[31] *Ibid.*, pp. 99, 106.

[32] Solomon Kobrin "The Chicago Area Project—a 25-Year Assessment," *Annals of the American Academy of Political and Social Science* (March 1959), p. 24.

[33] *Ibid.*, p. 26.

(2) campaigns for improving schools, traffic safety, sanitation, and property conservation; and (3)

. . . activity directed to the delinquent child, gangs of boys involved in delinquency, and, in some cases, adult offenders returning to the neighborhood from penal institutions. The activity includes helping police and juvenile court personnel develop plans for the supervision of delinquent youngsters; visiting boys committed to training schools and reformatories; working with boys' gangs in the informal settings of the neighborhood; and assisting adult parolees in their problems of returning to the community.[34]

While its sponsors (now the Illinois Youth Commission) stress community organization for its own sake and have made little attempt to prove its definite effects on delinquency, they are convinced of its benefits. Its greatest success occurred during the decade of the 1930's in Italian and Polish neighborhoods, presumably because these possessed social cohesion and strong local leaders (including politicians and racketeers). During the 1940's, however, population shifts moved the delinquency center of gravity to Negroes and Mexican-Americans, whose considerably lesser cohesion and almost total absence of leaders willing to work with the very poor were formidable obstacles to community organization. Without changing the basic CAP theories, the program was altered somewhat from a neighborhood to a wider community basis, with leadership obtained from the political and social elite in the larger community.

Conclusion

At the beginning of this chapter we asserted that crime-prevention programs leave untouched the basic criminogenic features of our culture and thus are dealing with excrescences rather than underlying causes. We will now speak briefly of the significance of this point to those concerned with the crime problem.

In Chapter 2 we outlined what appear to us to be the main attributes of American culture relevant to understanding the basic causes of crime. Among them were complexity, dynamism, materialism, impersonal relationships, restricted group loyalties, the survival of frontier values, and faith in the coercive power of law without expecting obedience to all laws. Some of these, certainly, are found in other Western cultures as well as in our own and are beginning to appear in those non-Western cultures adopting Western technologies, but their unique permutations within American cul-

[34] *Ibid.*, p. 26.

ture give our crime its distinctive properties. In the third chapter we indicated how values and practices of prestiged groups spread and set patterns for the rest of us including the criminal and potentially criminal. In attempting to characterize American culture, we naturally emphasized its criminogenic aspects, but it was also pointed out that man is as evidently social as antisocial, and that there are also values and practices which result in constructive, cooperative behavior rather than criminalistic or exploitative behavior. If the deeper roots of crime are to be cut, it would appear that a basic preventive program must be built upon our positive values and upon effort to change those values which are oriented toward crime. We are presumably quite willing to recognize the positive values and to try to stimulate them. We may not be quite so ready to recognize our criminogenic values and alter them, partly because they are often highly esteemed for themselves.

Let us merely sample a few of these positive values, and a few of what may be trends away from some of the more dangerous or negative ones. Life continues to become more and more impersonal, but there are efforts to repersonalize it and to create primary groups which nourish the social life of man. There is little evidence of lessening criminogenic group loyalty in the United States, but long-term trends may be in the opposite direction. Currently, for example, we observe significant trends away from race discrimination in spite of resistance to them. If the word "alien" still arouses some suspicion, millions have learned that in the concrete many aliens and their children are indistinguishable from Americans. The approval of cultural pluralism is coming somewhat to replace the demand that every displaced person or other immigrant seeking our shores become a complete replica of the typical native. Culture conflict is probably declining. If there have been incidents of bad faith in the field of sports, there has been reaction against them, and American good sportsmanship still is an important social value. Very likely the sex dilemma may be doomed by the very "new morality" which created it. There seems to be less hypocrisy and greater willingness to face the facts of life. This argues for stability on a new and more enduring and rational basis. The public has been aroused to demand more efficient police and court procedures which, though sometimes immediately hindering more basic attacks on crime, are increasingly combined with efforts at constructive delinquency prevention. Some newspapers are beginning to treat the crime problem more understandingly, and other papers and other media will increasingly follow when the public comes to appreciate the need. Social science spreads, and its implications, not yet fully realized, are promising. As we increasingly see criminals as products, the way toward crime prevention will be open, not merely because we can attack the problem effectively, but because the very realization that this is so tends to prevent those hostile, inhuman attitudes of greed and suspicion and prejudice which in a way *are* the crime problem. Our children are potentially criminal and exploitative, or noncriminal and cooperative. There is something of a foundation for basic crime prevention not only in the social nature of man, but in some of the attitudes, values, and trends in our society.

Yet if our analysis has been sound, crime prevention of a basic and enduring sort calls for changes in attitudes and values as well. Dangerous, deep-rooted values, some of which are almost sacred, require attention. Such changes would, however, involve tremendous difficulties. In the first place, they would require fuller knowledge than we now possess of the myriad effects of basic social change. In the second place, powerful interest groups are entrenched in some of the cultural roots of crime and will resist their uprooting. For example, business success depends upon the dominance of materialism and the continued acceptance of the principle of "rugged individualism." In the third place, some of the roots of crime are "sacred" in the minds of many of the general public. For example, group loyalties, race prejudice, and the illusions of self-direction and personal responsibility would be yielded with regret by many.

In terms of our analysis, it would seem that if our society is to move away from crime it should be less dynamic, more homogeneous, less intensively competitive and greedy for material gain, probably somewhat more planned and controlled. Such changes would seem to be needed to avoid such causes of crime as relative failure, city slums, struggle for speculative gains, monopolistic advantages, and various types of exploitation. We should need to restore the socializing influence of our declining primary groups. Though different in other respects, such a "crimeless" society would seem more nearly like primitive and peasant society than like modern society. The reader may well query, however, whether such a society would attract a population which has tasted the thrills and satisfactions of our modern, dynamic, complex, sensate, and crime-ridden existence. A crimeless society would be largely free from preferential group loyalties which we have found to be at once so cherished and so productive of strife and crime.

Perhaps the most basic change needed in the interest of crime prevention would be the incorporation in our culture of a genuinely scientific point of view which sees criminals and noncriminals as products. Such a society might not hold the criminal responsible, but would continue to hold him accountable for his crimes. It would use punishment when necessary, but only when necessary. It would have to justify punishment, not morally, but by objective evidence of its effectiveness.

Being aware, as are most sociologists, of both the extreme complexity of socio-cultural processes and of the technical difficulties encountered in manipulating for desired ends even limited portions of those processes, the present authors are not hopeful that the underlying causes of crime can be deliberately and significantly altered. Even if the technical difficulties could be overcome, there would remain the circumstance that removing the underlying causes as we see them would require such fundamental alterations in our way of life that it would no longer be our way of life. Are we willing to reduce the social complexity of America at the risk of creating thereby a blandly undifferentiated population? Would we gladly backtrack on our path toward ever greater reliance on mechanical aids to living in order to become less materialistic? Would we abandon the conveniences of large organizations for the sake of reducing impersonality? Would we forgo our present useful division of labor in order to reduce the restricted group loyalties which result in large degree from the division of labor? Would we tolerate law enforcement of a rigor sufficient to justify our faith in the law as an instrument of social control? Unless we are willing to pay such prices for its elimination, we may be obliged to accept our crime as an unavoidable cost of retaining the way of life we cherish.

Suggested Readings

Annals of the American Academy of Political and Social Science (March 1959). This excellent issue contains 16 articles on delinquency prevention.
Witmer, Helen L., and Tufts, Edith. *The Effectiveness of Delinquency Prevention Programs.* Washington, D. C.: U. S. Children's Bureau Publication No. 350, 1954. This careful evaluation concludes that certain counseling methods, psychiatric treatment, and conventional group-work programs are ineffective in preventing delinquency. Some child-guidance programs, area projects, and aggressive family casework, the authors feel, appear more hopeful.

Index of Names

537

Index of Subjects